Eighth Edition

HUMANITY

An Introduction to Cultural Anthropology

James Peoples

Ohio Wesleyan University

Garrick Bailey

University of Tulsa

WADSWORTH
CENGAGE Learning

Australia • Brazil • Japan • Korea • Mexico • Singapore • Spain
United Kingdom • United States

Humanity: An Introduction to Cultural Anthropology, **Eighth Edition**
James Peoples / Garrick Bailey

Anthropology Editor: Lin Marshall Gaylord

Assistant Editors: Jessica Jang, Liana Monari

Editorial Assistant: Paige Leeds

Technology Project Manager: Alexandria Brady

Marketing Manager: Meghan Pease

Marketing Assistant: Mary Anne Payumo

Marketing Communications Manager:
Tami Strang

Project Manager, Editorial Production:
Jerilyn Emori

Creative Director: Rob Hugel

Art Director: Caryl Gorska

Print Buyer: Paula Vang

Permissions Editor: Bob Kauser

Production Service: Joan Keyes,
Dovetail Publishing Services

Text Designer: Ellen Pettengell

Photo Researcher: Sarah Evertson

Copy Editor: Carol Reitz

Cover Designer: Larry Didona

Cover Image: © Prisma/SuperStock

Compositor: Newgen

For product information and technology assistance, contact us at
Cengage Learning Customer and Sales Support 1-800-354-9706.

For permission to use material from this text or product,
submit all requests online at **cengage.com/permissions**
Further permissions questions can be e-mailed to
permissionrequest@cengage.com.

Library of Congress Control Number: 2008920634

ISBN-13: 978-0-495-50874-8

ISBN-10: 0-495-50874-8

Wadsworth
10 Davis Drive
Belmont, CA 94002-3098
USA

Cengage Learning is a leading provider of customized learning solutions with office locations around the globe, including Singapore, the United Kingdom, Australia, Mexico, Brazil, and Japan. Locate your local office at **international.cengage.com/region.**

Cengage Learning products are represented in Canada by Nelson Education, Ltd.

For your course and learning solutions, visit **academic.cengage.com.**

Purchase any of our products at your local college store or at our preferred online store **www.ichapters.com.**

Printed in the United States of America
1 2 3 4 5 6 7 12 11 10 09 08

Brief Contents

1   The Study of Humanity 1

Part I Humanity, Culture, and Language 21

2   Culture 21

3   Culture and Language 44

Part II Theories and Methods of Cultural Anthropology 64

4   The Development of Anthropological Thought 64

5   Methods of Investigation 92

Part III The Diversity of Cultures 109

6   Culture and Nature: Interacting with the Environment 109

7   Exchange in Economic Systems 137

8   Marriages and Families 157

9   Kinship and Descent 184

10   Enculturation and the Life Course 208

11   Gender in Comparative Perspective 231

12   The Organization of Political Life 260

13   Social Inequality and Stratification 282

14   Religion and Worldview 304

15   Art and the Aesthetic 333

Part IV Anthropology in the Global Community 355

16   Globalization 355

17   Ethnicity and Ethnic Conflict 381

18   World Problems and the Practice of Anthropology 406

CONTENTS

Preface xi

1 THE STUDY OF HUMANITY 1

Subfields of Anthropology 2

Archaeology 2
Biological/Physical Anthropology 4
Cultural Anthropology 5
Anthropological Linguistics 8
Applied Anthropology 11

Careers in Anthropology 12

Cultural Anthropology Today 12

Understanding Human Cultures:
Anthropological Approaches 13

Holistic Perspective 13
Comparative Perspective 13
Relativistic Perspective 14

The Value of Anthropology 17

Concept review: Primary Interests of the Five
Subfields of Anthropology 3

A closer look: Six Million Years of Humanity 6

Globalization: A Short History of
Globalization 14

Summary 18

Key Terms 19

Suggested Readings 19

Media Resources 20

PART 1 HUMANITY, CULTURE, AND LANGUAGE 21

2 CULTURE 21

Introducing Culture 22

Defining Culture 23

Shared . . . 24
. . . Socially Learned . . . 25
. . . Knowledge . . . 26
. . . and Patterns of Behavior 27

Cultural Knowledge 29

Norms 29
Values 29
Symbols 30
Classifications and Constructions of Reality 32
Worldviews 33

The Origins of Culture 33

Culture and Human Life 36

Cultural Knowledge and Individual
Behavior 37

Is Behavior Determined by Culture? 37
Why Does Behavior Vary? 38

Biology and Cultural Differences 39

Globalization: Will Everyone Become a
Westerner? 26

Concept review: Components of Cultural
Knowledge 30

A closer look: The Cultural Construction
of Race 34

Summary 42

Key Terms 42

Suggested Readings 42

Media Resources 43

3 CULTURE AND LANGUAGE 44

Humanity and Language 45

Five Properties of Language 47

Discreteness 47
Arbitrariness 47
Productivity 48
Displacement 48
Multimedia Potential 48

How Language Works 48

Sound Systems 49
Words and Meanings 50
Nonverbal Communication 51

Language and Culture 53

Language as a Reflection of Culture 53
Language, Perceptions, and Worldview 55

Social Uses of Speech 57

Concept review: Five Properties of Language 49

A closer look: Indian Givers 52

Globalization: Globalization and Language 58

Summary 62

Key Terms 62

Suggested Readings 63

Media Resources 63

PART II THEORIES AND METHODS OF CULTURAL ANTHROPOLOGY 64

4 THE DEVELOPMENT OF ANTHROPOLOGICAL THOUGHT 64

Main Issues Today 65

The Emergence of Anthropology 66

Late-Nineteenth-Century Unilineal Evolutionism 68
A Science of Culture? 69

Anthropological Thought in the Early Twentieth Century 70

Historical Particularism in the United States (ca. 1900–1940) 70
British Functionalism, 1920s–1960s 74
The Tradition of Fieldwork 75

The Rebirth of Evolutionism in the Mid-Twentieth Century 76

Anthropological Thought Today: Divisions 78

Scientific Approaches 79

Evolutionary Psychology 80
Cultural Materialism 81

Humanistic Approaches 84

Interpretive Anthropology 85
Postmodernism 86

Either, Or, or Both? 87

Why Can't All Those Anthropologists Agree? 88

Globalization: Native Anthropology 76

Concept review: Comparison of the Scientific and Humanistic Approaches 79

A closer look: An Example of Materialism: Population Pressure and Cultural Evolution 83

Summary 89

Key Terms 90

Suggested Readings 91

Media Resources 91

5 METHODS OF INVESTIGATION 92

Ethnographic Methods 93

Ethnographic Fieldwork 93
Problems and Issues in Field Research 95
Fieldwork as a Rite of Passage 99
Ethnohistory 100

Comparative Methods 100

Cross-Cultural Comparisons 101
Controlled Historical Comparisons 104

Globalization: Ethics and Field Research 96

A closer look: Marshall Sahlins, Gananath Obeyesekere, and Captain James Cook 102

Concept review: Methods of Investigation 106

Summary 106

Key Terms 107

Suggested Readings 107

Media Resources 108

Part iii The Diversity of Cultures 109

6 Culture and Nature: Interacting with the Environment 109

Understanding Relationships with Nature 110

Foraging 112

Foraging and Culture 113
What Happened to Hunters and Gatherers? 117

Domestication 119

Beginnings of Domestication 119
Advantages and Costs of Cultivation 122

Horticulture 123

Varieties of Horticulture 123
Cultural Consequences of Horticulture 124

Intensive Agriculture 125

Varieties of Intensive Agriculture 126
Cultural Consequences of Intensive
Agriculture 127

Pastoralism 130

Environmental Advantages of Herding 130
The Karimojong: An Example from East
Africa 132

Nature and Culture 133

Globalization: Globalization and the Making of Indianness 118

A closer look: Domesticates in the Old and New Worlds 120

Concept review: Major Forms of Adaptation and Their Cultural Consequences 134

Summary 134

Key Terms 135

Suggested Readings 135

Media Resources 136

7 Exchange in Economic Systems 137

Economic Systems 139

Reciprocity 140

Generalized Reciprocity 140
Balanced Reciprocity 140

Negative Reciprocity 143
Reciprocity and Social Distance 143

Redistribution 144

Market Exchange 146

Money 146
On Market Economies 149
Peasant Marketplaces 153

Concept review: Three Forms of Exchange in Economic Systems 139

A closer look: "Insulting the Meat" Among the Ju/'hoansi 142

Globalization: Globalization and Markets 151

Summary 155

Key Terms 156

Suggested Readings 156

Media Resources 156

8 Marriages and Families 157

Some Definitions 158

Incest Taboos 159

Marriage 162

Defining Marriage 163
Functions of Marriage 164
Two Unusual Forms 165

Marriage in Comparative Perspective 167

Marriage Rules 167
How Many Spouses? 167
Marriage Alliances 172
Marital Exchanges 173

Kinship Diagrams 177

Postmarital Residence Patterns 177

Influences on Residence Patterns 177
Residence and Households 178

Family and Household Forms 179

Two-Generation Households 179
Extended Households 180

Concept review: Terms for Groups Formed on the Basis of Kinship Relationships 159

Globalization: Marriage and Family in Global Society 168

A closer look: Marriage and the Culture Wars 176

Summary 182

Key Terms 182

Suggested Readings 182

Media Resources 183

9 KINSHIP AND DESCENT 184

Introducing Kinship 185

Why Study Kinship? 185
Cultural Variations in Kinship 186

Unilineal Descent 187

Unilineal Descent Groups 189
Descent Groups in Action 192
Avunculocality Revisited 194

Nonunilineal Descent 196

Cognatic Descent 196
Bilateral Kinship 197

Classifying Relatives: Kinship Terminologies 198

Cultural Construction of Kinship 199
Varieties of Kinship Terminology 199
Why Do Terminologies Differ? 203

Globalization: Patrilineality and Globalization in China 190

Concept review: Forms of Descent and Kinship 198

A closer look: Influences on Kinship Systems 200

Summary 205

Key Terms 206

Suggested Readings 206

Media Resources 207

10 ENCULTURATION AND THE LIFE COURSE 208

Growing Up 209

Diversity in Child Care 210

Two African Examples 212

Aka 212
Gusii 214
Implications for Modern Parents 217

Life Course 218

Infancy and Childhood 218
Adolescence 220
Rites of Passage 220
Adulthood 224
Old Age 224

Globalization: Socialization, Shame, and Childhood Malnutrition on Mount Kilimanjaro 211

Concept review: Some Variations in the Life Course 219

A closer look: Aging Nations and Caring for the Elderly in Japan 226

Summary 228

Key Terms 229

Suggested Readings 229

Media Resources 230

11 GENDER IN COMPARATIVE PERSPECTIVE 231

Sex and Gender 232

Cultural Construction of Gender 233

The Hua of Papua New Guinea 234

The Sexual Division of Labor 237

Understanding Major Patterns 239
Understanding Variability 243

Gender Crossing and Multiple Gender Identities 245

Cross-Gender Occupation or Work Roles 247
Transvestism 248
Associations with Spiritual Powers 248
Same-Sex Relationships 248

Gender Stratification 249

Is Sexual Asymmetry Universal? 250
Influences on Gender Stratification 253
Gender Stratification in Industrial Societies 255

A closer look: Evolutionary Psychology and Sexual Double Standards 234

Concept review: Male/Female Differences Affecting the Major Patterns in the Sexual Division of Labor 241

Globalization: Bridal Photos in Taiwan: Globalization and Localization 256

Summary 258

Key Terms 258

Suggested Readings 258

Media Resources 259

12 THE ORGANIZATION OF POLITICAL LIFE 260

Forms of Political Organization 261

Bands 261
Tribes 264
Chiefdoms 265
States 266
International Governance 268

Social Control and Law 269

Social Control 269
Law 271

Legal Systems 272

Self-Help Systems 272
Court Systems 274

Concept review: Political Organization 263

Globalization: The Global Economy and the Future of the Nation-State 270

A closer look: Murder Among the Cheyenne 276

Concept review: Legal Systems 278

Summary 279

Key Terms 280

Suggested Readings 280

Media Resources 281

13 SOCIAL INEQUALITY AND STRATIFICATION 282

Systems of Equality and Inequality 283

Egalitarian Societies 284
Ranked Societies 285
Stratified Societies 286

Castes in Traditional India 287

Classes in Industrial Societies: The United States 290

Maintaining Inequality 294

Ideologies 295
American Secular Ideologies 296

Theories of Inequality 298

Functionalist Theory 298
Conflict Theory 299
Who Benefits? 301

Concept review: Systems of Equality and Inequality 284

Globalization: Globalization and Inequality 288

A closer look: The Forbes 400 293

Summary 302

Key Terms 303

Suggested Readings 303

Media Resources 303

14 RELIGION AND WORLDVIEW 304

Defining Religion 305

Beliefs About Supernatural Powers 305
Myths and Worldviews 306
Rituals and Symbols 309

Theories of Religion 310

Intellectual/Cognitive Approaches 311
Psychological Approaches 312
Sociological Approaches 314

Supernatural Explanations of Misfortune 315

Sorcery 315
Witchcraft 316
Interpretations of Sorcery and Witchcraft 317

Varieties of Religious Organization 318

Individualistic Cults 321
Shamanism 321
Communal Cults 322
Ecclesiastical Cults 323

Revitalization Movements 325

Melanesian Cargo Cults 326
Native American Movements 327

A closer look: Amish Communities in North America 307

Concept review: Varieties of Religious Organization 319

Globalization: Religious Diversity in the United States 329

Summary 330
Key Terms 331
Suggested Readings 331
Media Resources 332

15 ART AND THE AESTHETIC 333

The Pervasiveness of Art 335
Forms of Artistic Expression 336

Body Arts 336
Visual Arts 339
Performance Arts 345

Art and Culture 347

Secular and Religious Art 347
Art and Gender 349
Social Functions of Art 349

A closer look: Understanding Osage Art 342

Concept review: Forms of Artistic Expression 347

Globalization: Traditional Arts and the Global Economy 351

Summary 352
Key Terms 353
Suggested Readings 353
Media Resources 354

PART IV ANTHROPOLOGY IN THE GLOBAL COMMUNITY 355

16 GLOBALIZATION 355

The Development of Global Trade 356

European Expansion 357
The World and the Industrial Revolution 362

The Emergence of the Global Economy 365

Globalization: The Continuing Process 368

Population Growth and Inequalities in the Global Economy 370

Consequences of Globalization and the Global Economy 377

A closer look: Islamic Banking 369

Globalization: Religion and Politics: Globalization and the Rise of "Fundamentalism" 371

Summary 378
Key Terms 379
Suggested Readings 379
Media Resources 380

17 ETHNICITY AND ETHNIC CONFLICT 381

Ethnic Groups 382

Situational Nature of Ethnic Identity 383
Attributes of Ethnic Groups 383
Fluidity of Ethnic Groups 385
Types of Ethnic Groups 386

The Problem of Stateless Nationalities 387

Responses to Ethnic Conflict 396

Homogenization 396
Segregation 398
Accommodation 398

Concept review: Levels of Ethnic Identity 387

Globalization: A Clash of Civilizations? 388

A closer look: Ethnic and Religious Differences in Iraq 391

Concept review: Responses to Ethnic Differences 399

Summary 403

Key Terms 404

Suggested Readings 404

Media Resources 405

18 WORLD PROBLEMS AND THE PRACTICE OF ANTHROPOLOGY 406

Applied Anthropology 407

Population Growth 408

*Anthropological Perspectives on Population
Growth 408*

*Costs and Benefits of Children in North
America 409*

*Costs and Benefits of Children in the
LDCs 410*

World Hunger 412

Scarcity or Inequality? 413

Is Technology Transfer the Answer? 415

Agricultural Alternatives 416

Anthropologists as Advocates 418

Indigenous Peoples Today 418

Vanishing Knowledge 421

Medicines We Have Learned 423

Adaptive Wisdom 424

Cultural Alternatives 425

A closer look: The Declaration on the Rights of
Indigenous Peoples 422

Globalization: Globalization and the Question
of Development 426

Summary 427

Key Terms 428

Suggested Readings 429

Media Resources 429

Glossary 430

Notes 436

Bibliography 441

Peoples and Culture Index 453

Subject Index 455

PREFACE

A book with a title like *Humanity* might sound overly ambitious. The authors decided on this title back in 1985, when we began working on the first edition. We thought the title captures the most distinctive feature of the field called anthropology: of all disciplines in the social sciences, anthropology alone studies all the world's peoples. Anthropologists are interested in all humans who live on our planet, including those who lived in the prehistoric past, the historic past, and the present day.

Anthropology is not only broad in its scope. When we anthropologists do our work, we do it deeply as well: most research requires a commitment of years or even decades of detailed and intensive study. From such research, generations of anthropologists have discovered a vast amount of information about humanity. Paleoanthropologists are uncovering fossils and genetic relationships that are showing us how and when our species originated. Archaeologists are digging into information about how prehistoric peoples lived their lives.

Another subfield, cultural anthropology, is the main subject of this book. Cultural anthropology describes and tries to explain or interpret the fascinating cultural variability of the world's diverse peoples. In this text, we try to convey to students the life-enriching as well as the educational value of discovering this variability. In the process of discovery, we hope our readers will experience a change in their attitudes about other cultures and about humanity in general. We also hope the book leads readers to think about their own identities as individuals, as members of a particular society with its traditions and ways of thinking and doing things, and as participants in an increasingly worldwide human community. To achieve this last goal, we discuss anthropological insights into some of the major problems that afflict the world in the twenty-first century, such as ethnic conflicts, global inequalities, hunger, and the survival of indigenous cultures and languages. We also describe the diversity in various dimensions of human life, such as relations with the natural world, marriage, child care, gender, and religion, and we suggest the implications of such diversity for contemporary society. Last, we want students who are new to anthropology to grasp the full significance of the oldest anthropological lesson of all: that their own values, beliefs, and behaviors are a product of their upbringing in a particular human group rather than universal among all rational persons.

At the national level, alliances between nations have been newly formed or called into question since the 2001 attacks on the World Trade Center and the Pentagon. As we write in late 2007, the United States and a few of its allies are still involved in wars in Iraq and Afghanistan. Iran is alleged to be developing nuclear weapons—or maybe not. Russia was an enemy, then a friend, and now—it's hard to tell. Continued conflicts and threats lead some to believe that peoples of different nations, ethnicities, and religions can never live together in peace and security.

In the short term, wars and other forms of conflict separate the antagonists from one another. Yet, overall, the world's regions now interact more frequently and intensively than ever before. Unless there is a global economic collapse or a major war, this trend is probably not reversible. The main reasons for this increasing interdependence of peoples and nations include the increasing integration of the global economy, growing international migration, educational exchanges between countries and regions, the availability of the Internet, the worldwide spread of consumer culture, and the international media. Words like *multiculturalism* and *multinationalism* have become familiar to most people in just the past couple of decades. Anthropology has much to say about these changes. Just as important, anthropology helps us become more aware of how our own lives are affected by such changes.

New to the Eighth Edition

In the past 20 years, both the world and the discipline of anthropology have changed. More than any previous edition, this one both responds to and reflects on these changes.

First, because of developments in information technology, the increased international marketing of commodities, and the growth of travel for tourism and education, the interconnections among the world's peoples have increased. This globalization has many dimensions: cultural, economic, political, artistic, linguistic, and religious, just to name a few. For the first time, every chapter of *Humanity* now includes a Globalization box, with eight new discussions of various dimensions of globalization. Some discussions are mainly factually based, whereas others present anthropological insights into the process or the results of globalization. Each box, of course, is appropriate for the main subjects or themes of the chapter, but there also is a logical order to their sequence. For example, the Globalization box in Chapter 1 introduces the subject, and subsequent boxes deal with issues such as how globalization is affecting cultural diversity, language survival, anthropological research, family life, care of the elderly in Japan, inequality among nations, religious diversity in the United States, the production of art, fundamentalism, and development.

Second, the text of most chapters now contains more material that explicitly states the relevance of the subject for modern North America. Some insights are folded into the main text, whereas others appear in six new A Closer Look boxes, which examine relevant topics in more depth. In most chapters, we have condensed many sections, and several examples were shortened or eliminated to make room for new discussions.

To those instructors who have already used *Humanity,* the following chapter-by-chapter summary lists the major changes in this edition.

Chapter 1 introduces the subdisciplines and explains why anthropological perspectives, methods, and factual information are important. Material on biological anthropology is updated as of late 2007, including information on ape tool use and human evolution. At the request of reviewers, we added a section on careers in anthropology that undergraduates can pursue. The discussion of relativism retains the distinction between methodological and moral relativism, using female genital mutilation as an example of the complexity of the issue.

Chapter 2 (culture) contains an entirely new section on the origins of culture, using descriptions of the anatomy of speech and recent archaeological findings that indicate the use of symbols. We also redesigned and lengthened the discussion of subcultures, including noting some problems with the term itself. At the request of two reviewers, we present an explicit definition of the concept of *society.* Much of the wording of the chapter is streamlined, and we deleted some examples to make room for the new material.

We retained the organization of Chapter 3 (language) but shortened the section on structural linguistics, again at the advice of reviewers. In dealing with language and culture, our discussion of the linguistic relativity hypothesis incorporates recent empirical findings and ideas from the Max Planck Institute for Psycholinguistics. New examples are incorporated into this section, and we deleted the discussion of color terms. Overall, this chapter now emphasizes relationships between culture and language over the technical aspects of language.

Chapter 4 (theory) is the most thoroughly revised discussion in this edition. We retained its basic structure, although we gave some sections and subsections new headings. The focus remains on the distinctions between approaches that are broadly scientific and broadly humanistic. We shortened the material on nineteenth-century evolutionism and early-twentieth-century historicism and functionalism in favor of more thorough coverage of modern approaches: evolutionary psychology, materialism, interpretivism, and postmodernism. The concept of Other is incorporated, as are recent ideas about who speaks for Others, about agency, and about how the interactions of fieldworkers with communities shape ethnographic descriptions. We try to represent both sides of the (often implicit) dialogue fairly and objectively.

Chapter 5 (methods) is updated and a new Globalization box added. Anthropologists are increasingly involved in applied research for governmental agencies and private corporations. U.S. security agencies as well as the military are actively attempting to recruit cultural anthropologists. Thus, we thought it important to expand the discussion of professional ethics in the text.

In Chapter 6, we replaced the concept of adaptation with that of human-environmental relationships, based on a reviewer's suggestion. This alone resulted in many rewordings, but the chapter continues to provide an overview of foraging, horticulture, intensive agriculture, and nomadic pastoralism. We added new material on the changes in hunters and gatherers due to contact with other peoples, on how modern methods of using livestock contrast with those of pastoral peoples, and on the origins of agriculture in the New World.

Chapter 7 (exchange) is updated. The Globalization box discusses the consequences of ethanol production and covers more material on China.

In Chapter 8 (marriage and family), we kept the new material added in the seventh edition, including coverage of fictive kin, matrifocal families, and issues surrounding gay marriage in the United States. The introductory material, with several definitions, is updated and streamlined, as is coverage of the functions of marriage. We added an entirely new section on the incest taboo, listing four of the major hypotheses that try to explain

its universality. The new A Closer Look tells a personal story about intermarriages of several kinds and goes on to discuss how the postwar industrialization of Japan made it difficult for male farmers to find wives.

In Chapter 9 (kinship, descent, and terminology), we condensed the section on unilineal descent as much as possible while still retaining its content. A Closer Look and the Globalization box contain new material, including a description of how evolutionary psychology attempts to explain matrilineal descent (A Closer Look) and how patrilineal descent in China carried over into the preference for sons during the misnamed "one-child policy" (Globalization). In addition, the Globalization box discusses how today's pressures to succeed in education for both sexes result in serious stress for youngsters and parents.

Chapter 10 (enculturation and the life course) has a new organization of the section "Life Course" and expanded coverage of old age. The major changes, though, are new A Closer Look and Globalization boxes. A Closer Look describes how daughters-in-law continue to be important caretakers of elderly persons in Japan, although since the 1980s the government finances elder care institutions. The Globalization box is a case study of the relationships among child care norms and customs, parental shame, childhood malnutrition, and the global economy on Mount Kilimanjaro, Tanzania.

To Chapter 11 (gender) we added coverage of sexual dimorphism and a discussion of one explanation for the widespread double standard for extramarital sexual relations. The description of the Hua, used as an example of the cultural construction of gender, is condensed, as are some of the other ethnographic examples. At reviewers' recommendations, we reversed the order of two major sections and we introduced and applied the concept of sexual asymmetry. The new Globalization box discusses how modern Taiwanese brides are made over for wedding photos, which, although looking like creeping westernization, arguably is an example of localizing the global.

Chapter 12 (political life) now addresses the question of the effects of globalization on the existing nation-state level of government by including a short discussion of global governance. This more directly ties the text to the existing Globalization box entitled "The Global Economy and the Future of the Nation-State."

As in earlier editions, Chapter 13 (inequality) updates numerical data on the distribution of income and wealth in the United States, using statistics from 2006. We added recent material on the impact of globalization on inequality among and within nations, particularly China.

The section on secular ideologies contains a new discussion about biblical texts and related issues. The new A Closer Look describes the latest Forbes 400 list and some of its implications.

We condensed most of the conceptual discussions in Chapter 14 (religion) to create space for more coverage of religion in the United States. Shamanism and witchcraft are treated in less detail so that the new A Closer Look on the Amish in North America fits. The new Globalization box contains facts and ideas about religious diversity in the United States, using an example of accommodating members of the Muslim faith on a university campus.

Chapter 15 (art) has some modifications, including the Globalization box on "Traditional Arts and the Global Economy." This box now focuses on the decline in the production of the famous handmade Varanasi saris from northern India as a result of competition from machine-made products from China and other parts of India.

In Chapter 16 (globalization), we shortened some of the historical discussion and lengthened the discussion on the development of the global economy. Economic and demographic materials presented are updated in most cases. A Closer Look on "Islamic Banking" and the Globalization box on "Religion and Politics" are also updated.

For Chapter 17 (ethnicity), we included a new segment on terrorism in an expanded introduction. Discussions of the conflicts in Northern Ireland and between Israel and Palestine are updated. The section called "Solutions to Ethnic Conflict" from the seventh edition is retitled and refocused to "Responses to Ethnic Conflict." We also updated A Closer Look on Iraq.

Chapter 18 (world problems) is streamlined, and we include more recent developments in the cases of the Yanomamö, San, and Kayapó. A Closer Look is new because in September 2007, after more than 20 years of discussions, the United Nations passed "The Declaration on the Rights of Indigenous Peoples."

Pedagogical Features

New to this edition is a list of four or five key questions addressed by each chapter. The questions are the first thing readers see, so they can immediately know what the chapter is about and glimpse the kinds of things they should master from reading the material.

For the first time, in the eighth edition, every chapter contains at least two boxes: A Closer Look and Globalization. We continue to include Concept Reviews to condense ideas and make sharp distinctions in just a few

words. Also, each chapter contains a list of suggested readings, many of them new to this edition. About one-fourth of the photographs are new, scattered throughout the book to illustrate text discussions and make the book visually appealing.

In addition to these pedagogical aids, *Humanity* continues to include the following features to help students retain information and enhance understanding:

- A preview of each chapter's main content
- Clearly marked sections and subsections that organize the material logically and help students to see relationships between disparate topics
- Boldfaced key terms at their first mention in the text, accompanied by a list of key terms at the end of each chapter
- Point-by-point chapter summaries
- A Glossary that succinctly defines each key term
- Bibliographic notes by chapter
- Two indexes, one a traditional subject index and the other a list of peoples and cultures mentioned in the book
- Maps on the inside front cover that show the location of peoples and cultures mentioned in the book

Resources

Student Resources

For students who need or who welcome more help in mastering the material and studying for quizzes and examinations, Wadsworth offers the following student learning aids on line:

- Book-specific Premium Companion Website that includes interactive exercises, video exercises, flash cards, and quiz questions for each chapter.
- Discipline-specific Anthropology Resource Center with interactive exercises, map and video exercises, Meet the Scientist interviews, a Case Study Forum with critical thinking questions, and more.

The following are additional student resources:

- *Case Studies in Cultural Anthropology,* edited by George Spindler and Janice E. Stockard, offers a diverse array of case studies that emphasize culture change and the factors influencing change in the peoples depicted. New topics include five genders in Indonesia and Hawaiian fishermen.
- *Case Studies on Contemporary Social Issues,* edited by John A. Young, offers a variety of case studies that

explore how anthropology is used today in understanding and addressing problems faced by human societies around the world. Topics range from the cultural practices and politics affecting the spread of Ebola, to homelessness in New York City, and water resource management in Mexico City.

- Modules for cultural anthropology include *Human Environment Interactions* by Cathy Galvin and *An Introduction to Medical Anthropology* by Lynn L. Sikkink.

Instructor Resources

- Online Instructor's Manual and Test Bank. This instructor resource provides detailed chapter outlines, lecture suggestions, key terms, student activities such as exercises from the Anthropology Resource Center, and test questions that include multiple choice, true/false, fill in the blank, short answer, and essay.
- ExamView Computerized Test Bank. Create, deliver, and customize tests in minutes with this easy-to-use assessment and tutorial system. ExamView offers both a Quick Test Wizard and an Online Test Wizard that guide you step-by-step through the process of creating tests, while its unique WYSWYG capability allows you to see the test you are creating on screen exactly as it will print or display online. You can build tests of up to 250 questions using up to 12 question types. Using ExamView's complete word-processing capabilities, you can enter an unlimited number of new questions or edit existing questions.
- PowerLecture multimedia manager for Anthropology. This new CD-ROM contains digital images and Microsoft PowerPoint presentations for all of Wadsworth's 2009 introductory texts, placing images, lectures, and video clips at your fingertips. The CD includes preassembled Microsoft PowerPoint presentations and charts, graphs, maps, line art, and photos with a ZOOM feature from all Wadsworth © 2009 anthropology texts. You can add your own lecture notes and images to create a customized lecture presentation.
- Instructor Resources on the Anthropology Resource Center (ARC). Supplement your resources with a community share-bank of digital images organized by key course concepts, and a syllabus integrating the ARC with the eighth edition of *Humanity: An Introduction to Cultural Anthropology.*
- Wadsworth Anthropology Video Library. Qualified adopters may select full-length videos from an extensive library of offerings drawn from such excellent

educational video sources as *Films for the Humanities and Sciences.*

- ABC Anthropology Video series. This exclusive video series was created jointly by Wadsworth and ABC for the anthropology course. Each video contains approximately 60 minutes of footage originally broadcast on ABC within the past several years. The videos are broken into short, 2- to 7-minute segments, perfect for classroom use as lecture launchers or to illustrate key anthropological concepts. An annotated table of contents accompanies each video, providing descriptions of the segments and suggestions for their possible use within the course.

- A Guide to Visual Anthropology. Prepared by Jayasinhji Jhala of Temple University, this guide provides a compendium of 50 of the most outstanding classic and contemporary anthropological films. The guide describes the films, tells why they are important, and gives suggestions for their use in the classroom.

- AIDS in Africa DVD. Southern Africa has been overcome by a pandemic of unparalleled proportions. This documentary series focuses on the new democracy of Namibia and the many actions that are being taken to control HIV/AIDS. Included in this series are four documentary films created by the Periclean Scholars at Elon University: (1) *Young Struggles, Eternal Faith;* (2) *The Shining Light of Opuwo;* (3) *A Measure of Our Humanity;* and (4) *You Take Me Up,* a story of two HIV-positive women and their acts of courage helping other women learn to survive. Wadsworth is excited to offer these award-winning films to instructors for use in class. When presenting topics such as gender, faith, culture, poverty, and so on, you will find that the films are enlightening for students and will expand their global perspective of HIV/AIDS.

Acknowledgments

Since the first edition was published in 1988, the authors have benefited enormously from the reviewers of *Humanity.* Generally, the publisher solicits 10 to 15 reviews for each edition. Some reviewers are long-term users of the text, whereas others have never adopted it for their classes. Of course, we have never been able to incorporate all their suggestions for improvement, or the book would be twice as long as it is. But, over the last 20 years, we have added, subtracted, updated, rethought, and reorganized most of the book based on reviewers' comments. We thank all of them.

This edition incorporates many of the suggestions of the following reviewers:

Judith Brown, Oakland University
Beth Conklin, Vanderbilt University
Meghan-Tomasita Cosgriff-Hernandez, The Ohio State University
Susan Krook, Normandale Community College
Michael McDonald, Florida Gulf Coast University
Avis Mysyk, Cape Breton University
Francis Purifoy, University of Louisville
Gayatri Thampy, The Ohio State University
Adam Wetsman, Rio Hondo Community College
Anne Woodrick, University of Northern Iowa

Although we were unable to make all the changes suggested by these scholars, a great many of their suggestions are incorporated into the text. Their comments that the book needs to be more *explicit* about the relevance of anthropology in today's world were especially influential.

Both authors have also benefited from the suggestions of colleagues and friends. Jim thanks Mary Howard for her incredible support over the years as well as for her assistance in Chapter 10. Jan Smith and Akbar Mahdi have given numerous ideas over the last three years. Pamala Laucher makes everything work. Jim also thanks Stacia Bensyl and Brenda Robb Jenike for their help.

ABOUT THE AUTHORS

James (Jim) Peoples is currently Professor of Sociology/Anthropology and Director of East Asian Studies at Ohio Wesleyan University in Delaware, Ohio. Peoples has taught at the University of California at Davis and at the University of Tulsa in Oklahoma, among other colleges and universities. He received a B.A. from the University of California, Santa Cruz and a Ph.D. from the University of California, Davis. Within cultural anthropology, his research interests are cultural evolution, human ecology, cultures of the Pacific Islands, and cultures of East Asia. His first book, *Island in Trust* (1985), describes his fieldwork on the island of Kosrae in the Federated States of Micronesia. Since joining the faculty of Ohio Wesleyan University in 1988, he has taught courses about East Asia, the Pacific islands, human ecology, cultural anthropology, the anthropology of religion, world hunger, the prehistory of North America, and Native Americans of the southwestern United States. He just published a chapter on cultural anthropology in a volume that is translated for course use in China. His latest project is a coauthored book describing the prehistory, history, and contemporary culture of Kosrae island, Micronesia. When not teaching or writing, He enjoys fly-fishing, traveling, and gardening.

Garrick Bailey received his B.A. in history from the University of Oklahoma and his M.A. and Ph.D. in anthropology from the University of Oregon. His research interests include ethnohistory, world systems theory, and ethnicity and conflict, with a primary focus on the native peoples of North America. His publications include *Navajo: The Reservation Years* (with Roberta Bailey); *Changes in Osage Social Organization 1673–1906: The Osage and the Invisible World;* and *Art of the Osage* (with Dan Swan, John Nunley, and Sean Standingbear). Bailey has been a Senior Fellow in Anthropology at the Smithsonian Institution in Washington and a Weatherhead Resident Scholar at the School of American Research in Santa Fe. Actively engaged in contemporary Native American issues, he has served as a member of the Indian Health Advisory Committee, Department of Health, Education, and Welfare; of the Glen Canyon Environmental Review Committee, National Research Council; and of the Native American Graves Protection and Repatriation Act (NAGPRA) Review Committee, Department of the Interior, and is editor of *Indians in Contemporary Society,* Volume 2 of the *Handbook of North American Indians.* Bailey has taught anthropology at the University of Tulsa since 1968.

1 THE STUDY OF HUMANITY

Subfields of Anthropology

Archaeology

Biological/Physical Anthropology

Cultural Anthropology

Anthropological Linguistics

Applied Anthropology

Careers in Anthropology

Cultural Anthropology Today

Understanding Human Cultures: Anthropological Approaches

Holistic Perspective

Comparative Perspective

Relativistic Perspective

The Value of Anthropology

Cultural anthropologists are fascinated by the vast diversity of humanity. This fascination leads us to explore other peoples and places. Here anthropologist Margaret Kieffer interviews a Guatemalan woman weaver who is a member of the Mayan community.

Questions addressed in this chapter

What are the subjects of the five major subfields of anthropology?

How has cultural anthropology changed in the last several decades?

What is meant by the holistic, comparative, and relativistic perspectives, and why are they so important to anthropologists?

What wider lessons can we learn by studying anthropology?

What makes humans different from other animals? Do all people share the same human nature and, if so, what is it like? How and why do human groups differ, both biologically and culturally? How are people who live in industrialized, urbanized nations different from "traditional" or "indigenous" peoples? What are the social and cultural implications of living on a planet whose diverse peoples are now connected by multinational corporations and other global organizations? These are a few of the questions investigated by **anthropology,** the academic discipline that studies all of humanity.

Almost everything about people interests anthropologists. We want to know when, where, and how the human species originated and why we evolved into what we are today. Anthropologists try to explain the many differences between the world's cultures, such as why the people in one culture believe they get sick because the souls of witches devour their livers, whereas the people in another think that illness results from tarantulas flinging tiny magical darts into their bodies. We want to know why most Canadians and Australians like beef, which devout Hindus and Buddhists refuse to eat. We are interested in why some New Guineans often engorge themselves with the meat of pigs, which is the same animal flesh that some Middle Eastern religions hold to be unclean. In short, anthropologists of one kind or another are likely to investigate almost everything about human beings: our evolution, our genes, our emotions, our intellects, our art styles, our behaviors, our languages, our religions, and so forth.

Anthropologists, then, study many different things about humanity. In fact, perhaps the most distinguishing characteristic of anthropology—the one feature that makes it different from other fields that also include people as their subject matter—is its broad scope. Anthropologists are interested in *all* human beings, whether living or dead, Asian or African or European. We also are interested in many different *aspects* of humans, including their genetic makeup, family lives, political systems, religions, and languages. No people are too remote to escape the anthropologist's notice. No dimension of humankind, from skin color to art styles, falls outside the anthropologist's interest.

Subfields of Anthropology

Because anthropology is such a broad discipline, no single anthropologist can master the entire field. Therefore, modern anthropologists specialize in one of five principal subfields: archaeology, biological (or physical) anthropology, cultural anthropology, anthropological linguistics, or applied anthropology. (The Concept Review summarizes the primary interests of each of the five subfields.) Because cultural anthropology is the primary subject of this book, here we take only a brief look at the other subfields and some of their major findings.

Archaeology

Archaeology investigates the human past through the excavation and analysis of material remains. Modern archaeology is divided into two major kinds of studies: prehistoric and historic.

Prehistoric archaeology is the study of ancient, preliterate cultures—those that never kept written records of their activities, customs, and beliefs. Much information about the lives of prehistoric peoples can be recovered from the tools, pottery, ornaments, bones, plant pollen, charcoal, and other materials they left behind, in or on the ground. Through careful excavation and laboratory analysis of such material remains, prehistoric archaeologists reconstruct the way people lived in ancient times and trace how human cultures have changed over centuries and even over millennia. Contrary to the impression given by many television documentaries, the main goal of excavating a particular site is not to recover valuable treasures and other artifacts, but to understand how

PRIMARY INTERESTS OF THE FIVE SUBFIELDS OF ANTHROPOLOGY

Archaeology	Physical/ Biological	Cultural	Anthropological Linguistics	Applied
Excavation of material remains in prehistoric sites to reconstruct early human ways of life; study of remains in historic sites to learn more about historic, literate peoples	Comparisons of human anatomy and behavior with other primate species; physical (genetic) variation among human populations; biological evolution of *Homo sapiens*	Differences and similarities in contemporary and historically recent cultures; causes and consequences of sociocultural change; impacts of globalization and contacts on the world's peoples	General relationship between language and culture; role of language and speaking in cultural and social life of specific peoples; how language might shape perceptions and thoughts	Applications of anthropological skills, knowledge, concepts, and methods to the solution of real-world problems

© Robert Brenner/Photo Edit

▲ Prehistoric archaeologists investigate the remote past by the careful excavation of material remains.

people lived long ago. Indeed, research conducted by prehistorians provides our main source of information about how people lived before the development of writing.

Over decades of field research and laboratory work, prehistoric archaeologists have learned that agriculture first developed around 10,000 years ago, when some peoples of the Middle East began planting wheat and barley—for the first time, humans transformed certain wild plants into *crops*. Somewhat later, peoples of southern China, Southeast Asia, and West Africa domesticated other plants. On the other side of the world, in what we now call the Americas, different plants were brought under human control in southern Mexico and western South America. Surprisingly, most available evidence suggests that these six regions where agriculture developed were independent—meaning that the people of one region domesticated plants on their own, rather than learning the idea of agriculture from other peoples. Similarly, civilization (living in cities) developed in several different regions independently, beginning about 5,000 years ago.

To learn about the past in societies in which some people could read and write, historians study written materials such as diaries, letters, land records, newspapers, and tax collection documents. The growing field of **historic archaeology** supplements such written materials by excavations of houses, stores, plantations, factories, and other historic structures. For example, the cover story of the April 16, 2001, issue of *Time* magazine was titled "What Jesus Saw: Jerusalem Then and Now." Historic archaeologists worked with other scholars to reconstruct life in ancient Jerusalem, providing hard data on living conditions and other topics that are missing from written accounts.

Many archaeologists today are employed not in universities but in museums, public agencies, and for-profit corporations. Museums offer jobs as curators and researchers. State highway departments employ archaeologists to conduct surveys of proposed new routes in order to locate and excavate archaeological sites that will be destroyed. The U.S. Forest Service and National Park Service hire archaeologists to find sites on public lands so that the appropriate parties can make decisions about the preservation of cultural materials. Those who work in the growing field of *cultural resource management* locate sites of prehistoric and historic significance, evaluate their importance, and make recommendations about total or partial preservation. Since the passage of the National Historic Preservation Act in 1966, private corporations and government agencies that construct factories, buildings, parking lots, shopping malls, and other structures must file a report on how the construction will affect historical remains and on the steps taken to preserve them. Because of this law, the business of *contract archaeology* has boomed in the United States. Contract archaeology companies bid competitively for the privilege of locating, excavating, and reporting on sites affected or destroyed by construction. Hundreds of contract archaeology companies exist, providing jobs for thousands of archaeologists and students.

Biological/Physical Anthropology

Biological (also called **physical**) **anthropology** is closely related to the biological and zoological sciences in its goals and methods. It focuses on areas such as the anatomy and behavior of monkeys and apes, the physical (including genetic) variations between different human populations, and the biological evolution of the human species.

Within biological anthropology, researchers in **primatology** study the evolution, anatomy, adaptation, and social behavior of primates, the taxonomic order to which humans belong. Research on group-living monkeys and apes has added significantly to the scientific understanding of many aspects of human behavior, including tool use, sexuality, parenting, cooperation, male–female differences, and aggression. Field studies of African chimpanzees and gorillas, the two apes genetically most similar to the human species, have been especially fruitful sources of hypotheses and knowledge.

For example, in the 1960s, the famous British primatologist Jane Goodall observed toolmaking among African chimpanzees. Chimps intentionally modified sticks to probe the holes in termite mounds. When termite soldiers attacked the intruding objects, the chimps withdrew the probes and licked off the tasty insects. Goodall observed adult chimps teaching their young how to probe for termites, showing that humanity's closest animal relatives have at least a semblance of cultural tradition. Some chimpanzee groups wave tree branches in aggressive displays against other groups and wad up leaves to use as sponges to soak up drinking water. Working in West Africa, other researchers have observed some chimp groups using heavy round stones as hammers to crack open hard-shelled nuts. The chimps select stones of the proper shape and weight, control the force of their blows so that the nut does not shatter, and often leave the tools under nut trees for future use. Recently, observers have seen gorillas using sticks to gauge the depth of water and laying down a tree trunk to go across a deep pool. These and other observations have changed our understanding of human–animal differences: prior to such studies, making tools was widely considered to be one of the things humans could do that other animals could not.

Another type of biological anthropologist studies how and why human populations vary physically due to hereditary, genetic factors. This subfield is **human variation.** All humanity belongs to a single species, which taxonomists call *Homo sapiens.* One of the most important findings of anthropology is that the physical/genetic similarities among the world's peoples far outweigh the differences. Nonetheless, peoples whose ancestral homelands are in Africa, Asia, Europe, Australia, the Pacific islands, and the Americas were once more isolated than they are today. During this time, they evolved differences in overall body and facial form, height, skin color, blood chemistry, and other genetically determined features. Specialists in human variation measure and try to explain the differences and similarities among the world's peoples in these physical characteristics. (We discuss some major findings about "racial" variation in Chapter 2.)

Chapter 1 THE STUDY OF HUMANITY ■ 5

▲ Field studies by primatologists overturned some earlier notions about human uniqueness, such as the idea that humans are the only species to use and make tools. Here a young chimpanzee inserts a twig into a termite mound to probe for the nourishing insects.

Another aim of physical anthropology is to understand how and why the human species evolved from prehuman, apelike ancestors. The specialization that investigates human biological evolution is **paleoanthropology.** Over decades of searching for fossils and carrying out meticulous laboratory studies, paleoanthropologists have reconstructed the history of how the human anatomy evolved.

In the late 1970s, paleoanthropologists began to use new methods for investigating human evolution. Scientists in the field of molecular genetics can now sequence DNA—the genetic material by which hereditary traits are transmitted between generations. By comparing DNA sequences, geneticists estimate how closely different species are related. Studies comparing the genetic sequences of African apes with humans show that humans share 97.7 percent of their DNA with gorillas and 98.7 percent with chimpanzees and bonobos (also known as pygmy chimpanzees). DNA from modern humans and DNA sampled from the extinct human species *Neanderthal* are about 99.5 percent the same. Similarities in the DNA of two or more species are evidence that they share a common evolutionary ancestor. Also, the more similar the DNA between two or more species, the less time has elapsed since their divergence from a common ancestor. Thus, anthropologists study DNA sequences to estimate how long ago the species separated.

Through fossil analysis, DNA sequence comparisons, and other methods, the outlines of human evolution are becoming clear. Most scholars agree that the evolutionary line leading to modern humans split from the lines leading to modern African apes (chimpanzees and gorillas) at least six million years ago. (See A Closer Look for an overview of basic facts and the latest findings on human biological evolution.)

Most biological anthropologists work in universities or museums as teachers, researchers, writers, and curators. But many also apply their knowledge of human anatomy to solve modern problems. For instance, specialists in **forensic anthropology** work for or consult with law enforcement agencies, where they help identify human skeletal remains. Among their contributions are determining the age, sex, height, and other physical characteristics of crime or accident victims. Forensic anthropologists gather evidence from bones about old injuries or diseases, which are then compared with medical histories to identify victims. For example, forensic anthropologist Clyde Snow disinterred the bones of some of the northern Iraqi Kurds killed by Saddam Hussein's government in the late 1980s. In the 1990s, teams of forensic anthropologists exhumed remains from graves in Bolivia, Guatemala, El Salvador, and Haiti to identify victims of political assassination and determine the causes of their deaths.

Cultural Anthropology

Cultural anthropology (also called **social anthropology, sociocultural anthropology,** and **ethnology**) is the study of contemporary and historically recent human societies and cultures. As its name suggests, the main focus of this subfield is culture—the customs and beliefs of some human group. (The concept of culture is discussed at length in Chapter 2.)

As we'll see in future chapters, cultural anthropologists study an enormous number of specific subjects,

In his 1871 book, *The Descent of Man*, the British naturalist Charles Darwin proposed that humans and African apes (chimpanzees and gorillas) are closely related. Noting the anatomical similarities between humans and apes, Darwin argued that humans must have evolved from an apelike ancestor over eons of time. In his day, there was little evidence in the form of fossils that directly connected apes to humans, but Darwin realized that the many physical similarities among humans, chimps, and gorillas can best be explained by a common biological ancestry.

By the early 1900s, most scientists accepted Darwin's general theory of biological evolution as well as his specific hypothesis about the close relationship between humans and apes. In the twentieth century, biological anthropologists and archaeologists discovered thousands of fossils that confirmed the evolution of humanity out of an apelike ancestor. Before summarizing this evidence, we first describe briefly how scientists classify living organisms using the methods of taxonomy.

Even in Darwin's day, taxonomists recognized the similarity between African apes and humans. Both are classified in the same taxonomic superfamily (Hominoidea), though in different families (Pongidae for apes, Hominidae for humans). Below the family level, modern humans are classified in the genus *Homo* and in the species *sapiens*. Thus, you and I are *Homo sapiens;* the common chimpanzee is *Pan troglodytes;* the mountain gorilla is *Gorilla gorilla*. Generally, the criterion used to decide whether two very similar animals are in the same species is whether they mate and produce fertile offspring under natural conditions. All humans can do so.

Assigning an extinct animal known only from fossils to a species, or even to a genus, is often difficult. In human evolution, there are many ambiguities and uncertainties, many of which center around whether a particular fossil is or is not a direct ancestor of humans: for example, is a newly discovered bone or tooth one of a hominid, and, if so, was it a *Homo*, and, if so, to which species did it belong? These uncertainties are inherent in the fossil record; they are not, as some believe, "proof" that those who study human evolution are "just speculating."

Human Biological Evolution

Throughout the twentieth century, an enormous amount of evidence accumulated about the biological evolution of modern humans from an apelike ancestor over several millions of years. Below are some of the major general findings.

1. People did not evolve from chimpanzees or gorillas. Although these African apes are indeed our closest relatives in the primate family, humans did not evolve from them. Rather, modern humans and modern apes share a common ancestor that lived in Africa sometime between about five and eight million years ago. Metaphorically speaking, the living apes are our cousins, not our evolutionary grandparents. Your ancestors were not chimpanzees.

2. There is no longer a missing link. The term *missing link* used to refer to a fossil that is transitional between ape and human, combining some ape features with some human features. In Darwin's day, no such intermediate fossil had yet been discovered. Even today, some people who deny that humans evolved from some other life-form erroneously believe there is no fossil that directly connects *Homo sapiens* to an apelike ancestor. But, in fact, the first fossil link between apes and humans was discovered in South Africa back in the 1920s. Named *Australopithecus africanus,* its skull was much like that of an ape, but it walked bipedally (on two legs rather than four). Future discoveries showed that its pelvis, legs, and feet were much like those of modern humans. Later, paleoanthropologists found literally thousands of fossils linking *Homo sapiens* to apelike ancestors, representing hundreds of individuals who were hominids of one type or another. Today debate centers largely on how these hominids are related to one another and on which particular remains are directly ancestral to humans.

3. The main difference between apes and humans is bipedal locomotion. Most people think that brain size and intelligence are the main differences between humans and other animals. Certainly, the size of the brain distinguishes people and apes—a chimpanzee's cranial capacity averages around

far too many to list here. Here are some of their overall objectives:

- Study firsthand and report about the ways of living of particular human groups
- Compare diverse cultures in the search for general principles that might explain human ways of living
- Understand how various dimensions of human life—economics, family life, religion, art, communication,

and so forth—relate to one another in particular cultures and in cultures generally
- Analyze the causes and consequences of cultural change
- Enhance public understanding and appreciation of cultural differences and multicultural diversity

This last objective is especially important in the contemporary world, in which individuals with diverse cultural

400 cubic centimeters, a gorilla's around 500, and a human's around 1,300. And people are, in many ways, "smarter" than apes—humans use more sophisticated tools, speak complex languages, solve abstract problems, drastically modify their environments, and so forth. But the first change that began to split the evolutionary line leading to modern apes from the line leading to modern humans was not brain size, but the form of locomotion—human ancestors walked on two legs millions of years before their brains increased notably in size. Thus, evolutionarily speaking, it was bipedalism that set humanity on a different evolutionary path from modern apes. In fact, when biological anthropologists judge whether a disputed fossil fragment is or is not from a hominid, their main criterion is whether the fossil remains suggest that the animal regularly walked on two legs, not the size of its brain.

4. Nonhuman primates also make and use tools. Until the mid-twentieth century, scholars often said that tool use distinguished people from other primates. But others noted that many other animals also use objects as tools (e.g., sea otters use stones to break open abalone shells to get at the meat inside). Then some scholars claimed that humans are the only creatures to actually manufacture tools, meaning that only humans modify a natural object (a stone, a stick) into a particular shape to make it more useful. This too proved to be a misconception when, in the 1960s, Jane Goodall observed chimpanzees modifying sticks to make termite probes and using leaves to soak up water from hollow trees. Since then, other examples of toolmaking have been observed among chimps and even gorillas. So, toolmaking is not a uniquely human trait, although of course only humans are capable of taking technology to its more complex forms.

5. Humans are the most advanced or most evolved species. Actually, phrases like *most evolved* have little objective meaning in modern evolutionary science. Biologists and physical anthropologists speak of *differences* between species (such as between monkeys and apes and between apes and humans), but to speak of one species being more advanced than another involves value judgments. We can only say that humans and

apes evolved differently, depending on the specific kinds of pressures they encountered in their history, but we should not say that humans are more evolved.

Some Hominid Fossils and Dates

The first discovery of a fossil recognized as an early form of human occurred in 1856. In Germany's Neander Valley, quarry workers accidentally unearthed the first bones of the hominid that later was called Neanderthal Man. At the time, no one realized their significance, and there was debate about whether they came from a deformed European with a projecting face or whether they were human at all. Later, Neanderthal fossils were found in both Ice Age Europe and western Asia, along with convincing evidence that Neanderthals made stone tools, hunted large mammals, built shelters, used fire, and buried their dead. By the mid-twentieth century, many scientists thought that Neanderthal was our direct ancestor. (Perhaps it was comforting to think that modern humans evolved in Europe or in the Middle East.) By the late twentieth century, though, both fossil evidence and DNA comparisons demonstrated fairly clearly that *Homo neanderthalensis* is not a direct human ancestor but an offshoot that lived between 500,000 and 30,000 years ago.

Until the 1970s, most scholars thought that human evolution was essentially *linear;* that is, one hominid species arose from its ancestor, which quickly became extinct, perhaps because it could not compete. Linear evolution means that only one or, at most, two hominid species lived at the same time. In this view, an evolutionary line led from an apelike creature through various transitional forms (the "links" that people used to say were "missing") to modern humans.

For example, most researchers thought that two million years ago only two hominids coexisted, both found only in Africa. Both were members of the genus called *Australopithecus,* which at the time seemed to be the probable link between extinct apes and modern humans. The chimpanzee-sized *Australopithecus africanus* was mainly a meat-eater and eventually evolved into modern humans. The somewhat larger *Australopithecus robustus* was mainly a vegetarian and an

backgrounds regularly come into contact with one another in our emerging global society.

To some people, studies of other cultures seem esoteric—"interesting but of little practical value," they often say. Most anthropologists disagree. We think that what we learn by our descriptions, comparisons, and analyses of cultures helps to improve the human condition. We believe that our studies of other cultures will

help us understand our own way of life. And, as we shall see later, specific studies carried out by cultural anthropologists have helped solve practical problems in real human communities.

To collect information about particular cultures, ethnologists conduct **fieldwork.** Fieldworkers ordinarily move into the community under study so that they can live in close contact with the people. If practical, they evolutionary dead end that left no modern descendants. Both were considered hominids because both were bipedal. *Australopithecus africanus* was sometimes known as the "killer ape" because it was a predator, so killing animals for food was one of the things that began to differentiate hominids from pongids. Or this is what most paleoanthropologists believed.

Today, it is fairly well established that the human family tree is not linear but has *multiple branches;* that is, several species of early hominids existed at the same time, with most ending in extinction. Metaphorically, modern humans are but a small twig on the evolutionary tree of life. Discoveries since the 1970s have dramatically altered the linear view of the past, and today far more hominids are identified. The major issues are how they are related to African apes, to one another, and to modern *Homo sapiens.*

Many paleoanthropologists believe that the first hominid, living between about five and six million years ago in what is now Ethiopia, was *Ardipithecus. Ardipithecus* most likely was bipedal but resembled apes in most other features of the skeleton, skull, and teeth. A later form, *Australopithecus afarensis* (also known as Lucy) lived between about three and four million years ago. Lucy is most simply described as a hominid with an apelike head and humanlike limbs. Bones and teeth from about 300 individuals show pretty conclusively that Lucy's species was bipedal. In April 2006, paleoanthropologists published new information about the 4.2-million-year-old *Australopithicus anamensis* from Ethiopia, which many believe is the most likely link between *Ardipithecus* and *afarensis.*

Between about two and three million years ago, there were three or four hominids living at roughly the same time. One of them, *Homo habilis* (apparently the first hominid to make chopping tools out of stone), arose earlier than two million years ago and seems to have diversified. One of its several forms became a new species, *Homo erectus*, about two million years ago. So far as we know at present, *Homo erectus* was the first hominid that left Africa. Walking upright, *Homo erectus*

was in Georgia (the modern Asian nation bordering Turkey) by 1.8 million years ago. It migrated as far away from Africa as Indonesia (when first discovered, it was called Java Man) and China ("Peking Man"). Although its brain size averaged only about 900–1,000 cubic centimeters, *Homo erectus* was almost as tall as modern people and had a low forehead, prominent brow ridges, and a large but recognizably human face. This early form of humanity made sharp stone tools, butchered animals, and probably controlled fire.

In East Africa, some local populations of *Homo erectus* evolved into archaic *Homo sapiens* around 200,000 years ago. (*Archaic* is used to emphasize that there was great variety in the earliest *Homo sapiens* populations, with *Homo neanderthalensis* probably arising out of one form.) Evidence reported in early 2007 suggests that modern humans remained only in Africa until as recently as 60,000 years ago. By 50,000 to 45,000 years ago, modern humanity had moved into tropical southern Asia and reached Australia, presumably becoming the ancestral population of the indigenous people of Australia, the aborigines. If any local populations of *Homo erectus* were left in eastern and southeastern Asia, they were replaced by *Homo sapiens.* Somewhere around 40,000 years ago, *Homo sapiens* migrated into temperate Europe. From Siberia, people crossed the Bering Strait (then dry land because of the lower sea levels of the Ice Age) into the Americas, probably by 20,000 years ago. By 12,000 years ago, human beings had migrated to every landmass on Earth except Antarctica and the remote islands of the Pacific.

Notice how rapidly our species migrated to and colonized vast regions once we left our African homelands. In only about 50,000 years, humanity was found almost everywhere. Most scholars think that our remarkable success in colonizing new regions was due to a combination of our technological prowess, our ability to communicate complex messages through language, and the transmission of new ideas and behaviors to new generations through social learning—that is, through learning the culture of previous generations (see Chapter 2).

communicate in the local language. Daily interaction with the members of a community provides anthropologists with firsthand experiences that yield insights and information that could not be gained in any other way. Fieldworkers usually report the findings of their research in books or scholarly journals, where they are available to other scholars and to the general public. A written account of how a single human population lives is called an **ethnography,** which means "writing about

a people." (We have more to say about fieldwork in Chapter 5.)

Anthropological Linguistics

Defined as the study of human language, linguistics is a field all its own, existing as a separate discipline from anthropology. Linguists describe and analyze the sound patterns and combinations, words, meanings, and sen-

The relationship between early *Homo sapiens* and Neanderthals remains debatable. Some say that Neanderthals disappeared soon after the appearance of modern humans, with the last population surviving in Gibraltar until 28,000 years ago. Some studies comparing *Homo sapiens* and Neanderthal DNA suggest that modern humans once interbred with Neanderthals, but the evidence for interbreeding was challenged in 2007. It looks more and more like Neanderthals died out after modern humans moved into the regions Neanderthals once had all to themselves. DNA studies published in 2007 indicate, however, that sometime after migrating into northern Europe, Neanderthal was the first hominid to have light skin and red hair.

In 2004, the discovery of a tiny hominid on the Indonesian island of Flores caused a stir among paleoanthropologists. The first specimen was estimated to be around 18,000 years old and stood about 3½ feet tall. The international team that discovered it nicknamed it "The Hobbit," to the delight of the media. The team claimed that the hominid was a new human species, which they named *Homo floresiensis*. Soon other specialists disputed that the Hobbit was a new form of human, claiming instead that it was similar to nearby "pygmy" peoples and that it had a small brain (about 350 cubic centimeters versus about 1,300 for modern humans) because of the genetic disorder called microcephaly. Then, in 2005, seven more adults were described, along with a child's leg and arm bones, dating between about 74,000 and 12,000 years ago. This find supports the notion that *Homo floresiensis* was a distinct, and new, hominid that survived in isolation even after modern people had colonized most of the islands around it. But, for now, whether Hobbits were truly different from us is debatable.

Even more recently, in August 2007, a research team reported on two new fossils found near Lake Turkana, Kenya. One was a new *Homo habilis*, dating to 1.44 million years ago, later than all previously known *habilis* fossils. The other was a new fossil of *Homo erectus*, dating to 1.55 million years ago. If these discoveries and dates withstand the scrutiny of other researchers, then the two species coexisted in East Africa for several hundred thousand years. Most anthropologists had earlier thought *habilis* had simply evolved into *erectus*. The new findings suggest that the two species have a common ancestor, whose identity is presently unknown. It seems that the more we discover, the more complicated the evolutionary history of humanity becomes.

What Does All This Have to Do with You and Me?

What relevance does the evolutionary history of humanity hold for modern humanity—for humans as we are today? If evolution is accepted, then the characteristics of a living species are a product of the forces that shaped it in its past. So the way modern people are—human nature, some call it—might be more understandable if we can reconstruct our evolutionary past. For instance, many popular writers have claimed that humans are naturally aggressive, either because evolving into predators made us fierce or because our ancestors competed for resources so that early hominids had to fight to defend their territories. As evidence for their views, such writers cite research that allegedly showed that australopithecines were "killer apes," that *Homo erectus* ate their own kind, that Neanderthals made weapons used in violent encounters, and so forth. Modern humans are prone to violence and warfare because evolution made us this way, some claim. Implicit in the argument is that violence and warfare are so difficult to control because they are part of our genetic heritage.

Such arguments are not necessarily wrong, but the evidence about human evolution is subject to many interpretations. That humans evolved from apelike ancestors is practically indisputable, but researchers differ on details of the process. For example: Which early hominid is *the* earliest? Were the australopithecines our ancestors or just an evolutionary branch that died out? What are the details of how various ancient hominids are related to one another and to us? There are no generally accepted answers to such questions. Particular biological

tence structures of human languages. The ability to communicate complex messages with great efficiency may be the most important capability of humans that makes us different from primates and other animals. Certainly our ability to speak is a key factor in the evolutionary success of humans.

Cultural anthropologists are interested in language because of how the language and culture of a people affect each other. The subfield of **anthropological linguistics** is concerned with the complex relationships between language and other aspects of human behavior and thought. For example, anthropological linguists are interested in how language is used in various social contexts: What style of speech must one use with people of high status? Does the particular language we learned while growing up have any important effects on how we view the world anthropologists have their own opinions and publish them. Then others support or attempt to refute those ideas based on their views of what the evidence shows or, sometimes, based on their own biases or previous statements. If the interpretations of human *physical* evolution are contentious, then think about the uncertainties involved in trying to reconstruct the *behavior* (e.g., aggression) of an ancestor.

Some people, of course, do not accept evolution at all, and they especially do not accept the notion that humans evolved from any other so-called lower form of life. Those few who bother to read the scientific literature on human evolution misinterpret the many disagreements and contentious issues. "See," such skeptics often say, "those evolutionists can't even agree among themselves. Why should we believe them when they don't even believe one another?" But, fundamentally, evolutionists *do* believe one another. They disagree only on specific details and particular issues. They do not disagree on the fact that humans and apes shared a common ancestor some millions of years ago. Scholarly disagreement indicates that scholars are considering evidence and coming to different conclusions. It does not mean that the scholars are making things up. Indeed, it means only two very obvious things: The fossil record is incomplete and fragmentary, and bones do not speak for themselves.

Sources: Goebel (2007); Jurmain et al. (2008); Lalueza-Fox et al. (2007); Lordkipanidze et al. (2007); Moorwood et al. (2005); Spoor et al. (2007); Trinkhaus (2007); White et al. (2006); Wood (2002); Wood and Richmond (2002)

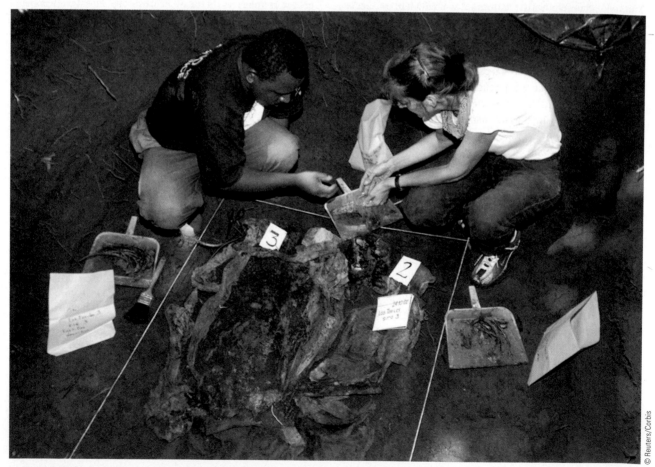

▲ Forensic anthropologists work with governments and international organizations to identify human skeletal remains and to help determine the causes of death. These forensic specialists are examining remains in El Salvador.

or how we think and feel? (Chapter 3 provides more information about language and social life.)

Applied Anthropology

In the past, most professional anthropologists spent their careers in some form of educational institution, either in colleges and universities or in museums. However, since about 1990, roughly half of those earning an anthropology Ph.D. have acquired jobs in some federal, state, or local governmental agency or in the private sector. Thousands of anthropologists now hold full-time positions that allow them to apply their expertise in governmental agencies, nonprofit groups, private corporations, and international bodies. Hundreds of others make their living as consultants to such organizations and institutions.

Applied anthropology uses anthropological methods, theories, concepts, and insights to help public institutions or private enterprises deal with practical, real-world problems. (A related area is sometimes called **practicing anthropology,** which includes professional anthropologists who hold jobs outside universities or other educational institutions.) Applied anthropology is generally seen as a fifth subfield of anthropology, but note that all applied anthropologists have been trained in one or more of the traditional four fields. In a sense, applied anthropology cuts across the other subfields and individuals in all subfields may also do applied work—that is, work that contributes directly to problem solving in an organization.

We discuss some of the ways applied anthropologists have contributed to the alleviation of human problems in later chapters. For now, a few examples illustrate some of the work they do.

Development anthropology is one area in which anthropologists apply their expertise to the solution of practical human problems, usually in the Third World. Working both as full-time employees and as consultants, development anthropologists provide information about communities that helps agencies adapt projects to local conditions and needs. Examples of agencies and institutions that employ development anthropologists include the U.S. Agency for International Development, the Rockefeller and Ford Foundations, the World Bank, and the United Nations Development Program. One important role of the anthropologist in such institutions is to provide policymakers with knowledge of local-level ecological and cultural conditions, so that projects will avoid unanticipated problems and minimize negative impacts.

Educational anthropology offers jobs in public agencies and private institutions. Some roles of educational anthropologists include advising in bilingual education, conducting detailed observations of classroom interactions, training personnel in multicultural issues, and adapting teaching styles to local customs and needs. Many modern nations, including those of Europe and the Americas, are becoming more culturally diverse due to immigration. As a response to this trend, an increasingly important role for educational anthropologists working in North America is to help professional educators understand the learning styles and behavior of children from various ethnic and national backgrounds.

Private companies sometimes employ cultural anthropologists full time or as consultants, creating a professional opportunity often called *corporate anthropology.* As globalization removes tariffs, quotas, and other barriers to international trade, people of different cultural heritages increasingly conduct business and buy and sell one another's products. The dramatic growth of overseas business activities encourages North American companies to hire professionals who can advise executives and sales staff on what to expect and how to speak and act when they conduct business in other countries. Because of their training as acute observers and listeners, anthropologists also work in the private sector in many other capacities: They watch how employees interact with one another, analyze how workers understand the capabilities of office machines, study how the attitudes and styles of managers affect worker performance, and perform a variety of other information-gathering and analysis tasks.

One growing field is **medical anthropology.** Medical anthropologists investigate the complex interactions among human health, nutrition, social environment, and cultural beliefs and practices. Because the transmission of viruses and bacteria is strongly influenced by people's diets, sanitation, sexual habits, and other behaviors, many medical anthropologists work as a team with epidemiologists to identify cultural practices that affect the spread of disease. Different cultures have different ideas about the causes and symptoms of disease, how best to treat illnesses, the abilities of traditional healers and doctors, and the importance of community involvement in the healing process. By studying how a human community perceives such things, medical anthropologists help hospitals and other agencies deliver health care services more effectively. Most medical anthropologists are ethnologists, but biological anthropologists also study disease patterns and how particular groups adapt to the presence of diseases, such as malaria and sleeping sickness. Language and communication also are important influences on health care delivery, so people trained in linguistic anthropology sometimes work in medical anthropology.

Applied anthropology is usually considered a separate subfield, but as the above examples show, those who do applied work are also educated in one or more of the other four subdisciplines. Speaking broadly, anthropologists are valuable to governments, international agencies, companies, and other organizations because they are trained to do two things very well: first, to observe, record, and analyze human behavior in very diverse settings; and, second, to look for and understand the cultural assumptions, values, and beliefs that underlie that behavior.

Careers in Anthropology

People who earn doctoral degrees in anthropology have a wealth of career options, as the preceding discussion shows. What are the opportunities for those with an undergraduate degree in anthropology? The following are a few of the many websites that describe the opportunities available.

- The American Anthropological Association (www .aaanet.org/careersbroch.htm) provides an excellent overview of the general kinds of jobs that can be pursued by people with a bachelor's degree.
- Brigham Young University's Anthropology Department (http://fhss.byu.edu/anthro) divides career paths into education, professional, nonprofits, government, private sector, and academic. Although designed with BYU students in mind, it provides specifics, including the general kinds of nonanthropology courses that students can take to increase their job prospects.
- The National Association for the Practice of Anthropology (www.practicinganthropology.org/employment/) posts a listing of current jobs for which anthropologists qualify. You can post your own resume for potential employers.
- For archaeology, the American Cultural Resources Association (www.acra-crm.org) lists jobs currently available in cultural resource management. The site also lists the names of firms engaged in CRM along with their URLs. This is an excellent site for students interested in CRM.

Generally speaking, in addition to learning to write, analyze, and think critically, students who study cultural anthropology are prepared to examine human life from many alternative perspectives, to study interactions between individuals and groups objectively and insightfully, to adjust to various social situations, to fit into diverse communities by respecting their ways of life, and to be sensitive to the multitude of differences between the world's peoples. Of course, along the way most students master other skills, such as statistical analysis or foreign languages, that demonstrate ability and establish credentials for a variety of career paths.

Cultural Anthropology Today

As our brief summary of the five subdisciplines confirms, anthropology is indeed a diverse field. Even by itself, cultural anthropology—the main subject of this text—is enormously broad: modern fieldworkers live among and study human communities in all parts of the world, from the mountains of Tibet to the deserts of the American Southwest, from the streets of Chicago to the plains of East Africa.

In the popular imagination, fieldworkers go to far-off places to study "native" peoples. Except for some common but mistaken stereotypes about "natives," this image was reasonably accurate until the 1970s. Until then, ethnology differed from sociology and other disciplines that studied living peoples mainly by the kinds of cultures ethnologists studied. Cultural anthropologists focused on small-scale, non-Western, preindustrial, subsistence-oriented cultures, whereas sociologists tended to study large Euro-American, industrial, money-and-market countries. Not too long ago, many cultural anthropologists sought untouched tribal cultures to study because living among the "primitives" usually enhanced one's reputation.

Today all this has changed. You are about as likely to find an anthropological fieldworker studying a Canadian medical clinic as a New Guinea village. A few subjects of recent studies in modern settings include American bodybuilders, the cultural significance of Elvis, British witches' covens, homeless persons, Appalachian towns, New Jersey fraternities, courts of law, the decline of the middle class, the U.S. Congress, and family life in Silicon Valley. In the early twenty-first century, anthropologists have published professional articles with titles such as "The Virtual Nuclear Weapons Laboratory in the New World Order." Book titles include *Junkie Business: The Evolution and Operation of a Heroin Dealing Network* (Lee Hofer, 2006) and *Behind the Gates: Life, Security, and the Pursuit of Happiness in Fortress America* (Setha Low, 2003). As these examples illustrate, cultural anthropologists are increasingly working "here at home" rather than far away.

Some studies done in the anthropologist's own country are of immigrant communities. North America—correctly said to be the continent of immigrants—includes people of diverse origins. Some immigrants become largely or partly assimilated: over a period of decades or generations they adopt many of the customs and beliefs of the so-called mainstream. In other cases, though, there is considerable cultural continuity with the past—immigrants continue their language, cuisine, family relations, wedding and funeral customs, and other practices and beliefs. For example, the U.S. government relocated thousands of Hmong, a people of highland Southeast Asia, into the Central Valley of California. Even after two or three decades of living in the United States, many immigrant Hmong still speak little English, bring large numbers of relatives to live with them in houses other Americans consider "single-family" dwellings, use their traditional methods of curing, and occasionally eat animals that Americans define as pets. Many people with Chinese, Japanese, Korean and, more recently, South Asian heritage maintain some traditions of their ancestral homelands to a surprising degree.

Even many anthropologists who work "far away" now conduct fieldwork in more than one place. This is largely because of the effects of **globalization**—the intermixing and migrations of peoples with diverse homelands, the multinational reach of communications media, the movement of production and services to overseas locales, the increase in international travel and tourism, and so forth. If an anthropologist wants to study "a people" and "their culture" in the world today, it is increasingly necessary to study them in all the places on our planet where they now live. Globalization itself is one of the most important areas of research in cultural anthropology. What are its impacts on people of all nations? Is a global megaculture developing that will someday make all humanity pretty much alike? (The Globalization box gives a first look at this topic, which runs throughout this book.)

As anthropologists have moved beyond their traditional focus on peoples of long ago and far away, the boundaries between cultural anthropology and other disciplines (especially sociology) are less clear-cut than they were even a few years ago. Most anthropological work, though, is still done in relatively small communities (on the order of a few hundred to a few thousand), where the researcher can interact directly with people and experience their lives firsthand. More than any other single factor, the intense fieldwork experience distinguishes cultural anthropology from other disciplines concerned with humankind. Also, cultural anthropology remains far more comparative and global in its scope and interests than the other social sciences and humanities. Even today, ethnologists are far more likely to conduct research in a country other than their own than are sociologists or psychologists.

Understanding Human Cultures: Anthropological Approaches

The main difference between anthropology and other social sciences and humanities is not so much the *kinds* of subjects anthropologists investigate as the *approaches* we take to studying human life. We believe it is important to study cultures and communities holistically, comparatively, and relativistically. Because it is these perspectives that make cultural anthropology distinctive, they need to be introduced.

Holistic Perspective

To study a subject holistically is to attempt to understand all the factors that influence it and to interpret it in the context of all those factors. The **holistic perspective** means that no single aspect of a human culture can be understood unless its relationships to other aspects of the culture are explored. Holism requires, for example, that a fieldworker studying the rituals of a people must investigate how those rituals are influenced by the people's family life, economic forces, political leadership, relationships between the sexes, and a host of other factors. The attempt to understand a community's customs, beliefs, values, and so forth holistically is one reason ethnographic fieldwork takes so much time and involves close contact with people.

Taken literally, a holistic understanding of a people's customs and beliefs is probably not possible because of the complexity of human societies. But cultural anthropologists have learned that ignoring the interrelationships among language, religion, art, economy, family, and other dimensions of life results in distortions and misunderstandings. The essence of the holistic perspective may be stated fairly simply: *Look for connections and interrelationships, and try to understand parts in the context of the whole.*

Comparative Perspective

Until the 1970s, anthropologists focused mainly on non-Western peoples, many of whom thought and acted quite differently from the citizens of the anthropologists' own nation. Anthropologists knew that the ideas and concepts they learned from their own upbringing and experience often did not apply to other peoples, whose cultural traditions were vastly different.

More than most people, anthropologists are aware of the diversity of the world's cultures. This diversity means that any general theories or ideas scholars might have about humans—about human nature, sexuality, warfare, family relationships, and so on—must take into account information from a wide range of societies. In other words, general theoretical ideas about humans or human societies or cultures must be investigated from a **comparative perspective.**

Globalization is one of those words that appear daily in the news media. The word means that the diverse nations and peoples of the world are increasingly interconnected by communication technologies, commercial relationships, political interests and conflicts, short-term travel and long-term immigration, and other forces. The Internet and mobile phones link people together to an unprecedented degree, facilitating the flow of information, ideas, and messages across national boundaries. The political impacts could be revolutionary, a fact recognized by the government of the People's Republic of China as it tries to control its citizens' access to websites. Huge container ships and lowered costs of sea transportation move billions of dollars worth of products across the Pacific, allowing North American consumers to benefit from the low labor costs of China and other nations when they shop at Wal-Mart, Toys"R"Us, and other stores. More people migrate between nations than ever before, which affects their home countries as well as those to which they relocate.

Of course, the mere fact of interconnectedness between world regions is not new. The ancient Silk Road linked China to Rome, the two greatest empires of 2,000 years ago. Along it flowed not just silk and precious metals, but ideas and inventions as well (the latter mostly from China to Europe). Islamic traders from Arabia proselytized their religion into both coasts of Africa as well as into much of the area that we know today as Southeast Asia. In the Americas, too, the Inca Empire stretched over most of western South America, and its runners/messengers carried commands from the Inca ruler to all parts of the world over which he ruled. These and other empires were far-reaching, but they were not truly global—neither communications nor transportation technologies were efficient enough to link most of the world's people to the major centers of global wealth and influence. And, until after Columbus's voyages in the 1490s, the peoples and cultures of the New and Old Worlds were mostly isolated from one another.

After Columbus, Europeans learned that they had contacted a world that was new to them, rather than discovering the alternative route to Asia that the Spanish monarchy had commissioned Columbus to find. In about 1500, vast quantities of gold and silver began to flow from the Americas to Europe, either looted from the Incas and Aztecs or mined with the labor of the "Indians." By three centuries later, millions of enslaved West Africans were working on the plantations of the American South, the Caribbean, and eastern South America. In the 1600s and 1700s, well-off Europeans developed a taste for the sugar, tobacco, and coffee from the Americas that the slaves produced for them. By the 1800s, African slaves in the American South were producing vast quantities of cotton fibers for Europe's Industrial Revolution, which was based on steam-powered looms for weaving clothing. The white owners of the large plantations became wealthy selling the products produced by "their" slaves, but the owners of clothing factories in the North also profited, as did those who wore the clothes.

During these same centuries, the European overseas trade with the East for spices, tea, silk, and porcelain brought India, China, and eventually the rest of Asia into world markets and ultimately into world conflicts. Catholic and Protestant missionaries usually accompanied or followed the contacts made to trade and build empires, further spreading the ideas and values of the West into other continents. For 500 years, then, various representatives of Western civilization have engaged other continents, incorporating most non-Western peoples into a larger, worldwide system. (As we discuss further in Chapter 4, anthropology itself grew out of the encounter of Western civilization with other continents and other peoples.)

The main reason anthropologists insist on comparison is simple: Many people mistakenly think that the customs and beliefs familiar to them exist among people everywhere, which is usually not the case. Anthropologists believe that the cultural ideas and practices of people living in different times and places are far too diverse for any general theory to be accepted until it has been investigated and tested in a wide range of human groups. The comparative perspective that anthropologists use to investigate their ideas may be stated as: *Do not make generalizations about humans without considering the full range of cultural diversity.*

Relativistic Perspective

Fundamentally, **cultural relativism** means that no culture—taken as a whole—is inherently superior or inferior to any other. Anthropologists adopt this perspective because concepts such as superiority require judgments about the relative worthiness of behaviors, beliefs, and other characteristics of a culture. Such judgments are usually rooted in one's own values, however, which, by and large, depend on the culture in which one was raised. (If you think there must be universal standards for judging cultures, you may be right. However, aside from such actions as homicide, people don't agree on what they are.)

Noting the half-millennium of such contacts between diverse peoples, some say there is nothing new about globalization. If globalization is only about the existence of "contacts between peoples" and "global interconnections," they are correct. But both the degree and the nature of contacts and interconnections are different in the twenty-first century. By *degree,* we mean that the intensity and importance of contacts and interconnections have increased dramatically in the past several decades; today the lives of more people are affected and are affected more thoroughly than, say, 50 years ago. By *nature,* we mean that the ways in which the world's peoples are interconnected are different than in the past. Two differences are especially important, each considered in more detail in later chapters.

First, the division of economic activities between nations and regions has changed. Until the mid-twentieth century, some nations and regions produced mainly food, metals, lumber, and other raw materials in plantations, mines, and forests. Generally, these nations and regions were known as "underdeveloped" or "Third World." The more industrialized, and mostly wealthier, countries bought most of these relatively low-value products, which their factories and laborers then turned into higher-valued, profit making products. Today, industrial production itself is increasingly globalized: in Latin America, Asia, and other regions, hundreds of millions of people now work in factories producing commodities for sale in international markets. More than ever before, there is an international market for labor, meaning that the industrial laborers of the countries we used to call "underdeveloped" are competing with the labor force of the "developed" countries. Whole industries have relocated. For example, the American textile industry has almost disappeared, its factories replaced by those in China, Indonesia, and other countries with far cheaper labor. Other industries that have moved offshore are toys, shoes, and consumer electronics. Some say that the globalization of factory production is leading to the decline of incomes among middle-class families and is largely responsible for the growing disparity of income and wealth between the rich and everyone else.

Second, things like DVDs, international migration, overseas travel, and the Internet have fostered increasing two-way cultural exchanges. Most people think that the media—an important carrier of music, tastes, styles, foods, ideas, beliefs, and the like—is rapidly transmitting the "culture" of the West to the rest of the world. A primary concern is that the North American and European culture (the "West") will erode and eventually destroy local traditions. We take up this and other issues about globalization in future chapters.

So, although the existence of interconnections among peoples and nations is not new, the impact of these connections on all peoples and nations and the way these interconnections work have changed in the last few decades. In the remainder of this book, we discuss globalization in boxes like this one as well as in the main body of the text itself. We emphasize the effects of globalization on all nations and regions, and not just how people like "Us" are affecting people like "Them," or how "They" threaten "Us."

Critical Thinking Questions

1. Being as specific as you can, how has globalization affected you personally?

2. In the future, will the "Us/Them" distinction be more difficult to make?

To see why a relativistic approach to studying cultures is important, contrast cultural relativism with ethnocentrism. **Ethnocentrism** is the belief that the moral standards, manners, attitudes, and so forth of one's own culture are superior to those of other cultures. Most people are ethnocentric, and a *certain degree* of ethnocentrism is probably essential if people are to experience the sense of belonging necessary for contentment and if their culture is to persist. Mild ethnocentrism—in which people are committed to certain values but don't insist that everyone else hold and live by those values—is unobjectionable and inevitable. But extreme ethnocentrism—in which people believe that their values are the only correct ones and that all people everywhere should be judged by how closely they live up to those values—leads to attitudes of intolerance and misunderstandings that anthropologists find objectionable.

Clearly, ethnocentric attitudes make objectivity difficult, and ethnographic fieldworkers should avoid evaluating the behavior of other people according to the standards of their own culture. Like the holistic and comparative perspectives, the essential point of cultural relativism may be stated simply: *In studying another culture, do not evaluate the behavior of its members by the standards and values of your own culture.*

Unfortunately, many people misconceive the word *relativism*. To anthropologists, relativism is a *methodological principle* that refers to an outlook that is essential for maximum objectivity and understanding when studying a people whose way of life differs from their own. As a methodological principle, relativism recognizes that behavior viewed as morally wrong (or sinful) in one society may not be wrong in another, such as polygamy or bare-breasted females. Unqualified condemnations of the actions or beliefs of some group of people have no place in anthropological research or in anthropological writings.

However, to a great many people, the term *relativism* means that "anything goes" with respect to individual behaviors. *Moral relativism* (relativism as a *moral principle*) implies that there are no absolute, universal standards by which to evaluate actions in terms such as right and wrong or good and bad.

Some people blame moral relativism for a host of social problems. In the early 2000s, many Americans worried about the morality and the long-term social effects of gay and lesbian relationships. When many gays and lesbians demanded the equal rights that they believe only marriage can grant, the legislatures of a number of states passed "defense of marriage acts" that define marriage as a relationship between a man and a woman. Others worry that society's acceptance of extramarital sex or tolerance for homosexuality erodes family values and increases divorce rates, or that the failure of public schools to inculcate patriotism and morality leads to delinquency and violence, or that the lack of public attention given to religious teachings is responsible for high crime rates. Such arguments and policies imply that there *are* absolute standards and clear rules about right and wrong or moral and immoral behavior. But moral relativism *taken to its extreme* says that there are few such standards or rules.

Newcomers to anthropology often confuse the two meanings of *relativism,* mistakenly believing that anthropologists promote both kinds of relativism. Most anthropologists are methodological relativists, but fewer are moral relativists. Anthropologists are as likely as anyone to consider oppression, slavery, murder, slander, and so forth as morally objectionable. The September 11, 2001, terrorist attack on the United States is viewed with as much horror by anthropologists as by most other people, although most of us seek to understand the historical background and sociocultural context that led to it rather than perceiving it simply as the incarnation of evil.

But the issues are not as simple in practice as the distinction between methodological and moral relativism implies. An example will illustrate. Most people have heard of the custom generally called *female circumcision* or *female genital mutilation.* The practice is widespread (but far from universal) in some regions of northern Africa. It varies in severity, ranging from removing the clitoris to stitching shut the labia until marriage. Cultural beliefs about the reasons for the custom also vary, but most often focus on controlling unmarried female sexuality and increasing a woman's desirability as a marriage partner. Further complicating the issue is that in many places a majority of older women support the custom, so it is not unambiguously an issue of male control or oppression of women. Often a girl or young woman herself considers it a symbol of her femininity and of her and her family's honor.

How should an anthropologist view this custom? Do we think of it as just another age-old tradition—like people eating with their fingers or men covering their genitals with only penis sheaths—that varies from people to people but is *inherently* neither right nor wrong? Surely not: This custom causes pain, exposes women to the dangers of infection and other complications, and is applied only to women because of their gender. In most cases, it is forced upon a girl at a certain age even if she objects. Because of its pain, danger, selectivity, and social enforcement, female circumcision is not comparable to customs surrounding food and home decoration, which vary from people to people but are generally "harmless."

Then, is female genital mutilation a form of oppression? And if so, by whom? Can culture itself oppress people? If it is oppression, does the anthropologist simply write about it, place it in its local cultural context, compare the cultures that practice it with other cultures that do not, develop an idea about its meaning and why it occurs, and then leave it alone? That is what many anthropologists believe we should do *as anthropologists*. Others disagree, believing instead that we should speak out against such practices, both as anthropologists and as human beings.

Then again, exactly what counts as "such practices"? Does eating dogs or cats or horses count? Does female footbinding in 1600s China count? Would tightly binding the waists of women in nineteenth-century Europe count? In North America, how are twenty-first-century breast augmentation or reduction, hip and thigh liposuction, face-lifts, and nose jobs different from female circumcision? Is it that they seem to be voluntary? If so, then when a North African woman consents to her circumcision, does her consent make the custom acceptable to us? And if a young North American woman feels constrained by the ideals of beauty as defined by the culture in which she grew up, is her liposuction or breast augmentation completely voluntary? Why do we hear so little about the removal of the foreskin of most American male infants, who have absolutely no choice when a physician mutilates their genitals?

Such answers are not at all obvious, which is our main point. Most anthropologists would probably be satisfied with the following solution: Relativism as a methodological principle is essential to anthropological research because it facilitates fieldwork and leads to greater objectivity. Moral relativism is a separate matter and depends largely on one's values. When an anthropologist encounters customs like female circumcision that rather clearly cause harm, then the matter becomes complex because it is difficult to remain morally neutral. In such cases, we need to examine the custom holistically to place it in its cultural context: perhaps the "victim's" perception of "harm" differs from ours, or perhaps the harm (like military casualties) is necessary to achieve some more important objective. We also need to consider comparable practices (such as breast augmentation) that might have a similar character or function within our own culture. After doing so, we might note that "we" sometimes do similar things as "them"—though we have trouble recognizing the similarity because it involves "us"—so that we need to examine ourselves when we condemn others. Such a view does not resolve the essential problem of cultural relativism, but at least it reminds us that all human groups believe and do things that some other human groups find abhorrent.

The Value of Anthropology

What insights does anthropology offer about humanity? What is the value of the information that anthropologists have gathered about the past and present of humankind? We consider these questions in future chapters. For now, we note some of the most general insights and contributions.

First, anthropology helps us understand the biological, technological, and cultural development of humanity over long time spans. Most of the reliable information available about human biological evolution, prehistoric cultures, and non-Western peoples resulted from anthropological research. This information has become part of our general storehouse of knowledge, recorded in our textbooks and taught in our schools. We easily forget that someone had to discover these facts and interpret their significance. For example, only in the late nineteenth century did most scientists accept that people are related to apes, and only in the late twentieth century did the closeness of this relationship become apparent.

Anthropology has contributed more than just data and facts. Anthropological concepts have been incorporated into the thinking of millions of people. To illustrate, in this chapter, we have used the term *culture,* confidently assuming our readers know the word and its significance. You may not know that the scientific meaning of this word, as used in the phrase *Japanese culture,* is not very old. Well into the nineteenth century, people did not fully understand the importance of the distinction between a people's culture (the *learned* beliefs and habits that made them distinctive) and their biological makeup (their *inherited* physical characteristics). Differences that we now know are caused largely or entirely by learning and upbringing were confused with differences caused by biological inheritance. Early-twentieth-century anthropologists such as Franz Boas, Alfred Kroeber, and Margaret Mead marshaled empirical evidence showing that biological differences and cultural differences are independent of each other. As this example shows, anthropologists have in fact contributed much to our knowledge of the human condition, although most people are not aware that these understandings and insights came largely from anthropology.

Another value of anthropology is that it teaches the importance of understanding and appreciating cultural diversity. Anthropology urges its students not to be ethnocentric in their attitudes toward other peoples. Cultural relativism not only is important to the objectivity of fieldworkers but also is one of the main lessons anthropology offers to the general public. Mutual respect and understanding among the world's peoples are increasingly important on our globalized planet, with its world travel, international migration, multinational businesses, and conflicts based on ethnic or religious differences. The world's problems will not be solved simply by eliminating ethnocentrism, but a relativistic outlook on cultural differences might help to alleviate some of the prejudices, misunderstandings, stereotypes, interethnic conflicts, and racism that cause so much trouble among people on all continents. Would America's reactions to the 9/11 attacks have been different if we had a better understanding of Iraq and Islam and the history of the relations between the Middle East and the West?

A related point is that anthropology helps to minimize the miscommunications that commonly arise when people from different parts of the world interact with one another. As we shall see in Chapter 2, our upbringing in a particular culture influences us in subtle ways. For instance, English people know how to interpret one another's actions on the basis of speech styles or body language, but these cues do not necessarily mean the same thing to people from different cultures. A Canadian businessperson selling products in Turkey may wonder why her host does not cut the small talk and get down to business, whereas the Turk can't figure out why the salesperson thinks they can do business before they have become better acquainted. A manager from a German firm may be unintentionally offensive when he shoves the business card of his Korean or Japanese counterpart in his pocket without carefully studying it. Anthropology teaches people to be aware of and sensitive to cultural differences—people's actions may not mean what we take them to mean, and much misunderstanding can be avoided by taking cultural differences into account in our dealings with other people.

Finally, because of its insistence on studying humanity from a comparative perspective, anthropology helps us to understand our own individual lives. By exposing you to the cultures of people living in other times and places, anthropology helps you see new things about yourself. How does your life compare to the lives of other people around the world? What assumptions do you unconsciously make about the world and other people? Do people in other cultures share the same kinds of problems, hopes, motivations, and feelings as you do? Or are individuals raised in other societies completely different? How does the overall quality of your existence—your sense of well-being and happiness, your family life, your emotional states, your feeling that life is meaningful—compare with that of people who live elsewhere? Anthropology offers the chance to compare yourself to other peoples who live in different circumstances. By studying others, anthropologists hope that people gain new perspectives on themselves.

Summary

1. The broad scope of anthropology distinguishes it from other disciplines in the social sciences and humanities. The field as a whole is concerned with all human beings of the past and present, living at all levels of technological development. Anthropology is also interested in all aspects of humanity: biology, language, technology, art, religion, and all other dimensions of human life.

2. Individual anthropologists usually specialize in one of five subdisciplines. Archaeology uses the material remains of prehistoric and historic peoples to investigate the past, focusing on the long-term technological and social changes that occurred in particular regions of the world. Biological/physical anthropology studies the biological dimensions of human beings, including nonhuman primates, the physical variations among contemporary peoples, and human evolution. Cultural anthropology is concerned with the social and cultural life of contemporary and historically recent human societies. Anthropological linguistics concentrates on the interrelationships between language and other elements of social life and culture. Finally, applied anthropology uses the concepts, methods, and theories of anthropology to solve real-world problems in such areas as development, business, education, and health care services.

3. Until around 1970, cultural anthropology concentrated on cultures known as "tribal" or "indigenous." This is not as true today, when many anthropologists conduct research in the urbanized, industrialized nations of the developed world. It is increasingly difficult to distinguish ethnology from the kindred discipline of sociology; however, firsthand, extended fieldwork in villages or relatively small towns or neighborhoods continues to be a hallmark of cultural anthropology. Also, ethnologists are far more comparative and global in their interests and research than other social scientists.

4. Cultural anthropologists approach the study of other cultures from three main perspectives. Holism is the attempt to discover and investigate the interrelationships among the customs and beliefs of a particular people. The comparative perspective means that any attempt to understand humanity or explain cultures or behaviors must include information from a wide range of human ways of life because anthropologists have learned that most customs and beliefs are products of cultural tradition and social environment, rather than of a universal human nature. Cultural relativism means that fieldworkers try to understand people's behaviors on their own terms, not those of the anthropologist's own culture. Most anthropologists consider themselves to be methodological relativists, but moral relativism is a separate, though related, matter.

5. Anthropology has practical value in the modern world. Most of the knowledge we have about human evolution, prehistoric populations, and indigenous peoples was discovered by anthropologists. Early anthropologists were instrumental in popularizing the concept of culture and in showing that cultural differences are not caused by racial differences. The value of understanding peoples of different regions and nations is another practical lesson of anthropology, one that is increasingly important as global connections intensify. The information that ethnographers have collected about alternative ways of being human allows individuals to become more aware of their own life circumstances.

Key Terms

anthropology
archaeology
prehistoric archaeology
historic archaeology
biological (physical)
  anthropology
primatology
human variation
paleoanthropology

forensic anthropology
cultural anthropology
  (social anthropology,
  sociocultural anthro-
  pology, ethnology)
fieldwork
ethnography
anthropological
  linguistics

applied anthropology
practicing anthropology
medical anthropology
globalization
holistic perspective
comparative perspective
cultural relativism
ethnocentrism

Suggested Readings

The following books are among the best introductions to the subdisciplines of anthropology:

Agar, Michael. *Language Shock: Understanding the Culture of Conversation*. New York: William Morrow, 1994.

Written in an informal style, this book is a readable first look at anthropological ideas about the relationship between language and culture.

Ervin, Alexander M. *Applied Anthropology: Tools and Perspectives for Contemporary Practice*, 2nd ed. Boston: Allyn & Bacon, 2004.

Thorough introduction to applied anthropology. Covers ethics, roles of anthropologists in policy formation and program assessment, and specific methods used in applied research.

Fagan, Brian. *People of the Earth: An Introduction to World Prehistory*. 12th ed. New York: Prentice Hall, 2006.

Comprehensive textbook written for undergraduates that covers the prehistory of all continents.

Jurmain, Robert, Lynn Kilgore, Wendy Trevathan, and Russel L. Ciochon. *An Introduction to Physical Anthropology*, 11th ed. Belmont, Calif.: Wadsworth, 2008.

A thorough introduction to primatology, human evolution, and genetic and physical variation among human populations.

Thomas, David, and Robert Kelly. *Archaeology*, 4th ed. Belmont, Calif.: Wadsworth, 2005.

Leading textbook by two eminent archaeologists. Focuses on methods rather than prehistory itself.

These three recent books are written for the general reader and cover human evolution:

Gibbons, Ann. *The First Human*. New York: Doubleday, 2006.

Describes the history of recent discoveries of hominids in Africa.

Morwood, Mike, and Penny van Oosterzee. *A New Human*. New York: HarperCollins, 2007.

Tells the story of the "Hobbit," including the political and interpersonal as well as the scientific dimensions of the discovery and interpretation.

Wade, Nicholas. *Before the Dawn*. New York: Penguin, 2006.

Comprehensive book on the last 50,000 or so years of the human past, including material on genetic adaptations, language development and diversity, the worldwide spread of humans, and the development of settled communities.

The following ethnographies are excellent for introducing the ways of life of various peoples around the world. All four are engaging.

Farrer, Claire R. *Thunder Rides a Black Horse: Mescalero Apaches and the Mythic Present.* 2nd ed. Prospect Heights, Ill.: Waveland, 1996.

Concise account of ethnographer's experience with the modern Apache. Focuses on girls' puberty ceremonies, interweaving Apache culture into the account.

Kraybill, Donald B. *The Puzzles of Amish Life.* Intercourse, Penn.: Good Books, 1990.

Focuses on how the Amish of Lancaster County, Pennsylvania, have maintained intact communities and their values by selectively using modern technologies.

Shostak, Marjorie. *Nisa: The Life and Words of a !Kung Woman.* New York: Vintage, 1983.

A fact-filled and readable biography of a woman of the !Kung (formerly called the Bushmen), a hunting and gathering people of the Kalahari desert in southern Africa.

Ward, Martha C. *Nest in the Wind.* 2nd ed. Prospect Heights, Ill.: Waveland, 1989.

A delightful account of a fieldworker's experiences and difficulties on a tropical Pacific island.

Media Resources

The Wadsworth Anthropology Resource Center
academic.cengage.com/anthropology

The Wadsworth discipline resource website that accompanies *Humanity: An Introduction to Cultural Anthropology*, Eighth Edition, includes a rich array of material, including online anthropological video clips, to help you in the study of cultural anthropology and the specific topics covered in this chapter. Other material includes a case study forum with excerpts from various Wadsworth authors, map exercises, scientist interviews, breaking news in anthropology, and links to additional useful online material. Begin by selecting Cultural Anthropology to take you to videos, research, and more. From the homepage, you may also select Applied Anthropology, which directs you to essays, glossary terms, the case study forum, and a list of internships and careers in anthropology.

2 CULTURE

Culture is the shared and learned ways of thinking, feeling, and acting found among a human society or other group. These people in Seoul, South Korea, are honoring the birthday of Buddha with prayers and gifts.

Introducing Culture

Defining Culture

   Shared . . .

      . . . Socially Learned . . .

   . . . Knowledge . . .

   . . . and Patterns of Behavior

Cultural Knowledge

   Norms

   Values

   Symbols

Classifications and Constructions of Reality

Worldviews

The Origins of Culture

Culture and Human Life

Cultural Knowledge and Individual Behavior

   Is Behavior Determined by Culture?

   Why Does Behavior Vary?

Biology and Cultural Differences

Questions addressed in this chapter

How do anthropologists define culture? How does this definition differ from other definitions of culture?

What is meant by cultural knowledge? How is it related to the behavior of individuals?

Why do most anthropologists claim that "race" is a cultural construct?

In what ways are humans dependent on the culture they acquire while growing up?

What are the relationships between biology and culture?

We hear the word *culture* almost every day. In one meaning, some people are "more cultured" than others. For example, you may think you enhance your "cultural sophistication" by going to a symphony or an art gallery. Perhaps you have heard someone complain about the "popular culture" of TV sitcoms, action movies, computer games, tongue and body piercings, and soap operas. Maybe you yourself use peoples' speech style or personal tastes as a basis for thinking that some individuals "have more culture" than others because of their ethnic identity, social class, or where they went to school.

Taken in context, these meanings of the word *culture* are fine. But anthropologists define and use the term in a different way. We want people to appreciate the full significance of culture for our understanding of humanity. In the anthropological conception, the distinction between "high culture" and "low culture" is meaningless, and it is impossible for one group of people to "have more culture" than another group.

In this chapter, we discuss the anthropological conception of culture. After giving the word a fairly precise definition, we cover some of its main elements, introducing some terms along the way. We then discuss why culture is so important to humanity. Finally, we explain the modern anthropological view of how cultural differences and physical/biological differences between human populations are related.

Introducing Culture

The Englishman E. B. Tylor was one of the founders of the field that was later to become cultural anthropology. In 1871, Tylor wrote *Primitive Culture,* in which he pulled together much of the information available about the native peoples of other lands (that is, places other than Europe). The book begins with a definition that many consider the earliest modern conception of culture. Tylor (1871, 1) wrote that culture is "that complex whole which includes knowledge, belief, art, morals, law, customs, and any other capabilities and habits acquired by man as a member of society." Notice that this definition is very broad, including almost everything about a particular people's overall way of life, from their "knowledge" to their "habits." Notice also that culture is something an individual acquires as "a member of society," meaning that people obtain their culture from growing up and living among a particular group.

Since Tylor's day, anthropologists have defined culture in hundreds of ways, although the main elements of Tylor's original conception of culture are still with us. Practically all modern definitions share certain key features. Anthropologists agree that culture:

- is learned from others while growing up in a particular human society or group
- is widely shared by the members of that society or group
- is responsible for most differences in ways of thinking and behaving that exist between human societies or groups
- is so essential in completing the psychological and social development of individuals that a person who did not learn culture would not be considered normal by other people

In brief, culture is learned, shared, largely responsible for group-level differences, and necessary to make individuals into complete persons.

Cultural anthropologists often use the term *culture* to emphasize the unique or most distinctive aspects of a people's customs and beliefs. When we speak of Japanese culture, for example, we usually mean the beliefs and customs of the Japanese that make them different from other people. How Japanese think and act differs in some ways from how North Americans, Iranians, Chinese, and Indians think and act, and the phrase *Japanese culture* concisely emphasizes these differences. So, to speak of the culture of a people is to call attention to all the things that make that people distinctive from others.

There are some things that anthropologists do *not* mean when we use the word *culture*. We do not mean that Japanese culture is better or worse than, say, French or Indian culture. We mean only that the three differ in certain identifiable ways. Anthropologists also do not mean that Japanese, French, or Indian culture is unchanging. We mean only that they remain in some ways distinct despite the changes they have experienced over the years from historical contact and globalization. Above all, anthropologists do not mean that Japanese, French, or Indian cultures are different because of the physical (biological) differences between the three peoples. We mean only that Japanese, French, and Indian children are exposed to different ways of thinking and acting as they grow up, so that they *become* Japanese, French, or Indian because of their upbringing in different social environments.

How do cultures differ? As a first look, cultures vary in their ways of thinking and ways of behaving. *Ways of thinking* means what goes on inside people's heads: how they perceive the world around them, how they feel about particular people and events, what they desire and fear, and so forth. *Ways of behaving* refers to how people commonly act: how they conduct themselves around parents and spouses, how they carry out ceremonies, what they do when they are angry or sad, and so forth. Obviously, thought and behavior are connected. How we act depends, in part, on how and what we think. In turn, the ways we think depend, in part, on how people around us behave because their behavior helps shape our thoughts.

Although ways of thinking and behaving are related, it is important to distinguish between them. To do so, we distinguish *mental* components and *behavioral* components of culture.

Culture's mental components include all the knowledge and information about the world and society that children learn while growing up. These components include attitudes about family, friends, enemies, and other people; notions of right and wrong (morality); conceptions about the proper roles of males and females; ideas about appropriate dress, hygiene, and personal ornamentation; rules about manners and etiquette; beliefs about the supernatural; standards for sexual activity; notions about the best or proper way to live (values); and perceptions of the world. The list could, of course, be expanded to include all other knowledge that the members of a society or other group have learned from previous gen-

erations. All these kinds of knowledge largely determine how the members of a culture think.

In this book, we use the phrase **cultural knowledge** to refer to the attitudes, ideas, beliefs, conceptions, rules, values, standards, perceptions, and other information stored in people's heads. There are two key points about cultural knowledge. First, ideas and beliefs are learned as a consequence of being born into and growing up among a particular group. This means that any information that people genetically inherit (such as "instincts") is not—by definition—part of culture because it is not learned. Second, an individual does not invent his or her culture. Rather, the members of any given generation are carriers of the cultural ideas and beliefs they have learned from previous generations and will pass along, with some modifications, to future generations. Some people, of course, have more influence on their culture than do others, but even very important people who are viewed as innovators are building on the cultural knowledge their group has learned from previous generations.

As for the behavioral components of culture, they include all the things people regularly do, or how they habitually act. As the terms *regularly* and *habitually* imply, members of the same culture generally adopt similar behaviors in similar situations (for example, in church, on the job, at a wedding or funeral, visiting a friend). Anthropologists are usually more interested in these regularities and habits—in what most people do most of the time in similar situations—than in the behavior of individuals. We are most concerned with **patterns of behavior.** To avoid repetition, we will use the terms *behavior(s)* and *action(s)* as synonyms for *behavioral patterns*.

Although we distinguish between the mental and the behavioral components of culture, the two are closely related and profoundly affect each other. To emphasize these interconnections, we speak of **cultural integration,** which means that the various elements of culture fit together in a more or less coherent way. Stated differently, cultural integration means that the various parts of culture are mutually interdependent. We use the phrase *cultural system* when we wish to emphasize the integration of culture.

Defining Culture

The concept of culture is so important that it is useful to have a formal definition of the term:

> The **culture** of a group consists of shared, socially learned knowledge and patterns of behavior.

For convenience, we discuss each major component of this definition separately.

Shared . . .

Culture is *collective*—it is shared by some group of people. The phrase "some group of people" is deliberately vague because the group that shares culture depends largely on our interests. The people who share a common cultural tradition may be quite numerous and geographically dispersed, as illustrated by phrases like *Western culture* and *African culture.* Although we use such phrases whenever we want to emphasize differences between Africans and Westerners, the people to whom they refer are so scattered and diverse that the term *group* has little meaning. On the other hand, the group that shares a common culture may be small. Some historic Pacific islands or Amazonian tribes, for instance, had only a couple hundred members, yet the people spoke a unique language and had distinct customs and beliefs.

Often people who share a common culture live in the same society. Although enormously difficult to define, a **society** has these characteristics:

- It is territorially defined, meaning that its members live in a contiguous physical space.
- Most members speak and/or can understand the same language, although the language may not be the language everyone learned from birth.
- Members share a sense of common identity relative to other societies, so they recognize their distinctiveness from other societies, usually because of distinctive customs and beliefs.
- Members are unified, although perhaps only temporarily and situationally, by an overarching organization that involves common activities or participation in public decisions.

The identification of a cultural tradition with a single society is sometimes convenient because it allows us to use phrases like *English culture, Chinese culture,* and *Navajo culture.* But there are many complexities.

We usually think of a modern nation as a single society, yet many cultural groupings, identities, and traditions coexist within the boundaries of most modern nations. The term **subculture** usually refers to cultural variations that exist within a single society. We are familiar with *regional subcultures.* Contrast the American states of Alabama and Connecticut, or the Canadian provinces of Quebec and British Columbia. Various *ethnic identities* live within national boundaries. Some North Americans think their countries are quite diverse, but many African

and Asian countries have dozens and dozens of languages and cultural identities because their national boundaries were drawn by Western colonial powers with little regard for tribal identities and boundaries. China recognizes more than 50 minority peoples, and some of them theoretically have traditional homelands called autonomous regions on maps.

Sometimes people extend the concept of subculture to refer to particular groups that recruit their members from the nation at large, as in phrases like *corporate cultures* or *occupational cultures* (which, technically, are subcultures). Particular religious denominations are sometimes called subcultures to emphasize contrasting worship rituals and values between churches, like Episcopalians and Southern Baptists. The word *subculture* is applied to people based on sexual orientation, as in the gay and lesbian subculture. Some people distinguish subcultures based on contrasts like rural and urban, public school and prep school, homemakers and professional women, and even male and female.

These examples show that culture is shared at various levels, which makes the concept of culture more complicated that it seems: At which level shall we speak of "a" culture or of "the" culture of people X? Generally, the words *culture* and *subculture* are useful if they contrast some group with another of the same kind—for example,

▲ By definition culture is shared by some human group, but the "group" is not always a society or nation. As this photo of Malaysian Muslims praying illustrates, the phrase *Islamic culture* does not refer to any particular society, but to the shared beliefs of people around the world who practice Islam.

West Europe/East Asia, English/French, Cherokee/Anglo, north/south, Catholic/Methodist. In most cases, the context of the discussion adequately defines the level.

The word *subculture* is often used too loosely, however. It is most useful when it points out distinctions that have many dimensions. For example, if gay subculture refers *only* to sexual orientation, then the word *subculture* is not very useful. It becomes more meaningful if it refers to broader contrasts between straights and gays in values and lifestyles. Also the more similarities there are between the members of the groups we wish to contrast, the less meaningful the concept of subculture becomes. Not just any difference between groups should be called *subcultural* (otherwise, even families could be subcultures), so distinctions based on criteria like occupation, employment status, type of school, or residence have limited usefulness.

In today's world, even the simple statement "Culture is shared among some group of people" has new complexities. Is it possible that our entire planet is heading toward a single global culture? (This issue is discussed in the Globalization box.)

Despite such complexities, when we say people *share culture,* we generally mean at least one of two things. First, the people are capable of communicating and interacting with one another without serious misunderstanding and without needing to explain what their behavior means. Second, the people share a **cultural identity:** they recognize themselves and their culture's traditions as distinct from other people and other traditions. Thus, not all Africans (or Westerners, or Native Americans) share culture by the first criterion, although in the modern era they do by the second.

. . . *Socially Learned* . . .

Individuals acquire their culture in the process of growing up in a society or some other kind of group. The process by which infants and children learn the culture of those around them is called **enculturation** or **socialization.** Learning one's culture, of course, happens as a normal part of childhood. To say that culture is learned from others seems obvious, but it has several important implications that are not so obvious.

If culture is *learned,* then it is not acquired genetically—that is, by means of biological reproduction. A people's culture does not grow out of their gene pool or biological makeup, but is something the people born into that group acquire as they grow up. Africans, East Asians, Europeans, and Native Americans do not differ in their cultures because they differ in their genes—they do not differ *culturally* because they differ *biologically.* Any human infant is perfectly capable of learning the culture of any human group or biological population, just as any child can learn the language of whatever group that child is born into. To state the main point in a few words: *Cultural differences and biological differences are largely independent of one another.*

To say that culture is *socially* learned is to emphasize that people do not learn culture primarily by trial and error. The main ways children learn culture are by observation, imitation, communication, and inference. One important way in which humans differ in degree, though not in kind, from other primates is their ability to learn by imitating and communicating with other humans. When you were an infant, you did not learn what is good to eat primarily by trying out a variety of things that might have been edible and then rejecting things that were not edible. Rather, other people taught you what is and is not defined as food. If you are a North American, you probably view some animals (cattle, fish) as food and others that are equally edible (horses, dogs) as not food. You did not discover this on your own but by learning from others what is edible, good tasting, or appropriate. This social learning spared you a lot of the costs (and possible stomachache and hazard) of learning on your own by trial and error.

Relying on social learning rather than trial and error gives humanity big advantages. First, any innovation that one individual makes can be communicated to others in a group, who thus take advantage of someone else's experience. If you recombine the elements of old tools to develop a more effective tool and share your knowledge, other members of your community can also use that better tool.

Second, each generation learns the culture of its ancestors and transmits it to the next generation, and so on to future generations. Thus, any new knowledge or behavior acquired by one generation is potentially available to future generations (although some of it is lost or replaced with each generation). By this process of repeated social learning over many generations, knowledge accumulates. People alive today live largely off the knowledge acquired and transmitted by previous generations. In modern societies, certain kinds of knowledge are transmitted through formal education in schools and colleges, as well as through informal teaching by parents, relatives, and community members.

Third, because culture is socially learned, human groups are capable of changing their ideas and behaviors very rapidly. Genetic change (biological evolution) in a population is slow because it relies on biological reproduction. In contrast, no genetic change and no biological

As global contacts become more common and intense, people in various places react differently depending on their own culture, the nature of the contacts, and their personal circumstances. The impacts on local cultures therefore differ widely. And those who are concerned about these impacts have opinions, often strong ones, on what the future holds for the cultural diversity on our planet.

First, some fear (while others hope) that the cultures of the most wealthy and militarily powerful regions will eventually become globally dominant, gradually displacing other traditions. This is what many North American travelers to Japan or India conclude when they see businesses like McDonald's or KFC doing well. It is what many Middle Eastern political and religious leaders fear when they ban movies with scantily clad women. Even some wealthy Western countries like Italy and France are concerned that their national traditions are being taken over by the "American culture of consumption." Some call the international marketing of products *cultural imperialism*, with companies from the United States usually identified as the main perpetrators—although Nokia (Finland), Nestlé (Switzerland), Samsung (South Korea), Panasonic (Japan), De Beers (the South African diamond company), and other companies with global markets and advertising are equally involved.

So, some people believe that what they call Western culture is becoming *the* global culture. This global cultural future is the one that is most commonly portrayed by the media. Some almost take it for granted or treat is as inevitable—for better or worse.

Alternatively, perhaps new forms of culture will arise out of the increased contacts between peoples that result from travel and migration. International travel for tourism or business exposes people to other places and peoples. At least some travelers go back home with new understandings and appreciation of the countries that hosted them. Temporary and permanent migration links peoples and traditions. Some countries are primarily destination countries for migrants. Most of the richest countries of Europe were formerly colonial powers. In some, large numbers of people from former colonies have immigrated, as in France (Algerians) and Britain (Pakistanis and Indians). In destination countries like Canada, the United States, and recently Australia, immigrants come mainly for jobs. But their traditions come along with their labor. Some citizens of destination countries worry about being culturally overwhelmed (and outvoted) by immigrants. They wonder whether "those people" can or even want to be culturally assimilated. Others who are more sympathetic to diversity note the new choices in food, films, music, and books immigrants bring with them, believing that immigration enriches their nations culturally.

Globalization has other effects on cultures. One is that some people feel culturally threatened by the frequency and intensity of contacts, which leads them to cling even more firmly to what they believe are their traditional values. In this case, globalization leads to greater attachments to a cultural past that is perceived as pure or uncorrupted by foreign influences. Outside influences are consciously rejected, sometimes with profound political consequences.

In countries with large numbers of immigrants, sometimes the newcomers are culturally and linguistically assimilated into the majority or so-called mainstream. Then future generations may not be recognized as immigrants and will be almost indistinguishable from others. Of course, "assimilated" groups usually bring new foods, drinks, and holidays (e.g., Italian food, Irish pubs, St. Patrick's day) to their new homelands. If these become mainstreamed, then the "assimilation" in reality is partly a "synthesis," meaning that the influences pass in both directions.

Alternatively, instead of assimilation, people from a given national background may establish permanent cultural enclaves

evolution have to occur for the knowledge and actions of a human population to be utterly transformed. Furthermore, your genetic makeup is more or less fixed at conception. During the course of your life, however, your ideas and actions are likely to change dramatically.

In sum, culture is learned, not inborn, which means that cultural differences cannot be explained by biological/genetic differences between groups of people. And the fact that culture is *socially* learned gives humanity some big advantages over other animals: innovations can spread, knowledge can accumulate, and peoples' ideas and actions can change rapidly.

. . . *Knowledge* . . .

When anthropologists use the phrase *cultural knowledge,* we do not mean that a people's beliefs, perceptions, rules, standards, and so forth are true in an objective or absolute sense. In our professional role, for the most part anthropologists do not judge the accuracy or worthiness of a group's in their new homelands. Festivals, cuisines, family and living arrangements, and languages are often preserved in these enclaves, which include various Chinatowns and Koreatowns in large cities, as well as small towns in California's Central Valley that some Anglos say are "just like Mexico." In these cases, as people of the past and present have migrated from their original countries, they have kept some of their traditions and maintained viable communities as ethnic enclaves within the larger society.

Each of these effects of globalization has occurred in some form in some places. There is no point in predicting which outcome will win out in the end, mainly because changes will continue in future decades and centuries so there will never be an "end." That is, there will not be a final outcome to cultural change once the global system has stabilized—because the global system will never stabilize.

It is worth pointing out, however, that when people discuss the worldwide spread of "culture," in many (not all) cases they are really talking and worrying about the external manifestations of culture. They are concerned about the observable, material trappings of culture rather than about *culture* as anthropologists usually use the term. For example, McDonald's originated in the United States, but does its presence in Japan and South Korea threaten those "cultures"? Is American culture threatened by Honda manufacturing plants in Ohio or by the NUMI (a joint venture between Toyota and General Motors) auto plant in Fremont, California? If you are an American citizen, did you feel your "culture" was threatened when a Chinese company bought IBM and started producing computers with the Lenovo label?

In fact, many things that people now believe are theirs originated elsewhere. The "English" alphabet came from the ancient Greeks, who adapted it from the even more ancient Phoenicians. "English" numerals (1, 2, 3, . . .) are in fact Arabic numerals. The English language itself originated in northern Europe out of the Germanic subfamily, which in turn is part of the widespread Indo-European language family. Canadian and American staples like bread, steak, and peas originated from other places. At least corn, tomatoes, beans, and chilis originated in North America, but actually those of us whose ancestors were early immigrants learned about them from the real Native Americans.

Also, it is worth countering the common view that the transmission of the material manifestations of culture has been in only one direction—from the West to the Rest. Certainly, American movies and music are popular in most of the world, as are Western clothing fashions, cosmetics, and a host of other trappings. But similar things have moved in the other direction. Japanese *anime* and *manga*, karaoke, sushi, and horror movies have made it big among North American young people. Indian and Chinese movies, *shisha* smoking from the Middle East, East Asian martial arts, tattoos engraved in Chinese characters, and salsa dancing and music also are doing well. In Honolulu, you can visit bars that serve kava (a mouth-numbing drink made from the root of a plant from the pepper family, which originated in Polynesia and other Pacific islands like Fiji, Vanuatu, and Pohnpei). And in most large North American and European cities, you can visit restaurants that will sell you food from . . . practically anywhere.

Critical Thinking Questions

1. Do you think consumer culture is taking over the world? Why or why not?

2. What will be the condition of Earth's cultures in the year 2100?

3. Do you agree that the worldwide spread of the material trappings of North American culture, like fast food and clothing styles, does not mean that North American culture is taking over the planet?

knowledge. We simply recognize that the knowledge of any cultural group differs to a greater or lesser degree from the knowledge of any other group. What is most important about cultural knowledge is not its truth value, but that:

- The members of a culture share enough knowledge that they behave in ways that are meaningful and acceptable to others so that they can avoid frequent misunderstandings and the need to explain what they are doing.
- The knowledge guides behavior such that the people can survive, reproduce, and transmit their culture.

In a few words, cultural knowledge must lead to behavior that is meaningful to others and adaptive to the natural and social environment. We consider some of this knowledge in the next section.

. . . and Patterns of Behavior

Even individuals who are brought up in the same culture differ in their behaviors. The behavior of individuals varies for several reasons. First, individuals have different *social identities:* males and females, old and young, rich and poor, family X and family Y, and so forth. Actions appropriate for people with one identity may not be appropriate for others. Second, the behavior of individuals varies with *context and situation:* a woman acts differently depending on whether she is interacting with her husband, child, priest, or employee. Third, each human individual is in some ways a *unique* human individual: even when brought up in the same society, we all differ in our emotional responses, appetites, interpretations of events, reactions to stimuli, and so forth. Finally, cultural standards for and expectations of behavior are often *ambiguous,* a point covered in more detail later in this chapter. For these and other reasons, it is a mistake to think of behavior as uniform within the same culture.

Despite such complexities, within a single cultural grouping, there are behavioral regularities or patterns. For instance, if you were to visit an Amazonian rain forest and encounter people known as the Yanomamö, you might be shocked by some of their actions. By most cultures' standards, the Yanomamö are unusually demanding and aggressive. Slight insults often lead to violent responses. Quarreling men may duel in a chest-pounding contest, during which they take turns beating one another on the chest, alternating one blow at a time. More serious quarrels sometimes call for clubs, with which men bash one another on the head. Fathers sometimes encourage their sons to strike them (and anyone else) by teasing and goading, while praising the child for his fierceness.

If, on the other hand, you visited the Semai, a people of Malaysia, you might be surprised at how seldom they express anger and hostility. Indeed, you might find them *too* docile. One adult should never strike another—"Suppose he hit you back?" they ask. The Semai seldom hit their children—"How would you feel if he or she died?" they ask. When children misbehave, the worst physical punishment they receive is a pinch on the cheek or a pat on the hand. Ethnographer Robert Dentan suggests one reason for the nonviolence of the Semai: Children are so seldom exposed to physical punishment that when they grow up, they have an exaggerated impression of the effects of violence.

The contrasting behavioral responses of the Yanomamö and Semai people illustrate an important characteristic of most human behavior: its social nature. Humans are supremely social animals. We seldom do anything alone, and even when we are alone, we rely unconsciously on our cultural upbringing to provide us with the knowledge of what to do and how to act. Relationships between people are therefore enormously important in all cultures. Anthropologists pay special heed to the regularities and patterning of these social relationships, including such things as how family members interact, how females and males relate to one another, how political leaders deal with subordinates, and so forth.

The concept of **role** is useful to describe and analyze interactions and relationships in the context of a group. Individuals are often said to have a role or to play a role in some group. Roles usually carry names or labels, such as *mother* in a family, *student* in a classroom, *accountant* in a company, and *headman* of a Yanomamö village. Attached to a role are the group's *expectations* about what people who hold the role should do. Learning to be a member of a group includes learning its expectations. Expectations include rights and duties. The *rights* (or privileges) defined by my role include the benefits the group members agree I should receive as a member. My *duties* (or obligations) include other group members' expectations of me.

Rights and duties are usually *reciprocal:* my right over you is your duty to me, and vice versa. My duties to the group as a whole are the group's rights over me, and vice versa. If I adequately perform my duties to the group, then other members reward me, just as I reward them for their own role performance. By occupying and performing a role in a group, I behave in ways that others find valuable, and I hope that some of my own wants and needs will be fulfilled. Conversely, failure to live up to the group's expectations of role performance is likely to bring some sort of informal or formal punishment. Among the Yanomamö, young men who refuse to stand up for themselves by fighting are ridiculed and may never amount to anything. The shared knowledge of roles and expectations is partly responsible for patterns of behavior.

Although defining culture as shared and socially learned knowledge and behavior seems pretty inclusive, some things most people commonly consider a part of culture are not seen as part of culture by many anthropologists. For example, many anthropologists do not see architecture and art objects such as paintings and sculptures as part of a people's culture. They are, rather, physical representations and material manifestations of cultural knowledge. They are products or expressions of culture rather than parts of culture. Thus, art expresses a culture's values, ideals of beauty, conflicts, worldviews, and so forth. Houses and public buildings are products of various aspects of culture, such as family life, sexual practices, political organization, ideas of beauty and symmetry, religious beliefs, and status distinctions.

Similar considerations apply to other kinds of physical objects and material things. For example, tools are physical manifestations of the ideas of their human makers and users, who have a mental template that determines the form of the tool. Even writing is not seen as "part of" culture by many anthropologists. Rather, writing is a means of storing knowledge, transmitting information, and—in the case of fiction—telling stories that are meaningful in the cultural group.

Cultural Knowledge

Cultural knowledge, then, includes a people's beliefs, attitudes, rules, assumptions about the world, and other mental phenomena. In this section, we discuss five elements of cultural knowledge: norms, values, symbols, classifications of reality, and worldviews. We cover these elements because they are among the most important components of cultural knowledge and because their anthropological meaning goes beyond that of everyday speech. The Concept Review previews the five major components in just a few words.

Norms

Norms are shared ideals (or rules) about how people ought to act in certain situations, or about how particular people should act toward particular other people. The emphasis here is on the words *ideals, rules, ought, should,* and *situations.* To say that norms exist does not mean everyone follows them all the time. Some norms are regularly violated, and what is normative in one situation need not be in other situations. *Norm* thus does not refer to behavior itself. Rather, *norm* implies that (1) there is widespread agreement that people ought to adhere to certain standards of behavior, (2) other people judge the behavior of a person according to how closely it adheres to those standards, and (3) people who repeatedly fail to follow the standards face some kind of negative reaction from other members of the group. Notice that we are able to make collective judgments about someone's personal morality or character because we share common norms. Notice also that shared expectations about how roles should be performed are one kind of norm.

Sometimes people feel that norms are irrational or arbitrary rules that stifle their creativity or keep them from doing what they want for no good reason. People may believe that some norms about proper conduct are confining, such as norms about how to dress correctly for special occasions, or about when and to whom we must give gifts, or about fulfilling familial obligations, or about when to have sex. But, in fact, norms make social interactions much more predictable and so are quite useful to us as individuals. It is mainly because we agree on norms that we know how to behave toward others and that we have expectations about how others should behave toward us in diverse social situations or settings.

For example, in the situation of a party where you do not know many people, you may feel a bit nervous. But people know how to introduce themselves, so soon you are introducing yourself, shaking hands, and asking the other guests what they do, what they are studying, and so forth. Here, and in many other cases in everyday life, we do not experience norms as oppressive. They serve as useful instructions on how to do something in such a way that others know what you are doing and accept you and your actions as "normal."

Values

Values consist of a people's beliefs about the way of life that is desirable for themselves and their society. Values have profound, though partly unconscious, effects on people's behavior. The goals we pursue, as well as our more general ideas about the good life, are influenced by the values of the culture into which we were born or raised. Values affect our motivations and thus influence the reasons we do what we do. Values are also critical to the maintenance of culture as a whole because they represent the qualities that people believe are essential to continuing their way of life. We may think of values as providing the ultimate standards that people believe must be upheld under most circumstances. People may be deeply attached to some of their values and, sometimes, be prepared to sacrifice their lives for them.

An excellent example of how values provide ultimate standards is the American emphasis on certain rights of individuals, as embodied in the Bill of Rights to the Constitution. No matter how much some Americans hate what the press prints, or despise what the conservatives or the liberals stand for, few believe that unpopular organizations or speech should be suppressed so long as they do not engage in or advocate violence. Freedom of the press, speech, and religion and other ultimate standards are supposed to supersede private interests and opinions.

Although people may say they cherish their values, it is easy to overemphasize their importance in peoples' lives. For one thing, to uphold one value sometimes leads us to neglect others (e.g., career enhancement versus family life). For another, our personal interests can lead us to ignore or downplay some values in some situations

Component	Definition	Example
Norms	Standards of propriety and appropriateness	Expected behaviors at weddings and in classrooms
Values	Beliefs about standards and worthwhileness	Individual rights
Symbols	Objects and behaviors with conventional meanings	Meanings of nonverbal behavior
Classifications	Divisions of reality into categories and subcategories	Kinds of persons and natural phenomena
Worldviews	Interpretations of events and experiences	Origin of good and evil

(e.g., remaining honest versus successfully competing). Finally, our fears, loves, hates, and other emotions can lead us to ignore our values in favor of other concerns. For example, most people in the United States agree that persons accused of crimes have rights to a trial and an attorney. But perceived threats from real and imagined terrorists led some Americans to agree that these values should be ignored at Guatanamo Bay, Cuba. Prisoners of war should not be tortured. But what actions constitute "torture" became a political issue in the Senate hearings to confirm the U.S. attorney general in late 2007.

Symbols

A **symbol** is something (like an object or an action) that represents, connotes, or calls to mind something else. Just as we learn norms and values during socialization, so do we learn the meanings that people in our group attach to symbols. And just as norms and values affect patterns of behavior, so do the understandings people share of the meanings of symbols. Our common understandings of the meanings of actions allow us to interact with one another without the need to explain our intentions, or to state explicitly what we are doing and why.

For the most part, the understandings that the members of a culture share about the meanings of actions and objects are unconscious. We can speak to inquiring strangers about our values and explain to them why we believe they are important. But it is nearly impossible to tell someone why a particular gesture, a way of walking, a style of dress, or a certain facial expression carries the meaning it does rather than some other meaning. We "just know." "Everyone knows," for such things are common knowledge and maybe even common sense—to people who share the symbols.

Two important properties of symbols are that their meanings are arbitrary and conventional. *Arbitrary* in this context means that there are no inherent qualities in the symbol that lead a human group to attribute one meaning to it rather than some other meaning. Thus, the wink of an eye that often means "just kidding" in some cultures is—literally—meaningless in other cultures. *Conventional* refers to the fact that the meanings exist only because people implicitly agree they exist. Thus, at an intersection, a red light means "stop," but only because all drivers agree that it does.

Words provide a familiar example of the arbitrary and conventional nature of symbols. In English, the word for a certain kind of large animal is *horse,* but in Spanish, the same animal is called *caballo,* in German *pferd,* in Arabic *hisanun,* in French *cheval,* and so on for other languages. The meaning "horse" is conveyed equally well by any of these words, which is another way of saying that the meaning is arbitrary and conventional.

The shared understandings that allow people to correctly interpret the meanings of behaviors are enormously important. Because you assume that the people you interact with share your understandings, in most situations you know how to act and what to say so as not to be misunderstood. Culture, in other words, includes common understandings of how to interact with one another appropriately (i.e., according to shared expectations) and

▶ When we interact with one another, we communicate meanings by our facial expressions, body language, and even how much space we maintain between one another. By North American standards, these Moroccan men probably are standing too close together.

© Anders Ryman/Corbis

meaningfully (i.e., in such a way that other people usually are able to interpret our intentions).

Nonverbal communication provides a fine example of these understandings. When you interact with someone face to face, the two of you are engaged in a continual giving and receiving of messages communicated by both speech and actions. Spoken messages are intentionally (consciously) sent and received. Other messages—including body language, facial expressions, hand gestures, touching, and the use of physical space—are communicated by nonverbal behavior, much of which is unconscious. Nonverbal messages emphasize, supplement, or complement spoken messages. We are not always conscious of what we are communicating nonverbally, and sometimes our body language even contradicts what we are saying. (Is this how your mother often knew when you were lying?)

The general point is that cultural knowledge conditions social behavior in ways people do not always recognize consciously—at least until someone's behavior violates our understandings. Furthermore, many gestures and other body movements with well-known meanings in one culture have no meaning, or have different meanings, in another culture. On a Micronesian island studied by one of the authors, people may answer "yes" or show agreement by a sharp intake of breath (a "gasp") or by simply raising the eyebrows. One may also answer "yes" by the grunting sound ("uh-uh") that carries exactly the opposite meaning to North Americans. Pointing out a direction is done with the nose, not the finger. You would signal "I don't know" or "I'm not sure" by wrinkling your nose, rather than by shrugging your shoulders. It is rude to walk between two people engaged in conversation; if possible, you walk around them; if not, you say the equivalent of "please excuse me," wait for permission, and then bend at your waist while passing between them.

Aside from showing the social usefulness of shared understandings of symbolic behavior, these examples of personal space and gestures illustrate one way misunderstandings occur when individuals with different cultural upbringings interact. Raised in different cultures in which spacing and gestures carry different meanings, individuals (mis)interpret the actions of others based on their own culture's understandings, often seeing the others as rude, unfriendly, insensitive, overly familiar, and so forth. Arabs and Iranians often stand "too close" for the Canadian and American comfort zone. In South Korea, it is common to see two young females holding hands or with their arms around each other while walking. But their touching symbolizes nothing about their sexual orientation, nor does two men holding hands in parts of the Middle East. Japanese are less likely than North Americans to express definite opinions or preferences or to just say no. To outsiders, this reluctance often comes across as uncertainty, tentativeness, or even dishonesty, whereas the Japanese view it as politeness. The common American tendency to be informal and friendly is viewed as inappropriate in Japan and many other cultural settings where outward displays of emotions are not shown to mere acquaintances.

In a world where the globalization of trade and international travel are commonplace, it is worth knowing that much of what you "know" is not known to members of other cultural traditions, just as what they "know" may be unfamiliar to you. Think before you take offense at their actions. And think before you give it.

Classifications and Constructions of Reality

The members of a cultural tradition share ideas about what kinds of things and people exist. They have similar **classifications of reality,** meaning that people generally agree on how nature, objects, groups, individuals, and other phenomena should be divided into categories. Another phrase for this is the **cultural construction of reality:** from the multitude of differences and similarities that exist in some phenomena, a culture recognizes (constructs) only some features as relevant in making distinctions. The cultural construction of reality implies that different peoples do not perceive the human and natural worlds in the same ways.

For instance, all cultures recognize kinship relationships, but they classify relatives in diverse ways. What kind of "blood" relative someone is to you might seem to depend on how that person is related to you biologically. But how you conceive of your relatives and how you place them into named categories like *uncle* and *cousin* are not determined strictly by how they are related to you biologically. English speakers think of the sisters of both our mother and our father as a single kind of relative, and we call them by the same kinship term, *aunt.* But in some cultural traditions, the sister of your mother is considered one kind of relative and the sister of your father a different kind, and you would call each by a separate kinship term.

Thus, people of different cultural traditions vary in the way they conceive of their societies as divided up into kinds of people. The phrase *kinds of people* also refers to how the members of a culture classify one another into categories loosely referred to as *racial.* Probably most people think of the members of one race as physi-

cally more similar to one another than they are to members of different races—thus, the "white race" and the "black race" are physically distinct. In fact, though, most anthropologists agree that race is culturally constructed rather than biologically given (see A Closer Look).

Similar considerations also apply to how a people divide up plants, animals, landscape features, seasons, and other dimensions of the natural world. In turn, how people culturally construct their environment influences how they define and use natural resources (which, therefore, are not entirely natural). Plants, animals, minerals, waters, and the like are classified not just into various kinds but also into various categories of usefulness. For example, what one group considers *food* is not necessarily defined as *food* by another group. Muslims and Orthodox Jews consider pork unclean. Traditional Hindus refuse to consume the flesh of cattle, their sacred animal. The fact that a given animal or plant is edible does not mean that people *consider* it edible (or else more North Americans would eat dogs, as do many East and Southeast Asians, and horses, as do many French).

Even a people's conception of time is, in part, culturally constructed. Consider the units of time used by most of us in the modern world: seconds, minutes, hours, days, weeks, months, years, decades, centuries, millennia. Of these, only days, months, and years are in any sense "natural," meaning that they are based on natural occurrences (sunrises, moon phases, seasonal changes). Even these natural occurrences do not correspond with our cultural units: Days do not run from sunrise to sunrise but begin at midnight; months no longer reflect lunar phases; new years begin in January rather than at solstices or equinoxes. The other units by which we divide the passage of time are entirely culturally constructed, meaning that although we have instruments to record them precisely, they exist only because we classify time using these units.

Finally, people of different cultures differ in their beliefs about the kinds of things that do and do not exist. For instance, some people believe in witches who use malevolent supernatural powers to harm others. Traditional Navajo believe that witches can change themselves into wolves, bears, and other animals. The Tukano people of the Bolivian rain forest think that a spirit of the forest controls the animals they depend on for meat. So a Tukano shaman periodically makes a supernatural visit to the abode of the forest spirit. He promises to magically kill a certain number of humans and to send their souls to the forest spirit in return for the spirit's releasing the animals so the hunters can find game.

In sum, not only do different cultures classify objective reality in different ways, they also differ on what reality *is:* One culture's definition of reality may not be the same as that of another culture.

Worldviews

The **worldview** of a people is the way they interpret reality and events, including their images of themselves and how they relate to the world around them. Worldviews are affected by cultural constructions of reality, which we have just discussed. But worldviews include more than just the way a culture carves up people and nature. People have opinions about the nature of the cosmos and how they fit into it. All cultures include beliefs about spiritual souls and include more beliefs about what happens to souls after bodies are lifeless. People have ideas about the meaning of human existence: how we were put on Earth, who or what put us here, and why. They have notions of evil: where it comes from, why it sometimes happens to good people, and how it can be combated. They have beliefs about what supernatural powers or beings are like, what they can do for (or to) people, and how people can worship or control them. Everywhere we find myths and legends about the origins of living things, objects, and customs. (We have more to say about such topics in Chapter 14.)

These examples all seem to be based in a group's religion. But it is important not to confuse worldview and religion, and especially not to think that *religion* and *worldview* are synonymous. Although religious beliefs do influence the worldview of a people, cultural traditions vary in aspects of worldview that we do not ordinarily think of as religious.

For instance, the way people view their place in nature is part of their worldview: Do they see themselves as the masters and conquerors of nature, or as living in harmony with natural forces? The way people view themselves and other people is part of their worldview: Do they see themselves, as many human groups do, as the only true human beings, and all others as essentially animals? Or do they see their way of life as one among many equally human but different ways of life? Most modern scientists share a similar worldview: They believe that all things and events in the universe have natural causes that we can discover through certain formal procedures of observation, experimentation, and systematic logic.

The Origins of Culture

Like so much else about the early past of humanity, when we began to depend on culture is unknown and, perhaps, unknowable. Most ethnologists think that the essence of culture—without which everything else about culture could not exist—is the ability to create and understand symbols. If so, then somehow researchers must find a way to date the development of the cognitive capacity needed to understand symbols, the meanings of which are arbitrary and conventional rather than inherent in their physical properties. Obviously, determining when humanity developed this capacity is difficult.

One way to investigate the origin of culture is to look at the anatomy needed to produce speech. Language is almost entirely symbolic (see Chapter 3), so estimating when the ability to speak language evolved is one indication of when humanity became dependent on culture. Indeed, culture as we know it could not exist without language. Philip Lieberman is one scholar who investigates this topic. The mouth, tongue, larynx, and other parts of the human vocal tract are biologically evolved for speech. The vocal tract of apes and other animals are incapable of producing the full array of sounds humans use to speak, making humans the only speaking animal. By measuring parts of the hard anatomy (bones) of modern humans and comparing them to the anatomy of prehistoric hominids, Lieberman concludes that the full capacity for language probably evolved between about 90,000 and 50,000 years ago. Of course, very few fossils are available for such a study, so Lieberman's conclusions are tentative, and future research is more likely to make the estimated dates earlier rather than later.

Archaeology provides another possible way to investigate the origin of culture. Perhaps evidence of the ability to understand symbols exists in the archaeological record. It is difficult to know whether some long-gone people had the ability to create and understand symbols because material evidence of this ability is seldom preserved in the archaeological record. For example, artifacts like spear points were made for practical purposes—that is, to produce a useful product like food or shelter. Tools are not *inherently* symbolic, as shown by the fact that other animals make and use them. Their shape or style may have had symbolic components, but often it is difficult to know whether ancient toolmakers chose a particular shape or style because it was "efficient" or because it was "meaningful." Good material evidence of prehistoric symbolic capacity should be objects that have no obvious or probable use in producing something. There are plenty of such objects in late prehistory. For example, as early as 32,000 years ago, prehistoric people made paintings on the walls of more than 300 caves in France and Spain. Some other objects were fairly clearly produced for their aesthetic/artistic value, like clay and stone sculptures of humans and animals, but they too are relatively late.

Even today race is an explosive topic. In the United States, political liberals think that affirmative action policies based in part on race are necessary to redress centuries of discrimination against "racial minorities." Conservatives argue that "race-based" hiring and admissions practices deny opportunities to qualified white people, many of whom come from socioeconomic backgrounds that are just as deprived as those of many minorities. Someday soon, the Supreme Court will decide about affirmative action, but the debate will still not be over.

Most people who debate such public issues assume that race is an objective, natural category into which most individuals with certain observable physical characteristics can be placed. If you can't say what race you are, it is probably because you are of "mixed race." We can observe the racial differences between humans by visiting almost any large city in North America, where members of different races mingle. Race seems real. Race even seems obvious.

Most anthropologists disagree. They argue that race is not, in fact, an objective and natural category, but a cultural classification of people based on perceptions and distinctions that arise more from culture than from biology. Race, they believe, is a cultural construct rather than a biological reality. What does this mean, and why do most anthropologists believe it?

First, genetic studies show that the genetic variation within a given race far exceeds the variation between races. Two randomly chosen individuals within the same racial category are about as likely to be as different from each other in their total genetic makeup as are two individuals of different races. So, genetically, races are not discrete populations. This is because fully modern humans—*Homo sapiens*—evolved only during the last 100,000 years or less, and our species probably left Africa even more recently. Significant genetic divergences have not had very long to evolve.

Second, most differences that we attribute to race are only skin deep. When we place people into racial categories, we generally focus on certain visible physical traits: skin color, facial features, hair characteristics, and so forth. If we looked beyond observable traits to consider other (invisible or less visible) traits, different racial categories would result. For example, a racial classification of the world's people based on blood groups (ABO, rH, and other factors) would yield a different classification than one based on skin color. The same applies to a racial classification based on the shape of teeth or jaws, or on the ability to digest lactose (a milk enzyme). In short, the traits we use to define races lead to one kind of racial classifi-

cation, but we would have a different classification if we used different traits. We define some physical features as relevant, whereas others are unrecognized (unperceived) or irrelevant. Also, note that it does not take very much ancestry to classify individuals as members of a minority racial category such as African American or East Asian. Barack Obama is viewed as black by most blacks and whites, despite the fact that his mother is white.

Third, just how many "races" are there? Most elderly people raised in North America would say three, which used to be called Mongoloid, Negroid, and Caucasoid. This threefold classification of humanity is based on the history of contacts between Europeans and certain peoples of Africa and Asia. But why only three? The so-called Pygmies of central Africa are quite different physically from their Bantu neighbors, as are the once-widespread Khoisan peoples of southern Africa. The indigenous peoples of New Guinea, Australia, and the surrounding islands are quite different not only from many of their neighbors but also from some Africans whom they outwardly resemble in their skin coloration. Many people of southern Asia have skin as dark as some Africans, although in some other physical characteristics they resemble Europeans. Why don't we place these groups into their own racial categories?

Along the same lines, different cultures sometimes develop different racial classifications of people. In Brazil, people use a multitude of terms for people whom they classify as different. Based on his fieldwork, Conrad Kottak reported that in a single village in northeastern Brazil, 40 different terms were used in a racial classification! To non-Japanese, Japan appears to be a racially homogeneous country. Yet many Japanese recognize and emphasize the differences between native Japanese and descendants of immigrants from Korea. Some Japanese are prejudiced against the Burakamin, the modern descendants of groups whose ancestors are believed to have engaged in low-level occupations. Yet Burakamin are so indistinguishable physically that those "pure" Japanese who care about such things have to investigate the ancestry of potential spouses to be sure they are not Burakamin.

Fourth, racial classifications change over time even within the same cultural tradition. In the Americas, people who are today considered to be indistinguishable racially once were widely viewed as members of different races. When large numbers of Irish immigrated to the Americas after the potato blight struck Ireland in the mid-nineteenth century, they were considered a race by many other Americans whose ancestors had lived here somewhat longer. Jews were also seen by many as a distinct racial group. Such distinctions sound absurd today—to most North Americans, at any rate. Will present-day racial divisions seem just as absurd in the next century?

The difficulty of determining how many races exist, the fact that different cultures disagree on the number and definition of races, and the varying ways that race has been viewed historically—all cast doubt that races are objectively definable biological groupings.

So, do some anthropologists actually deny that there are important physical differences between populations whose ancestors originated in different continents? No. What they deny is that these differences cluster in such a way that they produce discrete biological categories of people (i.e., races). Individual human beings differ from one another physically in a multitude of visible and invisible ways. If races—as North Americans typically define them—are real biological entities, then people of African ancestry would share a wide variety of traits while people of European ancestry would share a wide variety of *different* traits. But once we add traits that are less visible than skin coloration, hair texture, and the like, we find that the people we identify as "the same race" are less and less like one another and more and more like people we identify as "different races." Add to this point the fact that the physical features used to identify a person as a representative of some race (e.g., skin coloration) are continuously variable, so that one cannot say where "brown skin" becomes "white skin." Although the physical differences themselves are real, the way we use physical differences to classify people into discrete races is a cultural construction.

For these and other reasons, most anthropologists agree that race is more of a cultural construction than a biological reality. Indeed, the American Anthropological Association recommends eliminating the word *race* from the 2010 American census.

Why does it matter whether race is a cultural construction rather than a biological reality? So long as people can avoid viewing some "races" as inferior to others, why is it so important that we see race as a cultural construct?

It might matter a great deal, given the past and current realities of racial divisions. Racial terms (e.g., *brown, black, white*) carry connotations, making it very difficult for most people to use such terms in a neutral manner. Once a culture has classified people into kinds or types, it is difficult to avoid ranking the types according to some measure of quality, goodness, or talent. Familiar qualities include intelligence, work ethic,

athletic ability, and musical ability. Some people believe that Asians are smart and work hard, whereas African Americans are better natural athletes and more musically talented. From such seemingly innocent stereotypes, we too easily conclude that it is natural talent that puts many Asians near the top of their class, and some African Americans near the bottom academically. Books such as *The Bell Curve* (1994) argue that genetically based intellectual abilities explain much of the differential success of different "races" in America today. Such arguments are moot if race is indeed a cultural construction.

There is another reason to view race as culturally constructed: Doing so helps to avoid confusing "race" with other kinds of differences that have nothing to do with physical differences. Most North Americans do not distinguish—at least not consistently—differences due to "race" from differences due to language, national origin, or cultural background. The latter differences, of course, are based on culture and/or language, not on physical characteristics. Too easily, race is confused with ethnicity. For example, many people view Native American and Hispanic as the same kind of identity as race. But Hispanics may be black or white or brown or any other humanly possible color, and many people who identify themselves as Native American based on their origins and culture are indistinguishable physically from Americans with European ancestry.

Last, race is currently a part of the way people identify themselves to one another. It is an important part of an individual's social identity. Another person's perception of you—and your perception of yourself—is affected by your assumed membership in some racial category. Such identities often carry a great degree of "racial pride." Racial pride may be a positive force in the lives of people who have suffered the effects of prejudice and discrimination, as older African Americans who were part of the 1960s Black Power movement will appreciate. Yet racial pride cuts both ways, as people who are familiar with the beliefs and activities of the Aryan Nation and other such groups dedicated to maintaining "racial purity" know. Although race may be a source of pride, it is also a major—perhaps *the* major—source of conflict and cause of division in many of the world's nations. Political leaders and opinion shapers in the popular media can and do manipulate the opinions of one "race" about other "races" to further their own political and social agendas. Depending on your own "racial" identity and values, it may be either comforting or disconcerting to realize that race is a cultural construction and therefore a division of our own making.

In 2007, archaeologists reported evidence that early *Homo sapiens* from North Africa created objects that carried a meaning beyond their physical properties. An international team of archaeologists excavated marine shell beads that ancient people of Morocco manufactured around 82,000 years ago. Many beads were perforated and had wear patterns indicating that they had been strung and worn on the body. Some were coated with a mineral called red ochre, showing that the makers altered the natural color of the shells. Most likely, people were decorating their bodies with the beads. Bodily decorations imply that others understood the beads as symbols of beauty, status, family or group identity, or the like. The beads communicated meanings that were not determined by their appearance or other physical properties; that is, the beads were symbols.

Probably culture as we socially learn and experience it today originated earlier than its physical manifestations in the form of beads or other symbolic objects. But so far, all we can say is that humanity had the capacity for culture by around 80,000 years ago. Perhaps this helps explain why current evidence suggests that *Homo sapiens* did not leave our African homeland until around that time.

Culture and Human Life

Anthropologists believe that culture is absolutely essential to humans and to human life as it is usually lived—in association with other people, or in social groups. Those who study animal behavior know that living in social groups does not require culture. Many species of termites, bees, ants, and other social insects live in quite complex groups, yet they have no culture. Gorillas, chimpanzees, baboons, macaques, and most other primates are also group-living animals. Primatologists have shown that chimpanzees learn to use and make simple tools, share food, communicate fairly precise messages, have intergroup conflicts in which animals are killed, and form relationships in which two individuals who are physically weaker cooperate to overpower a stronger animal. Yet few anthropologists claim that chimpanzee groups have culture in the same sense as all human groups do. (Some use the term *protoculture* to emphasize that many animal behaviors are socially learned rather than instinctive.) If other group-living social animals cooperate, communicate, and survive without culture, why do people need culture at all?

The main reason boils down to this: The culture of the society or other group into which people are born or raised provides the knowledge (information) they need to survive in their natural environments and to participate in the life of groups. This knowledge, which infants begin to socially learn soon after birth, is necessary because humans do not come into the world equipped with a detailed set of behavioral instructions inherited genetically from their parents. Rather, people are born with *a propensity to learn the knowledge and behaviors of the group they were born into from observation, interaction, and communication with members of that group.*

Culture is necessary for human existence in at least three specific ways:

1. Culture provides the knowledge by which we adapt to our natural environment by harnessing resources and solving other problems of living in a particular place. As they grow up, children socially learn skills for tracking game, gathering wild plants, making gardens, herding livestock, or finding a job, depending on how people make their living in a particular society. Because most human populations have lived in the same environment for many generations, if not centuries, the current generation is usually wise to take advantage of the adaptive wisdom learned and passed down by its cultural ancestors. Culture is so important to a human group's ability to survive in a particular place and time that some anthropologists believe adaptation is the most essential purpose of culture itself (others disagree, however, as discussed in Chapter 4).

2. Culture is the basis for human social life. It provides ready-made norms, values, expectations, attitudes, symbols, and other knowledge that individuals use to communicate, cooperate, live in families and other groups, relate to people of their own and opposite sex, and establish political and legal systems. As they grow up, people learn what actions are and are not acceptable, how to win friends, who relatives are, how and whom to court and marry, when to show glee or grief, and so forth.

3. Culture affects our views of reality. It provides the mental concepts by which people perceive, interpret, analyze, and explain events in the world around them. Our culture provides a filter or screen that affects how we perceive the world through our senses. Some objects "out there" in the world are sensed; others are not. Some events are important; others are ignored. During socialization, people learn the categories, symbols, worldviews, and other knowledge that filter their perceptions of reality and give meaning to things and events. Growing up in a given culture thus leads people to develop shared understandings of the

world (keep in mind that "shared understandings" do not imply Truth).

In sum, culture is essential to human life as we experience it because it provides us with the means to adapt to our surroundings, form relationships in organized groups, and interpret reality. Adaptation, organization, interpretation—these are three of the main reasons culture is essential to a normal human existence. In later chapters, we look at some of the diverse ways in which various cultures have equipped their members to adapt to their environment, organize their groups, and understand their world.

Cultural Knowledge and Individual Behavior

How are the shared ideas and beliefs of a group of people related to the behavior of individuals? This question is important not only for studying other cultures but also for learning how people think about their own lives and their relationship to society.

Is Behavior Determined by Culture?

Some believe that culture largely determines or dictates behavior, a view known as **cultural determinism.** If this idea is strictly and literally true, then personal freedom is an illusion, as is the exercise of free will. We only *think* we are free and have free will, but actually culture is pulling our strings.

Many anthropologists of the past (and a few in the present) believed that culture is, in effect, all powerful in the lives of individual human beings. They view culture as existing independently of individuals, who were treated merely as culture's carriers and transmitters. Some claim that "culture has its own laws," implying that people themselves have little ability to alter the future of their societies.

According to cultural determinism, culture provides rules or instructions that tell individuals what to do in particular situations: how to act toward friends, co-workers, and mothers-in-law; how to perform roles acceptably; how to worship; how to have weddings; how to settle quarrels; and so forth. Any "deviants" who do not follow the rules of their culture are usually brought back into conformity, ostracized, or eliminated. In this view, it is the normative dimensions of culture that are emphasized. Norms tell us how to do things: usually we

do them in these ways; when we do, we receive rewards; when we don't, we are punished.

This view applies to some actions, but recall that cultural knowledge consists of far more than just rules or instructions. It consists of values that provide only rough and sometimes conflicting guidelines for behavior. It includes shared constructions of reality and worldviews, which certainly influence our behavior, but only indirectly (by affecting how we perceive and interpret the world) rather than directly (as instructions). Finally, cultural knowledge includes attitudes, understandings of symbols, and other kinds of ideas and beliefs that affect how people act, but not in the same way that rules do. The effects of these and other mental components of culture are too subtle and complex to think of them as rules or instructions.

Besides, most people do not experience their culture as all powerful. Although it *could* be true that your mind is mainly a vessel that carries your culture, you probably think there is a lot more to you than that. Most modern anthropologists agree, and they reject notions of extreme cultural determinism. Culture does shape individuals, but it is also shaped by individuals.

In most situations, people have some leeway to choose between alternative courses of action. In their everyday lives, most people do not blindly follow the dictates of their culture. They scheme, calculate, weigh alternatives, and make decisions. For those actions that are important in their own lives or in the lives of others they care about, they plan ahead and consider the possible benefits and costs before they act. In deciding how best to approach the relationship between knowledge and behavior, we must take into account people's ability to think ahead, plan, and choose.

One way to do this is to realize that formulating plans and making choices involve both rational thought and emotional dispositions. Therefore, they take place within the existing framework of cultural knowledge. Planning and choosing involve at least the following procedures: deciding on one's goals (ends); determining the resources (or means) available to acquire these goals; considering which specific actions are likely to be most effective; calculating the relative costs (in time and/or resources) and benefits (rewards) of these alternative actions; and, finally, choosing between alternative behaviors.

Culture affects every step of this choice-making process. Norms force individuals to take into account how others are likely to react to their behavior. Values affect the goals that people have and help prevent them from acting in ways that infringe on the rights of others. Choices are affected by the existing cultural constructions of people and things, worldviews, and individuals' anticipation of how others will interpret the meaning of their actions.

Culture thus affects goals, perceptions of appropriate and effective means, relative weighting of costs and benefits, and so on. So important is the effect of cultural knowledge on individual decisions that one influential anthropologist long ago defined culture itself as "standards for deciding what is, . . . what can be, . . . how one feels about it, . . . what to do about it, . . . and how to go about doing it" (Goodenough 1961, 552).

So, one important way cultural knowledge affects actions is by its profound influences on choices individuals make about what to do in various situations. One way to say this is that cultural knowledge supplies "boundaries" for behavior. Speaking metaphorically, culture draws the lines that behavior usually does not cross, meaning that culture determines which behaviors are likely to be proper or acceptable or understandable to others. Within these boundaries, people are free to choose between alternative actions. Most people do not violate these cultural boundaries because they believe in the moral correctness of norms and values, because they fear negative reactions from others, or because doing so would involve actions that others might misinterpret.

Why Does Behavior Vary?

The complexity of the relationship between knowledge and behavior is one reason we distinguish knowledge from behavior. Shared ideas and beliefs affect individual actions, but for the most part they do not determine them in detail. In fact, ideas and beliefs sometimes do not predict behavior very well at all, and what is expected is often not what occurs. There are several major reasons the actions of individuals often depart from expectations.

The most obvious reason is that no two individuals have exactly the same life experiences, even though they are brought up in the same cultural tradition. A related reason is that no two individuals (except identical twins) have the same genetic makeup, and our genes affect how we react to our life experiences. Different life experiences and biological uniqueness make individuals different (to greater or lesser degrees, of course) in their reactions and actions.

Other reasons for variations in behavior are more subtle. Norms and values are not always consistent and do not always provide unambiguous guidelines for behavior. Generally, you should not tell lies, but sometimes a small lie is necessary to preserve a personal relationship or to avoid hurting someone's feelings. Small lies sometimes avoid greater harms. Often, too, small lies are so useful to achieve our personal goals that our private interests take precedence over the anti-lying norm.

In many situations, pursuing one worthwhile goal or upholding one value conflicts with pursuing another goal or upholding another value, so people must choose between them. You may believe in the work ethic, value success and getting ahead on the job, and want to be a good parent. You hold these beliefs, values, and goals simultaneously—you "want it all." But jobs and career advancement may reduce the time we can devote to the pursuit of our "family values," so we must decide how to allocate our time and energy between activities that are all culturally defined as worthwhile.

Also, people find ways to justify (to themselves and to others) violations of norms and accepted moral standards when such norms and standards conflict with their interests. You may rationalize stealing from your employer by the "fact" that you are underpaid. Your boss may justify having you work overtime for no extra pay because he is "pressured" from his own boss. Your company may lay off its workers and move its operations overseas because it must operate in a "highly competitive global environment." Your classmates may rationalize cheating on a test because the instructor is "boring" and the course is "all B.S. anyway."

Finally, people receive contradictory messages about what actions are proper and morally right. Sometimes ideal models for behavior are contradicted by the messages and models people receive from the actions of their parents, relatives, friends, political leaders, and the media. Most agree that extramarital affairs and violence are wrong, for example, but we gain the impression from many sources that they are common and almost to be expected. Older generations want us to uphold their standards of sexual morality, but when we watch TV, DVDs, and movies, we are exposed to conflicting values.

We chose the preceding examples because they are familiar to most readers. But the main point of the examples is this: All cultures have abstract public values and publicly acknowledged norms that distinguish right from wrong, appropriate from inappropriate, and so forth. But all people recognize that real-world situations are complicated. Real-life individuals have personal goals to pursue and sometimes yield to temptation. People have to choose between values and norms that conflict at least sometimes and in some circumstances.

In sum, all humans and all groups periodically deal with the complicated conflicts between private interests and public duties. The actions of individuals are often an uneasy compromise between the two. Although our behavior is embedded in the context of cultural knowledge, its relationship to this context is complex and variable. All of us recognize that this applies to ourselves. We should realize that it applies to others as well.

Biology and Cultural Differences

In many ways, humans are like other mammals. Biologically, we must regulate our body temperatures, balance our energy and liquid intake and expenditures, and so forth. But anthropologists say that humans are special mammals because we rely so heavily on culture for our survival and sense of well-being. How, then, are humanity's biology and culture related?

Although we cannot discuss this issue in depth, it is necessary to address one important question about this relationship: Do biological/genetic/physical differences between groups of people have anything to do with the cultural differences between them? To rephrase the question so that its full implications are apparent: Is there any correlation between cultures and human physical forms, or "races," as they are usually called? (See A Closer Look for why the whole concept of race is problematic.)

Before the twentieth century, many people believed that the physical differences between groups of people explained differences in how they thought, felt, and behaved. That is, many people believed that "racial" differences partly or largely accounted for differences in culture. According to this notion, now called **biological determinism,** cultural differences have a biological basis, meaning that groups of people differ in how they think, feel, and act because they differ in their innate biological makeup.

Biological determinism is potentially a convenient theory about what makes people different from one another in their beliefs and actions. It is simple to understand. It can be a politically or economically useful idea, especially when combined with ethnocentric attitudes about the superiority of one's own culture. If French or German culture is superior to African or Native American culture, then it might be because the French or Germans are biologically superior to Africans or Native Americans. Colonial rule, the expropriation of land and other resources, slavery, genocides and attempted genocides, and other practices often were justified by the idea that groups of

▲ Race and culture vary independently of each other because members of different "racial" categories can share the same culture. This multiethnic crowd in Miami Beach is watching a performance.

people differed in their customs and beliefs—and also in their intelligence—because of their physical differences. If who comes out on top in competition among individuals and groups is biologically determined, then the status quo is justified—and even inevitable.

With few exceptions, modern ethnologists reject biological determinism. We believe that genetic differences between human populations do not cause cultural differences. The diverse cultures of Africa did not and do not differ from the cultures of Europe or Asia because the peoples of these continents differ biologically. Nor do the cultures of different ethnic groups within a modern nation differ because these ethnic groups differ physically: African Americans, European Americans, and Asian Americans do not differ in their beliefs and actions because of their different genetic makeup.

To claim that physical differences are irrelevant as causes for cultural differences might seem like a sweeping overgeneralization. Certainly, it is difficult to prove. But this claim is based on evidence, most of which is quite familiar. Consider the following three unquestionable facts:

1. Individuals of any physical type are equally capable of learning any culture. For instance, the North

American continent now contains people whose biological ancestors came from all parts of the world. Yet modern-day African, Chinese, South Asian, Irish, and Italian Americans have far more in common in their thoughts and actions than any of them have in common with the peoples of their ancestral homelands.

2. An enormous range of cultural diversity was and is found on all continents and regions of the world. For example, most West Africans are biologically similar, yet they are divided into dozens of different cultural groupings. The same disjunction between physical characteristics and cultural diversity applies to people of northern Asia, southern Asia, Europe, and other regions. There is far too much diversity within populations that are biologically similar for biological differences to be a significant cause of cultural variation.

3. Dramatically different ways of thinking and behaving succeed one another in time within the same biological population and within the same society. Cultures can and regularly do undergo vast changes within a single human generation. Changes within one generation cannot possibly be due to genetic changes in the population.

Because of these and other kinds of evidence, most cultural anthropologists feel justified in reaching the following conclusion: Physical (including "racial") differences between human populations are largely irrelevant in explaining the cultural differences between them. So, if we want to explain the differences between the Kikuyu culture of East Africa and the Chinese culture of East Asia, we ignore the physical and genetic differences between the Kikuyu and the Chinese. We might argue that differences between the Kikuyu and Chinese natural environment and contacts with surrounding peoples make their cultures different. But for the most part we ignore the possibility that genetic differences between groups explain cultural differences between groups.

Most cultural anthropologists strongly oppose biological determinist notions. In fact, in the early decades of the twentieth century, some anthropologists, such as Franz Boas, fought such ideas by marshaling evidence that—to state the point simply—culture is not determined by race.

This conclusion does not imply that biological factors are irrelevant to cultural anthropologists. Human beings have physiological needs and biological imperatives just like other animals. Food, water, shelter, and the like are necessary to sustain life. Sexual activity is pleasurable for its own sake as well as necessary for reproduction. People become sick and may die from disease, so coping with the effects of viruses, bacteria, and other microorganisms is a biological necessity. Finally, no human society can survive unless its females give birth and its members effectively nurture and enculturate their children. To persist over many generations, all groups develop means of meeting these biological needs and coping with these environmental problems; those that have failed to do so are no longer around.

It is one thing to hold that the biological imperatives humans all *share* are important in shaping culture. It is quite another thing to claim that the biological *differences* between populations are important determinants of the cultural differences between these populations. The first point is generally accepted, although its implications are disputed (see Chapter 4). The second statement is generally rejected, although conceivably recent research on the human genome may lead us to reconsider it.

Because humans are both cultural and biological beings, much of what we do is oriented around the satisfaction of biological needs for food, shelter, reproduction, disease avoidance, and so forth. Such imperatives must be dealt with in all societies. It is partly because of these problems that anthropologists have discovered **cultural universals,** or elements that exist in all known human cultural groupings.

Some cultural universals are obvious because they are requirements for long-term survival in a species that relies on social learning, material technology, and group living. Such universals include tools, shelter, methods of communication, patterns of cooperation used in acquiring food and other essential resources, ways of teaching children, and so forth. There is no great mystery about why all human groups have such things.

Other cultural universals are not so obvious. They do not seem necessary for the physical survival of individuals or groups, but they are nonetheless present in all cultural traditions. Among these are:

- ways of assigning tasks and roles according to age, gender, and skill
- prohibitions on sexual relations (incest taboos) between certain kinds of relatives
- organized ways of sharing and exchanging goods
- games, sports, and other kinds of recreational activities

© Bruce Connolly/Corbis

▲ It is not clear whether music somehow helps people survive or performs essential functions for societies and cultures, but it nonetheless is a cultural universal. These Chinese are skilled drummers.

- beliefs about supernatural powers and rituals that are used to communicate with and influence them
- decorative arts
- singing and other forms of music
- customary ways of handling the dead and expressing grief
- myths, legends, and folklore
- rites of passage that ceremonially recognize the movement of people through certain stages of life

We could list more cultural universals. But our point is that all human cultures share certain characteristics whose universal existence is not explained by the fact that they are obviously necessary for the short- or long-term biological survival of populations. Perhaps these universals exist because they are a necessary product of a culture-bearing, language-using, symbol-understanding species.

Or perhaps there is in fact an inborn genetic basis for sexual rules, religion, play, kinship, art, and other cultural universals. If so, it is still true that the precise forms that these and other universal elements take vary from culture to culture. For instance, all human societies have beliefs about the supernatural (religion), but the nature of these beliefs varies enormously among cultures, as seen in Chapter 14. Likewise, people in all societies keep track of their family and kinship relationships, but they do so in a wide variety of ways, as documented in Chapters 8 and 9. Male–female differences are important among all peoples but in highly diverse ways, as described in Chapter 11. Music and art exist universally, but this tells us little about musical tastes or artistic styles, discussed in Chapter 15. Most of the rest of this book deals with these and other cultural variations.

Summary

1. In anthropology, *culture* refers to the whole way of life of some society or group. To describe and analyze culture, we distinguish between its mental and behavioral components, or between cultural knowledge and patterns of behavior. *Culture* is here defined as the shared, socially learned knowledge and behavioral patterns characteristic of some group of people. The term *group* may refer to an entire society, an ethnic group, or some kind of subculture, depending on the context of the discussion.

2. Cultural knowledge is not true in any objective sense, but it must at least allow a society to persist in its environment and it must enable people to interact appropriately and meaningfully. Cultural knowledge has many components, some of which are norms, values, common understandings of the meanings of symbols, classifications and constructions of reality, and worldviews. Because these and other components of cultural knowledge are products of social learning—not inborn—we must learn them during enculturation, although they may seem natural or commonsensical.

3. How, why, and when the human species first developed culture is uncertain, but the capacity to engage in symbolic actions existed by about 80,000 years ago and probably earlier. Among modern humans, culture is essential to our existence because of its adaptive, organizational, and interpretive functions.

4. Some say that cultural knowledge determines the actions of individuals, but this view is simplistic. Cultural ideas and beliefs serve as more than just rules or instructions for actions. A more useful and realistic view is that cultural knowledge affects the choices people make about how to act in particular situations. Cultural knowledge limits and influences behavior but does not determine it in detail because people's actions most of the time are not simply programmed by their culture.

5. Biological determinism is the notion that the culture of a human population derives in part from biological or "racial" factors. If true, then biological differences are relevant in explaining cultural differences between human groups. This idea is rejected by nearly all ethnologists, who consider the biological differences between groups largely irrelevant as explanations for cultural differences. The shared biological heritage of the human species does affect culture, however, because how people meet their biologically given needs is reflected in their culture. The existence of cultural universals also suggests that the shared genetic heritage of all humanity affects the kinds of cultures that are possible in the human species.

Key Terms

cultural knowledge	enculturation	classifications of reality
patterns of behavior	(socialization)	(cultural constructions
cultural integration	roles	of reality)
culture	norms	worldview
society	values	cultural determinism
subculture	symbols	biological determinism
cultural identity		cultural universals

Suggested Readings

Brown, Donald E. *Human Universals.* New York: McGraw-Hill, 1991.

   A description and analysis of cultural universals.

Cronk, Lee. *That Complex Whole: Culture and the Evolution of Human Behavior.* Boulder, Colo.: Westview, 1999.

   A readable yet sophisticated book addressing the relationship between culture, biology, and human nature. Author's views are controversial.

Hooker, John. *Working Across Cultures.* Stanford, Calif.: Stanford University Press, 2003.

   Applies the anthropological concept of culture to issues of conducting business in other countries, including

Mexico, northern Europe, India, China, Turkey, and Zimbabwe.

Middleton, DeWight R. *The Challenge of Human Diversity: Mirrors, Bridges, and Chasms.* Prospect Heights, Ill.: Waveland, 1998.

Brief discussion of anthropological concepts used to describe and understand cultural diversity. Includes

examples of interactions between people of different cultural backgrounds.

Spradley, James, and David W. McCurdy, eds. *Conformity and Conflict: Readings in Cultural Anthropology.* 11th ed. Boston: Allyn & Bacon, 2003.

Collection of interesting essays for introductory students.

Media Resources

The Wadsworth Anthropology Resource Center
academic.cengage.com/anthropology

The Wadsworth discipline resource website that accompanies *Humanity: An Introduction to Cultural Anthropology*, Eighth Edition, includes a rich array of material, including online anthropological video clips, to help you in the study of cultural anthropology and the specific topics covered in this chapter. Other material includes a case study forum with excerpts from various Wadsworth authors, map exercises, scientist interviews, breaking news in anthropology, and links to additional useful online material. Begin by selecting Cultural Anthropology to take you to videos, research, and more. From the homepage, you may also select Applied Anthropology, which directs you to essays, glossary terms, the case study forum, and a list of internships and careers in anthropology.

3 CULTURE AND LANGUAGE

Symbolic language is one of human-ity's most remarkable capabilities. These Japanese farm women com-municate verbally by speech and nonverbally by facial expressions and gestures.

Humanity and Language

Five Properties of Language

Discreteness

Arbitrariness

Productivity

Displacement

Multimedia Potential

How Language Works

Sound Systems

Words and Meanings

Nonverbal Communication

Language and Culture

Language as a Reflection of Culture

Language, Perceptions, and Worldview

Social Uses of Speech

Questions addressed in this chapter

Why is the ability to speak and understand language so remarkable?

How does human language differ from the ways other animals communicate?

How are words formed from sound combinations, and why is every meaningful string of sounds not a "word"?

What are some ways the language of a people reflect their culture?

What is the Sapir-Whorf hypothesis?

What are some ways speech is affected by social context?

As children grow up, they socially learn the sounds, words, meanings, and grammatical rules they need to send and receive complex messages. Language is the shared knowledge of these elements and rules. Along with our heavy dependence on culture, our ability to communicate complex, precise information is the main mental capability that distinguishes humans from other animals.

We begin this chapter by discussing briefly a few of the many reasons language is so remarkable. Then we describe some features of language that make it more sophisticated than the communication systems of other animals. We show how people send and receive messages by following unconscious rules for combining sounds and words in ways that other people who know the language recognize as meaningful. People also communicate by nonverbal means, including bodily movements and spatial relationships. Cultures vary in how they interpret these elements of communication, although some expressions and movements seem to carry similar meanings universally. Finally, language is related to many aspects of culture, and speaking is itself a culturally conditioned behavior.

Humanity and Language

Although we talk to one another every day, we seldom consider how remarkable it is that we can do so. Yet the ability to speak and comprehend the messages of language requires knowledge of an enormous number of linguistic elements and rules. Language and culture together are critical to the development of human individuals—without them, our psychological and social development is incomplete. In all probability, without them, we would be unable to think, as the word *think* is generally under-stood, because language and culture provide our minds with most of the concepts and terms for thought itself. Thus, the workings of the human mind depend crucially on the knowledge of some language.

Several points reveal the importance of language for human life. First, *Homo sapiens* is the only animal capable of speech and the only animal biologically evolved to speak and understand true language. Other animals—including honeybees, social species of ants and termites, some whales and dolphins, gorillas, and chimpanzees—are capable of impressive feats of communication, but only humans have language in a fully developed form. With the aid of intensive training from humans, chimpanzees and gorillas can learn to use sign language or to manipulate symbols standing for words and concepts into sentences. With no human interference, one chimp taught sign language to another and later they used it to communicate. Despite these feats, no great ape is capable of responding to this simple request: "What do you plan to do next week?"

In fact, language is so critical to humanity that it helped shape our biological evolution. This includes, of course, the speech regions of our brain, but it also includes our vocal tract. The human *vocal tract* consists of the lungs, trachea (including vocal cords), mouth, and nasal passages. The vocal tract is biologically evolved for speech. It is a remarkable resonating chamber.

Here are some examples. You make different vowel sounds by raising and lowering the tongue or parts of the tongue. The position of the tongue modifies the shape of the mouth and hence produces sounds of different wavelengths, which human ears recognize as different sounds (compare where your tongue is for the vowels in *sit* and *set*, in *far* and *fur*, and in *teeth* and *tooth*). You produce most consonants by interrupting the flow of air through

▶ Successful attempts have been made to teach sign language to a few chimpanzees and gorillas. These apes have learned signs for things, actions, and even emotional states, and they can combine these signs into meaningful sentences. However, they are not capable of mastering language in its fully developed forms.

© H. S. Terrace/Animals Animals

the mouth. The initial sound of the word *tip* is formed by bringing the tip of the tongue into contact with the alveolar ridge just behind the teeth and then releasing the contact suddenly. You change *tip* to *sip* by blowing air through your mouth while almost, but not quite, touching the tip of your tongue to your alveolar ridge, thus making the initial sound a brief hissing noise. Your vocal cords interact with other parts of your vocal tract. They either vibrate and produce a buzzy sound (say "mmmm"), or they remain open and allow air to flow into your mouth freely (contrast the sound *h* in *how* with the first *w* in *wow*). You change *tip* to *dip* by vibrating your vocal cords with the first sound of *dip*. The other vowels and consonants of English and other languages are made by articulating various parts of the vocal tract in contrasting ways.

You move all these parts of your vocal tract unconsciously with astonishing speed and precision. Each sound is possible because the chamber formed by the mouth, throat, and nasal passages, and the muscles of the tongue and lips, are biologically evolved to allow us to produce it. There is a good reason chimpanzees cannot speak human words: Their vocal tract is not evolved to do so. Yet, with training, any human can utter the sounds found in any language.

Second, language makes it possible for people to communicate and think about abstract concepts as well as about concrete persons, places, things, actions, and events. Among these abstractions are *truth, evil, god, masculinity, wealth, values, humanity, zero, law, democracy, jihad, universal, space,* and *hatred.* Humans all understand such abstractions. Indeed, without the ability to conceptualize such abstractions, culture as we experience it could not exist. Further, our everyday behavior is greatly affected by abstract ideas such as *friend* and *enemy, food* and *poison, beautiful* and *ugly, play* and *work.*

Third, the social learning by which children acquire culture would be impossible without language. Language makes it possible for the knowledge in one person's mind to be transmitted into the mind of another person. During enculturation, not only do we learn "facts" and "lessons" about the world, but we also hear (or read) stories and myths, whose lessons are only implicit. The worldview of a culture is communicated (and perhaps even shaped) by language.

Finally, language allows humanity to enjoy the benefits of the most complete and precise form of communication in any animal. We can communicate incredibly detailed information about past, present, and future events.

In fact, we can learn about events that happened far away and long ago and speculate about events that could possibly happen tomorrow but probably won't. We can tell lies. We can discuss plans, contingencies, and possible courses of action, based on our expectations about what might happen in the future. All these are things humans do so routinely that we consider them ordinary.

In brief, language is powerful. It makes abstract thought possible. It allows the relatively quick and easy transmission of information from one individual (and generation) to another. It allows the communication of complex and precise messages, including speculations and lies.

Five Properties of Language

Back in 1960, linguist Charles Hockett identified 13 properties that distinguish language from the communication abilities of other animals. Only 5 of the 13 are important for our purposes.

Discreteness

Discreteness means that when we speak we combine units (sounds and words) according to shared and conventional rules. Knowing a language means knowing both the units and the rules for combining them. Words are composed of discrete units of sound (e.g., *j, u, m, p*) that are combined to communicate a meaning (*jump*). Similarly, we apply rules to combine discrete units of meanings (words) to form meaningful sentences.

Alphabets are possible because of discreteness. In alphabetic writing, people combine the letters of their alphabet to form words. The letters of the English alphabet symbolize discrete sounds, and originally each sound was pronounced in a similar way in all the words in which it appeared. For example, the letter *t* appears in *student, textbook, eat,* and *today,* and so does the sound we symbolize as *t* in the English alphabet. The same applies to other letters in an alphabet.

In English writing, most letters no longer represent a single sound. The letter *a,* for example, is pronounced differently in the words *act, father, warden, assume,* and *nature.* The same is true for other letters that represent English vowels. Some single sounds in English are rendered in spelling as two letters, such as *th, ng,* and the *gh* in *rough.* Why doesn't English spelling always reflect the way these words are pronounced? Basically, because changes in how words are spelled have lagged behind changes in pronunciation since the invention of the printing press.

By themselves, most sounds carry no meaning: The three English sounds in the word *cat,* for example, are meaningless when pronounced by themselves. But by combining this limited number of sounds in different ways, we form words, and words do communicate meanings. Thus, the three sounds in *cat* can be put together in different sequences to form the words *act* and *tack.* Words, then, are composed of sound combinations that have recognized, conventional meanings in a speech community.

Just as all languages use a small number of sounds to make a large number of words, words are combined according to the grammatical rules of the language to convey the complex messages carried by sentences. By mastering their language's words and their meanings, and the rules for combining words into sentences, speakers and listeners can send and receive messages of great complexity with amazing precision (e.g., "From the basket of apples on your left, hand me the reddest one on the bottom.").

Discrete sounds are sometimes said to be the building blocks of language. By recombining them in different sequences and numbers, speakers can pronounce an infinite number of words (although most languages have only thousands of words).

Arbitrariness

The relationship between the sound combinations that make up words and the meanings these words communicate is *arbitrary,* so words are symbols (see Chapter 2). As children learn to speak and understand, they learn the combinations of sounds that are permissible according to the rules of their language. For instance, in English, *mp, nt,* and *ld* are all possible combinations, but *pm, tn,* and *dl* are not (although these combinations are used by other languages). Children also learn to match certain sound combinations (words) with their meanings. By the age of 1 or 2, most children have learned the meanings of dozens of words. They have mastered many words that refer to objects (*ball*), animals (*doggie*), people (*mama*), sensory experiences (*hot*), qualities (*blue, hard*), actions (*eat, run*), commands (*no, come here*), emotions (*love*), and so forth. The child learns to associate meanings with words, even though the specific sound combinations that convey these various meanings have no inherent relationship to the things themselves. Thus, the feelings aroused by "I love you" in English are also aroused by "Te amo" in Spanish, although the sounds of the message are different.

Because the relationship between meanings and words or sentences is arbitrary, our ability to communicate linguistic messages is based entirely on conventions shared by the sender and receiver of a message. When we learn a language, we master these conventions about meanings, just as we master pronunciations and other things.

Productivity

Productivity refers to a speaker's ability to create totally novel sentences and to a listener's ability to comprehend them. Productivity means that a language's finite number of words can be combined into an infinite number of meaningful sentences. The sentences are meaningful because the speaker and listener know what each word means individually and the rules by which they may be combined to convey messages. The amazing thing is that individuals are not consciously aware of their knowledge of these rules, although they routinely apply them each time they speak and hear. For example, unless you have linguistic training, you probably do not know that you form an English plural by adding one of *two* sounds (either *–z* or *–s*) to the end of a noun (contrast the last sounds of *beans* and *beats*).

Displacement

Displacement refers to our ability to talk about objects, people, things, and events that are remote in time and space. Language has this property because it uses symbols (words and sentences) to transmit meanings, so things and people do not have to be immediately visible for us to communicate about them. We can discuss someone who is out of sight because the symbols of language (in this case, a name) call that person to mind, allowing us to think about him or her. We can speculate about the future because, although its events may never happen, our language has symbols that stand for future time, and more symbols that allow us to form a mental image of possible events. We can learn about events that happened before we were born, such as wars in Korea and Vietnam.

Because of the displacement property, we can describe things that may not even exist, like ghosts and ghouls. We tell one another stories about events that never really happened, and thus create myths, legends, and folklore. People can learn of events and things far away in space, such as fighting in Afghanistan and Iraq, explorations of the moon and Mars, and factories in China and India. Political leaders can mislead citizens, and be misled themselves, about weapons of mass destruction and terrorist connections in distant lands. Much that is familiar in human life depends on this important property—including the ability to lie.

Multimedia Potential

Messages use some medium for their transmission from sender to recipient. For example, writing is the medium in which the messages of this book are transmitted. When you speak, the medium for your message is speech, transmitted to the ears of your listeners by sound waves. Gestures and bodily movements are communications media that are received by the sense of sight rather than hearing. Messages can also be transmitted through other media, including touch and even chemicals, whose odors carry meaning for animals such as ants and dogs.

Unlike most other ways of communicating, language has *multimedia potential,* meaning that linguistic messages can be transmitted through a variety of media. The original medium for language, of course, was speech. But when the ancient Sumerians, Egyptians, Chinese, and Mesoamericans found it useful to keep records of taxes, labor, oracles, the passage of time (through calendars), and military conquests, they developed the medium of writing. Over several centuries, writing techniques spread to other regions such as the Greek islands, southern Asia, Japan, Korea, and western Europe. American Sign Language is a medium for the hearing impaired. Even touching and the resulting nerve signals can be a medium for language. Helen Keller, both blind and deaf, communicated and received linguistic messages by touch. Morse code, signing, and the Internet are all possible because of language's multimedia potential.

The Concept Review summarizes these five important properties of language. Together, discreteness, arbitrariness, productivity, displacement, and multimedia potential make language the most precise and complete system of communication known among living things. Because of them, you understand the following lie perfectly although you've never read or heard it before: "Last Tuesday at 7:02 P.M., I saw you chase my neighbor's dog around the yard and bite its ear."

How Language Works

As children learn the language of their community, they master an enormous amount of information about sounds, sound combinations, words with meanings, and rules for combining all of these. **Grammar** refers to all the knowledge shared by those who are able to speak and understand a given language: what sounds occur, rules for combining them into sequences, meanings that are conveyed by these sequences, and how sentences are constructed by stringing words together according to precise rules.

FIVE PROPERTIES OF LANGUAGE

Discreteness	Arbitrariness	Productivity	Displacement	Multimedia potential
Minimal units of sound and meaning may be combined in different ways to communicate messages.	Sounds and words are independent from their meanings.	A finite number of words can be combined into an infinite number of novel sentences.	Language can be used to discuss objects, persons, and events that are not immediately present or that are imaginary, future, or only possible.	Messages can be transmitted through many media (sound, print, sight, electronic).

Grammatical knowledge is *unconscious:* those who share a language cannot verbalize the nature of the knowledge that allows them to communicate with one another. It also is *intuitive:* speaking and understanding are automatic, and we ordinarily do not need to think long and hard about how to speak or understand linguistic messages.

This scientific use of *grammar* differs from the everyday use of the term, as often taught in language courses. In everyday speech, we judge people partly on the basis of whether we consider their grammar proper. In the United States, there are several dialects, or regional variants, of English. One, called *Standard American English* (SAE)—the dialect we usually hear in the national news media—is culturally considered the most "correct." Other dialects, especially those spoken by many African Americans and by southern or Appalachian whites, are looked down on by many of those whose dialect is SAE.

But there is no such thing as a superior and inferior dialect (or language) *in the linguistic sense.* That is, each language, and each dialect, is equally capable of serving as a vehicle for communicating the messages its speakers need to send and receive. So long as a person successfully communicates, there is no such thing as "bad grammar" or people who "don't know proper grammar." If Jennifer says, "I ain't got no shoes," you will have a different impression of her than if she says, "I have no shoes." But the first Jennifer's speech is perfectly good English—to members of certain subcultures who speak one English dialect. If speakers communicate their intended meaning to listeners, then the words they use or the ways they construct their sentences are as valid linguistically as any other. The evaluations we make of someone else's grammar or overall style of speech, then, are *cultural* evaluations. They are based on some peoples' cultural norms of correct grammar, values about the kinds of people who speak in a certain way, and so forth.

With this important point about the essential equality of languages and dialects in mind, here we briefly cover two aspects of grammar: (1) sounds and their patterning, and (2) sound combinations and their meanings.

Sound Systems

When we speak, our vocal tract emits a string of sounds. The sounds of a language, together with the way these sounds occur in regular and consistent patterns, make up the *phonological system* of the language. The study of sound systems is called **phonology.**

The particular sounds that speakers of a language recognize as distinct from other sounds are called **phonemes.** Phonemes are individual sounds that make a difference in the meanings of words. Linguists use slash marks / / to show that a particular sound is a phoneme in a given language. Thus, a few English consonants are / f /, / t /, / b /, / n /, / z /, and / l /. Some English vowels are / a /, / i / (pronounced "ee"), / o /, and / u /. Thus, words consist of a string of phonemes, like / mi / and / yu / (although there is an *o* in the way we spell *you,* phonologically the "o" is absent).

Of course, languages have different phonemes, and the phonemes of some do not appear in others. If you know Spanish, then you know that / v / does not exist in that language, which is why native speakers of Spanish may pronounce *very* as *berry.* Japanese has no *r* or *l* sound, which is why Japanese people have trouble distinguishing them when they speak English. On the other hand, the Japanese language distinguishes sounds that English does not. Japanese has double consonant sounds that make a difference in the meanings of words, like / t / versus / tt / or / p / versus / pp /. Thus (using English spelling), *kite* means "come" and *kitte* means "stamp," but English speakers trying out their Japanese must practice a lot lest they mistakenly say at the post office, "Please give me a come."

Further, differences that one language recognizes in sounds are not always recognized in other languages. English speakers hear differences between consonants that are voiced (your vocal cords vibrate to make a buzzy sound, as in / v /) and voiceless (your vocal cords do not vibrate, as in / f /). Thus, in English, *vat* and *fat* are different words, as are *bat* and *pat.* But in Kosraen, a language of Micronesia, the sound differences between / v / and / f /, / d / and / t /, / b / and / p /, and / g / and / k / make no difference in meaning. It is as if English speakers could not distinguish between *veal* and *feel,* between *dan* and *tan,* between *big* and *pig,* and between *got* and *cot.* In English, whether a consonant is voiced or voiceless makes a different in the meanings of words in which they occur; in Kosraen, it does not.

One of the most interesting ways languages differ in phonology is using the pitch of the voice to convey meaning. (The *pitch* of a voice depends on how fast the vocal cords vibrate: The higher the frequency of vibration, the higher the pitch of the voice.) English speakers use pitch to convey different meanings, as you can see by contrasting the following sentences:

She went to class.
She went to class?

The first statement is turned into a question by altering the pitch of the voice. In the question, the pitch rises with the word *class.*

Speakers of English use pitch changes over the whole sentence to communicate a message; that is, the voice pitch falls or rises mainly between words, rather than within a word. There are many other languages in which a high, medium, or low pitch used within an individual word, or even in a syllable, changes the fundamental meaning of the word.

Languages in which the pitch (or tone) with which a word is said (or changes in the voice pitch during its pronunciation) affects the meaning of a word are known as **tone languages.** Tone languages are widespread in Africa and in southeastern and eastern Asia. Chinese, Thai, Burmese, and Vietnamese are all tone languages (Japanese and Korean are not), which is why they have a musical quality to ears accustomed to English. As an example of how pitch can affect meaning, consider these words from Nupe, an African tone language:

bá (high tone) to be sour
bā (mid tone) to cut
bà (low tone) to count

© Steve Raymer/Corbis

▲ In tone languages, the voice pitch a speaker uses when speaking a word, or changes in the pitch within a word, makes a difference in the meaning of the word. Vietnamese is only one of many tone languages.

Here, whether *ba* is pronounced with a high, mid, or low tone changes its meaning. Because the tone with which a word is pronounced changes its meaning, the pitch of the voice is a kind of phoneme in tone languages. It has the same effect as adding / s / in front of the English word *pot,* which totally alters its meaning to *spot.*

Words and Meanings

Words are combinations of phonemes to which people attach conventional meanings. Any language contains a finite number of words, each matched to one or more meanings.

Morphology is the study of meaningful sound sequences and the rules by which they are formed. Any sequence of phonemes that carries meaning is known as a **morpheme.** Why not just call them "words"? Because in analyzing meanings, morphologists need a more precise concept than *word*. For example, you know the meanings of the following sound sequences, none of which is itself a word:

un	ed
pre	s
non	ing
anti	ist

Both the prefixes in the first column and the suffixes in the second alter the meaning of certain other morphemes when they are attached to them.

Sound sequences like these are "detachable" from particular words. For instance, adding the suffix *-ist* to *art* and *novel* creates new meanings: "a person who creates art" and "one who writes novels." That *-ist* has a similar meaning whenever it is a suffix is shown by the word *cram;* by adding *-ist* to it, you instantly know that a *cramist* is "a person who crams."

To analyze such compound words and their meanings, linguists have a concept that includes prefixes and suffixes such as *uni-, -ing,* and *-ly.* There are two kinds of morphemes in all languages. **Free morphemes** are any morphemes that can stand alone as words—for example, *desire, possible, health, complete,* and *establish.* **Bound morphemes** are attached to free morphemes to modify their meanings in predictable ways—for example, *dis-, bi-, un-, -er, -ly,* and *-ed.* Thus, by adding bound morphemes to the free morphemes in our examples, we get

desires	desirable	undesirable
possibly	impossible	impossibility
healthy	healthful	unhealthy
completed	incomplete	uncompleted
establishing	establishment	antiestablishment

Just as phonemes are a language's minimal units of sound, morphemes are the minimal units of meaning. Thus, we cannot break down the free morphemes *friend, possible, vocabulary,* and *run* into any smaller units that carry meaning. Nor can we break down the bound morphemes *non-, -ish,* and *tri-* into any smaller units and still have them mean anything in English.

We make new compound words by applying a rule of compound-word formation, not by learning each compound word separately. For instance, take the English rule for forming a plural noun from a singular noun. It is usually done by adding either the bound morpheme / z /, as in *heads, colors,* and *eggs,* or / s /, as in *lamps, steaks,* and *pots*—all meaning "more than one." Children learn the rule for plural formation at an early age, but it takes them a while longer to learn the many exceptions. Adults think it's cute when children apply the morphological rules

of English consistently to all words, saying "childs," "mans," "foots," "mouses," and "deers" for plurals and using "goed," "runned," "bringed," and "doed" to make a present-tense verb into a past-tense verb. But, of course, children are just applying the rules they have inferred from many other words.

Of all linguistic elements, free morphemes are the most easily transmissible across different languages. When groups who speak different languages come into contact, one or both groups often incorporate ("borrow") some of the foreign words. Incorporation is especially likely to happen if one language's words have no counterparts in the other, as is commonly the case for many nouns. Because of the spread of world trade and political systems during the last five centuries, English words have spread widely into other languages. Japanese and Korean have incorporated hundreds of English words, many from the realm of technology and commodities. In France, the use of English words became such a hot political issue that the government outlawed the "importation" of further English words.

Lest English speakers become too proud of the spread of "their" words, it should be noted that English (a Germanic language) itself has, over the centuries, adopted words from the Romance languages (which originated from Latin), as anyone who has studied French, Spanish, Portuguese, Italian, or other Romance languages knows. Less well known is that the early English colonists who settled in the Americas adopted lots of words from Native Americans—words that are now incorporated into English (see A Closer Look).

Nonverbal Communication

People send and receive messages using more than just phonemes, morphemes, and sentences. Facial expressions are enormously important in conveying emotions and intentions. We also routinely send both conscious (intentional) and unconscious (implicit) messages by how we move our bodies or parts of our bodies. *Kinesics* studies the role of bodily motions in communication. We can convey feelings and other emotions and messages by touching another person.

Some nonverbal facial expressions and bodily movements convey the same messages among all peoples, so presumably they have a biological basis. Pleasure, sadness, anger, puzzlement, and some other emotional responses are shown by similar facial expressions everywhere, so they convey similar meanings universally. Notice, though, that facial expressions can be used to deceive, as with phony smiles and feigned anger. Also, frequently a given

The earliest European settlers of eastern North America came from the British Isles. Except for French-speaking Quebec and parts of California, Texas, and the Southwest, most citizens of Canada and the United States speak English as their native language. Few of us know about the influence of the original native languages of North America—those spoken by American Indians—on the English vocabulary. Many familiar English words, phrases, and place names are derived from one or another Native American language.

The earliest Spanish and Portuguese explorers were surprised at how many of the plants and animals in the "New World" (North and South America and the Caribbean) were unknown to them. A few animals, such as deer and wolves, were enough like familiar European fauna that European words were applied to them. Others, however, had no European counterparts. Terms taken from North American Indian languages were adopted for many of these, including *cougar, caribou, moose, raccoon, chipmunk, opossum, skunk,* and *chigger.* Other "English" terms for animals are taken from the languages of South American peoples: *condor, piranha, tapir, toucan, jaguar, alpaca, vicuña,* and *llama.* Plants, too, were unfamiliar, and Native American words were adopted for *saguaro, yucca, mesquite, persimmon, hickory,* and *pecan,* to name only some of the most common derivatives.

As we shall see in Chapter 6, Indians of the Americas were the first to domesticate numerous food plants that now have worldwide importance. All the following crop names have Native American origins: *squash, maize, hominy, avocado, tapioca* (also called *manioc* and *cassava,* both words also taken from native languages), *pawpaw, succotash, tomato,* and *potato.* Indian words for natural features other than plants and animals also were adopted by European immigrants: *bayou, muskeg, savanna, pampas, hurricane,* and *chinook.* Terms in various Native American languages for clothing, housing, and other material objects have made it into English: *igloo, tepee, wigwam, moccasin, parka, poncho, toboggan, husky, canoe, kayak,* and *tomahawk. Caucus* and *powwow,* for meetings, are two other English words with native origins.

People everywhere name geographical locations. The earliest European settlers often named American places to honor important people in their home countries—for example, Charleston, Albuquerque, Columbus, Carolina, and Virginia (the latter named after the supposed condition of England's Queen Elizabeth I). Other American place names are derived from European geography—Nova Scotia (new Scotland), New Hampshire, Maine (a province in France), and, of course, New York and New England.

Native American peoples had their own names for places and landscape features, and often these names were the ones that endured and appear on modern maps. River names with Indian origins include Mississippi, Ohio, Yukon, Missouri, Arkansas, Wabash, Potomac, Klamath, Minnesota, and Mohawk, to mention just a few of the most familiar. The lakes called Huron, Ontario, Michigan, Oneida, Tahoe, and Slave have Indian names, as do hundreds of other bodies of water in Canada and the United States. Whole states are named after Indian peoples, such as the Illini, Massachuset, Ute, Kansa, and Dakota, whereas names of other states and provinces are derived from native words, such as Manitoba, Ontario, Saskatchewan, Texas, Oklahoma, Ohio, Minnesota, Iowa, and Nebraska. A few large cities with names derived from Indian languages are Tuscaloosa, Tallahassee, Natchez, Tulsa, Cheyenne, Miami, Chicago, Saskatoon, Ottawa, and Omaha. Seattle was named after a particular Indian leader, Seal'th, of the West Coast. Finally, the names of two whole countries on the North American continent have Indian roots: *kanata* (Canada) is an Iroquoian word meaning village (although it now is applied to a much larger community), whereas the area formerly known as New Spain took a name meaning "the place of the Mexica" (another name for the Aztecs) after winning its independence in 1823.

Aside from the inherent interest in the historical fact that many words in the English vocabulary have Indian origins, the adoption of words is a reminder of another, wider point: The culture of those of us who live in the modern world is the product of interaction among a wide diversity of peoples. In the past five centuries, increasing contact among the major regions of the planet has led to the spread of cultural beliefs and ideas. Like our languages, our cultural traditions have multiple origins.

Sources: Nestor (2003), Weatherford (1991)

---

facial expression is normatively appropriate (as in greeting someone), so the expression occurs regardless of the actual internal emotional state of the person.

We also communicate nonverbally by using space, meaning how closely people who are interacting space themselves apart when standing or sitting or walking.

Proxemics studies the meanings conveyed by space and distance. Edward Hall, who pioneered the field of proxemics with his books *The Silent Language* and *The Hidden Dimension,* noted that in the United States people communicate messages by how far apart they stand or sit while interacting. There is intimate distance (up to about 18 inches), personal distance (more than 2 feet to 4 feet), and social distance (over 4 feet), the latter applying mainly to formal situations. (Try violating these conventions by standing a bit too close to an acquaintance; just be sure to do so in an area where the person can back away from you.) It is usually offensive or a sign of aggression "to get in someone's face," as illustrated by barroom quarrels and player–umpire altercations.

Like speech, most forms of nonverbal communication are symbolic: A particular bodily motion or distance does not inherently convey a certain message, but does so only because of conventions, or common understandings. Because much nonverbal communication is arbitrary and conventional, there is great potential for misunderstanding when people do not share understandings about nonverbal messages—that is, when people have learned different conventions. Probably the potential for misunderstanding is even greater with nonverbal messages than for spoken language. In speaking to a "foreigner," both of you generally know that you don't understand the other's language, so at least both of you are aware of your ignorance. But with nonverbal messages, both of you are more likely to think you do understand, so one or both of you might give or take offense when none is intended.

Miscommunication is especially likely with touching, the unspoken rules for which vary greatly from people to people and even from individual to individual. On one Micronesian island, married, engaged, or romantically involved couples never walk hand in hand, although close friends of the same sex frequently do so (carrying no implication of sexual preference). Public hugging, even in greeting or to say goodbye, is seldom seen; according to islander cultural norms, handshakes are sufficient. Touching someone on the head—including what North Americans consider an affectionate rub or friendly pat—is offensive. Imagine the snickers (which in part covered embarrassment) when a visiting Anglo couple were seen kissing.

Some scholars who study nonverbal communication distinguish "low touch" and "high touch" cultures. Such dichotomies are usually simplistic, but it is true that cultures vary greatly in how they define situations in which touching is normatively desirable or appropriate. There is often an implicit power dimension to physical contact as well: High-status people are much more likely to affectionately touch subordinates than the reverse—affectionate (or "phony affectionate") touching symbolizes familiarity, and touching by lower-status individuals is often seen as "too familiar."

Similar ideas apply to the use of space. Again, the possibilities for miscommunication are great when people with different cultural upbringings interact. Sometimes Middle Easterners or Latin Americans stand too close for North Americans' comfort zones. Simply becoming aware that cultural norms about body motions, touching, distance, and so forth differ from people to people can help us all avoid taking offense when none is intended. In a world where international migration, tourism, global business, and other forms of intercultural contact are exploding, awareness of such differences is both personally useful and socially valuable.

Language and Culture

The major interest of anthropological linguists is how the culture a group of people share is connected to the language they speak. This topic can be technical, so in this section we focus on only two areas that might tie language and culture together. First, some parts of language reflect social relationships and the importance people culturally attach to different things or categories. Second, possibly language shapes a people's perception of reality and even their entire worldview.

Language as a Reflection of Culture

Most anthropological fieldworkers try to learn the language of the community in which they work. For one thing, speaking in the local language facilitates interaction and may help create relationships of trust. But fieldworkers also know that learning language helps them understand the local culture, because many aspects of a peoples' language reflect their culture.

For instance, a complex classification tends to develop around things that are especially important to a community. If people frequently communicate about objects, qualities, actions, or persons, they are likely to have many names or labels for them and to divide and subdivide them into many detailed categories. Consider different occupational categories in North American society, such as automobile or carpentry tools. A professional mechanic or carpenter identifies hundreds of different tools; the Saturday-afternoon home mechanic or handy spouse identifies perhaps several dozen; and the rest of us don't know what a feeler gauge or miter saw looks like. Numerous other examples could be cited, of course, but there are no surprises here.

Notice, though, that not all specialized vocabularies are developed just to meet the needs of some people to converse easily or precisely about things that matter to them. They also serve as status markers for professions and other groups. Lawyers speak "legalese" only partly because they need to make fine distinctions between points of law that are obscure to the rest of us. Legalese is a secret—as well as a specialized—vocabulary. Entry into the select group of attorneys depends in part on mastery of an esoteric vocabulary with all its nuances of meanings. Of course, it is helpful to the profession that the general population cannot understand real estate agreements and other contracts (like software agreements) written by attorneys. Others have to pay for an attorney's special knowledge to interpret important documents written by other attorneys.

You might have noticed that college professors, when acting out their professional roles, sometimes use esoteric words, complex sentence constructions, and "sophisticated" speech styles. (Even textbook authors sometimes do the same thing with their word choices and writing styles.) This is partly to increase the precision of communication, but it also serves to distinguish them from other people with less (or different forms of) education.

Members of various ethnic and "racial" categories often have their own ways of pronouncing words or styles of speaking. Speakers learn dialects based on ethnic identity at a young age from family and friends. But there may be more to speaking a dialect than simply speaking the way you learned while growing up. In Canada and the United States, many African and Hispanic Americans adopt a speech style as a symbol of pride in their identity. To show they are cool, some young Anglos adopt phrases they hear from the media or from persons with African or Hispanic heritages. Hip-hop and rap have become mainstreamed because of their use of language as well as rhythm. In Hawaii, some Haoles use the word *brudda* to address native Hawaiians, thus demonstrating that they know the local lingo.

In sum, in a diverse society, occupational, ethnic, and other kinds of groups develop vocabularies and speech styles to facilitate communication, to help ensure the continuation of their privileges and rewards, to mark themselves off from everyone else, to symbolize cultural and racial pride, to show how cool they are, and so on. What about differences *between* whole languages, spoken by members of *different* cultures? Similar ideas apply. To understand them, the concept of **semantic domain** is useful. A semantic domain is a set of words that belongs to an inclusive class. For example, *chair, table, ottoman,* and *china cabinet* belong to the semantic domain of "furniture." "Color" is a semantic domain that some cultures divide up endlessly, like blue with its many shades and red with all its hues.

In a similar way, different languages vary in the semantic domains they identify, in how finely they carve up

these domains, and in how they make distinctions between different members of a domain. Some differences are obvious. For instance, tropical lowland peoples are not likely to have the semantic domains we call "snow" or "ice" in their native language, whereas some Arctic peoples have an elaborate vocabulary about snow and ice conditions. Further, the degree to which some semantic domain has a multilevel hierarchical structure depends on the importance of the objects or actions in people's lives: island, coastal, or riverine people dependent on fish are likely to have many categories and subcategories of aquatic life, fishing methods, and flood and tide stages, for instance. Can we go beyond such fairly obvious statements?

For some domains, we can. Some things or qualities seem to be "natural domains," meaning that the differences between their elements seem to be so natural that they are obvious to any people. The differences may even seem to be inherent in the things themselves. We therefore expect that people everywhere would carve up these domains in similar ways. For instance, the wavelength and amount of light reflected from an object determine its color, so color is an inherent (natural) quality of a thing. Surely, anyone can recognize that blue and green are different colors, but, as you might expect, not everyone does.

Likewise, biological kinship is a natural relationship, in the sense that who an infant's parents are determines who will and will not be the baby's genetic relatives. Obviously, aunts and uncles are fundamentally different kinds of relatives from parents. But not all peoples recognize such differences and make them culturally significant, so "relatives" is not a natural domain. Because we return to this subject in a later chapter, here we want to show only that different cultures do not in fact make the same distinctions between relatives; that is, the way relatives are culturally classified varies somewhat from people to people.

Consider the relatives that English-speaking people call *aunt, first cousin,* and *brother.* An aunt is a sister of your mother or father; a first cousin is a child of any of your aunts and uncles; and a brother is a male child of your parents. These individuals are all biologically related to you differently, so "naturally" you place them into different categories and call them by different terms.

But other distinctions are possible that you do not recognize as distinctions and that are not reflected in the kinship terms you use. Not all your aunts are related to you in the same way: some are sisters of your mother; others are sisters of your father. Why not recognize this difference by giving them each their own term? Similarly, your first cousins could be subdivided into finer categories and given special terms, such as terms meaning *child of my father's sister, child of my mother's brother,* and so on. And since we distinguish most other categories of relatives by whether they are male or female (e.g., brother versus sister, aunt versus uncle), why don't we apply the sex distinction to our cousins?

How do we know that the way a people divide the domain of relatives into different categories is cultural rather than natural? Because different cultures divide the domain in different ways. People in many societies, for instance, call their mother's sister by one term and their father's sister by another term (although English speakers collapse both into one term, *aunt*). It is also common for people to distinguish between the children of their father's sister and their father's brother, calling the first by a term we translate as "cousin," the second by the same term they use for their own brothers and sisters. Even stranger, from the English language's perspective, are peoples who call the daughters of their maternal uncles by the term *mother* (just like their "real mother"), but not the daughters of their paternal uncles, for whom they use the term *sister.* (These various ways of categorizing kin, by the way, are not random; such labels are related to other aspects of a people's kinship system—see Chapter 9.) Obviously, the way various peoples divide the seemingly "natural domain" of biological relatives is not the same the world over.

We could provide other examples, but the overall point is clear. Cultures divide up the world differently, forming different categories and classifications of natural and social reality out of the "natural" properties of things and people. The implications of this point are more important than you might think. If you know a word for something—an object, a kind of person, an emotion, a natural feature of the landscape—then you tend to think it is real. Giving something a label tends to make us think of it as a single "thing." These kinds of "things" *are* real in one sense: the word refers to *something* in the mind of the speaker, even if only to emotions or abstractions. But this reality might differ for someone who speaks a language that reflects a different culture. You may think you know the meanings of *democracy, family, law,* and *religion,* but do other peoples mean the same things when they translate these words into their own language?

Language, Perceptions, and Worldview

We've seen that many aspects of a language reflect the culture of the people who speak it. Could the converse also be true? Is it possible that knowing a given language predisposes its speakers to view the world in certain ways? Could it be that the categories and rules of their

language condition people's perceptions of reality and perhaps even their worldview?

Language could shape perceptions and worldviews both by its vocabulary and by the way it leads people to communicate about subjects such as space and time. Any language's vocabulary assigns labels to only certain things, qualities, and actions. It is easy to see how this might encourage people to perceive the real world selectively. For instance, as we grow up, we learn that some plants are "trees." So we come to think of *tree* as a single kind of thing, although there are so many kinds of trees that there is no necessary reason to collapse all this arboreal variety into a single label. But we might perceive the plants our language calls *trees* as more similar than do people who speak a language that makes finer distinctions among these plants. In such cases, language might affect our cultural classifications of reality.

Further, language might force people to communicate about time, space, relationships between individuals and between people and nature, and so forth in a certain kind of way. Potentially, this constraint on the way people must speak to be understood by others can shape their views of what the world is like.

The idea that language influences the perceptions and thought patterns of those who speak it, and thus conditions their worldview, is known as the **Sapir-Whorf hypothesis,** (or the **linguistic relativity hypothesis**) after the two anthropological linguists who proposed it. One of the most widely quoted of all anthropological passages is Edward Sapir's statement, originally written in 1929:

> [Language] powerfully conditions all our thinking about social problems and processes. Human beings do not live in the objective world alone, nor alone in the world of social activity as ordinarily understood but are very much at the mercy of the particular language which has become the medium of expression for their society. . . . The fact of the matter is that the "real world" is to a large extent unconsciously built up on the language habits of the group. . . . The worlds in which different societies live are distinct worlds, not merely the same world with different labels attached. (Sapir 1964, 68–69)

Sapir and Whorf believed that language helps define the worldview of its speakers. It does so, in part, by providing labels for certain kinds of phenomena (things, concepts, qualities, and actions), which different languages define according to different criteria. Some phenomena are therefore made easier to think about than others. The attributes that define them as different from other similar things become more important than other attributes. These attributes provide a filter that biases our perceptions.

In brief, the linguistic relativity hypothesis holds that people's perceptions, the verbal categories they use to think about reality, and perhaps their entire worldview are related to the language they learn while growing up.

In the 1930s and 1940s, Benjamin Whorf suggested that language conditions a people's conceptions of time and space. He noted that English encourages its speakers to think about time using metaphors derived from space. For example, we say "a long time" and "a long distance," although time is not really "long" or "short" in the same sense as distance. Also, English-speaking people talk about units of time using the same concepts with which they talk about numbers of objects. We say "four days" and "four apples," although it is possible to see four objects at once but not four units of time. Finally, English-speaking people classify events by when they occurred: those that have happened, those that are happening, and those that will happen.

Because they share a different language, however, the Native American Hopi speak about time and events differently, Whorf believed. With no tenses exactly equivalent to our past, present, and future and no way to express time in terms of spatial metaphors, Hopi speak of events as continuously unfolding, rather than happening in so many days or weeks. Whorf argued that the Hopi language led the Hopi people to a different perception of the passage of time.

The units of time sequence of the English language are a good example of the issue. Units that appear on calendars—days, months, and years—are based on natural cycles (although months are not precisely based on lunar phases). But decades, centuries, and millennia are linguistic categories with no natural basis. Units used on watches—seconds, minutes, and hours—are purely linguistic units as well. How much is the perception of time affected by such arbitrary divisions imposed on our minds by language? Do the time units of calendars and watches "create" our views of time?

What shall we make of the Sapir-Whorf hypothesis? Certainly, none of us as individuals creates the labels our language assigns to reality, nor do we create the constraints our grammar places on the way we talk about time and space. Rather we learn them from our linguistic ancestors of previous generations, and we must adhere to these labels and rules if we are to be understood. Surely, this necessity biases our perceptions *to some degree*. The question is, how much? More precisely, how important is language as opposed to other influences on perceptions and views of reality?

For decades, the Sapir-Whorf hypothesis was not generally accepted, although most scholars found the idea that language shapes thought intriguing and significant. The idea implies that without knowing it, our perceptions and thought processes are shaped by the language community into which we happen to have been born, so the world is not *directly* perceptible through our ordinary senses. Potentially, this "fact" makes it difficult for anyone (including even scientists) to know anything for sure. And, taken seriously, it would mean that human rational thought and reason are partially an illusion because individuals can reason only with the subjective concepts and patterns their language provides. Finally, if language does, in fact, significantly affect how a people perceives and thinks about the world, then if some given language were to become truly global, that language's ways of perceiving and thinking would also dominate. (We present more facts and ideas on language and globalization in the Globalization box.)

Despite these important implications, most scholars have reason to be skeptical about linguistic relativity. First, if language significantly shapes the way its speakers perceive and think about the world, then we would expect a people's perceptions and worldviews to change only at a rate roughly comparable to the rate at which their language changes. But worldviews are capable of changing much more rapidly than language. Although the English language has changed in the past century as new words have been added and pronunciations of old words have altered, the changes have not matched the dramatic alterations in the perceptions and worldviews of most of its speakers. Also, religious traditions such as Islam and Christianity have spread beyond their original linguistic homes and become part of the culture of people with enormously diverse languages (although these traditions changed as they diffused).

Second, many linguistic differences that one would think affect perceptions and views of reality do not, in fact, seem to do so. A familiar example is the classification of nouns in some languages as either "feminine" or "masculine." As children learn these languages, they learn that different nouns require different articles (as opposed to the English articles *a* and *the,* which are gender neutral) and that adjectives acquire different endings depending on whether they refer to nouns that are masculine or feminine. The Romance languages (including Spanish, French, Italian, Romanian, and Portuguese) classify objects in this way, whereas English does not. The Sapir-Whorf hypothesis seems to imply that the speakers of Romance languages somehow view gender as a more significant or permeating distinction than do speakers of other languages: Every time people speak, they use gendered terms, which should reinforce the significance of gender in their minds. But there is no evidence that speakers of Romance languages have more "gendered" views of reality than do speakers of English or other languages that do not classify nouns as feminine or masculine. Conversely, Chinese uses the same personal pronoun when referring to both women and men, yet traditional China was rather patriarchal.

Still, linguistic relativity is such an intriguing idea that a few scholars since the 1990s have reconsidered it. They suggest that one problem with the original ideas of Sapir and Whorf is that they were too grandiose. Perhaps language does not affect perceptions, thought processes, and worldviews as sweepingly and thoroughly as linguistic relativity claims, but only selectively and with more modest impacts. That is, specific aspects or domains of a language influence how individuals perceive and think about reality in those aspects or domains—for example, about space or number. Researchers in this field now investigate specific domains in which language most powerfully shapes perceptions.

Researchers at the Max Planck Institute for Psycholinguistics have investigated how speakers of different languages talk about space and location. (Here we greatly simplify their complicated and technical findings.) English speakers talk about space in multiple ways. Space can be relative to the location of the speaker or hearer—for example, "on my left" or "above you." Note that if you turn around, what was just on your left is now on your right. We also talk about space using absolute locations, especially when we discuss long distances—for example, "head north to get there" and "south of town." These "cardinal directions" do not depend on which way an individual is now facing. When we provide someone with directions, we often combine relative and absolute references—for example, "turn left on Main Street and go west for about two miles." One Australian aboriginal language called Guugu Yimithirr uses only absolute references, comparable to English's cardinal directions. Thus, they might say, "There's a fly on your northern knee" (quoted in Brown 2006, 109). If you are a longtime resident of Hawaii, you probably know that directions are sometimes given with the Hawaiian words *mauka* (toward the mountains) and *mukai* (toward the ocean). These words are not equivalent to cardinal directions because whether *mauka* is north or south of you depends on which side of the island you are on. In southern Mexico, a community of Mayans speaks a language called Tzeltal. Their main spatial reference is in terms of "uphill" and "downhill," but these are more like cardinal directions to them because the overall slope of the land is consistent and they are seldom on the other side of mountaintops.

So Tzeltal speakers describe movements on the landscape in terms of "ascending," "descending," or "going across." If an object is on the ground, something else is located "uphill," "downhill," or "acrossways" from it. They have no left/right distinction, so a translation of the location of a house might be "to the downhill of you." Apparently, language does affect their perceptions: when shown two mirror-image photographs, Tzeltal speakers usually say they are exactly the same.

Research on linguistic relativity is ongoing. Perhaps someday it will uncover unexpected and important effects of language on perception and even on worldviews.

Social Uses of Speech

Part of socialization is learning how to communicate appropriately in given social situations. Different situations require different verbal and nonverbal behavior because how you speak and act varies with who you are talking to, who else is listening, and the overall situation in which the interaction is occurring. Much of your speech behavior is an aspect of the role you assume relative to other people, such as friends, bosses, children, siblings, and teachers.

To speak appropriately, people must take the total context into account. First, they must know the various situations, or social scenes, of their culture: which are solemn, which are celebrations, which are formal versus informal, which are argumentative, and so on. Cultural knowledge includes knowing how to alter one's total (including verbal) behavior to fit these situations. Second, individuals must recognize the kinds of interactions they are expected to have with others with whom they have particular relationships: Should they act lovingly, jokingly, contemptuously, or respectfully and deferentially toward someone else? Cultural knowledge thus also includes knowing how to act (including how to speak) toward others with whom an individual has certain kinds of relationships.

These two elements—the particular culturally defined situation and the specific individuals who are parties to the interaction—make up the *social context* of verbal and nonverbal behavior. The field of **sociolinguistics** investigates mainly how speech behavior is affected by social context.

How the speech of the parties to a social interaction reveals and reinforces the nature of their relationship is seen clearly by terms of address. Whether you call someone by a first name or a title like "doctor" varies with the social context. Higher-ranking people are more likely to address lower-ranking individuals by their first name, or

The migration of peoples is one of the most important facts about humanity's past. When people move to a new region, they carry lots of "baggage"—not just their possessions, but also their genes, cultures, and languages. Until several hundred years ago, migration was the main way languages spread to new regions. For instance, when one people of China (who call themselves Han, speaking the language usually called Mandarin) developed a politically complex form of culture around 3,500 years ago, they began to conquer their neighbors to the south and west, and many Han migrated to new regions. By about 1,000 years ago, Han occupied most of the country we now call China. Their Mandarin language spread with them, displacing other peoples and their languages or assimilating them culturally and linguistically as they conquered them politically. Even today, China's 1.3 billion people speak more than 200 languages, including Mandarin, Cantonese, Hunanese, Tibetan, and several other provincial languages with millions of speakers, as well as numerous languages of indigenous peoples.

In the past 500 or so years, large-scale migrations have continued. Indeed, the largest-scale migrations in known history are the ones that brought the bodies, cultures, and languages of western Europeans to the Americas, which to the Europeans was a New World. A great many of the several hundred indigenous languages of North and South America disappeared between the 1500s and the 1900s, as the people who spoke them either died out from new diseases and violence or became linguistically assimilated into whichever European ethnic group came into political and economic dominance. Today, the vast majority of people who live in the Americas speak English, Spanish, Portuguese, or French. Most of those who speak some indigenous Native American language also speak one of these four languages as a second language.

On a global level, no one knows how many languages spoken a few hundred years ago are extinct today. A recent estimate is that between 4,000 and 9,000 languages have disappeared since the fifteenth century. One estimate is that at least half of all languages were extinguished in the last 500 years. The United Nations estimates that roughly half of the remaining languages are endangered. In some cases, as among Native North Americans and the Australian aborigines, the main reason for linguistic extinction was the biological extinction of the speakers from disease and violence. In other cases, although the people whose ancestors once spoke their own language are alive today, the languages have died as the groups became assimilated culturally and linguistically into their nation's majority.

To see how a language can wither away over several generations, consider the languages of immigrants. Some second- and third-generation immigrants continue to know the language of their ancestral land, but after that few descendants are likely to speak it. Once a language is no longer spoken in the home, it takes a conscious and dedicated effort to learn it, and over time fewer and fewer children will do so. If children are exposed to only the majority language in formal school settings as well as in their peer groups, their chances of learning the language of their ancestors dwindles. Only if there is an entire community of speakers—who use the language among themselves, who serve as linguistic models for young children, and who reward youngsters for speaking it well—is a language likely to survive. In present-day North America, the Amish are one such community, as are various big-city "Chinatowns," "Koreatowns," and numerous Latino communities. Cities like Vancouver, San Francisco, and Los Angeles include tens of thousands of Chinese who form enclaves where Cantonese or Mandarin is spoken as the first language. In the future, there will probably be many more such linguistic communities, such as the Hmong (refugees from Southeast Asia who were resettled in the United States in the 1980s), South Asians (in Silicon Valley, California), and Somalis (in central Ohio).

The Summer Institute of Linguistics in Monterey, California, publishes *Ethnologue,* a rich source of information on the world's languages. According to *Ethnologue,* there are about 6,900 languages in existence, of which 4,400 are spoken only in Asia and Africa. One 2001 study notes that the vast continent of Asia—which contains two-fifths of the earth's land surface and three-fifths of its people—still contains thousands of languages, but most are very localized, and more than half of Asia's languages have fewer than 10,000 speakers. *Ethnologue* estimates that more than 500 of the remaining languages are nearly extinct, meaning that only a few elderly people still speak them. In Africa, where humanity began and where our species acquired the capacity for language, 46 languages are

even by their last name used alone. Not only does this nonreciprocal use of address terms reflect social inequality, but it also reminds people of it each time they speak. Spanish speakers have a similar understanding with polite address terms such as *Don* or *Señora.* They also have to choose between two words for *you:* the formal (*usted*) or the informal (*tú*), depending mainly on relative status.

Speech style and habits depend on status and rank in other ways. For example, there used to be greater nearly extinct. In Canada and the United States, about 260 indigenous (Native American) languages are still spoken. This sounds like a respectable number, but 85 of them have only a few elderly speakers and so are likely to be gone soon. In Brazil, where there were once probably hundreds of indigenous languages, at least 42 are extinct and 29 others are endangered, according to *Ethnologue*.

Modern-day globalization has a linguistic dimension. When companies from two nations trade, either they need to use translators or someone has to learn the other's language. When people on remote Pacific islands or in mountain villages of Southeast Asia rent videotapes, they are exposed to new languages. Globalization thus promotes the success of a few languages—namely, those used in the global arena. Over time, communication in one of these languages becomes more and more useful. If, at the same time, the linguistic community that once sustained the local language is disintegrating, the local language may become endangered.

Contrary to most English speakers' linguistic chauvinism, today Mandarin has more native speakers than any other language, around 900 million. But English is now the language most widely used in worldwide commerce, the international mass media, and globally popular culture. More than any other single language, English is learned as a second language in diverse countries from Japan to Mexico. In fact, more people now speak English as their second language (about 350 million) than as their first language (about 320 million). In places like southern Asia and the Pacific, where there are many hundreds of localized indigenous languages, English is usually the *lingua franca*—the language that people learn as their second language so that they can communicate widely with one another. And English nouns are commonly used for modern objects and technology.

That English is so widely spoken as a second language is a result of the history of colonialism and the twentieth-century economic and political dominance of the United States in world affairs. It is certainly not because English is a superior language or because it is easy to learn as a second language. Some countries known for their strong national identity resent the influx of English words—notably France, which actually has laws against the use of certain English words.

Some think that eventually the world's peoples will all speak only a few languages. For example, Andrew Dalby believes that within the next couple hundred years, only around 200 languages will survive. Surviving languages will include those like English and Spanish that are now in global use as well as others that are or will become the national languages of their countries. All indigenous languages will be gone, including languages like Irish and Welsh.

But perhaps not. In many regions, people want to reaffirm their national or ethnic identities, and learning to speak the ancestral language of their homelands is one symbolic means of doing so. Schools in Wales now require Welsh. The desire to preserve the language of one's native land is a mark of national or ethnic identity. It is a symbol of a political or social commitment to the broader goal of preserving identities.

Thus, speaking a particular language can do more than send the messages encoded in the words and sentences. With the spread of globalization, speaking a native tongue can tell people that you are proud to be who you are. In Europe, many people learn several languages because languages are emphasized in schools and because so many Europeans travel widely on their continent. Such multilingualism is almost certainly a positive force in the world. Perhaps more American school districts should realize that learning "foreign languages" is not a costly luxury in today's world.

Critical Thinking Questions

1. Sometimes breakdowns in communication lead to misunderstandings and conflicts between individuals and nations. Given this fact, is the development of a single language that would reduce miscommunication necessarily a bad thing? Or is breakdown in communication really an important reason for conflicts, compared to other reasons?

2. Whether the widespread use of English as a second language will endanger other languages is debatable because language can be a major source of ethnic or national identity and pride. Under what future circumstances is English likely to rise to worldwide dominance?

Sources: Dalby (2003), Sampat (2001), Gordon (2005—online version: http://www.ethnologue.com/), Walsh (2005)

differences between the speech of men and women in North America than there are today. Because of their fear of being considered unladylike, women were less likely to use profanity, at least in public. Men, likewise, were expected to avoid using profanity in the presence of women, so they would not "offend the ladies." Certain words were regarded as more appropriate for women's use than men's, such as *charming, adorable,* and *lovely.* In modern times, there are fewer differences between women's and men's vocabularies, largely as a consequence

▶ Japanese honorifics include rules about formality and politeness, many of which are related to the relative status of the individuals interacting.

© Nick Clements/FPG/Getty Images

of the women's movement and the popular media. Even today, though, some people make judgments about a stranger's sexual orientation by how he or she speaks.

Other cultures exhibit customs in speech behavior with which most English-speaking people are unfamiliar. Here are some examples:

- Some languages accentuate the difference between the sexes more than English does. In languages such as Gros Ventre (of the northeastern United States) and Yukaghir (of northeastern Asia), men and women pronounced certain phonemes differently. In Yana, an extinct language spoken by a people who formerly lived in northern California, many words had two pronunciations, one used by men and one by women. In a few languages, the vocabularies of men and women differ, with men using one word for something and women using a different word. In a language spoken by the Carib, who formerly inhabited the West Indies, the vocabularies of men and women differed so much that early European explorers claimed (mistakenly) that men and women spoke different languages. In many languages, the speech of women and men differs in other respects, such as the degree of forcefulness, whether they avoid confrontational speech, and their tone of voice.

- In parts of Polynesia and Micronesia, there used to be a special *respect language,* with which common people had to address members of the noble class. On some islands, the respect language had not only a different speech style but also different words. Often there were severe penalties for commoners who erred in addressing a noble, including beatings or worse if the offender was judged to have been intentionally disrespectful or challenging.
- On the Indonesian island of Java, there are distinct "levels" of speech involving different pronouns, suffixes, and words. A speaker must choose between the three levels—plain, more elegant, and most elegant. The speech style the parties to the interaction use depends on their relative rank and on their degree of familiarity with one another. In choosing which style to use with a specific person, a Javanese communicates not only the message of the sentence but also information about the quality of the relationship. Accordingly, changes in the relationship between two individuals are accompanied by changes in speech style.
- In Korean and Japanese, a complicated set of contextual norms (called *honorifics*) governs the degree of formality and politeness people normally use to show respect to those of higher social position. For

instance, verbs and personal pronouns have alternative forms that speakers must choose between in addressing others. Relative status is the main determinant of which form to use. In Japanese, one verb form is used when the speaker is of higher status than the listener, another form when the two are of roughly equal status, and yet another when the speaker is a social inferior. Even today, honorifics sometimes apply when women and men address each other. Japanese and Korean use different forms of personal pronouns (like *I* and *you*) to reflect the relative status of the parties. For example, when a social superior is addressing an inferior, he or she often does not use the pronoun *I* as a self-reference but instead refers to his or her status relative to the person being addressed. For instance, a higher-status person may say "Look at teacher" instead of "Look at me," or "Listen to father" instead of "Listen to me." Reciprocally, one usually does not use the pronoun *you* with one of higher status but replaces it with a term denoting the superior's social position—for example, "What would teacher like me to do now?" and "Would father like me to visit?" Confused foreigners trying to learn the subtleties of Korean and Japanese speech etiquette are usually advised to use the honorific forms to avoid giving offense unintentionally. Today, to a large extent, knowing how to speak is a matter of politeness and decorum, but in traditional Korea and Japan, honorific speech was socially and even legally enforced.

• All societies have customs of taboo, meaning that some behavior is prohibited for religious reasons or because it is culturally regarded as immoral, improper, or offensive. There are linguistic taboos also. Some words cannot be uttered by certain people. For instance, the Yanomamö of the Venezuelan rain forest have a custom known as *name taboo*. It is an insult to utter the names of important people and of deceased relatives in the presence of their living kinfolk. So the Yanomamö sometimes give names like "toenail of sloth" or "whisker of howler monkey" to children, so that when the person dies, people will not have to watch their language so closely. Other name taboos are enforced only against specific individuals. Among the Zulu of southern Africa, for example, a woman was once forbidden to use the name of her husband's father or any of his brothers.

As the preceding examples show, speech is affected by the social context, including how situations are culturally defined and the particular individuals who are speakers and listeners. Norms partly explain why people's use of language varies with context—you are not expected to act and speak the same way at a party as you do in church or at work, for instance, and you know intuitively and unconsciously how to adjust your behavior to these different social scenes.

The choice of speech style, words, and phrases is governed by more than just norms, however. People have personal goals, and speaking in a certain way can help them get what they want. In everyday life, we strive to present the image of ourselves that we want someone else to perceive. The opinions that employers, friends, lovers and hoped-for lovers, coworkers, roommates, and even parents have of us depend partly on how we speak—our use of certain words and avoidance of others, the degree of formality of our style, whether we try to hide or to accentuate regional dialects, and so forth. How we speak is an important part of what social scientists call our *presentation of self*. It is part of how we try to control other people's opinions of us. Like other ways we present ourselves—including the jewelry we wear, how we sit and walk, how we design our hair or shave our head, where and what tattoos to place on our bodies—the way we speak is part of the way we tell others what kind of a person we are. Almost without knowing it, we adjust our speech style, mannerisms, and body language to manage the impressions other people have of us. Our cultural knowledge of these adjustments is mostly routine and usually unconscious (except at job or college interviews!).

We noted early in this chapter that language is composed of symbols that convey conventional meanings. We can now add that the act of speaking itself is a powerful symbol for communicating other kinds of implicit meanings. Just as the morphemes of language communicate messages, so do the multitude of ways in which we communicate using them. Like the clothes we wear, the foods we eat, and the cars we drive, the way we speak is part of the way we present ourselves to the world. Others read meanings into not only our words and sentences but also our style of speech and body language. If we can adjust our style and body language, we can to some extent control the implicit messages we communicate about ourselves. (Today, if you have enough money you can buy the instruction of professional specialists to correct your bad speech and habits and improve your self-presentation.) The act of speaking, then, conveys messages beyond the meanings of the words and sentences themselves. Consciously or unconsciously, every time we speak we tell the world who we are.

Summary

1. Along with culture, language is the most important mental characteristic of humanity that distinguishes us from other animals. Language shaped our biological evolution, allows us to communicate abstract concepts, is necessary for complete social learning, and enables us to rapidly and precisely send and receive complicated messages.

2. Five properties of language differentiate it from other systems of communication. It is composed of discrete units (sounds, words) that are combined in different sequences to convey different meanings. It relies on the shared, conventional understanding of arbitrary and meaningful symbols. Language is productive, allowing us to intuitively and unconsciously combine sounds and words creatively to send an infinite number of messages. It enables humans to communicate about things, events, and persons that are remote in time and space. Its multimedia potential allows communicating in writing and movements (e.g., signing).

3. *Grammar* refers to the elements of language and the rules for how these elements can be combined to form an infinite number of meaningful sentences. Grammatical knowledge is enormously complex, yet it is both unconscious and intuitive. Linguists divide the study of language into several fields.

4. Phonology is the study of the sounds and sound patterns of language. Only some of the sounds humans are able to make with their vocal tracts are recognized by any specific language. The features of sounds that speakers recognize as making a difference in the meanings of words in which they occur vary from language to language and are called phonemes. Among many other phonological differences, languages vary in the way they use voice pitch to convey meanings, as illustrated by tone languages.

5. Morphology studies meaningful sound sequences and the rules by which they are formed. Any sequence of phonemes that conveys a standardized meaning is a morpheme. Free morphemes can stand alone as meaningful sequences, whereas bound morphemes are not used alone but are attached to free morphemes during speech. When people learn a language, they learn its free and bound morphemes and their meanings along with the rules by which bound morphemes can be attached to free morphemes.

6. Some aspects of language reflect the cultural importance of subjects, people, objects, and natural phenomena. The need to converse easily about some subject leads to the elaboration of semantic domains connected to that subject. In other domains, such as relatives, anthropologists have discovered surprising diversity in how various peoples classify kin and give them different labels according to different principles. The words and categories of language are thus related to a culture's classifications of reality.

7. The linguistic relativity hypothesis claimed that the language a people speak predisposes them to see the world in a certain way by shaping their perceptions of reality. Vocabulary and other features of language might influence perceptions by leading its speakers unconsciously to filter out certain properties of reality in favor of other properties. The conventions of language also might force individuals to talk about subjects such as time and space in a certain way if they are to be understood. Although language does, in some ways and to some degree, shape perceptions and worldviews, the notion that language shapes perceptions and thought processes to a significant degree is not accepted by most modern scholars. Recent research concentrates on how specific linguistic domains affect perception and thought.

8. Sociolinguists study how speech is influenced by cultural factors, including culturally defined contexts and situations, the goals of the speaker, the presence of other parties, and so forth. Speech style and body language mark differences in rank and status, as between ethnic groups, classes or statuses, and males and females. Speech formality and overall style are parts of a person's presentation of self; speaking communicates many meanings beyond the words themselves.

Key Terms

grammar	morpheme	Sapir-Whorf hypothesis
phonology	free morpheme	(linguistic relativity
phonemes	bound morpheme	hypothesis)
tone languages	semantic domain	sociolinguistics
morphology		

Suggested Readings

Bauer, Laurie, and Peter Trudgill, eds. *Language Myths.* London: Penguin Books, 1998.

Highly readable volume with chapters that correct common misconceptions about language.

Crystal, David. *English as a Global Language.* 2nd ed. Cambridge: Cambridge University Press, 2003.

Discusses the rise of English in the global arena, with a discussion of future possibilities.

Fromkin, Victoria, Robert Rodman, and Nina Hyams. *An Introduction to Language.* 8th ed. New York: Heinle, 2002.

Excellent and witty textbook, readily understandable despite the technical chapters, with many examples.

Lakoff, Robin. *The Language War.* Berkeley: University of California, 2000.

An influential linguist shows how language is used in political conflicts and intrigues.

Salzmann, Zdenek. *Language, Culture, and Society: An Introduction to Linguistic Anthropology.* 2nd ed. Boulder, Colo.: Westview Press, 1998.

An introductory text describing language as a system of communication as well as how language use is affected by social context, nonverbal communication, and other interconnections between language and culture.

Media Resources

The Wadsworth Anthropology Resource Center
academic.cengage.com/anthropology

The Wadsworth discipline resource website that accompanies *Humanity: An Introduction to Cultural Anthropology*, Eighth Edition, includes a rich array of material, including online anthropological video clips, to help you in the study of cultural anthropology and the specific topics covered in this chapter. Other material includes a case study forum with excerpts from various Wadsworth authors, map exercises, scientist interviews, breaking news in anthropology, and links to additional useful online material. Begin by selecting Cultural Anthropology to take you to videos, research, and more. From the homepage, you may also select Applied Anthropology, which directs you to essays, glossary terms, the case study forum, and a list of internships and careers in anthropology.

4 THE DEVELOPMENT OF ANTHROPOLOGICAL THOUGHT

Anthropology arose in the nineteenth century as a result of contacts between the West and peoples of other lands. How were Polynesians related to other peoples and to Europeans? How does this drawing from the mid-1800s portray them?

Main Issues Today

The Emergence of Anthropology

Late-Nineteenth-Century Unilineal Evolutionism

A Science of Culture?

Anthropological Thought in the Early Twentieth Century

Historical Particularism in the United States (ca. 1900–1940)

British Functionalism, 1920s–1960s

The Tradition of Fieldwork

The Rebirth of Evolutionism in the Mid-Twentieth Century

Anthropological Thought Today: Divisions

Scientific Approaches

Evolutionary Psychology

Cultural Materialism

Humanistic Approaches

Interpretive Anthropology

Postmodernism

Either, Or, or Both?

Why Can't All Those Anthropologists Agree?

Questions addressed in this chapter

What global forces contributed to the emergence of the field of anthropology?

What were the main ideas of the unilineal evolutionists?

How did American historical particularism and British functionalism challenge nineteenth-century evolutionism?

What are the main differences between the scientific and the humanistic approaches to anthropological thought today?

The discipline that today we call anthropology developed out of the contact between Europeans and the rest of the world. As Europeans walked, rode, and sailed to the Middle East, Asia, the two Americas, and the islands of the Pacific Ocean, they ran into people who did not look, act, and think in familiar ways. Especially in the centuries after Columbus's voyages, European intellectuals struggled to understand these peoples and their strange and "barbaric" ways of living. At first, their interpretations were based on their own Judeo-Christian worldview. But by the last few decades of the nineteenth century, advances in knowledge and the changes in worldview that we call science resulted in new ways of understanding humanity and all its diversity. It was then that anthropology became a full-fledged field of academic study in the United States and Europe.

As we will see in this chapter, at its birth, cultural anthropology was distinct from other fields because of its focus on the peoples and cultures of other (non-European) lands. Interest in such peoples and cultures was increasing due to new global contacts, and no existing discipline concentrated on them. Today, it is popular to call far-away peoples with other ways of living "the Other" in contrast to Ourselves—the cultures of the West, as we say today. Although the word is somewhat problematic (*Other* is a bit ethnocentric—Other to whom? to Us, of course), we use it in this chapter because it is a convenient shorthand for the non-Western peoples on which anthropology used to concentrate. Also, it is a common word used by contemporary ethnologists to draw contrasts.

Main Issues Today

In one chapter, it is impossible to discuss all the issues that concern cultural anthropologists in the twenty-first century. We must concentrate on only some of the major questions of today, questions that also run throughout the history of the field: Can and should cultural anthropology be a science, in the same sense that biology is a science? What are the most useful concepts and theoretical orientations to use in studying human cultural diversity? When we study another culture during fieldwork, whose representations should we use? Should the anthropologist/ethnographer decide what's important; that is, should anthropologists define the questions and propose the answers? Or, should the views of the Others themselves take precedence; that is, should the native point of view take priority?

Generally, those who think anthropology is a science try to collect "data" about the Others to describe and explain cultures, much as biologists collect data to explain the diversity of life. The primary goal of scientific anthropologists is to find the general principles that influence cultures—that cause them to be the way they are. Scientific anthropologists often claim that the main goal of their discipline is to explain cultural differences and similarities. In addition to collecting data through fieldwork, scientific types believe that we must compare and contrast cultures of the past and present to discover these general principles. For the most part, they think the aims of science ought to guide our investigations. Quite often, they claim that the views of the people whose cultures they study are not adequate explanations for their own actions, thoughts, and feelings.

In contrast, other modern ethnologists are less concerned—in many cases, not at all concerned—with whether their field is a science. They tend to treat each culture as a unique product of such a vast number of influences that there really are no "general principles" that "cause" differences and similarities. Rather, each culture is a product of its own unique and specific past. Although the phrase is not perfect, here we call them "humanistic anthropologists." Humanistic types tend to focus on portraying specific cultures with sensitivity. One issue humanistic anthropologists are concerned with today is *representation*: Who can legitimately speak for the Others? Should the anthropologist's account of a culture be based on her or his own questions, or should the anthropologist serve more as a translator whose writings allow the Voices of Others to be heard and understood by Ourselves?

The Emergence of Anthropology

Until a few centuries ago, the vast majority of Earth's people had no knowledge of any people or any culture other than the one into which they themselves were born. Of course, there were some exceptions. In the fifth century B.C.E., the Greek historian Herodotus wrote about the peoples of Persia, northern Africa, and nearby regions. Much later, in the 1200s, the Venetian trader Marco Polo reached China (then called "Cathay") via the ancient Silk Road that had connected Rome and China since before the time of Christ. Marco Polo's descriptions of his adventures in China made his book popular among the European literary elite. Descriptions like those of Herodotus and Marco Polo were rare and often treated skeptically, however. Some parts of Marco Polo's account were so surprising to his European readers that many of them did not believe his tales, such as the one about the Chinese burning black rocks as fuel.

Only in the 1500s did the nations of Europe begin to send large numbers of traders, missionaries, military personnel, and officials to other continents. During the next 400 years, Spain, Portugal, Britain, France, and other European nations established formal colonies in large parts of Africa and Asia and in all of the Americas. European visitors and residents of other lands published hundreds of written descriptions about the customs and beliefs of the peoples of the Americas, Asia, Africa, and scattered islands of the Pacific. From these accounts, scholars learned that vast continents across the lands and oceans existed and that they were populated by people who were definitely Other in their customs and beliefs.

Between around 1500 and the mid-1800s, most Western scholars believed in the essential accuracy of the story of creation recounted in the Judeo-Christian Bible. In the biblical account, Earth was only a few thousand years old; one biblical scholar claimed that Earth was created in 4004 B.C.E. Because God created everything in only six days, humanity was the same age—just as old as Earth itself. Further, the biblical creation story contained no substantial reference to any land occupied by the kinds of Others that Europeans were encountering. So who were all these people of the Americas and Africa? How could Western thinkers make sense of these "savages" and their ways of living? What implications did their existence have for the understanding of Ourselves and other human beings? Did their existence challenge the worldview derived from Judeo-Christian teachings?

By the mid-1800s, other puzzles had sprung up. For example, in Europe and North America, people discovered stone tools and other signs that ancient people had lived there. Some tools were side by side with animals that were long extinct, suggesting that those people and animals were contemporaneous. In Germany's Neander Valley, a partial skeleton of a humanlike creature was unearthed. Who made these ancient, prehistoric tools? Were they made by people like those of today? Were the Neanderthal bones human, and, if so, what did they mean?

In Europe, some people (early archaeologists) noted that there seemed to be a regular sequence of toolmaking: the earliest were made of stone, later tools included some of bronze, and still later iron was used. This sequence came to be known as the Three Ages: Stone Age, Bronze Age, and Iron Age. Each age had a greater variety of tools than the preceding age, and the materials used in each stage seemed superior to those of the earlier age. It looked like the lands where the advanced civilizations of the West arose once contained "ruder, simpler, and more primitive" peoples. In the United States, early Anglo settlers of Ohio and surrounding states commented on the existence of large earthen mounds, wondering who could have constructed these ancient monuments—certainly not the ancestors of the "Indians" who lived in these regions today! (Of course, future work showed conclusively that the mounds were made by "Indians," whose cultures later proved to be about as complicated as those of Europe itself.)

Until the mid-1800s, the Judeo-Christian worldview framed most interpretations of contemporary primitives and archaeological remains. Perhaps the "savages" of other lands were the degenerated descendants of Noah's errant son, Ham. Or, maybe they were remnants of one of the lost tribes of Israel, as some scholars claimed about the Polynesians. Possibly, the Devil buried the Neander bones and prehistoric artifacts to undermine believers' faith. Whatever the specific explanation, the customs and beliefs of distant, unfamiliar peoples generally were interpreted in terms of the biblical account of world creation and human history.

Then, beginning in the middle of the nineteenth century, in geology and biology a new set of beliefs about how

◄ This painting by Raphael shows the expulsion of Eve and Adam from Paradise. Well into the nineteenth century, the biblical account of history provided the dominant framework explaining the existence of "natives" in other lands and the nature of their culture.

to understand the world emerged. We generally call these ideas *science*. In fact, the findings of geology and biology led to a whole new worldview about Earth, life in general, and human life in particular, which is now accepted by the majority of scholars from all continents. Geology and biology helped bring humanity within the grasp of the scientific worldview, in which human beings and human cultures are understood to be the result of some process that is entirely natural rather than supernatural.

In geology, James Hutton and Charles Lyell demonstrated that Earth itself was not merely thousands but many millions of years old (today, we know that our planet is about 4.5 billion years old). In biology, Charles Darwin revolutionized popular ideas about life. Rather than each plant and animal being separately made by a Creator, Darwin proposed that one species arose out of another by an entirely natural process. He documented this process in his 1859 book, *On the Origin of Species*.

Darwin's natural process is *evolution*. Evolution means that over a long period of time, one species changes into a new species or into several new species. Some species die out altogether, leaving no descendant species. But often, before its own extinction, a new species changes (evolves) into one or more other species. Thus, multiple new species evolve, and they eventually change into even more species. Given enough time, all the diversity of life on Earth can be explained by this process of natural transformation. From simple beginnings, the natural process of evolution created all the forms of life that surround us today. All it takes is time—millions and millions of years of time. When geology demonstrated the age of Earth, it showed that our world was old enough for diverse and complicated life-forms to evolve from simple beginnings.

Of course, Darwin's main impact was on biology and the field now called paleoanthropology. Darwin established the possibility that the human species evolved from an apelike ancestor, and his idea was confirmed in the twentieth century (see Chapter 1). Darwin's ideas about change in nature influenced how Western intellectuals viewed human *cultural* existence as well as *biological* existence. If biological life-forms could evolve, then could cultural forms also have arisen through a process of change? Simple forms of organic life had transformed into more complex forms of life. Analogously, in cultural existence, some scholars reasoned that later, more complex ways of living had developed out of earlier, simpler ways of living.

During these same centuries in Europe and North America, the Industrial Revolution and the Enlightenment (the Age of Reason) brought about a general belief in progress—the notion that human life has gotten better and better over the course of many centuries. Darwin and some of his followers wrote of the "struggle for survival" and "survival of the fittest." To some, the idea of struggle suggested that progress occurred because stronger individuals and groups succeed by outcompeting weaker individuals and groups. Could the struggle for survival also apply to human societies?

Thus, nineteenth-century scholars interested in human culture had access to two major kinds of information: (1) written accounts left by Westerners who visited other lands, including the colonies of the European nations, and (2) tools that ancient, long-disappeared peoples from Europe and North America had left in the earth. They also were exposed to ideas about origins, evolution, and progress. Logically enough, many believed that there was a relationship between the various peoples in the written accounts and the ancient people who had made the prehistoric tools and monuments. The long-disappeared prehistoric peoples of Europe and the Americas were in some ways similar to the peoples described in the accounts of Western visitors to other continents. Just as stone tools were the earliest form of technology, so some peoples still alive in the nineteenth century (like the aborigines of Australia and Tasmania) were examples of the earliest forms of culture.

Late-Nineteenth-Century Unilineal Evolutionism

In accord with the intellectual climate of the late nineteenth century, a few scholars became interested in how and why cultures had changed over the course of many millennia. The ideas of evolution, progress, stages, and survival were the keys. Just like plants and animals, cultures had evolved. The earliest "simple" (or "primitive") cultures had given rise to ever more "complex" ("more advanced") cultures. For the most part, this evolution represented progress or development: later cultures were, in some *objective* sense, superior to earlier cultures. (Here *objective* means that there is a universal standard by which superiority can be judged, an assumption that later anthropologists questioned.)

Briefly stated: As human cultures evolved, they passed through a series of stages. Examples of each stage could be found in the peoples described in all those written accounts and also in the artifacts that prehistoric people had left behind, in or on the land. Although nineteenth-century Western civilization represented the highest stage of cultural evolution, in many other places lived peoples whose cultures remained in earlier stages. The cultures of these peoples had survived into the present because they had not yet evolved, or they had evolved at

slower rates than the cultures of more advanced peoples. These peoples were survivors of earlier stages of culture, meaning that they were remnants or relics from humanity's distant past.

Today we call the approach of these early anthropologists **unilineal evolutionism.** At the time, the anthropologists who adopted this approach could not have known that future generations of anthropologists would challenge most of their goals and methods.

For example, the evolutionists thought that survivors of the very earliest stages of cultural evolution still exist in Australia and Polynesia. In other places, remnants of later, intermediate stages can be found: the people of the Pacific islands called Fiji and the Iroquois Indians are living representatives of the middle stage of cultural evolution, which one scholar called *barbarism.* In still other regions, later stages exist: the Incas of South America and the Chinese, Koreans, and Japanese are "civilized" people. Civilization is a higher cultural stage than the stage represented by the Fijians and Iroquois. By carefully studying and comparing peoples who exemplified all the stages, evolutionists believed they could reconstruct the nature of the various stages and figure out what had led one stage to progress to the next.

The unilineal evolutionists are usually considered to be the first true cultural anthropologists. They had a subject matter that was by and large separate from that of other disciplines—the cultures and societies of peoples who lived in foreign lands (the "Others"). They had a reasonably coherent objective—to reconstruct and understand the stages through which human cultures had traveled on their long road to civilization. They used a methodology that was then in its infancy—comparing and contrasting peoples in various stages of development to discover the nature of the stages and the relationships between them. In brief, cultural anthropology became an academic discipline in the West because it had its own subject matter, objectives, and methods.

Consider just one example of unilineal evolutionism. In 1871, the Englishman E. B. Tylor published the landmark book *Primitive Culture.* In it, he investigated the origins and development of religious beliefs. Where did religion come from? Tylor argued that religious beliefs originated out of peoples' attempts to explain certain experiences. For example, immediately after someone dies, the physical body still exists even though the life of the person has ended. What explains the difference between a living and a dead person? Being ignorant of the actual causes of death, early humans reasoned that living people have a spiritual essence (a "soul") that animates or gives life to the physical body. When the soul leaves the

◀ In their effort to see how all the Other cultures related to one another and to the West, unilineal evolutionists arranged cultures into a sequence of stages. One scholar placed the Fijians of the Pacific in the middle stage called *barbarism*. This 1840 drawing is of a Fijian "Club Dance." Notice how the drawing does make the people of Fiji look barbaric.

body, the person stops breathing and moving and, hence, dies. Also, people have dreams, trances, and visions in which they see images of all kinds of things and events. Logically, but falsely, early peoples concluded that the things are real and that the events actually occurred. Tylor called the form of religion that this reasoning produces *animism*, which is the belief that the world is inhabited by spiritual beings of many kinds, such as nature spirits living in mountains, trees, water, heavenly bodies, and animals; spirits of deceased persons (ghosts); spirits that cause illness; spirits that possess someone and make them insane; and a multitude of other spirits.

For Tylor, animism was the earliest form of religion. It was the primeval, simplest, most primitive religion from which all others arose. Tylor thought that living peoples who still had animistic beliefs were survivors of this earliest religion. Anthropologists could learn about the earliest form of religion by studying peoples who were still animistic. How did animism evolve into its later forms? Over time, people reasoned that some of the spirits were more important or influential than others. Eventually, such spirits were elevated to higher positions. They became gods of various things and activities, such as gods of sun, moon, sky, rain, earth, clans, war, agriculture, love, fertility, and so forth. There were at one time many such gods, well known from Greek and Roman mythology. This stage of religion is called *polytheism*, meaning religions that include a belief in many gods, each with his, hers, or its own sphere of influence.

What about *monotheism*? This form of religious belief was represented by the Judeo-Christian heritage of the West. It was also familiar from Islam, which had been known to Europeans for more than a millennium. Tylor argued that monotheism evolved when one of the gods of polytheism acquired dominance over other gods. Eventually, over centuries, the other gods came to be seen as false gods or not to exist at all.

Tylor's three stages of religion—animism, polytheism, and monotheism—illustrate the main ideas of the unilineal evolutionists. Examples of each stage survived in many scattered places—in fact, on all continents. One stage evolved into another, not just in one region or continent, but in many. For example, animistic religions evolved into polytheistic religions among many peoples, and, in turn, polytheism evolved into monotheism several times. The fact that the same sequence of stages occurred again and again among widely scattered peoples seemed to imply that human cultures developed in regular, recurrent patterns. If so, then human cultural evolution followed some sort of "law," meaning that some similar process was resulting in similar changes, analogous to Darwinian evolution.

A Science of Culture?

Following this logic, most unilineal evolutionists thought that the new field of anthropology could and should be a science. They believed that the development of culture could be explained much as biology explains the evolution of living organisms. Thus, Tylor (1871, 2) wrote that human "thoughts, wills, and actions accord with laws as definite as those which govern the motion of waves, the combinations of acids and bases, and the growth of plants and animals."

Few anthropologists of today agree with this statement because, unlike waves and chemicals, humans have active minds of their own and do not always think and act in ways that follow laws or general principles. Many contemporary thinkers do not believe that what Tylor called a "science of culture" is possible. Some do not think it is even desirable, because humans have minds and feelings that are unlike those of other living things.

The unilineal evolutionists nevertheless made significant contributions to the development of anthropology. Thanks largely to their writings, by the early twentieth century, anthropology became a full-fledged academic discipline. Scholarly fields that investigate various aspects of humankind were already established in European and American universities as departments or schools of religion, theology, art, philosophy, classics, history, anatomy, and so forth. But a discipline whose focus was the physical and cultural diversity of humanity was not recognized until the last decades of the 1800s. In the United States, the first anthropology course was taught in 1879 at the University of Rochester. In 1886, the first anthropology department was founded at the University of Pennsylvania. It was followed near the turn of the century by university departments at Columbia, Harvard, Chicago, and California (Berkeley).

Anthropological Thought in the Early Twentieth Century

Despite their contributions, many assumptions and facts of the unilineal evolutionists were rejected in the early decades of the twentieth century, partly because their methods were flawed and much of their information was erroneous. Anthropologists in America and Great Britain set out in different directions, as we now discuss.

Historical Particularism in the United States (ca. 1900–1940)

At the end of the 1800s and for the next three or four decades, the American anthropologist Franz Boas and his students questioned the methods and the findings of unilineal evolutionism. Boas was so influential in the United States that he is often called the "father of American anthropology." In his view, each and every culture has its own separate past and each culture is "one of a kind"—that is, different from all others. Because each culture was affected by almost everything that had happened to it in the past, and because different things had happened to different cultures, each culture is unique. This approach is usually called **historical particularism** (or **historicism**). Notice that if it is true that each culture is the distinctive product of its own history, then it is difficult to identify any general principles that affect all cultures. Rather, each culture must be studied on its own terms.

Clearly, the unilineal evolutionists did not study each culture "on its own terms." In making their comparisons and formulating their stages, they imposed their own "terms" (e.g., complexity, progress, stages) on other cultures. Take the notion of complexity in the realm of technology, for example. Most people *might* agree that guns and bullets are more complex than bows and arrows, which, in turn, are more complex than spears and throwing sticks. But what can *complex* mean when applied to other customs and beliefs, like those about marriage, political organization, or religion? In what sense is the marriage form called "monogamy" more complex than forms called "polygamy"? Boas realized that such features are merely *different* from culture to culture. By any *objective* criterion, one form of marriage or religion does not represent "progress" over another.

The stages of the nineteenth-century evolutionists derived from ethnocentric assumptions, Boas thought. They placed their own cultural existence at the top of the cultural ladder, looked around for peoples whose cultures represented the "earlier stages," gave the stages labels like "savagery," slotted particular cultures into their preconceived classifications, and then concluded that they were discovering the laws of cultural development using the methods of science.

As an example of Boas's point, consider the American unilineal evolutionist Lewis Henry Morgan. Morgan identified three stages of cultural evolution, which he labeled "savagery," "barbarism," and "civilization." He viewed civilization as the highest form, of course. It was Morgan who had placed the Fijians and Iroquois in the middle stage of "barbarism." But many peoples, such as Japanese, Koreans, and Chinese, would have said that it was Morgan's own people who were the "barbarians." So, although it might be possible to speak of progress in technology, it is difficult to do so for cultures as wholes. Does monotheism represent "progress" over animism or polytheism? Perhaps it does, but you are more likely to

▲ Often considered the "father of American anthropology," Franz Boas challenged the unilineal evolutionists' concept of stages. In doing so, he made many lasting contributions, including popularizing the notion of cultural relativism and marshaling evidence that cultural differences and biological differences are largely independent of each other.

think so if your own religion is monotheistic. And if your criteria for defining "progress" were ethnocentric, then your concept of "stages of progress" obviously is almost useless.

These arguments seemed to mean that the unilineal evolutionists were wrong: Cultures do not develop along a single series of progressive stages, culminating in nineteenth-century Western civilization. Instead, each culture changes along its own unique path, depending on the particular influences that affect it. To understand a culture, therefore, we must study it *individually,* not as a representative of some hypothetical stage, which Boas thought existed only in the minds of the evolutionists. Anthropologists must free themselves from preconceived

ideas and assumptions and give up speculative schemes of evolution and ethnocentric definitions of progress.

The historical particularists also pointed out that that it is very difficult to place the customs and beliefs of *different* peoples into the *same* stage of progress. In most cases, the customs and beliefs of widely scattered peoples only appear to be similar, although they are, in fact, different. For example, Tylor probably would have said that Japanese Shinto and Chinese Daoism are both examples of animism because both religions believed in a multitude of spirits. In contrast, the ancient religions of both Greece and Polynesia had many gods and so would be classified as polytheistic. But are Shinto and Daoism the same "form" of religion just because Shintoists and Daoists believe in many spirits? And how can you claim that the religions of ancient Greece and Hawaii have the same "form" and therefore belong in the same "stage"? What would the Chinese and Japanese, or the ancient Greeks and the Hawaiians, themselves say about such comparisons?

In short, to say that the customs and beliefs of two or more Other cultures are the "same" or "similar" because they look the same to Us is to ignore a host of differences between these cultures. The Greeks and Hawaiians had different gods, who did different kinds of things to and for people, and for the historicists, this is enough to consider them different forms of religion. (Carried to an extreme, of course, this means that every religion has a different form from every other religion, which makes every religion unique.) The only way to get a valid notion of stage would be to study the development of each religion separately, which might lead to the discovery of the stages of evolution for each religion. But these stages, if found, would probably not be universal. The same applies to other elements of culture, Boas thought.

These simple points had major implications for how Westerners studied all those Others. If it is true that each culture is unique, then it is difficult to compare cultures to one another. If every culture has a past that is fundamentally different from the past of every other culture, then it is not likely that general laws or principles exist that apply everywhere. This would make a genuine science of culture difficult because science attempts to find general principles or processes that explain human cultures.

Boas thought the basic assumptions of the evolutionists were flawed, mainly because their ideas about progress and stages were ethnocentric. But he also noted that the ways the evolutionists investigated other cultures—their methods—led them to errors. Today, nineteenth-century evolutionists often are called "armchair anthropologists" because they themselves had not lived among any of those "savages" and "barbarians" (with a few exceptions like Morgan, who actually studied the Iroquois firsthand). Instead, for the most part, they relied on descriptive accounts written by people who too often were untrained, who presented their "impressions" rather than "hard facts," and who were biased in their perceptions of Others.

Boas thought that professional anthropologists must abandon the comforts of their armchairs and engage in firsthand interactions with members of other cultures. The main need of the infant field of anthropology was more factual information about other cultures, not endless speculations in faculty offices and classrooms. Anthropologists themselves must conduct *ethnographic fieldwork.* This was the only way they can be somewhat confident that they have their facts correct. And only after anthropologists are sure that their facts are correct should they begin to even try to make general statements or to theorize about cultures. Boas, in brief, wanted more and better descriptions of more cultures.

Boas thought it essential that fieldworkers remain objective as they observe and record the customs and beliefs of other cultures. Fieldworkers must enter the communities and lives of the Others with an open mind. Above all, they should not be ethnocentric because ethnocentrism inevitably leads to errors in fieldwork. If a fieldworker visits another people with an attitude of superiority, he or she is not likely to come away with accurate, objective information. Fieldworkers who go into the field with preconceived notions are likely to observe and report on things that are consistent with their own preconceptions and not notice or report on contradictory things.

According to Boas, fieldworkers should adopt an attitude of cultural relativism. While living among Others, we must temporarily suspend our own values, morality, standards of hygiene, ways of interpreting actions, and so forth. We must not apply our own standards and beliefs to evaluate the standards and beliefs of Others. Not only does a relativistic attitude help us fit into the community, but it also minimizes the chances that we will misinterpret or misunderstand people because we see them through the filter of our own culture's perceptions and biases.

Boas himself conducted firsthand fieldwork among two Native American peoples, the Inuit and the Kwakiutl. He sent many of his students at Columbia University out for fieldwork experiences, including Margaret Mead, who became famous for her 1928 book, *Coming of Age in Samoa.* Because of the influence of Boas and his students, in American anthropology of today, living among and participating in the lives of the people under study is the main method by which one becomes a professional

and acquires a positive reputation in the discipline. The tradition of fieldwork is one of Boas's lasting legacies.

In addition to learning more about cultures, firsthand fieldwork has another benefit. The traditional customs, beliefs, and languages of many of the world's peoples had already disappeared because of diseases, genocide, assimilation, and other effects of global contacts. Surviving cultures and languages were vanishing or changing rapidly. Boas believed it was the duty of anthropologists to record disappearing traditions before they were gone forever. Many students of Boas, like A. L. Kroeber and Robert Lowie, did fieldwork among Native American peoples, whose cultures they believed were especially endangered.

Aside from giving us the doctrine of cultural relativism, Boas did as much as anyone to show that biological differences and cultural differences are largely independent of each other; that is, the culture of a human group is a product of learning and tradition, not of genetic heritage (see Chapter 2).

In sum, historical particularism made four enduring contributions to modern anthropology: (1) it discredited the overly speculative schemes of the unilineal evolutionists; (2) it insisted that fieldwork is the primary means of acquiring reliable information; (3) it imparted the idea that cultural relativism as a methodological principle is essential for the most accurate understanding of another culture; and (4) it demonstrated and popularized the notion that cultural differences and biological differences have little to do with each other. These contributions helped to shape modern cultural anthropology.

Historical particularism gave rise to other movements in the first half of the twentieth century, all of which shared its emphasis on cultural uniqueness and relativism. One of the most influential is called **configurationalism.** One of Boas's students was Ruth Benedict, whose 1934 book, *Patterns of Culture,* is considered a classic. Benedict argued that, from the vast array of humanly possible cultures, each particular culture develops only a limited number of "patterns" or "configurations" that dominate the thinking and responses of its members. Each culture develops a distinctive set of feelings and motivations that orients the thoughts and behaviors of its members. (Note the emphasis on cultural uniqueness.) These configurations give each culture a distinctive style, and the thoughts and actions of its members reflect its configurations. Behavior that one people consider crazy or abnormal might be acceptable or even ideal among another people. (Note the emphasis on cultural relativism.)

For example, Benedict wrote that the Kwakiutl of the Northwest Coast of North America are individualistic, competitive, intemperate, and egoistic. This cultural configuration affects Kwakiutl customs. They stage ceremonies known as *potlatches,* in which one kin group gives away enormous quantities of goods to another. The aim is to shame the rival group because if the rival is unable to return the presentations on certain occasions, its members suffer a loss of prestige. In fact, to avoid losing prestige, the recipient group is obliged to return gifts of even greater value. Over time, the presentations might snowball until the members of one group, in their ceaseless quest for prestige, are materially impoverished (or so Benedict imagined). The whole complex of behaviors connected to the potlatch reflects the cultural configuration of the Kwakiutl—the Kwakiutl are so caught up by the prestige motivation that groups impoverish themselves to achieve this goal. To describe the Kwakiutl, Benedict used the term *Dionysian,* after the Greek god known for his drinking, partying, and other excesses.

Benedict contrasted the Kwakiutl configuration to the Zuni of the North American Southwest. Zuni control their emotions, she claimed. They are moderate, modest, stoical, orderly, and restrained in their behavior. They do not boast or attempt to rise above their peers but are social and cooperative. This "Apollonian" cultural theme, as Benedict called it, permeates all of Zuni life. Unlike a Kwakiutl leader, a Zuni man does not seek status; indeed, a leadership role practically has to be forced on him. So, according to Benedict, each culture has its unique patterns and themes, which makes it possible for a person that culture A labels a megalomaniac to be culture B's ideal person.

Although modern anthropologists agree that different cultures emphasize different themes or patterns, most think that Benedict overemphasized the effect of culture on the thoughts, feelings, and actions of its members. It is misleading to characterize cultures in simple terms, such as that Kwakiutl are Dionysian (given to excess), whereas Zuni are Apollonian (moderate in all things). To do so easily leads one people to develop stereotypes about the "personality" or "character" of another people. For example, some Americans say the Japanese have "authoritarian" personalities because they seem to submit to the authority of their bosses and to be devoted to their companies. In most such opinions, one's own culture is assumed to be the standard, and others are judged on the basis of that reference point. Thus, Italians are "excitable" to North American perceptions because they seem to be so enthusiastic about love, food, and family. Similarly, according to common American stereotypical labels, Irish have fiery tempers, Swiss are humorless, and Swedes are sensual. But "the" Zuni, "the" Irish, and

▲ Ruth Benedict, here shown with two Native Americans of the Blackfoot tribe, was one of Boas's most influential students. Among her writings was *The Chrysanthemum and the Sword,* a 1946 book that tried to elucidate Japanese culture to the West shortly after World War II.

"the" members of other human communities are not simple products of their culture's "configurations." Rather, the personality and character of the members of a culture are highly variable, and the relationship between culture and the behavior of individuals is complicated (see Chapter 2).

Historical particularism greatly changed the way anthropologists thought about culture and conducted research, but it has limitations. Think about the claim that each culture is unique—like no other. Certainly, if differences between cultures are what we are most interested in, we can always find them. Then we can go on to claim that no two cultures are alike. So at some level, the claim that "each culture is unique" is correct. So also is the claim that no two individuals brought up within the same culture are exactly alike. Yet they *are* alike in some ways. So, *in some ways,* no culture is like any other. But also, *in some ways,* a given culture does have things in common with some other cultures. More generally speaking, there are similarities as well as differences between ways of life. Historical particularists tended to overlook the similarities and to neglect the investigation of factors that might explain them.

Consider also the claim that, because each culture is the unique product of its particular past, one cannot generalize about the causes of cultural differences. Most particularists said that there was no small set of factors that were generally important causes of cultural differences. Rather, which factors are "causes" and which "effects" depends on the particular culture and its history. But others disagree. To say that the natural environment is most important in culture X, art styles in Y, values in Z, and so forth, is to say little more than that everything is related to most everything else. The holistic perspective (see Chapter 1) assumes that culture is "integrated." But it is possible that some influences are more important than other influences in all or most human populations; for example, it is possible that how people interact with their natural environment is *generally* more important than art or values in causing a people to live the way they do. Recognizing interrelationships and integration does not imply that every factor has equal weight as a causal influence.

By the 1940s, the interests of many American anthropologists returned to discovering the general principles of human cultural existence. Meanwhile, another way of studying human societies and cultural diversity developed in Europe.

British Functionalism, 1920s–1960s

At about the same time that historicism was popular in the United States, a very different approach developed in Great Britain. Generally called **functionalism**, its main tenet was that social and cultural features should be explained mainly by their useful functions to the people and to the society—that is, by the benefits they confer on individuals and groups. Because humans are above all social beings who live in families, communities, and other kinds of organized groups, most aspects of their culture and society serve to help individuals meet their needs and/or to contribute to the maintenance of the society itself.

One British functionalist was Bronislaw Malinowski. He emphasized the needs of individuals. To him, the main purpose of culture is to serve human biological, psychological, and social needs. What are these needs? Most of the biological needs are rather obvious: nutrition, shelter, protection from enemies, maintenance of health and—if the society is to persist—biological reproduction. Humans also have psychological and social needs, such as the needs for love and affection, for security, for self-

expression, and for a sense of belonging. The purpose of culture is to fulfill these needs. Unlike other animals, humans have few inborn instructions or instincts that tell us how to meet our needs. Instead, as we grow up in our culture, we learn the behaviors, social rules, values, and ways of perceiving the world that guide our actions and our thoughts. Some parts of culture meet individual needs directly, such as knowledge of how to acquire food or make shelter. Other aspects function to raise and socialize new generations of group members, such as educational practices and family life. Still others encourage people to adhere to group values and rules that make cooperation possible, such as religious beliefs and practices and creative arts. Thus, even if a given feature of culture does not *directly* serve individual needs, it still contributes to the maintenance of the entire cultural system without which human survival would be difficult (see Chapter 2).

Of course, no one can deny that an important function of culture is to help people meet their "needs." But, in some kinds of societies, some individuals and groups have their needs met more completely than others. Further, culture itself can create perceived needs (you can think you need something when you don't really). And the social and economic conditions under which people live make them need some things that people of other times and places did not need. If you were an attorney in Britain or a college student in Japan in the 1960s, you would not need a computer, but you would today, if you are to be successful. Finally, it is likely that "needs" grow as the capacity for meeting them increases, as all economists know. Thus, the idea of "needs" is more of a problem than it appears to be, since "needs" do vary from place to place and time to time. Further, although it is correct to say that our culture helps us meet our needs, this statement does not take us very far in understanding culture. It hardly tells us anything useful about cultural *differences*.

Another influential functionalist from Great Britain was A. R. Radcliffe-Brown. Instead of emphasizing the needs of individuals, Radcliffe-Brown focused on the needs of societies. For him, maintaining orderly social relationships—between family members, friends, members of the same village or town, leaders and followers, and the like—is the main function that must be met if societies are to exist and persist. He imagined that a human society is like a living organism in which each organ has a function to fulfill that contributes to the life of the whole body. In studying a body, a physiologist not only looks at each organ individually, but also considers its role in the life process of the whole organism. Just as organisms cannot stay alive for long unless their organs function properly, so a society cannot persist unless its

◄ Bronislaw Malinowski was an influential British functionalist. He is best known for his ethnographies about the Trobriand Islanders. Like the American Franz Boas, Malinowski insisted that cultural anthropologists conduct firsthand fieldwork themselves.

© Mary Evans Picture Library/Alamy

various institutions play their proper roles in social life. Radcliffe-Brown felt that most customs and beliefs a people share help their society remain in *equilibrium* (a steady state, with not too much conflict or rapid change).

From today's perspective, it is clear that societies are not very much like living organisms. Individuals have minds and motives of their own, unlike cells and organs. And few societies are in equilibrium for very long. Societies change constantly. The rate of change and the direction of change vary, and functionalism had relatively little of lasting value to say about change.

Despite these shortcomings, the British functionalists did make lasting contributions to anthropology. By emphasizing the importance of social relationships between individuals and of living in organized groups, they led anthropologists to pay more attention to how groups are organized and how they relate to one another. Their emphasis on equilibrium led us to pay more attention to how the parts of a society and culture fit together, and therefore made us attentive to integration.

The Tradition of Fieldwork

Like the American historicists, the British functionalists helped establish the tradition of firsthand fieldwork. Malinowski is famous mainly because of his fieldwork and ethnographic writings about the Trobriand Islanders of the western Pacific. Some of his books, like *Argonauts of the Western Pacific* and *The Sexual Life of Savages,* are ethnographic classics. Not only is fieldwork the best means of obtaining reliable information about a people,

but it is also a necessary part of the training of anthropologists, Malinowski believed. We cannot claim to understand people, or the diverse cultures in which people of various places grow up, until we have immersed ourselves in the experience of some culture other than our own.

Malinowski thought the main objective of fieldwork is to see the culture as an insider to the culture sees it. In an often-quoted passage from his famous 1922 ethnography *Argonauts of the Western Pacific,* Malinowski (1922, 25) wrote: "[T]he final goal, of which an Ethnographer [*sic*] should never lose sight . . . is, briefly, to grasp the native's point of view, his relation to life, to realise *his* vision of *his* world." This idea of what fieldwork is all about remains influential—though controversial—today.

In order to "grasp the native's point of view," fieldworkers usually make visits that last at least a year, and they often return to the community many times. Also, fieldwork involves deep involvement in the daily lives of the people. Where possible, fieldworkers should master the local language, live with the local people, participate in games and voyages, become familiar with how members of families relate to one another, observe lots of ceremonies and rituals, record myths and legends, and—generally—learn all they can about a culture from interacting with people and participating in their lives. This way of learning about another culture is generally called *participant observation,* and it is the most important method for many fieldworkers.

Because of the influence of early-twentieth-century anthropologists like Boas and Malinowski, the fieldwork experience is today an essential part of the graduate

As we've seen, anthropology arose after Western Europeans contacted Other peoples—natives, as the British often called them—of Africa, Asia, Australia, the Americas, and the Pacific. For nearly a century, the theoretical and field research of most Western anthropologists occurred with little regard for how the Natives would react to the research and its publication. For the most part, the neglect of local reactions was not because researchers did not care about the people, but because so few of them were literate enough to read our writings. Most theorists, of both the scientific and humanistic camps, were interested in what Malinowski called the "native's point of view," but they did not worry too much about the natives' views of the scholarly books and articles anthropologists wrote about them.

Today anthropology itself has globalized. Countries whose peoples we study have universities with their own anthropologists who write about their own country or their own people. National or regional governments are sometimes reluctant to allow Western fieldworkers to come in. Many people who appear in our ethnographies now read what we write and are often critical of our findings and, occasionally, of how they are used. Some are resentful because their customs, beliefs, opinions, and Voices are represented by outsiders rather than by themselves. Some believe (usually mistakenly) that anthropologists grow wealthy by writing about them, while they are paid relatively little when they assist us. To phrase the general point as a question: What happens to anthropology when its subjects begin investigating themselves? (One answer: Invite them to investigate Us—Our families, religions, politics, education, medical practices, and the like.)

The Japanese anthropologist Takami Kuwayama discusses these and related issues in his 2004 book, *Native Anthropology*. He points out that most academic disciplines have spread across national boundaries, thus becoming global. As this happens, unequal relationships develop between those scholars born in Western nations in which the disciplines originated and scholars from other regions.

A major issue for a global anthropology is *representation*: Who is best qualified to describe the culture of a people, to translate their customs and beliefs into a form that is intelligible to outsiders? Some anthropological scholars from the West are reluctant to give up their claim to represent the Others, even when educated Others challenge their findings. Kuwayama notes that because the most well-endowed and prestigious universities (and, we might add, individual scholars) are in Western Europe and North America, the representation that prevails is as likely to be based on political concerns as on concerns about accuracy or completeness. That is, because of the history of relationships between the West and the Others, the scholarly voices and research of Westerners are often more authoritative than the voices and research of Others.

training of almost all cultural anthropologists. Fieldwork demonstrates that you can *do* anthropology yourself as well as *study* the anthropological research and theories of your teachers. It shows that you can contribute original knowledge about Others, and in most colleges and universities, making new contributions is essential for success in one's academic career.

Until 20 or 30 years ago, most fieldworkers were from either North America or Western Europe. As a consequence, most ethnographies describing the ways of life of diverse peoples were written by Western anthropologists, who for the most part were trained in Western universities. But anthropology today has gone global. People of many nationalities representing many cultures are now anthropologists, interested in writing about the very people whom Western ethnographers used to monopolize. This has led to new issues, and in the future new ways of representing Other cultures are likely to emerge (see the Globalization box).

For many, fieldwork transforms them as persons. After being intensively exposed to another way of living, we often come away with a different perspective on Ourselves. Even anthropologists have trouble overcoming their own biases and not looking at Others through ethnocentric lenses. Fieldwork is the closest most of come to dissolving the differences between Us and Others. This is another reason most professional anthropologists conduct fieldwork. That, and the fact that most of us like it.

The Rebirth of Evolutionism in the Mid-Twentieth Century

The objections of Boas to unilineal evolutionism were powerful ones, but other studies of cultural evolution (though not the unilineal kind) came back into fashion in the 1940s. The problems with the "old" evolutionism were its flawed assumptions and inadequate methods.

For example, simply because Western ethnographers are outsiders to local cultures, they sometimes claim to be more objective than Native anthropologists, who tend to see their own customs and beliefs through their own cultural lenses. Or, Westerners may say that Native anthropologists have an interest in making their own people look good to outsiders, so they romanticize local customs by de-emphasizing facts that they fear will leave readers with negative impressions. In brief, some claim that a Native is more likely to have a political agenda to pursue, while outsiders supposedly are more interested in accuracy.

You can imagine what most Native anthropologists think of such opinions, which make it seem that they are the only ones with axes to grind. This dilemma seems unresolvable. As we discuss later in this chapter, some modern anthropologists say that the Voices of the Natives should usually carry more weight. Others claim that anthropology is a science that seeks to generalize through comparisons, and there is no reason to think that any Native is better qualified to compare than an outsider.

Kuwayama offers a solution to the dilemma of writing about cultures in a global community. He proposes that anthropology develop a forum in which all opinions about an issue of fact or interpretation can be aired on an equal footing. At present, if you are to speak authoritatively (have others take your views seriously), you must publish. You must write scholarly books and find someone to publish them. Better, you must get your articles published in scholarly journals that are peer reviewed (that is, the article is critically analyzed by others who are recognized experts in the subject, who decide whether your article is meritorious enough to be published). Many Native anthropologists have less access to the world of publishing than most scholars in the major universities. Therefore, the information they gather and the opinions they offer are usually underrepresented in the global community of anthropological scholars. The fact that English has become the primary language of discussion does not help the situation. Finally, in publishing as in other realms of life, sometimes it's whom you know rather than what you say that determines whether something you write appears in print.

Kuwayama suggests that more people be given an opportunity to have their Voices heard. Exactly how this opportunity will be offered is unclear, even to Kuwayama. But he notes that worldwide access to the Internet is increasing dramatically and that it is more inclusive than other forums because anyone can post to it. (Interestingly, this is exactly the reason so many scholars mistrust the Internet: except for the restrictions placed on content from countries such as China, there are few controls over it, so "anyone can post to it," which is why so much of it is "garbage.") Someday there may be a wiki-anthropology.

Source: Kuwayama (2004)

Some mid-twentieth-century scholars thought they corrected the assumptions and adopted more sophisticated methods. They developed a "new evolutionism," or **neoevolutionism**, so called because their objectives were much the same as the objectives of the nineteenth-century evolutionists, but their methods and specific theories were different. Two North American anthropologists were the most influential neoevolutionists.

Writing mostly in the 1940s–1960s, Leslie White thought that the nineteenth-century evolutionists got some things right after all. The technologies (tools, technical knowledge, skills) that people use to acquire nature's resources have, in fact, improved over the centuries. "Improved" how? Improved in the sense that people with better technologies are able to harness more energy per person per year. That is, some technologies are more productive or efficient than others, so people can produce more useful products with them. White held that it is, in fact, possible to measure cultural evolution *objectively:* Cultural evolution occurs as the amount of energy harnessed from the natural environment increases. So, in principle, it is possible to define cultural evolution without resorting to questionable criteria, which, if true, overcomes one of historical particularism's objections.

White went further. Over long periods of time, as humans discovered and invented new technologies that increased energy capture, changes in the organization of societies and in the ideas and beliefs of their members followed. To use White's own terminology, changes in the "social system" and the "ideological system" occur as a consequence of improvements in the "technological system." Generally speaking, over time, the social and ideological systems have grown more complex. But what does *complex* mean? Complex means that the scale (size) of societies increases dramatically, occupational specialization develops, large-scale trade and long-distance exchange grow, political centralization occurs, and inequality between classes becomes greater. Again, White argued that all these social changes are largely independent of the anthropologist's own prejudices and preconceptions, so they also are objective measures of evolution.

For example, most people who live by hunting and gathering wild resources live in small, mobile groups in which there is little division of labor except by sex, in which leadership roles are nonexistent or weak, and in which all families have access to about the same amount of food and other valued products. In contrast, soon after a new source of food energy—namely, the cultivation of domesticated foods (crops) and the raising of domesticated animals (livestock)—came into existence several thousand years ago, new forms of culture evolved. People started living in larger, more settled communities (villages), some people took up new activities like making pottery or creating art, more powerful leaders emerged, and some families had access to more food or other valued goods than others. After a couple thousand years, the new technology became so productive and its social and ideological consequences came to be realized in a completely new form of society—civilization. Civilization evolved in regions like Mesopotamia, Egypt, southern Asia, eastern China, Mesoamerica, and western South America.

White believed that the increased energy capture made possible by improved technology *caused* most important changes in human cultures. The transition to agriculture caused civilization to develop in some regions, and the discovery of how to use the energy of burning coal to power looms caused the rise of industrial society in Great Britain. For this reason, White is often called a *technological determinist*, meaning he believed that technology causes ("determines") most everything else in culture that is important. What causes changes in aspects of culture like family organization and political structures? To White, these were part of the "social system" and, hence, largely responded to changes in technology. What about aspects of culture like religion, philosophy, worldview, and art? To White, these were part of the "ideological system," and by and large they changed to reflect and justify changes in the social system.

In summary, White generalized that as technology develops, culture evolves to take advantage of the increased energy available and new ideologies arise to explain and justify the new technological and social arrangements. For White, the evolution of civilization everywhere resulted from increased energy capture, and in a broad view all civilizations had similar social and ideological systems. So, cultural evolution is in fact a regular, patterned process about which anthropologists can generalize. We can make comparisons and contrasts. Each culture is not entirely unique, and we can legitimately provide explanations that do not depend on the "native point of view." White agreed with E. B. Tylor that anthropology should be "the science of culture," and White made this the title of a book published in 1949.

Another neoevolutionist, Julian Steward, agreed with White that how people acquire natural resources and cope with their environment is the most important part of a people's way of life. But, more than White, Steward's theory emphasized the natural environment, which provided food and other necessary resources. Steward's ideas eventually gave rise to the modern field of cultural ecology, which studies how humans relate to the environment. We discuss such studies in Chapter 6.

Men like White and Steward made attempts to explain culture in scientific terms respectable again in American ethnology. For White, the general principle needed to explain cultural evolution is technological determinism. For Steward, interactions between humans and their environments are the most important causes of cultural differences and similarities (although these interactions are quite complicated). White and Steward are two of the most important intellectual ancestors of the various scientific approaches in Western anthropology today.

Anthropological Thought Today: Divisions

Boas's early criticisms of the unilineal evolutionists illustrate a division within cultural anthropology that continues to this day. First, the evolutionists thought ethnology should be like the natural sciences in its goals. But Boas thought it was mainly a "historical science" or a "descriptive science." By these phrases, Boas meant that anthropologists should try to give complete and objective *descriptions* of different cultures, but that developing general *theories* about culture was premature and possibly would never happen.

Second, the evolutionists wanted to establish the general principles that governed cultural development. But the historicists mistrusted most generalizations, especially broad and sweeping ones like "all cultures pass through similar stages." The closer you come to getting inside another culture, they argued, the more details you perceive and, hence, the more different it looks from other cultures. Most similarities are only superficial, like the "similarity" between Hawaiian and Greek polytheism.

Third, the evolutionists uncritically placed similar cultures in the same stage of progress (like the Iroquois and the Fijians, both in barbarism). But the historicists

COMPARISON OF THE SCIENTIFIC AND HUMANISTIC APPROACHES

Scientific Approach	Humanistic Approach
Primary goals are explaining cultural differences and similarities and why and how cultures change.	Main goal is describing and interpreting particular cultures, to achieve an insider's view and/or give people their Voices.
Humans are part of nature, different only in degree from other animals; emphasizes relationships with environment.	Humans are unique because they are cultural and linguistic beings, different in kind from other mammals; emphasizes symbols.
Regularities and consistent cross-cultural patterns exist, which can be discovered through empirical observations and systematic comparisons.	Particular cultures are so complex that each must be understood on its own terms; comparisons distort the cultures that are compared.
Methods emphasize observation of group patterns and comparisons; the ethnographer determines what is important for the purposes of scientific generalization.	Field methods emphasize participation and relationships with local people; descriptions emerge out of interactions between fieldworkers and so are never completely objective.

insisted that the evolutionists' idea of progress was ethnocentric and that therefore stages were artificial creations. If there are no universal stages, or even common stages, then the regularities of cultural development that the nineteenth century scholars perceived were not real, but only the result of their assumptions and methods.

Fourth, the evolutionists compared and contrasted cultures from all parts of the world and found the "same" customs among widely scattered peoples. But the historicists reasoned that because each culture's history is different from the history of every other culture, it follows that each culture is unique and distinctive. This means that it is very misleading to place several cultures into the same category because there are always differences between them. For example, if you say that the ancient Hawaiians and Greeks have the "same" religion, which *you* label as polytheism, then that label is *yours*, not theirs. To call the two religions the same is to misrepresent and distort them. It denies the religion, and the people who believe and practice it, their distinctiveness. It denies the Others their own Voices. It privileges the voice of the anthropologist, meaning that it assumes the anthropologist's ideas are more valid than the ideas of Others about what they do and how they think.

The Concept Review compares some of the main differences between the scientific and the humanistic approaches. Notice that they differ in their conceptions of goals, human uniqueness, the validity of comparisons among cultures, and the methods used in fieldwork.

The same general kinds of issues persist in Western ethnology today. There are many, many contemporary schools of thought, which we cannot cover. Despite this diversity, one important division today is cultural anthropologists whose interests and methods are more similar to science versus those whose interests and methods are more humanistic.

Scientific Approaches

Those who adopt one of the **scientific approaches** to the study of Other cultures seek to discover the general forces that make cultures the way they are; that is, they want to *explain* human ways of life. They are interested in big questions: What are the primary causes of social and cultural differences and similarities? What makes societies and cultures change and/or change at different rates? What are the relationships among the major components of a peoples' way of life, such as resource acquisition, family organization, political structure, and religious beliefs and rituals? When two cultures come into contact, what kinds of forces affect the outcome?

Given the complexity of the human species, and even of a single society, it might seem that the answer is always going to be: "It all depends." Scientifically oriented scholars ask, "On what, mainly"? If the answer turns out to be "on everything else" (and this is exactly what some modern scholars say), then the scientific approach probably will not be able to achieve its goals. There can never be a "general theory" that answers their big questions because the word *theory* implies that only a small number of general principles are responsible for most of the important differences, changes, relationships, and other phenomena. *Theory* implies that there are only a few underlying causes or principles or forces. If societies are indeed products of "everything that happened to them in the past," then we cannot point to a few events or processes and say that these are *generally* important in *most* societies *most* of the time. Human existence would be too chaotic and random to be explained by any general theory.

As an example of the word *theory*, recall the ideas of Leslie White. He argued that technological improvements over centuries of human history were largely responsible for most important changes in societies and ideologies. White's idea of technological determinism is, at best, incomplete, partly or largely because he did not give adequate attention to the natural environment. Complete or not, White's ideas represented a *theory,* as we use the word here: he pointed to a small number of important factors that caused changes in other parts of a cultural system. He thought that systematic cross-cultural comparisons were essential to develop and test his theory—a view that is shared by most scientific approaches today.

Evolutionary Psychology

As one example of the scientific approach, in the late 1970s, some anthropologists adopted a theory then known as **sociobiology.** Social scientists now usually call it **evolutionary psychology.** It emphasizes the similarities between humans and other animals, arguing that humans are subject to the same kinds of processes that operate in other parts of nature. Harvard biologist Edward O. Wilson was instrumental in the development of this theoretical framework in the biological sciences. He was interested in animal social behavior—that is, in why many animals (e.g., lions, ants, many ungulates) live in herds or other groups whose members help one another in such ways as cooperating in hunting or emitting alarm calls that warn the group of a nearby predator.

Why are such behaviors puzzling? In the animal kingdom, most biologists have long believed that natural selection usually produces organisms that are genetically *selfish*, meaning that unselfish *(altruistic)* behavior in animals is rare, existing only under very special circumstances. For instance, most cooperative social behaviors and alarm calls appear to be costly to the individual animal, yet the benefits accrue to the entire group. A prairie dog calling to alert its neighbors to a predator might call the predator's attention to itself and thus stand a greater chance of getting eaten. How could natural selection produce animals that act altruistically, when altruistic behavior is so costly to the altruistic animal? Natural selection should select against altruism because an altruistic animal will have less chance of survival and reproduction than the selfish ones.

Wilson, along with other biologists such as Richard Dawkins and William Hamilton, solved this puzzle by noting that the unit of "selfishness" is not individual organisms, but genes. Because genes are the units that are transmitted to offspring through reproduction, only genes that make more copies of themselves in the next generation can survive. Genes, sociobiologists argue, largely program the bodies that temporarily house them to act in ways that improve their biological *fitness*—in ways that increase their frequencies in the next generation. To paraphrase Dawkins, a body and its behavior are a gene's way of making more copies of itself. Some evolutionary psychologists claim that this statement applies to humans as well as to other animals. Taken seriously, this means that *your* body and behavior are your genes' ways of making more copies of themselves.

The main contribution of sociobiology was the insight that related individuals share a greater proportion of their genes with one another than they do with nonrelatives of the same species. For example, a female can potentially increase the fitness of one or more of her genes if she aids her brother, if that brother carries the same genes. By helping her brother, she herself may reproduce less, but this cost can be more than offset if her help improves her brother's fitness enough to offset her own loss of fitness. Thus, natural selection increases the fitness of any gene that programs its body to help a relative if the cost in fitness (to the gene) is lower than the benefit to the same gene housed in the relative's body. So, an individual animal can behave altruistically after all, but only if the benefit of the altruism helps a relative far more than it costs the "altruist" (note that the behavior is not truly altruistic because it increases the fitness of the gene).

Some anthropologists believe that such ideas contribute to explaining human social behavior. For example, you and I have a genuine interest in the welfare of our relatives. All else equal, the more closely related we are, the more we care for them, and people care most for those individuals who are the main vehicles for transmitting their genes—their own offspring and offspring's offspring. We care little, or less, for nonrelatives and will assist them only if they somehow return benefits to us or to our relatives. They do this mainly by reciprocity; that is, they return our help immediately or at some later time if we can count on their presence in the future. Evolutionary psychologists claim that selfishness motivates most human actions, although the selfish motive is sometimes disguised when we help family members or friends in expectation of future returns.

◄ In the 1970s, the work of Harvard's Edward O. Wilson and other sociobiologists became influential in ethnology. Famous for his work on ants and other social insects, Wilson argued that human behaviors and beliefs are shaped by natural selection. Human societies and cultures therefore can be explained by evolutionary processes similar to those operating in other animal species.

© Rick Friedman/Corbis

More generally, evolutionary psychologists note that, for most of human history, the most important social groups (bands, discussed in later chapters) were largely composed of relatives who cooperated in foraging, food sharing, child care, and other activities. They also point out that far more human societies allow a man to have several wives than allow a woman to have several husbands, which is consistent with sociobiology, for reasons we discuss in Chapter 8. They claim that evolutionary psychology explains many of the following widespread human behavioral and mental predispositions:

- Xenophobia—We may hate or mistrust strangers because, as obvious nonrelatives, they cannot be trusted.
- Warfare—Braver men who protect the group are more likely to attract more wives and/or have more sex and hence more offspring.
- Male unfaithfulness to wives or promiscuity—Males get more children and therefore more fitness without the costs of raising the children.
- Female preference for marrying high-status/wealthy males—Women get access to more resources through such marriages, thus improving the fitness of their offspring.

Critics of such ideas charge that these and other so-called predispositions are more the product of enculturation than of genes because they vary markedly from people to people. Even if evolutionary psychology "helps"

in understanding such widespread patterns, critics say that it tells us little or nothing about the reasons different peoples exhibit them strongly, only weakly, or not at all. So, this "help" is minimal at best and may even be harmful if it makes us falsely believe we now understand something. And, at any rate, the insights of sociobiology apply mainly if "all else is equal," which it never is in human societies. Finally, many self-sacrificial acts of devotion by individuals, such as suicide bombers and *kamikaze* pilots who are devoted to their faith, values, or homelands, are a problem for evolutionary psychology.

There are numerous other arguments both for and against evolutionary psychology, some of which we cover in later chapters. For now, note that it is an excellent example of the scientific side of ethnology: it holds that people are subject to the same principles and pressures as other animals—most important, to the forces of natural selection.

Cultural Materialism

Another modern scientific approach—more popular than evolutionary psychology—is **cultural materialism** (or just **materialism**). It claims that the satisfaction of human material needs and desires is the most important influence on how societies are organized and what people think and believe. People face the same kinds of material needs as all mammals: we must receive adequate intakes of food and water, regulate our body temperature (by building shelters and wearing clothing), reproduce, cope with organisms that cause disease, compete successfully, and so forth. To satisfy these needs efficiently, people have to organize their societies in certain ways to cooperate or to succeed in competition with other societies. Many other elements of a people's culture are determined by or are greatly influenced by how people organize their activities to survive and persist in their environments. In essence, materialists think that how a people make their living in their environment is the most important influence on the rest of their cultural existence.

If one thinks that relationships with the environment and acquisition of material resources are primary, then those aspects of culture that help people get resources will strongly affect all other aspects. More than any other animal, people depend on *technology* to exploit resources, compete, and cope with other problems of environmental adaptation. Technology includes not just the physical *instruments* (the tools) used to produce food, provide shelter, and generally manipulate the environment. Equally important, technology includes the *knowledge* (skills) about the environment, about resources, and about the manufacture and effective use of tools that people have acquired by learning from previous generations.

Because humans rely on tools and knowledge to acquire food and harness other resources, technology is among the most important aspects of culture everywhere. Materialists believe that a peoples' technology strongly affects other parts of their culture, including family life, political organization, values, and even worldviews, much as White argued in the 1940s. Yet most materialists of today disagree with White's view that increased energy capture made possible by technological improvements has generally made human life better, leading to cultural progress. In contrast to White, most modern materialists believe that technological changes have improved the lives of *some* people in *some* respects, but that changes in technology have had mixed results overall.

Because the main purpose of technology is to enable people to make a living in their environment, materialists recognize that the natural environment and technology together strongly affect culture, just as Steward said. In applying their technology in their environment, over time people may discover new resources or learn that certain resources are preferable to others. The environment poses certain problems and hazards with which people have to cope, such as drought, unpredictable rainfall, excessive cold or heat, diseases, pests, and soil nutrients.

Population size and the rate of population growth are also important causal forces because they affect technology, resources, conflicts, working hours, and other things. Some materialists believe that long-term population growth and the changes it forces groups to make in their relationships with the environment and with other human groups are the most widespread cause of cultural evolution (see A Closer Look).

In their emphasis on the importance of physical/biological needs, technology, environment, and population size, modern materialists resemble earlier thinkers such as Malinowski, White, and Steward. Modern materialists are more sophisticated than their precursors, however. For example, for the most part, early theories about causation were *linear,* meaning that one thing makes another thing the way it is; thus, A "causes" B, or A "determines" B. But modern materialists are more likely to view technology, environment, population, and culture as having *feedback* relationships with one another. That is, as their numbers increase and people interact with their environment using their technology, they change the environment. In turn, these changes lead people to alter their technology and continue population growth, which then further alters the environment, and so on. For example, as people exploit a resource, they may deplete its supply. Future generations must then either work harder to acquire the resource, develop a new method of acquiring it, or switch to an alternative resource. Other cultural changes accompany these changes in resources.

Following this line of argument, one of the founders of cultural materialism, the late Marvin Harris, proposed that many important changes in human cultures result from a process known as *intensification.* Although human populations have various ways of limiting population growth, over the long term in many regions, human numbers have increased. As population grows, people overexploit and deplete resources, which leads to degradation of their environment. This forces them to use their environment more "intensively": they turn to resources they previously ignored, which requires them to devote more time and energy (labor) to acquire energy and materials, which leads them to develop new technologies to harvest and process resources. As human numbers continue to increase, people must continue to intensify their use of resources by working longer hours to acquire more resources; taking more land out of its natural state and controlling the plants and animals that live on it; developing new technologies like irrigation and fertilization to squeeze more product out of nature; and even warring against neighbors to take over their lands. Both population growth and intensification lead to new social relationships and organizations, which develop to

AN EXAMPLE OF MATERIALISM: POPULATION PRESSURE AND CULTURAL EVOLUTION

Until about 10,000 years ago, humans lived in small mobile groups, eating only wild plants and game animals. People cannot digest many wild foods such as the leaves of trees and grasses, so the wild foods that we are able to eat were widely scattered. Consequently, the human population was sparse and people spread out over the land in small groups to exploit food and other resources without getting in other groups' ways. There were individual quarrels and violence over personal grievances, but relatively little serious, prolonged conflict between groups over valuable resources.

If human numbers increase over many decades or centuries in a given region, each person and each group will have less and less food and fewer resources unless they take steps to cope with their growing population. Materialists call this *population pressure*, which exists whenever populations increase enough to force people to change how they use resources and to invent different technologies.

In humanity's prehistoric past, in most regions, population growth leveled off when the available land could not support more people: group members either died, migrated out, or limited the number of children they had. In other regions, though, the natural environment was able to produce more resources if people worked harder or longer, if they discovered new technologies to increase production, or if they learned to eat new foods or to domesticate plants and animals. In brief, in some places, the environment responded to human work, or to technological innovations, or to efforts to control the food supply. There were five or six such regions (discussed in Chapter 6) where people responded to population pressure by developing new technologies and devoting most of their work to cultivate only a few species of plants and animals. After many centuries, these plants became crops and these animals became livestock, and agriculture began.

Once agriculture developed, the land could support even more people, so populations continued to grow. Again, only a few environments were able to sustain growth for many centuries. These environments were most commonly the valleys of large rivers that flood seasonally and deposit fertile silt carried downstream from highlands and mountains, such as the rivers of ancient Mesopotamia and the Nile of Egypt. Flooding renewed the soil, so by careful management and irrigation, these people produced enough food to feed their ever-growing numbers.

In those few places where population growth continued for many centuries, the land filled up with more people and more settlements. Eventually, some group or its leaders calculated that they could benefit by engaging in threats or aggressive fighting with their neighbors in order to add new territories and acquire more resources. Organized group fighting (warfare) became more frequent and intense and eventually led the cultures of the entire region to change. Once one local group engaged in aggressive warfare, others had to take defensive measures to protect themselves. They began living in even larger settlements so they could mobilize more warriors more quickly. They made alliances with some neighboring groups to deter aggression from enemies, thus enlarging the size of the social unit whose members cooperated for purposes such as warfare and trade. Political leaders became more powerful to control the allocation of resources or to assume leadership in warfare or both. Chiefs and eventually kings and emperors rose to power, and strong class distinctions emerged. This process led to the cultural evolution of the form of society we know as civilization. The effects of civilization on human life were mixed: some classes and individuals grew wealthy and powerful, while the majority in lower classes suffered deprivation, forced labor, war deaths, and diseases.

Notice that the word *progress* does not apply to the development of civilization in this theory: some people became better off, some worse off than in precivilized societies. Notice also that this particular theory of cultural evolution holds that one force—population pressure—caused most of the important changes in human ways of living. As we shall see, other contemporary anthropologists believe that theories like this one are far too simple and dehumanize people by seeing them as "results" of some larger process rather than as active agents in creating their own cultures.

Sources: Cohen (1977), Harris (1979)

facilitate the new ways of exploiting nature. In turn, new social arrangements require new worldviews, values, and norms to reinforce them. If human numbers continue to increase, the process of intensification will necessarily continue until completely new forms of society and culture develop (e.g., civilizations, nation-states, industrial societies, global economies).

We discuss some of these processes in later chapters. For now, note three of the main arguments of materialists: (1) Many customs and beliefs of a particular culture can be explained by how they help people live in the natural world; (2) population growth and intensification are major factors that drive cultural evolution; and (3) generally, and in the long run, material forces like overall environment, resources, technologies, and population densities are more important than ideas and beliefs like religion and worldview, values, and symbols.

Humanistic Approaches

Some aspects of both evolutionary psychology and cultural materialism are not seriously questioned. Most people do transmit their genes by having children, and most of us are more likely to help relatives than strangers. But whether the biologically determined "predispositions" identified by evolutionary psychology are all that important is debatable. Some deny that such universal human predispositions exist at all. Or, if they do exist, then trying to explain them has the effect of "justifying" (in the disguise of "explaining") racial hatreds, violence, sexual inequalities, and the like. The notion that human beings are innately selfish is odious to many and probably to most anthropologists.

Likewise, no one denies that people have material needs. But whether such needs are "basic" and "shape" all of human existence is debatable. Some think that humans differ from other animals in that these needs can be satisfied in such a multitude of ways that cultural differences cannot possibly be reduced to "material need and want satisfaction." They deny that material factors can explain any specific culture, much less cultural differences and similarities and long-term changes. In fact, they doubt that culture has any *general* explanation. Many believe that any scholar who tries to "explain" culture or cultures dehumanizes people by treating them as objects.

Most scholars who adopt the **humanistic approach** doubt or deny that any general theory can "explain" culture in the same way that evolutionary theory explains life or that Einstein's relativity theory explains the physical world. Humanistic anthropologists are skeptical of general theories for many reasons. One is that humanity's social and cultural worlds are just too complicated for one "theory" to "explain" them. All those cultures of all those Others cannot be reduced to a single formula, they claim.

Humanistic scholars say that another reason for rejecting general theories is that humans are such unique animals. *Homo sapiens* is such a special kind of animal that the methods and analysis that biology uses to explain other life-forms do not apply to us in any significant respect. Human uniqueness, as we already know, lies mainly in our heavy dependence on social learning and our capacity for complex communication—that is, in both culture and language.

Other animals live entirely in the natural world, with its food sources, predators, mates and potential mates, and so forth. Of course, humans also have to eat, drink, sleep, and excrete. But, humanists point out, we also live in a cultural world: what, when, and how we eat, drink, sleep, and excrete are largely determined by the culture into which each of us happens to have been born. People live in the world, but they have a "worldview," and their view of the world is about as important in affecting their behaviors, thoughts, and feelings as the real world itself.

Language also makes us unique, humanists say. Language provides words with which we classify and categorize objects, people, events, actions, qualities, and so forth. Because of language, we construct categories of events, people, groups, objects, plants, and so on. These categories vary from culture to culture and are entirely learned, not at all natural. Not only do these words and categories not reflect what the natural world is really like, but also language provides us with words for things that have no material existence at all, such as ghosts and demons. If the Sapir/Whorf hypothesis (see Chapter 3) has any validity and generality, then our language conditions our perceptions of the world itself, so every people live in a perceived world that is like that of no other people. Last, language allows us to lie to one another, which makes it possible for some people to manipulate and control other people. These features of language are all unique to humankind, and because of them we create our own reality as well as respond to actual reality.

All this means that human reactions to the world (to nature) and human beliefs about the world are products of culture and language. If true, this implies that, at most, material factors like environment, technology, and population affect culture only by *limiting* (constraining) how a people act, think, and feel. Material factors cannot *determine* (cause) actions, thoughts, and feelings because these factors themselves are in part products of actions, thoughts, and feelings. Neither causes or "explains" the other, which makes untangling causes and effects pretty much impossible.

When cultural materialists claim that nature's resources are very important influences on cultures and societies, a critical humanist may respond that resources are not entirely natural. Consider food resources, for instance, which materialists think are so important. Influenced by religious prohibitions and cultural notions of what's edible and what's too disgusting to consume, various peoples of the world refuse to eat cattle, pigs, dogs, horses, and insect larvae—exactly the same flesh that is considered so delicious by many other peoples. If food and other resources are culturally defined and culturally

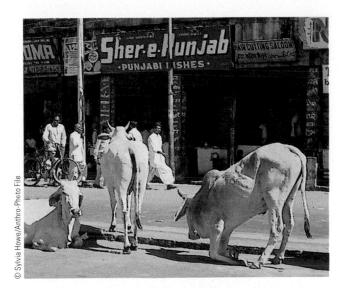

© Sylvia Howe/Anthro-Photo File

▲ Cultural materialists often hold that how people harness and utilize resources is the main influence on their culture. Humanistic anthropologists counter that whether something found in nature is a resource and, if so, how that resource is used vary from culture to culture. The sacred cattle of Hinduism, for example, are not the same kind of food resource in India as are cattle in North America or Africa.

meaningful as well as simply biological nutritious, then in human life resources are both cause *and* effect. Long ago, our cultural ancestors built (culturally constructed) the cultural world in which we live our lives. We live this cultural world as well as in the natural one.

Thus, some humanistic anthropologists think that Tylor's and White's "science of culture" is not possible: humans and their societies are too complex and too diverse, and humans live partly in worlds that their language and culture construct for them.

Other humanists do not believe that anthropology should even *try* to be scientific. In their view, scientific anthropology "objectifies" cultures; that is, in its efforts to generalize, science places cultural features into categories (e.g., forms of marriage, types of religions) that are the categories of the anthropologist, not those of the people themselves. Humanists often make this point by saying that scientifically oriented anthropologists "rob people of their voices." They mean that scientific anthropologists are arrogant to the extent that they believe they know better than the Other people themselves what is important in their lives and what was important in shaping their culture.

A similar objection by some humanists is that scientific approaches "deny that people are agents." This

means that scientific anthropologists by and large view people and groups as merely *responding* (in predictable ways) to conditions, not as *actively* trying to come up with new ways of responding to conditions. Materialists treat people, and especially "Other People," as automatons who pretty much act in ways that are determined by their natural environment and other people around them.

Thus, some humanistic anthropologists believe that the scientific perspective is not only mistaken but also not desirable. It treats Others as mere objects, often ignoring their views of what they are doing and falsely treating them as automatons rather than agents. In a sense, they say, the scientists deny the Others their humanity. At least, these are some things that many humanistic anthropologists *claim* is true for materialists and other scientific anthropologists.

You might well wonder: *If* all this is true, how is it that materialist scholars have been so misguided about the importance of environment, technology, adaptation, and so forth? Some humanists claim that materialist thinking is a product of Western cultural values and beliefs. Because the West places such high value on material welfare and consumption, materialists mistakenly impose these same values and beliefs on other cultures. Living in a competitive and capitalistic society predisposes cultural materialists to see "economic man" in cultures where he does not exist. The materialist theory is a kind of ethnocentrism, they claim.

Some materialists respond in kind. They point out that most academics are members of the privileged class, in status, wealth, or both. Because most academics (including humanistic anthropologists) so seldom have to worry about filling their stomachs, or sheltering themselves from heat, snow, and rain, or protecting themselves from enemies, it is easy for them believe that such concerns are not important in other cultures either. The humanists' failure to realize the broad importance of material factors is related to their own wealth and privilege. The humanistic approach is a kind of ethnocentrism, some claim.

Even more than the scientific approach, it is difficult or impossible to collapse humanistic anthropology into a few schools or ways of approaching Others. Here we discuss only two. Interpretive anthropology has been around for several decades, whereas postmodernism has become popular in anthropology only since the 1980s.

Interpretive Anthropology

Like other humanistically oriented anthropologists, **interpretive anthropologists** emphasize the uniqueness and individuality of each human culture. Every culture has its own ways of doing things, its own worldview, its own values, and so forth. Even if two or more cultures look similar, close examination usually shows that the meanings they attach to behaviors, objects, and concepts are different. This uniqueness makes comparisons between different cultures misleading. And because science attempts to generalize through comparisons and contrasts, it follows that anthropology is more of a humanistic discipline than a scientific one. It has more in common with literature and art than with biology or psychology, according to the interpretive approach.

Interpretive anthropologists emphasize the symbolic dimensions of culture. All social behavior has a symbolic component, in the sense that participants constantly must behave in ways that others will understand. All social interaction, therefore, is symbolic and meaningful. Meanings exist only by virtue of common agreement among the parties to the interaction—whether the interaction involves making conversation, making change in a store, or making bumpers in an auto plant. Neither participant can tell an observer how he or she knows what the other participant "means" by this or that behavior. Yet participants consistently behave in ways that others understand, and they consistently interpret the behavior of others correctly.

The job of the anthropologist is not to explain elements of a culture but to explicate one element through others. That is, the anthropologist shows how one thing in a cultural system makes sense in terms of other things in the same system, because interpretation *is* seeing how things make sense when understood in their context. (Analogously, a dictionary explicates the meanings of words in terms of other words. Only if one knows the meanings of many words in the dictionary can one use them to decipher the meanings of unknown words.) We seek to understand a people's way of life as they understand it. In the words of the late Clifford Geertz (1983, 58), who shaped the entire approach, we seek to grasp "the native's point of view," "to figure out what the devil they think they are up to." This involves acquiring intimate knowledge of a particular culture so that the ethnographer can make sense of the culture for those who do not know it.

According to many interpretive anthropologists, the search for generalized explanations of human ways of life is futile. So many factors contributed to the formation of a culture, and these factors interacted in such complex and unpredictable ways, that we must concentrate on understanding the unique elements of each way of life. In this respect, interpretive anthropologists exemplify the humanistic perspective.

Postmodernism

Postmodernists generally believe that the methods and assumptions of all science—including fields such as biology—are themselves culturally situated and culture bound. This means that science, as most people understand it, is not objective in its theories and even in its facts ("data"). Rather, it is carried out by scientists who themselves are products of a particular cultural upbringing. Like all knowledge, scientific theories are affected by conditions in the scientists' own culture.

For example, postmodernists might say that the claim of materialists that material needs and wants are important causal forces is culture bound: materialists live in a culture that values material things, so their theory assumes the primacy of material factors. Evolutionary psychologists were brought up in cultures that practically celebrate selfishness. In free-market economies, everyone is supposed to be looking out for themselves and consuming and competing, so the evolutionary psychologists raised in this economic system impose these alleged biological imperatives on humanity in general. Such theories are culture bound, in the same way Boas showed that unilineal evolutionism was culture bound—although Boas used the term *ethnocentric*.

How can this be? Postmodernists point out that scientific thinking and methods became prominent during the Enlightenment period (also called the Age of Reason) of late eighteenth- and nineteenth-century western Europe. Enlightenment philosophers emphasized rational thought as the key to advancing knowledge about the world, from the solar system to humanity. Tradition and especially religion were viewed as impediments to discovering Truth. Emotions could also get in the way, especially if they keep otherwise rational thinkers from accepting the reality of a fact or principle just because they don't like it or its implications. For example, if you are a male, you might refuse to accept evidence showing that not all societies are patriarchal. You reject or discount the evidence because it is not consistent with what religion has taught you and it makes you feel guilt or other kinds of emotional distress. Your refusal to accept the evidence is not "rational," so it gets in the way of improving your knowledge. This would not matter very much for your society unless, of course, men hold the power in that society and most of them feel and believe as you do. Enlightenment thinkers tried to free thought from the shackles of religion and emotion, so that Reason and Science could reveal the world to us as it really is.

Postmodernists do not think there is anything very special about this kind of rational thought. They say that all of human knowledge originates in a particular social, economic, and political context. *Scientific* knowledge is no exception: because science is a product of a particular cultural tradition—that of the West—it reflects the economy, family organization, political ideology, worldview, and so forth of Western society. Science, in fact, is just one among hundreds of other systems of cultural knowledge. Many postmodernists hold that science has little more claim to absolute Truth than do the ideas and beliefs of other peoples. All are valid on their own terms, but none is "privileged" or has any exclusive claim to objectivity. If scientists themselves don't realize this, it is because they are inside the knowledge system and so do not grasp the implicit assumptions of their rationalistic and mechanistic worldview.

Postmodernists also think that the most important thing about the context of knowledge is power relationships. Prevalent beliefs and ideas in a community reflect lines of power, largely because those with power have the most influence on which ideas and beliefs become "prevalent." To illustrate with a modern example, most North Americans believe in things like private property, free-market capitalism, democracy, and various individual rights and freedoms. These beliefs reflect, and support, the interests of some people over other people. Much scholarly knowledge—the kind taught in colleges and universities—is like this, postmodernists claim. For example, evolutionary psychology is often taught as a credible or even correct theory in biology courses, although postmodernists hold its theories support sexism and patriarchy.

In anthropological fieldwork, there is often a power dimension to the relationship between the fieldworker and the local people. Most fieldworkers are able to command more resources and thus can influence people to talk about things they'd rather not discuss (although there are ethical standards in fieldwork, covered in Chapter 5). Postmodernists mistrust most older ethnographies, and generally they prefer accounts in which the fieldworkers openly discuss their personal relationships with members of the community. They also prefer ethnographies in which the ethnographer gives her or his readers access to the local Voices.

As mentioned, postmodernism penetrated anthropology in the 1980s and has attracted more converts in our discipline than in any other social science. One reason for the popularity of this perspective in anthropology is its apparent consistency with cultural relativism. However, critics of the approach became vocal in the late 1990s. Do postmodernists adopt the tenets of their own ideas in their personal lives? If science is "just another" kind of knowledge, do postmodernists refuse to ride in airplanes

or use microwaves? How have their own ideas escaped the influence of power relationships? And are *their* ideas also culture bound?

Postmodernism reminds us that rationality and science do not provide all the answers and do not ask all the necessary questions. It leads us to ask where our ideas come from and who might gain and lose from them. Perhaps most important, it warns anthropological thinkers of the dangers of becoming arrogant about our objectivity. Scientifically oriented theorists can easily forget that they themselves are cultural beings and that their own ideas about the human world are culturally conditioned.

Either, Or, or Both?

The differences between the scientific and humanistic orientations are sometimes presented as conflicting: Humanists often accuse scientists of dehumanizing people in their effort to explain them, whereas scientists claim that humanists are deceiving themselves if they think they can get inside some Other culture.

To some extent, different approaches exist because of the differing interests of anthropologists. For example, scholars whose research areas include subjects such as human adaptation, economic systems, or long-term evolutionary changes in societies are likely to find a materialist approach useful. Those who study dimensions such as mythology, art, oral traditions, or worldviews are more likely to fall into the humanistic camp. So, in part, the diversity of modern approaches reflects the fact that human beings and their cultures are complex and multifaceted, so the orientation most useful to understand one facet (e.g., subsistence) may not prove very useful to understand another (e.g., worldview).

In the interest of balance, in the remainder of this book, we try to avoid choosing between the two orientations by taking the following approach. Like evolutionary psychologists and cultural materialists, we think that *it is important* that people are part of nature. But we recognize that different elements of a culture are influenced to different degrees by material conditions. The way an economy is organized is greatly influenced by the local environment, by climate, by technology, and by the size and density of the human population. But the ways the members of a culture resolve their disputes, raise their children, perform their rituals, or act toward their fathers in law are less influenced by material conditions or are influenced by them only indirectly. The legends they recite, the specific objects they use as religious symbols, and the way they decorate their bodies may have little to do with material forces. Such elements of a cultural system may be only loosely tied to the natural world and to material needs and wants. If so, we cannot account for them without considering people's desires for a meaningful existence, for an emotionally gratifying social life, for an intellectually satisfying worldview, for creative self-expression, and so forth.

So, we avoid the either/or dilemma by pointing out that different orientations are useful for studying different dimensions of culture. Still, people who are new to anthropology are often puzzled by the diversity of approaches within the field. We therefore conclude this chapter by suggesting answers to the following question:

Why Can't All Those Anthropologists Agree?

Physicists, geologists, and other natural scientists generally agree on a set of laws or principles that govern the world. In geology, for example, processes such as sedimentation, plate tectonics, volcanic eruptions, fossilization, and so forth are fairly well understood and account for the main geological features of our planet. Biologists, likewise, believe that the process of evolution produced the diversity of all life on Earth, although the relative importance of natural selection and random events in this process remains uncertain.

Cultural anthropology lacks a comparable set of general principles (as do the other social sciences except economics). Consider one basic question scientifically oriented ethnologists ask: What are the important causes of the differences and similarities among the world's known cultures? If you could ask 100 ethnologists this question, you would get a multitude of answers. Cultural materialists would mention forces such as climate, resources, population sizes, and technology. Humanistically oriented scholars would say that the question itself is wrongheaded because anthropologists should be trying to interact with members of particular cultures and gain an insider's view of them—not to "explain" them. Many would respond that there is no generalized explanation because cultures are so complex and diverse that the most important causes in culture X are not at all important in culture Y. Still others would hold that the question is ethnocentric, and in some cases racist, because it reduces people in other cultures to the status of "objects" of our explanations.

Why don't anthropologists agree about the answer to this question and numerous other basic questions about humanity? Several factors contribute to the absence of consensus.

First, we humans are conscious and self-aware beings who state a variety of reasons for why we do and think what we do and think. The zoologist studying an animal's behavior observes and records the behavior, and then typically tries to identify the elements of the natural and social environment to which the behavior is adapted. But anthropologists must listen to the reasons people themselves give for their behavior. People talk back, and anthropologists must take their talk, as well as their patterns of behavior, into account.

Second, for ethical reasons, anthropologists do not set up controlled experiments to study how people respond. Suppose—following Steward's lead—we want to study how the natural environment affects cultures. We cannot hold everything constant except the supply of food, water, or shelter and then see how people react when the supply of food, water, or shelter is varied. The only way the anthropologist can "control" conditions is by looking around the world for "natural experiments"—places where the natural environment is similar and peoples with different histories live. We can choose a sample of peoples who live in environments that appear to be similar and then see whether the peoples who live in these places have similar cultures. For example, we might compare indigenous peoples who live in the world's deserts: the Sahara of northern Africa, the Kalahari of southern Africa, the American Southwest, the Gobi of northeast Asia, and so forth. To conduct such a comparative study, we would have to rely on the ethnographic reports written by a multitude of earlier ethnographers, whose reports resulted from their observations and discussions with peoples in the various deserts.

Suppose our comparative study finds, as it will, that the cultures are similar in some respects but different in others. Then other problems arise: Natural environments are only similar, never identical. Did we fail to detect a small but critical difference in the environment that might explain the cultural differences? Or, are the differences due to nonenvironmental factors? Likewise, cultures are only similar, never identical. Shall we call customs and beliefs that differ in minor ways between the cultures the "same," or are the subtle differences between them sufficient to call them "different"? Suppose we decide that some behavior, like sharing food within a village, is the "same" behavior in the cultures. But then we discover that people in several of the cultures give different reasons for the behavior—in culture X, people say they want to help one another, whereas in culture Y, they say they give only because they expect to get something back later. Are both of these behaviors still "sharing food"? Or, should we consider them different because people's stated motivations differ? Or, did the various ethnographers falsely believe a certain behavior was "food sharing" when in fact it was something else? Such questions are *inherently* difficult to answer when dealing with human beings, and anthropologists cannot sort them out in laboratories or other experimental settings.

Third, fieldworkers study members of their own species. Because they are human, fieldworkers enter their research experience with a culture of their own. This culture inevitably affects their objectivity and, hence, their interactions with the community, their perceptions of what is important, and so forth. Conversely, individuals in the community itself have their own perceptions, opinions, and biases about the fieldworker. Among the many factors that affect how the community reacts are the fieldworker's physical characteristics, gender, and personality as well as the kinds of questions asked and the historical experience of the community with individuals of the anthropologist's own society. Although most fieldworkers attempt to overcome their own cultural biases and to fit into the community, complete objectivity is impossible. In fact, some contemporary anthropologists—especially postmodernists—write ethnographies that focus far more on their interactions with local people than on the culture of the people themselves. They think that any ethnography is a "construction"—built out of interactions that another fieldworker would not experience—not a simple report on "facts" about a given group. (We have more to say on such issues in Chapter 5.)

There is another possible reason anthropology lacks a common theoretical orientation and an agreed-upon set of principles. It is quite likely that people become anthropologists for a wider variety of reasons than people become, say, physicists. Some of us study anthropology because of our curiosity about why the human species is so diverse culturally. Others go into the field to further the cause of social justice—by educating themselves and others about racism, ethnocentrism, colonialism, or sexism, for example. Some want to immerse themselves in travel and interaction with people who are different from themselves, and they become anthropologists because the field provides them with such opportunities. The very broad scope of anthropology (see Chapter 1) helps account for the variety of reasons people choose it as a career: you can study agriculture, family life, political organization, medicine, art, religion, folklore, and almost anything else having to do with humankind. Naturally, people who study topics as diverse as these are unlikely to agree on their theoretical orientations to the field as a whole. Indeed, many of them consciously reject any form of theoretical orientation, preferring to concentrate on researching particular cultures.

In sum, there are four major reasons modern cultural anthropologists have such varied orientations to the study of culture:

1. Our subjects—other human beings—are themselves conscious beings who are aware of their own behavior and state their own reasons they do what they do. Human subjects talk back.
2. Anthropologists cannot set up experiments that enable them to control the conditions under which people live, allowing their behavior to be manipulated. Anthropologists observe people as they live their everyday lives.
3. Complete objectivity is impossible to achieve when a researcher is studying humans, both because researchers themselves are culture-bearers and because the subjects of the study react to fieldworkers in varied ways. Ethnographers are different, and they encounter different problems as they work in different places.
4. The broad scope of the field itself and the enormous diversity of reasons people study anthropology make it unlikely that consensus will emerge. Cultural anthropologists are among the most diverse of scholars.

Summary

1. Anthropology originated as a distinct academic discipline in the late nineteenth century, after colonialism intensified contact between peoples of European ancestry and the indigenous peoples of Africa, Asia, the Americas, and the Pacific. Darwin's theory of evolution was one of the main notions that allowed Western intellectuals to make sense of the peoples and cultures of other lands. It seemed to imply that the history of life on Earth was progressive, with simpler organisms evolving into more complex ones.

2. In the nineteenth century unilineal evolutionists applied the notion of evolution to cultures. Using written accounts as their main source of information about

Other cultures, they arranged cultures into a sequence of progressive stages, from simple to complex, with Western civilization at the pinnacle. Anthropology thus began as the academic field that studied how humankind progressed out of rude beginnings into a more "civilized" cultural existence.

3. In the early twentieth century, both American and British anthropologists developed new approaches. The American historical particularists, led by Boas, demolished the speculative schemes of the unilineal evolutionists by arguing that concepts such as "complexity" depend on one's point of view and thus have little objective meaning. Boas popularized the notion of cultural relativism that remains a hallmark of ethnology today. In Great Britain, functionalists such as Malinowski and Radcliffe-Brown tried to show how the various parts of a culture and its social system serve to meet the needs of individuals and society. By emphasizing the interrelatedness of cultural systems, functionalism strengthened the holistic perspective. Both the historical particularists and the functionalists emphasized the importance of firsthand fieldwork as the surest path to objectivity and as essential for the training of anthropologists.

4. In the middle decades of the twentieth century, neoevolutionists like White and Steward returned to cultural evolution, avoiding most mistakes of the nineteenth-century scholars. White emphasized the importance of technology, Steward of adaptation to the local environment, in making cultures the way they are. Both men thought that a people's methods of acquiring resources (energy, food, and so forth) from nature are the main influences on culture. Both also believed that anthropology is a science, whose main objective is to explain cultural differences and similarities.

5. Contemporary cultural anthropologists are diverse in their theoretical orientations. One very broad modern division is whether ethnology is a scientific enterprise or a humanistic study.

6. Two examples of scientific approaches are sociobiology/evolutionary psychology and cultural materialism. Sociobiology emphasizes that humans are part of nature and that, like other animals, most of our behavior helps us transmit our genes to future generations. Materialists argue that how a given people organize their groups and pattern their activities to acquire energy and materials from their natural environment is the major explanation for other aspects of their cultural system. To materialists, cultural differences and similarities ultimately can be explained by factors such as environment, technology, population pressure, and economic organization.

7. In contrast, humanistically oriented anthropologists mistrust all generalized explanations of cultural phenomena. Interpretive anthropologists emphasize the uniqueness of each culture and favor studying, appreciating, and interpreting each culture individually. They claim that scientific approaches illegitimately try to speak for Other cultures and falsely assume that people simply respond to external forces instead of creatively engaging them. Postmodernists think that science in general has no particular claim to Truth and that many scientific ideas taught by schools and colleges reflect power relationships in the wider social and cultural context.

8. Contemporary anthropologists thus do not agree among themselves on many fundamental questions, including even the major objectives of their field. Their lack of consensus is understandable, given that their (human) subjects are self-conscious and willful beings; that anthropologists cannot experiment with people's lives; that total objectivity in fieldwork is impossible; and that the field itself studies such diverse subjects that a single theoretical orientation is unlikely to be able to encompass all of them.

Key Terms

unilineal evolution
historical particularism
  (historicism)
configurationalism
functionalism
neoevolutionism

scientific approach
sociobiology (evolutionary psychology)
cultural materialism (materialism)
humanistic approach

interpretive anthropologists
postmodernists

Suggested Readings

Among the volumes that cover the history of anthropological thought are:

Erickson, Paul, and Liam Murphy. *A History of Anthropological Theory.* 2nd ed. Calgary: Broadview Press, 2003.

An overview of anthropological thought.

Erickson, Paul, and Liam Murphy, eds. *Readings for a History of Anthropological Theory.* 2nd ed. Calgary: Broadview Press, 2006.

Contains original articles on key anthropologists.

McGee, R. Jon, and Richard L. Warms, eds. *Anthropological Theory: An Introductory History.* 3rd ed. New York: McGraw-Hill, 2003.

A comprehensive reader containing important writings of all the thinkers covered in this chapter, and more.

Moore, Jerry D. *Visions of Culture: An Introduction to Anthropological Theorists and Theories.* 2nd ed. Walnut Creek, Calif.: AltaMira Press, 2004.

This slim volume contains chapters on most of the major thinkers right up to today.

To understand the contemporary divisions between the scientific and humanistic approaches, consult some of the following works:

Geertz, Clifford. *The Interpretation of Cultures.* New ed. New York: Basic Books, 2000 (originally published in 1983).

Collected articles by the key founder of the interpretive approach. Three articles are especially well known: (1) "Thick Description: Towards an Interpretive Theory of Culture," (2) "The Impact of the Concept of Culture on the Concept of Man," and (3) "Deep Play: Notes on the Balinese Cockfight."

Geertz, Clifford. *Local Knowledge: Further Essays on Interpretive Anthropology.* New York: Basic Books, 2000.

Another compendium of some of Geertz's best-known essays.

Harris, Marvin. *Cannibals and Kings.* New York: Random House, 1977.

Harris explains and illustrates his Intensification hypothesis. Easy reading and an excellent example of materialist thought.

Johnson, Allen W., and Timothy Earle. *The Evolution of Human Societies.* 2nd ed. Stanford, Calif.: Stanford University Press, 2000.

Sophisticated theoretical and factual treatment of cultural evolution, focusing on changes that resulted in increasing societal complexity over time.

Sanderson, Stephen. *Evolutionism and Its Critics.* Boulder, Colo.: Paradigm, 2007.

A history of ideas about cultural evolution that also defends the perspective from its old and recent critics.

Media Resources

The Wadsworth Anthropology Resource Center
academic.cengage.com/anthropology

The Wadsworth discipline resource website that accompanies *Humanity: An Introduction to Cultural Anthropology,* Eighth Edition, includes a rich array of material, including online anthropological video clips, to help you in the study of cultural anthropology and the specific topics covered in this chapter. Other material includes a case study forum with excerpts from various Wadsworth authors, map exercises, scientist interviews, breaking news in anthropology, and links to additional useful online material. Begin by selecting Cultural Anthropology to take you to videos, research, and more. From the homepage, you may also select Applied Anthropology, which directs you to essays, glossary terms, the case study forum, and a list of internships and careers in anthropology.

5 METHODS OF INVESTIGATION

Margaret Mead's highly innovative field studies in Samoa and New Guinea made her one of the most widely read anthropologists of the twentieth century.

Ethnographic Methods

Ethnographic Fieldwork

Problems and Issues in Field Research

Fieldwork as a Rite of Passage

Ethnohistory

Comparative Methods

Cross-Cultural Comparisons

Controlled Historical Comparisons

Questions addressed in this chapter

What are the objectives of cultural research?

What methods do researchers use to study the culture of living peoples, and what problems do researchers have in conducting field research?

What methods do researchers use to study past cultures, and what are the major problems involved in ethnohistoric research?

What is the purpose of comparative research, and what methods do researchers use in these studies?

Anthropological research has two purposes: (1) to collect and record new data about specific people (ethnography), and (2) to expand our theoretical understanding of human cultural systems in general through comparative analysis. We first discuss the methods used to describe a single people, called **ethnographic methods,** and then we summarize how anthropologists use descriptive accounts to test hypotheses through the use of **comparative methods.**

Ethnographic Methods

There are two sources of cultural data about a particular people: the living members of the society and written accounts or other records about that group of people. Collecting cultural data by studying and interviewing living members of a society is called **ethnographic fieldwork.** Studying a people's culture using written accounts and other records is termed **ethnohistoric research.**

Ethnographic Fieldwork

Ethnographic fieldwork involves the collection of cultural data from living individuals. The researcher lives with or close to the people being studied and interacts with them on a day-to-day basis for a long period, usually a year or more. Not infrequently, the anthropologist has to learn the group's language and behave according to the group's social norms. By its very nature, fieldwork fosters a close personal relationship between the researcher and members of the society being studied. This social closeness between researchers and the people they study distinguishes anthropologists from other social scientists.

Anthropologists have always used fieldwork as the primary method for collecting cultural information. Over the past century, the objective of fieldwork has changed and with it the data-gathering techniques. Today, a number of techniques are used in the course of any research project.

Interviewing is the most basic method of collecting cultural data. The anthropologist asks questions and elicits answers from members of the society being studied. Interviews may be structured or unstructured. A *structured interview* consists of a limited number of specific questions. It may take the form of a questionnaire that the researcher fills in as the questions are answered. This type of interview is best suited for collecting general quantitative data about the group. For example, most research begins with a census of the community: the number of people in each family, their ages and relationships, and basic economic information about the family. In this manner, the researcher constructs demographic and economic profiles of the group. Structured interviews are also used to create genealogies. Most research requires a clear knowledge of how group members are related to one another. Genealogies are important in understanding the social and economic behavior of individuals beyond the immediate family. There are, however, limits to the utility of structured interviews.

In *unstructured interviews,* the researcher asks open-ended questions, hoping that the respondent will elaborate on the answers. The questions may be general, about family life, marriage, a particular religious ritual, or economic activity. Most cultural data are collected through unstructured interviews. In these interviews, the researcher learns the cultural explanations for information collected in the structured interviews.

Although it is the source of most cultural data, interviewing has severe limitations. The problem usually is not with the answers given by the members of the group, but rather with the questions asked by the researcher. What is relevant or irrelevant to the proper understanding of a particular cultural phenomenon depends on the culture of the individuals involved. Initially, the researcher does not understand the cultural context of the data and thus does not know what questions need to be asked and answered. The early stages of a research project are often characterized by "shotgun" questioning as the anthropologist seeks to learn enough about the culture to ask the right questions. Through interviewing, a researcher can gain a good basic knowledge of a culture's major structural features. However, no matter how knowledgeable and willing the respondents might be, verbal descriptions in themselves are incomplete and do not enable the researcher to gain an in-depth knowledge of the people or an understanding of the true dynamics of their culture.

To understand the limitations of interviewing, ask yourself this question: If an anthropologist from another culture asked you to describe a baseball game, what would you say? How complete would your description be? Chances are, if you are an avid fan, you could relate enough information for the anthropologist to gain a basic understanding of the game. You could tell how many players are on each side and explain the basic rules about balls, strikes, runs, errors, and innings. From memory alone, it is highly unlikely that you would explain everything that might occur during a game. You would probably give the researcher an idealized model of a baseball game. Certain facts would be left untold, not because you were hiding them but because they are either so commonplace or so unusual that they are not part of your consciousness concerning the game. Interviews alone can give the researcher only a simplified overview of a particular cultural phenomenon, an idealized model.

If researchers want to truly understand baseball, they cannot simply talk to someone about it; they need to see a game. In fact, researchers should observe several games and discuss what occurred with a knowledgeable person. It would be even better for researchers to participate, at least in a minor way, in a game. Only by combining interviewing with observing and participating can one begin to understand the rules and dynamics of the game. So it is with the study of any cultural phenomenon.

During the late nineteenth and early twentieth centuries, anthropologists relied primarily on interviews to collect cultural data. This technique was well suited to the anthropological objectives of that time. The traditional lifestyles of non-Western peoples were rapidly changing in many parts of the world, and anthropologists were concerned about collecting as much cultural data as possible before knowledge of these ways of life disappeared. This was particularly true in North America, where Native American groups had already been placed on reservations, and their economies and cultures had drastically changed. Anthropologists wanted to learn about earlier Native American lifestyles before all knowledge of the pre-reservation period was lost. The only way the pre-reservation culture of these peoples could be studied was by interviewing individuals who had grown to adulthood before the reservations were created. In a relatively short period, anthropologists were able to collect, and thus preserve, a vast body of general descriptive data on Native American cultures.

In the 1920s, anthropologists' interest began to shift from just recording descriptions of the general culture of a society to attempting to understand the basic dynamics of cultural systems. In other words, anthropologists wanted to see how these systems worked and how their parts fit together. A leader in this change was Bronislaw Malinowski, mentioned earlier in the discussion of functionalism in Chapter 4, who popularized a new data-collection technique called **participant observation.** Anthropologists no longer merely recorded and analyzed people's statements. To a greater or lesser extent, they took up residence with the people they were studying and began trying to learn about the culture by observing people in their daily lives and participating in their daily activities.

Participant observation has often been misinterpreted, even by some anthropologists who have taken it too literally. It does not mean becoming a full participant in the activities of the people—in other words, "going native." The emphasis of this technique is more on observation than on participation. Participant observation usually does require that one live in the community because only by doing so can one observe and record the behavior of individuals as they go about their daily work, visit their friends, interact with their relatives, participate in rituals, and so on. These observations of behavior serve to generate new questions. Why does a man share food with some families but not with others? Why do some women wear their hair in a particular style? Does a particular color of clothing have any meaning? Some behaviors have significance; others do not. For example, variations in hairstyles may be merely the result of personal preferences, or they may reflect status differences. Color may or may not have special significance. In American society, black symbolizes mourning, but in other societies, covering one's body with white clay symbolizes the same emotion. Participant observation allows the researcher to collect more detailed data than does interviewing alone, and thus it makes possible a deeper understanding of inter-relationships between cultural phenomena.

Firsthand observations of the members of a society also enable the researcher to see how people diverge from the culturally defined, idealized model of behavior. An incident that occurred while Malinowski was work-ing in the Trobriand Islands illustrates the divergence between cultural norms—the way people say they ought to behave—and the way they actually behave. One day Malinowski heard a commotion in the village and dis-covered that a young boy in a neighboring village had committed suicide by climbing a palm tree and flinging himself onto the beach. In his earlier questioning of the islanders, Malinowski had been told that sexual relations between a man and his mother's sister's daughters were prohibited. On inquiring into the suicide of the young boy, Malinowski found that the boy had been sexually involved with his mother's sister's daughter, and that in fact such incestuous relationships were not rare. So long as such liaisons were not mentioned in public, they were ignored. In this particular case, the girl's ex-boyfriend had become angry and publicly exposed the transgres-sion. Although everyone in the village already knew of this incestuous relationship, by making it public the ex-boyfriend exposed his rival to ridicule, thus causing him to commit suicide. It is doubtful that such behavior could have been discovered by only interviewing individuals.

Problems and Issues in Field Research

Every fieldwork experience is, to some extent, unique. Specific problems differ, depending on the individual characteristics of the researcher, the nature of the com-munity, and the particular questions being studied. There are, however, three difficulties that, to varying degrees, affect virtually every field research situation: (1) stereo-typing, (2) defining the fieldworker's role in the com-munity and developing rapport, and (3) identifying and interviewing consultants.

Stereotyping. When we think of stereotypes—pre-conceived generalizations concerning a particular group of people—we usually think only of their effects on the perceptions of one party of a relationship. Anthropolo-gists ask themselves how they can overcome their own stereotypes and cultural biases about the people they study. Stereotyping, however, is a two-way street. Every society has stereotypes concerning members of other so-cieties and of ethnic and racial groups. Thus, although the goal is for anthropologists to put aside their personal stereotypes sufficiently to research the cultural system of another people with some degree of objectivity, those with whom the ethnographer will be living and working will not have shelved their own stereotypes. Although most anthropologists have been and still are of European ancestry, most subjects of anthropological research are non-European peoples. Even if a particular anthropolo-gist is of Asian, African, or Native American ancestry, a similar problem exists because anthropologists seldom belong to the local community they study and thus are outsiders. As a result, an anthropologist who enters an-other community must contend with local stereotypes about the ethnic or racial group with which the anthro-pologist is identified.

In the case of anthropologists of European ancestry, local stereotyping has most frequently been derived from contact with only a limited range of individuals, such as missionaries, soldiers, government officials, tourists, or people involved in economic development projects. Re-gardless of the nature and intensity of this contact, most non-Western peoples have a well-developed idea about the expected behavior of such individuals. The tendency of local people to fit the ethnographer into one of their stereotypical categories can at times prove a burden for fieldworkers. Anthropologists' behavior seldom conforms to the model that the local people have developed. Previ-ous contacts with Europeans and Euro-Americans have often been structured in a manner that places the "na-tive" in the position of social inferior. Thus, an anthro-pologist attempting to gain social acceptance in such a society is typically met with suspicion, if not with hos-tility. The types of questions anthropologists ask about behavior and beliefs frequently arouse suspicions further and elicit guarded answers. Why does this researcher want to know about our family structure, our political organization, our ritual secrets? What is the person go-ing to do with this information? While the anthropologist is trying to understand the community, the members of the community are attempting to understand the anthro-pologist's motives. Depending on the nature of previous contacts, some types of questions may provoke more suspicion than others. For example, a minority or tribal group involved in some illegal or illicit activity—such as smuggling, poaching, or growing drugs—may wonder

To attempt to fully understand the culture of a community, anthropologists delve into the public and private lives of individuals and witness events that are private and personal. The researcher learns things about both the community and the individuals within it that few, if any, outsiders know. Not infrequently, the researcher gains knowledge of highly sensitive activities or events that, if known to others, could potentially do harm to either individual members of the community or the community as a whole. In the most extreme cases, the researcher may even have knowledge of activities that may be considered illegal or criminal by others. As a result, researchers in few disciplines face the range of ethical and moral dilemmas that frequently confront anthropologists.

Not surprisingly, the American Anthropological Association (AAA) has devoted a great deal of thought to the complex issue of professional ethics. The AAA approved a Code of Ethics in June 1998 and endorses various Statements on Ethics. The full text of the Code and Statements as well as discussions of specific cases are found on the AAA website. The AAA Code covers anthropology in general and also archaeological, biological, linguistic, and cultural anthropology. Here we quote only the main points relevant to cultural field research. First, the Code states that because "anthropologists can find themselves in complex situations and subject to more than one code of ethics, the AAA Code of Ethics provides a framework, not an ironclad formula, for making decisions."

"A. Responsibility to people . . . with whom anthropological researchers work and whose lives and cultures they study.

1. Anthropological researchers have primary ethical obligations to the people . . . they study and to the people with whom they work. These obligations can supersede the goal of seeking new knowledge, and can lead to decisions not to undertake or to discontinue a research project when the primary obligation conflicts with other responsibilities, such as those owed to sponsors or clients. These ethical obligations include:

- To avoid harm or wrong, understanding that the development of knowledge can lead to change which may be positive or negative for the people . . . worked with or studied.
- To consult actively with the affected individuals or group(s), with the goal of establishing a working relationship that can be beneficial to all parties involved.

2. Anthropological researchers must do everything in their power to ensure that their research does not harm the safety, dignity, or privacy of the people with whom they work, conduct research, or perform other professional activities.

3. Anthropological researchers must determine in advance whether their host/providers of information wish to remain anonymous or receive recognition, and make every effort to comply with those wishes. Researchers must present to their research participants the possible impacts of the choices, and make clear that despite their best efforts, anonymity may be compromised or recognition fail to materialize.

4. Anthropological researchers should obtain in advance the informed consent of persons being studied. . . . Informed consent, for the purposes of this code, does not necessarily imply or require a particular written or signed form. It is the quality of the consent, not the format, that is relevant.

5. Anthropological researchers who have developed close and enduring relationships . . . with either individual persons providing information or with hosts must adhere to the obligations of openness and informed consent, while carefully and respectfully negotiating the limits of the relationship.

6. While anthropologists may gain personally from their work, they must not exploit individuals [or] groups. . . . They should recognize their debt to the societies in which they work and their obligation to reciprocate with people studied in appropriate ways."

The vast majority of anthropological field researchers have been and are involved in pure academic re-

whether the anthropologist will inform government authorities. Members of groups that have been exposed to Western culture frequently assume that the ethnographer's objective is to make money and that researchers become wealthy by publishing books.

In other cases, members of the community may be aware that Europeans and Euro-Americans do not approve of or believe in certain types of behaviors, and few people will disclose information on topics they think

will be met with disapproval or scorn. This reticence is particularly evident for certain types of religious beliefs and practices. As a result of the extensive activities of Christian missionaries, most non-Western peoples are well aware that Westerners usually deny the validity of witchcraft and the existence of werewolves. Members of societies that hold such beliefs are usually hesitant about discussing these subjects with Westerners. They are understandably reluctant to talk openly about an uncle who search. However, over the past 50 years or so, cultural researchers have increasingly become involved in what is termed "applied anthropological research" (see Chapter 1). This change is not surprising. Anthropology is the only academic discipline that focuses on understanding non-Western peoples. Prior to globalization, the cultures of most people studied by anthropologists were, at least in the minds of many Western government and business leaders, politically and economically irrelevant. Anthropological knowledge and research, though possibly interesting, were considered by many to be of limited or no real value in developing policies and programs. With globalization, anthropological knowledge of non-Western peoples has become not only valuable but also increasingly relevant in many areas of concern, such as health care, multicultural education, economic development, and international marketing. Developmental anthropologists, for example, now work for the World Bank, the United Nations Development Program, and the U.S. Agency for International Development as well as private foundations and corporations.

As we discussed in Chapter 1, since 1990 about half of all those who have earned Ph.D. degrees in anthropology have found employment in either government agencies or the private sector as "applied anthropologists." Recognizing that increasing numbers of anthropologists are today involved in applied research raises new ethical issues, and the AAA Code of Ethics includes a section on such research. The most relevant statement is: "In working for government agencies or private businesses, they [the researchers] should be especially careful not to promise or imply acceptance of conditions contrary to professional ethics . . . ."

The involvement of applied anthropologists in nonacademic research often raises ethical questions not confronted by academic researchers, but the potential involvement of anthropologists in national security issues raises even more ethical concerns within the profession. During World War II, anthropologists were actively involved with government intelligence agencies, particular in Asia and the Pacific. During the so-called Cold War that followed, however, the profession as a whole took a strong position against attempts by various government agencies to recruit anthropologists to collect political and military intelligence data. The reason for this was simple: If some anthropologists were involved in intelligence gathering, then all anthropologists would potentially become viewed as government agents. This would endanger not only their research but also themselves as individuals. As a result, government intelligence agencies, both civilian and military, have had to rely on political scientists, economists, sociologists, and psychologists to serve as policy consultants as well as to gather and analyze intelligence data.

Noting that the recent failures, both politically and militarily, in Iraq were due to "intelligence failures," meaning that Americans did not understand the culture of the Middle-Eastern peoples, U.S. security and intelligence agencies are again attempting to recruit cultural anthropologists. This has raised serious concerns within the profession. In what capacity, if any, can an anthropologist work within an intelligence agency and still adhere to the AAA Code of Ethics?

Critical Thinking Questions

1. What are some ethical problems an applied cultural anthropologist might face in working for a private corporation or governmental agency?

2. Why might anthropologists be opposed to working in military intelligence-gathering activities?

3. Can an ethical distinction be made between general consulting on national security issues and direct involvement in field research to collect security data?

---

they believe can turn himself into a deer or a snake with someone who will probably view what they say as ridiculous. Likewise, they probably would not say that their father had been killed by a witch if they thought that the researcher did not believe in witchcraft.

Developing a role and rapport. Often against a background of suspicion and distrust, an anthropologist has to develop a rapport with the members of the community. *Rapport* in this sense means acceptance to the degree that a working relationship is possible, although ethnographers are rarely, if ever, totally accepted by the people among whom they work. Over a period of time, however, most anthropologists succeed in gaining some degree of trust and friendship, at least with a few members of the group.

The particular role or roles that anthropologists eventually define for themselves within a society vary

▲ Among the earliest anthropological researchers and writers was Francis LaFlesche (1857–1932), an Omaha Indian from Nebraska.

greatly with the circumstances of the particular situation. Depending on the amount and nature of research funding, an anthropologist may be an important economic resource for the community, paying wages to interpreters and assistants or distributing desirable goods as gifts. Anthropologists who have a car or truck frequently find themselves providing needed transportation for members of the community. Ethnographers may also provide comic relief by asking "silly questions," behaving in a funny manner, making childlike errors in speaking the language, and generally being amusing to have around. Researchers may also be a source of information about the outside world, disclosing information to which local people would not otherwise have access. Sometimes community members are as curious about the anthropologist's society as the anthropologist is about theirs. Or the anthropologist may be considered just a harmless nuisance. During the course of research, the typical fieldworker adopts all these roles plus many others.

Identifying and interviewing consultants. Ethnographers learn a good deal about people simply by living among them and participating in many of their activities. This rather casual, informal participant observation provides a good feel for the general pattern of life. But for most purposes, observation and participation alone are insufficient. We want to know not only what people are doing but also why they are doing it. Because certain realms of culture are not observable (e.g., religious beliefs, myths, stories, and social values), the researcher has to interview members of the group.

An individual who supplies the ethnographer with information is called a **consultant** or **informant.** Field research involves the help of many consultants, who sometimes are paid for their services. Just as no one individual is equally well informed about every aspect of our own cultural system, so no one person in another society is equally knowledgeable about every aspect of that society's way of life. Women are more knowledgeable than men concerning certain things, and vice versa. Shamans and priests know more about religious rituals than other people do. The elderly members of the community are usually most knowledgeable about myths, stories, and histories. Thus, the anthropologist has to attempt to identify and interview those people who are most knowledgeable about particular subjects. Individuals whom the local community considers to be expert in some particular area are known as **key consultants** or **key informants.**

A number of factors affect the quality and accuracy of the data collected through interviewing. The people being studied seldom understand fully what the anthropologist is trying to accomplish. In some instances, especially among minority populations, there may be a deliberate attempt to deceive the researcher. For example, collecting livestock-ownership data on the Navajo reservation can at times prove difficult. The total number of livestock on the reservation is controlled by the tribe, and individual stockowners have a permit that allows them to keep a certain number of animals. Because some people keep more stock than their permits allow, they are reluctant to disclose the actual number in their herds. There is also the problem of humorous deception. Osage men wear a roach made out of deer tail and turkey beard or porcupine hair on their heads at dances. During a dance, an Osage was overheard telling an inquisitive visitor that these roaches were made of horse tails, and that a young Osage male proved his manhood by cutting the hair for his roach from the tail of the meanest horse he could find. In this case, the Osage was simply having fun at the expense of a visitor, but anthropologists also encounter this problem. To get around these and other difficulties, anthropologists try to interview a number of individuals separately about specific points to gain several independent verifications.

Cultural barriers also make it difficult to collect certain types of data. For example, collecting genealogies is not always as easy as it might seem because in many societies it is customary not to speak the names of the dead. Among the Yanomamö of Venezuela and Brazil, not only is it taboo to speak the names of the dead but it is also considered discourteous to speak the names of prominent living men, for whom kinship terms are used whenever possible. When ethnographer Napoleon Chagnon persisted in his attempts to collect genealogies, the Yanomamö responded by inventing a series of fictitious genealogical relationships. Only after five months of intensive research did Chagnon discover the hoax. When he mentioned some of the names he had collected during a visit to a neighboring village, the people responded with "uncontrollable laughter" because his informants had made up names such as "hairy rectum" and "eagle shit" to avoid speaking the real names.

Fieldwork as a Rite of Passage

Fieldwork is important to cultural anthropologists not just because it is the major source of our data on human cultures but also because it is a key aspect of the anthropologist's education. It is one thing to read ethnographies about other ways of life, but it is something quite different to live among and interact with individuals from another cultural tradition daily for a year or longer. As we have seen, anthropologists usually live in the native community, submerging themselves in the social life of the people, living in native dwellings, eating local foods, learning the language, and participating as fully as an outsider is allowed in daily activities. Living as social minorities, usually for the first time in their lives, anthropologists depend on the goodwill of people whose norms and values they neither totally understand nor completely accept. Under these conditions, participant observers have to adjust their behavior to fit the norms and behavior patterns of the people they are studying. This modification of the fieldworker's own behavior is a necessary part of learning about the community. Because fieldworkers usually work alone, they are socially and physically vulnerable to members of the community. During the course of their research, anthropologists will violate, or at least be perceived as violating, some of the societal norms of behavior. Such incidents may destroy the rapport gained with some key consultants or result in the researcher being ostracized. In serious cases, the fieldworker may become the target of physical violence.

When in the field, except on rare occasions, the anthropologist is the uninvited guest of the community. Regardless of how researchers may rationalize their work as being for the long-term good of the community or humanity, they are basically there to serve their own needs and interests. If a serious problem develops between the anthropologist and members of the community, the fieldworker must bear the primary responsibility and blame.

The fieldwork experience tests and taxes the attitude of cultural relativity (as discussed in Chapter 1) that anthropologists teach in their classrooms. It is easy to discuss the concept of relativity in a university setting, but it is more difficult to apply this concept to one's own situation. Regardless of which society it is, certain cultural aspects will offend one's own cultural norms and values. For example, according to the anthropologist's own social norms, some local people might "abuse" certain family members or certain powerful leaders might "exploit" lower-ranking members of the society. As the fieldworker develops friendships, this "abuse" or "exploitation" frequently becomes personalized. Under what circumstances, if ever, an anthropologist should attempt to intervene and try to impose her or his cultural standards on the members of another society poses a real and personal dilemma. In theory, such intervention is never permissible, but in real-life situations, the answer is not always so clear.

Many people experience a kind of psychological trauma when surrounded by people speaking a language they cannot fully understand and can speak only imperfectly, eating foods that are strange, seeing architecture that is alien, and observing people using gestures and behaving in ways they either do not comprehend or do not approve of. The strange sounds, smells, tastes, sights, and behaviors result in disorientation. Out of their normal cultural context, fieldworkers do not understand what is happening around them, yet realize that their own actions are often being misunderstood. The symptoms of **culture shock** are psychological and sometimes even physiological: paranoia, anxiety, longing for the folks back home, nausea, hypochondria, and, frequently, diarrhea.

The attempts by ethnographers to maintain their relativistic perspective and objectivity in their daily interaction with members of the other society usually compound the normal trauma of culture shock. Socially isolated and unable to release their frustrations and anxieties through conversations with sympathetic others, they often have to cope with their psychological difficulties alone.

For many anthropologists, much of their time in the field is extremely traumatic, and as a result, most anthropologists view fieldwork as a rite of passage. More than any other aspect of their training, fieldwork transforms students of anthropology into professional anthropologists. Although many overemphasize the importance of fieldwork, it is undeniably a significant educational experience. Most individuals return from their fieldwork with a different perspective on themselves and their own culture. Fieldwork often teaches us as much about ourselves and our own culture as about the culture of the peoples we are studying.

Ethnohistory

The study of past cultural systems through the use of written records is called **ethnohistory.** Since the late nineteenth century, anthropologists have used written materials in their studies, but the importance of this research has been widely recognized only since the 1970s. The growing interest in ethnohistory has come with the realization that non-Western societies have changed far more dramatically over the past few hundred years than had previously been thought.

Like historians who study their society's past, ethnohistorians make use of such materials as published books and articles, newspapers, archival documents, diaries, journals, maps, drawings, and photographs. Not surprisingly, many scholars treat history and ethnohistory as if they were synonymous. There are, however, critical—yet frequently overlooked—differences between ethnohistory and history.

- An ethnohistorian is primarily interested in reconstructing the cultural system of the people. The actual historical events themselves are of interest only because they cast light on the cultural system or changes in the system.
- Historical events have little significance outside the cultural context of the peoples involved. Ethnohistorians study nonliterate peoples. Thus, whereas historians can use accounts recorded by members of the society being studied, ethnohistorians have to use accounts recorded by members of other literate societies. As a result, the problem of interpreting accounts is usually more difficult for the ethnohistorian than for the historian.

The problem of interpretation raises an additional question about the validity of particular reports. Not only do we have to ask about the accuracy of the account, but we also have to ask how knowledgeable the recorder was about the cultural context of the events. Ethnohistorians use certain criteria to evaluate the potential validity of an account. How long did the writer live among these people? Did the observer speak the language? What was the observer's role? Soldiers, missionaries, traders, and government officials have different views, biases, and access to information.

The difficulty with ethnohistory is that no hard-and-fast rules can be used in evaluating these data. The lon-

ger an individual lived among members of a particular society and the better the person spoke the language, the more reliable the account should be; however, this cannot be automatically assumed. In some cases, the writer may have had little interest in the people, perhaps because the contacts were only related to a job. This attitude is evident in the accounts of many traders and government officials. In other cases, the account may be self-serving, with individuals attempting to enhance their careers. Thus, sometimes soldiers and government officials falsified their official reports. Ethnocentrism is still another factor. Missionary accounts, in particular, often demonstrate overt bias against local customs and beliefs; one has to remember that individuals become missionaries because they are avid believers. Nevertheless, some of the most objective accounts of other societies were written by missionaries who were scholars themselves.

Thus, in ethnohistoric research, there is no simple way to evaluate a particular document or account. At best, a single event may be recorded in several independent accounts that can each be used to verify the accuracy and interpretation of the others. Unfortunately, multiple observations are the exception, not the rule.

A final limitation on the use of ethnohistoric materials is that seldom are all aspects of a particular society evenly reported. For example, data on economic activities may be the most abundant, whereas information on religious ceremonies and beliefs may be absent or limited. As a result, ethnographic studies based on ethnohistoric research alone usually lack the depth and balance of studies gained from field research. Despite its problems and limitations, however, ethnohistoric research provides us with the only clues we have to the past of many societies, as well as the key to a vast store of cultural data hitherto untapped.

Comparative Methods

So far we have discussed only how anthropologists collect cultural data on peoples, past and present, using fieldwork and historical materials. We have some cultural data available on more than 1,200 societies. As shown in the following chapters, anthropologists have used these data to demonstrate a wide range of cultural variability among human populations. However, we are not interested in merely describing particular cultural systems and the range of variability they display. We are also interested in attempting to explain why these differences exist. In other words, anthropologists want to make generalizations concerning cultural systems. Generalizations cannot be made based on the study of a single society; we need methods by which many societies can be compared in a systematic way. The objective of comparative studies is to test hypotheses.

Cross-Cultural Comparisons

The most frequently used comparative method is **cross-cultural comparison.** In this method, hypotheses are tested by examining the statistical correlations between particular cultural variables, using synchronic data drawn from a number of societies. Historical changes in the societies examined are ignored; the societies are compared at whatever period they were studied. This research method involves three steps. First, the researcher must state the idea as a hypothesis—that is, state it in such a way that it can be supported or not supported ("tested") by data drawn from a large number of human populations. Second, the ethnologist chooses a sample of societies (usually randomly) and studies the ethnographies that describe their way of life. Third, the data collected from these ethnographies are classified and grouped in such a manner that the correlations between variables may be shown statistically. What the researcher is attempting to find is the pattern of association: Do two or more cultural variables consistently occur together or not? In most cases, these tasks are far more difficult than they may sound.

To illustrate how the cross-cultural method is used to test a hypothesis, we shall examine the relationship between sorcery and legal systems within a group of societies. Sorcery is discussed in some detail in Chapter 13. Here it is sufficient to know that sorcery is the belief that certain people (sorcerers) have power, either supernatural or magical, to cause harm to others. Some anthropologists believe that sorcery serves as a means of social control in societies that lack a formalized legal apparatus—courts, police, and so forth—to punish wrongdoers. They argue that people will be reluctant to cause trouble if they believe that a victim of their troublemaking has the ability to use supernatural power to retaliate against them. Overall, societies without a formal legal system should have a greater need for a mechanism such as sorcery to control behavior. So, if the hypothesis that sorcery is a mechanism for social control is correct, we ought to find that sorcery is more important in societies that have no formal means of punishment than in societies with a specialized legal system.

To see whether this hypothesis is true across a variety of societies, we use the cross-cultural method. We determine for many societies (1) the relative degree of impor-tance of sorcery, and (2) whether the society has a formal apparatus for punishing wrongdoing. We make a table in which all the possible combinations of the two cultural elements are recorded:

Sorcery	Specialized Legal Apparatus Absent	Present
Important	A	B
Unimportant	C	D

In the cells of the table, we record the number of societies in which the four possible combinations are found. If the hypothesis is supported, we should find that cells A and D contain the greatest number of societies. If the hypothesis is not supported, we should find that the distribution of societies in the cells is random, or that cells B and C contain the greatest number of societies, or some other distribution.

In 1950, Beatrice Whiting conducted such a study by surveying the ethnographic literature for 50 societies. Her results were as follows (Whiting 1950, 87):

Sorcery	Specialized Legal Apparatus Absent	Present
Important	30	5
Unimportant	3	12

On the basis of this comparison, we might conclude that the hypothesis is supported because most of the societies fall into the cells predicted by our hypothesis. We would not worry about the eight societies (the "exceptions") that appear in cells B and C. The hypothesis did not claim that social control was the *only* function of sorcery, so the importance of sorcery in the five societies in cell B might be explained by some other factor. Nor did we claim that sorcery was the *only* way that societies lacking a specialized legal apparatus had to control their members, so the three societies in cell C might have developed some alternative means of social control. (Although outside the scope of this text, statistical tests are available that show how confident a researcher can be that such associations did not occur by chance.)

Some confusion is caused by cross-cultural tabulations such as this. One of the most common is to mistake correlation for causation: Simply because two cultural elements (X and Y) are usually found together does not mean that one (X) has caused the other (Y). Y could have caused X, or both X and Y could have been caused by some third element, W. In the preceding example, it

In January 1778, two British ships under the command of Captain James Cook discovered the Hawaiian Islands. They stayed only three days before continuing on to the northern Pacific. In the winter of 1778–1779, they returned and for seven weeks sailed among the islands without making landfall. Finally, on January 17, 1779, they landed on the large island of Hawaii. This second landing was greeted by thousands of Hawaiians, including King Kalani'opu'u. Cook was presented with a great feathered cloak and cap and was greeted with rituals, including a multitude of people prostrating themselves before him and chanting "Lono." On February 4, Cook and his ships departed with a spectacular sendoff. However, the weather quickly turned bad and one ship sprung its mast, forcing the expedition to return to the island for repairs. The Hawaiians did not welcome this return. Hostilities soon developed, and a battle took place in which Cook was killed.

Scholars have long thought that the Hawaiians identified Cook's visit as the return of their god Lono. Using ethnohistoric and ethnographic data, Marshall Sahlins reexamined this interpretation in his 1981 study, *Historical Metaphors and Mythical Realities,* and reached the same conclusion.

Lono was a mythical god-king who the Hawaiians believed periodically returned to the islands and ruled in human form, usurping power from the earthly kings who were representatives of the rival god Ku. Several earlier Hawaiian kings had been identified as Lono ruling on Earth. Every year, during a period called *Makahiki,* a series of rituals were performed and dedicated to Lono. Lono symbolically returned to the islands at the beginning of Makahiki, at which time the priests of Lono took control of the temples from the priests of Ku. During the four lunar months that followed, the priests of Lono were in charge of rituals. Makahiki ended with Lono being symbolically sacrificed and returning to the sky. With Lono gone, control returned to the king and the priests of Ku, the earthly representatives of Ku.

Sahlins found that as Cook sailed among the islands for seven weeks, the timing and direction of his movements coincidentally corresponded with the mythological movements of the god-king Lono. His landing on January 17 took place at the start of Makahiki; his departure on February 4 corresponded with the end of Makahiki. According to Sahlins, the Hawaiians identified Cook as the personification of Lono, an interpretation further strengthened by Cook when he told them during his departure that he would return the next year.

Cook's untimely return to repair one of his ships was ominously interpreted by the king and priests of Ku as Lono returning to claim earthly powers. Not surprisingly, the Hawaiian priests had him killed and viewed the killing as the ritual sacrifice of the rival god-king Lono, which they symbolically reenacted every year.

When Gananath Obeyesekere, a Sri Lankan anthropologist, first heard Sahlins present this interpretation of Cook, he was "taken aback." Why would the Hawaiians think that this European was a god? Drawing from his own knowledge of southern

was assumed that the absence of formal legal punishments "caused" many societies to need some other social control mechanism, and that sorcery became important to meet this need. On the basis of the data in the table, we might also conclude that societies in which sorcery is important have little need for a formal legal apparatus, so they fail to develop one.

To acquire the data needed to test her hypothesis, Whiting read through ethnographic information on all 50 societies in her sample. This approach suffers from several disadvantages. It is so time consuming that only a small number of societies can be included in the sample. There is also the problem of bias by the researcher, who must decide, for example, whether sorcery should be considered "important" or "unimportant" among some people. Borderline cases might get lumped into the category that supports the researcher's hypothesis.

Thanks largely to a lifetime of work by George Murdock, another method is available to modern researchers that partially overcomes these two problems (although it has troubles of its own, to be discussed shortly). In the *Ethnographic Atlas,* Murdock and his associates summarized information on more than 1,200 societies in the form of coded tables. Each cultural system has codes that show its form of kinship, marriage, economy, religion, political organization, division of labor, and so forth. Contemporary cross-cultural researchers no longer need to search through ethnographies for information relevant to their investigations; rather, they use the information already coded and analyze the results by using a computer. This reduces the bias of the researcher because whoever coded the information on a particular society had no knowledge of the hypothesis under investigation. It also allows a larger number of societies

Asian peoples, he could not think of a single example of Sri Lankans or other southern Asian peoples seeing the newly arrived Europeans as gods. To Obeyesekere this was an example of European myth building, in which the European explorer/civilizer becomes a "god" to the natives.

In 1992, Obeyesekere published *The Apotheosis of Captain Cook: European Mythmaking in the Pacific,* in which he challenged Sahlins's interpretation. In his criticism of Sahlins and other Western scholars, Obeyesekere touches on a broad range of theoretical and substantive issues. We cover just two of the major points.

Obeyesekere argues that it was the English themselves who first mythologized Captain Cook. He had already made two successful and daring voyages into the unknown waters of the Pacific. Because of published accounts of these trips Cook had become—in the eyes of the British—the very image of the ideal explorer/civilizer. A competent, courageous, generous, decent, and humane individual who understood and was well liked by the native peoples he encountered, Cook embodied all the qualities and greatness of civilized humanity. His violent death at the hands of a strange and savage people to whom he had brought the prospects of civilization served only to enhance his mythic stature. In his research, however, Obeyesekere found that Cook, particularly on his third and final voyage, was not the Cook of British mythology. Cook could be brutal with both the natives and his crew, as well as arrogant and not always competent. Obeyesekere also found little

contemporary evidence that the members of the crew thought the Hawaiians viewed Cook as a god. The idea that Hawaiians identified Cook with Lono dates from early-nineteenth-century accounts that were compiled long after the events themselves.

Obeyesekere further argues that still prevalent in Western academic thought is the idea that non-Western peoples, such as the Hawaiians, think differently. According to Obeyesekere, "Implicit . . . is a commonplace assumption of the savage mind that is given to prelogical or mystical thought and in turn is fundamentally opposed to the logical and rational ways of thinking of modern man." Thus, the "childlike" natives lacked rational reflection. Even when anthropologists accept the idea that other people can act rationally, rationality is constrained by the boundaries of their own cultural beliefs; "their thought processes are inflexible; [and] they cannot rationally weigh alternative or multiple courses of action." Thus, Obeyesekere further argues that these implicit and sometimes explicit assumptions about the nature of other peoples underlie the interpretation that Hawaiians thought Captain Cook was a god and that that god was Lono.

In his critique of Sahlins, Obeyesekere raises a critical issue. Does anthropology reflect a Western cultural bias? Are anthropological interpretations of other peoples' behavior a reflection of implicit Eurocentric beliefs about others?

Sources: Sahlins (1981), Obeyesekere (1992), Sahlins (1995)

to be included in a sample because the data can be retrieved far more quickly.

Using cross-cultural methods to see whether some specific hypothesis applies to a large number of societies is thus easier today than ever before, but some difficulties still exist. One seems to be inherent in the method itself, which dissects whole cultures into parts ("variables," as we called them) and assigns a value (or "state") to each part. In the preceding example, the variables were sorcery, which had two states (important, unimportant), and specialized legal apparatus, which also had two states (present, absent). To test the hypothesis that the states of these two cultural elements are consistently related, we ignored everything else about them. We also ignored everything else about the societies in the sample, such as their family systems and their economies.

A more familiar example makes the point clearly. One element of cultural systems is the number of gods in whom people believe. For purposes of some specific hypothesis, the possible states of this variable might be monotheism (belief in one god), polytheism (belief in many gods), and no gods. Any researcher who included modern North America in the sample would probably consider our primary religion—Christianity—as monotheistic. Most of the Middle East also would be considered monotheistic. The problem is: Can North American monotheism be considered equivalent to Middle Eastern monotheisms? If we consider them the same, we ignore the differences between the worship of the Christian God, the Jewish Yahweh, and the Islamic Allah. When we lump these three varieties of monotheism together into a single kind of religion, we distort them to some degree.

© Gideon Mendel/Corbis

▲ Christianity, Judaism, and Islam are all monotheistic and have common historical roots. But Christians and Jews do not pray by prostrating themselves toward Mecca, as these Muslims in South Africa are doing. Should cross-cultural researchers consider all of them one kind of religion, or not?

Cross-cultural studies examine data ahistorically, or without reference to time. In other words, the cultural system of a particular society is treated as timeless or unchanging. Thus, in cross-cultural studies and the *Ethnographic Atlas,* there is "a" cultural system coded for the Cheyenne: Cheyenne cultural system circa 1850. However, the cultural system of a society is never stable but constantly changing. For example, today the Cheyenne live in houses, drive cars and trucks, and participate in a wage-money economy. In 1850, the Cheyenne lived in hide-covered tepees, rode horses, and hunted buffalo. In 1650, the Cheyenne lived in permanent earth lodge villages, traveled by foot or canoe, and depended on farming and hunting for their subsistence. Although Cheyenne cultural systems have continuity, all aspects of their culture have changed, to some degree, over the period just described. Thus, in reality, there is no stable Cheyenne culture, but an ever-changing system. The

ahistorical studies used in cross-cultural research create an artificial picture of the cultural system of a society.

Controlled Historical Comparisons

Only in the past 30 years have anthropologists attempted **controlled historical comparisons.** Unlike cross-cultural studies, controlled historical comparisons use changes in particular groupings of societies over time to define general cultural patterning and to test hypotheses. Controlled historical comparisons, like cross-cultural studies, are usually extremely complex. We illustrate this method by a simple example.

As we discuss in Chapter 9, people organize their family lives in various ways. Two common ways are matrilineal descent and patrilineal descent. In matrilineal societies, family group membership is inherited through your mother; you belong to your mother's family. In patrilineal societies, group membership is inherited through your father; you belong to your father's family. Anthropologists have long attempted to explain why some societies are matrilineal and others patrilineal. Cross-cultural research has shown that a relationship exists between matrilineality and patrilineality and the relative economic importance of males and females in the society. However, cross-cultural studies can show us only correlations between descent and other synchronic aspects of the cultural system. For example, these studies can tell us what types of economic systems are most frequently found with matrilineal or patrilineal societies. Cross-cultural studies cannot measure the long-term effects of external changes on matrilineal or patrilineal societies. Is matrilineality or patrilineality more adaptive in some situations than in others? If so, what types of situations favor matrilineal societies, and which favor patrilineal societies? To examine this question, we must turn to controlled historical comparisons.

Michael Allen (1984) has asserted that matrilineal societies in the Pacific were more successful than patrilineal societies in adapting to European contact. Is there a way to test Allen's assertion? First, we must restructure this statement as a testable hypothesis. What do we mean by success? The term *success* is subjective and cannot be directly measured. We have to convert this term into some measurable quantity. One quantifiable measure of the success of a particular system is the relative ability of a society to maintain or expand its population over time. Thus, our hypothesis would be: Given the same degree of disruptive external pressures, matrilineal societies maintain their population levels better over time than patrilineal societies. Now we need to find a group of matrilineal societies and patrilineal societies that experienced a comparable intensity of external contact over a period of time and compare their relative populations at the beginning and end of the period. If Allen is correct, the matrilineal societies should have a larger population at the end of the period than the patrilineal societies.

The farming Native American tribes of the eastern United States present an almost ideal case for testing Allen's assertion. They had similar cultural systems, except that some were matrilineal and others were patrilineal. Their collective histories of contact with Europeans were also basically the same. During the historical period, all these societies suffered the effects of epidemic diseases, warfare (with Europeans as well as intertribal), severe territorial dislocation, political domination, and social discrimination.

Now the problem is determining an appropriate time frame to examine and finding comparable population data. One problem with ethnohistoric research is that the researcher is forced to use the data available in the records. It is not until about 1775 that sufficient population data are available in missionary, military, and explorer accounts to estimate the populations of all these tribes with any accuracy. In 1910, the U.S. Bureau of the Census conducted a special Native American census, which was the first truly comprehensive census of Native American societies in the United States. Thus, the time frame we will use is from 1775 to 1910. Using ethnographic data, we can then classify particular societies as either matrilineal or patrilineal and determine their populations at the beginning and end of this period:

	1775	1910	Percent
Matrilineal societies	88,590	82,714	93
Patrilineal societies	36,400	13,463	37
Totals	124,990	96,177	77

From this table we can see that during this 135-year period, the matrilineal societies declined by only about 7 percent of their total population, whereas patrilineal societies lost 63 percent of their population. If maintenance of population is a measure of a society's success, then matrilineal societies in the eastern United States were more successful than patrilineal societies.

As is the case with all comparative studies, findings such as these raise more questions than they answer. Are these population figures and the historical experiences of these societies truly comparable? If they are comparable, is the significant factor differences in descent form, or is it some other cultural factor we have not considered? We need to add at this point that not all matrilineal societies in this study were equally successful in maintaining their population levels, and that a few patrilineal societies studied increased in population during this period. There is room, then, for argument. If, in the final analysis, however, we decide that our findings are valid and that matrilineal societies are, under certain conditions, more adaptive than patrilineal societies, we still cannot directly say why.

Cross-cultural comparisons and controlled historical comparisons give us distinctly different measures of cultural phenomena. They address different questions and test different hypotheses. They are complementary, not competitive, methodologies.

Some anthropologists (especially idealists—see Chapter 4) believe that both kinds of comparative studies distort each cultural system in the sample so much that the whole method is invalid. They think that ripping each element out of the particular context in which it is

Ethnographic methods	The collection of cultural data on a particular society or group of societies. The primary purpose is the collection of descriptive data.
Ethnographic fieldwork	The collection of cultural data from living individuals. This usually requires that the researcher live with or close to the people being studied.
Ethnohistoric research	The study of the past cultural system of a people through the use of written records.
Comparative methods	The comparative study of the cultural systems of a number of different societies. The objective is to test hypotheses so that we can explain why differences exist.
Cross-cultural comparisons	The testing of hypotheses by using synchronic data drawn from a number of different societies.
Controlled historical comparisons	The comparative use of historically documented changes in particular groupings of societies over time to define general cultural patterning and to test hypotheses.

embedded robs it of its significance because each element acquires its meaning only in its local historical and cultural context.

Despite these and other problems, comparative methods are the only practical means available for determining whether a hypothesis is valid among human cultural systems. Those who use these methods are aware of the difficulties, yet they believe that the advantage of being able to process information on large numbers of societies outweighs the problems.

Summary

1. Anthropological methods fall into two overall categories. Ethnographic methods involve the collection of information on a specific cultural system, whereas comparative methods are used to test hypotheses or to investigate theoretical ideas by comparing information on numerous cultural systems.

2. The basic aims of ethnographic methods are descriptive, whereas comparative investigations aim to determine whether some hypothesis or theoretical idea is supported by the accumulated data on human cultures.

3. The kinds of ethnographic methods used by anthropologists depend on whether they are investigating a contemporary or a past way of life.

4. Research into the past way of life of a people usually involves ethnohistory (perusal of written documents). This method requires considerable interpretation by the researcher. Sometimes those who wrote the documents used in ethnohistoric reconstructions misinterpreted events because of their cultural backgrounds and ethnocen-

trism. The contents of documents are often affected by the private interests of their authors.

5. Fieldwork is the primary method of acquiring data about the culture of a living people. Fieldworkers usually live among those they study for at least a year, conducting formal interviews and surveys and engaging in participant observation. The difficulties of conducting fieldwork vary with the personality and gender of the fieldworker and with the people and specific topic being studied.

6. There are four problems that all fieldworkers must face. First, not only must fieldworkers fight against their own ethnocentrism and tendencies to stereotype the people they study, but they must also overcome the stereotypes local people have developed about outsiders. Second, it is often difficult to establish a rapport with local people because they may have had no previous experience with the kinds of questions fieldworkers ask. Third, identifying reliable informants and finding people willing to participate in intensive surveys may pose a serious problem. Fourth, sometimes people deliberately deceive anthropologists because they mistrust their motives, do not want certain facts to become public, or are culturally forbidden to give away secrets of their religion.

7. Fieldwork is viewed as an essential part of the graduate education of anthropologists and almost a prerequisite for professionalism. It is, in some respects, a rite of passage.

8. Comparative methods involve ways of systematically and reliably comparing massive amounts of information collected by previous ethnographers. The use of comparative methods presents many difficulties, including stating the research hypothesis in such a way that it is testable, reliably defining and measuring the variables of interest for many societies, deciding whether similar cultural elements from two or more societies are the "same" or "different," and contending with unintentional researcher bias. The results of comparative studies can be difficult to interpret. Correlation is often confused with causation.

Key Terms

ethnographic methods
comparative methods
ethnographic fieldwork
ethnohistoric research
interviewing
participant observation

stereotyping
consultant (informant)
key consultant (key informant)
culture shock
ethnohistory

cross-cultural comparisons
controlled historical comparisons

Suggested Readings

Works that deal with research methods and problems include:

Agar, Michael. *The Professional Stranger: An Informal Introduction to Ethnography.* New York: Academic, 1980.

Quite good for the beginning student. Tells how ethnographers do their work, with lots of examples taken from the author's own field experiences.

Bernard, H. Russell. *Research Methods in Anthropology: Qualitative and Quantitative Approaches.* 3rd ed. Walnut Creek, Calif.: AltaMira Press, 2001.

Now in its third edition, this work has become the standard reference for research methods in anthropology.

Brown, Michael F. *Who Owns Native Culture?* Cambridge, Mass.: Harvard University Press, 2003.

This book is concerned with the issue of native rights and culture, important issues of which every culture researcher should be aware.

Emerson, Robert M., Rachel I. Fretz, and Linda L. Shaw. *Writing Ethnographic Fieldnotes.* Chicago: Guides to Writing, Editing, and Publishing. Chicago: University of Chicago Press, 1995.

This is a how-to manual for individuals involved in field research.

Martin, Calvin, ed. *The American Indian and the Problem of History.* New York: Oxford University Press, 1987.

In this edited work, anthropologists, historians, and Native Americans discuss the problems in trying to objectively interpret the cultural history of Indian America. This is a critical book for any ethnohistorian studying Native American culture.

Obeyesekere, Gananath. *The Apotheosis of Captain Cook: European Mythmaking in the Pacific.* Princeton, N.J.: Princeton University Press, 1992.

In part, this study attacks Marshall Sahlins's interpretation of the Cook murder, accusing him of Eurocentric bias. Obeyesekere shows the difficulty in attempting to objectively analyze historical documents.

Spradley, James P. *The Ethnographic Interview.* New York: Holt, Rinehart and Winston, 1979.

Spradley, James P. *Participant Observation*. New York: Holt, Rinehart and Winston, 1980.

Two books that complement each other, one focusing on structured interviewing of informants, the other on detailed observation.

A number of books deal with the actual experiences of ethnographers in the field. They are valuable for conveying the feeling of fieldwork, problems ethnographers encounter, relating to local people, and so forth.

DeVita, Philip R., ed. *The Naked Anthropologist: Tales from Around the World*. Belmont, Calif.: Wadsworth, 1992.

A collection of 27 personal accounts of fieldworkers discussing the situations, issues, and problems they encountered.

Dumont, Jean-Paul. *The Headman and I*. Prospect Heights, Ill.: Waveland Press, 1992.

Account of a fieldworker's relationships with the Panare people of the Venezuelan Amazon.

Freilich, Morris, ed. *Marginal Natives: Anthropologists at Work*. New York: Harper & Row, 1970.

Ten anthropologists discuss the problems of fieldwork.

Golde, Peggy, ed. *Women in the Field: Anthropological Experiences*. Chicago: Aldine, 1970.

Twelve female ethnographers discuss special difficulties they encountered because of their gender.

Hayano, David M. *Road Through the Rain Forest*. Prospect Heights, Ill.: Waveland Press, 1990.

Describes the fieldwork experiences of Hayano and his wife among the Awa, a people of the highlands of Papua New Guinea.

Medicine, Beatrice. *Learning to Be an Anthropologist and Remaining "Native."* Urbana: University of Illinois Press, 2001.

In these selected writings of one of America's foremost Native American scholars and anthropologists, there are a number of excellent discussions of being both a "native" and an anthropologist.

Rabinow, Paul. *Reflections on Fieldwork in Morocco*. Berkeley: University of California Press, 1977.

An interesting discussion of the author's experiences in Morocco.

Ward, Martha C. *Nest in the Wind*. Prospect Heights, Ill.: Waveland Press, 1989.

Wonderfully readable account of Ward's personal experiences and fieldwork difficulties on Pohnpei Island, Micronesia.

Media Resources

The Wadsworth Anthropology Resource Center
academic.cengage.com/anthropology

The Wadsworth discipline resource website that accompanies *Humanity: An Introduction to Cultural Anthropology*, Eighth Edition, includes a rich array of material, including online anthropological video clips, to help you in the study of cultural anthropology and the specific topics covered in this chapter. Other material includes a case study forum with excerpts from various Wadsworth authors, map exercises, scientist interviews, breaking news in anthropology, and links to additional useful online material. Begin by selecting Cultural Anthropology to take you to videos, research, and more. From the homepage, you may also select Applied Anthropology, which directs you to essays, glossary terms, the case study forum, and a list of internships and careers in anthropology.

6 CULTURE AND NATURE: INTERACTING WITH THE ENVIRONMENT

Getting food is perhaps the most important way that people interact with their environments. This Somali woman is hoeing her field. Cultivating the soil is only one way of producing food.

Understanding Relationships with Nature

Foraging
Foraging and Culture
What Happened to Hunters and Gatherers?

Domestication
Beginnings of Domestication
Advantages and Costs of Cultivation

Horticulture
Varieties of Horticulture

Cultural Consequences of Horticulture

Intensive Agriculture
Varieties of Intensive Agriculture
Cultural Consequences of Intensive Agriculture

Pastoralism
Environmental Advantages of Herding
The Karimojong: An Example from East Africa

Nature and Culture

Questions addressed in this chapter

How does the relationship between humans and the environment differ from the relationships of other animals with the environment?

What are the main ways various peoples live on the land?

What are the costs and benefits of agriculture and herding?

What are the most important ways various adaptations affect human cultural existence?

What new forms of society arose soon after the development of intensive agriculture?

In this chapter, we explore some of the ways human groups interact with the natural environment and the cultural consequences of these interactions. Human–environment interactions are an appropriate topic to begin our discussion of cultural diversity because many anthropologists (materialists) believe that how people interact with nature is the primary cause of cultural differences and similarities and the prime mover of cultural change. Future chapters deal with other dimensions of cultural diversity: marriage and family life, kinship systems, relationships between the sexes, socialization, political organization, religion and worldview, and artistic expression.

First we provide some concepts that are useful in studying and comparing human–environment interactions. Then we discuss hunting and gathering (foraging), which nourished humanity for most of our existence. In several parts of the world, how people made their living was dramatically altered between 10,000 and 6,000 years ago, when people first domesticated plants and animals. Agriculture and herding imposed new requirements and opened up new opportunities for human groups, resulting in major changes in cultures, as we shall see.

Understanding Relationships with Nature

In biology and ecology, *adaptation* refers to how organisms develop physiological and behavioral characteristics that allow them to survive and reproduce in their environment. *Adaptation* thus refers to the adjustments organisms make to their surroundings. Like other animals, humans adapt to their natural surroundings. However, to emphasize that human groups—to greater or lesser degrees—alter their environments in the process of living in them, we prefer the term *interaction* to *adaptation*. Of course, in many ways, other animals also alter their environments, as when beavers build dams and earthworms aerate and create soil. But, both prehistorically and historically, humans have altered nature in the process of adapting to it more than other organisms. *Interaction* emphasizes this alteration.

For the human species, the way any given generation relates to the environment is strongly conditioned by the environmental changes that previous generations have caused. That is, human groups adjust to the natural environment that is in part created by the actions of previous generations. This is especially relevant in recent centuries and will be increasingly relevant in the future, with global warming and other impacts of industrial and consumer society. But it has been true for a great many societies, at least since the development of agriculture several thousand years ago.

In studying human–environment interactions, we focus on two important features. First, the environment (or *habitat*) includes *natural resources* that people harness to meet their material needs and wants: food, water, wood and leaves for shelters and fires, stones or metals for tools, and so forth. Second, the environment poses certain *problems* that people must solve or overcome: resource scarcity, excessively low or high temperatures, parasites and diseases, rainfall variability, deficient soils, and so forth. In interacting with nature, people must harness resources efficiently and cope with environmental problems adequately.

Like other species, humans are affected by the environment both physiologically and genetically. For example, bacteria, viruses, and parasites kill or sicken susceptible individuals, but those who are genetically resistant survive, reproduce, and pass more of their genes along to the next generation. By means of natural selection, over many generations human populations become more resistant to the life-threatening microorganisms to which they are exposed—even as the microorganisms evolve better means of attacking us. Natural selection acting on our genes helps us to adjust to the environments in which we live, just as for other organisms.

One way humanity differs from other species, however, is that we adjust and adapt to changes in our environments *mainly*—not exclusively—by cultural rather than biological/genetic means. If the climate grows colder or if a group migrates to a colder area, humans cope mainly by lighting fires, constructing shelters, and making warm clothing, not mainly by evolving physiological adaptations to cold. Humans hunt animals by making weapons and mastering techniques of cooperative stalking and killing, not by biologically evolving the ability to run faster than game. Group cooperation and technology (including both the tools themselves and the knowledge required to make and use them) allow humans to adapt to a wide range of environments without undergoing major alterations in their genetic makeup.

The transmission of socially learned knowledge and behavior enabled humanity to colonize all of Earth's terrestrial habitats, from tropical rain forests to Arctic tundra, from the vast grassy plains of central Asia to tiny Pacific atolls. Our ability to live in diverse habitats by means of technology and group living surely is one of the secrets of the success of the human species—in 2007, 6.6 billion strong and growing.

As Leslie White noted (see Chapter 4) in the 1940s, one of the most important ways people interact with nature is by harnessing energy (e.g., food, fuel) and raw materials (e.g., minerals for tools, wood for shelters). Acquiring energy and materials from the environment is part of *production*—the patterned, organized activities by which people transform natural resources into things (products) that satisfy their material needs and wants. Indeed, those modern anthropologists who follow the materialist orientation think that the process of production is so important that many other aspects of a group's culture are shaped by it.

Production has three components. People apply (1) their own time and energy (*labor, work*) and (2) the tools and knowledge (*technology*) available to them to (3) the *resources* available in their environment. Labor, technology, and resources (which economists call the *factors of production*) are combined in various ways to produce food, shelter, and other material products that people need and desire.

These concepts are easy to grasp, but there are a few complexities. Many complications arise from the fact that humans are social animals (see Chapter 2), who live in groups of various sizes and compositions. Because of group living, we have to organize ourselves to produce what we need and want. For example, individuals have to know what to do and what to expect others to do, and they have to know when and where to work so they do not come into conflict or violate one another's rights. The *organization of production* solves problems such as who will do which productive tasks, when, where, and how. Three main factors are involved in the organization of production.

1. People try to use their labor efficiently. Usually, they work most efficiently by dividing tasks among themselves according to factors like sex, age, and skill. The allocation of work to different kinds of people is called *division of labor*. Ideally, but not always in practice, tasks are allocated according to ability.
2. Groups usually use labor and harness resources most efficiently if their members cooperate. For example, several hunters may have a better chance of spotting, tracking, and killing large game. Net fishing may be more productive if people work together. Because cooperation is usually more efficient than working alone, a group's *patterns of cooperation* are an important part of how it organizes itself for production.
3. Groups often face the problem of conflict over access to resources: Which people have the right to use a particular resource at a particular time and place? As they interact with nature, communities find ways of defining their *rights to resources*. Generally, some group or individual has rights to a given area of land or territory, along with its resources, whereas others are prohibited from doing so or may do so only with permission. Industrialized, market societies solve such problems by defining some people as *owners* of productive property, based in large part on their ability to purchase or lease (or their luck in inheriting) such property. Preindustrial cultures have property rights also, but they often differ from those of industrialized nations. To capture these differences, anthropologists distinguish *ownership rights* from *use rights*, and *group rights* from *individual rights*. A territory and its resources are most frequently "owned" by some kind of group—most often a family unit of some kind or a residential group—that has collective rights to use the resources. The group's leader (e.g., the family head, the village chief) allocates the use of the resources among the members. Group members have rights to use the

▶ Production is usually an organized social activity. As among these African net fishers, cooperation usually increases the efficiency of labor.

© Charles Hughes/Documentary Educational Resources

resources, so long as they do not violate the rights of other group members to use them also. Commonly, the group "owns" and its members "use" resources, according to local norms. Thus, the "property rights" of individuals are always limited by the rights of others.

To summarize: Productive activities are one important way people interact with their environment. Production involves the application of labor and technology to natural resources. Because humanity is a social species, production is an organized social activity, involving the division of labor, patterns of cooperation, and the allocation of rights to resources.

These concepts are useful in comparing some of the ways various peoples interact with their environments by harnessing resources and coping with problems. Anthropologists generally divide preindustrial peoples into three major categories, based largely on how they produce their food:

1. **Hunting and gathering** (also called **foraging**), in which people exploit the *wild* plants and animals of their territory for food
2. **Agriculture** (or **cultivation**), in which people intentionally plant, care for, and harvest *crops* (domesticated plants) for food and other uses
3. **Herding** (or **pastoralism**), in which people tend, breed, and harvest products of *livestock* (domesticated animals) for food, trade, and other uses

It is *very* misleading to view these categories as mutually exclusive. (Note, incidentally, that anthropologists use these three categories for our own purposes; like other cultural categories, they do not faithfully depict the complex realities of human–environment interactions.) For example, before contact with Europeans, many Native Americans cultivated crops like corn and squash, but relied on wild game for most of their meat supply because they had no livestock. Many African people today farm some of their lands, but also raise cattle and other livestock on lands that are less suitable for agriculture. In fact, since agriculture began several thousand years ago, most peoples have relied on a combination of production strategies, depending on their technologies, local environments, and what their neighbors are doing.

In the rest of this chapter, we describe these ways of relating to nature and discuss some of the main ways they affect culture.

Foraging

Foragers, or hunter-gatherers, get their food from collecting (gathering) the wild plants and hunting (or fishing for) the animals that live in their regions. Foragers do not attempt to increase the resources found in their environments by growing crops or intentionally breeding livestock for meat and other products. But many foragers

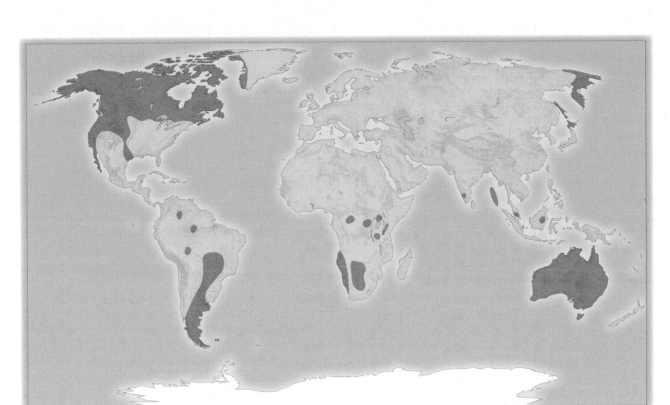

▲ **Figure 6.1** Principal Regions of Foragers at the Time of First Contact with Europeans.

do attempt to control resource availability in other ways. For example, some Native American peoples periodically burned forests and grasslands to attract game or increase the supply of sun-loving wild berries or other plants.

On current evidence, *Homo sapiens* has existed for about 100,000 years (see Chapter 1). But no one on Earth farmed crops or herded livestock until about 10,000 years ago, and most people continued to live off wild plants and animals until a few thousand years ago. The foraging adaptation thus supported humanity for the first 90 percent of our existence as a unique species. After Western exploration and colonialism brought so many indigenous people into larger systems, many hunters and gatherers survived, even into the twentieth century in a few places (see Figure 6.1).

Compared to farmers and herders, hunters and gatherers do not modify their natural environments very much, but instead take what nature offers. If edible wild plants are available only in particular places during particular seasons, foraging groups must move to those places at those times to harvest them. If major game animals live in large migratory herds, hunters must follow them or else hunt other animals when that game has left their region. A brief statement will help understand both the for-

aging adaptation and how it affects culture: To acquire resources efficiently, foragers must organize themselves to be in the right place at the right time with the right numbers of people.

Foraging and Culture

Anthropologists classify hunting and gathering as a single "type" of adaptation, and in the minds of many people, all foragers seem pretty much alike. (This is why you may have heard "When we were all hunters and gatherers on the savannah . . .") But foragers living in different habitats differ dramatically, partly because environments vary in the kinds and quality of food resources they contain. For example, peoples of the resource-rich environment of the American Northwest Coast lived a fairly sedentary existence in large permanent settlements, whereas the Shoshone of the arid and resource-sparse American Great Basin roamed in small bands or individual families. In spite of such differences, most—but not all—foraging peoples share certain cultural similarities. Our main goal in this section is to describe how the adaptive requirements of hunting and gathering affect the cultures of most foraging peoples.

Division of labor by age and sex. Among foraging peoples, the division of labor is largely along the lines of age and sex, although special knowledge and skill also serve as a basis for assigning tasks. In the great majority of foraging peoples, men do the bulk of the hunting and women most of the gathering of plants. However, it is not unusual for either sex to lend a hand with the activities of the other. For example, among the BaMbuti of the tropical forest of Zaire, the women and children help the men with hunting by driving game animals into nets. In general, however, hunting is men's work.

Seasonal mobility. Most foragers move across the landscape to cope with seasonal changes. None of Earth's environments offers the same kinds and quantities of resources year round. In most places, there are seasonal differences in precipitation. Outside the tropics, there usually are marked seasonal variations in temperature as well. Ordinarily, game animals are available in some places and not others at different seasons, and nuts and fruits tend to be available at only certain times of the year.

Foragers migrate to where food or water is most plentiful or easiest to acquire during a given season. For example, the Hadza people of Tanzania lived in an arid region with distinct wet and dry seasons. In the rainy months, the Hadza dispersed around the many temporary water holes that formed, living on the wild plants and animals in the immediate vicinity. At another time of the year, when these ponds evaporated, they lived in large camps clustered around the few relatively permanent water sources.

Seasonal congregation and dispersal. To exploit plants and animals efficiently, most hunters and gatherers adjust the sizes of their living groups to match the seasonal availability and abundance of their food supply. At some times of the year, it is most efficient to disperse into small groups, which cooperate in the search for food. During other seasons, these groups come together in larger congregations.

The Western Shoshone live in the arid Great Basin of what is now Nevada and Utah. Until white settlers disrupted their traditional adaptation in the mid-nineteenth century, the Shoshone lived off wild plants and animals. Most of their meat came from deer, antelope, and small mammals such as rabbits and squirrels. Plant foods included roots and seasonally available seeds, berries, pine nuts, and other wild products.

For most of the year, the Shoshone roamed the dry valleys and slopes of the Great Basin in tiny bands consisting of a few nuclear families, or even single families. Families occasionally gathered for cooperative hunting of antelopes and rabbits, which they drove into corrals and nets. But a more permanent aggregation of families was difficult because a local area did not have enough resources to support large numbers of people for more than a few days.

One important plant food became available in the fall, and in most years it was capable of supporting many families throughout the winter. Around October, the cones of the piñon trees on the high mountains ripened and produced large, nourishing pine nuts. During their travels in late summer, Shoshone families noticed which specific mountain areas had the most promising pine nut harvest. They arranged their movements to arrive at these productive areas in the fall. Ten to twenty families camped in the same region, harvesting and storing pine nuts. During favorable years, the pine nut harvest supported these large camps throughout most of the winter. Spring found the families splitting up again, reliving the pattern of dispersal into tiny groups until the next fall. No family had exclusive access to any particular territory in any season. Rights to resources were essentially based on first come, first served, meaning that whichever group arrived at an area first was free to harvest its plants and animals.

Bands. In most environments, to hunt and gather efficiently, foragers live in small, mobile groups of 50 or fewer, so as not to exhaust the supply of wild foods too quickly. To distinguish these living groups from the settled hamlets, villages, towns, and cities found among other peoples, anthropologists call these mobile living groups *bands*. (Chapter 12 discusses the political aspects of band life.) All or most members of a single band are relatives or are married to relatives. Kinfolk or not, members cooperate in production and usually share rights to harvest the wild resources of a given territory. In most foraging communities, the size of bands is flexible, with the numbers adjusted according to the availability of the food supply. Further, individuals are not attached permanently to any band, but have many options about where to live and whom to live with.

The Ju/'hoansi (also known as the !Kung) of southern Africa illustrate band organization. Living in what is now southeast Angola, northeast Namibia, and northwest Botswana, the Ju/'hoansi are the most thoroughly studied of all hunter-gatherers. The northern part of their environment is an arid tropical savanna, which turns into the Kalahari desert in the south. Until the twentieth century, the Ju/'hoansi exploited this habitat entirely by

▲ Gathering plant foods is mainly women's work among foraging peoples. This Ju/'hoansi woman is bagging mongongo nuts, a nourishing staple.

foraging. They gathered more than 100 species of plants and hunted more than 50 kinds of animals, including mammals, birds, and reptiles. Plant foods consisted of nuts, fruits, berries, melons, roots, and greenery. A particularly important and nourishing food was the mongongo nut, which ripens in around April and provided about half the people's caloric intake.

Because their habitat received so little rainfall and then only seasonally, the availability of water greatly affected the annual rhythm of Ju/'hoansi lives. From about April to October (winter in the Southern Hemisphere), there was little precipitation, and practically no rain fell between June and September. During this dry season, water for people and animals was available only at a few permanent water holes, around which many families congregated into relatively large settlements of 20 to 50 individuals, and often more. When summer rainstorms created temporary water holes between November and March, the people traveled in smaller camps to exploit the more widely distributed wild resources. But rainfall

in this part of southern Africa is not reliable from year to year or place to place. In some years, up to 40 inches of rain falls during the wet months; in other years, as little as 6 inches. Precipitation is also spatially unpredictable: one local area may receive severe thunderstorms, while 20 miles away there is no rain at all.

The overall aridity, seasonality, and variability in precipitation influenced how the Ju/'hoansi organized their bands. During wet months, people spread out among the temporary water holes in camps numbering about 10 to 30. When they moved to a water hole that had not been occupied recently, game was relatively plentiful and a wide variety of plant foods were easily available. But the longer a band remained, the more its members exhausted the resources surrounding the water hole. The men had to roam farther away from their camps while hunting, and the women had to travel longer distances while collecting plants. After several weeks, a camp reached the point at which its members judged that the costs of continuing to forage in the area were not bringing adequate returns in food. They then moved to a new wet-season camp. One ethnographer, Richard Lee (1969, 60), succinctly notes that the Ju/'hoansi "typically occupy a camp for a period of weeks or months and eat their way out of it."

As the months passed and the land dried up, people made their way back to one of the permanent water holes, where several dozen people congregated. By the end of the dry season, the supply of mongongo nuts and other preferred plant foods was exhausted around the permanent water holes and the people ate the less tasty bitter melons, roots, and gum. The Ju/'hoansi considered this a relatively hard time of the year, and they anticipated the November rains, when they could again disperse into the smaller wet-season groups.

Reciprocal sharing. It is mutually beneficial for foraging peoples to share food and other possessions, both within and between families. The sharing is more or less on the basis of need: those who have more than they can immediately use share with others. For example, among the Ju/'hoansi, on any given day only some people actually go out gathering and hunting. But plants and especially animals brought back to camp are widely distributed, so even families who did not work that day usually receive a share. The fact that most or all members of a single band are relatives further encourages the sharing of food.

Reciprocal sharing applies especially to meat. Successful hunters returning to camp share the kill with other families, including those who have not participated in the day's hunt. One reason for the special emphasis on the equitable sharing of meat is the uncertain returns of hunting compared to gathering. Among the Ju/'hoansi, on most days women return to camp with their carrying bags full of nuts, roots, fruits, and other wild plants. Men's chances of capturing game, however, are smaller: Richard Lee estimates that only about two out of five hunting trips capture animals large enough to take back to camp. Men who are successful one day may be unsuccessful the next, so they give today so that they can receive tomorrow.

Sharing is *normatively expected* behavior, so people who regularly fail to share are subjected to ridicule or other kinds of social pressures. Going along with the expectation of sharing is a positive cultural value placed on equality of personal possessions (property) and even of social status. Families who attempt to hoard food or other products may be ostracized. Men who try to place themselves above others socially by boasting about their hunting skills or other accomplishments are soon put in their place. The result is that there is both economic and social equality between the families of most hunting and gathering bands.

Rights to resources. It is beneficial to have familiar, patterned ways of allocating natural resources among individuals, families, and other kinds of groups. Many hunters and gatherers have developed similar ways of determining such rights: who can harvest which resources, where, and when.

One way to organize rights over a territory and its resources is for each group to establish and maintain *exclusive* claims to particular territories. Cultural ideas about the relationship between people and territory might be, for example, that this area is *mine* or *ours*, whereas that area is *yours* or *theirs*. Among foragers, exclusive access would mean that each band has rights to remain in a specific area during a particular season. One benefit of allocating rights in this way is that the members of each band would know they alone can harvest the foods found in particular places at definite times. Another advantage is that bands would not interfere in each other's hunting and gathering activities.

Despite these (apparent) benefits, most foragers organize rights to resources quite differently. Among the Ju/'hoansi, for instance, particular families tended to return to the same territories year after year. Over time, others came to recognize them as the "owners" of the area. Commonly, the reliable water holes together with the wild resources around them were "owned" by a set of siblings whose rights grew stronger as they grew older.

But by merely asking permission—seldom refused—anyone with a kinship relationship to one of the "owners" could come and visit and use the area's food and water. Because most Ju/'hoansi had many relatives and in-laws who were "owners" of various places, each family had many options about where and with whom they would live, work, relax, and socialize. So, who was living and foraging together fluctuated radically because each band received visitors several times a year. Instead of establishing exclusive claims to particular places, Ju/'hoansi families were attached only loosely to territories and for the most part came and went according to their preferences and circumstances. If a quarrel or dispute occurred, one of the parties could simply leave to join another group temporarily. Most other known hunter-gatherers had similar ways of allocating rights to resources.

To sum up, most foraging peoples were similar in the following respects:

- Division of labor based mainly on sex and age
- High mobility
- Congregation and dispersal of groups, especially from season to season
- Life in bands of varying size and flexible composition
- Strong values of reciprocal sharing and of equality in personal possessions and social status
- Loose attachment of people to territory and flexible rights to resources

You can see how these similarities helped foragers harness resources and cope with problems. But, although these characteristics describe most hunter-gatherers reasonably well, we must keep in mind that foragers are diverse. Not all have this set of cultural features.

In fact, in some environments, foragers lived quite differently. Along the Northwest Coast of North America (roughly from Oregon into the Alaskan panhandle), food resources—especially fish—were exceptionally abundant, and the Native Americans who lived there were able to smoke and preserve a supply of fish that lasted for many months. Also, salmon and other fish were more reliably abundant on the Northwest Coast than in most other environments where foragers lived—in most years, people could count on fish swimming up the rivers to breed in the fall, and in the bays and estuaries year round. Because of abundance, reliability, and long-term food storage, there was not much need for seasonal mobility or small living groups. Most Northwest Coast people settled in villages, where many families lived in spacious and often elaborately decorated wood-plank houses. Resource abundance and reliability also affected property notions along the coast. If a food resource is so abundant and reliable that you can usually count on its availability, then it makes sense for you to stay close to it and defend it against other groups that might desire it as well. So, people of the Northwest Coast developed more defined property rights: particular groups were more closely associated with particular locations than were people such as the Shoshone or Ju/'hoansi.

Another place where the culture of foragers was different was the North American Great Plains after about 1600. Technically speaking, Native Americans of the Plains were hunters and gatherers because they did not farm and they kept no domestic animals except dogs and horses. However, their main food resource was unusually abundant, and during the spring and summer it gathered in huge herds that were most effectively hunted cooperatively by dozens of mounted men. This resource, of course, was bison, tens of millions of which once grazed the tall grass prairies of central North America. In most areas of the Plains, grasses grew luxuriantly in the spring and early summer, leading the bison to congregate in herds of thousands. As the summer progressed, the land became drier and the grass patchier, so the bison broke up into smaller herds for the fall and succeeding winter months.

The Cheyenne are a Plains people. In the early and mid-nineteenth century, the Cheyenne lived mainly on bison meat, so they tracked the seasonal movements of their principal food source. From June until late summer, as the bison gathered in huge herds, the people lived as a single tribe in an enormous camp of several thousand. Men on horseback used bows and arrows and, later, rifles to hunt the animals for their meat and hides. As the bison herds split up in the fall, so did the tribe because it was too difficult for the people to remain together as a single enormous camp when their food supply was so widely scattered. By breaking up into smaller bands during the fall and winter, each with its own name and identity, the Cheyenne gained other advantages. Their numerous horses, which were their main source of wealth and pride, had more grass to graze on. Fuel for fires during the freezing winter was easier to acquire; dried animal dung was the primary fuel in this place of few trees.

The Plains peoples were unusual foragers in many ways. One way was the size of their summer settlements, which usually numbered in the hundreds, as compared to the maximum band size of 50 to 100 among peoples such as the Ju/'hoansi and Shoshone. Another was that they had formal political leaders ("chiefs"), as discussed in Chapter 12. So, like the Northwest Coast cultures, the Plains Indians are a useful reminder of the dangers of overgeneralizing about foragers.

The most little-known fact about the Native Americans of the Great Plains is that the way they were living when Anglos encountered them in the 1700s was not their ancient, "time immemorial" way of life. In fact, many or most cultural features of the Plains Indians did not exist until after the introduction of the horse into North America, and this did not happen until the 1600s (see the Globalization box).

What Happened to Hunters and Gatherers?

For tens of thousands of years, hunting and gathering worked well. The human population grew to several million. Further, foraging is a flexible adaptation, meaning that it can be applied to any environment with a sufficient quantity of wild, edible plants and animals. Foraging can and has supported people in rain forests, grasslands, tundras, mountains, and even on Arctic ice during winters. Human ingenuity and rapid communication by social learning allowed hunter-gatherers to migrate into all the continents except Antarctica by around 15,000 years ago. Even then, humanity was a successful species.

In fact, most research suggests that hunter-gatherers enjoyed a relatively high quality of life. Richard Lee's quantitative studies of the Ju/'hoansi in the 1960s show that they worked only about two and a half days per week to acquire their food supply. Even adding in time spent in other kinds of work, such as toolmaking and housework, they worked only about 42 hours per week. Most modern-day adults would be happy to have such a short workweek! Further, the Ju/'hoansi's relatively modest work efforts were sufficient to keep them well fed most of the time: Adults consumed an average of 2,355 calories and 96 grams of protein per day, more than sufficient for their bodily needs. Robert Kelly compared figures on other foragers living in various environments. He found that working hours about like those of the Ju/'hoansi were common in reasonably productive environments, but quantitative studies are few and of uncertain reliability.

Evidence also indicates that foraging peoples enjoyed a diverse diet and were healthy compared to farmers. Hunters and gatherers live from plants and animals that naturally occur in their habitats and that are well adapted to periodic droughts and other hazards. In most places, their diets were diverse compared to those of farmers and herders, who focused their attention and efforts on only a few crops and livestock. Foraging bands were small and moved often, which reduced the incidence and spread of infectious diseases. There are, of course, exceptions, but the bulk of the evidence suggests that hunter-gatherers

To the Anglo-American public, no Indian people typifies Native American life more than the Plains tribes, such as the Blackfoot, Cheyenne, Comanche, Crow, Dakota, and Mandan. Thanks partly to Hollywood, these tepee-dwelling, buffalo-hunting, horse-mounted warriors of the grasslands have come to represent the very essence of "Indianness." When Anglos visualize "traditional" Indian ways of life, they may imagine Red Cloud, Black Kettle, Sitting Bull, or some other Plains leader dressed in beaded buckskin clothing, wearing a feathered "war bonnet," and seated on a horse, most likely in front of a tepee. Few of us know that this way of life was largely a product of the coming of Europeans.

Indeed, it had to be, because the adaptation of the Plains Indians as most Anglos know them rested on the horse, and there were no horses in the Americas between about 11,000 years ago and the 1500s. Along with many other large mammals (mammoths, giant sloths, oversized bison, saber-toothed cats, and others), horses became extinct in the Americas about 11,000 years ago, at the end of the last Ice Age. With no way to hunt the bison effectively, the open grasslands of the Great Plains held relatively little attraction for American Indians. Not only were bison difficult to hunt for people on foot, armed with only a bow and arrow or spear, but transporting meat any distance over the vast grasslands was physically arduous. American Indians had to carry food and other possessions either on their own backs or on the backs of their dogs, for which they developed harnesses. Before the 1600s, the Great Plains were inhabited mainly by widely scattered small bands of nomadic foragers who probably depended more on wild plants than on the vast herds of bison.

Ten thousand years after their extinction, horses were reintroduced into the Americas by the Spanish invaders and colonists in the 1500s. Horses were instrumental in defeating and conquering the two great civilizations of the Americas: the Aztecs of central Mexico and the Incas of western South America. Horses gave the small number of Spanish soldiers big advantages in combat. The mere sight of these huge unknown animals mounted with men wearing armor intimidated the Aztec and Inca foot warriors. Horses reached the Great Plains in sizable numbers only in the late 1600s and early 1700s. It took Native peoples only a few decades to make effective use of their new domesticated animal in hunting and warfare.

Horses revolutionized the cultural existence of some tribes. Not only could a hunter on horseback armed with bow and arrow kill enough bison within a few months to feed his family for a year, but he could also pack the meat on horseback for long-distance transport and trade. Families could transport more possessions; they could have larger tepees and more (and more finely decorated) clothing and other items. Groups that formerly had to be widely scattered could now gather in large encampments, numbering in the thousands, during favorable seasons.

did not have a particularly hard life. Some anthropologists go so far as to call them "affluent," although this does not mean the same as contemporary affluence.

Once plant and animal domestication developed, however, agricultural and herding peoples increased in numbers and expanded their territories. Over several millennia of expansion, cultivators and herders pushed many foraging peoples into regions that were ill suited to crops and livestock. As a result, when European contact with people of other continents intensified after about 1500, hunters and gatherers already lived primarily in regions too cold or arid to support agriculture (see Figure 6.1). Since 1500, even more foragers have lost their lands as they died from diseases and warfare, yielded their territories to outsiders for plantations and mines, relocated onto reservations, and/or gave up foraging voluntarily for the attractions of introduced ways of making a living.

By the beginning of the twentieth century, most foragers had died out altogether or had become assimilated into some other society. Contact was especially hard on Native Americans, who lived on lands highly coveted by Anglo, Spanish, French, and Portuguese settlers and who were susceptible to a host of diseases brought by Europeans and the Africans they enslaved. Most scholars who have looked seriously at the impact of diseases on Native Americans estimate that 80–90 percent of Indians died from epidemics. Europeans did indeed conquer and subdue many Native peoples, but not in the way most people imagine: bacteria and viruses were more important than guns and bullets.

Only a few foragers preserved their way of life into the twentieth century. By the twenty-first century, foraging among these peoples too was endangered. The Ju/'hoansi of southern Africa were surrounded by herders, and many had taken up raising livestock. Governments curtailed their old freedom of movement by fencing off lands. Some left the Kalahari to work for wages in mines or, in the 1960s and 1970s, to serve as trackers for the military in South Africa. Some voluntarily settled down at government-funded stations, where they

Horses also altered the relationship between the groups that had them and those that did not. Residents of the Plains were now capable of rapidly assembling large parties of horse-mounted young warriors who could raid nearby farming villages with near impunity. Within a few decades, small nomadic bands were transformed into aggressive raiders of their farming neighbors. In response, some farming peoples who lived along the fringes of the Plains took up the mounted nomadic way of life themselves. For example, until the 1600s, the Cheyenne lived mainly by farming corn in the region that is now Minnesota, but by the late 1700s, they too had turned into "Plains Indians." Some of the Dakota also abandoned the sedentary life and became seminomadic, horseback-mounted, bison-hunting, tepee-dwelling people.

As other peoples moved onto the Plains, eventually they challenged the original Plains tribes for dominance over critical hunting resources, which intensified competition and intergroup conflict. As a result, warfare and the warrior tradition became an integral part of Plains Indian values and social organization. For many Plains peoples, a major way a young man could make a name for himself was by raiding neighboring tribes and taking a few horses. Another way is what Anglos know as "counting coup": a man would bravely ride into a throng of enemies and tap one or more of them with his lance.

All of this sounds utterly "traditional." Yet the Plains Indian culture (as Anglos imagine it) emerged well after contact with outsiders in a world that was already being transformed by global forces such as conquests and large-scale migrations. Given the diverse cultural origins of the various Plains tribes, they developed a remarkably homogeneous way of life within a short period: elaborately equipped tepees, beaded (with European trade beads) clothing, the Sun Dance, and the emphasis on the male's role as a warrior. It was not until the latter half of the nineteenth century that Euro-Americans seriously challenged the Plains Indians for control of the Great Plains, three centuries after they had first begun acquiring horses. Because the Plains peoples were the last major tribes to resist Euro-American military dominance, it is not surprising that the wider society mistakenly thinks of them as the "essence of Indianness."

Critical Thinking Question

1. The discussion argues that the culture of the Plains Indians was not fully indigenous, but was a result of how the horse interacted with preexisting cultural traditions. How often do you suppose we mistakenly believe customs or beliefs are "indigenous" when in fact they are products of interactions between peoples?

Sources: Ewers (1955), Hoebel (1978), Lowie (1954), Oliver (1962)

began eating large quantities of corn porridge, drinking alcohol, and catching new diseases (including HIV). Recently, governments realized that they could earn money from tourists by turning much of the Ju/'hoansi territory into game parks, and even the people themselves have become tourist attractions. The Hadza are one of the few remaining East African foraging people who still get much of their food from gathering and hunting. They now find that the royal family of the United Arab Emirates wants to pay big dollars to the government of Tanzania to lease part of their land for safaris.

Domestication

Domestication is the intentional planting and cultivation of selected plants and the taming and breeding of certain species of animals. Its main beneficial effect is to increase the supply of the selected species by controlling their location and numbers. Controlling part of nature requires new technologies and, in most circumstances, additional labor inputs compared to foraging. With respect to plants, in this book we are concerned with *food crops,* or those species that people intentionally select, plant, care for, harvest, and propagate for purposes of eating. People also grow plants for other purposes, such as for fibers (cotton, flax, hemp) or for drugs (tobacco, coca leaf, opium poppy). With animals we are concerned with *livestock,* or those species that people raise, control, and breed to provide food (meat, dairy products) or other useful products (hides, wool), or for performing work (pulling plows, carrying people and possessions). People keep animals for other reasons also, such as companionship (pets).

Beginnings of Domestication

Detailed coverage of the origins of plant and animal domestication is outside the scope of this text. (See A Closer Look for information on the world regions where

The domestication of plants and animals occurred independently in the Old World (Europe, Asia, and Africa) and the New World (North and South America and the Caribbean). Before European colonization, the crops grown in the two hemispheres were completely different.

Old World Crops

The earliest plant domestication occurred in the region around what is now Jordan, Israel, Syria, eastern Turkey, and Iraq, known to prehistorians as the Fertile Crescent. Wheat, barley, lentils, peas, carrots, figs, almonds, pistachios, dates, and grapes were first grown here. Oats, cabbages, lettuce, and olives were first domesticated in the Mediterranean. In West Africa, sorghum, finger millet, watermelons, and African rice were domesticated; sorghum and finger millet still feed millions of people on the African continent. Eggplants, cucumbers, bananas, taro, and coconuts originated in southern Asia and Southeast Asia. Soybeans, Oriental rice, millet, citrus fruits, and tea were domesticated in ancient China. Taro (a root crop widely grown in Southeast Asia and the Pacific) and bananas were probably first cultivated in New Guinea or the islands around it. Sugarcane may come from the same area. We get our morning caffeine from coffee, first domesticated in the Ethiopian highlands.

New World Crops

Maize, tomatoes, several varieties of beans, red peppers, avocados, and cacao (now used in the making of chocolate) originated in Central America and Mexico, in either the highlands or the coastal lowlands, or both. Various members of the squash family (squash, pumpkins, and gourds) were first intentionally grown in the same region, although squashes probably also were grown in eastern North America. From Peru came numerous crops that are still important to the region and to the world, including potatoes, sweet potatoes, and lima beans. From lowland South America came manioc (cassava), peanuts, pineapple, and cashews. Chili peppers originated in South America also, but were taken back home by Europeans, where they later gave heat to food in southern China, India, Thailand, and other parts of the Old World. Only as recently as the 1980s did research show that the prehistoric Native Americans of the eastern United States domesticated several crops, including sunflower, gourds and squash, marshelder, and goosefoot. The Native peoples apparently abandoned the last two, grown for their tiny seeds, when maize and beans from Mesoamerica became available, with their larger seeds and better yields. A couple of crops that were important in the diet of the Indians at the time of contact with the Spanish were amaranth and quinoa, but the Spanish outlawed them because of their use in "pagan" ceremonies.

Some plants were domesticated not just once but several times in various parts of the world. Squash may have had independent origins in Mesoamerica, the Andes, and eastern North America. Separate species of rice were domesticated in Africa and Asia, apparently independently. Cotton was domesticated independently in three places: South America, Central America, and either India or Africa. Three yam species were grown in West Africa, Southeast Asia, and tropical South America.

Old World Livestock

In the Old World, the earliest animals were domesticated at about the same times and in the same places as crops were first grown. In the Middle East, the wild ancestors of the most important livestock lived in large herds, including sheep, goats, and cattle. These animals were and are kept for their hides, wool, meat, and milk. Another large mammal, the horse, was first domesticated on the Asian grasslands around 5,000 years ago. When mounted, horses greatly increased the speed of long-distance travel and, of course, increased the mobility of warriors and soldiers. For thousands of years, from Central Asia to North Africa, camels have made it possible for people and products to cross vast stretches of arid land. Along with asses, donkeys, and South Asian yaks, horses and camels enabled people to carry heavy loads long distances, increasing the possibilities and profits of trade. When harnessed to the plow, cattle, horses, and Asian water buffalos supplemented human labor in farming. Their dung added nutrients to agricultural fields and gardens. Finally, pigs—first brought under human control in Southwest Asia and perhaps eastern Asia—are

particular crops and livestock were first domesticated. It also shows how much you owe to peoples who lived thousands of years ago.) In the Old World, crops were grown and livestock kept by around 10,000 years ago in the Middle East and by about 9,000 years ago in eastern Asia. Over the next several thousand years, adaptations based on domesticated plants and animals developed or spread into most African, Asian, and European environments that could support either or both farming and herding. In the New World, a completely different set of an outstanding source of protein and today remain the major source of meat in China and non-Muslim Southeast Asia.

New World Livestock

Compared to ancient Old World peoples, Native Americans domesticated few livestock. In the Andes, llamas and alpacas (related to camels) were used for meat and transportation. Their thick, long hair was also woven into beautiful clothing by weavers of the ancient Andean civilizations. In South America, people still raise guinea pigs for their meat. Elsewhere in the Americas, turkeys and Muscovy ducks were the only animals domesticated for food, and these only in a few areas. Dogs, present also in the Old World, were used in hunting and often as food.

Why did American Indians domesticate so few animals compared to Middle Easterners and Asians? The answer is uncertain, but one important reason may be that so many of the large herd animal species in the Americas became extinct shortly after the end of the Pleistocene epoch, about 11,000 years ago. Members of the horse and camel family, in particular, all disappeared (except in the Andes). Horses did not return to the Americas until the Spanish brought them in the 1500s. Jared Diamond (1997) argues that the large herd mammals such as bison and caribou that remained after the New World extinctions were not amenable to human control. Certainly, it was not the capabilities or the intelligence of the prehistoric Indians that explains why they domesticated so few animals.

What's Cooking?

Soon after Spain, Portugal, France, Britain, and the Netherlands began exploring and establishing colonies on other continents, crops and livestock began to spread from continent to continent. Many New World crops were taken to various parts of the Old World, where they became important foods for millions of people. Manioc (or cassava, as it is commonly known) from Amazonia became a staple in tropical Africa and Asia. Mexican corn spread widely, especially in Africa, Mediterranean Europe, and eastern Asia. After initial resistance, the Andean potato became a staple food in Russia, northern Europe, and—especially—Ireland. Imagine Italian food without the Mexican tomato! Over the centuries, Native American cultivators had become master farmers, and food crops are one of the greatest gifts they bestowed upon the rest of the world.

Crops and livestock moved across the Atlantic Ocean in the other direction also. European colonists took Old World wheat, oats, barley, grapes, and other crops to temperate zones of the Americas. In parts of the Americas with more tropical climates, rice, bananas, and coconuts became important foods. But livestock were the most important food introduced from the Old World. Pigs, cattle, sheep, and horses were introduced very soon after the European encounter with the New World. Over the next couple of centuries, they multiplied rapidly and spread widely. Old World livestock greatly eased the life of the European colonists—pigs and cattle thrived and multiplied in the Americas and became enormously abundant by the time European settlers began spreading over the landscape. Plentiful, familiar cattle, pigs, and sheep helped attract European colonists to the Americas in the 1700s and 1800s. Plows pulled by horses, mules, and oxen turned over heavy soils and broke up the matted roots of grasses, enabling settlers to farm the rich earth of the American Midwest and Plains for the first time and making this region the breadbasket for the rest of the country.

Very few of us recognize our debt to the prehistoric Middle Easterners, Asians, Africans, Andeans, and Mexicans who domesticated the plants and animals we eat daily. Yet most North American meals include foods brought to the continent from all over the world centuries ago. If you're an all-American, steak-and-potatoes kind of person, only the potatoes are truly American—and they (like another of your favorites, beans) came from well south of the border. Today, there is an ecological movement to "eat local" because a lot of energy can be saved from transportation costs if people in New York eat, say, apples from their own state rather than those grown in Washington. Eating local is a fine idea. But it's enlightening to know that the foods that we now grow locally came from all over the globe.

Sources: Fagan (1986), Crosby (1972), Diamond (1997), Dillehay et al. (2007), Pickersgill (2007), Pope et al. (2001)

plant species was domesticated in Mexico by about 7,000 years ago, and in the Andes region of South America by the same time or even earlier.

In the Old World, people domesticated several animal species at about the same time they began to farm.

Livestock probably were an efficient complement to farming. The availability of livestock meant that men eventually gave up hunting, putting their labor into farming, crafts, warfare, metallurgy, ruling, and other activities instead. Later, strong animals like oxen,

▶ The most important benefit of agriculture compared to foraging is that agriculture produces far more food per area of land. This Chinese peasant is working in a field of wet rice, one of the most productive agricultural systems in the world.

© Michael S. Yamashita/Corbis

horse, and mules pulled the plows that helped increase yields. In the New World, however, except for residents of the Andes, most peoples who relied on the cultivation of crops for their food got all or most of their meat from deer, antelope, small mammals, fish, and other wild animals. Most New World peoples, then, got the bulk of their meat from wild, not domesticated, animals, even though many of them were farmers.

Plant and animal domestication probably had more long-lasting and dramatic effects on cultures than any other single set of changes in peoples' relationship with nature—except, perhaps, industrialization. For example, once certain plants evolved by human selection into crops, people produced more food in a given area of land. Increased production allowed them to remain in one place for long periods—over time, groups became more *sedentary*. They could also live in much larger settlements than the bands of most foragers—groups settled in *villages* and, later in some places, in *towns* and *cities*.

Advantages and Costs of Cultivation

If it is true that prehistoric hunters and gatherers lived fairly well, then why did so many humans take up farming? In trying to account for why agriculture developed at all, most archaeologists point to two factors that led prehistoric foragers to gradually begin cultivating crops. The first is climate change: in the Eastern Mediterranean, where agriculture developed earliest—around

10,000 years ago—the climate became warmer at about the same time people began domesticating plants and animals.

The second factor is growing human populations. Although prehistoric hunters and gatherers lived well, once their numbers began to increase substantially, wild plants and animals could no longer support the population size in a region. Agriculture can and nearly always does support far more people per unit of territory. Planting and cultivating crops give a group greater control over the numbers of *edible* plants that exist in their environment, raising the ability of the land to support people. If a field is planted in wheat, or rice or corn, then nearly all the plants growing there produce foods that humans can digest. If the field is left in its natural state, only a fraction of the wild plants are digestible and, hence, edible.

How these two factors interacted, and the importance of other factors, is one of the most controversial issues in modern archaeology, but most believe the single greatest advantage of agriculture over foraging is that agriculture supports far more people. Only in the most favorable environments does the population density of foragers exceed one or two per square mile. In contrast, agricultural peoples typically live at densities of dozens or hundreds per square mile.

Supporting higher population densities does entail some costs, however. Creating and maintaining the artificial community of plants that make up a garden or farm require labor, time, and energy. First, the plot must be prepared for planting by removing at least some of the vegetation that occurs naturally in the area. In some kinds of agriculture, people modify the landscape itself by constructing furrows, dikes, ditches, terraces, or other artificial landforms. Second, the crops must be planted, which requires more labor. Third, natural processes continually encroach on the artificial plant community and landscape that people have created: weeds invade and compete for light and soil nutrients, animal pests are attracted to the densely growing crops, and rainfall and flood may wash away physical improvements. Periodically cultivators must "beat back nature" by removing weeds, protecting against pests, rebuilding earthworks, and so forth. Fourth, the act of farming itself reduces the suitability of a site for future harvests, by reducing soil fertility if nothing else. In future years, the farmers must somehow restore their plots to a usable condition or their yields will fall. All these necessities require labor and other kinds of energy expenditures.

So, farming is a lot of work, and much evidence suggests that most people who make their living by agriculture work at least as long and hard as most foragers. Cultivation also led to other changes—in settlement size and permanence, in ownership of resources, in political organization, and in many other dimensions of life—that culminated in the evolution of whole new forms of culture, as we shall see.

Preindustrial farming systems are conveniently divided into two overall forms, based partly on the energy source used in farming and on how often a garden or field is cultivated. The forms are usually called *horticulture* and *intensive agriculture*. Both have many, many varieties—far too many for us to even mention most of them.

Horticulture

In **horticulture,** people use mainly or exclusively the energy (power) of their own muscles to clear land, turn over the soil, plant, weed, and harvest crops. There are no plows pulled by draft animals (like horses or oxen) to help prepare the soil. Instead, hand tools such as digging sticks, shovels, and hoes are used for most tasks. Farmers may clear new fields by burning the natural vegetation. Some horticultural people fertilize their gardens with animal or human wastes or with other kinds of organic matter. If irrigation is necessary, they usually hand-carry water from nearby rivers or streams. Figure 6.2 shows the most important regions where the horticultural adaptation existed at the time of contact by the West.

Varieties of Horticulture

One type of horticulture is *shifting cultivation* (also called *slash and burn*). Once very widespread, in modern times it is limited to pockets of remote tropical rain forests in Central and South America, Southeast Asia, and central Africa. Shifting cultivators farm the forest in a cycle. Using axes, knives, and other hand tools, they first remove a small area of forest. After the wood and leaves dry out, they burn the refuse to recycle valuable plant nutrients. Generally, a given garden plot is cultivated for only two or three years before its fertility declines and it is gradually abandoned. Then another plot is cleared; a new garden is planted, tended, and harvested until its productivity declines. It too is abandoned, and its natural vegetation regrows until it recovers its ability to produce an adequate harvest, which typically takes 10 or more years.

Shifting cultivation works well so long as population density (the number of people who live in an area of a given size) does not grow too large. For every plot of land under cultivation at any given time, several plots are *fallowed*—they have been left alone for the forest to regrow and the land to recover. If, for every acre of land being cultivated, 10 acres are under fallow, then far fewer people could be supported per acre than if only half the land were fallowed at any one time. This is one reason that, in most regions, shifting cultivation has given way to intensive agriculture (discussed later).

Another example of horticulture is *dry land gardening.* It is defined by the main climatic factor with which cultivators have to cope: low, erratic, and unpredictable rainfall. Like other horticulturalists, dry land gardeners use no plow; simple hand tools—hoes, spades, and so forth—powered by human muscles are the characteristic technology. Dry land gardening occurs in the American Southwest, in arid parts of Mexico, in some of the Middle East, and in much of sub-Saharan Africa. In the more arid regions of Africa, it is sometimes supplemented by cattle keeping because rainfall is too low and unpredictable for people to depend entirely on their crops.

Cultivation in arid lands is risky: even if rainfall and harvests are adequate in most years, there is a chance that in any given year not enough rain will fall. Therefore, people who cultivate in dry regions have developed various gardening techniques to cope with the possibility of drought.

The Western Pueblo peoples—the Hopi and Zuni—of the North American Southwest illustrate one way to cope with aridity. In this region, annual rainfall averages only about 10 inches, concentrated in the spring and late summer. Further, in this high country, the growing season for

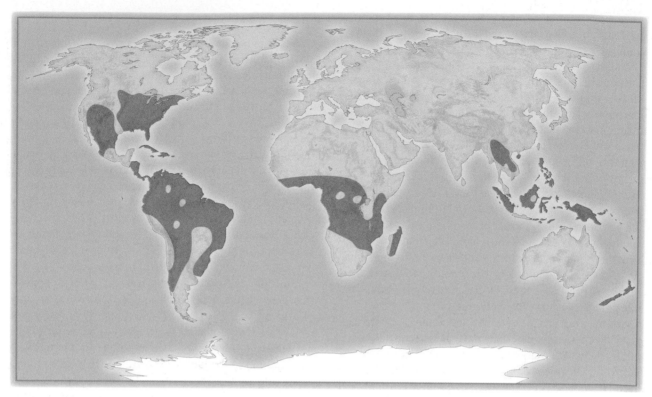

▲ **Figure 6.2** Principal Regions of Horticulture at the Contact Period.

corn—the major food—is only about four months long. The people are faced with extreme uncertainty: if they plant too early, a spring frost may kill their crops; if they wait too long, they will lose some of the critical moisture from the spring rains.

Traditionally, the Western Pueblo handled risk by planting some crops in those areas most likely to flood, where soil moisture usually lasts until harvest time. Yet, in some years, the unpredictable rains are so torrential that runoff washes away the crops. To cope with such natural hazards, the people diversify both the place and the time of their planting. They plant the seeds of corn, squash, beans, and other crops in several locations so that, no matter what the weather, some fields produce a harvest. Gardens in low-lying areas may be lost during an unusually wet year, but upland gardens still yield a crop. Staggering the time of planting likewise lowers the risk of cultivation; by planting crops weeks apart, the risk of losing all of a planting because of an untimely frost is reduced. Thus, by mixing up where and when they plant, the Pueblo peoples reduce the risk of cultivation in an arid, highly seasonal environment.

Cultural Consequences of Horticulture

Both shifting cultivation and dry land gardening methods represent successful efforts to increase the amount of food that can be produced in an area if people harvest only wild resources—productivity is much greater than what would naturally be available to foragers. And even though some people say that horticulture is "rudimentary" agriculture, people still must remove most of the natural vegetation from the land to plant their crops—and they still have to know when and what to plant, so their knowledge is not at all "rudimentary." Finally, horticulture requires that people invest labor in their gardens or fields (by clearing, planting, and weeding) in expectation of a later return (the harvest). Foragers, as you recall, seldom do such things.

Thus, horticulture improves the productivity of land, modifies the natural environment, and requires people to make labor investments in their lands. These facts alone affect the cultural systems of horticulturalists. How do their cultures differ from those of foragers? Subsequent chapters address this question more thoroughly. For now, we note two of the most important ways in which the horticultural adaptation shapes the cultures of people who live by it.

First, the size and permanence of settlements increase. Rather than living in bands or camps of 20 to 50, most horticulturalists aggregate into *villages,* sometimes with hundreds of residents. And rather than moving every few weeks, people become more *sedentary,* remaining in the same location for years, decades, or sometimes even longer. Villages are more permanent, both because effective adaptation does not require people to move frequently and because families who have cleared and planted plots want to stay around at least long enough to recoup their labor investment.

Second, rights to resources differ from those found among most hunter-gatherers. Among horticulturalists, rights to land are better defined, meaning that particular individuals, families, and other groups are more attached to specific places where they or their ancestors have established a claim.

The main reason for more definite claims to resources is as follows. (For now, we assume that the family is the group that cooperates in food production.) When a family invests its labor in clearing, planting, and improving its plots or fields, that investment of labor establishes the family's *claim* to the land. Families that have claims to specific fields pass their rights on to their children, most of whom marry and transmit the rights to their own children. Over several generations, families become the recognized owners of particular plots of land. (Of course, land rights may be disputed, and not every family's rights are regarded as legitimate by everyone else, which leads to "political problems." Thus, societies find it valuable to develop structured ways of resolving conflicts, as discussed in Chapter 12.) In the present generation, then, any given individual or family has ownership rights to a specific parcel, which usually includes the gardens they are actually cultivating. Rights often extend to abandoned plots that they or their ancestors cultivated in the past and to which they or their children may return in future years.

Among horticultural peoples, then, ownership rights over well-defined parcels of land are usually held by families or some other kind of kinship group. In contrast, foragers most commonly have use rights over large territories with only vaguely defined boundaries. Further, horticultural families usually claim ownership over the land itself, because the soil may be made productive by planting crops on it. For foragers, use rights are typically exercised over only the wild resources of a territory.

In sum, two major ways the cultures of horticulturalists differ from those of foragers are: (1) living groups (villages) are larger and more permanently settled, and (2) families have more definite rights of ownership over particular pieces of land. These two factors have other effects on cultures. For example, if people are sedentary, they can store possessions rather than having to carry them around, raising the potential for wealth accumulation. More definite land rights raise the possibility that some families will inherit or otherwise acquire more productive resources than others. These and other effects are considered in later chapters.

Intensive Agriculture

In the farming system known as **intensive agriculture,** farmers keep their fields under cultivation far longer than horticulturalists. Indeed, some intensive agriculturalists have their lands under almost continuous cultivation— the same fields are farmed year after year, with only brief fallow periods. This is what is meant by using land more *intensively:* to produce higher yields, farmers work the land (and usually themselves) harder. (Figure 6.3 shows the major regions where intensive agriculturalists lived at the time of contact with Europeans.)

Intensification is possible only if people are able to maintain the productivity of their land year after year. In various regions, to maintain productivity people fertilize (generally with the dung of livestock), rotate crops, weed carefully, turn over the soil prior to planting, and add compost (organic matter) to the soil. For some of these tasks, a new tool, the plow, and a new source of energy (power), draft animals, are useful. Using plows pulled by horses, oxen, water buffalo, or other draft animals, a farmer can more quickly prepare the soil. In addition to traction for the plow, livestock provide many other useful products: meat, milk and other dairy products, manure, hides, and transportation. After harvest, livestock may be turned loose to graze on the unharvested stalks of crops, fertilizing fields in the process. In some regions, animal muscle powers the mechanical pumps that carry irrigation water to the fields.

For all these reasons, intensive agriculture is substantially more productive per area of land than horticulture. An acre of land produces greater yields and, hence, is capable of supporting far more people—5, 10, and even 20 times the numbers of most horticultural adaptations. Supporting more people is probably the main advantage of intensive agriculture over horticulture.

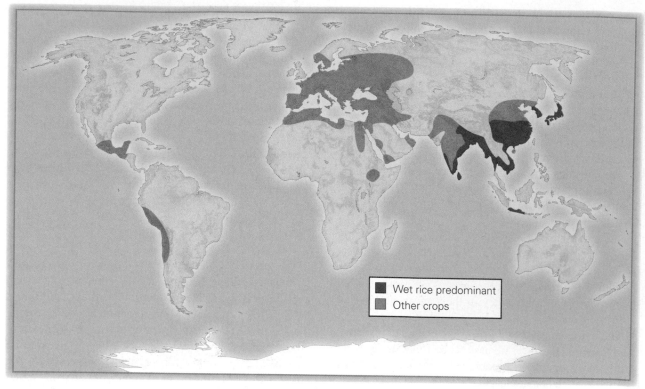

▲ **Figure 6.3** Principal Regions of Intensive Agriculture at the Contact Period.

Varieties of Intensive Agriculture

In the Old World, especially in parts of Asia and Europe, intensive agriculture included plowing the land. But before the coming of Europeans, New World peoples had no domesticated animals suitable for pulling plows. Indeed, except in the Andes of South America, the only animals domesticated by Native Americans were dogs, turkeys, and Muscovy ducks. Andean people also had llamas and alpacas, but these were not harnessed to plows.

Despite this limitation, Native American peoples in places such as the valley of Mexico (land of the Aztecs) and the Andes found ways of increasing yields by intensifying their production efforts. In the valley of Mexico, for example, people transformed swamps and the margins of lakes into productive fields called *chinampas* by constructing raised fields in which they planted crops like tomatoes, squash, and corn. By continually adding new organic materials from the lake bottoms, they kept gardens under almost continuous cultivation. In the Andes, stepped terraces were constructed to reduce erosion, and an incredible variety of potatoes and other crops were grown during the summer. Andean peoples

also developed a variety of methods for coping with frost in their mountain homelands.

Another method of increasing yields is to augment the water supply by artificial means. Farmers around the world use many ingenious irrigation methods. Some dam streams to conserve runoff and dig ditches to transport water to the fields. In many Asian river valleys, channels transport water and fertile silt to fields during the annual monsoons, when rivers overrun their banks. In many mountainous regions of Southeast Asia and China, the level of water in hillside rice fields is controlled with an elaborate system of terraces. Rice is produced through a highly coordinated system to supply water in these *wet rice* regions.

In sum, compared with horticulture, intensive agriculture produces more food per unit of land. Its high productivity is due to factors such as using shortened fallow periods, preparing the land more thoroughly prior to planting, removing weeds, adding manure and other organic matter to preserve fertility, and manipulating the supply of water. These (and other) inputs give people greater control over conditions in their fields, leading to higher yields per unit of land.

◄ Wet rice is a very productive form of intensive agriculture that has supported large populations in Asia for many generations. If necessary, humans can construct artificial terraces even on steep slopes, as these Indonesian terraces illustrate.

Cultural Consequences of Intensive Agriculture

The development of intensive farming eventually had dramatic cultural consequences in many regions, mostly resulting from its relatively high productivity. A single farm family using intensive methods can usually feed many more people than just its own members. Far more than either foragers or horticulturalists, intensive farmers can produce a **surplus** over and above their own subsistence (food) requirements. This surplus can be used to feed other people, families, and groups, who no longer need to produce their own food.

What happens to this surplus? Many things, depending on circumstances. Farmers trade excess food for other useful products like pottery, tools, wood, and clothing. If the community uses money (see Chapter 7), families may produce surplus food for sale and use the money to buy other goods. If the village or other settlement has a strong political leader, such as a chief, he can collect the surplus from his subjects and use the food to pay laborers who work on public projects such as trails, temples, and irrigation works. If the community is part of a larger, more encompassing political system, with a ruler and a governmental bureaucracy, then the government may collect part of the surplus as a tax. Political officials then use the tax for public purposes (e.g., support of armies, the judiciary, and the religious hierarchy) and/or to further its own political interests.

All these possibilities illustrate a central fact about most peoples who depend on intensive agriculture: Most are not politically independent and economically self-sufficient communities but are instead incorporated into some kind of large organization. Their villages or towns are part of a more inclusive political system that dominates or rules them in some way. Their surplus is traded, sold, or taxed (or all three) and supports people who do not themselves do farm work—people such as rulers, aristocrats, bureaucrats, priests, warriors, merchants, and craft specialists.

Intensive agriculture, then, is strongly associated with large-scale political and economic organization: Local-level farmers in villages produce food and other products for people who live elsewhere, and they, in turn, receive things (products, services) from the larger system. The association of intensive agriculture with large-scale political organization is ancient, going back more than 5,000 years in parts of the Old World and more than 2,000 years in two regions of the New World.

In a few parts of the world, within a few centuries or a millennium after the development of intensive agriculture, the socially and politically complex society we call **civilization** (including, among other things, the first cities) emerged. Civilizations have a form of government known as the *state* (discussed further in Chapter 12), contrasting markedly with the egalitarian groups of foragers. *States* are large-scale political units that feature a ruler, a governing bureaucracy, class distinctions

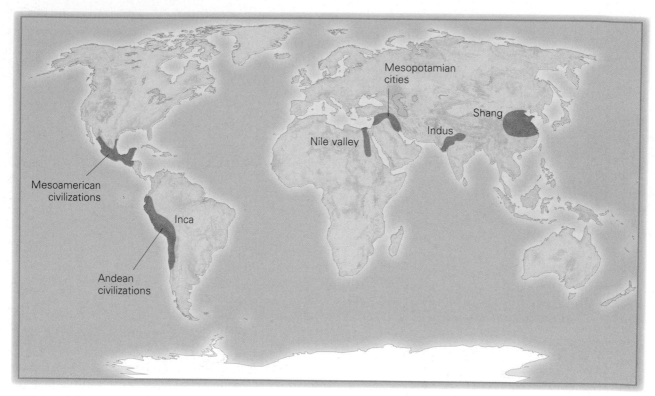

▲ **Figure 6.4** Ancient Civilizations.

between the elite and common people, and methods of extracting labor and surplus products from those who are responsible for farming the land.

In ancient times, intensive farmers were incorporated into the four major civilizations of the ancient Old World: the valley formed by the Tigris and Euphrates rivers of Mesopotamia, the Nile valley of Egypt, the Indus River valley of Pakistan, and the vast empire of China. In the New World, too, agricultural peoples were part of large-scale political units, such as the Mayans, Toltecs, and Aztecs of Mesoamerica, and the Incas of the Andean coast and highlands (see Figure 6.4).

All these early civilizations were supported by intensive agriculture based on large-scale irrigation and water control facilities. Intensive farmers produced the food supply and paid tribute or taxes to support the rulers, priests, armies, and officials who staffed the government, protected the city, organized the worship of gods, and performed other roles that had now become necessary. So far as we know, intensive agriculture is virtually a prerequisite for civilization because no civilization ever developed out of a foraging or horticultural adaptation. (The Mayan civilization was once thought to have been

an exception, but recent evidence shows that the Mayans, too, used intensive farming methods.)

By 1,000 years ago, other states developed in Old World places like Korea and Japan (both influenced by China), southern India, much of Southeast Asia, parts of Africa, and most of Europe. In subsequent centuries, the entire world would be dramatically affected by states, which tend to expand to incorporate more people and resources.

In the world we live in today, virtually every human community is politically and economically incorporated into larger organizations—namely, into nations and the global economic system. Rather than producing largely for their own subsistence, most modern farmers produce for sale on local or international markets. Methods of farming the land have changed dramatically in recent decades. In most industrial nations of Europe, the Americas, and East Asia, farming with animal-powered plows has been replaced by mechanized agriculture, with its tractors, combines, and other machinery powered by gasoline and other kinds of energy derived from fossil fuels. Economically, most small, family-owned farms in Canada and the United States must invest heavily in

▲ Even today, in many Asian nations, millions of peasants live in rural regions. These Vietnamese peasants in the Mekong Delta are using the road to dry their rice.

machinery and other technologies to keep their farms productive because their livelihood and standard of living are based on their yields and the prices they receive for their crops, livestock, and other products.

Intensive farming methods do survive even in the twenty-first century, especially in the developing regions of southern Asia and Southeast Asia, Latin America, and Africa. Economically, farming communities often fit into their nations as **peasants**, a term that anthropologists use for rural people who live by a combination of subsistence agriculture and market sale. Peasants are integrated into a larger society both politically (i.e., they are subject to laws and governments imposed by their nations) and economically (i.e., they exchange products of their own labor for products produced elsewhere). In many developing countries, peasants are a numerical majority of the population and produce much of the food consumed by town and city dwellers. Peasants produce goods that are sold for money, traded or bartered, paid to a landlord as rent, and rendered to a central government as taxes.

So far as we know, there were no peasants until the emergence of the ancient civilizations just mentioned. The farm work of prehistoric peasants fed the craft workers, the merchants, the state-sponsored priests, the political elite, the warriors, and the builders of palaces and temples. The tribute or tax (paid in food, crafts, labor, or all three) rendered by peasants was extracted from them by armed force or threat of force. The peasantry of medieval Europe, for example, eked out a meager living, paying a substantial portion of their annual harvest to their lords or working many days a year on their lord's estate.

Given this information, we might well wonder whether the development of intensive agriculture benefited the peasants who actually farmed the land. True, the high productivity of intensive agriculture allowed the specialized division of labor that led to writing, metallurgy, monumental architecture, cities, and the great religious and artistic traditions we associate with civilization. But how about the peasants who produced the food that made such "progress" possible? For them, writing meant that more accurate accounts could be kept of their taxes or the number of days they worked for overlords. Iron and other metals meant that peasants had better farming tools; yet for the most part they were not allowed to use them to ease their own work but instead only to produce more surplus for others to appropriate. Metal also meant that weapons became more deadly and armies more dangerous, allowing one state to make war against other states more effectively. Most peasant families continued to live in hovels, even while engineers designed great palaces, religious structures, and walled cities and towns that were built using peasant tax-labor. Throughout history, most peasants the world over were denied the benefits offered by technological progress, although the food they produced made much of this progress possible.

Pastoralism

Most farmers also keep domesticated animals. Southeast Asian and Pacific horticulturalists raise many pigs and chickens. Intensive agriculturalists raise livestock, such as horses, oxen, water buffalo, and cattle, that pull their plows, fertilize their fields, and provide dairy products and meat. Livestock do not merely "supplement" the adaptation of farming peoples: because of the meat, eggs, milk, hides, wool, transportation, fertilizer, and horsepower they provide, they are usually critical to the nutritional and economic welfare of cultivators. The income earned by selling livestock or their products is often the main source of cash for many farmers in the developing countries.

However, cultivators do not depend on their domesticated animals to the same extent or in the same way as do peoples known as *pastoralists,* or herders. Herders acquire much of their food by raising, caring for, and subsisting on the products of domesticated animals. With few exceptions, the livestock are gregarious (herd) animals. Cattle, camels, sheep, goats, reindeer, horses, llamas, alpacas, and yaks are the common animals kept by herders in various parts of the world.

Agriculture and pastoralism are not mutually exclusive ways of living on the land because many pastoral peoples also farm. In saying a people are "pastoralists," we do not mean merely that they keep livestock. More important, the needs of their animals for naturally occurring food and water greatly influence the seasonal rhythms of their lives.

The key phrase is "naturally occurring." Most farmers raise crops that they feed to their livestock and/or maintain fields in which their animals graze. In general,

pastoralists do neither of these. Their herds graze on natural forage and therefore must be moved to where the forage naturally occurs. Some or all of the people must take their livestock to wherever the grasses or other forage is available in a given season. This high degree of mobility, known as **nomadism,** characterizes the pastoral adaptation. Most commonly, pastoralists are seasonally nomadic—they do *not* wander aimlessly. Their migrations are often "vertical," meaning that nomads take their animals to highland areas to graze during the hottest season of the year.

Environmental Advantages of Herding

For the most part, herders live in only certain kinds of environments. (Figure 6.5 shows where pastoralists lived prior to European expansion.) The pastoral adaptation occurs mainly in deserts, grasslands, savannas, mountains, and the Arctic tundra. Obviously, these environments are diverse, but they do share a common feature: Cultivation is impossible, extremely difficult, or highly risky because of inadequate rainfall or wide yearly fluctuations in rainfall (as in deserts or savannas) or very short growing seasons (as in mountains and tundras). As always, there are exceptions to our generalizations, but most herders live in regions that are not well suited to cultivation.

In such arid or cold environments, herding offers several advantages over farming. First, most of the vegetation of grasslands and arid savannas (grasses and shrubs) and of tundras (lichens, willows, and sedges) is indigestible by humans. Livestock such as cattle, sheep, and reindeer are able to eat this vegetation and transform it into milk, blood, fat, and muscle, all of which are drunk or eaten by various pastoral peoples. Thus, in some areas, livestock allow people to exploit indirectly certain wild plant resources that are not directly available to them. Livestock convert inedibles into edibles.

Herding also levels out fluctuations in the food supply. In areas with low and unreliable rainfall, crops often fail because of drought. Livestock provide an insurance against periodic and unpredictable droughts and accompanying crop failures. In high-altitude mountains, frosts threaten crops. Not only do livestock store food "on the hoof," but they can also be traded or sold to neighboring peoples for cultivated foods. Livestock reduce risks.

Finally, a big advantage of livestock is their mobility. Herders can move their animals to areas with the freshest or lushest pasture or to sources of water. People can move their herds away from neighbors who have grown too aggressive or away from easy contact with national governments that often want the nomads to settle down

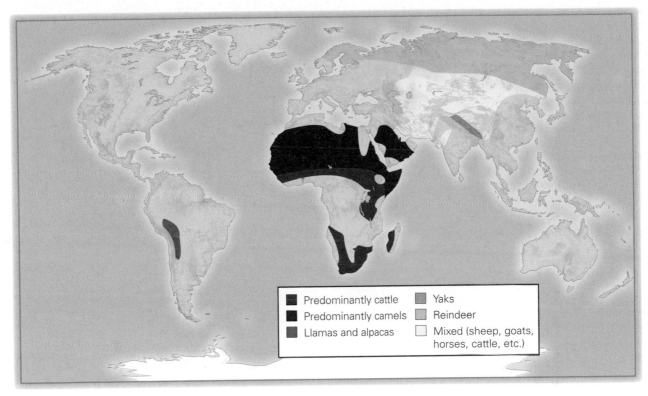

▲ **Figure 6.5** Principal Regions of Pastoralism at the Contact Period.

so they can be taxed, formally educated, or better controlled. Livestock make it relatively easy to move either voluntarily or when necessary.

With advantages like these, you may well wonder why pastoralism was and is not more widespread. Why didn't the herding adaptation spread to areas where cultivators lived? Part of the reason is that environmental conditions are not conducive in many regions. For example, until recently pastoralism seldom developed in tropical forests, largely because of lack of suitable forage. (Today, enormous tracts of tropical forest in Central and South America are cleared and replanted in grasses suitable for cattle grazing.) Livestock diseases also limit the distribution of pastoralists. For example, much of eastern and southern Africa is occupied by cattle herders (most of whom also farm, however). Herders would presumably be even more widespread on the continent were it not for the limitations imposed by the presence of the tsetse fly, which transmits the debilitating disease sleeping sickness to cattle.

Another factor limiting the distribution of pastoralism is that herding is not the most productive way of using resources in those areas in which agriculture can be carried out reliably. The best way to understand why is to apply the ecologists' "10 percent rule." The food energy produced by green plants lies at the base of all terrestrial ecosystems. In the presence of sufficient water, carbon dioxide, and minerals, plants convert the energy of sunlight into simple sugars. Herbivores (plant-eating animals) consume the vegetation and use it to maintain their own bodies and produce offspring. Carnivores (animal-eating animals), in turn, feed on herbivores. At each of these levels of the food chain, most of the energy is lost as it is carried to the next level. Thus, herbivores transform only about 10 percent of the plant energy they consume into their own flesh; and only around 10 percent of the energy carnivores acquire by eating herbivores is available to make more carnivore flesh. At each level, 90 percent of the energy consumed is lost to respiration, waste production, and other processes. The 10 percent rule says that only about 10 percent of the energy locked up in living matter at one level is available to the next level.

Now we can see why herding is not as efficient as farming if the environment supports crops reliably: overall, pastoralists eat higher on the food chain. People can obtain more total food energy from an environment by farming because they can gain much more energy from (cultivated) plants than from (herded) animals. This does

► Most pastoralists live in regions that are too cold or too arid for agriculture. The Nenet, reindeer herders in the western Siberian tundra, live partly from eating reindeer meat and trading the products of their herds. They also use the animals as beasts of burden for long-distance travel.

not imply that people first figured out that they could most productively use the land by growing crops rather than raising animals, and then opted for cultivation. More likely, farming won out over herding—in areas that are suitable for both—because of its greater labor productivity. Further, the 10 percent rule translates into higher potential (and actual) population densities for cultivators, who in some regions outcompeted pastoralists for those territories that both could exploit.

It is informative to compare how most pastoral nomads use livestock with how livestock are raised and fattened in North America, Japan, and most of Europe. Pastoralists teach us that livestock are most efficiently used as converters of inedibles to edibles. If you take something that people can eat and feed it to livestock, you lose most of the energy, vitamins, and protein to the bodily functions of the animal. In North America, most soybeans and corn are grown as fodder for livestock such as pigs, cattle, and fowl (although the ethanol industry is changing that for corn). When you eat a pound of flesh, you are eating several pounds of corn and soy. You also are consuming the energy used to process the "food" into the "fodder." And, of course, you are supporting the industries that produce the fertilizers, herbicides, and insecticides used to produce the crops that make our livestock so juicy and tender—that is, so fatty. So enjoy your dinner—some ear of corn gave its life for it!

Forces such as "efficiency" do not tell us everything about where pastoral people live. Some herders could cultivate their lands, and they do know how to farm, but they consciously choose not to grow crops. The cattle-herding Maasai of Kenya and Tanzania are an example. In some parts of the Maasai territory, cultivation is possible, and, in fact, most neighboring tribes combine cattle herding with cultivation of sorghum and other crops. The proud Maasai, however, look down on cultivation because their herds represent wealth and are the main symbol of their cultural identity relative to their neighbors. Maasai, therefore, live largely off the products of their cattle—blood, milk, curds—and trade with their neighbors for the cultivated foods they do eat. The reasons they continue their pastoral adaptation are, therefore, as much "cultural" as "ecological."

The Karimojong: An Example from East Africa

The Karimojong of Uganda illustrate many features of nomadic pastoralism. Living on an arid savanna with marked seasonal differences in rainfall, well into the twentieth century they subsisted by a combination of horticulture and cattle herding. The Karimojong numbered about 60,000 when Rada and Neville Dyson-Hudson studied them in the 1960s.

Questions addressed in this chapter

What are the three main forms of exchange?

How does the form of reciprocity between people vary with social distance?

What is the relationship between redistribution and political life?

What are the benefits and costs of market economies?

How do peasant marketplaces differ from market economies?

In the mid-1970s, when one of your authors (J. P.) conducted fieldwork on a Micronesian island called Kosrae, a man in his 60s told me he had heard that many people in "Merike" (America) had no land. "Is this true?" he wanted to know. I assured him it was. "But if they have no land, where does their food come from?" "We buy it in stores," I answered. Being familiar with stores, jobs, wages, and money, he nodded. "But where do people live?" He also understood my explanation of rent and the buying and selling of land. "How much does a house cost?" I estimated that he could buy a small house in California (where I then lived) for around $40,000 but that few people had that amount of money on hand and would have to borrow most of it. "Does everyone have to do this in Merike?" "Almost everyone," I replied. He was astonished. "On Kosrae," he said, "everyone gets land from his father [and/or mother, he should have added] and we build our own houses."

The Micronesian was surprised not only because $40,000 was far more money than he would make in his life, but also because almost all Americans have to buy or rent land to live on. The people of Kosrae did sometimes sell land to one another, but those who sold the land they inherited were regarded as unfortunate or shortsighted. In his experience, land was not simply a "commodity" to be bought and sold routinely, like clothing or detergent. A family's land helped define their identity; sometimes people referred to a family by the name of the shared estate it had inherited from its ancestors. Although unmarked, the boundaries that separated one person's land from another's were widely known or, in cases of dispute, debated. How could so many Americans not have any land at all, and how could they pay so much for it?

By mid-2007, the median price of an American house was $220,000. In the San Francisco Bay Area, in 2006 the median price of a small lot with a house built on it was $550,000, up almost 14 percent from the previous year and 14 times more than in the mid-1970s, when I talked to the man from Kosrae. In Merike, "homes" are the main "asset" of most families and "homeownership" is part of the "American Dream." If you rent when you can afford to buy, you are just "giving money to your landlord," rather than building up "equity" and reaping the benefits of the "tax break" from the "interest" you pay over the "amortized life of the loan."

The American Dream is to own the land that the Kosraen man took as his normal birthright. Many American families reasonably conclude that soon they will be priced out of their Dream. By the summer of 2007, so many people had bought houses they could not afford (for many of them, "a house they could not afford" was any house at all) that a financial crisis threatened to cause a recession—a slowdown of the buying and selling that most people believe is essential for their quality of life. Where did all these risky borrowers get the loans? From lenders who did not worry about whether new homeowners could pay them back because most of them sold the loans to another financial institution.

How, indeed, did land come to cost so much, and why is a place to live something you must buy from someone else? The answer, of course, is that Americans live in an economy in which land *is* a commodity, whose price is theoretically determined by supply and demand. Californians (and Texans and Albertans and Londoners and Japanese) may complain about the "ridiculous" price of land and housing, but it seems no one can do too much about it. Supply and demand are "impersonal," and land prices are set by something called the "market." In a market economy, human wants and productive and consumptive activities create prices, yet (paradoxically) they are not controlled by anyone.

7 EXCHANGE IN ECONOMIC SYSTEMS

Economic Systems

Reciprocity

Generalized Reciprocity

Balanced Reciprocity

Negative Reciprocity

Reciprocity and Social Distance

Redistribution

Market Exchange

Money

On Market Economies

Peasant Marketplaces

In the twenty-first century, global markets are integrating nations and regions into a single exchange system. This is the Ginza shopping district of Tokyo, where you can buy nearly anything, especially if it's expensive.

© Jim Peoples

Reciprocity	**Redistribution**	**Market**
Back-and-forth exchange of products, gifts, and objects; symbolizing relationships as well as satisfying material needs and wants	Collection of products and valuables by a central authority, followed by distribution according to some normative or legal principle	Free exchange of products (P_1, P_2) and services (S_1, S_2) for money ($) at prices determined by impersonal forces of supply and demand

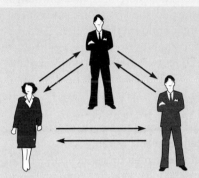

Economic Systems

The term *economics* has a multitude of meanings. Here we use it in its everyday meaning: Economics is how people make their living. There are three parts to making a living. First, someone has to work and use technology to transform nature's resources into useful *products*. Second, someone *consumes* the products by eating, living in, driving, wearing, or sometimes merely displaying them. Third, between the time they are produced and consumed, many products change hands, or are *exchanged*. In economies like those of foragers or horticulturalists, often the producers and the consumers are the same people (usually, family members), but nonetheless exchange exists in these and all economies. In modern market economies, the producers and the consumers are nearly always different people (or groups), so practically every product is exchanged. And most people in developed market economies do not "produce" anything tangible, but make their living from jobs that provide services or communicate information that others are willing to pay for.

In fact, in modern market economies, most products are produced entirely for exchange (sale on the market), and once the value acquired from the market exchange (money) has been gained, the producer has little further interest in the product. But markets are only one way of organizing exchange. In subsistence-based economies, families or other kinds of kinship groups produce mainly for their own needs, not for sale on the market. And rather than exchanges based on supply, demand, and prices, exchanges are organized around other principles. This chapter considers some ways in which these exchanges are structured and how they differ from the buying and selling of market-based exchange.

Anthropologists usually classify various forms of exchange into three major modes or types:

1. **Reciprocity,** in which individuals or groups pass products back and forth, with the aim of helping someone in need by sharing with him or her; creating, maintaining, or strengthening social relationships; or obtaining products made by others for oneself
2. **Redistribution,** in which the members of an organized group contribute products or money to a common pool or fund that is divided (reallocated) among the group as a whole by a central authority
3. **Market,** in which products are sold for money, which in turn is used to purchase other products, with the ultimate goal of acquiring more money or accumulating more products or both

The Concept Review illustrates the three forms of exchanges.

Most products (including land and labor) are exchanged through the market mode in modern industrial economies, but reciprocity and redistribution also exist. Examples of reciprocity are various gifts we give and receive on holidays, birthdays, weddings, baby showers, and other culturally special occasions. If you are employed, every pay period you participate in redistribution because federal, state, and local governments collect a portion of your wage or salary as taxes, which they spend on public purposes, like wars or roads, or transfer to other members of society, like the elderly and the poor.

All these exchange forms thus exist in modern societies, but not all preindustrial peoples have all three. Reciprocity in one form or another occurs in all human populations. But redistribution requires a central leader(s) whose role(s) carries authority to organize the collection of resources from the group and to make decisions about how they will be reallocated. Redistribution, therefore, is an insignificant exchange mode in societies that lack strong leaders who make decisions on behalf of the group. The market mode of exchange requires money, private property, and certain other features that are absent in nonmarket economies.

Reciprocity

In subsistence economies such as those based on foraging, horticulture, and pastoralism, families and households are commonly capable of producing most of the food and other products they consume. That is, most families are *potentially* self-sufficient in the sense that they own or have access to the land, labor, tools, and other resources necessary for survival.

However, in no known society are families, households, or other kinds of social groups self-sufficient *in fact.* Everywhere, such groups exchange products with other groups. Most anthropologists say that this is because families and other groups need or want to maintain relationships with other families and groups, and exchange is necessary to create and sustain these relationships. Examples of why groups need such relationships include ensuring long-term economic security, acquiring spouses, maintaining political ties, and strengthening military alliances.

The form of exchange used for such purposes is *reciprocity,* defined as the mutual transaction of objects without the use of money or other media of exchange. Reciprocity takes several forms: sharing with those in need, providing hospitality, giving gifts, engaging in mutual feasting, and bartering. Obviously, each form is motivated by different considerations and values, so we distinguish three forms of reciprocity: generalized, balanced, and negative.

Generalized Reciprocity

The defining feature of **generalized reciprocity** is that those who give goods do not expect the recipient to make a return at any definite time in the future. Generalized reciprocity occurs between individuals who are (or at least are normatively expected to be) emotionally attached to one another and, therefore, have an obligation to help one another on the basis of relative need. Parents who provide their children with shelter, food, vehicles, and college educations are practicing generalized reciprocity. Giving without expectation of definite return also should occur between parties to certain other kinds of social relationships, such as wives and husbands, siblings, and sometimes close friends.

Because it includes various forms of sharing with relatives and other people who are defined as close by cultural norms, generalized reciprocity is found in all societies. Among some peoples it is the dominant form of exchange, however, meaning that more resources are distributed using this form than any other form.

For example, most hunter-gatherers expect their band mates to share food and be generous with their possessions, partly because most members of a band are relatives of some kind (see Chapter 6). Among the Ju/'hoansi, the band is a social group within which food sharing is culturally expected or even mandatory. Those who are stingy with possessions or who fail to share food with others are ridiculed or socially punished in some other way. Generalized reciprocity ensures an equitable—if not entirely equal—distribution of food among the band's families. It also maintains social and economic equality between the families that make up the band. In fact, the Ju/'hoansi have a custom they call "insulting the meat" that seems designed to keep even the best hunters from becoming too proud and boastful (see A Closer Look).

Balanced Reciprocity

In **balanced reciprocity,** products are transferred to someone (the recipient) and the donor expects a return in products of roughly equal value. Over the long run, the value of the products exchanged should be close to equivalent. The return may be expected soon, or whenever the donor demands it, or by some specified time in the future. With generalized reciprocity, the giver continues to provide assistance even when the receiver is unable to return anything for a long time. With balanced reciprocity, the giver tries to apply some kind of sanction against the receiver if the latter does not reciprocate

◀ Each member of this Inuit ("Eskimo") whaling crew will receive a share of the whale meat and blubber. Sharing the fruits of cooperative efforts is one form of generalized reciprocity.

within the appropriate time period. Donors may become angry if there is no reciprocation, may complain or gossip to others, may try to force a return, or may suspend all relations until things of appropriate value are returned.

Although the value of the objects exchanged is supposed to be about equal, balanced reciprocity is characterized by the absence of bargaining between the parties. In some preindustrial economies, the exchange of objects without having to negotiate for each transaction (How much of A will you give me for my B?) frequently is organized by a special relationship between two individuals known as a *trade partnership*. Individuals of one tribe or village pair off with specific individuals (their "partners") from other regions with whom they establish long-lasting trade relationships.

For instance, in the Trobriand Islands off the eastern tip of the island of New Guinea, there was a form of balanced reciprocity called *wasi*. Residents of coastal villages traded fish for yams and other garden crops produced in the mountainous interior. The exchange was formalized: A coastal village paired off with an interior village, and within each village individuals formed trade partnerships. The rates at which garden produce was exchanged for fish were established by custom, so there was no haggling at any particular transaction.

In *wasi,* each trade partner received foods not readily available locally, so parties to the transaction gained a material benefit. In other cases, trade partnerships have social as well as material benefits. For example, the Ju/'hoansi have a gift exchange custom called *hxaro*. In *hxaro,* the gift exchange is delayed (those who receive a product are not expected to return anything for an indefinite but often long period of time) and nonequivalent (even when a return is made, the value of the object need not be equal to the one received). *Hxaro* partners rely on one another for mutual support in other contexts, such as when one partner asks to forage in the territory of another. The social relationship created and reinforced by *hxaro* matters more to people than the objects given and received.

In *hxaro,* gifts make friends and vice versa, so gifts have *symbolic value*. More generally, when two people exchange gifts, ideally both gain something more than the sum total of the economic worth of the objects. On your friend's birthday, instead of giving her a CD in exchange for a gift of about equal value on your own birthday, you both could save the cost of wrapping paper and cards by buying the objects yourselves. But then neither of you would enjoy the symbolic value that is added when the exchange of "things" becomes an exchange of "gifts" on culturally appropriate occasions. As material symbols of good relations, gifts both create and sustain feelings of solidarity and relations of mutual aid between individuals and groups. This is why, cross-culturally, gift-giving ceremonies are frequently part of peacemaking between formerly hostile groups; the gifts symbolize in a tangible form the beginning of a new period of peaceful coexistence.

Many gathering and hunting peoples have cultural mechanisms that cut proud and boastful people down to size, reminding them that they are no better than anyone else. A fascinating example of such a mechanism is found among the Ju/'hoansi, the foragers of southern Africa described in Chapter 6. The Ju/'hoansi call their custom "insulting the meat," referring to the practice of ridiculing successful hunters' contributions. Their goal is to keep skilled hunters modest because modesty is an important value in their culture. In the following extract, Richard Lee describes this custom in his ethnography, *The Dobe Ju/'hoansi*.

> When a hunter returns from a successful hunt, or when meat is brought into a camp, one would think that this would be met with open glee and the hunter praised for his skill. Quite the contrary: The people often display indifference or negativity at the news of a successful kill, and I was surprised to see the lowkey way in which the hunters would break the news of their success. /Xashe, an excellent hunter for /Xai/xai, put it this way:
>
> When you come home empty-handed, you sleep and you say to yourself, "Oh, what have I done? What's the matter that I haven't killed?" Then the next morning you get up and without a word you go out and hunt again. This time you do kill something, and you come home. My tsu ("older kinsman") sees me and asks: "Well, what did you see today?" "Tsutsu," I reply, "I didn't see anything."
>
> I am sitting there with my head in my hands but my tsu comes back to me because he is a ju/'hoan. "What do you mean you haven't killed anything? Can't you see that I'm dying of hunger?" "Well, there might be something out there. I just might have scratched its elbow."
>
> Then you say, as he smiles, "Why don't we go out in the morning and have a look." And so we two and others will bring home the meat together the next day.

Men are encouraged to hunt as well as they can, and the people are happy when meat is brought in, but the correct demeanor for the successful hunter is modesty and understatement. A /Xai/xai man named /Gaugo said:

> Say that a man has been hunting. He must not come home and announce like a braggart, "I have killed a big one in the bush!" He must first sit down in silence until I or someone else comes up to his fire and asks, "What did you see today?" He replies quietly, "Ah, I'm no good for hunting. I saw nothing at all . . . maybe just a tiny one." Then I smile to myself because I know he has killed something big.

The theme of modesty is continued when the butchering and carrying party goes to fetch the kill the following day. Arriving at the site, the members of the carrying party loudly express their disappointment to the hunter:

> "You mean you have dragged us all the way out here to make us cart home your pile of bones? Oh, if I had known it was this thin I wouldn't have come."
>
> "People, to think I gave up a nice day in the shade for this. At home we may be hungry, but at least we have nice cool water to drink."

To these insults the hunter must not act offended; he should respond with self-demeaning words:

> "You're right, this one is not worth the effort; let's just cook the liver for strength and leave the rest for the hyenas. It's not too late to hunt today, and even a duiker or a steenbok would be better than this mess."

The party, of course, has no intentions of abandoning the kill. The heavy joking and derision are directed toward one goal: leveling potentially arrogant behavior in a successful hunter. The [Ju/'hoansi] recognize the tendency toward arrogance (/twi) in young men and take definite steps to combat it. As /Tomazho, the famous healer from /Xai/xai, put it:

> When a young man kills much meat, he comes to think of himself as a chief or a big man, and he thinks of the rest of us as his servants or inferiors. We can't accept this. We refuse one who boasts, for someday his pride will make him kill somebody. So we always speak of his meat as worthless. In this way we cool his heart and make him gentle.

Insulting the meat is one of the central practices of the Ju/'hoansi that serve to maintain egalitarianism. Even though some men are much better hunters than others, their behavior is molded by the group to minimize the tendency toward self-praise and to channel their energies into socially beneficial activities. As a result, the existence of differences in hunting prowess does not lead to a system of Big Men in which a few talented individuals tower over the others in terms of prestige.

Source: Excerpt from *The Dobe Ju/'hoansi,* 2nd ed., by Richard B. Lee, pp. 54–55, copyright © 1993 by Holt, Rinehart and Winston, Inc., reprinted by permission of the publisher.

So, the transaction of material symbols (gifts) is one of the ways people express positive social relationships. But gifts are also used to create social bonds that are useful to the giver, and to obligate people from whom the giver wants something. Gift giving makes someone indebted to you and therefore can be used to create an obligation to return a favor. Lobbyists and sales representatives know that balanced reciprocity can serve one's self-interest.

Among some peoples, balanced reciprocity takes the form of mutual exchanges of gifts or invitations for political purposes. For an example of how balanced reciprocity creates and sustains political alliances, we turn to the Maring, a horticultural people of the mountainous interior of Papua New Guinea. In the 1960s, when they were first studied by Roy Rappaport, the Maring lived in settlements composed of clusters of kin groups. Each settlement was engaged in periodic warfare with some of its neighbors. Unless a settlement was unusually large, its members formed a political alliance with one or more nearby settlements. When warfare occurred, the warriors of each settlement relied on their allies for military support and, in the case of defeat, for refuge.

An important expression of continued goodwill between allied groups was periodic invitations to feasts, accompanied by exchanges of pigs and wealth objects. Every few years, whenever they accumulated enough pigs, the members of a settlement invited their allies to an enormous feast, appropriately called a *pig feast*. At the pig feast, which was attended by hundreds of people, allies brought large quantities of wealth objects to exchange and pay off debts; they consumed enormous quantities of pork provided by their hosts; they were on the lookout for potential spouses and sexual partners; and they aided the host settlement in the ceremonial dancing that the Maring believed ritually necessary for success in the fighting that soon occurred. The host group used the occasion of their pig feast to gauge the amount of military support they could expect from their allies: The more people who attended the feast, the more warriors the host settlement could put on the battleground. Later, the guests accumulated enough pigs to reciprocate by hosting a pig feast of their own.

A Maring community sponsored a pig feast to compensate its allies for their previous military aid as well as to reciprocate previous pig feasts. The failure to organize a pig feast large enough or soon enough to compensate allies could result in an alliance weakening and even ending. Thus, mutual invitations to feasts were essential to the military success and continued survival of a Maring settlement. Here, and among many other peoples, the reciprocal flow of products, of invitations and return invitations, and of other forms of give-and-take, are essential for well-being and even survival.

Negative Reciprocity

The distinguishing characteristic of the third kind of reciprocity known as **negative reciprocity**—is that both parties attempt to gain all they can from the exchange while giving up as little as possible. Negative reciprocity is usually motivated largely by the desire to obtain

material goods at minimal cost. Insofar as it is motivated by the desire for material goods, negative reciprocity is like market exchange; it is different mainly because no money changes hands between participants.

In economies with no money, negative reciprocity is an important way for individuals and groups to acquire products that they do not produce themselves. Few communities are entirely self-sufficient: some foods they like to eat are not found where they live; some materials they need to make tools are not found locally; or they lack the skill to produce some of the objects they use. To acquire these things, people produce other goods to exchange for "imports."

Barter is one form of negative reciprocity. In the interior highlands of Papua New Guinea, many indigenous peoples manufactured money or wealth objects by stringing shells together into long chains or belts. Because these shells did not occur naturally in the interior, they were traded from people to people until they reached their final destination. Salt was also a trade object because it was found in only a few areas. Similarly, in western North America, the obsidian (volcanic glass) used to make stone tools was found in only a few areas; other peoples acquired it through trade. In some cases, these trade routes stretched for hundreds of miles, with the obsidian passing through the hands of numerous middlemen before finally being made into a tool.

Reciprocity and Social Distance

Each type of reciprocity tends to be associated with certain kinds of social relationships. As Marshall Sahlins, who first distinguished the three varieties, noted, the kind of reciprocity that occurs between individuals or groups depends on the **social distance** between them. Social distance is the degree to which cultural norms specify persons should be intimate with or emotionally attached to one another. A given mode of reciprocal exchange is normatively appropriate only with certain kinds of social relationships.

This is illustrated in North American cultural norms. You should practice generalized reciprocity with your children and perhaps with siblings and elderly parents. Others may judge you as uncaring or selfish if you refuse to offer help that is genuinely needed. But, if a middle-income person repeatedly lends money to a cousin or puts a niece through college, you are likely to regard the person as either unusually generous or perhaps a bit foolish for having extended generalized reciprocity beyond the range of relatives to whom it seems appropriate.

A normative association between exchange and social distance applies to market transactions, the equivalent of negative reciprocity in modern monetary economies. In buying and selling, people are supposed to be "looking out for themselves" and "trying to get the most for their money." We regard this as fine—in fact, as smart shopping—with transactions between strangers in a car lot, when everyone is supposed to bargain. But when the seller and buyer are friends or relatives, it is difficult for them to disentangle their economic transaction from their personal feelings for each other. Bonds between relatives and friends cannot easily be combined with market exchange: kinship and friendship are supposed to have an element of selflessness, whereas buying and selling are assumed to have selfish motives. You might buy a used car from your friend, but chances are both of you feel anxious about the transaction: Will our relationship be damaged if the car is a lemon?

As our social relationships with other people change, so does the kind of reciprocity we practice with them. For example, as we grow up, our increasing independence from our parents is manifested by a change in the way we exchange goods with them. We go from being the recipients of generalized reciprocity to more of a balanced reciprocity as we become more independent, and finally—at least until the advent of Social Security—to being the provider of generalized reciprocity.

Finally, changing one form of reciprocity into another can be a way of changing the nature of a social relationship. Because the form of reciprocity two people practice is related to the degree of social distance between them, one party can increase or decrease the social distance by initiating a new form of exchange. Or someone can signal his or her wish to draw another person closer by tentatively initiating a relationship of balanced reciprocity.

I can let you know that I want to become your friend by giving you an unexpected gift or inviting you to dinner. In turn, you let me know whether you share my feelings by whether you return my gift on an appropriate occasion, repeatedly find reasons to refuse my dinner invitation, or come to dinner several times at my place without reciprocating. If we both use this "strategy of reciprocity," neither of us needs to be put in a potentially embarrassing position of verbalizing our feelings. I signal my wish by my initial gift or invitation, and you decline or accept my offer of friendship by your response. Reciprocity thus is often a symbolic act, conveying messages about ideal social relationships, hoped-for social relationships, and even rejected social relationships. Because we routinely use reciprocity as a way of conveying feelings and sending social messages, some anthropologists view the exchange of material goods as a form of communication.

Redistribution

The major difference between reciprocity and redistribution—the second major form of exchange—is how the transfer of products and other resources is organized. With reciprocity, resources pass back and forth between two participants, with no third party to act as intermediary. With redistribution, resources collected from many individuals or groups are taken to a central place or put into a common pool or fund. Some overarching authority (empowered to make decisions on behalf of those who contributed) later draws from this pool or fund and returns public goods and services to allegedly benefit the group as a whole.

In modern nations, the resource (money, in this case) that is redistributed takes the form of taxes on wages, profits, retail sales, property, interest, and other income and assets. Consider how national tax systems are supposed to operate in most modern nations. The national government redistributes tax revenues in two main ways. First, revenues are distributed in such a way as to benefit the whole country. Citizens receive police protection, law enforcement, national defense, infrastructure (e.g., dams, roads, airports), regulation of polluting industries, and so forth. Here, resources collected from the citizenry are expended on public goods and services. Second, taxes provide assistance for individuals in need. In the United States, these are "transfer payments" in the form of Social Security, Medicaid and Medicare, disaster relief, children's services, and so forth. Such public expenditures are based on moral norms and cultural values about social justice, equal opportunity, and helping those in need. Redistribution systems around the world are used for similar purposes: to provide public goods and services and to provide assistance to individuals and groups in need.

But there is another side to redistribution, a side with which we are also familiar. First, there is often conflict over who should provide the public resources, how the resources should be expended, and how much of a share should be given to those who collect and distribute them. One common social and political problem with redistribution is political disagreement: When many individuals have contributed to the public pool or fund, not everyone is likely to agree on how the "public resources" should be spent for the "public good." Much of the conflict between

▲ Gift exchange is a familiar form of reciprocity. Here in Narita, Japan, two men formally exchange gifts before an important festival.

political parties in modern industrial democracies is rooted in disagreements over who should be taxed and how much, and over how government revenues should be spent. Parties and various interest groups are, in many cases, quarreling over redistribution: Who pays? Who gets what? And how much?

Second, elected officials and other officeholders who make important decisions about redistribution sometimes use public resources to further their own interests and ambitions, rather than to benefit the entire country or to help those in greatest need. In the United States, for instance, elected officials make "pork barrel" deals to allocate federal tax dollars to finance highway construction in their districts. Congestion might be reduced for a while, but the real purpose is to provide jobs for their constituencies or to serve special-interest groups who contribute to their reelection. Balanced reciprocity between members of Congress often integrates well with redistribution: "You vote for my bridge reconstruction; I'll vote for your wetlands reclamation." Speaking more

generally, political interests—in addition to concern for the public welfare—enter into decision making about redistribution.

A common form of redistribution in the preindustrial world is **tribute.** The subjects of a chief or other title holder contribute products (usually including food) into a common pool under the control of the central authority. Often the tribute is culturally viewed as a material symbol that the subjects continue to acknowledge the chief's sacred authority. Some of the accumulated products are consumed by the chiefs and their relatives, some are distributed to support the work of crafts specialists (e.g., weavers and potters), and some are redistributed to the whole population at public feasts, celebrations, and ceremonies.

Examples of redistribution systems using tribute payments exist on many of the islands of Polynesia and Micronesia in the Pacific. On many islands, the entire population was divided traditionally into two ranks or classes, noble and commoner (Chapter 13 has more about rank and class). Members of the nobility did little agricultural or other manual work, but instead managed the political system and organized religious ceremonies. Commoners produced the food for themselves and their families and performed most physical labor.

On some islands, the king or principal chief was viewed as the ultimate owner of the land and its resources. Nobles generally had ritual functions, including prayers and sacrifices to deities and ancestors. On most islands, commoners paid periodic tribute to families of noble rank, whether in return for their use of the land or as a sacred obligation, or both. Tribute fed the nobility and their families and supported specialists. The tribute rendered by commoners was used partly for public purposes, such as feeding people who worked on trails and public buildings, providing relief from temporary food shortages, and publicly celebrating special events. On a few of the larger, resource-rich islands such as Hawaii and Tahiti, the nobles were sufficiently powerful to become materially wealthy from tribute: they lived in the best houses, slept on the softest woven mats, wore special clothing, had numerous servants, and ate only the finest foods.

Market Exchange

To say that objects or services are exchanged "on the market" means that they are bought and sold at a price measured in money. Person A possesses goods that person B wants to acquire; B acquires the goods by giving A whatever amount of money both A and B agree on; A then uses the money to acquire more goods from other people.

Because we are so familiar with markets, this exchange form sounds obvious. But notice that it requires four things:

1. Some object that serves as a medium of exchange—that is, *money*
2. A rate at which goods and services are exchanged for money—that is, *prices*
3. Prices that are determined by *supply and demand*
4. *Privately owned property*

Related to the third point, markets imply the absence of coercion: if prices are set by supply and demand, then neither party to a transaction can be forced to buy or sell from the other party. Everyone has alternative ways of spending their money. This is a *free market*—no third party (a government, for example) sets prices or forces anyone to buy or sell from anyone else, and no single

supplier of a good (a monopolist) controls enough of the market to force people to buy from him, her, or it (in the case of firms). Related to the fourth point, private property does not mean that there are no restrictions on how owners can use it because even private property is subject to public laws and regulations. One important feature of market economies is that *productive property* is in private hands, including the hands of shareholders for companies whose shares are traded on stock exchanges. This kind of property (or *capital*) is used to produce goods or services and then sold for a price with the goal of making profit.

In market economies, governments protect and enhance the market. Governments print money and control the money supply; protect private property by means of laws, police, and courts; break up some monopolies; pay for public goods and infrastructure such as highways, ports, and airports; regulate polluting industries; prohibit insider trading in stock markets; and in many other ways allow markets to work smoothly. Governments are more directly involved in the economy also: if recession threatens, the government may act; if too many banks are in trouble, the government may bail them out to avoid a financial collapse; if wages do not keep up with inflation, the government may raise the minimum wage. In brief, the market is "free" only in part.

Because markets require money, we discuss some of the diversity in money objects and money uses.

Money

Money is another of those things we take for granted, so much so that it seems like a simple idea. Actually, the idea of money presupposes a lot of other ideas, so money is actually rather complicated.

Money is objects that serve as *media of exchange* in a wide range of transactions of goods, services (including labor), or both. If an economy uses money, person A can acquire something from person B without having to return an object desired by B—that is, without having to barter. B can then use the money to buy a chosen object or service. Because you sell your time and skills for money, the value of your labor is expressed in terms of money ("wages" and "salaries"). This facilitation of exchange is the main function of money. Money greases the wheels of commerce.

Other characteristics of money are derived from its function as a medium of exchange. For example, money serves as a *standard of value*: we can compare the values of the goods and services that can be exchanged for money because money serves as a common measure of

▲ The market form of exchange requires money, prices determined by supply and demand, and private ownership of most resources and technology. Ownership shares of companies are bought and sold by licensed brokers on the floor of the New York Stock Exchange.

how much things are worth. This makes it a lot easier for you to decide whether to buy new outfits or a new HDTV; you can compare their values (i.e., their prices) and thus determine how many outfits you would be giving up for the new HDTV.

Money is also a *store of value:* because you can use it any time to purchase a wide range of goods, it stores your wealth, often in a portable form that can be carried in pouches or pockets. If you are rich and don't want anyone to know it, don't buy anything that displays your wealth; just keep the money, because you can transform it into goods that you can display later if you wish. Or if you want to defer immediate consumption so that you can get something really expensive later, just save your money, since it stores your resources indefinitely (unless, of course, inflation is high; then, without you doing anything at all, your money becomes worth less).

Notice also that money takes on *symbolic significance.* Money is both a standard and a store of value, and people have different amounts of it. So, we can use it as a way to evaluate people, especially if we don't already

know them. We all know that clothing, jewelry, cars, houses, and so forth aren't really indicators of moral character, but they are still signals about how much individuals or families are "worth." (If you doubt this, ask what criteria you use to judge people you don't know.) Money can even symbolize national identity or independence: some citizens of England still resist adopting the pan-European currency (the Euro) because they see it as a threat to their sovereignty.

These and other characteristics mean that not just any object is suitable to be used as money. Obviously, money objects must be *durable.* This is why hard objects such as modified stones, shells, and metals often serve as currency.

Money is more useful as an exchange medium if it is *divisible,* so sometimes different kinds of objects serve as denominations of money—equivalent to nickels, quarters, dollar bills, and thousand-dollar bills. Among the Kapauku, a people of the rugged interior of Papua, small cowrie shells imported from the coast serve as money. As the shells circulate, their natural polish wears off,

▶ One of the more unusual forms of money is the stone money of Yap in the Federated States of Micronesia.

© Paul Chesley/National Geographic Image Collection

and since the older ones are more scarce, they are worth more than the newer ones—thus, the "age" of the money serves as a kind of denomination.

The supply of the money object must be *controllable* because if people can get all they want of it, its value inflates and it becomes worthless as an exchange medium: Who would give you anything in exchange for it? The monetary supply can be controlled by a government, which manufactures the only "legal tender" in the society. Or the supply can be controlled by using only imported or rare objects as money. Shells imported from far away frequently serve as money because of their scarcity and durability. The money supply can also be controlled by using a currency that requires a lot of labor to make. Minerals or shells can be ground into shapes, drilled with holes, and strung into necklaces. In such cases, money remains scarce because it takes a lot of time to make it.

Most money is *portable* for convenience. In different cultures, you can stick it in your pocket, carry it around your neck or waist, wrap it in a bundle, roll it up, or wear it around your arm. On the island of Yap in Micronesia, however, huge stone disks weighing hundreds of pounds serve as a kind of money. Yapese stone money is seldom moved; rather, the ownership of it is transacted so that the money stays in one place even when its owner changes.

As the stone money of Yap illustrates, an enormous variety of objects serve as money in one or another region of the world. In preindustrial economies, the kinds of monetary objects are surprisingly diverse. In Africa, for

example, the following objects served as money in some part of the continent: iron, salt, beads, cowrie shells, cloth, gin, gold dust, metal rods, brass bracelets, and livestock. Among the Aztecs, cacao beans served as currency.

The range of goods that can be acquired with money varies greatly. In some economies, the range is broad. Many kinds of resources and goods can be bought and sold, including labor, land, tools, and sometimes even people (slaves). In these systems, money serves as a *generalized medium of exchange;* that is, it can be used to acquire many kinds of goods and services. Of course, there are always some things that money just can't buy. Love is the classic example, but if you have enough money, it is not hard for you to *think* everyone loves you.

In many preindustrial economies, the range of money uses is relatively narrow. Only a few categories of products may be purchased with money. For example, it may be possible to buy food, clothing, and a few other goods, but land is not available for sale at any price and labor is almost never sold. Economic anthropologists sometimes call this **limited-purpose money.**

A famous example of limited-purpose money comes from the Tiv of Nigeria, studied by Paul Bohannan. Tiv money consisted of metal rods, but the rods could not be used as an exchange medium for all other goods. For one thing, land could not be sold, and labor was exchanged among relatives based on the principle of generalized reciprocity. For another, among the Tiv, goods circulated in different *exchange spheres.* Certain kinds of products could only be exchanged for certain other kinds of products. Products were culturally classified into categories, within which they were freely exchangeable, but between which exchange was difficult.

The "subsistence sphere" category included cultivated crops, chickens and goats, and some tools and household goods. Goods within this sphere were exchangeable for one another by means of barter. The "prestige sphere" included slaves, cattle, a special kind of white cloth, and metal rods. Within the prestige sphere, metal rods functioned as an exchange medium: one could sell cattle for metal rods and then use the rods to acquire white cloth or slaves, for example, but the monetary function of metal rods was normally limited to the prestige sphere.

However, it was possible to acquire subsistence goods in exchange for metal rods, but these transactions were rare for two reasons. First, few people were willing to trade their metal rods for subsistence goods. This is because goods that circulated in the prestige sphere had much greater cultural value to Tiv than subsistence goods. Second, metal rods were worth an enormous amount of subsistence goods. Yet metal rods had no denominations; that is, unlike dollars and cents, they were not divisible into fractions. So for a Tiv to try to exchange one metal rod for subsistence goods would be like an American taking a thousand-dollar bill into a grocery store to buy food, with the clerk unable to make change. As a result of these two factors, Tiv metal rods were largely limited-purpose money.

The Tiv example reminds us that just because we find it convenient to call some object like metal rods "money" does not mean that the object has all the characteristics of our own currency. Indeed, some anthropologists believe that money objects are lacking in preindustrial economies and that money is a Western concept that we should not attempt to apply to other cultures. This problem is mainly semantic, however. If we define money simply as a medium of exchange, then it is found in many other economies. To avoid confusion and false impressions, we always need to specify its uses and its cultural meaning to local people.

On Market Economies

The phrase *market economy* means that practically the whole economy is organized on *market principles*. Briefly, here are the most important of these principles:

- Practically all privately owned goods and services have a monetary price: they can be bought and sold on the free market.

- Most people make their living by selling something on the market. Some people make their living by selling goods or services to consumers. But most people are workers: they make their living by selling their labor to a group (such as a firm or public agency). Workers have to do this because most of them do not own the natural resources and capital with which to make their own living.

- The factors of production are allocated by the market. Because privately owned resources, capital (including technology and equipment), and labor are bought and sold, the supply of and demand for these factors of production determine the uses to which they are put. In theory, the market allocates them so that they are used in ways that bring the highest return (profit).

- The economy is self-regulating. The impersonal forces of supply and demand set prices and therefore regulate the kinds of economic activity that occur.

Economies organized by market principles have a lot of advantages for individuals—you can shop around until you find the best deal, and you are not tied to any particular place or employer. And there is no doubt that an economy organized on free-market principles is tremendously productive, as Karl Marx—the nineteenth-century archenemy of capitalism—himself recognized.

Still, it's worth considering some of the ways that living in a market economy affects people and society. For example, compare a market economy in which most people sell their labor to a firm or an agency to an economy in which people themselves own or have access to everything they need to survive and do well (by their standards, of course). Because we have described the hunting and gathering Ju/'hoansi of southern Africa extensively, we'll use them for comparison and we'll assume (falsely) that they still live a traditional lifestyle by using the present tense.

Work. You probably do not have what you need to survive on your own. You must get a job. On the job, for the most part your working days and hours are set by your employer. (You have some flexibility, but exercising it too often endangers your job.) How much income you earn and how much job security you have vary, but both are highly dependent on your employer. In turn, the employer reacts to impersonal market forces: You may lose wages, benefits, or the job itself if your company decides to "outsource" your job to "remain competitive in global markets."

If you are a Ju/'hoansi, by virtue of being born into a given family, you have access to a territory that supplies

▶ A main characteristic of market economies is that most people do not own what they need to survive; they sell their time and skills for a wage or salary.

© Sean Gallup/Getty Images

you with almost everything you need. You have to work for your food and other things, of course, but when you have acquired all you and your group need or want, you can stop working. If you take a day off, someone else will give you and your family enough food for that day. You have no concept of wage or job security, but you do think about subsistence security: Will there be a drought or other kind of natural calamity? Droughts are as "impersonal" as market forces—and just as unpredictable. But everyone knows this from generations of living in the same place, so you have alternatives: You can go live with your husband's brother's band for a while until natural conditions improve.

Family. When you go to work every day, chances are you leave your family. If you have children, your job will compete with your family for your time and probably for your mental energy. It will be hard for you to balance these demands and preferences. Your boss is sympathetic, and even your boss's boss understands when you have to take personal days because she knows you personally. But people higher up on the corporate ladder don't know you at all, and all your bosses are ultimately answerable to them. Really, you are interchangeable; someone else can do what you do about as well. So get used to balancing your personal life and work requirements.

If you were a Ju/'hoansi, you have no boss, although other people in your band exert some influence over what you do. Everyone knows you, and you know everyone, so within reason everyone can take everyone else's personal

situations into account. You don't care too much about getting ahead. Of whom? For what?

Values. You find a lot of things and qualities important and desirable: family, freedom, and fun, just to name a few factors that start with *f.* In fact, so many different kinds of things and qualities are important and desirable that you cannot possibly satisfy them all. When you get one thing, some other desire springs to the forefront to take its place on your wish list. And just in case you should ever come close to satisfying one category of desire—the desire for material goods—advertising will remind you that you want things you never even knew existed. There is never enough. It's a good thing, too, because growth in the economy would cease if too many people decided they have enough, found a way to cut back on their work hours, and stopped spending.

If you are a Ju/'hoansi, you also care about family, freedom, and fun. You value equality, meaning not that everyone is "equal" (which is a social impossibility) but that it is distasteful when some people have full bellies while others go hungry. You really don't like it when someone you know brags about himself, so you join others in cutting such people down to size. Since you know that the other people with whom you have spent most of your life feel the same way, you remain outwardly modest. No one in your camp has very many material possessions—they are too hard to carry around, and if someone has something she doesn't really need, someone else will probably ask her for it. When you get enough things, and everyone

In late 2007, the world price of oil soared to $95 per barrel. The price of gasoline exceeded $3 per gallon in the United States. Once again, Americans realized they were "too dependent" on foreign oil. Fortunately, technological developments in the 1970s have allowed us to make fuel from corn—and American farmers can produce a lot of corn, especially when American taxpayers subsidize both farmers and giant agricultural corporations to produce it. After it has been processed into ethanol, mixed with real petroleum, and pumped into fuel (not "gas") tanks, corn can both reduce gasoline prices at the pump and free us from having to deal with people who don't like us, and vice versa. Everyone benefits.

Not quite. Demand for corn by ethanol-processing plants rose so much that the market price of corn nearly tripled between the end of 2005 and 2007. Corn syrup (fructose) is used to sweeten so many products that there was a general increase in the prices of food—including beef, chicken, and pork, which (while they were alive) feed partly on processed corn. So, if we save some money on fuel for our cars, we lose some of it in the prices we pay for our snack foods, soft drinks, and other fructose-laden products. Further, at most, ethanol yields only about 30 percent more energy than the energy needed to produce it, and some researchers claim its energy balance is negative. (The Brazilians produce ethanol from sugarcane, which yields 800 percent more energy than is required to produce it.) Most researchers doubt ethanol will reduce our dependence on foreign oil. Finally, the market for corn is a global market. American increases in the demand for ethanol led to an increase in the price of corn in Mexico—and the price of corn tortillas, a staple of the Mexican diet, rose.

The impact of increased ethanol demand on Mexican corn prices is an example of market globalization: the entire world is increasingly integrated into a single economic system organized by market principles. Labor, capital, technology, consumer products, and services move with few restraints across national boundaries. Theoretically, if the entire world would become a single integrated megamarket, then subsistence maize farmers in Uganda would compete with American corn farmers to sell their products in both Kampala and Chicago. Obviously, the implications of such a global market would be profound for Americans, Ugandans, and the rest of the world.

Market globalization has multiple dimensions, each related to the others. First is the *internationalization of capital and labor*. Corporations in the developed world move their production facilities to other, poorer nations, where they employ people who will work for a fraction of North American, European, and Japanese wages. There are many advantages for companies that relocate factories in regions where the labor force is relatively poor. Wages are far lower. Factory safety regulations are less constraining. Rents are cheap. Environmental laws are relatively lax or unevenly enforced. Unions are nonexistent or poorly organized. All in all, these and other advantages lower production costs and, therefore, raise the profits of corporations that locate factories in less developed regions.

Second is the *globalization of consumer products* along with *marketing efforts*. Products produced in one country are sold in other countries with few or no restrictions. In Europe, the European Union agreement finalized in the 1990s ended all tariffs and quotas on consumer goods among its member nations, and the free flow of products was further streamlined with the adoption of the Euro as the common currency. In the Americas, the North American Free Trade Agreement (NAFTA) will eventually make Canada, the United States, and Mexico into a single market. North Americans and Europeans can easily see the impact of consumer globalization. Go to your closet and try to find a garment or pair of shoes manufactured in your own country. Check out your DVD, gaming console, TV, CD player, and other electronic equipment. Where were they manufactured? What do you suppose you would have paid for them if they had been made in Toronto, London, Tokyo, or Chicago?

International markets are not new, but their size and reach expanded dramatically in the late twentieth century. In the 1960s, for example, an agreement between the United States and Mexico allowed U.S. corporations to set up factories (called *maquiladores*) in Mexico along the border region with Texas. The plants produced massive quantities of clothing and consumer electronics for American consumers. Garment companies sent cloth to the *maquiladores* to be cut and sewn into clothing sold to American consumers. Electronics firms sent components south to be soldered and assembled. Products were then brought back to the United States for final finishing and sale. There were no tariffs (import taxes) on the finished products, and Mexico allowed North American companies to retain ownership of assembly plants on its soil in return for the jobs and training received by its citizens. Most Mexican employees of these multinational firms are unmarried women, who come from all over the country to get jobs in the assembly plants. The Americans and Europeans made similar arrangements with Asian countries like Taiwan, Singapore, and South Korea.

Since the early 1980s, wage levels in these countries have climbed and their governments have instituted more workplace and environmental regulations. In order to remain competitive by controlling labor and other production costs, corporations relocated production facilities to other countries that had fewer regulations and lower prevailing wages. Countries in Southeast Asia (like Malaysia, Indonesia, and the Philippines),

(continued)

the Caribbean, and Africa have invited foreign companies to establish factories to provide jobs for their people and tax revenues for their governments.

The two most important countries to expand opportunities for foreign investment in the past 20 years are India and the People's Republic of China. China's population of 1.3 billion is more than four times that of the United States (300 million). Now that the Chinese Communist Party has relaxed some of its restrictions on rural-to-urban migration, its huge and growing cities soak up the labor of tens of millions of former peasants. The new, privately owned factories turn out clothing, toys, machinery, home electronics, housewares, and other products at rock-bottom production costs. In the 1990s, tens of thousands of Chinese grew wealthy, and tens of millions became middle class.

But problems loom. More tens of millions of rural Chinese are left out, and many have had their land confiscated for all those new developments. Will their patience wear out and be expressed as demonstrations or even rebellions, leading to political instability that will crush China's industries and exports? The new factories churn out air pollution and water contamination as well as toys, socks, and other products. In its contribution to global warming, China will soon match the United States. Will the Chinese environment—and the rest of our planet—absorb the impacts? In the summer of 2007, Mattel announced the recall of 19 million toys made in China because samples revealed that they contained unsafe amounts of lead. What hazards do consumers in the richer countries face when they pay so little for products produced in the global factories? In short, in the global marketplace, poverty becomes even more of a global problem, global environmental consequences increase, and cheaply produced products can harm consumers all over the globe.

Why have global markets experienced this expansion? There are a host of reasons, which vary greatly according to who is providing the explanation. High labor costs, environmental regulations, and occupational safety restrictions in the developed countries are some reasons. Why pay an American garment worker $10 per hour when a Mexican woman will do the same work for $2, and without many of those aggravating labor negotiations and environmental laws?

Technological advances are another reason. Giant freighters hauling hundreds of containers greatly reduce the costs of transporting products from where they are extracted or processed to where they are ultimately sold and consumed. Today electronics can be assembled and clothing can be stitched and sewn in Southeast Asia or Africa, then shipped or flown to North America or Europe, and still produce large profits for factory owners and retailers. Advances in mining and timber extraction make it possible to economically extract minerals and lumber from places where it was too expensive a few decades ago. Modern agricultural technology, with its chemicals and machinery, is applied to land in Mexico and Latin America to supply North American consumers with tomatoes and grapes in January and bananas and mangoes all year round.

Globalization is likely here to stay, barring a worldwide economic collapse. Its consequences are debated by news media, government officials, labor unions, companies, and consumers. The most important questions focus on its costs and benefits, especially the question of who loses and who gains. Nearly everyone agrees that corporations win from globalization, mainly because of reduced labor costs and less restrictive environmental and workplace regulations. Consumers in the rich countries also probably win because prices for many

else around you has about the same things, and no media bombard you with images that make you think you are not sexy enough—well, then enough really is enough.

None of the preceding comparisons is meant to disparage market economies, which have done much to improve the lives of millions of people around the world. At any rate, the economies of most of the world's nations are increasingly integrated into a single global market economy, which seems far more likely to expand than contract for the foreseeable future (see the Globalization box).

Our main point is this: Some scholars, talk-show hosts, elected officials, and others have completely bought into (pardon the pun) market principles and market economies. They talk and act and support policies as though

the costs of markets are so low as to be negligible. But they're not:

- Unlike the Ju/'hoansi, you probably won't move your family in with your husband's brother if times get tough because it would be humiliating. Relatives care about and care for one another, but not in that way. Markets encourage individual achievement, but with some social costs.
- Because modern technology has made everyone's labor so productive, theoretically we could all be working less. That's probably what a Ju/'hoansi would do. But the same force (market competition) that fosters technological improvements also means that production

products—from shoes to computers—are lower. But we don't know how many hazardous products like the lead in Mattel's toys will show up in the future.

What about the workers who used to work in the factories in the developed countries, whose formerly high-paying jobs were replaced by people who live half a world away? Many are the victims of "restructuring" and "increasing efficiency" because their employers must "lower costs" to "compete in the global market" in order to "be responsible to their stockholders." Those who favor globalization point out that laid-off and fired North American workers have found other jobs and, at any rate, have benefited as consumers from the lower prices made possible by cheap overseas labor. Critics of globalization claim that most of these new jobs are lower-paid jobs in service industries and that the alleged decline of the American middle class is due largely to globalization.

And what about the workers in the new global production system, whose globally competitive labor provides low-priced products for sale to consumers buying on the global marketplace? Views diverge on their welfare also. Critics of globalization claim that such workers are exploited. Rich companies take advantage of their poverty and lack of alternative economic opportunities by offering low wages and deplorable working conditions in terms of working hours, health, and safety. Those who favor the expansion of global markets respond that these workers are being paid more than they would otherwise be paid, that they receive job experience and training, that their countries receive the taxes paid on their wages, and so forth. Critics fire back that if things are getting so much better in places like Mexico and Central America, then why are so many Mexicans and Central Americans still illegally entering the United States in search of well-paying jobs?

Finally, what about the effects of globalization on the maintenance of cultural heritages? Is there to be a global cultural melting pot? Will there be a global megaculture if the diverse peoples of the world buy and sell on the global megamarket? People who fear the effects of globalization point out that advertising has infiltrated even remote places such as the interior mountains of New Guinea. Is a culture devoted to megaconsumption the kind of world we want to live in? they ask. Those who favor globalization believe that countries will take what they want and leave the rest. They also hold that companies that sell in particular countries will have to adapt their products and advertising to local cultural preferences. Thus, McDonald's franchises in India accommodate Hindu traditions with burgers made from something besides beef, and you can buy falafelburgers at McDonald's in parts of the Middle East. France has fought what it considers cultural imperialism by passing laws against the use of certain English words in the interest of preserving the French language.

Critical Thinking Questions

1. The short-term costs and benefits of market globalization are discussed above. What do you think the world economy will look like in 2020?

2. Are those who claim that globalization threatens local traditions and cultural heritages giving too little credit to those whose cultures they say they want to preserve?

Sources: Shapouri et al. (2002); *Time* 170(12):50–51 (September 17, 2007)

---

has to increase to stay competitive. So, productivity gains are used mainly to increase output, not to reduce working hours. Markets encourage people and companies to be competitive, not to take it easy.

- Probably you will try to live what your culture considers the good life. And your culture's definition of the good life is affected by the market economy itself, which requires ever-increasing consumption fueled partly by advertising and the media. Because most people tend to admire others who live out their culture's values, to get their admiration you'll probably buy a lot of stuff. Unlike the Ju/'hoansi, you've got a place to put it. Unlike the Ju/'hoansi, no one—not even your brother—is likely to ask you for it. Markets encourage continual growth in consumption, which is hard to resist.

If you were raised in a market economy, you may think that such things are not "costs" at all, or that they are costs that are worth bearing. But consider the possibility that the *only* reason you think that is because you were enculturated inside a market economy with its norms, values, and worldview.

Peasant Marketplaces

Those of us who live in industrialized market economies purchase most of what we need and want in restaurants, car lots, supermarkets, and shopping malls. We earn

► In peasant marketplaces like this one in Oaxaca City, Mexico, vendors themselves often produce the food and wares they sell.

money from our jobs and spend the money on goods and services, relying on other organizations (mainly companies) to sell us the products we wish to buy.

Even in the twenty-first century, millions of rural peasants (see Chapter 6) do not live completely in the global marketplace. Rather than selling their labor to others in return for a wage, they work the land and fish the waters to supply food for their families directly. Rather than producing goods that they turn around and sell at a price to others, families consume most of what they produce themselves. There are places in such communities where goods are bought and sold—there are *peasant marketplaces.* But people do not rely on marketplaces for most of what they consume, nor do they spend most of their working hours producing goods to sell at the marketplace.

Peasant marketplaces are ancient and especially important in West Africa, southern and Southeast Asia, the Caribbean, and Central and South America. Peasant vendors sell food, cloth and clothing, pottery, leather products, livestock, and other goods produced by their families. Traveling merchants (middlemen) bring commodities imported from the developed world or from elsewhere in the region to sell to local people at the local marketplace.

Despite all the buying and selling, peasant marketplaces are not the same as modern shopping malls or department stores. There are some notable differences. First, the kinds of products sold at the marketplace are limited, and most families rely on the market only for those products they cannot produce for themselves efficiently. Most people do not make most of their living by selling things (products, labor) on the market.

Second, producing and marketing goods for monetary profit are part-time activities for many vendors (sellers). Many marketplaces are staffed mainly by peasants, who sell small quantities of food, pottery, furniture, fibers, crafts, or other objects they have produced with family labor. Indeed, marketplaces often are *periodic,* meaning that they do not open every day, but only a day or two a week. Traveling merchants typically visit several markets in different regions in a single week, often buying products for sale at one market and reselling them at a distant market a day or two later.

Third, peasant vendors usually sell products that they or their family members, rather than hired laborers, produce. This means that any single vendor offers to sell only a few kinds of goods in limited quantities. Most marketplaces also feature products sold by people who specialize in buying them wholesale and selling them retail. Such people are dependent on the market—with all its insecurities and risks—for their livelihood. They therefore have developed various strategies to reduce the risks they face.

When we who live in a market economy visit a marketplace—a store or car lot, for instance—we typically buy goods from total strangers. We pay the same price as everyone else. We expect sellers to be looking out for themselves, just as sellers expect us to be trying to get the most for our money. This characteristic is referred to as the "impersonality of the marketplace," which is nicely expressed by the old saying: "One person's money is as green as anyone else's."

In contrast, in the small towns and villages of peasant communities, vendors sometimes develop personal and intimate relationships with some of their customers. For example, in a Philippine marketplace studied by William Davis, vendors establish relationships called *suki* with "special customers," people who regularly buy their wares. The sellers' goal is to reduce their risks by gradually building up a steady, large clientele of customers, rather than by squeezing all the money they can out of each individual transaction. From the *suki,* the customer receives credit, favorable prices, extra quantities of goods at a given price, the best quality of goods the seller has to offer on a particular day, and certain services. The vendor benefits as well: Their *suki* are expected not to buy from any other suppliers of the goods they carry. This is helpful in calculating the quantities of goods they will be able to sell and, hence, helps prevent them from overstocking their stalls.

As *suki* in this Philippine marketplace illustrates, the impersonality of the marketplace can be modified by the formation of personal ties between buyers and sellers. Supply and demand operate to affect prices, yet people may recognize that charging as much as the market will bear on any given day is not necessarily in their long-term interest. This is not surprising in communities in which most people know most other people. Those who have things to sell are often selling them to people whom they know in other, nonmarket and noneconomic contexts.

Summary

1. *Exchange* is the patterned ways products are transferred between the time they are produced and the time they are consumed. Anthropologists classify the variety of exchanges in human economies into three major modes or types: reciprocity, redistribution, and market.

2. Reciprocity is the giving and receiving of objects or services without the transfer of money. One form, generalized reciprocity, usually occurs between parties who are normatively obliged to assist one another in times of need, such as relatives and sometimes close friends. With balanced reciprocity, the return of an object of equivalent value is expected within a reasonable time. The goal of balanced reciprocity may be the acquisition of goods for their utility, as in Trobriand *wasi.* More often, it is motivated by the desire to create or sustain good relationships between individuals (as in gift giving) or political alliances between groups (as with the Maring pig feast). Negative reciprocity is characterized by the desire of both parties to acquire as many goods as possible while giving up as few as possible, as in barter.

3. The kind of reciprocity that exists between individuals and groups depends on the normatively appropriate social distance between them. Exchange relationships alter as social relationships change. Conversely, one party can attempt to alter a relationship by offering an object (or invitation), and the other party can signal acceptance or rejection by a particular response. In effect, a reciprocal exchange of goods (and, for that matter, services) can serve as an exchange of messages about feelings and relationships. Reciprocity thus has symbolic as well as material content.

4. In redistribution, the members of a group contribute products, objects, or money into a pool or fund, and a central authority reallocates or uses them for public purposes. Taxes in modern nations and tribute in chiefdoms are examples. Normatively, redistribution is supposed to provide resources to increase public welfare, either to provide public goods or to support those in need. In fact, there is much debate over collection and allocation, and those officials who do the collecting and allocating frequently use their authority for their private ambition rather than the public interest.

5. Market exchange involves buying and selling commodities. It therefore requires money, prices determined by supply and demand, and privately owned property. Money makes the exchange of goods and services more convenient and also facilitates the making of profit and accumulation of wealth. Money functions as a medium of exchange, a standard of value, and a store of value. These functions mean that money objects generally (but not always) have the characteristics of durability, divisibility, limited supply, and portability. The range of goods and

services that can be bought with money varies among economies. In market economies, money is a generalized exchange medium, but it has more limited uses in many preindustrial societies, as illustrated by Tiv metal rods.

6. Market economies allow us to be free to choose where to shop and work, and they are also enormously productive and expansive. Some people believe that this advantage is so overwhelming that the costs are negligible. But perhaps these people think this way because they were enculturated into the norms, values, and worldviews that characterize a market economy.

7. Rural peasants of many countries do not completely rely on markets; they produce most of their food themselves and shop at local marketplaces for only some of their needs and wants. In peasant marketplaces, most vendors are small-scale and part-time. In many regions, they develop special relationships with sellers to reduce their risks, as illustrated by *suki* in the Philippines.

Key Terms

reciprocity	generalized reciprocity	social distance
redistribution	balanced reciprocity	tribute
market	negative reciprocity	limited-purpose money

Suggested Readings

Plattner, Stuart, ed. *Economic Anthropology.* Stanford, Calif.: Stanford University Press, 1989.

A collection of articles on economic systems.

Sahlins, Marshall. *Stone Age Economics.* New York: Aldine, 1972.

Deals with the organization of production and modes of exchange in preindustrial economies.

Weatherford, Jack. *The History of Money: From Sandstone to Cyberspace.* New York: Crown, 1997.

Compares money from a historical perspective.

Wilk, Richard R. *Economies & Cultures: Foundations of Economic Anthropology.* Boulder, Colo.: Westview Press, 1996.

A readable and thoughtful overview of economic anthropology, focusing on major issues and debates.

Media Resources

The Wadsworth Anthropology Resource Center
academic.cengage.com/anthropology

The Wadsworth discipline resource website that accompanies *Humanity: An Introduction to Cultural Anthropology,* Eighth Edition, includes a rich array of material, including online anthropological video clips, to help you in the study of cultural anthropology and the specific topics covered in this chapter. Other material includes a case study forum with excerpts from various Wadsworth authors, map exercises, scientist interviews, breaking news in anthropology, and links to additional useful online material. Begin by selecting Cultural Anthropology to take you to videos, research, and more. From the homepage, you may also select Applied Anthropology, which directs you to essays, glossary terms, the case study forum, and a list of internships and careers in anthropology.

8 MARRIAGES AND FAMILIES

The family is a fundamental social unit in all societies, although its forms and functions vary from people to people. This Indian nuclear family is on the move in the city of Indore in the state of Madya Pradesh.

Some Definitions

Incest Taboos

Marriage

Defining Marriage

Functions of Marriage

Two Unusual Forms

Marriage in Comparative Perspective

Marriage Rules

How Many Spouses?

Marriage Alliances

Marital Exchanges

Kinship Diagrams

Postmarital Residence Patterns

Influences on Residence Patterns

Residence and Households

Family and Household Forms

Two-Generation Households

Extended Households

Questions addressed in this chapter

What are the main theories about incest taboos?

What are the major forms of marriage?

Why are marriage alliances important in so many societies?

What are the main types of postmarital residence, and how do anthropologists try to explain them?

What are the main household forms in human societies? What are some of the main influences on household forms?

When American politicians proclaim that "the family is the backbone of our nation" and that their own policies promote "family values," they can hardly go wrong. After all, how many voters see themselves as antifamily? Certainly, the bonds of marriage and family are among the central social relationships of most societies. For one thing, a married couple, aided by some kind of extended family, is usually the social group that nourishes and socializes new generations. For another, family ties are the basis of residential groups that not only live together but often own property together, play together, work together, and worship together.

Families, we all recognize, do a lot of things that are helpful to their members and to society at large. So, when studies show that American divorce rates hover around 50 percent and that about 30 percent of American children live in households with only one parent present, we believe that something is amiss. We fear that broken homes and single-parent families will cause harm to children, communities, and the whole nation. Worrying that marriage between people of the same sex will erode the "sacred institution" of marriage, in 2004 the American president and some members of Congress attempted (unsuccessfully) to include the one man–one woman marital norm in the Constitution.

In this chapter, we look at some of the main ways cultures differ in their marriage practices and in the organization of their families and households. Before doing so, though, we need to define some terms that are used in this and subsequent chapters.

Some Definitions

Anthropologists distinguish between two kinds of relatives. **Consanguines** are "blood" relatives—people related by birth. **Affines** are "in-laws"—people related by

marriage. So, your *consanguineous relatives* are all of your blood relatives—your parents, siblings, grandparents, parents' siblings, and cousins. Your affines are all of your relatives by marriage—such as your sister's husband, wife's mother, and father's sister's husband.

Both consanguineous and affinal relationships can, in theory, serve as the basis for all kinds of social groups. When people form an organized, cooperative group based on their kinship relationships, anthropologists call it a **kin group.** The **nuclear family,** which consists of a married couple together with their unmarried children, is one kind of kin group. Its members live together, share the use of family wealth and property, rely on one another for emotional support, pool their labor and resources to support the family, and so on.

Larger groups can be formed out of kinship relationships. People everywhere keep track of distant relatives who are part of their **extended family.** Most North Americans recognize extended family ties, if only when cousins, aunts and uncles, and other distant relatives gather for holidays, family reunions, weddings, and funerals. Theoretically, the number of people who make up your extended family could go on "forever" to include third cousins and beyond. Extended families do not have clear social boundaries; rather, recognized relationships are likely to wither and eventually disappear as relatives become more and more distant. You may know and occasionally interact with all of your first and second cousins, but beyond that range, whether you even know their names depends mostly on circumstances such as whether they live in your town or state.

In contrast, in more traditional societies, most of the important relationships in the lives of individuals are defined by extended kinship ties, so most of a person's relationships with other people depend on whether, and precisely how, they are related. Extended families (and even larger groupings of relatives) are far more important in

Term	Meaning
Kin group	A social group formed on the basis of recognized (including fictive) kin relationships between its members
Nuclear family	A married couple and their unmarried children
Extended family	Culturally recognized relatives of varying degrees of distance
Household	A domestic group, or people who live in the same place and share assets and certain responsibilities

the lives of individuals: You live in the same household with them, you count on them for economic support, you share access to land with them, you and they have common religious duties, and so forth. In such societies, nuclear families are important, but they are embedded in larger, more inclusive kin groups. Some of these groups are enormously large, consisting of hundreds of members, as we see in the next chapter. In this chapter, we focus mainly on domestic groups, especially on nuclear and extended families and the ties that create and bind them.

A **household** (or *domestic group*) is a kin group of one or more nuclear families who live in the same physical space. Among their many functions, households usually have primary responsibility for nurturing and enculturating children. North Americans usually think of the members of a household as living in a single dwelling, such as an apartment, condo, townhouse, or detached single-family dwelling. In some other societies, the nuclear families that together make up a single household live in separate dwellings on land they own jointly. So long as the families use common property like land and tools, cooperate in work, share income or wealth, and recognize themselves as having distinctive identities, they belong to a single *household* even though they live in separate *houses*. We consider types of households later.

The preceding terms referring to groupings based on family and kinship seem simple enough. But it is easy to use one term when technically you mean another, which can lead to confusion. The Concept Review may provide some help.

Households are not always formed exclusively by family or marital ties, as gay and lesbian couples, heterosexual unmarried couples living together, and various other roommates and housemates illustrate. In fact, in a great many societies, people incorporate unrelated

people into their family and household, acting and feeling toward them in the same way as they do consanguineous relatives. This practice is widespread enough that ethnologists have a phrase for it: **fictive kinship,** in which individuals who are not actually biological relatives act toward one another as if they were kin. Adoption is the most familiar example. In many islands of the Pacific, it is very common for a couple to adopt (or foster) one or more children, whether or not they have parented children themselves. Unlike in most Western nations, usually the adopted children keep up ties with their biological parents, who are often relatives of their adopted parents. For many purposes, such children in effect have two sets of parents to support them emotionally and economically.

This chapter mainly concerns the diversity in marriage and family among humanity. But before continuing, we note that everywhere there are rules that govern who may and may not marry. The most universal of these rules is the *incest taboo,* which is so basic that we discuss it first.

Incest Taboos

Rules against sexual intercourse between relatives are called **incest taboos.** Incest taboos are cultural universals (see Chapter 2), but there are some qualifications to this generalization. For one thing, the specific relatives to whom the taboos apply vary from people to people. Some societies prohibit sex and marriage between all first cousins, whereas others not only allow but prefer marriage among certain cousins. We cover such cases later.

For another thing, nearly every society prohibits sex between nuclear family members, but there are three documented cases in which sexual intercourse between siblings was permitted: the ancient Hawaiians, the pre-historic Incas, and the civilization of Egypt. Among the Hawaiians and Incas, incest was allowed only to members of the royal family and existed to preserve the spiritual purity of the royal ancestral bloodline. In ancient Egypt, even common people sometimes married (and presumably had sex with) their own siblings. Everywhere else in the known world, mating between siblings and between parents and children is culturally forbidden (which is not the same as saying it does not occur). In most cultures, the incest taboo is extended beyond the nuclear family to prohibit sex between uncles and nieces, aunts and nephews, and some kinds of cousins. Other than the widespread extension to these relatives, cultures vary in the categories of kinfolk with whom sex is tabooed.

Anthropologists have wondered a lot about why nuclear family incest is almost universally taboo. This wonder sometimes surprises people who are not anthropologists, who usually think that intercourse within the family is universally prohibited because inbreeding is genetically harmful to the children. Indeed, in Euro-American societies, incest is illegal because science has demonstrated that the offspring of incestuous matings have a significantly higher chance of exhibiting harmful recessive genes. But humans had laws or enforced norms against incest long before genetic science even existed, so clearly biomedical knowledge is not the primary explanation for the universality of the incest taboo.

What, then, are some other reasons for the nuclear family incest taboo? There are four major explanations.

The first two explanations begin with the assumption that many or most people have sexual desire for their close relatives. Because acting on these desires would somehow harm others in their family or other group, the incest taboo exists to help groups control such behavior. In many cultures, adults teach children that incest is one of the most reprehensible crimes, and this culturally imposed prohibition forces people to repress their own desire. Several specific hypotheses make these assumptions, but we discuss only two of the most credible.

"Marry Out or Die Out" is the idea first proposed by E. B. Tylor, one of the nineteenth-century evolutionists we introduced in Chapter 4. Tylor noticed that a rule prohibiting marriage between close relatives forces people to seek their mates outside their domestic groups. These marriages force families to establish relationships with one another—relationships that widen the scale of economic and political cooperation. Over time, groups that marry out had an advantage over those that did not, so eventually all groups developed incest taboos.

As we note later, Tylor's idea contains an important insight: Outmarriage does indeed offer advantages to those domestic groups that practice it. Unfortunately, this insight does not pertain to the incest taboo. There is no necessary reason a successful family could not allow sexual relations between its members but forbid them to marry one another. This hypothesis thus confuses the incest taboo ("Thou shalt not have sexual intercourse within thine own domestic group") with outmarriage rules ("Thou shalt not marry within thine own domestic group").

The "Peace in the Family" hypothesis, also called the *family disruption hypothesis,* argues that nuclear family incest would lead to intrafamilial sexual rivalry and competition. It would interfere with the normal and essential functions of the family, such as economic cooperation and enculturation. It also might undermine the authority of the parental generation of the family, who would be constantly challenged by their children. Brothers might be brought to blows over their sisters, and vice versa. And imagine the status and role confusions: for example, if a man had children by his daughter, the daughter's children would also be her half-siblings, and the father's children would simultaneously be his grandchildren.

This hypothesis is plausible but difficult to evaluate. We do not know whether sexual relations in the family would threaten the family's peace because the nuclear family incest taboo is well-nigh universal. Would brothers and sisters peacefully wait their turns? Probably they would not, but we have no way of testing the hypothesis. At any rate, the incest taboo is sometimes extended to very distant relatives who hardly know one another, and family disruption cannot explain these extensions.

The other two explanations both assume that the majority of people have little sexual desire for their close relatives. The two hypotheses are closely related and, indeed, complementary. Also, the same objection apples to both: If there is so little sexual desire between close relatives, then why do people need a taboo at all?

"Inbreeding Avoidance" is the cultural rationale for the taboo that is familiar to most of our readers. Both genetic theory and experimentation have firmly established that offspring of sexual unions between close relatives have a significantly higher probability of inheriting homozygously recessive harmful alleles that show up phenotypically; that is, incest is bad for the children and the "gene pool." The inbreeding avoidance explanation simply states that the incest taboo exists to reduce the incidence of mating between close relatives.

Why, then, do anthropologists not embrace the notion that avoiding intercourse with one's close relatives has the biological function of preventing the harmful genetic effects of inbreeding? One reason has already been mentioned. Many preindustrial peoples are unaware of these harmful genetic effects, so these effects cannot consciously be the reason for the taboo. This objection, however, is not fatal to the inbreeding-avoidance idea because the hypothesis does not require awareness that "it's bad for the children." Nonhuman primates do not "know" that inbreeding increases the expression of deleterious alleles, but they act as if they know: they generally do not mate with close genetic relatives. We need only postulate that throughout humanity's evolutionary history, those individuals who mated with their close relatives left fewer surviving and reproducing offspring than those who did not. The genes of those who did not interbreed with their close relatives would have spread within the population. Evolution then "built in" a lack of sexual desire for close relatives over a long time span; our knowledge is instinctive, not conscious. This idea about the incest taboo, of course, is consistent with evolutionary psychology (see Chapter 4), the general theory that humanity's behavior has been shaped by genetic evolution. (Notice that evolution would also have had to build in knowledge of who one's close relatives are, or who they are most likely to be.)

Another objection is more serious: Many peoples do not apply the taboo to the kinds of relatives that inbreeding avoidance predicts they should. For example, some peoples allow or encourage marriage (which normally involves reproduction) between one set of cousins but prohibit both marriage and sexual intercourse with another set of cousins who are equally closely related genetically. Among certain populations, it is quite common for a man to marry his mother's brother's daughter, but for his father's brother's daughter to be prohibited as both a sexual and marriage partner. Yet among other peoples, a man is encouraged to marry his father's brother's daughter. Now why should some populations prohibit sex with one kind of cousin and others encourage it? In other words, the inbreeding-avoidance theory does not explain the cross-cultural variability in the kinds of relatives to whom the taboo applies. It predicts (or seems to predict) that all peoples ought to prohibit the same relatives.

The "Familiarity Breeds Disinterest" explanation holds that males and females who are closely associated during childhood have little sexual desire for one another when they grow up. Also called the *childhood familiarity hypothesis,* this hypothesis was first proposed by a nineteenth-century scholar named Edward Westermarck. It was rejected for decades but became popular again in the 1970s because of some ethnographic studies that seem to support it.

One study is from the *kibbutzim,* an agricultural collective first established in Israel in the 1950s. Nearly all *kibbutzim* are now disbanded, but in the past children were raised not in families by their parents but in communal peer groups by specialists in child care. Several infants of similar age were placed in a common nursery soon after birth. They were nourished and enculturated

◄ On the kibbutzim of Israel, children raised in communal nurseries tended not to be interested in one another sexually, supporting the "familiarity breeds disinterest" theory of the incest taboo. Here four kibbutz children are getting ready for bed after their baths.

as a group, with more children joining them later around our kindergarten age. A peer group of 10 to 20 children was raised together until adolescence, more or less as if they were siblings. Boys and girls raised in the same peer group were not forbidden to marry and in fact were often encouraged to get together. But people raised together almost never married, although they had plenty of opportunities to get to know one another. Their behavior thus supports the "familiarity breeds disinterest" idea.

Arthur Wolf's study of marriage in Taiwan also supports the childhood-familiarity theory. Some Taiwanese couples with male children "adopted" girls to be reared and trained in their households as future wives for their sons. In each family, a boy and girl grew up together in the same household—in most respects just like brother and sister—and were expected to marry. If it is true that children raised together have little sexual interest in one another, then there should be less sexual activity and greater marital difficulties for these couples than for other Taiwanese. Wolf found that, in fact, these couples had fewer children, higher rates of divorce, and more extramarital sexual activity than other couples.

Finally, evidence from an Arab village in Lebanon studied by Justin McCabe supports Westermarck's hypothesis. For a variety of reasons, it is fairly common in the Middle East for a man to marry one of his father's brother's daughters. In fact, in the village studied, about 20 percent of all marriages were between men and women whose fathers were brothers. These cousins were in constant childhood association with one another because of the close personal relationship between their fathers. If childhood familiarity does indeed produce adult sexual disinterest, then it should be revealed in these marriages. In fact, it is: these cousin marriages had three times the divorce rate and produced fewer children than other kinds of marriage.

So, some ethnographic research suggests sexual disinterest between individuals who have intimate childhood associations. This lack of desire cannot be universal, or there would never be any nuclear family incest. And the disinterest is not absolute, or the unusual marriages in Taiwan and Lebanon just described would have no children at all. However, the childhood-familiarity hypothesis does explain why most people do not commit incest within the nuclear family—they have no desire to do so.

Further, if childhood familiarity does lead to erotic disinterest as adults, then the inbreeding-avoidance explanation is also supported. To avoid inbreeding, people must have some way of recognizing their close relatives.

In general, my close relatives are likely to be those with whom I was raised, so if I avoid mating with my childhood associates, I generally will not be inbreeding. Both these hypotheses taken together are capable of explaining why nuclear family incest is uncommon.

Notice, though, that neither the inbreeding-avoidance nor the childhood-familiarity hypothesis explains why nuclear family incest is usually *punished* whenever it does occur. It is easy to see why, for example, a sister would rather reproduce with a nonrelative than with her brother (at least it is easy to see if we think she lacks desire for her brother!). But how does the lack of desire by individuals become a punishable offense or, in many cultures, a capital crime? Why should anyone else care?

Some scholars have used the very existence of a taboo on incest to argue against both the inbreeding-avoidance and childhood-familiarity explanations. Their argument is that if people generally do not have erotic feelings toward close relatives, then cultures do not need a taboo. The fact that there is a taboo at all shows sexual desire for close kin, for why prohibit an action that people have no desire to commit? But this objection is unfair because neither explanation denies that some people have sexual desire for their relatives. There is merely evidence suggesting that *most* people do not. We can see why this objection is unfair with an analogous legal prohibition: Few people argue that a legal prohibition on murder or assault proves that most people want to commit these acts.

To return to our overall discussion, notice that three of the four hypotheses account mainly for the incest prohibitions within the nuclear family. They therefore cannot explain everything about incest taboos because in most human populations incest prohibitions are extended to more-distant relations. Only the "marry out or die out" hypothesis explains the extension of the incest taboo beyond the nuclear family. But, as we saw earlier, this hypothesis explains only why people marry outside the domestic group, not why cultures prohibit incest within domestic groups. This point leads naturally into marriage.

Marriage

Biologically speaking, procreation creates the family relationships of an individual: who your parents are determines your grandparents, your aunts and uncles, your cousins, and so forth. To the extent that a procreating couple are married, marriage and its resulting family relationships seem pretty basic. How many ways can people marry and have families? Quite a few, it turns out. We begin with marriage.

Defining Marriage

What is marriage? Persons with little knowledge of cultural diversity might say that marriage is a relationship between a woman and a man involving romantic love, sexual activity, cohabitation, child rearing, and shared joys and burdens of life. People trained in law might also note that marriage has legal aspects, such as joint property rights and child care obligations. Religious people may want to include their beliefs that marriage is a relationship sanctioned by God, a relationship that should last until the parties are separated by death. Gay, lesbian, and bisexual people will want to add their own provisions.

Although broadly applicable in many modern nations, the preceding definitions obscure the diversity in marriages that anthropologists have uncovered. For example, choosing one's spouse is not always a private matter to be decided by the couple. In many cultures, marriage is likely to be a *public* matter that involves a broad range of relatives who must consent to or even arrange the marriage.

Further, as often as not, romantic love is not considered necessary for marriage, and sometimes it is not even relevant to the relationship. Couples do not marry because they "fall in love." For example, in traditional China, Korea, and Japan, a man and a woman seldom had a chance to fall in love before they married because they usually hardly knew each other and often had not even met. Sometimes boys and girls were betrothed at birth or as children. Even when couples married as adults, the marriage was arranged by their parents with the aid of a matchmaker, usually a female relative of the groom's family or a woman hired by them. She tried to find a woman of suitable age, wealth, status, and disposition to become a wife for the young man. The matchmaker would "match" not only the couple to each other, but also the woman to the husband's parents. Once she married, the wife would be incorporated into her husband's family; her labor would be under the control of her husband's parents, especially her mother-in-law; she would worship the ancestors of her husband's family, not those of her own parents; her behavior would be closely watched lest she disgrace her in-laws; and her children would become members of her husband's kin group, not her own.

Even cohabitation in the same house does not universally accompany marriage. In many villages in Melanesia, Southeast Asia, and Africa, the men sleep and spend much of their time in a communal house (called, appropriately, the *men's house*), while their wives and young children live and sleep in a separate dwelling.

Other Western cultural notions of and customs about marriage do not apply elsewhere. Sex is not always confined to the marriage bed (or mat). There may or may not be a formal ceremony (wedding) recognizing or validating a new marriage. The marital tie may be fragile or temporary, with individuals expecting to have several spouses during the course of their lives. Or the tie may be so strong that even death does not end it. For example, in parts of old India, there were strict rules against the remarriage of a higher-caste widow, and such a widow often followed her husband to the grave by throwing herself onto his cremation fire (a practice now illegal in India).

Finally, in case you are wondering, there are culturally legitimate marital relationships that are not between a man and a woman. Among the Nuer of the southern Sudan, sometimes an older, well-off woman pays the bridewealth needed to marry a girl. The girl then takes male lovers and bears children, who are incorporated into the kin group of the older woman. The pastoral and horticultural Nandi of Kenya allow marriage between women. Some men have more than one wife, and at her husband's death surviving wives normally receive a share of his cattle, which they, in turn, pass along to their own sons. When a married woman grows too old to bear children and happens to have no sons to inherit the cattle given her by her husband, she may take a younger woman as her wife, thus becoming a "female husband." She picks a sexual partner for her young wife, whose male children then become the heirs of the "female husband." The two women, however, are not supposed to be sexually active after the birth, with other men as well as with each other. Regina Smith Oboler, who worked among the Nandi, reported that the relationship was almost identical to that between a married woman and a man. (We have more to say on same-sex relationships in Chapter 11.)

Because of all this diversity, formulating a definition of marriage that encompasses all the cross-cultural variations in the relationship is hard because there will always be a society that does not fit the definition. As you can imagine, numerous definitions have been offered, but there is still no agreement on the "best" one. Most anthropologists agree, however, that marriage in *most* human societies involves the following:

- A culturally defined relationship between a man and a woman from different families, which involves and regulates sexual intercourse and legitimizes children

- A set of rights the couple and their families obtain over each other, including rights over children born to the woman
- An assignment of responsibility for nurturing and enculturating children to the spouses and/or to one or both sets of their relatives
- A creation of variably important bonds and relationships between the families of the couple that have social, economic, political, and sometimes ritual dimensions

When we define marriage in this way, do all societies have some form of marriage?

This question is tricky, and not just because the definition above is problematic. But the answer appears to be no. Consider the Na, an ethnic group of Yunnan Province in the south of China. (The Na are ethnically distinct from the Han, China's majority population.) A typical Na adult woman remains at her home, living with her siblings and other members of her consanguineous family. Men visit her at night for sexual intercourse, but there is no "commitment" or "obligation"; both people have multiple sexual partners, often simultaneously. The man does not spend the night and seems to have no obligation to his children, or even to recognize them as his. Children are raised by their mother and her own family, so the Na have no nuclear families. Either the woman or her male visitor may initiate the communication that leads to their relationship, but it is always the man who visits and the woman who stays at home. The Na, therefore, lack all four aspects of the definition of marriage given above, so they have no marriage as we define the term, nor do they have marriage as most people understand it. Cai Hua, the Han Chinese ethnographer, says that the Na show that marriage and nuclear families are not universal human institutions. (Where, we might ask, is the "backbone" of Na society?)

The Na are very unusual. Nearly all other peoples have some institution that is recognizably "marriage."

Functions of Marriage

The near-universality of marriage suggests that marriage does important and useful things for individuals, families, and/or society at large. Three functions are among the most important.

1. Marriage forms the social bonds and creates the social relationships that provide for the material needs, social support, and enculturation of children. Most cultures recognize that forming a (variably) stable bond between a woman and her husband is an important reason to marry. In the human species, the tie between mothers and fathers is more important than in most other animals because of the lengthy dependence of children on adults. Until age 10 or older, children are largely dependent on adults for food, shelter, protection, and other bodily needs. Equally important, children need adults for the social learning that is crucial to complete their psychological and social development. It is theoretically possible that children *need* only one adult, the mother. But, generally, children benefit from multiple caretakers and supporters, and marriage helps to create and expand relationships that help children.

2. Marriage defines the rights and obligations a couple have toward each other and toward other people. Some rights and obligations, of course, concern sex. The marriage bond reduces (but does not eliminate) potential conflicts over sexual access by defining and limiting adult sexual access to certain individuals (normatively or legally, at any rate). Extramarital sex is not, of course, prohibited to the same degree in all cultures, but limitations are placed on it, and usually it is punished formally or informally. In the vast majority of societies, the nurturing and care of young infants are entrusted mainly to mothers, so mothers need to be supported for some variable period after childbirth by their husbands or relatives. Other rights and duties concern the allocation of work and other activities. All cultures divide up work by sex and age in some way: Men do some kinds of tasks, women other kinds. Although the work usually overlaps, there is enough differentiation in most communities that the products and services produced by women must somehow be made available to men, and vice versa. Marriage helps define these rights and duties and establishes the household within which family members do things for one another.

3. Marriage creates new relationships between families and other kinds of kin groups. In a few societies, nuclear families are physically able to produce what they need to survive with their own labor and resources. But the incest taboo forces individuals to marry someone other than their immediate relatives. Every such marriage creates a potential new set of (affinal) relationships between the relatives of the couple. The importance attached to these affinal relationships varies cross-culturally. At the very least, the families of the wife and husband have a common interest in the children. In addition, a great many societies use the relationships created by intermarriage to establish important trade relationships or political alliances, as we see later.

Because marriage—and the new nuclear family each marriage creates—is useful to individuals and to societies in these and other ways, a relationship like marriage and a group like the family are almost universal among the world's cultures. However, no particular *form* of marriage or *type* of family is universal. Cultures evolved various marriage and family systems to perform these functions. To show how diverse these systems can be, we now consider two unusual systems.

Two Unusual Forms

"Marriage" among the Nayar of southern India.

Before Great Britain assumed colonial control over their part of India in 1792, the Nayar were a warrior caste (see Chapter 13). Because so many Nayar men served as soldiers for several surrounding Indian kingdoms, they were away from their homes and villages much of the time. Frequent male absence affected marriage and

▲ Human children are dependent on adult care for many years, as this photo of a Laotian woman and her children reminds us. Providing for the physical and emotional needs of children is everywhere a major function of families.

family life. The Nayar almost certainly lacked nuclear families, in the sense of a couple and their offspring living together and sharing responsibilities. Depending on how we define marriage, they may have had no marriage either. Yet Nayar people managed all the "functions" of marriage listed above. How did sexuality and provision for children work in such circumstances?

Nayar villages were composed of a number of kin groups. At birth, most children became members of the kin group of their mother. Each group was linked for certain ceremonial purposes to several other groups, either from its own or from neighboring villages. Both Nayar women and men known to engage in sexual relations with anyone in their own kin group were put to death because such behavior was considered incest. Restrictions on Nayar women were even more severe: Under penalty of death or ostracism, they had to confine their sexual activity to men of their own or a higher subcaste.

Every few years, all the girls of a kin group who were nearing puberty gathered for a large ceremony, the purpose of which was to ceremonially "marry" these girls to selected men from the linked kin groups. At the ceremony, each "groom" tied a gold ornament around the neck of his "bride." Each couple then went to a secluded place for three days, where they may have had sexual relations. Afterward, the "grooms" left the village, and none had any further responsibilities to his "bride"; indeed, he might never even see her again. For her part, the "bride" and the children she would later bear had only to perform a certain ritual for her ceremonial "husband" when he died. The ritual tying of the ornament by a man of a linked kin group did, however, establish a girl as an adult, able to have sexual liaisons with other men when she matured.

After her "marriage," each girl continued to live with her own consanguineous relatives. When she reached menarche, she began to receive nighttime male visitors from other kin groups. She established long-lasting relationships with some of her partners, who were expected to give her small luxury gifts periodically but did not live with her. None of her partners supported her or her children in any way other than these occasional gifts; indeed, they also visited other women and fathered other children. The food and clothing of a woman and her children were supplied by her brothers and other members of her family, who also provided an inheritance for her children. So, a woman looked to her own sisters and brothers rather than to her sexual partner(s) for most of the economic support for herself and her children.

A Nayar woman's early "marriage," then, did not establish a nuclear family, nor did her later sexual partners live with her or support her children. There was only one other thing a woman required from her partners: When she got pregnant, one of them had to admit that he could have been the father of her child by paying the fees for the midwife who helped deliver the baby. If none of her partners did so, it was assumed that she had had sexual intercourse with someone of a lower caste. She, and sometimes her child, would be expelled from her kin group or killed.

Cross-generational marriage among the Tiwi of northern Australia.

In most societies, people who marry are comparable in age. Often the husband is older, sometimes significantly older. The Tiwi, who traditionally lived on the Bathurst Islands just off the coast of northern Australia, were unusual because both sexes frequently married people of markedly different ages—in fact, most spouses belonged to different generations. Ethnographer C. W. M. Hart worked among the Tiwi in the late 1920s, and Arnold Pilling worked there in the early 1950s. Jane Goodale's later work focused on Tiwi women.

Like other aboriginal peoples of Australia, the Tiwi were exclusively hunters and gatherers. Male elders made most of the important decisions in a band, including decisions about foraging activities and the distribution of food. Many elderly men were polygynous—that is, they had more than one wife. Polygynous men had access to lots of food from their wives' gathering and fishing, and they could acquire prestige by distributing the food widely to other families. Other male elders were desired as allies, and allies could be acquired by food distribution and by another means to be discussed in a moment. Tiwi prized meat, but as men reached their 50s and 60s, they were unable to hunt effectively. To hunt meat, they needed sons, which they generally had, and sons-in-law, which they could get by marrying off their daughters.

Tiwi marriage is unusual because of two rare customs. First, when a girl was born, she was almost immediately promised as a wife to some other man. This is "infant betrothal," with the husband selected by the infant's father. Second, there was a cultural requirement that all females be married virtually all their lives. So after her betrothal, an infant girl was considered already married. And when a woman's husband died, she remarried almost immediately, which we call "widow remarriage."

An astute Tiwi father did not marry his infant daughter to just anyone. He used her marriage to win friends and gain allies. The allies who were most valuable were

men of about his own age, so naturally he tended to marry his daughters to these men. But the relationship created by one such marriage was often reciprocated—if you married your daughter to a friend, you would likely receive his daughter, sooner or later. So a man might gain a wife in return for a daughter.

If a man's wives had daughters when he was in his 40s and 50s (which was common because wives were so young), then he married some of them to men his own age. Not all of them, though, because a man also wanted sons-in-law to come live in his band and help supply meat. An elder would look around for a man in his 20s who seemed like a diligent and skillful hunter and a promising ally. He married some of his daughters to these younger men. When his daughters grew up, his sons-in-law would supply him and his household with meat.

A girl growing into womanhood would already have a husband, most likely one who was perhaps 20 or 30 years older than herself. Of course, this meant that most wives outlived their husbands but did have children by them. By Tiwi custom, widows had to remarry. But to whom? Some young men in their 20s had failed to attract the notice of the elders and therefore had no wives of their own. But they still could be friends and useful allies of the sons of these widowed women. So at the death of her husband, her sons (usually with her consent and approval) married their mother to a man 20 or 30 years her junior. That way, she would have the support of a strong hunter as she aged, and her sons would strengthen a friendship and gain an ally. (Incidentally, Tiwi wives might seem like "pawns," but in fact they were active participants in marital machinations, as Jane Goodale documented in her book, *Tiwi Wives*.)

If you had visited the Tiwi during their traditional life, what would you have observed? Many elderly men had several wives, many of whom were 20 to 30 years younger than themselves. Young men had either no wife at all or only one wife, and that one wife was probably at least 20 years older than her husband. Elderly men were married to women in the prime of their lives, whereas many younger men in their "prime" had wives who were old enough to be their mother. Looked at from the point of view of a typical female's life cycle, she is first a co-wife of a much older man; then after he dies she and her male children arrange for her to marry a man who is young enough to be her son.

We emphasize again that both the Nayar and the Tiwi had unusual marriage systems. (Both systems are no longer operating.) Of course, it is unlikely that either people viewed their marriage practices as "unusual." It was just what they did. Perhaps they even thought it was only natural. Maybe they even considered it the backbone of their societies.

Marriage in Comparative Perspective

The relationship we call marriage varies enormously among cultures. For one thing, most cultures allow multiple spouses. For another, the nature of the marital relationship—living arrangements, what wives and husbands expect from each other, who decides who marries whom, authority patterns, how the relatives of the couple relate to one another, and so forth—differs from people to people. Some of this diversity is described in this section.

Marriage Rules

Everywhere, the choice of a spouse is governed by norms that identify members of some social groups or categories as potential spouses and specify members of other groups or categories as not eligible for marriage. One set of rules is called **exogamous rules.** Exogamy ("outmarriage") means that an individual is prohibited from marrying within her or his own family or other kin group or, less often, village or settlement. Because the incest taboo applies to those people whom the local culture defines as close relatives, members of one's own nuclear family and other close kin are almost everywhere prohibited as spouses. (Recall, incidentally, that the incest taboo prohibits *sex*, whereas rules of exogamy forbid *intermarriage.*)

Other kinds of marriage rules are **endogamous rules.** Endogamy ("inmarriage") means that an individual must marry someone in his or her own social group. The classic example of an endogamous group is the caste in traditional Hindu India (see Chapter 13). Other kinds of endogamous categories are found in orthodox Jews, races in the American South during slavery, and noble classes in many ancient civilizations and states.

Endogamous rules have the effect of maintaining social barriers between groups of people of different social rank. Rules of endogamy maintain the exclusiveness of the endogamous group in two ways. First, they reduce the social contacts and interactions between individuals of different ranks. Intermarriage creates new relationships between the families of the wife and husband and potentially is a means of raising the rank of oneself or one's offspring. Endogamy has the effect of keeping af-

final relationships within the caste, class, ethnic group, race, or whatever; this reinforces ties *within* the endogamous groups and decreases interactions *between* the groups. Second, endogamy symbolically expresses and strengthens the exclusiveness of the endogamous group by preventing its "contamination" by outsiders. This is most apparent with Indian castes because the cultural rationale for caste endogamy is to avoid ritual pollution: the Hindu religion holds that physical contact with members of lower castes places high-caste individuals in a state of spiritual danger, precluding the possibility of marriage between them.

Technically, the term *endogamy* applies only to cultural rules (or even laws) about confining marriage to those within one's own group. But it is important to note the existence of *de facto endogamy,* meaning that although no formal rules or laws require inmarriage, most people marry people who are like themselves. De facto racial and social class endogamy exists in most modern nations, including North America. This is partly because opportunities for members of different classes to get to know one another are often limited. For instance, members of different classes often go to different kinds of schools and often hang out with different sets of friends. Such practices decrease social interactions between classes and thus reduce the possibility that people of different classes will meet and fall in love. De facto endogamy also exists because of powerful norms against marrying outside one's own "kind." Members of elite classes (and parents and other relatives of young people) may worry that would-be spouses of lower-class standing would not fit in with their social circle (to phrase their objection politely). Likewise, interracial couples are warned about the social stigma attached to their relationship and about the "problems" they and their children will encounter. Of course, these problems exist largely because some people continue to think that interracial marriages are problematic! Racial and ethnic barriers to marriage seem to be breaking down in many regions due to improved education and increased interactions between peoples due to globalization. Globalization is changing popular attitudes and affecting marriage and family in some obvious ways, but also in more subtle ways (see the Globalization box).

How Many Spouses?

One way cultures vary in marriage practices is in the number of spouses an individual is allowed to have at a time. There are four logical possibilities:

As interactions between people of diverse nationalities and cultural traditions increase, we have increased opportunities to get to know one another. Students cross national and cultural boundaries in search of better educations or new cultural experiences. Employees of multinational companies fly all over the world buying and selling. Migrants settle in new homelands. Tourists go abroad to see the world or just to increase their stock of travel stories and photos to show and tell their friends.

There are many outcomes of increased global interactions. One is cross-cultural (or transnational) marriages and adoptions. Allow one of your authors (J. P.) a personal story. In the 1950s, my great-uncle married a Japanese American woman. He was a tobacco country boy from North Carolina, born into a family that included die-hard racists among its members. She was a California girl whose family had been in an internment camp for Japanese Americans during World War II. Both families objected strenuously to the marriage, though for different reasons, and ostracized the couple for years. (Eventually, the families accepted the relationship.) In the 1980s, my first cousin married an African American woman who had two daughters, and they soon had a daughter of their own. In the 1990s, another of my first cousins married a man from the Philippines. No one from either family thought much about it, and both families now dote on their two grandsons. In the early 2000s, another of my first cousins (an unmarried man with the same parents as the African American and Philippine American intermarriages) adopted a one-year-old boy from a Chinese orphanage. Everyone in the family is delighted. So, at family reunions, I see black Americans, white/black Americans, two Philippine American boys, and a 5-year-old Chinese-looking boy named Jake—all now members of an extended family whose (Anglo) grandparents were semiliterate tobacco sharecroppers in North Carolina until the 1940s. My own son graduated from college in 2007. His first college girlfriend was from China, his second from India. Who knows if there will be a third and, if so, from where? If none of this seems unusual to you, then you were probably born in the *late* twentieth century.

In the old times, when discussing such relationships, many racially or culturally intolerant people talked about "sticking with your own kind." More polite people discussed all the "problems" such marriages would have because of "society's attitudes."

Such attitudes are still around, of course, but interracial, intercultural, and international marriages are becoming so common that soon almost everyone will know someone who has married inter-someplace. Perhaps we will someday live in a world where most people think that everyone is their "own kind."

Some effects of globalization on marriage and family are more indirect and, therefore, more subtle than my family's story. Take Japan, for example. Japan has been buying from and, especially, selling to the global marketplace since the late nineteenth century, when the nation was "opened up" by the Americans under threat of force. After losing World War II and having two cities destroyed by the only nuclear weapons ever detonated against civilian targets, Japan recovered within two decades. It already had many advantages over countries that Westerners then called *underdeveloped*. It was predominantly urban, and most of its citizens were very well educated. It had been industrialized for decades and was reindustrialized in the 1950s and 1960s. It was comparatively homogeneous linguistically and culturally as well as "racially," so most Japanese agreed on their values and goals. It did not have a lot of political instability and crime.

By the 1970s, Japan was such an economic powerhouse that American car makers and electronics manufacturers justifiably felt threatened. In the postwar (World War II, that is) era, Japan was the first non-American, non-European nation to develop its economy from global trade. As it grew wealthy by exporting its autos, motorcycles, consumer electronics, and other high-tech products, more and more of Japan's rural people left the family farm in search of a better life in the city. This is a common, predictable effect of development: people migrate from farms to cities because of job opportunities and other attractions of city life. Urban households buy their food from farms, theoretically increasing the income of rural people with their purchases.

But a marriage and family problem developed in the Japanese countryside. There was an ancient custom known as *primogeniture,* in which the eldest son inherits the family farm, including the farmhouse, equipment, any livestock, and the land. Younger sons made their own ways, perhaps working for their eldest brother on the family estate, joining a monastery, or moving to another region. What about the women? If a woman's parents were able to arrange her marriage to an eldest son, then she moved in with her husband's family, to live with

1. **Monogamy,** in which every individual is allowed only one spouse
2. **Polygyny,** in which one man is allowed multiple wives
3. **Polyandry,** in which one woman is allowed multiple husbands

4. **Group marriage,** in which several women and men are allowed to be married simultaneously to one another

The last three possibilities are all varieties of **polygamy**—"plural spouses." Notice that the three types of her father- and mother-in-law. Usually, marrying an eldest son was a desirable match for a woman with rural parentage—she would have to work hard serving her husband's parents as well as working on the land of her husband, but she had considerable security for herself and her children, and eventually *she* expected to become the mother-in-law of her eldest son's wife. Then she could take life a bit easier.

As Japan's economy grew after the war and rural-to-urban migration picked up, younger sons from the farm migrated and provided much of the unskilled labor in factories, low-level services, and the enormous construction industry. There was still considerable family pressure on eldest sons to remain behind on the family farm. Land is scarce and valuable, and many Japanese value what's left of their countryside and rural life. Parents, grandparents, and other relatives did not want land that had been in their family to be sold off. Japanese people love rice for its symbolic value as well as for its nutritional value. The dominant political party did not want to see the country become even more dependent on imported foods, so it limited rice imports by various means and heavily subsidized Japan's remaining rice farmers. So, you might think that the eldest sons were doing well.

Unfortunately, few Japanese women were interested in marrying an eldest son. Farm work is hard, and small farm towns are boring. Many Japanese city women have never been to a farm, and most who have would never dream of moving there. A farm wife probably will live with her husband's parents, with little privacy, and will have to care for them when they grow old. Throughout the countryside, new marriage norms eroded the ability of parents to control the marriages of their daughters, so even most young, rural women were unwilling to marry a farm boy. Better to marry a "salaryman"—a man with a reliable and well-paying job in Tokyo or Kyoto or Osaka or one of more than a dozen other Japanese cities with a million or more people. The husband would work long hours and might not come home until midnight, but until recently Japanese wives expected much less socially and romantically from their husbands than Western wives. Odds are, a Japanese husband will turn control over his salary to his wife, who can use it for household expenses and save for their children's education.

In the view of many rural Japanese, the shortage of wives for farmers became a crisis. In one village in the late 1980s,

of unmarried persons between ages 25 and 39, 120 were men and only 31 were women, a ratio of 4:1. Some Japanese villages began to organize for the purpose of finding wives for their unmarried men, not all of whom were still young. One mountain village placed newspapers ads, promising free winter skiing vacations to all young women who visited and agreed to meet its men. Over a five-year period, 300 women responded, but none became wives as a result. In another mountain village of 7,000, there were three bachelors for every unmarried woman, so the local government became a marriage agent. It brought in 22 women from the Philippines, South Korea, Thailand, and other Asian countries to marry its men, many in their 40s and 50s. Some marriages endured, but others ended in divorce because of the labor demands of farm life, the burden wives bore in caring for their husband's elderly parents, and cultural differences. Small businesses developed that offered counseling services for bicultural couples and served as marriage brokers to match Japanese men with foreign women.

Even today, many Japanese farm men remain bachelors. Farming in Japan is now primarily a part-time occupation—farmers find off-season jobs in construction or other tasks, unable to make an acceptable living even with government subsidies. And farming is now largely performed by older persons. For example, in one important rice-growing area, between 1980 and 2003, the number of people making most of their money from farming fell by 56 percent, and the number of people between ages 15 and 59 fell by 83 percent. There was one increase, though: there were 600 more farmers older than 70 in 2003 than in 1980.

Critical Thinking Questions

1. Do you know people who have married interculturally or interracially? Do they have any special problems?

2. The Japanese government could stop supporting Japanese farmers and let the Japanese people buy most of their grains in the international market. Is this a good idea?

Sources: Bernstein (1983); James Brooke, "Japan Farms: An Old Man's Game," *New York Times,* November 7, 2003, Kunio (1988); Joji Sakurai, "Japan Looks to Foreign Brides to Save Its Villages," *Delaware Gazette,* May 19, 1997, p. 12

polygamy refer to the number of spouses *allowed* to a person, not necessarily to how many spouses most people have. For example, in polygynous cultures, men are permitted more than one wife, but only a minority of men actually have more than one.

It may surprise members of monogamous societies to learn that most of the world's cultures historically allowed polygamy. The most common form of plural marriage is polygyny. In the past, before colonialism had affected most of the world's peoples, about three-fourths of all societies allowed a man to have two or more wives. Today, polygyny is allowed in many modern nations in the Middle East, and it remains common among indigenous tribal peoples of Africa, Southeast Asia, and Amazonia. Recent American news stories leave the impression that many Mormons still practice polygyny, but in fact the church outlawed it in the nineteenth century, and the vast majority of Mormon faithful disavow the practice.

Polyandry is rare. It is documented in fewer than a dozen societies—less than 1 percent of the world's cultures. Group marriage, so far as we know, has never been a characteristic form of marriage in a whole human society. Indeed, most anthropologists believe that group marriage, where it has occurred, has been a short-lived phenomenon brought about by highly unusual circumstances.

Many Westerners misunderstand the nature of polygamous marriages, seeing them mainly as attempts, usually by men, to get access to more sexual partners. We fail to recognize the social and economic conditions that make these forms of marriage advantageous. We now look at these conditions for polygynous and polyandrous societies.

Polygyny. Even in societies that allow polygyny, only a minority of men actually have more than one wife. Thus, polygyny exists as an alternative form of marriage, rather than the predominant (most common) form. In those societies that allow it, polygyny ordinarily is the preferred form of marriage, at least for men. Speaking generally, men of high rank and status or wealthy men are the ones who have plural wives, although there are many exceptions.

Even with only a minority of men married polygynously, an obvious problem exists for some other men: If some men have two or more wives, this reduces the number of marriageable women so that some other men cannot marry. This is, in fact, often the case. In other cases, this problem is not as serious as one might think, because in many populations, there are more marriageable women than men at any one time. More males than females may die prematurely because they engage in hazardous activities, such as warfare and hunting. Higher male death rates increase the number of men who are able to find wives, even though some men are polygynous.

From the female perspective, in many societies polygyny has the beneficial effect of ensuring that virtually all women find husbands. Becoming married is often important for a woman's welfare because marriage legitimizes her children, and in many cultures children are her main or only source of social security—they are the people she depends on to support her in old age. There is another reason a woman wants to marry: to ensure that her children are well provided for. In the majority of polygynous societies, inheritance of land, livestock, and other wealth and productive property passes from fathers to sons. A woman need not marry to bear children, but she does

▶ Polygyny is allowed as a form of marriage in many of the world's cultures. This is a Maasai man with his wives and children. Maasai are a cattle-herding people of Kenya and Tanzania.

want a husband to ensure that her sons have an adequate inheritance (her married daughters usually acquire their resources from their own husbands). Thus, in societies in which for some reason there are more adult women than men, polygyny provides a means for almost all women to gain the benefits of husbands for both themselves and their children.

For their part, most men prefer to have two or more wives. Men usually have both social and economic incentives for marrying several women. Socially, a man's status commonly is directly related to the size of his family and, hence, to the number of his wives and children. Also, when a man marries more than one woman, he acquires a new set of affines—fathers- and brothers-in-law whom he can call on for support, trade, or political alliances. Economically, there are also short- and long-term benefits, especially in horticultural and pastoral adaptations, where a woman's labor is important in providing food and wealth to her family. The more wives and children a man has, the larger the workforce available to his household. In pastoral societies in Africa and elsewhere, polygyny enables a man to increase the size of his herds because he has more herders (wives and children) to tend livestock. Similarly, in those farming societies in which female labor is important, a polygynous man has more family members to tend fields and harvest crops. As he grows older, he will have more children and grandchildren to look after his herds or work his fields and care for him. Thus, as long as he has the resources to support them, a man usually tries to acquire additional wives.

What determines whether a particular man is *able* to acquire more than one wife? The answer is usually wealth: only well-to-do men are able to afford more than one wife. "Afford," however, does not mean what North Americans might think; it is often more a matter of being able to *acquire* additional wives than of being able to *support* them. Most polygynous peoples have the custom of bridewealth (discussed later), which requires a prospective groom and his relatives to give livestock, money, or other wealth objects to the kin of the bride. Although fathers and other relatives are typically obliged to help a young man raise bridewealth for one wife, only a minority of men can get together sufficient resources to provide bridewealth for additional wives.

There may be social and economic advantages for the cowives of a polygynous man. Many North Americans think that, given a choice, no woman wants to be part of a "harem." But the most prestigious marriage for a woman is to a husband of wealth and status—the type of man who is most likely to have married other women.

Not only will the woman herself be better provided for, but her children may also receive larger inheritances of land, livestock, wealth, or other property. In addition, cowives may lighten a woman's workload. Cowives usually work together and cooperate on chores such as producing, processing, and preparing food, tending livestock, and caring for children. Thus, in many societies, it is not unusual for a wife to encourage her husband to take additional wives to assist her in her chores.

Despite their advantages for both men and women, polygynous marriages have inherent problems. A common problem is rivalry between cowives and favoritism by husbands. Several strategies are used in polygynous societies to minimize friction within these families. One way is for a man to marry women who are sisters, a widespread practice known as *sororal polygyny*. The rationale for sororal polygyny is that sisters are raised together, are used to working together, have preexisting emotional bonds, and are likely to be less jealous of one another. Sisters are, therefore, likely to be more cooperative than wives who are not related to one another—a point consistent with evolutionary psychology (see Chapter 4).

In most cultures in which a man marries a number of women who are unrelated, each wife usually has her own separate dwelling, which helps to minimize conflict among the cowives. Also, cowives are usually allocated different livestock to care for, and they may have separate gardens to tend and harvest. The effect of such practices is that each wife, together with her children, is semi-independent from the other wives. Despite such practices, rivalry and jealousy among cowives are problems in many polygynous marriages.

Polyandry. Polyandry, the marriage of one woman simultaneously to two or more men, is a documented practice in only about a dozen societies. Much has been written about this unusual form of marriage, but ethnologists have not yet satisfactorily explained it. Some believe that female infanticide is partly responsible, arguing that the death of large numbers of girls would produce a shortage of adult women, which would lead several men to be willing to share a wife. All else being equal, female infanticide does indeed have the effect of decreasing the number of marriageable women, but far more human groups allow many of their female infants to die than practice polyandry. Female infanticide is not a *general* explanation for polyandry.

Rather than discussing general explanations, we note that wherever polyandry exists, it does so as an alternative form of marriage. Like polygyny, polyandry is *allowed,* but it is not the *predominant* form of marriage; most couples are monogamous even where polyandry is allowed. Therefore, to understand the reasons for polyandry, we indicate some of the special conditions that lead some people (namely, husbands and their joint wife) to choose to join in a polyandrous marriage.

The insufficiency of a family's land to support all its heirs is one such condition. Many families in farming communities have faced the following dilemma: Our land is barely adequate, and all available farmland is already owned by another family or by a landlord, so we cannot provide all our children with enough land to support them and their families. Many European peasants faced this problem during the Middle Ages and even into the nineteenth century. In Ireland and some other parts of Europe as well as Japan, one solution was *primogeniture,* or inheritance by the eldest: the oldest son inherited the farm and most of its property, and the younger sons had to find other ways of supporting themselves. Younger sons served in the army or became priests or found some other occupation. Daughters who did not marry usually either remained at home or joined a nunnery. After the Industrial Revolution in the late 1700s, many migrated to cities and went to work in factories.

Some peoples of the Himalayas developed another solution—polyandry. The rugged topography and high altitude of Tibet and Nepal sharply limit the supply of farmland. A farm may be adequate to support only a single family, but many couples have three or more sons. If the sons divide their inheritance by each taking his own wife, the land would become so fragmented that the brothers' families would be impoverished. To solve this problem, sometimes all the sons marry one woman. This form of polyandry, called *fraternal polyandry,* helps to keep the farm and family intact and limits the number of children in the family. Although the oldest son usually assumes primary responsibility for the wife and children, the joint wife is not supposed to favor him or his brothers sexually. When children are born, ideally each brother treats them as if they were his own, even if he knows that a particular child was fathered by one of his brothers.

What are the benefits of fraternal polyandry? For the brothers, sharing a wife preserves the family property, keeping the land, the livestock, the house, and other wealth together. Also, one brother can stay in the village and work the family land during the summer, while another brother takes the livestock to high mountain pastures and a third brother (if present) visits towns in the lowlands to sell the family's products. This system also

has advantages for the wife, who has multiple husbands to work for her and help support her and her children. Her life is usually less physically strenuous, and she usually has a higher standard of living than a woman married to only one man.

Although Himalayan polyandry has economic advantages, problems can arise. A younger brother can decide at any time to end the arrangement, claim his portion of the family property, marry another woman, and establish his own family. The oldest brother does not have this option because, as head of the family, he bears primary responsibility for supporting the wife and children.

Marriage Alliances

Cultures vary in the importance they attach to the tie between wives and husbands. In some cultures, there is no formal wedding ceremony. Instead, a couple is socially recognized as "married" when they regularly live together and as "divorced" when one of them moves out. Each partner retains her or his own separate property, so the separation or divorce is not very "messy." In the contemporary United States, the wedding ceremony is often a big and expensive affair, marriages are supposed to endure, and couples usually own houses, furniture, and other property jointly. Yet about half of all new American marriages will end in divorce, many quite messy because of conflicts over property and custody of the children. For many Americans, monogamy turns out to be *serial monogamy,* meaning only one legal spouse at a time.

Many cultures consider the marital relationship to be far more serious. In many, marriage establishes lasting social relationships and bonds not just between the couple but also between their families and other relatives. The affinal ties between kin groups created by intermarriage are frequently important not only socially but also economically, politically, and often ritually. Marriage establishes an *alliance* between the members of two kin groups, and in many cultures, **marriage alliances** are critical for the well-being and even survival of the intermarried groups. This appears to have been the case among the ancient Israelites because Moses says in Genesis (34:16): "Then we will give our daughters unto you, and we will take your daughters to us, and we will dwell with you, and we will become one people."

A good example of how intermarriage creates and maintains ties between kin groups is provided by the Yanomamö, a horticultural and hunting tribe of the Amazon rain forest of South America. Most Yanomamö villages feared attacks by enemies, so a village had to be prepared to defend itself. Also, men of each village periodically went on raids intended to capture the women and resources of their enemies. It was, therefore, advantageous for villages to establish and maintain military alliances for mutual defense and offense, because the more men a village could mobilize as warriors, the more likely it was to be successful in conflicts. Smaller villages almost had to form alliances or they would be victimized by their more numerous enemies. Having allies was also helpful in case of military defeat: a defeated group could take refuge with an allied village, whose members would feed and protect the refugees until they could establish productive gardens in a new location.

Marriage was a key strategy in creating and maintaining these alliances. When the men of a Yanomamö village wanted to form an alliance with another village, they began by trading. For instance, one village might tell the other it needed clay pots and would be willing to trade its bows for them, or it might say it needed hallucinogenic drugs used in shamanistic curing and would trade its hammocks for them. The people of each village were capable of making all these products for themselves, but trade provided the excuse for visiting one another to begin forming an alliance. If no trouble broke out during the trading—for a Yanomamö village did not even trust its longtime allies, much less its prospective allies—the relationship might extend to mutual invitations to feasts. If the feasts did not turn violent, the men of the two villages would agree to give some of their "sisters" (female relatives) to one another. This was considered the final stage of alliance formation; once the villages had exchanged women, the alliance was—by Yanomamö standards—secure.

The Yanomamö illustrate how intermarriage creates bonds and establishes important political relationships between villages. Among many peoples, these bonds and relationships are important to families or entire communities. If marriages are a means of establishing ties that are critical to a group's material well-being or survival, then the choice of which group to marry into may be too important to be left entirely up to the woman and man whose marriage creates the relationship. Older, wiser, and more responsible people should be making such critical decisions.

Understanding that who marries whom is so important to families and even larger groups helps to explain one widespread custom—*arranged marriages*—that many Westerners view as an infringement on a person's freedom to choose. To offer an alternative view, a couple's freedom to choose their own spouse is an infringement on the freedom of their parents and other relatives to form advantageous relationships with other families. How serious this infringement is, and whether the "freedom" of one party or another takes precedence, is not absolute but depends on circumstances. Perhaps some of our readers will find arranged marriages less offensive when they realize that a poor marital choice often puts more people at risk than just the couple themselves.

The importance of the intergroup ties created by intermarriage is also revealed by two other widespread customs. In one, called the **levirate,** if a woman's husband dies, she marries one of his close kinsmen (usually a brother). The relationships between the intermarried kin groups are too valuable for a woman to be returned to her own family because then she might marry into another kin group. Therefore, a male relative of her deceased husband takes his place. Because both her dead husband and her new husband belong to the same kin group, the relationship between the two groups remains intact. The converse custom, the **sororate,** also preserves the affinal ties between kin groups. If a woman dies, her kin group is obliged to replace her with another woman from the group, and no additional bridewealth is transferred. The Zulu of southern Africa, as well as many other African peoples, practiced both the levirate and the sororate. In societies with these customs, marriages—and the affinal ties they create—endure even beyond death.

Marital Exchanges

In most cultures, the marriage of a man and a woman is accompanied by some kind of transfer of goods or services. These *marital exchanges* take numerous forms, including the North American custom of wedding showers and wedding gifts. In these, the presents given by relatives and friends supposedly help the newlyweds establish an independent household. We give things that are useful to the couple jointly, with food-preparation and other household utensils the most common type of gift. Many couples even register at stores so that their relatives and friends will provide the items they want.

Comparatively speaking, the most unusual feature of North American marital exchange is that practically nothing is transferred between the relatives of the groom and bride: the couple treats the gifts as their private property. Like most of our other customs, this seems natural to us. Of course, the gifts go to the couple—what else could happen to them?

Plenty else, as we describe in a moment. For now, notice that the fact that the couple receives the gifts fits with several other features of Euro-American marriage. First, in addition to creating new nuclear families, marriage is the bond through which new independent households are started. So, the husband and wife "need their own stuff." If, in contrast, the newlyweds moved in with one of their relatives, they would not have as great a need for their own pots and pans, wine glasses, silver candlesticks, dishes, and other household items.

Second, our marriage-gift customs fit with the value our culture places on the privacy of the marital relationship: It is largely a personal matter between the husband and wife, and their relatives should keep their noses out. If the in-laws get along and socialize, that's great, but our marriages generally do not create strong bonds between the families of the bride and groom. (In fact, the two families often compete for the visits and attention of the couple and their offspring.) As we saw in Chapter 7, gifts make friends, and vice versa; the fact that the in-laws do not exchange gifts with each other is a manifestation of the absence of a necessary relationship between them after the wedding. If, in contrast, the marriage created an alliance between the two sets of relatives, then some kind of an exchange would probably occur between them to symbolize and cement their new relationship.

Third, the gifts are presented to the couple, not to the husband or wife as individuals, and are considered to belong equally and jointly to both partners. But there are marriage systems in which the property of the wife is separate from that of her husband; if divorce should occur, there is no squabbling over who gets what and no need for prenuptial legal contracts.

With this background in mind, what kinds of marital exchanges occur in other cultures?

Bridewealth. **Bridewealth** is the widespread custom that requires a man and/or his relatives to transfer wealth to the relatives of his bride. It is easily the most common of all marital exchanges, found in more than half the world's cultures. The term *bridewealth* is well chosen because the goods transferred are usually among the most valuable symbols of wealth in the local culture. In sub-Saharan Africa, cattle and sometimes other livestock are the most common goods used for bridewealth. Peoples of the Pacific islands and Southeast Asia usually give their bridewealth in pigs or shell money and ornaments.

One of the most common rights a man and his relatives acquire when they transfer bridewealth to his wife's family is rights over the woman's children. Reciprocally, one of a wife's most important obligations is to bear children for her husband. This is well exemplified by the Swazi, a traditional kingdom of southern Africa. A Swazi marriage is a union between two families as well as between the bride and groom. The payment of bridewealth—in cattle and other valuables—to a woman's relatives establishes the husband's rights over his wife. A woman's main duty to her husband is to provide him with children. If she is unable to do so, her relatives must either return the bridewealth they received for her or provide a second wife to the husband, for which he need pay no extra bridewealth. Reciprocally, a man must pay bridewealth to gain rights of fatherhood over the child of a woman, even though everyone knows he is the child's biological father. If he does not do so, the woman's relatives will keep the child; if the woman herself later marries another man, her new husband will not receive rights over the child unless he pays bridewealth.

Brideservice. **Brideservice** is the custom in which a husband is required to spend a period of time working for the family of his bride. A Yanomamö son-in-law is expected to live with his wife's parents, hunting and gardening for them until they finally release control over their daughter. Among some Ju/'hoansi bands (see Chapters 6 and 7), a man proves he can provide by living with and hunting for his wife's parents for 3 to 10 years, after which the couple is free to camp elsewhere.

Brideservice is the second most common form of marital exchange; it is the usual compensation given to the family of a bride in roughly one-eighth of the world's cultures. Sometimes it occurs in addition to other forms of marital exchange, however, and occasionally it can be used to reduce the amount of bridewealth owed.

Dowry. A marital exchange is called **dowry** when the family of a woman transfers a portion of its own wealth or property to the woman (their daughter) and/or to her husband and his family. The main thing to understand about dowry is that it is *not* simply the opposite of bridewealth; that is, it is not "groomwealth." The woman and her family do not acquire marital rights over her husband when they provide dowry, as they would if dowry were the opposite of bridewealth; rather, the bride and her husband receive property when they marry, rather than when the bride's parents die. By providing dowry, parents give their female children extra years of use of the property and also publicly demonstrate their wealth.

Sometimes dowry is the share of a woman's inheritance that she takes into her marriage for the use of her new family. Dowry may represent an occasion for a family to display their wealth publicly by ostentatiously moving furniture and clothing from their house to that of their daughter's husband. Among other peoples, the family of a man will not allow him to marry a woman unless she and her family are able to make a dowry payment. Typically, the cultural rationale is that women do not contribute as much to a family as do men, so a family must be compensated for admitting a new female member. (Interestingly, this rationale is usually found among societies in which the domestic labor of the female is both difficult and valuable.)

Historically, dowry transfers were common in Eurasian (Europe, southern Asia, and the Middle East) cultures. Most peoples that practiced it were intensive agriculturalists and had significant inequalities in wealth. It has always been a relatively rare form of marital exchange, occurring in only about 5 percent of the societies recorded by anthropology.

Although a minority of societies practice dowry, some of these societies are quite populous. Dowry is common today in parts of southern Asia (India, Bangladesh, and Pakistan), where dowry includes jewelry, household utensils, women's clothing, and money. Much of the dowry is presented to the bride on her wedding day, but her parents and maternal uncle often provide gifts periodically throughout the marriage.

In recent decades, the demands of Indian families for dowry have led to thousands of tragic deaths. Rather than a one-time marital exchange, some Indian families demand additional, continual payments from the parents of a woman who has married one of their sons. They ask for large sums of cash, household appliances like refrigerators and televisions, motorbikes, and other consumer goods. If the wife's family refuses, their daughter may be severely injured or even killed by burning (in "accidental kitchen fires"), beatings, withholding food, falls, or other retaliations. About 7,000 Indian women suffered "dowry deaths" in 2003, according to official figures, but the actual number is likely much higher. If these numbers sound large, be aware that India has more than a billion people, so dowry deaths are not common statistically.

There are other forms of marital exchanges, including some in which both sets of relatives exchange gifts as a material symbol of the new basis of their relationship. And the three forms discussed above are not mutually exclusive. For example, in most of traditional China, both bridewealth and dowry occurred at most marriages. The groom's family would make a payment to the bride's, and the bride's family would purchase some furniture and other household goods for their daughter to take with her when she moved into her husband's household. For wealthier families, dowry was usually displayed as it was transported ostentatiously through the streets between the houses of the bride and groom. Dowry thus became a Chinese status symbol. Sometimes, if the bride's family was substantially poorer than the groom's, part of the bridewealth payment would be spent on purchasing goods for the woman's dowry. This was legal and common until after the Communist Revolution in 1949, when Communist Party leaders outlawed both bridewealth and dowry, with only partial success.

Although the preceding information about marriage rules, forms, alliances, and exchanges has barely introduced these complicated topics, enough has been presented for you to glimpse both the cross-cultural diversity of marriage customs and the societal importance of marriage. Marriage is tied up with adaptation, with economics, and, quite obviously, with politics and religion. Similar interrelationships among marriage, politics, and religion are seen in the contemporary United States, as the recent political wars over gay marriage illustrate (see A Closer Look).

▲ In most societies that have the dowry custom, a woman takes wealth from her family into her marriage. This jewelry-bedecked Pakistani bride is waiting for her wedding.

© Ed Kass / CORBIS

In early 2004, the newly elected mayor of San Francisco began issuing marriage licenses to gay couples. In May, the state of Massachusetts legalized same-sex marriages. Alarmed at the prospect of other states passing similar legislation, President George W. Bush and conservatives in the U.S. Congress pressed for an amendment to the U.S. Constitution. After several rewrites, when brought to a vote on July 14, 2004, the amendment read:

Marriage in the United States shall consist only of the union of a man and a woman. Neither this Constitution, nor the constitution of any state, shall be construed to require that marriage or the legal incidents thereof be conferred upon any union other than the union of a man and a woman.

In the vote, the proposal failed to gain even a majority in the U.S. Senate, where a two-thirds vote is required for passage of a constitutional amendment. Leftists, liberals, and most moderates opposed the amendment. Liberals saw it as either the latest attempt at gay-bashing or just another symbol of cultural intolerance. Some viewed it as a shameless effort by neo-conservatives and religious fundamentalists to gain political support in the November 2004 elections by forcing their opponents (mainly Democrats) to vote yes or no, which would then allow them to claim that the "no" voters were antifamily and didn't share mainstream values. Even some conservatives opposed it because they believed it infringed on states' rights. Even without the amendment, 11 states passed amendments to their constitutions to ban gay and lesbian marriages.

Why did gay marriage become so politicized? The short answer is that the issue is part of the American "culture wars." Among the battles are whether there are absolute standards of right and wrong; the role that Christian teachings should have in schools, courtrooms, and other public institutions; whether individuals are morally responsible for all their actions; and how much multicultural diversity "one nation under God" can absorb without tearing itself apart from within. Same-sex marriage provides ammunition for the culture warriors: Is it "immoral" or merely another "alternative lifestyle"? Given that many Protestant denominations welcome gays and lesbians and some even allow their ordination, is it against biblical teachings? Are homosexual desires (like heterosexual desires) rooted in genes and hereditary, or is being openly gay a "choice"? Is being lesbian or gay a "mental disorder," and, if so, can you be "cured"? What would happen to the nation as a whole if diverse forms of marriage were legalized? If same-sex marriage is legalized, will polygamy be next?

By mid-2007, 10 states had passed laws allowing gay and lesbian domestic partners to adopt children together, rather than as individual parents. This means that one partner can become the legal parent of the adoptive child of the other. Perhaps these laws mean that more Americans are willing to accept gay marriage, and indeed a 2006 Pew Center poll reported that opposition to gay marriage fell from 65 percent in 1996 to 51 percent in 2006. Alternatively, the laws may mean only that legislators in the 10 states are anxious to find homes for the 120,000 or so American babies who need them. The Catholic Church and conservative Protestants remain opposed to gay adoption, with one Protestant leader saying it harms kids "because it intentionally creates motherless or fatherless families." And, if 10 states have laws allowing joint adoptions, it means that 40 do not.

Many who object to lesbian and gay adoption insist that children need both a mother and a father, and no substitutes will do. And strong opponents of same-sex marriage hold that marriage between one woman and one man is the bedrock of human society, so changing it is likely to endanger social order in lots of unpredictable ways. In July 2004, in a Saturday radio address supporting the proposed amendment, President Bush said, "The union of a man and a woman in marriage is the most enduring and important human institution. . . ." Obviously, the president meant that *one form of marriage*—monogamy ("a man and a woman")—is the most enduring and important institution. On this point, at least, he was mistaken, for polygyny is widespread and even polyandry exists.

At any rate, no matter how fiercely culture wars are fought to preserve the marriage practices that are normative and valued by most North Americans, these practices are sure to change and then change again. Whether people can marry outside their race or ethnicity, what goes on during courtship, how people choose their spouse, what they expect from marriage, what obligations wives have toward husbands, how enduring marriages will be, how the children resulting from the "union" of a man and a woman are raised—all these and most other features of marriage as we know it today would be viewed with consternation and even horror by North Americans of a century ago. No doubt at least some of them would have foretold the horrific effects on society if blacks and whites were ever allowed to marry, if premarital sex were to become common, if many women were the main family breadwinners, if half of all marriages ended with divorce, and if large numbers of couples entrusted their preschool-aged children to something called "day care centers" for 40 hours a week.

Sources: San Francisco Chronicle, Monday, July 12, 2004, pp. A1, A8; Thursday, July 15, 2004, pp. A1, A14; Tim Padgett, "Gay Family Values," *Time,* July 16, 2007, pp. 51–52

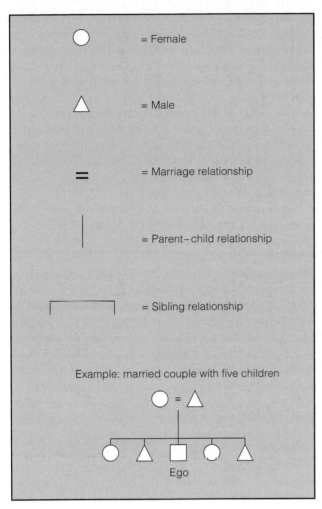

▲ **Figure 8.1** Symbols Used on Kinship Diagrams.

Kinship Diagrams

At this point, we need to introduce a set of notational symbols used in the remainder of this chapter and the next. This notation allows us to express diagrammatically how any two persons are (or believe themselves to be) related by bonds of kinship. The symbols are shown in Figure 8.1, along with how they are used to show a married couple with five children. By stringing a number of symbols together, we can make a complete chart—called a *genealogy*—that shows all the relatives of a given individual and how they are related to that individual. In these charts, or kinship diagrams, it is useful to have a reference individual, or a person to whom everyone on the chart is related. It is customary to call this reference

individual "ego." In Figure 8.1, ego is symbolized by a square to show that his or her gender is irrelevant for the purposes of the genealogy. (If ego's gender mattered, we would symbolize him or her with either a triangle or a circle.)

Postmarital Residence Patterns

In modern Euro-American societies, most newly married couples establish a new domestic group (household) in their own apartment, condo, or house. Elsewhere, couples do not set up a new household but more often move into an existing household—that of either the husband or the wife. Where most newly married couples in a society establish their residence is known as the **postmarital residence pattern.** Cross-cultural research shows that our own pattern, in which couples form new households separate from their parents, is uncommon.

What are the common patterns? By splitting enough hairs, we can identify a dozen patterns, but here we present only six (in order from most to least frequent):

1. **Patrilocal**—Couples live with or near the parents of the husband.
2. **Matrilocal**—Couples live with or near the wife's parents.
3. **Ambilocal**—Couples may choose to live with either the wife's or the husband's kin; roughly half of all couples choose each.
4. **Bilocal**—Couples move back and forth between the households of both sets of parents according to preferences and circumstances.
5. **Neolocal**—Couples live apart from both parents, establishing a separate dwelling and independent household.
6. **Avunculocal**—Couples live with the maternal uncle of the husband.

About 70 percent of all societies have patrilocal residence as the predominant pattern. Thirteen percent have matrilocal residence. Bilocality, ambilocality, neolocality, and avunculocality together account for the remaining 17 percent.

Influences on Residence Patterns

What sorts of factors affect postmarital residence patterns? What determines whether newly married couples live separately or move in with some kind of relatives? And, if most couples co-reside with some relatives, as they do in most societies, what affects which set of relatives?

There is no simple answer, but property rights and inheritance forms are important influences on postmarital residence. In societies in which men own the most important productive property and inheritance passes from fathers to sons, brothers have good reasons to join their fathers (and each other) in a common household to cooperate and protect their interests in land, livestock, or other wealth. When the sons of most families in a society bring their wives and children into their father's existing household, this pattern of behavior leads to the residence anthropologists call *patrilocal*. Where important resources are controlled or owned by women, and especially if female labor is important in supplying food for their families, then sisters tend to live and work together, and *matrilocal* residence is most likely to develop as sisters bring their husbands to live with them.

Ambilocal and bilocal patterns are most common in societies in which inheritance of important resources passes through both sexes and the labor of both women and men is important to household subsistence. Most hunter-gatherers have one of these two patterns. As explained in Chapter 6, most families in a foraging band need or want to maintain access to several territories, so the rights to gather and hunt in a particular area are flexible. Nuclear families may live off and on with the husband's and wife's bands, depending on sentimental ties or short- or long-term availability of resources. If all or most couples do this, the result is bilocal residence. Or, the couple may settle with whichever parental family has the most resources or with whichever they have good relations, leading to ambilocality.

Modern industrialized nations are usually neolocal for two major reasons. First, job availability forces many couples to move away from their home town. This is especially true for "upwardly mobile" couples seeking higher incomes, better opportunities, and the more materially rewarding lifestyle valued by many. Second, in industrialized countries, most workers do not rely on their family connections for access to their livelihood but instead sell their labor on an impersonal market to an employer they have never met. In other words, most ordinary citizens do not inherit productive property from their parents and do not rely on their parents for their livelihood, so they establish independent domiciles free from parental control and interference. The result is neolocal residence and an emphasis on nuclear family ties.

Although control over resources and form of inheritance are important overall influences, no single factor "determines" postmarital residence. For instance, if most couples rely on the wife's family for access to the resources they need to survive and raise children, then most couples will live with the wife's family and matrilocal residence will be the pattern. But a multitude of other factors also affect residence choices. In fact, in some societies, even though women have much control over land, residence is not matrilocal because these other factors are locally more important than keeping sisters together in a common household. Similar complexities apply to the other residence patterns, so there is no single explanation.

We conclude this section by pointing out a few more complications that make generalizations difficult. For one thing, there are many exceptions to almost all generalizations about humanity: for example, the Tiwi of Australia (discussed earlier) are patrilocal, although they are foragers. For another, a great many peoples do not have a single residence pattern; rather, where people live varies over time. Among some Inuit ("Eskimo") peoples, often couples lived neolocally in the summer and patrilocally in the winter. Among western Shoshone, most families lived neolocally during the dry summers but came together with other relatives during the fall and winter. Last, even within a single society, different families make different choices. For example, China's industrial economy is growing at a staggering rate, and its residence is transforming from the pre-twentieth-century patrilocal pattern to a neolocal pattern. Yet many rural couples live with the husband's family, and even many young urban couples live with relatives because of housing shortages and the (ever-weakening) obligation to support one's elderly parents.

The subject of postmarital residence might seem trivial. What difference does it make whether newly married couples live alone or with one set of parents?

Residence and Households

In fact, there are good reasons for our interest in residence patterns: they greatly affect the kinds of family relationships that are most important in a human community.

A moment's reflection reveals that both matrilocal and patrilocal residences place a new nuclear family (usually created by a new marriage) with one set of relatives rather than the other set. In turn, whom a newly married couple lives with influences whom they will cooperate with, share property with, feel close to, and so forth. If postmarital residence is patrilocal, for instance, then the husband lives with and works with his own consanguineous relatives (his father and brothers, paternal uncles and cousins *through his father*). The wife is likely to cooperate in household chores, gathering, gardening, and doing other tasks with members of her husband's family, more than with her own.

Postmarital residence also affects the relatives with whom children are most likely to develop strong emotional bonds. If residence is matrilocal, for example, then the children of sisters (who are cousins *through their mothers*) live together in a single household (much like biological sisters and brothers) and are likely to view their relationship as being like real siblings. The children of brothers, on the other hand, will live in different households and are less likely to play together and develop strong emotional attachments.

Most important, the prevailing form of residence affects the kinds of household and family units that exist among a people. Consider neolocal residence, for example. If all or most newlyweds set up their own households, distinct from and independent of that of either of their parents, then a new household and family unit is established with each new marriage. This pattern emphasizes the social and economic importance and independence of nuclear families because mothers and fathers—and not more distant relatives—are most likely to be the main teachers of their children and breadwinners for the household. The couple maintains relationships with their parents, siblings, and other relatives, of course, but neolocal residence tends to lead to an emphasis on nuclear families as the most culturally important and stable family unit.

Comparing neolocal to the other forms of postmarital residence might lead you to think differently about some statements of North American political leaders. For the most part, when politicians worry about the decline or breakup of "the" American or Canadian family, they are usually talking about the nuclear family. "The" family is threatened by high divorce rates, unmarried couples living together, absent or deadbeat fathers, high illegitimacy rates, gay and lesbian lifestyles, and so forth. In recent years, so many families have split up that family stability has become a major social problem. But the disintegration of *extended family* relationships is treated differently: No one worries much about the separation of adult married children and their parents, or about how many married siblings have not seen one another for years. We consider it normal—not a social problem—when married children move out of their parents' homes and away from their siblings. Indeed, most view it as unfortunate if newlyweds live with either set of parents; surely only economic necessity could force them to do so. Perhaps you join many of your peers in

thinking young marrieds who visit or seek advice from their parents too often are a little strange. Why can't they make their own choices and break away from their mom and dad?

In the United States, marital residence has economic consequences. In the last half of 2007, the practice of making loans at subprime rates of interest caused so many homeowners to default on their home mortgage payments that the housing market was negatively affected. (By *negatively affected,* we mean that home prices declined. Only homeowners think that lower prices are negative, however; lower prices are favorable for those who are seeking to buy a house and qualify for a loan.) Economists, the media, and politicians worried that falling home prices, losses by lenders, lack of new construction, and lower stock prices would bring about a recession. Homeowners worried that they would not be able to make as much money when they sold their houses as they had anticipated from past experience or forecasts. If loan defaults can have such widespread effects on the housing market, think what would happen to the market if huge numbers of newly married Americans began moving in with one of their parents—thus practicing some form of residence other than neolocal.

Family and Household Forms

One of the most important differences in households is the number of generations they include. Nuclear families include only two generations (parents and children), whereas extended families often include three or more generations.

Two-Generation Households

Some people believe that the nuclear family is the basic unit of kinship. (Notice that "individuals" cannot be the basic unit of kinship because kinship is inherently about *relationships* among individuals.) Other kinds of kin groupings arise when nuclear families associate together in patterned ways. For example, patrilocal residence associates the nuclear families of brothers with one another in the same household. Neolocality does not associate nuclear families with one another *residentially,* although, of course, related nuclear families have other kinds of socially and emotionally important ties.

Possibly, though, those who think the nuclear family is somehow "basic" believe this only because they live in a society in which a couple and their offspring are the most visible family form. Perhaps they view other forms as morally perverse or as unfortunate compromises a particular nuclear family has to make due to special circumstances such as lacking the income to live in a place of their own.

There is another view: that the "basic unit" of kinship is a woman and her offspring. People who think this point out that fathers are more frequently separated from their children than are mothers. Fathers may separate temporarily or permanently for many reasons. In subsistence economies, men may be absent for long periods hunting, herding, trading, raiding, or carrying out other duties. In communities—and in modern countries—where most families depend on wage labor, husbands/fathers may take jobs in distant cities or countries for many months or even years. The money they send back to their families at home (called *remittances*) is surprisingly large: in 2004, around 10 million migrants (predominantly men) from Mexico and other Latin American countries remitted $30 billion to their home countries.

Historically, male absence for extended periods was especially common in regions that were colonies of a major world power. In sub-Saharan Africa, especially, European colonial powers imposed taxes on men or introduced new commodities that soon became virtual necessities, such as kerosene lanterns, nails, metal tools, and cooking utensils. In order to earn money to meet expenses, married men went to work for foreign companies on distant diamond or gold mines or left their families to work on plantations owned by Europeans. This pattern continues in much of Africa and other regions even today. For the families left behind, the result is the **matrifocal family,** where a mother (with or without a husband) bears most of the burden of supporting her children economically and nurturing them emotionally and intellectually.

Matrifocal families occur in modern industrial societies as well, whenever households are "female-headed," as the U.S. Census Bureau calls them. About half of all African American children live in households with a female head. Some say that matrifocal families are an important cause of poverty, crime, and other social problems today. Adult men would act more responsibly if they had jobs that supported their nuclear families, they say. Sons need male role models and supposedly find them elsewhere if their fathers are not around. Mothers would be much better mothers if they didn't have to struggle so hard to pay the bills.

In modern nations, it is true that poor families are more likely to be female-headed than affluent families.

But this does not mean that matrifocal households are a significant cause of poverty and other social ills. Matrifocal families are also a consequence of poverty: lack of job skills or other factors lead to high unemployment among men, causing many women to decide that having a permanent male presence is too costly. Female-headed households in the United States and elsewhere are not necessarily the result of men's refusal to act responsibly or of women's moral choices: they also are adaptations that people make to their economic and social environment.

Extended Households

Extended families are made up of related nuclear families. Because the related nuclear families usually live in a single household, here we use *extended family* and *extended household* as synonyms. Extended households typically include three and sometimes four generations of family members.

Many anthropologists think that the form of family (household) that is prevalent in a society depends on its postmarital residence pattern. For example, with patrilocal residence, the married sons of an older couple remain in the household of their parents. Alternatively, each son builds his own house on his parents' land, near their dwelling, but they cooperate with one another and pool or share resources. As they grow up and marry, the daughters depart to live with their husbands' parents. If all the sons and daughters of a couple do this, the resulting household type is called *patrilocally extended*— brothers live in a single household with their own nuclear families and parents (see Figure 8.2a). If all families in the village, town, or other settlement follow this pattern, then the settlement consists of patrilocally extended households. Notice that the residents of each household are related to one another through males. The married women of the community live scattered in the households of their husbands. Perhaps many of them have married out of the community altogether.

The converse occurs with matrilocal residence. The mature sons leave as they marry, and the daughters bring their husbands to live with them in or near their parents' households. The household type formed by the co-residence of daughters and sisters with their parents is called the *matrilocally extended household* (see Figure 8.2b). The sons of an elderly couple are scattered in the households of the women they have married, either in their own home community or in another community. If most people follow this residence pattern, then the community consists of numerous households, each of which

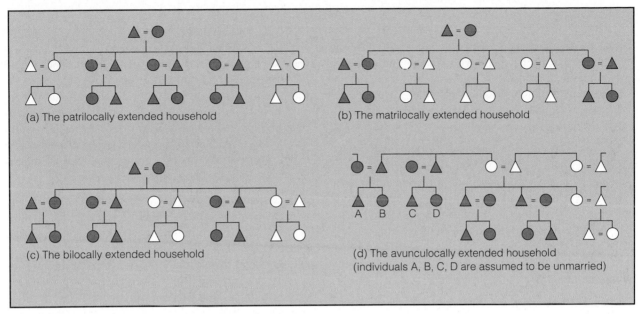

(a) The patrilocally extended household

(b) The matrilocally extended household

(c) The bilocally extended household

(d) The avunculocally extended household
(individuals A, B, C, D are assumed to be unmarried)

▲ **Figure 8.2** Household Forms. The shaded individuals are members of a single household.

is lived in by women related through females, plus their husbands and children.

The same relationship between residence and prevalent household form applies to the other residence patterns. With bilocal and ambilocal residence, there is no consistency in whether households are made up of people related through males or females. Some couples live with the husband's family, others with the wife's family. The household type is *bilocally* (or *bilaterally*) *extended* (see Figure 8.2c). The community's households are a mixture of people related through both sexes, in roughly equal frequency. With neolocal residence, the settlement—be it village or modern suburb—consists of relatively small domestic units made up of nuclear families.

The avunculocal residence pattern associates nuclear families with the husband's mother's brother. If every one resided this way (which they usually do not), then the settlement would consist of households composed of older men (the household heads) and the families of their sister's sons. This is called the *avunculocally extended household* (see Figure 8.2d). It includes men (and their wives and children) who are related to one another through women (their mothers). (Confused by this one? In Chapter 9, we explain why avunculocal residence makes good sense in many societies that trace their main kinship relationships through women.)

We can now see the main reason postmarital residence patterns are important: They give rise to various household and family forms. The kinds of family and domestic groups found among a people result from where newly formed families go to live. Stated differently, the prevalent household type in a human community represents the crystallization of the pattern of postmarital residence. And who lives with whom—the household type—is important because households so often hold property in common, cooperate in production and other economic activities, enculturate children together, and sometimes even worship the same ancestral spirits.

In this chapter, we have given an overview of some variations in domestic life. If this book were about industrial, market-economy societies, we might stop our discussion of groupings formed on the basis of kinship relationships at this point. This is because, among the industrialized, urbanized portion of humanity, other kinds of relationships and groupings—economic, educational, political, religious, and so on—are organized by relationships other than kinship—by specialized firms, schools, parties, governments, churches, and so on. But, as we discuss in Chapter 9, in preindustrial cultures, kinship principles are used to form much larger kin groups that organize and perform a wide range of other activities.

Summary

1. The incest taboo is a culturally universal rule that regulates who may have sex with whom. The taboo is more puzzling than it seems, and there are four main hypotheses that try to account for it: "Marry Out or Die Out," "Peace in the Family," "Inbreeding Avoidance," and "Familiarity Breeds Disinterest."

2. The wide diversity in marriage customs and beliefs makes marriage difficult to define, but there is some agreement on its major functions for both individuals and societies. Some form of marriage is nearly universal, although the particular form of marriage, the kinds of rights and duties it establishes, and many other aspects of the marital relationship vary. The Nayar and Tiwi illustrate unusual forms of marriage, and the Na of southern China seem to have no marriage at all.

3. Marriage is everywhere governed by rules, two of which are exogamy and endogamy. Marriage systems are commonly classified by the number of spouses an individual is allowed: polygyny, monogamy, polyandry, and group marriage, in order of relative frequency in human societies. In preindustrial societies, marriage is often the cornerstone of alliances between families or larger kin groups. The Yanomamö illustrate the use of strategic marriages to create and sustain military alliances, a practice quite common in the preindustrial world. The levirate and sororate are customs that preserve affinal relationships even after the death of a spouse.

4. New marriages are usually accompanied by the exchange of goods or services between the spouses and the families of the bride and groom. The most common forms of marital exchange are bridewealth, brideservice, and dowry. These exchanges are used to create affinal relationships, compensate a family or larger kin group for the loss of one of its members, provide for the new couple's support, or provide a daughter with an inheritance that helps her attract a desirable husband.

5. *Postmarital residence patterns* refers to where newly married couples establish their residence. From most common to least common, the patterns are patrilocal, matrilocal, ambilocal, bilocal, neolocal, and avunculocal. There are many influences on which of these forms will be most prevalent in a given community, including economic forces and inheritance patterns. But no single factor is adequate to explain the cross-cultural variation in residence patterns.

6. Anthropologists are interested in postmarital residence patterns mainly because where a newly married couple goes to live influences which kinship relationships are most emphasized in a society. In particular, the prevalent forms of family and domestic groups in a community arise out of many couples living with one or another set of relatives. Patrilocally, matrilocally, bilocally, and avunculocally extended families are often interpreted as the crystallization of postmarital residence patterns.

Key Terms

consanguines	monogamy	dowry
affines	polygyny	postmarital residence pattern
kin group	polyandry	patrilocal residence
nuclear family	group marriage	matrilocal residence
extended family	polygamy	ambilocal residence
household	marriage alliances	bilocal residence
fictive kinship	levirate	neolocal residence
incest taboo	sororate	avunculocal residence
exogamous rules	bridewealth	matrifocal family
endogamous rules	brideservice	

Suggested Readings

Collier, Jane F. *Marriage and Inequality in Classless Societies.* Stanford, Calif.: Stanford University Press, 1988.

Compares marriage systems and marriage exchanges in small-scale societies from a theoretical perspective, discussing their impact on male–female relationships.

Stockard, Janice E. *Marriage in Culture: Practice and Meaning Across Diverse Societies.* Fort Worth, Tex.: Harcourt College Publishers, 2002.

Describes and compares postmarital residence and marriage in four cultures: Ju/'hoansi, traditional China, Iroquois of around 1800, and the polyandrous Nyinba of Nepal. One of the best brief (129 pages) recent comparative treatments of marriage.

Stone, Linda. *Kinship and Gender: An Introduction.* 3rd edition. Boulder, Colo.: Westview Press, 2005.

Introduction to diversity in kinship, gender, and marriage, rich in illustrative case studies.

Suggs, David N., and Andrew W. Miracle, eds. *Culture and Human Sexuality: A Reader.* Pacific Grove, Calif.: Brooks/Cole, 1993.

A collection of articles dealing with sexuality and related topics from a cross-cultural perspective. Includes both case studies and theoretical articles.

Most ethnographies contain a description of the domestic life of the people studied. Here are three ethnographies that focus narrowly on domestic life:

Levine, Nancy. *The Dynamics of Polyandry: Kinship, Domesticity, and Population in the Tibetan Border.* Chicago: University of Chicago Press, 1988.

Case study of fraternal polyandry in the Himalayas.

Shostak, Marjorie. *Nisa: The Life and Words of a !Kung Woman.* New York: Vintage Books, 1983.

A wonderfully readable biography of a !Kung woman, much of which focuses on her relationships with family, husbands, and children.

Wolf, Margery. *The House of Lim.* Englewood Cliffs, N.J.: Prentice Hall, 1968.

An ethnographic study of family life in a Taiwanese Chinese farm family.

Media Resources

The Wadsworth Anthropology Resource Center
academic.cengage.com/anthropology

The Wadsworth discipline resource website that accompanies *Humanity: An Introduction to Cultural Anthropology,* Eighth Edition, includes a rich array of material, including online anthropological video clips, to help you in the study of cultural anthropology and the specific topics covered in this chapter. Other material includes a case study forum with excerpts from various Wadsworth authors, map exercises, scientist interviews, breaking news in anthropology, and links to additional useful online material. Begin by selecting Cultural Anthropology to take you to videos, research, and more. From the homepage, you may also select Applied Anthropology, which directs you to essays, glossary terms, the case study forum, and a list of internships and careers in anthropology.

9 KINSHIP AND DESCENT

Kinship relationships are important both in the lives of individuals and for the well-being of society. This large Jewish family shares food and drink during a holiday.

Introducing Kinship

Why Study Kinship?

Cultural Variations in Kinship

Unilineal Descent

Unilineal Descent Groups

Descent Groups in Action

Avunculocality Revisited

Nonunilineal Descent

Cognatic Descent

Bilateral Kinship

Classifying Relatives: Kinship Terminologies

Cultural Construction of Kinship

Varieties of Kinship Terminology

Why Do Terminologies Differ?

Questions addressed in this chapter

How do societies differ in their kinship systems?

What are the differences among the four major forms of descent and kinship?

What are some widespread functions of kinship groups and relationships?

What is the relationship between the form of descent and kinship terminologies?

Humans are among the most social of all mammals. We are born into, live with, and die among other people. Young children rely totally on parents and other adults for the food, shelter, protection, and socialization needed to raise them to social maturity. Even as adults, we rely on cooperation with others for survival, economic well-being, and emotional gratification. When we die, many members of the groups to which we belonged mourn our passing.

Of the many kinds of organized groups in society, those based on kinship, or culturally recognized biological ties, are among the most important. In many cultures, the specific persons with whom one cooperates in everyday life are relatives of some kind. The groups that organize large-scale cooperative activities are established on the basis of kinship ties. Within those groups, the nature of individuals' relationships with one another depends largely on what specific kinds of relatives they are.

In this chapter, we cover how kinship relationships are used in a variety of ways by different peoples to organize relationships and create cooperative groupings. We also describe some of the main ways that members of different cultures define and classify their relatives into labeled categories.

Introducing Kinship

Like relationships established by marriage and family/household forms, relationships and groups defined by kinship organize a variety of tasks and activities. The kind of tasks and activities, and the kinds of relationships and groups, vary from people to people, as you have come to expect.

Why Study Kinship?

Why are anthropologists concerned with kinship? In Western society and that of developed nations, kinship relationships certainly are important in individuals' lives. But, compared to many other peoples that anthropologists work among, kinship is not an important *organizing principle* of society as a whole. Instead, different kinds of specialized groups organize different kinds of activities. We have economic groups (corporations), religious groups (churches, synagogues, mosques, temples), and educational groups (schools, colleges), each of which specializes in different realms of our lives. Each of us is a member of a number of such groups and associations. You might belong to formal groups such as a university, conservation organization, church, political party, and a business. (Here *formal* means that the group is *organized as a group,* with officers, membership criteria, explicit goals, rules, and so forth.) At the same time, you are active in many informal *networks* made up of fellow students, neighbors, friends, and those of your coworkers with whom you associate after work, with whom you socialize or share common interests. (The members of your social *network* do not necessarily have any relationship to one another, but you have personal relationships with each of them as individuals.)

Notice two important characteristics of these groups and networks. First, they are *voluntary:* if your interests change, or if you find another group or network that satisfies you more, you are free to change jobs, churches, neighborhoods, and friends. Second, for the most part, the groups have *nonoverlapping membership:* each group typically consists of a different collection of people. We cooperate and interact with different individuals in the various groups to which we belong. Members of each group have varying and sometimes contradictory expectations about how we should behave because we perform different roles in each. Our behavior differs according to the identity and expectations of the particular persons (the *social context*) we are associating with at the moment—we act one way at home, another at church, and yet another at work. (Our fellow church members might be surprised if they could see how we act on the job, but—probably fortunately—ordinarily they do not.)

In contrast, among many indigenous peoples, one lives with, works with, socializes with, and often worships with the same people, most of whom are relatives. Kin groups and kin relationships are *multifunctional*, meaning that the same groups organize many aspects of peoples' life, such as who cooperates in labor, who owns what lands, who carries out rituals together, and who quarrels with whom. Most of the activities organized by the firms, schools, governments, churches, and other specialized groups in an industrial society are organized by one or another kind of kin group. We can no more understand such societies without studying their kinship systems than we could understand modernized nations without knowing about businesses, schools, and laws.

Cultural Variations in Kinship

In more than a century of studying kinship systems and analyzing their role in cultures, anthropologists have discovered surprising variations. Among the most important variations are the following.

Ways of tracing kinship ties. In most of North America and Europe, most people believe they are related equally and in the same way to the extended families of both their mother and their father. Particular individuals may develop closer ties with one or another side of their family according to circumstances and personal preferences, such as whether only one set of grandparents live nearby. But there is no systematic *cultural pattern* of feeling closer to or socializing with relatives according to whether they are paternal or maternal kin.

In contrast, most other peoples place primary importance on one side of the family—either the paternal or the maternal side—in preference to the other. For example, in many cultures, most individuals become members of only their father's kin group. In such systems, relatives through one's mother usually are considered to be kin, but kin of a fundamentally different and less important kind than paternal relatives. There are also systems in which kin groups are organized around maternal relationships, and paternal kin are culturally deemphasized.

Normative expectations of kin relationships. The kinds of social relationships a people believe they should have with various kinds of relatives are part of the norms of kinship. Kinship norms are surprisingly variable from people to people. There are kin systems in which brothers must strictly avoid their sisters after puberty; in which sons-in-law are not supposed to speak directly to their mother-in-law; in which a boy is allowed to joke

▲ One way kinship systems vary is in whether the most important relationships are traced through males, females, or both sexes. On this Micronesian woman's home island, relationships through females are emphasized.

freely with and appropriate the property of his maternal uncle but must show utmost restraint and respect toward his paternal uncle; and in which people are expected to marry one kind of cousin but are absolutely forbidden to marry another kind of cousin. In brief, many social behaviors toward relatives that members of one culture regard as normal are different in other cultures.

Cultural classifications of relatives. Except for fictive kinship (see Chapter 8), kinship relationships are created through biological reproduction. When a woman gives birth, her relatives and those of her mate become the biological relatives of the child; for example, your mother's brother's children automatically are your "first cousins." Thus, the kinship relationship between any two people depends on how these individuals are related biologically.

Yet anthropologists claim that kinship is a cultural—as opposed to a biologically determined—phenomenon. Societies differ in the way they use the biological facts of kinship to create groups, allocate roles, and classify relatives into various kinds. In our own kinship system, for example, whether a woman is our maternal or paternal aunt makes no difference: we still call her *aunt* and think of both our maternal and paternal aunts as the same kind of relative. But the side of the family makes a difference in some other kinship systems, where the father's sisters and mother's sisters are completely different kinds of relatives and are called by different terms.

Keeping this overview of kinship diversity in mind, let's look at kinship in more detail.

Unilineal Descent

Consider what it means to be consanguineous relatives. If "kin" are defined in strictly biological terms, then someone is your relative because you and that person share a common ancestor in an earlier generation. Thus, your sister is the female child of your parents; your aunts and uncles are the children of your grandparents; your first cousins are the grandchildren of your grandparents; and your second cousins have the same great-grandparents as you. Stated differently, a man is your biological relative if you and he are *descended* from a common ancestor who lived some number of generations ago. The greater the number of generations back this common ancestor lived, the more distantly you and the man are related.

Notice that you are descended from 4 grandparents, 8 great-grandparents, 16 great-great-grandparents, and 32 great-great-great-grandparents. Everyone alive today who is descended from these 32 people is related to you to some degree. Going back in time, the number of your ancestors doubles every generation. So, even if you count back only four or five generations, you have an enormous number of living *biological* relatives who are descended from those ancestors. (This is why it's not unusual if you are "descended" from George Washington.)

Obviously, no society keeps track of all biological kin. From the total range of potential relatives, all cultures consider some kinds of relatives as more important than others. The number of relatives is reduced in two main ways: (1) by forgetting or ignoring the more remote kinship relationships, and (2) by emphasizing some kinds of kinship relationships and deemphasizing others. All peoples use the first method, or they would recognize tens of thousands of relatives. In the West, most people have little reason to keep track of relatives more distant than second cousins because there is so little interaction with them. (As an exercise, try to name your second cousins.)

Many peoples also use the second method: they place more importance on some relatives than on others. The most common way of doing this uses the sex of connecting relatives as the basis for defining which kin are close

or most socially important. For example, if a given culture places more importance on relatives traced through males, then individuals will think that their father's relatives are more important than their mother's relatives—for some purposes at least. Relationships through females will be deemphasized and perhaps forgotten in two or three generations. If you lived in such a culture, your second cousins on your father's side might quite important relatives, but you might barely know your second cousins through your mother.

Culturally speaking, then, kinship relationships are defined by how people trace their descent from previous generations. How people in a given culture trace their descent is called their **form of descent**. Descent can be traced through males, females, or both sexes.

Cultures in which peoples trace relationships through only one sex have **unilineal descent**: people place importance on either their mother's ancestral line or their father's ancestral line, but not both. There are two categories of unilineal descent:

1. **Patrilineal descent**—People trace their primary kinship connections to the ancestors and living relatives of their father. In cultures with patrilineal descent, a person's father's relatives are likely to be most important in his or her life. Individuals are likely to live among their father's kin, and most property is inherited by sons from fathers.
2. **Matrilineal descent**—People trace their most important kinship relationships to the ancestors and living relatives of their mother. In matrilineal descent, it is the mother's relatives who are most important in a person's life. People are most likely to live with or near their mothers' relatives and usually inherit property from their mother or mother's brothers.

Of these two forms of unilineal descent, patrilineal is the most common. There are about three times as many patrilineal as matrilineal cultures.

Let's look at each form of unilineal descent more closely to see which relatives are considered most important for an individual. In Figure 9.1, the patrilineal relatives of the person labeled *Ego* are shaded. The kinship diagram shows that Ego's patrilineal kin include only those relatives related to Ego through males. For instance, Ego's father's brother's children are related to Ego through males, whereas Ego's other first cousins (through Ego's mother or father's sister) are not.

Looking at patrilineal descent another way, we see that Ego's patrilineal kin include all the people descended *through males* from the man labeled *Founder* in Figure 9.1. In fact, any two individuals shaded in the

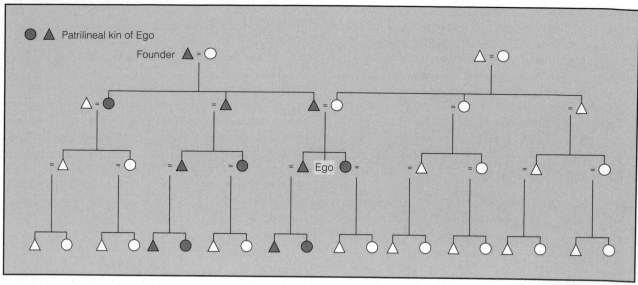

▲ **Figure 9.1** Patrilineal Descent.

diagram are related to each other through males. Women as well as men are patrilineal kin, but the children of women are not related through males and, therefore, are not patrilineal kin. Why aren't the children of the women counted? Because in most patrilineal cultures, sex between patrilineal relatives is incestuous, so the women's children become members of their fathers' patrilineal group.

How does patrilineal descent affect behavior between different relatives? In all sorts of ways, but widespread and important effects are the inheritance of property and obligations to relatives. In patrilineal societies, property is passed down through the male line or, in other words, from fathers to sons. We can see the significance of this effect by contrasting it with inheritance in North American society. You do not distinguish between your two grandfathers but think of yourself as related in the same way to both. But if you lived in a patrilineal society, your father's father would play a far more significant role in your life, and it would be from him and your father that you would expect to inherit wealth or receive land rights. Your mother's father would pass his property on to his sons and sons' sons—not to you because you are related to him through his daughter, not his son. A similar distinction would exist between paternal and maternal uncles: paternal uncles would be far more important.

In patrilineal kinship systems, individuals (of both sexes) have greater obligations to patrilineal relatives. People know their mother's family, of course, and often have close emotional ties with them depending on resi-

dence and individual circumstances. But one's primary duties are to kin through the father, not through the mother. For example, if you are a man, you mainly work the land or care for the livestock of your father's family, you remain with or near your father's household through most of your life, you are obliged to care for your parents in their older years, and so forth. Because most patrilineal peoples are also patrilocal, most often a woman leaves her own family when she marries to join her husband's family. In regions like east and most of southern Asia, families who had daughters brought them up only to have them leave upon marriage, so a great many families preferred male children to female children. The Globalization box discusses some consequences of the preference for sons in China's recent history.

Similar considerations apply to matrilineal descent. If you lived in a matrilineal society, your most important relatives would be your mother, mother's mother, mother's mother's mother, plus the daughters of all these women and their children. In Figure 9.2, Ego's matrilineal relatives are shaded. Note that only one set of cousins—Ego's mother's sisters' children—is shaded in the diagram. They are all related to Ego through female links, and therefore Ego is likely to have closer relationships with them than with other cousins. Property is most likely to be inherited from one's mother and maternal grandmother and from the brothers of these women. In matrilineal societies, men usually leave most of their property not to their own children but to their sister's children. As a result, maternal uncles (mother's brothers)

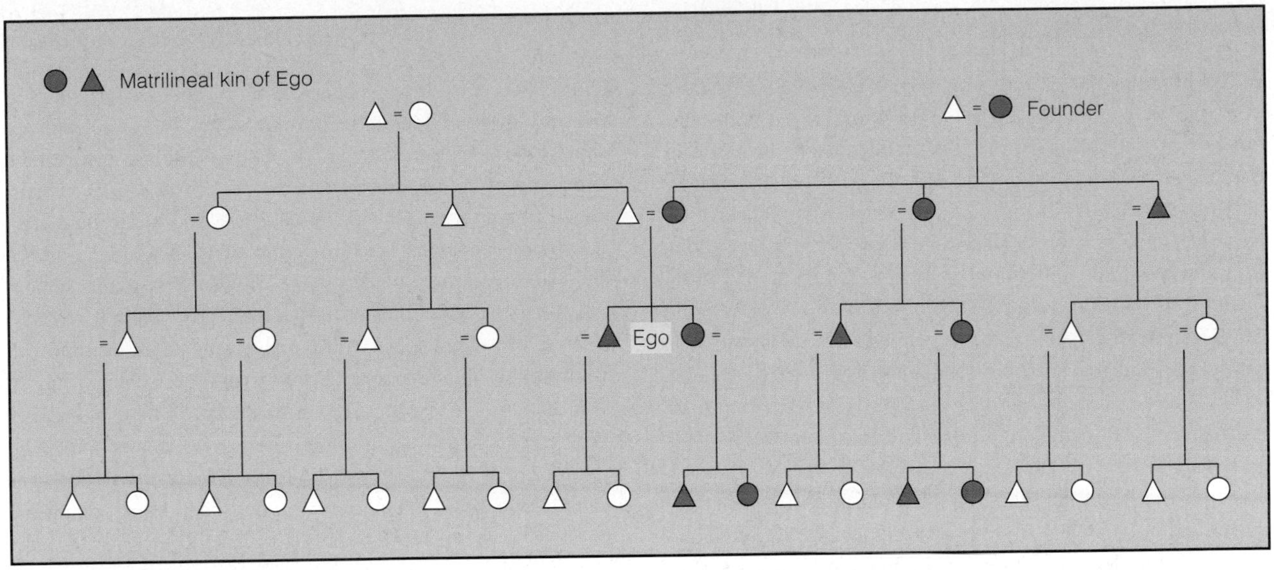

▲ **Figure 9.2** Matrilineal Descent.

are important figures in one's life, and in some respects they assume the role with its rights and duties that we usually associate with fathers.

In unilineal descent systems, relationships such as aunt, uncle, and cousin differ from those to which most of our readers are accustomed. Some cousins, in particular, are more important relatives than other cousins: father's brothers' children in patrilineal systems, mother's sisters' children in matrilineal systems. Not all cousins are culturally perceived as the same kinds of relatives in unilineal societies. This fact has led anthropologists to distinguish between *parallel cousins* and *cross cousins*. Two sets of cousins are parallel cousins if their parents are siblings of the same sex, so your parallel cousins are your mother's sisters' children and your father's brothers' children. People are cross cousins if their parents are siblings of the opposite sex, so your cross cousins are your father's sisters' children and your mother's brothers' children. The significance of this distinction is that in unilineal descent systems, one set of parallel cousins always belongs to the same kin group as Ego, as you can see by contrasting the cousins shaded in Figures 9.1 and 9.2. On the other hand, no cross cousin is ever in Ego's kin group in a society with a unilineal descent form.

Unilineal Descent Groups

In Chapter 8, we saw how various peoples form household groups by associating nuclear families together in patterned ways. Much larger kin groups of people—also

known as **descent groups**—can be established on the basis of kinship ties.

Take matrilineal descent, for example. A matrilineal descent group exists when people who are descended from the same woman through females recognize their group identity and cooperate for some purposes. When a matrilineal rule of descent establishes a group of people all related to one another through females, we say that the group is created using the *matrilineal principle*. We can state the matrilineal principle as "everyone joins the descent group of his or her mother." Alternatively, we can say, "only children of the female members of a group become members." Looking back to Figure 9.2, we see that all the individuals in the diagram are members of a single descent group. (Recall that the children of the group's men join the descent groups of their own mothers, which usually are a different group because incest taboos and exogamy rules usually prohibit sex and marriage between any of the group's members.)

Conversely, groups can develop by repeated application of the *patrilineal principle:* In any given generation, only males transmit their membership in the group to their offspring. The result of applying this principle for several generations is a group of people related to one another through males, as you can see in Figure 9.1. Assuming the patrilineal kin group is exogamous, the children of the group's women become members of their father's patrilineal group.

A **unilineal descent group** is a group of relatives all of whom are related through only one sex. A *matrilineal*

China has one of the oldest civilizations, going back at least to the Shang dynasty of about 3,500 years ago. For most of its history, the Han Chinese, the most numerous cultural/ethnic and linguistic group, were rather rigidly patrilineal and patrilocal—and patriarchical also. Property inheritance, family names, responsibilities to honor ancestors, the main bonds of obligation to others—all these and more passed from fathers to sons. Women left their own homes and families upon marriage. When they moved into their husband's family, they became subject to the authority of his parents (as was he) and worked hard to keep the family prosperous (as did he). Although not completely separated from her own biological family—she was allowed to visit them, provided it was not too often and she didn't remain too long—the wife's main duty was to her husband's family. This was symbolized by her bowing before the ancestral shrine and tablets of his family after they married. If he was wealthy enough to support them, a man could take concubines into his household and his wife was not supposed to object provided he live up to his obligations to support her and her children. All these practices and beliefs were reinforced by the philosophical tradition called Confucianism, and some scholars even call the above characteristics the "Confucian family."

Going along with the kinship system was a strong cultural preference for sons. Girls were only a "small happiness" to a family. They were expensive to raise and could not carry on the family name. The resources and time expended on their childhood usually brought little return when they married out. Male children were strongly desired—so much so that the failure to bear a son was one of seven reasons a man could divorce his wife (but usually he took concubines in the hope that one of them would produce a male heir).

Global trade with the West and Japan intensified in the 1800s and 1900s, which did not bring prosperity to most of China's peasants. After decades of political disorder and poverty, in 1949 Mao Zedong's Communist forces won a civil war. The Chinese Communist Party soon instituted government ownership of land and most other productive property. Chairman Mao's reforms did help restore law and order, he undertook specific policies to improve the lives of women, and the Chinese government placed great emphasis on public education for both sexes. In the last half of the twentieth century, the lives of women (relative to those of men, at least) improved substantially. This happened even in rural areas, according to anthropologist Yunxiang Yan. Young women have a stronger voice in choosing their husbands and now usually make the final decision about whom to marry, if only by vetoing her parents' selections. Couples can go out together, which means that marriages are more likely to be based on romantic love. Women's education exposes them to new ideas and gives many of them new economic opportunities by helping to level the playing field in the competition for jobs.

After Mao's death in 1976, his successor, Deng Xiaoping, began the economic reforms that led to China's phenomenal growth by exporting factory goods to the global economy. China's powerful leaders had long realized that they had to do something to reduce the rate at which the nation's population was growing if China was to avoid a food crisis and develop its economy. In 1979, they instituted a law that became known as the "one-child policy." Under it, couples who lived in cities could have only one child. Rural couples were allowed two children, and the law was further relaxed for minority peoples. Knowing the continued cultural preference for sons, in practice officials in some regions allowed a couple to try again for a boy if the first child was female. But there were penalties for having extra children: state-owned employers penalized people in pay and promotions, extra fees were imposed for health care and education, fines could be

descent group is a group whose members are (or believe themselves to be) related through females, or who trace their descent through female links from a common female ancestor. A *patrilineal descent group* comprises people who trace their descent through males from a common male ancestor.

Unilineal descent groups can be small or enormous, depending mainly on the genealogical depth of the group—that is, on how far back in time any two members of the group must go to trace their relationships to each other. A small matrilineal group with a few dozen members might consist of people descended matrilineally from a woman who lived four or five generations ago. A large matrilineal group with many hundreds of members might consist of people who trace their ancestry back to a woman who lived nine or ten generations ago. Anthropologists often use genealogical depth as a way to define different kinds of unilineal groups. From imposed, and extreme social pressure was applied to encourage conformity.

But the old preference for sons remained, so in the 1980s and 1990s, many couples found ways of eliminating unwanted female pregnancies and children. These included abortions, hiding second pregnancies from officials, and leaving one's community during late pregnancy to have a secret baby that, if female, was often placed in an orphanage. In the 1980s and 1990s, significantly more boys than girls were born. As a consequence, projections suggest that by about 2020, China will have approximately 30 million more males than females. Where these men will find their spouses is a problem that receives little Western media coverage, but it is potentially important to China's future stability.

The one-child policy helped lower China's population growth, although other factors also contributed heavily to couples' choice to have fewer children. The policy also led to tens of millions of Chinese who are only children, with no sisters or brothers. The publicity campaign that accompanied the policy, along with a multitude of other factors, significantly raised the status of females in China. Today, whether you have a boy or girl matters much less than it used to—what matters most now is that your only child receives the education that will allow her or him to get ahead in their careers. Many parents, along with grandparents, are quite attentive to their only son or daughter, leading some Chinese to call the only children "little emperors," especially if they are boys, suggesting extreme parental indulgence.

On the other hand, unlike real emperors, children are under a lot of pressure to succeed in school and to pass the national exams that lead to placement in Chinese colleges. Obligations to live up to parental expectations generally are greater among Chinese than among North Americans, and this extends to parents' wishes about colleges and careers. What Chinese call the "4-2-1" phenomenon cuts both ways: 1 child is the center of attention of 2 parents and 4 grandparents, but the same 6 adults have such high expectations for success that many children who don't measure up feel terrible about disappointing their older relatives. Parents care about their children's success because they love their little emperors, of course, but also because they rightly expect that their children will become their main source of support in their elder years. As Vanessa Fong discusses in her 2004 book, *Only Hope*, rising expectations for upward mobility by both parents and children results in intense competition in schools, but also in new frustrations when rising hopes are not realized.

As is also true in Japan and South Korea, Chinese parents make large sacrifices to maximize the life chances of their children. Some spend hours a week going over lessons. They try to get their 6-year-olds into the best elementary schools so they will have a head start. They pay big bucks to send their children to cram schools, which offer extra lessons after the regular school day that will give a leg up on the intense competition over the college entrance exams. Private companies, both Chinese and foreign, specialize in selling educational materials to Chinese families. Learning English is viewed as one key to a successful future. In 2003, Disney was selling packages titled "Magic English" and "Baby Einstein," and Time-Warner was market-testing a 40-CD interactive set of English lessons in Shanghai that sold for around U.S.$3,300.

Critical Thinking Question

1. Why do Chinese parents and grandparents seem so concerned that their children do well in school?

Sources. China Daily (November 5, 2003); Fong (2004); Jackson and Howe (2006); Yan (2006)

"shallowest" to "deepest," these groups are called unilineally extended families, lineages, and clans. (There are other types, but they are not discussed here.)

Unilineally extended families consist of people who cooperate and have mutual obligations based on their descent from an ancestor who lived only three or four generations ago. Extended families may be defined either patrilineally or matrilineally. Such families may or may not live in the same household (see Chapter 8), but they recognize their close ties, may hold common property, may cooperate in work, and may have shared ritual responsibilities.

Lineages are unilineal groups composed of several unilineally extended families whose members are able to trace their descent through males or females from a common ancestor who typically lived four or five or more generations in the past. By the conventional definition, the extended families that make up the group must be able to state how they are related to one another for anthropologists to call the group a lineage. Lineages may be either patrilineal (patrilineages) or matrilineal (matrilineages), depending on the form of descent prevalent among a given people.

Clans are unilineal descent groups whose members believe they are descended from a common ancestor through either the male line (*patriclans*) or the female line (*matriclans*). The major difference between a clan and a lineage is generational depth. With clans, the common ancestor lived so far in the past that not all the members of the clan are able to state precisely how they are related to one another. Like lineages, clans are usually exogamous. Members of the clan think of themselves as relatives and frequently refer to one another as "clan brother" or "clan sister." In many societies, clans own or control land and other forms of property. Generally, each clan is further subdivided into two or more lineages.

Among many peoples, clans are *totemic,* meaning that their members are symbolically identified with certain supernatural powers associated with particular animals, plants, and natural forces such as lightning, the sun, and the moon. Clans commonly take the name of their primary totemic symbol, and thus have names such as the bear clan, the sun clan, the reed clan, and the eagle clan. The association with particular supernatural powers often gives specific clans control over particular religious rituals. Although the function of clans varies from one society to another, they are usually among the most significant economic, social, and political units in the society.

Often people need to call upon different numbers of relatives for different purposes. A woman may need help with her gardening chores and will ask her extended family members for help. Or a group may need to defend itself against enemies, for which purpose they need to mobilize dozens or even hundreds of men to serve as warriors, so they call upon their lineagemates or clanmates for aid. Unilineal descent is a useful organization for these and many other purposes because it allows people to mobilize varying numbers of their relatives when they need assistance. Using one of the unilineal descent principles, smaller kin groups can be nested inside larger ones.

For example, in a patrilineal society, a nuclear family is a part—a "segment"—of a patrilineally extended family. In turn, the extended family is a segment of a larger group (a small patrilineage), while the small patrilineage is a segment of a larger patrilineage, which in turn is a segment of a patriclan. Using this *segmentary organiza-*

▲ In patrilineal societies, relationships traced through males can be used to form large groups of people, such as lineages and clans.

tion, dozens, hundreds, or even thousands of relatives can be mobilized, depending on the circumstances. The flexibility of segmentary unilineal descent systems makes them useful for many economic and political purposes (see Chapter 12).

Descent Groups in Action

The preceding description of descent forms and groupings is abstract. But, like families, descent groups are made up of living people who work in gardens, conduct rituals, teach their children, construct their dwellings, and carry out innumerable other activities together. If people are to work together for common purposes, they must have ways of creating groups and ensuring their continuity over time; they must have ways of assigning group members to roles and allocating tasks to them; they must have ways of making decisions that affect the members. In a word, they must be *organized.* More often than not, descent groups and kinship relationships provide the organizational basis on which various cooperative activities are carried out.

Two examples illustrate how unilineal descent principles organize cooperative activities. One is a patrilineal people of a Pacific island who call themselves the Tikopia. The second is the Hopi, a matrilineal Native American people of the Southwest.

Tikopia: A patrilineal society. Tikopia is a western Pacific island with only 6 square miles of land area. In the late 1920s, when Raymond Firth studied it, Tikopia had a population of about 1,200. Tikopians trace their descent patrilineally, and all Tikopians belong to one of four patriclans, each with it own name. Each patriclan is subdivided into several patrilineages, averaging 30 to 40 members. The members of each patrilineage trace their descent in the male line back to a common ancestor—the founder of the patrilineage—who lived four to six generations ago. The oldest male member of a patrilineage is usually its head, who makes certain decisions for the lineage as a whole. Lineages are exogamous, so the children of a lineage's women do not become members of it.

What sorts of activities do Tikopian lineages and clans organize? The lineage controls rights to land and certain other kinds of property. Each lineage owns house sites and several parcels of land planted in crops, including yams, taro, coconut, and breadfruit. The families of the lineage have the right to plant and harvest crops on lineage land. They cannot, however, sell, trade, or give it away to members of other lineages. The patrilineage, then, owns land and allocates use rights to parcels among its members, and each family acquires most of its food through farming the land of their lineage.

Ordinarily, each nuclear family cultivates mainly the lineage land of its husband-father. In Tikopia, the female members of a patrilineage retain their use rights to lineage land even after they marry. When a woman marries, a parcel of the land of her lineage is divided off for her own and her husband's and children's use. A woman may not, however, pass any of her rights to this land along to her children; when she dies, the use of the parcel reverts back to the patrilineage into which she was born. Thus, each patrilineage allows the female members who marry out of it to use plots of land for subsistence during their lifetimes but not to transmit rights to the land to their offspring.

The social rank of individuals is also determined largely by their lineage membership and their status within it. One lineage of each clan is considered the senior lineage. Because its living members are believed to be descended (through males) from the founder of the clan, it is the highest-ranking lineage of that clan, so its members receive certain kinds of respect from their clanmates. The senior lineage of each clan also has the right to select one of its male members to serve as the clan chief. Tikopian kinship thus has a political dimension because authority over others is granted or denied to an individual or group largely through the descent group's membership and rank.

Like people everywhere, Tikopians believe in supernatural powers. These beliefs are also tied to the kinship system because each clan has specific ritual duties to perform. Each of the four clan chiefs serves as the religious leader and organizer of certain religious ceremonies. Each clan has its own ancestral spirits, which were the deceased former chiefs of the clan. Each clan also has its own gods, with whom its chief acts as intermediary.

One religious duty of clan chiefs is to carry out rituals that ensure the availability of food. Each of the four major subsistence crops is mystically associated with one of the clans. The gods of this clan control the crop. The clan chief performs the rituals that ensure the continued supply and fertility of whichever crop "listened to" (as the Tikopia phrase it) the gods of his clan. Thus, each clan—in the person of its chief—has ritual responsibilities toward the other three clans. A patrilineage, too, has an ancestral home with sacred shrines where its members gather to honor their ancestors.

Tikopians exemplify the diverse functions that are often assigned to kin groups. Patrilineages control use rights to land and some other kinds of property and influence an individual's social rank. Patriclans have political functions, and their chiefs carry out rituals that Tikopians believe are essential for the well-being of all islanders.

Hopi: A matrilineal society. In northeastern Arizona live a matrilineal people known as the Hopi. The Hopi divide themselves into about 50 exogamous matriclans (some of which are now extinct). Clans are not residential groups; most have members who live in more than one of the Hopi's nine *pueblos*. A Hopi pueblo, or village, often is a single large apartment-like building divided into many rooms in which families reside. Each clan is subdivided into several matrilineages. The female members of a Hopi matrilineage usually live in adjoining rooms within a single pueblo.

Traditionally the Hopi are matrilocal, so after marriage a man usually joins his wife, her sisters, and her other matrilineal relatives to form a matrilocally extended household. Most Hopi extended families consist of one or more older women, their daughters together with their husbands, and sometimes even their granddaughters and their husbands. Because of lineage and clan exogamy and matrilocal residence, husbands are outsiders, and—as the Hopi say—their real home is with their mother's extended family. The residential core of a matrilineage thus consists of its women, who live close to one another throughout most of their lives. The married men of the lineage are scattered among the households of their wives, although they frequently return to their matrilineal home for rituals and other responsibilities or in case of divorce.

Most property, both secular and ceremonial, is inherited matrilineally. Living space, for instance, is passed from mother to daughter. Farmland, on which the Hopi formerly depended for more of their subsistence, is owned by a clan, with each lineage having use rights over particular parcels at any one time. The husbands of the lineage's women do most of the farming to support their families, although they themselves do not own the land.

Membership in a matriclan also establishes one's relationships with the supernatural world. Each clan is mystically associated with a number of supernatural powers called *wuya*. Clans usually take their name from their principal *wuya*, such as bear, rabbit, corn, badger, snake, cloud, sun, and reed. The members of a matriclan pray to their *wuya*, asking for protection and for bountiful harvests.

Hopi religion features a ritual calendar that includes a large number of annually required ceremonies. In most cases, each ceremony is "owned" by the members of a certain clan, meaning in Hopi culture that this clan has primary responsibility to see that the ceremony is performed on time and in the proper manner. Every clan represented in a village has a clanhouse, in which the masks, fetishes, and other sacred items used in the ceremonies it owns are kept when not in use. The clanhouse usually consists of a room adjoining the dwelling of the senior female member of the clan. This woman, the *clan mother,* is in charge of storing ritual objects and seeing to it that they are treated with the proper respect. There is also a male head of each clan whose duties likewise are partly religious because he is in charge of performing the ceremonies owned by his clan. A male clan head passes his position, together with the ritual knowledge required to hold it, down to either his younger brother or his sister's son. In this way, culturally important ritual knowledge is kept within the clan.

Among the Hopi, as with most other matrilineal systems, the roles of father and husband differ from those in patrilineal systems. As we have seen, a husband moves in with his wife and her relatives after marriage. Traditionally, a man brings little property into the marriage other than his clothing and a few personal items. The house, its furnishings, the food stored there, and other goods remain the property of his wife's family. A man provides food for himself and his family by working in the fields of his wife, but the products of his labor belong to his wife.

The combination of matrilineal descent and matrilocal residence profoundly affects relationships between fathers and children. Children's relationship with their father is usually close and tolerant. A man seldom punishes his own children. Culturally, this is not considered his appropriate role because—after all—children and fathers belong to different descent groups. The father's sisters and brothers likewise exhibit warm feelings for their nieces and nephews, often providing them with gifts and affection. The main disciplinarians of children are their mother's brother and other members of their mother's kin group. This is partly because a child's behavior reflects well or poorly on the kin group of the mother, so members of this group have the primary duty of monitoring and correcting children.

The Hopi illustrate how the matrilineal principle recruits individuals into kin groups in which they perform various economic, religious, and social roles. They also show how the form of descent found among a people influences interpersonal relationships between relatives, including between fathers and children and maternal uncles and their nieces and nephews.

Neither the Tikopia nor the Hopi system "typifies" patrilineal and matrilineal kinship. A wide range of diversity occurs in patrilineal and matrilineal systems. The two peoples do illustrate some of the main differences between patrilineal and matrilineal peoples, however, with respect to recruitment into groups, allocation of roles, nature of emotional attachments, and organization of common activities. They also exemplify a fundamental organizational feature of many preindustrial societies: Multifunctional kin groups carry out most of the cooperative activities that more specialized groups perform in industrialized nations.

Avunculocality Revisited

Comparatively speaking, Hopi women have a great deal of influence on domestic life and control over property—land in particular. (As we discuss in Chapter 11, Hopi women owe their relatively high status partly to

© Bettmann/Corbis

◄ The unmarried status of these young Hopi women is shown by their hairstyle. In Hopi villages, traditionally the husbands of women worked the land of their wives' families and moved into their wives' households. Hopi matrilineages and matriclans also organize many other economic and ceremonial activities.

their control over land and partly to matrilineality and matrilocality.) Because they are a matrilocal people, sisters live together and their husbands live apart from their matrilineal relatives for as long as the marriage lasts.

Not all matrilineal people are matrilocal, however. A common pattern of postmarital residence among matrilineal peoples is avunculocality, in which married couples live with or near the husband's mother's brother (see Chapter 8). More than one-third of all matrilineal societies have avunculocal residence as the predominant pattern. Most of the others are matrilocal or patrilocal. Now that we are aware of matrilineal descent groups and know that they often control property, we can understand this unfamiliar residence pattern.

First, the fact that a people are matrilineal does not necessarily mean that women control property and politics. That is, *matrilineality*—descent through females—should not be confused with *matriarchy*—rule by women or dominance by women over men. Even in most matrilineal societies, men control and make decisions about the use and allocation of land and other forms of wealth and have more of a say than women do in public affairs. The oldest competent man of a lineage usually has the greatest control over life-sustaining or culturally valuable property in a matrilineal society. Of course, in contrast

to patrilineal peoples, in a matrilineal society, a lineage elder has authority over his sister's children rather than his own children. This is because a man's children supposedly have their property and loyalties with the group of their mother.

How can a male lineage elder have his sisters' sons living with or near him, where he can keep an eye on them, and where they can look after their own interest in land and common property? The answer is avunculocal residence (see Figure 8.2d in Chapter 8). If a man's sisters' sons bring their wives to live with them in a common residence, then the elder and young male members of a single matrilineage live in a single place. The married women of the matrilineage are scattered among the households of their own husbands' mothers' brothers. The children of the matrilineage's women are likewise scattered among the households of their fathers, so long as they are unmarried. But as they marry, they return to their own mother's brothers' households—the place of their own lineage.

In short, avunculocal residence has the effect of localizing male matrilineal relatives who have a common interest in land, wealth, or other material property and/or who share ritual responsibilities. It therefore makes perfect sense once we see how the matrilineal principle forms kin groups that hold common property, and once we realize that men have control over wealth and public affairs among most matrilineal peoples.

Nonunilineal Descent

Once you understand how people become members of various kinds of unilineal groups, they seem simple enough. If your society is matrilineal, for instance, you and everyone else joins their mother's kin groups, and as a consequence everyone in your lineage or clan is related through females.

But human social life is rarely so clear-cut. In real societies where either unilineal principle is the norm, the actual membership of lineages and clans is not as well defined as the principles make them appear. For instance, in matrilineal systems, circumstances vary and change: adoptions, childless women, inability to get along with one's matrikin, insufficiency of land owned by the matrigroup, and other factors make it likely that some individuals will join a group other than that of their mother. Thus, even in unilineal systems, there is often some degree of choice about which group to join, depending on personal preferences and circumstances. Still, there is a norm or rule about what "should" happen.

In societies with **nonunilineal descent,** individuals do not regularly associate with either matrilineal or patrilineal relatives, but make choices about whom to live with, whose land to use, and so forth. There are different forms of nonunilineal descent, two of which are most common: cognatic and bilateral.

Cognatic Descent

Cultures with **cognatic descent** have no formal principle or rule about whether individuals join the group of their mother or father. Some people join with their father, others with their mother, entirely or largely according to preferences and circumstances. A **cognatic descent group** consists of all the individuals who can trace their descent back to the common ancestor (founder) of the group through both female and male links.

More than in unilineal systems, in cognatic descent, people make choices about the groups they want to join. The choice is commonly based on factors such as one's chances of inheriting rights to land use or other forms of property or wealth, the desire to associate with a relative of high status or rank, childhood residence, and emotional ties. For example, in a cognatic system, you might decide to reside and cooperate with your mother's relatives if her kin group has a lot more land available for you

to cultivate than does your father's group. Or if a coveted political office or honorific title is about to become vacant in your father's group, you might decide to try to acquire it by moving in and working with his relatives.

Cognatic descent is found in all world regions, but it is especially prevalent among Polynesians, including Samoans, Hawaiians, Tahitians, and New Zealand Maori. Details vary from island to island, but generally speaking, people can join any cognatic group or groups to which they can trace ancestry. Membership in the group bestows rights to agricultural land, house sites, and some other kinds of property.

In cultures with unilineal descent, individuals ordinarily become a member of only one group—their father's or their mother's. With cognatic descent, everyone potentially belongs to several groups because everyone has the opportunity to join all the groups to which their parents belong, and each parent is probably a member of at least two groups.

So, cognatic descent groups have *overlapping membership.* This potentially poses a problem for access to land and other culturally valued things. For example, if all members of a group have rights to the land collectively owned by this group, and if one-half or more of the entire population potentially has such rights, then the "right" does not mean much.

In the cognatic societies of Polynesia, most people keep up their membership in several groups simultaneously by contributing labor and foods to feasts sponsored by the groups and generally showing their interest in and commitment to the groups. The islands of Samoa provide an example. Each Samoan village has a council that plans public activities, levies fines, and performs other functions for the whole community. Each village includes several cognatic kin groups known as *'aiga.* Although each *'aiga* has branches represented in several villages, every *'aiga* has an ancestral village that its members consider their homeland. In its homeland village, each *'aiga* has the right to select one or more of its men to hold important titles. These title holders serve as the *'aiga*'s representatives to the village council. Acquisition of such a title carries great honor as well as authority to regulate use of the *'aiga*'s land, resolve disputes among the *'aiga*'s members, organize feasts and ceremonial gifts, and assess the members for contributions to marriages, funerals, and other events.

When a title becomes vacant because of death or some other reason, all members of the entire *'aiga* have a voice in choosing the new holder of the title, whether they live in the homeland village or not. Because people belong to several *'aiga* at the same time, they have a voice in choosing the new title holder for several groups, although

▲ In bilateral societies, kindred are ego-focused and usually come together only on special occasions, such as weddings, funerals, and, as here in Maine, family reunions.

they do not necessarily exercise their rights in every *'aiga* to which they belong. Because men belong to several groups, they have the right to compete for and gain a title in these groups. A young man might anticipate a future title vacancy in one of his *'aiga* and decide to move to the village where that *'aiga* is represented on the council to concentrate his energies on acquiring that particular title. This general kinship and village-level political organization persists in much of rural Samoa to this day.

The Samoan *'aiga* illustrates some of the common functions of cognatic kin groups: They can hold property and regulate access to land, organize cooperative activities, and serve as the basis for acquiring honored and authoritative political roles. In these respects, they are similar to the lineages and clans of unilineal systems. But in cognatic systems, the range of individual choice about group membership is much wider than in unilineal descent.

Bilateral Kinship

Bilateral (two-sided) **kinship** systems differ from unilineal descent in that bilateral kinship relationships are traced through both genders. Individuals regard their relatives through both parents as equal in importance. All cousins are the same kind of relative, for instance, regardless of whether they are related to Ego through the mother or the father.

Bilateral kinship, as you recognize, exists in most contemporary Western countries, but it is also common in other parts of the world. Bilateral kinship differs from both unilineal and cognatic descent in that no large, well-defined, property-holding groups exist. Rather than lineages and clans, the tracing of kinship relationships bilaterally produces networks of relatives known as the **kindred.** A kindred consists of all the people that a specific person recognizes as relatives through both sides of the family.

To understand bilateral kinship and the kindred, imagine a Canadian named Liz. Liz recognizes her relatives through her father and mother as equivalent and interacts with them in much the same way (unless she has established strong bonds with someone because he or she lives close by, or for some other reason). The more distant the relationship, the less likely Liz is to interact with or even know who her relatives are. The only times she is likely to see many of her kindred in the same place are at events such as weddings, funerals, and family reunions. Many of Liz's relatives do not know one another (her cousins on her mother's side are unlikely to know her cousins through her father, for example). All the members of her kindred do not consider themselves relatives, and they certainly do not own any common property. The only thing that ever brings them together is the fact that they are related to Liz.

Forms	Characteristics	Associated Kin Groups
Unilineal		
(a) Patrilineal	through male line	(patri)lineages and (patri)clans
(b) Matrilineal	through female line	(matri)lineages and (matri)clans
Nonunilineal		
(a) Cognatic	through either male or female line	cognatic descent groups
(b) Bilateral	through both parents of Ego	none: individuals belong to the kindred of Ego but associate only temporarily, on Ego's behalf

As this hypothetical example shows, a kindred is *ego-focused,* meaning that each individual is the center of his or her own set of relatives. Only you and your siblings share the same kindred; your mother has a different kindred, as do your father and all your cousins. Both unilineal and cognatic descent groups, in contrast, are *ancestor-focused,* meaning that people are members of a descent group by virtue of the fact that they recognize descent from a common ancestor whose identity is known or assumed.

The Iban, a people of the tropical island of Borneo in Malaysia, provide a non-Western example of bilateral kinship. The Iban are shifting cultivators who traditionally lived in longhouses subdivided into numerous apartments. Each apartment is occupied by a single ambilocally extended family (see Chapter 8) called a *bilek.* Most *bilek* include three generations: an elderly couple, one of their married sons or daughters and spouse, and their children. The *bilek* owns the section of the longhouse where its members live. Each *bilek* owns separate land, farmed largely in rice by its members.

The *bilek* is the main residential and property-owning group among the Iban. Compared with unilineal and cognatic descent groups, the *bilek* is relatively small, averaging only six or seven members. When an individual Iban needs more people for some purpose, he can ask for help from his kindred, people who are related to him through bilateral ties. In organizing hunting or periodic long-distance trading or warfare expeditions, for example, a man would call out dozens of his first and second cousins to get enough people together to help him for this specific purpose. In other words, a man *mobilized* his kindred to help him accomplish some particular task or achieve some goal. The bilateral relatives he mobilized, however, came together and cooperated only occasionally. They did not constitute a permanent kin group and did not hold any common property because the *bilek* was the property-holding unit.

The Concept Review will help you keep track of the various forms of descent and the kinds of groups that are associated with each.

We have presented four of the major forms of descent and kinship found among humanity. This diversity is surprising and puzzling. Surprising, because genetically your biological relatives are determined by your parentage, so why would some peoples emphasize their mother's line, others their father's line, and others both lines equally? Puzzling, because although there have been many attempts, so far no satisfactory explanation of descent and kinship has emerged. Asking the people themselves why they have one kind of kinship rather than another usually does not help. If you are from a Western nation, you will see this by trying to answer the following question: Why doesn't your society attach more importance to relatives through mothers than through fathers? A Closer Look presents some of the most influential ideas about the causes of diversity in kinship and descent.

Classifying Relatives: Kinship Terminologies

In Chapter 2, we noted that one of the major components of cultural knowledge is the way a people construct (classify) natural and social reality. Kinship relationships and groups are a major part of social reality in all human cultures. Just as cultures differ in the ways they trace their descent and form social groupings of relatives, so do they differ in how they place relatives into types, or labeled categories. The labeled categories are called **kin terms,** and the ways in which people classify their relatives into these categories are called their **kinship terminology.**

Most people think that the kin terms they use to refer to different relatives reflect the way those relatives are related to them biologically (genetically). In English, this is true for *some* terms: *mother, father, sister, brother, son,* and *daughter* all define individuals related to you in distinct (unique) biological ways. For example, no other female relative other than your *sister* shares your parentage (setting aside considerations of fictive kinship, such as adoption, foster parenting, and step relatives).

However, there are other English kin terms that do not faithfully reflect genetic relatedness. Consider *uncle* and *aunt.* They refer to siblings of your parents, distinguished only by their gender. But the individuals you call *aunt* and *uncle* are related to you in four different ways: your father's siblings, your mother's siblings, your father's siblings' spouses, and your mother's siblings' spouses. Note that both consanguineous and affinal relatives are included in the English terms *uncle* and *aunt.* The same idea applies to some other terms: A particular term may group together several individuals related to you in different ways. Thus, *grandfather* includes both mother's father and father's father; *grandmother* is used for both mother's mother and father's mother; and *first cousin* refers to a wide range of people who are connected to you biologically in different ways.

Thus, a people's kinship terminology only imperfectly reflects the biological relationships among individuals. More fundamentally, kin terms reflect the various norms, rights and duties, and behavioral patterns that characterize social relationships among kinfolk. Speaking broadly, collapsing relatives of different kinds into a single term reflects the cultural fact that people think of them as the same kind of relative. In turn, people conceive of them as the same kind of relative because they have similar kinds of relationships with them. Thus, the men we call *uncle* have the same general kinds of social relationships with us regardless of whether they are our mother's or our father's brothers or are the husbands of the many women we call *aunt.*

Cultural Construction of Kinship

Because the way people classify various relatives into labeled categories does not perfectly reflect the degree of genetic relatedness between them, anthropologists commonly say that kinship terminologies are *culturally con-*

structed. The **cultural construction of kinship** implies two things: (1) as children grow up in a certain community, they socially learn the logic by which their culture classifies "relatives" into categories, and (2) those categories do not simply reflect biological/genetic relationships. (If they did, we might be justified in saying that kinship is *biologically determined.*) In fact, as we'll see in a moment, the labeled categories of kinship sometimes hardly match up at all with biological relationships.

Before we can discuss particular kinship terminologies, we need to understand the logic by which they are culturally constructed. By "logic" we mean the principles that people use to distinguish one kind of relative from others. There are many principles, but only four are relevant for our purposes.

First, every kin term has a reciprocal term. For example, the reciprocal of *grandfather* is either *granddaughter* or *grandson.* If you call a woman *mother,* she will call you *son* or *daughter.*

Second, for some terms, the gender of the individuals to whom the term applies makes a difference. In English, gender matters for terms like *brother* and *sister, uncle* and *aunt,* and *grandfather* and *grandmother.* Indeed, gender is the only criterion that distinguishes the relatives just mentioned from one another. Gender is irrelevant, however, for another of our kin terms, *cousin.*

Third, kinship terms usually reflect whether the individual referred to is of the same or a different generation than Ego's. In English, specific terms are used for relatives in Ego's own generation (like *cousin*), in Ego's parents' generation (*aunt*), and in Ego's children's generation (*niece*). In describing kinship terminologies, we call Ego's parents' generation the *first ascending generation* and Ego's children's generation the *first descending generation.* Although the terms used in most kinship terminologies reflect generational differences, some systems use terms that transcend generations.

Side of the family is a fourth criterion by which kin terminologies are constructed. In English, side of the family is irrelevant: your relatives through your mother receive the same terms as relatives through your father. As we know, many other cultures place special emphasis on relationships through females (mothers—matrilineal) or males (fathers—patrilineal). As you suspect, this emphasis is reflected in terminological systems.

Varieties of Kinship Terminology

By using these and other principles in different ways, the world's diverse peoples have developed many ways of classifying relatives into labeled categories. The

Anthropologists have wondered for decades why cultures have the form of kinship they do. Why are the Tikopia patrilineal, the Hopi matrilineal, the English bilateral? Are there any general explanations? So far no one has identified a single factor or even a small number of factors that account for why different cultures develop different kinship systems. There are, however, a number of factors that *influence* (as opposed to *cause*) which form of kinship a people will have.

One influence is how people relate to their environment. For example, about 60 percent of all foraging cultures are nonunilineal. Why? Nonunilineal kinship gives individuals and nuclear families a lot of choice about which of their many kin relationships to activate at any given time. The Ju/'hoansi (see Chapter 6) and most other foragers must adapt to seasonal, annual, and spatial fluctuations in wild food availability. So it is beneficial to keep your options open by maximizing the number of people to whom you can trace kinship connections, which is done with nonunilineal kinship. Note that this influence is consistent with materialist approaches (see Chapter 4).

Relationships with the environment affect other descent forms also. About three-fourths of pastoral societies are patrilineal. According to one hypothesis, nomadic herding is associated with patrilineal descent because livestock are most commonly owned by men, although wives and daughters often actually care for the herds or flock day by day. To conserve labor in protecting and moving animals to seasonally available pastures, brothers often combine their animals into a single herd. This is one reason ownership of animals typically passes from fathers to sons. Brothers tend to stay together to cooperate in herd management and look after their common inheritance; therefore, they will reside patrilocally. Patrilocal residence associates male relatives together in a single location, whereas it disperses females. Over many generations, patrilineal descent

develops as a consequence because men who stay together through most of their lives tend to form close relationships and to pass ownership along to sons.

Patrilineal descent has also been viewed as a way to improve success in intergroup warfare among people. Examples include the Maring of New Guinea (see Chapter 7) and the Yanomamö of the Amazon (see Chapter 8). Patrilineal descent encourages male solidarity (bonding) and thereby increases their willingness to cooperate in battles, as well as decreases the chances of male relatives becoming antagonists. Evolutionary psychology (see Chapter 4) might explain patrilineal descent in these terms. Several cross-cultural studies have found an association between patrilineal descent and warfare frequency. But exactly why this correlation exists is a subject of much dispute, especially because war is important in many matrilineal societies.

What sorts of factors influence the formation of matrilineal descent? Some anthropologists think it is connected to the way peoples acquire their food. Matrilineal descent is more likely to be found among horticultural peoples than among foragers or intensive agriculturalists (see Chapter 6); nearly 60 percent of matrilineal cultures are horticultural. This association is probably related to the fact that women perform so much of the daily subsistence work in most horticultural populations, as we discuss in Chapter 11.

A cross-cultural study by Melvin Ember and Carol Ember suggests that horticulture plus long-distance warfare or trade often leads people to develop matrilineal descent. The reasoning is that if men are far away fighting or trading much of the time, they have less time for garden work, so women take over most of the garden labor. Women are more likely to work effectively if they cooperate with close female relatives than if they are working with or for their husbands' relatives. Also, a middle-aged or elderly couple will want to keep their daughters

classification systems have names like Eskimo, Hawaiian, Sudanese, Iroquois, Omaha, and Crow. (Don't be misled by the names of these systems. The American anthropologist Lewis Henry Morgan developed the classification system for kinship terminology in 1871. He named each system after the first people among whom he encountered it. In fact, all the systems are found on many continents, although four of them were named after the Native American peoples that Morgan learned about.)

Here we cover only four systems: Eskimo, Hawaiian, Iroquois, and Omaha. We further simplify things by considering only terms used for consanguineous relatives in Ego's generation and in Ego's first ascending (parental) generation. To make these systems easier to understand, we translate the terms into their closest English equivalents. Keep in mind that these translations are only rough approximations, and that some terms have no exact English equivalents.

around after they marry, to work their land and help support them in their old age. So postmarital residence is typically matrilocal in horticultural cultures in which men are often absent. Matrilocality places a group of sisters and other female matrikin in a single household or village. Their brothers move away after their marriage, and the children of these brothers develop closer relationships with their mother's family than with their father's relatives. This ultimately leads to the tracing of descent through females. This hypothesis seems to work reasonably well for some matrilineal cultures, such as the Iroquois and the Huron of North America and the Nayar of south India (see Chapter 8).

For evolutionary psychology (sociobiology), the most puzzling aspect of matrilineal descent is that most men give more material support to their sister's children than to their own children. This is "puzzling" because ordinarily men are more closely related to their own children than to the children of their sisters, and evolutionary psychology predicts that people are more likely to help closer genetic relatives than more distant ones. Back in 1974, Richard Alexander suggested that matrilineal descent can be explained by sociobiology. When will an average man be more closely related genetically to his sister's children than to his own? The answer: when the "probability of paternity" falls below about 0.25—that is, when an average man is only about 25 percent sure that the children of his wife are, in fact, his children. The mathematics of this are outside our scope. But the idea is that a man and his sister know that they have the same mother, so they automatically have some genetic relatedness even though there is good chance they have different fathers. Therefore, a man knows that his sister's children are related to him. But if there is about a 75 percent chance that he is not the father of his wife's children, then few of his own children are genetic relatives. Therefore, it pays off genetically to support his sister's children rather than those of his wife.

Around one-sixth of human societies are matrilineal. Is it likely that there are this many societies with a paternity probability lower than 0.25? No, because this assumes that in the matrilineal one-sixth of all societies, a woman is roughly three times more likely to be impregnated by a man other than her husband. Although sexual behavior, and especially extramarital sexual behavior, is difficult to research, this number is unrealistic.

However, evolutionary psychology can *potentially* help us understand why there are so many societies whose social organization is based on kinship, as we said earlier. Groups that own resources, cooperate in labor, raise children together, go to war together, and the like are most often relatives in preindustrial societies, which is consistent with evolutionary psychology. Critics of the approach argue against this idea in several ways, most notably that humans are more likely to cooperate with people they trust. We tend to trust people we know well, and whom do we know better than those we were raised with, regardless of whether they are our biological relatives?

As you can tell, there is a lot of controversy about the causes of kinship systems, and probably most anthropologists doubt that there is any universal explanation. It may be that crosscultural variations in kinship are influenced by so many kinds of complex factors that no generalized explanation is possible. Or, perhaps anthropologists have not yet looked in the right places for causes.

Sources: Aberle (1961); Alexander (1974); Divale (1974); Divale and Harris (1976); C. Ember (1974), Ember and Ember (1971); Ember, Ember, and Pasternak (1974)

Eskimo. **Eskimo terminology** is the easiest for English speakers to understand because this is the system most of us are familiar with (see Figure 9.3). In this system, Ego's biological mother is called *mother,* and Ego's biological father is called *father.* These are the only two persons to whom these terms apply. The term *aunt* is used for both Ego's father's sister and Ego's mother's sister, and the term *uncle* is used for Ego's father's brother and mother's brother. The terms *brother* and *sister* are used for only the children of Ego's mother and father. The term *cousin* is used for all children of Ego's uncles and aunts.

Hawaiian. **Hawaiian terminology** uses the fewest terms (see Figure 9.4). All of Ego's relatives in the first ascending generation are called either *mother* or *father:* the term *mother* is extended to include Ego's mother's sister and Ego's father's sister, and *father* is extended to

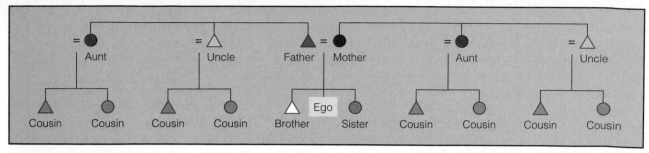

▲ **Figure 9.3** Eskimo Kinship Terminology.

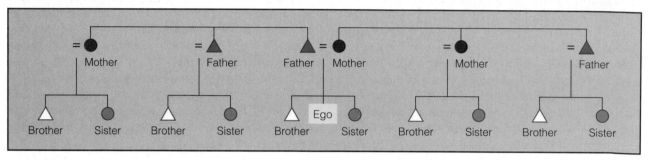

▲ **Figure 9.4** Hawaiian Kinship Terminology.

include father's brother and mother's brother. In Ego's own generation, all relatives are called either *brother* or *sister*. Thus, Hawaiian terminology includes no terms equivalent to the English terms *uncle, aunt,* and *cousin.* Although the Hawaiian system extends the terms *mother* and *father,* this does not mean that individuals are unable to distinguish their biological parents from their other relatives of the parental generation.

Iroquois. People who use the **Iroquois terminology** categorize relatives very differently than the Hawaiian and Eskimo systems (see Figure 9.5). The term *father* includes father's brother but not mother's brother. *Mother* includes mother's sister but not father's sister. Mother's brother and father's sister have their own unique terms. Looking at Ego's own generation, we also see a difference. The children of father's brother and mother's sister are called *brother* and *sister.* The children of mother's brother and father's sister are called by a term that might be translated as *cousin.*

Although this distinction may seem unusual to us, it also exists in the Omaha system, so we need to understand the logic behind it. Peoples who use the Iroquois system distinguish between parallel and cross cousins. They give their parallel cousins the same terms they use

for their own brothers and sisters. They distinguish cross cousins from parallel cousins, calling cross cousins by a unique term (here we translate the term as *cousin,* although obviously it has no English equivalent).

To understand the logic behind calling parallel cousins *brother* and *sister* and cross cousins by a different term, go back to the terms used for Ego's parents' siblings. Ego's father's brother and mother's sister are called *father* and *mother,* respectively. Thus, it is logical to call their children *brother* and *sister.* (After all, what do you call the children of the people you call *mother* and *father*?) Ego calls his father's sister by a term that might be translated as *aunt,* although the indigenous term is often something close to "female father." Ego's mother's brother is *uncle* (or "male mother"). So it is logical to call their children (who are Ego's cross cousins) by another term we might translate as *cousin.*

Omaha. **Omaha terminology** is difficult for English speakers to grasp (see Figure 9.6). The terms used in the first ascending generation are identical to the terms in the Iroquois system, and parallel cousins are called *brother* and *sister.* The difference between Iroquois and Omaha is how cross cousins are treated. Omaha terminology has no term similar to English *cousin.* In addition, in Omaha

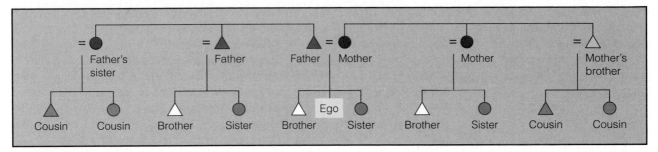

▲ **Figure 9.5** Iroquois Kinship Terminology.

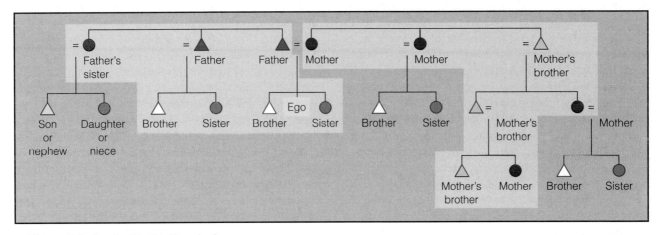

▲ **Figure 9.6** Omaha Kinship Terminology.

terminology, a distinction is made between cross cousins on the mother's side (the children of mother's brother) and cross cousins on the father's side (the children of father's sister). Mother's brothers' daughters are called *mother,* and mother's brothers' sons are called *mother's brother.* Thus, Ego's maternal cross cousins are grouped with individuals in Ego's parents' generation. For Ego's paternal cross cousins, the term depends on Ego's sex. If Ego is a male, he calls his father's sisters' children *niece* and *nephew.* If Ego is a female, she calls her father's sisters' children *son* and *daughter.*

Why are there two separate terms for father's sisters' children, depending on the sex of Ego? This distinction is perfectly logical. Remember that kinship terms are reciprocal and that Figure 9.6 shows only the terms used by Ego. To understand why the sex of Ego is important in this relationship, ask: What would father's sisters' children call Ego? In Figure 9.6, you see that Ego is their mother's brother's child. Thus, if Ego is female, they would call her *mother,* and she would reciprocate by

calling them *son* or *daughter.* If Ego is male, they would call him *uncle,* and therefore he would call them *niece* or *nephew.*

There are other systems, but these four are the most common and widespread. This diversity is surprising, and some of the ways of classifying relatives are puzzling. Can we account for them?

Why Do Terminologies Differ?

In previous chapters, we emphasized that cultures are integrated: one aspect "fits" with others and sometimes makes sense only when understood in context. Kinship terminology systems are an example of cultural integration.

A good way to begin is by noting that the four terminologies described can be separated into two types. In the Eskimo and Hawaiian, the side of the family does not matter in classifying relatives; in the Iroquois and Omaha, it does. Stated another way, among the diverse peoples who use the Eskimo or Hawaiian system, the principle of distinguishing relatives according to the side of Ego's family is irrelevant; they *could* recognize the distinction between mother's and father's kin, but they do not. Among the many cultures who use the Iroquois or Omaha system, the principle of distinguishing relatives according to family side *is* relevant. Why should the side of the family matter in some terminological systems but not in others?

As you've guessed, the side of the family matters in some terminologies because some people trace their descent through only one of their parents. The side of the family makes no difference in other systems because these populations trace their kin connections equally through both parents. *In general*—there are exceptions—the way a people trace their descent affects the relationships between kin, which affects the terms used to refer to various kin.

Consider the Eskimo classification. Comparing it with the other terminologies, we see that it differs in two main ways: (1) it makes no distinctions between Ego's father's and mother's relatives, and (2) no other relatives of any kind are lumped together with nuclear family relatives. Assume that these two features mirror people's ideas about how various kin are related. We might conclude that people think (1) that both sides of the family are of equal importance to an individual (or, rather, there is no systematic *social pattern* of importance through one side over the other), and (2) that nuclear family relatives are somehow special and thought of differently than are other kinds of relatives. In the case of North America, our surnames are inherited mainly through males, but other than this, we are no more likely to have special relationships with our kin through our fathers than through our mothers. And, generally, the members of our nuclear families *are* special: We do not expect to inherit much, if anything, from other relatives; we usually do not live in extended households; kin groups larger than the nuclear family do not usually own property in common; and so on.

More generally, we expect the Eskimo classification of relatives to be associated with cognatic or bilateral kinship. And usually it is: about 80 percent of all societies that use the Eskimo terminological system have either bilateral or cognatic kinship. This is because neither side of the family is consistently emphasized, so people do not think of their mother's or father's relatives as being any different. The absence of a special relationship with kin through either parent is reflected in the terminology.

What about the Hawaiian system? As in the Eskimo system, family side is irrelevant. Logically, then, it ought to be associated consistently with cognatic or bilateral kinship. The fact that it lumps other relatives with nuclear family members seems to indicate that the nuclear family is submerged or embedded in larger extended households. Ego should have important relationships with the siblings of his or her parents and with their children. Despite this logic, the Hawaiian terminology is not as consistently associated with cognatic or bilateral kinship as is the Eskimo terminology; in fact, about 40 percent of societies with the Hawaiian classification are unilineal. The Hawaiian system is apparently also compatible with unilineal descent.

And the Iroquois? Ego's father and father's brother are assigned a single term, which is different from mother's brother. Mother and mother's sister are given the same term, which is not the same term that Ego uses for father's sister. Thus, Ego distinguishes between maternal and paternal aunts and uncles in the first ascending generation. The fact that the side of the family matters in this generation seems to imply unilineal descent. And, in fact, the Iroquois system is usually found among peoples who trace their descent unilineally: about 80 percent of all Iroquois terminologies occur in unilineal descent forms. If you look back at Figure 9.5, you will see that Ego classes with his own brother and sister the children of relatives he classes with his mother and father. This certainly makes logical sense—if you call someone *mother,* it follows that you will call her son *brother.* The cross cousins have a separate term because their parents are not classed with Ego's own biological parents, which again is logically consistent.

The Omaha system carries the distinctions between the mother's and father's side "down" into Ego's own generation. If you compare Figures 9.5 and 9.6, you will see that the Omaha differs from the Iroquois by distinguishing cross cousins according to whether they are related to Ego through Ego's mother or father. Mother, mother's sister, and mother's brother's daughter are lumped together, although they are members of different generations. Mother's brother and mother's brother's son likewise are lumped together under a single term.

What can explain this way of classifying relatives? The fact that these relatives are all related to Ego through Ego's mother must mean something, and the fact that they are classified together and distinguished only by their gender must be significant. Indeed, both these features are clues to the logic behind the Omaha terminology. It is found among peoples who use the patrilineal principle to form kin groups.

How does patrilineal descent make sense of the Omaha system? In Figure 9.6, we have lightened the background around those relatives in the diagram who belong to Ego's own patrilineal group. Notice that the cousins in Ego's group are called *brother* and *sister,* to reflect that they are in Ego's own lineage. We have also lightened the background of those relatives who are members of Ego's mother's patrilineal group. Notice that all the members of this latter group are assigned only two terms—one for the male members of the group and one for the female members of the group. The two terms have no English translation, but they mean roughly "female member of my mother's group" and "male member of my mother's group." Their common *social identity* as members of Ego's mother's kin group overrides the *biological fact* that they are members of three generations. If you have followed the argument, you will agree that the Omaha system makes perfect sense, provided it is associated with patrilineal descent forms. And, indeed, more than 90 percent of all cultures that use the Omaha terminological system are patrilineal.

Another system, the Crow, is essentially the mirror image of the Omaha. You will not be surprised to learn that the Crow system is strongly associated with societies that have the matrilineal form of descent.

Thus, terminological systems make sense once we understand that they reflect the prevalent relationships and groupings produced by various ways of tracing kinship connections. The ways in which various people classify and label their relatives reflect the social realities of their kinship system, though not perfectly. These ways look mysterious until we understand these classifications and labels in the context of the kinship systems that give rise to them. The Eskimo terminology used by Americans would probably look strange to people who use, say, the Omaha terminology. Our failure to distinguish between relatives through one's mother and father would be strange because to them these relatives are clearly differentiated, given the way their kinship systems place people in different kin groups.

The various peoples who use one or another of these kinship classification systems cannot state the logic of their classifications in the same way we just did. For instance, people who use the Omaha terminology cannot tell you why they label their relatives as they do because they lack a comparative perspective of their own kinship system. To them, their mother, mother's sister, and mother's brother's daughter are called by the same term because all these women are the same kind of relative, just as *aunts* are all the same kind of relative to us. They do not realize that in Eskimo systems these females all have separate terms; nor are they aware that their terminology reflects the groupings and relationships of their kinship system.

But then again, people who use the Eskimo system cannot account for our own classification system either, until, of course, they become aware of the diversity in human kinship systems discovered in the past century by anthropologists. The way people—including you and me—classify their kinfolk seems quite natural to them until they learn that other people do it differently.

Summary

1. Relationships and groups based on kinship are important in the social organization of preindustrial peoples. Kinship is based on biological relatedness, but societies vary in their kinship systems. There is diversity in the kinds and sizes of groups formed using kinship principles, in the norms attached to kin roles, and in the way people culturally categorize their relatives.

2. One variation is in how people trace their relationships back to previous generations—in how they trace their *descent.* In unilineal descent, relationships traced only through one sex are emphasized. Unilineal descent groups may be formed using the matrilineal or patrilineal principle, which yields kin groups composed of people related through females and males, respectively. In order of increasing inclusiveness and genealogical depth, the main kinds of descent groups are extended families, lineages, and clans. The multifunctional nature of descent groups and the diverse kinds of activities organized by such groups are illustrated by the patrilineal Tikopia and the matrilineal Hopi. The avunculocal residence pattern is understandable once we realize that it consistently occurs in matrilineal cultures.

3. In cognatic descent, people trace their ancestry through both males and females. Cognatic descent groups exist that own common property and cooperate in various contexts, but individuals are able to join all the groups to which they can trace ancestry and can choose those groups with which they want to associate closely. The Samoan *'aiga* illustrates the functions of cognatic descent groups.

4. People who trace their kinship relationships bilaterally have no kin groups larger than extended families because the kindreds of different individuals overlap so much. In most industrialized nations, kinship is bilateral, and individuals trace their bilateral relatives outward from themselves. Unlike unilineal descent, kindreds are ego-focused, and large numbers of Ego's relatives are likely to congregate only on certain occasions, such as weddings, funerals, and family reunions. Individuals in preindustrial bilateral societies, such as the Iban, mobilize their kindreds to help them in various tasks, such as hunting, trading, and construction.

5. Kinship is culturally constructed, meaning that people culturally classify their relatives into labeled categories by recognizing some differences between relatives and ignoring others. This classification gives rise to various systems of kin terminology, of which we discuss four: Eskimo, Hawaiian, Iroquois, and Omaha. Very generally speaking, the ideas people have about how they are related to one another are strongly influenced by how the descent form of their society sorts people into groups and establishes relationships of one or another kind between kinfolk.

Key Terms

form of descent	lineage	kinship terminology
unilineal descent	clans	cultural construction of
patrilineal descent	nonunilineal descent	kinship
matrilineal descent	cognatic descent	Eskimo terminology
descent groups	cognatic descent group	Hawaiian terminology
unilineal descent group	bilateral kinship	Iroquois terminology
unilineally extended	kindred	Omaha terminology
families	kin terms	

Suggested Readings

There are a number of texts and collections of readings on kinship, descent groups, and the classification of relatives:

Collier, Jane F., and J. Yanagisako, eds. *Gender and Kinship: Essays Toward a Unified Analysis.* Stanford, Calif.: Stanford University Press, 1987.

Collection of articles focusing on relationships between the sexes and kinship.

Fox, Robin. *Kinship and Marriage: An Anthropological Perspective.* New York: Cambridge University Press, 1984.

Comparative introduction to marriage forms, kinship systems, and their causes and consequences. Was for years the standard text in this technical subject.

Schneider, David M., and Kathleen Gough, eds. *Matrilineal Kinship.* Berkeley: University of California Press, 1961.

Contains a description of nine matrilineal systems and an analysis of some dimensions of variation in matrilineal societies. Introductory essay by Schneider is a good overview.

Stone, Linda. *Kinship and Gender: An Introduction.* 3rd ed. Boulder, Colo.: Westview, 2005.

As the title suggests, looks at the interrelationships between kinship systems and gender. Many case studies illustrate the author's general points. Includes discussion of new reproductive technologies.

The following ethnographies include descriptions of specific kinship systems:

Chagnon, Napoleon A. *Yanomamö.* 5th ed. Fort Worth, Tex.: Harcourt Brace Jovanovich, 1997.

Description and interpretation of a patrilineal horticultural and hunting people of the Brazilian and Venezuelan rain forest. Shows how conflict and cooperation are based

SOCIALIZATION, SHAME, AND CHILDHOOD MALNUTRITION ON MOUNT KILIMANJARO

The Chagga live on the slopes of Mount Kilimanjaro in the African nation of Tanzania. Once relatively prosperous because of their agricultural skills and the fertile soil on the mid-altitude lands of the mountain, in the 1970s and 1980s thousands of Chagga families became so poor that their children suffered from malnutrition and many died from hunger-related diseases. Yet most of these poor families lived near relatives who were relatively affluent from wage labor in the service economy and from the coffee they produced and sold on global markets. Traditionally, Chagga were normatively obliged to help their needy relatives, and many did offer such assistance. But others failed to provide adequate assistance. In fact, they joined the health care and nutritional professionals who were supposed to help malnourished children in blaming the parents—especially mothers—for the hunger of their children. The mothers, many of the professionals told them, needed to learn how to feed their kids a balanced diet. This made the parents ashamed of their poverty and of their "failure" to provide their children with enough food. How did this happen?

In their 1997 book, *Hunger and Shame,* Mary Howard and Ann Millard describe and analyze the relationships among child malnutrition, child care ideas and practices, and the global economy for the Chagga people. Superficially, the causes of childhood hunger were not hard to determine: in the 1970s, Tanzania was beset by a combination of drought, a disease of the coffee plant (the main cash crop, produced for export), a worldwide drop in coffee prices, and other external factors over which the Chagga themselves had no control.

When we look deeper, though, the causes were less obvious. The drought was widespread and hurt all farmers, but it hit some families much harder than others. Falling income from coffee production did not directly put children in danger. Indeed, to some extent, the land that Chagga had planted in coffee over the decades reduced the amount of land that could be used to produce food. But the Tanzanian government had a policy of increasing exports and made it illegal to uproot coffee trees, even if the land was replanted with food crops in a time of decreasing prices for coffee. Population growth in the twentieth century reduced the amount of land available per person, and over time competitive pressures left some families landless or nearly so. These families had little choice but to try to support themselves by wage labor, but there were many of them and few jobs, so wages were low on the few coffee plantations and in the local Catholic missions. Population growth meant that the land available to Chagga had to support more people even as more and more land was planted in coffee and the income earned from coffee exports was falling. No wonder some families were unable to make a living and became impoverished.

Why did people blame poor Chagga parents for the malnutrition of their children? The answer lies in the interrelationships among the breakdown of old political and social relationships, the incorporation into the global economy, and Chagga child care ideas and practices, plus some influences of the Catholic Church.

In earlier years, Chagga had hereditary chiefs who collected tribute but also had responsibilities to care for the poor through redistribution (see Chapter 7). The wealth of chiefs and other persons was mainly in cattle, cloth, beads, and a few other items. Families of different social ranks could and did accumulate these valuables, but accumulation was limited by mutual obligations. One responsibility of chiefs was to care for the needs of the poor through hospitality, use of lands, and redistribution of food. And even wealthy commoners needed the labor of their less-well-off relatives to help care for their cattle and help work their land. In short, there was economic inequality, but it was balanced by obligations of redistribution and reciprocity.

Money, though, can be accumulated in unlimited amounts and, unlike cattle, it can be hidden away and hoarded out of sight of needy kinfolk. Also, money can buy labor on the impersonal market, so when the cash portion of the economy grew large enough, old obligations broke down as more and more people looked outside their local community for their economic welfare and security. Many Chagga poor no longer had the traditional social safety net to fall into when times got tough because of weather or markets. There was still a sense of duty toward poorer relatives, but generally assistance would be offered once and not again.

Like many other East African peoples, for Chagga the ideal interval between births was two to four years, so most women tried not to have another baby until their last-born child was 2 to 4 years old. There were spiritual beliefs about the relationship between an infant and a child still in her or his mother's womb. Mothers were not supposed to become pregnant until they had weaned their infants. If they did, then the unborn baby or its patrilineal ancestors would cause the older child to become sick and possibly die. The birth interval had the useful consequence of reducing the rate of overall population growth. It also meant that a couple would not have too many young mouths to feed or to compete for mother's breast milk. Birth spacing occurred by means of reducing the amount of sexual intercourse between husbands and their wives who were still nursing their babies. But by the middle of the twentieth century, efforts to space births increasingly were ineffective. There were several reasons for this, but one was Catholic teachings that all birth-control methods except the rhythm method were

(continued)

sinful, which, one woman said, "did not work when her husband was drunk" (Howard and Millard 1997, 122).

The symptom of childhood illness caused by babies born too close together was swelling of the belly, which actually is the medical condition called *kwashiorkor,* or protein-calorie undernutrition; that is, children were not getting enough food. Well-off Chagga, including even the relatives of couples with sick, hungry children, often blamed the parents for improper birth spacing, thus shaming them in the eyes of the community. Likewise, when families of sick, hungry children sought help at a government-funded clinic, the medical staff usually thought the problem was the mothers' lack of education about the proper foods to feed their children. For example, the flyer that announced the opening of the clinic contained statements like these:

2. If [the mother] prepares the right food for the child and if the child eats enough of this good food, he will be a healthy child again.

3. The mother must *learn* exactly what good food is, how to prepare it and how to give it to the child.

4. [At the clinic] the mother is therefore shown in detail how to cook good food. She will learn what kind of food that [*sic*] is good for building the child's body strength. She will also learn what kinds of foods give energy and which foods protect the body from certain diseases.

5. The mother will be shown how much to take of each kind of food, how to mix the food and how to cook it. She will also be told how often the child needs food. . . .

13. If the mother has been through all the lectures and knows well how to cook and care for her child, she will get a certificate at the end of her training. She can bring this home to show to her family and it will remind her of the weeks she has spent at the unit treating her own child. We hope she will feel happy. (Howard and Millard 1997, 184–185)

Obviously, the clinic felt that a Chagga mother who visited it did not know how to feed the proper food, in the proper mixture, in the proper amounts to her sick, hungry children. Once she had become educated, she would be given a certificate to take home to show that she recognized her earlier mistakes.

The shame that she and her husband felt over their failures would be made even more public. This was supposed to make her feel "happy."

But most Chagga women know, as they have always known, how to feed their children. Their "techniques," their "backwardness," their "lack of education" were not to blame. Their lack of access to resources was the main problem. "Without money, what can we do?" one Chagga woman asked (Howard and Millard 1997, 187). And resource shortages were due largely to factors outside the control of families, including the drought, past population growth, and how these factors related to the global market for coffee, the world price of which fluctuates notoriously.

There are wider lessons in the story of the Chagga's hungry children. When we see or hear of poverty, hunger, or—for that matter—homelessness in the United States, it is too easy to blame such problems on the personal characteristics of individuals. If children are hungry, it is the fault of their lazy, ignorant, uncaring, and/or abusive parents. If someone is homeless, it is because of the person's drug/alcohol abuse, unwillingness to get a job, lack of education, mental condition, or some other aspect of the person him/herself. Are we wrong? Not necessarily, but problems like hunger and homelessness are rooted in social and economic conditions as much as in choices individuals make. The "choices" made under conditions of deprivation may be merely ways of coping with these conditions. Sometimes, at least, we act like those Chagga whose cultural assumptions led the parents of undernourished children to feel shame.

Critical Thinking Question

1. Chagga cultural beliefs and practices interacted with forces from the global market to affect families in different ways. Can you think of other ways "inside forces" might interact with "outside forces" to affect local communities?

Source: Howard and Millard (1997)

Two African Examples

We could continue with generalizations like those above. But as an illustration of differences in socialization, we consider two African peoples in some detail: the Aka of the rain forest of central Africa and the Gusii of Kenya. Their comparison makes the point we mentioned earlier: how a people raise and enculturate their children depends on more than just their ideas and beliefs. Equally,

or more important, it depends on the conditions of their wider society, such as economic and political conditions.

Aka

The Aka are one of several short-statured ("pygmy") groups who have lived in the African rain forest for centuries. Like other Pygmies, Aka are mainly foragers who exploit the natural products of the forest by a combination

▲ Compared to most other peoples, Pygmy fathers are heavily involved in the care of infants and young children.

of hunting, fishing, collecting honey, and gathering fruits, roots, and leaves of plants. Although they do not plant gardens for themselves, for three or four months of each year the Aka trade with and work in the fields of their agricultural neighbors in exchange for manioc (cassava) and other cultivated foods. Most of the year, though, they live largely on the animals and plants of the forest.

Barry Hewlett, who studied the Aka in the 1970s and 1980s, reports that Aka parents are indulgent toward infants and children. Infants have physical contact with a parent or other caregiver most of the time. Mothers and fathers deal with infants' crying almost immediately. Whenever children wish, their mothers nurse them, and nursing continues until the child is 3 or 4 years old or until the mother becomes pregnant again. Infants sleep with their parents, as do other dependent children. Parents do not worry about spoiling their children or creating too much dependency. Children crawl and walk whenever they are ready; Aka do not believe children have to be systematically taught how to do such things.

After infants learn to walk and talk, they assume some tasks and responsibilities. Parents may ask them to gather firewood or fetch water, for example. But the Aka place great value on individual autonomy, even of children, so parents usually do not enforce their commands. Like parents in most groups, they may yell at their kids, but corporal punishment is rare—indeed, if one parent strikes an infant, that is reason for the other parent to ask for a divorce. By accompanying adults on their gathering and hunting trips, 7- or 8-year-old children learn the tasks needed to assume adult roles. Generally speaking, boys learn from their father and girls from their mother, but there is considerable overlap between the two.

Aka infants typically have many caregivers. As foragers, the people travel in small groups that average about 25 or 30 members. Most adults in the camp are relatives of the children. Aunts, uncles, grandparents, and older siblings care for infants much of the time, actually holding them more often than their own mothers while they are resting in camp. Despite this pattern, caregiving is not "communal" because the mother and father are considered to have the main responsibility for nurturing and teaching children.

Aka fathers are heavily involved in the care of their infants and young children. On the basis of his detailed field study, Hewlett reports that the Aka have the highest degree of father participation and involvement in infant care of any known human group. Fathers of infants younger than 4 months old hold or carry their babies one-fifth of the time when they are in camp, even though the infants are dependent on their mothers for nourishment. Fathers also make it a point to be generally available to their infants and children. Far from the role of remote but respected disciplinarian found in many other cultures, Aka fathers are emotionally intimate with their babies. As a result, older children become attached to their father and report having as warm feelings toward him as toward their mother, Hewlett says.

The reasons a particular people raise and socialize their children in a particular way are complex. Is the main factor their worldview? Their values? How they make their living? Their family organization? Obviously, all these and many other forces matter to different degrees among different peoples.

In the case of the Aka, how their bands are organized is one of the important factors. Married couples have their own sleeping huts, but the entire band of about a dozen families live in close proximity, with little domestic privacy. Both men and women are needed to get food for the family, and in fact mothers and fathers contribute about equal amounts to the daily food supply. Cooperation beyond the range of the nuclear family is essential. Often the entire band, including women and men, cooperate in hunting with nets. From the child's perspective, both the mother's and the father's sides of the family are about equally important. There is almost no difference in access to valued resources within an Aka band. Sharing is so ingrained as a norm that Hewlett calls it "demand sharing," meaning that an individual will give up an object if someone else asks for it. Finally, like the Ju/'hoansi, who have the custom called "insulting the meat," the Aka avoid showing off. No one brags about his or her accomplishments or skills, and, in fact, a man who shows a tendency to flaunt his talents may find other men and women putting him in his place by joking about the shape and size of his genitals.

Gusii

The Gusii's child-care beliefs and behaviors contrast with those of the Aka. The million or so Gusii live in the highlands of southwest Kenya. Unlike the hunting and gathering Aka, the Gusii traditionally made their living by growing crops and herding livestock (cattle, sheep, and goats). In recent times, many Gusii men began working for a wage. Women now improve their own economic welfare by selling grain at local markets. Robert A. LeVine, Suzanne Dixon, Sara LeVine, and their collaborators studied infant and child care among the Gusii for a period of 17 months in the 1970s. Their 1994 book, *Child Care and Culture: Lessons from Africa*, focuses especially on children from birth until about 30 months of age.

Gusii care of infants and small children differs both from the Aka and from those practices familiar to most Westerners. Most North Americans observing Gusii mothers interacting with infants would find the mothers very attentive to their children in some respects, but lacking in other maternal qualities considered essential or desirable for childhood development in Europe, Canada, or the United States.

In providing for the physical needs of their infants, Gusii mothers are diligent. Infants are rarely allowed to cry for more than a moment before the mother nurses or soothes them. This is easy for a mother because she and her baby are in nearly constant contact—mothers carry infants with them almost everywhere, either in their arms or tied into a sling on their back. Even when a woman is working in her garden, her baby is on her back or on a mat beside her. Infants sleep with their mother every night because on-demand nursing is customary and no decent mother would fail to nurse her demanding child during the night. A mother continues to nurse her child for the first 16 to 20 months, with no fear of making the baby too dependent on herself. Aside from nursing and comforting, mothers are careful that their children avoid physical danger, such as fires and animals.

On the other hand, a Westerner might feel that the Gusii mother–infant relationship is deficient in stimulation and emotional attachment. Gusii think that a mother can take good care of her baby without engaging in much "baby talk," playful interaction, and frequent affectionate touches and loving caresses. Crying babies are always calmed, but intellectual stimulation, smiles, and excitement are not important goals of the mother during infancy. Language development, too, does not seem high on a Gusii mother's priorities: When babies "babble," mothers do not encourage it with baby talk of their own, but tend to avert their gaze to avoid exciting the infant.

After an infant has grown into a toddler, mothers ease off in their attention. A Gusii woman, after all, has a lot of work to do. There are fields to plant and weed, grain to harvest, meals to cook, and firewood to gather. There are likely to be other children to attend to, since most women bear several children during their lifetime. After the phase of high physical dependency has passed in the life of her child, a mother resumes her full workload in the house and garden. When she is away, the 1- to 2-year-old child is left behind in the care of older siblings, some of whom are only 5 or 6 years old themselves.

Westerners might consider such "infant day care" under the supervision of children a kind of parental neglect, but it is normal in Gusii families and in most other parts of Africa. Older sisters are responsible for much socialization. They assist their younger siblings in language, work skills, and social development.

A Gusii woman in her 30s or 40s typically has several children. A mother continues to do garden work and other physical labor, but as her children grow up, more of her time is spent managing their activities and supervising their work. For the most part, she issues commands and assigns tasks, which children are expected to complete—although actual task completion varies a lot. Mothers seldom give detailed instructions or show their youngsters how to do something, although their older siblings do. Nor do mothers provide much encouragement or praise for a task well done. Mothers who praise their kids are felt to be encouraging selfishness, disobedience, and overly large egos. Apparently, the development of their children's self-esteem is not high on a Gusii mother's priority list. She becomes a more authoritarian presence as her children grow up, although she remains diligent in supplying them with food.

By the time they are in their early teens, most daughters will marry and move in with their new husband. When they become strong and responsible enough by the teen years, sons will join young men at the cattle camps—small roaming groups of young males that tend and protect cattle. Later, when they marry in their 20s, most sons will bring their wives to live with them near their mother because sons are a woman's primary support in old age.

So far, we have said nothing about Gusii fathers. This is because most Gusii men are barely involved in caring for their children, and most are seldom around even when their wife is caring for an infant. The Gusii and Aka live only about 1,200 miles away from each other on the African continent. But in the degree of father involvement, the two peoples are worlds apart. To understand the difference between their child-care practices, we must consider additional facts about the Gusii way of life. We must put them in the total context of the way the people live.

The most relevant facts are these: The Gusii are a patrilineal, polygynous, patrilocal, decentralized tribal people with high fertility and child mortality rates. How does this context affect Gusii child rearing?

Because of patrilineal descent, a male inherits most of his land and livestock from his father and father's father. Men are clearly the heads of Gusii extended family units, or homesteads. Normatively speaking, a wife obeys her husband, but she often responds to his demands by assigning tasks and responsibilities to her children. Family life, then, is fairly hierarchical and authoritarian, compared to that of the Aka (and to that of most Western nations, at least in modern times).

Polygyny is much less common today, but in the 1950s about 60 percent of Gusii women were cowives. Which men have more than one wife? Basically, those who can come up with the resources (in livestock, mainly cattle) to pay the bridewealth for several wives. Accumulating so many livestock takes time, so it is mainly older men who can afford to be polygynous. Most men's first marriage is in their early 20s, but most women marry much younger.

Because Gusii are patrilocal, a wife goes to live on the family lands of her husband. In fact, by the time they are in their early teens, most daughters have married and moved in with their new husband. A polygynous man has an obligation to provide each wife with a separate dwelling for her and her children, with garden land and a few livestock for milk. The mini-household where a wife-mother lives with her own children is called by a term that translates as "house," indicating that it is culturally regarded as semi-independent from the larger, extended household. Generally, wives provide for their own offspring, although cowives may help one another and share some tasks.

Decentralized tribal people means that Gusii have no formal chiefs or other kind of political authority that issues commands, settles disputes, or prevents warfare among Gusii themselves or between Gusii and neighboring tribes. Defense is up to the younger men of the settlement, so they must be available and willing to fight to defend themselves, their families, their livestock, and their local community against attack. Being a willing warrior was a valued male role. Any group whose men did not fight back and retaliate would be considered weak and would be repeatedly attacked and have its livestock stolen.

High fertility means that a woman has many children during her childbearing years. An average woman has eight or nine children between her marriage in her teens and menopause. For most of her reproductive life, she is pregnant, nursing, or looking after young children.

Indeed, she expects to become pregnant again soon after she has weaned her last infant. If her husband doesn't visit her often enough, she may even demand one of her rights as a wife—that her husband impregnate her.

High child mortality means that many children die during their first two years of life. About 1 in 10 babies dies before the age of 2. If a baby survives the first year or two, the mother considers it to be relatively safe. Most who survive the first couple of years grow into adulthood, although in olden times young male lives were at risk from violent clashes.

These factors interact in complex ways, but here the key point is to understand how Gusii care of infants and children makes sense in light of the overall context of Gusii life.

Why are Gusii families so large? The short answer is that children are "valued." This is true, but there are good reasons Gusii value having lots of children. A man prefers to have several wives (though most cannot afford to do so) because he wants his wives and their future children to work the land and tend the livestock that are his main forms of material wealth and the main source of economic security for himself and his relatives. His sons will tend his animals when they grow up and protect them from theft, while his daughters will bring in additional livestock from the bridewealth he receives when they marry. He wants his patrilineal family line to continue and to prosper in future generations, for which large numbers of sons are useful. When a man dies, he wants his sons to bury him—an important custom in the Gusii worldview—and his later descendants to pay homage to his memory. A man also enhances his status and reputation by having several wives and many children.

As for a woman, she also wants many children to assist her with her work and to help her meet her husband's demands. Further, because a woman lives on her husband's land, she finds that having many sons is economically beneficial in her old age: Her daughters will marry and move out, but her sons will bring their wives near where she lives to help her with her work and provide her with food. Also, because child mortality rates were so high (though they have declined in recent decades), a woman needs to have several children to make sure she has enough surviving sons. If a woman is a cowife, it is useful for her to have many sons to help protect her interests against her husband's other wives, who are in some ways rivals.

In sum, Gusii parents do value large families, but the value they place on children is sensible and rational to both mothers and fathers, given the way Gusii live.

Why are Gusii mothers so attentive to their infant's physical needs, yet leave their toddlers in the care of

▲ In Africa and on other continents, young children frequently assist with the child care of their younger siblings, as this Baggara girl of Sudan is doing with her baby sister.

their older children? Because so many children die before the age of 2, the main goal of a mother for her infant is simple survival, not providing a warm and nurturing social environment to improve the child's intellectual and emotional development. For those women who have been married long enough to have several children, spaced two to four years apart, older siblings are available to look after toddlers. It is good training for their own parenting skills, and LeVine and his colleagues believe that the toddler has few problems. Assuredly, in a culture such as Gusii, it is not a form of child neglect, as it would be considered in North America.

Why are Gusii fathers hardly involved in child care, in sharp contrast to Aka fathers? There are several reasons:

- Aka mothers and fathers regularly work together to acquire food by cooperative net hunting. Gusii couples rarely work together. This allows Aka fathers to be more continuously available to their infants.

- Aka couples live in the same hut along with their children. If married to a polygynous man, a Gusii wife has her own house and semi-independent household, and the husband-father does not live with her on a permanent basis.

- Among the foraging Aka, wild resources are not privately owned. In contrast, some Gusii men have more land and livestock than others. Their land can be worked and their herds increased by having a lot of dependents—that is, wives and children. So the most successful Gusii men have several wives and too many children to be as attentive as Aka fathers.

- Aka share objects and food widely and almost daily within the band, whereas Gusii men gain social advantages by engaging in balanced reciprocity with other men to make alliances. Exchanging and feasting take a lot of organizing. Children enjoy benefits from their father's success, especially when it is time to inherit his wealth, but it reduces his contact with them.

- Aka do occasionally have physical fights with one another, but living in the rain forest, they have no true enemies against whom they must mobilize for defense. Gusii have land and livestock that are sometimes coveted by other Gusii as well as by other tribes, so they have to be ready and able to defend themselves from attack and theft. This takes time and energy away from fathering.

Some readers may conclude that Aka men are "better fathers" than Gusii men. But this view ignores the different ways of life of the two peoples. Good Gusii fathers look after the welfare of their children in their own customary and culturally appropriate way. They provide their wives with land, livestock, a house site, and other resources to support herself and their children. When their sons are ready to marry, Gusii fathers give them an adequate inheritance and assistance with bridewealth. They provide all their family dependents with protection from enemies. Good Gusii fathers try to increase the size of their herds so that their sons will inherit more animals and thus have better chances to succeed in life. All this is facilitated by having a large family and political connections and alliances, and maintaining such connections and alliances consumes much of a Gusii man's time.

Implications for Modern Parents

Aka and Gusii children are brought up in different cultural worlds. Different kinds of knowledge and personal qualities are needed for success, so naturally child-care and enculturation practices are not the same. Notice also that the different degrees of paternal care among the two peoples are not *simply* determined by their ideas and beliefs about the proper way to care for and teach children.

Consider Gusii fathers, for example. Surely some fathers wish they could remain physically and emotionally close to their children. But protecting their property, providing an adequate inheritance for their sons, and achieving success in the wider society do not allow them to achieve their ideal parenting goals. A Gusii father's circumstances—the conditions to which he must adjust his fathering behavior—do not allow him to act as he wishes.

Likewise, many factors affect how a Gusii mother relates to her children. She has ideas and beliefs about the proper way to treat and teach her children. She acquired these ideas in her own childhood and from a lifetime of talk, observation, and other kinds of social learning. But she also encounters circumstances and conditions as she lives her own life and tries to be a good mother. These are external factors or constraints that affect a mother's actual child-care behavior (see Chapter 2 on the relationship between cultural knowledge and behavior).

A mother's beliefs and circumstances both affect how she raises her children. Because of her *beliefs,* she thinks certain ways are better than others. Because of her *circumstances,* she finds certain behaviors to be necessary or more feasible than others. The mother may prefer to remain as attentive to her 2-year-old child as she is to her newborn, but her circumstances do not allow this: she has obligations to her husband, to other relatives, and to her older children, so she cannot always do what she prefers.

The wider message is that economic, social, and political factors beyond the control of parents and other caretakers are *universally* important influences on how parents rear their children. Many employed parents in twenty-first-century industrial nations bemoan their inability to spend as much time with their children as they believe is necessary for their children's emotional well-being or intellectual development. To make up for the hours spent on the job instead of at home with the kids, modern parents believe in devoting "quality time" to their children. The implication is that in the past no one had to worry about such things.

But parents everywhere have to cope with conditions that affect how they rear children. Societies have adjusted to these conditions, they have readjusted as these conditions have changed, and they will continue to adjust. Thus far in the United States, working parents themselves have had to make most of the familial rearrangements needed to find child care. Although this is changing, only a small percentage of companies offer on-site day care or help parents through flexible work scheduling. Given all the emphasis on family values in the United States, perhaps it is time for more employers to find new ways of accommodating the child-care needs of their employees. Maybe family-values politicians will encourage them.

Life Course

A person's **life course** consists of the culturally defined age categories through which he or she passes between birth and death. It includes stages such as infancy, childhood, sexual maturation (puberty and subsequent adolescence), adulthood, and old age. At specific ages, a particular person will be a member of one of these age categories, whereas at other times, she or he is in between the various categories and stages of life.

The labeled age categories of other cultures are variable. Individuals everywhere go through changes that are biologically similar, but how people define and treat changes in the life course varies. A Gusii female, for example, passes through the following culturally defined age categories: infant, uncircumcised girl, circumcised girl, married woman, female elder. At each age level, certain events should happen in a female's life, and she is concerned if the events do not happen within the appropriate time frame. Thus, to become a "female elder," a woman must have married children, and so women worry about the number of their children and whether their sons and daughters will marry early enough.

So all peoples have age categories, but societies vary in the number of categories they recognize, the sharpness with which they define the categories, the importance of the categories relative to other distinctions such as sex, and the roles members of the category are expected to adopt.

Transitions between stages may take place gradually and not receive any special notice. In all cultures, though, transitions between at least some stages of life are sharply and formally defined by a rite of passage. A **rite of passage** is a public ceremony that marks, recognizes, celebrates, or is believed to actually cause a change in a person and her or his status, usually brought about or related to increasing age. Examples of rites of passage that most North Americans experience include birth ceremonies, birthday celebrations, graduation ceremonies, weddings, and funerals. Other familiar rites of passage are baptisms, bar and bat mitzvahs, baby and wedding showers, and installations of officials (inaugu-

rations). All of us enjoy (endure?) such rituals that mark new stages of our lives, but, as we shall see, some human groups "ritualize" certain kinds of transitions to extraordinary degrees.

Physical changes are visible evidence of some life course transitions, such as puberty and, in a few cultures, menopause. Here again, physical and biological markers of maturation and aging are interpreted differently and made culturally meaningful in a host of ways. Stages in the life course are intertwined with physical maturity, but in many cultures, an individual does not pass through a certain stage until something has happened to him or her. A person may not become an "adult" with all the rights and responsibilities the culture associates with "adulthood" until the person has married, for example. In many cultures, an initiation ritual is necessary to make a boy into a man or a girl into a woman, as we shall soon see with some examples. People do not grow up on the basis of physical changes alone. Maturation is a cultural as well as a biological process, so details of the life course vary from people to people. (The Concept Review provides a brief overview of a few of these variations.)

As individuals move through the stages of their lives, their overall role in society changes. Here we consider four stages that all societies recognize to greater or lesser degrees: infancy and childhood, adolescence, adulthood, and old age. These stages serve as a convenient way to organize our discussion of the life course, but it is important to recognize that cultures vary in how they conceive of these stages and in how transitions from one to another are recognized and marked.

Infancy and Childhood

It seems obvious that infancy begins at birth. But actually the stage of infancy is more complex because peoples differ in their beliefs about when life begins. Like other phases of the life course, "infant" is a culturally defined category of person in addition to being a physiological stage of physical and mental development. For example, does one become a human person at the time of conception, at some later phase in the mother's pregnancy, at birth, or at some time after birth?

Anthropologists often use the phrases *social birth* and *social person* to recognize that not all newborns are viewed as completely human in some cultures. Obviously, there are important consequences of beliefs about when human status is attained. Parents and families may not mourn the death of a newborn who they do not believe is yet fully human. In the wider society, an individual

Stage	Some Cross-Cultural Variations
Infancy	"Human status" begins at or after birth? Timing and significance of naming?
Childhood	Domestic and subsistence work responsibilities? Degree of separation of boys and girls?
Adolescence	Responsibilities and privileges relative to adults? Presence, elaboration, and significance of initiation rituals?
Adulthood	Defined by age or by life events and experiences?
Old Age	Degree of respect received from younger people? Degree of control over family resources? Provisions made for support?

may not be granted legal protection until he or she is culturally considered a living human being. The American legal system has struggled with this issue for years: people of different religious beliefs, ethnic affiliations, and political persuasions do not agree on when human life begins: at the time of conception, late in pregnancy, or at birth itself. Among the Cheyenne of the American Great Plains, children in the womb were thought to be completely human and were accorded legal protection. A woman who aborted her child was considered a murderer. She might be banished for a while because taking a life polluted the whole group.

In other cultures, though, even birth itself does not automatically confer the rights that come with human status. Where infant mortality rates are high, sometimes it is too painful for mothers and fathers to become emotionally attached to newborns. Northeast Brazil is one of the poorest regions of the Americas. Here many children are born into matrifocal families, and many mothers are unable to care adequately for some of their babies. To become social persons, babies must exhibit signs that they are likely to survive. Infants who are small and weak, who do not nurse vigorously, and who are frequently ill are believed to "want to die" and to become angels who fly up to heaven. There is little ceremony at their burial, their graves are unmarked, and the mother does not show much grief. (If a mother weeps, her tears dampen the wings of the little angel, so he or she cannot fly to heaven.) Nancy Sheper-Hughes, who worked among these women, sees the mothers' reaction as a response to their desperate circumstances: women cannot afford to invest financially and emotionally in babies who probably will not live.

In most cultures, an infant receives a name at birth. The act of assigning a name to a child is one symbol that she or he is recognized as a social person. The formal naming of a child is often the first rite of passage. For the Osage, a matrilineal Native American people now living in Oklahoma, the naming rite bestowed human status on the individual. Osage parents often waited several months—in the case of a sickly child, possibly more than a year—before naming a child. A child who died before acquiring a name was quietly buried, and the family did not have to observe a year of mourning. After they were convinced the infant was going to survive, parents began to prepare for a naming ritual. A ritual specialist called a "little-old-man" from the child's father's clan organized and directed the ceremony. Little-old-men representing all 24 Osage matriclans gathered in a ritual lodge to hold the ceremony. Each little-old-man recited a long prayer asking God's blessing for the child. After all clan prayers were recited, the child was handed to each of the little-old-men, who in turn blessed the child with water, cedar, corn, and other symbolic substances. Then the baby was given a name belonging to the child's clan by the leader of the ceremony, which symbolized the acceptance of the child as a member of a particular clan. The ritual participation of members of the other 23 clans indicated the acceptance of the child as an Osage. Only after the naming ritual did Osage infancy truly begin.

At some point, infants begin to toddle around, stop nursing, learn the proper places and techniques for eliminating their bodily wastes, speak long sentences, and so forth. Such events usually mark the passage into childhood, the period when people begin to acquire technical and mechanical skills. In most societies, learning technical skills begins early by Western standards, by about age 5 or 6. Simple tasks not demanding great strength are done even earlier—3-year-olds may sweep the house, feed the animals, wash the baby, pick up in the yard, run errands, deliver messages, and so forth.

In industrial societies, much technical learning takes place in schools, where trained specialists provide instruction in the skills needed to succeed in life. Among many preindustrial peoples, children learn most skills informally by watching and imitating adults and following their instructions. For example, among the Navajo of New Mexico and Arizona, 6- and 7-year-old boys and girls begin helping with the herds of sheep and goats. While Navajo boys learn the technical skills needed by men, girls learn the skills of women, helping their mothers prepare wool for weaving, grinding corn, making clothing, and caring for their younger brothers and sisters.

Adolescence

Most people experience physiological puberty between ages 12 and 16. In most societies, sexual maturation alone does not convey full adult status, with all its rights and responsibilities. Biologically determined sexual maturation usually precedes culturally defined social maturation, especially for males.

This intermediate stage of transition from childhood to adulthood is what we call *adolescence*. An earlier generation of anthropologists debated whether all peoples culturally recognized a stage of life comparable to adolescence: Do some peoples go directly from childhood to adulthood, with no transition period for training in fully adult roles and for achieving emotional maturity? Certainly, not all peoples have a word for adolescence in their language. Certainly, too, in many societies, girls are married before or very shortly after their first menstruation and so early on assume the role of wife. But neither of these facts means that adolescence is absent as a cultural concept, though its length may be short and its importance slight.

For males in many cultures, adolescence is a period when they prove their worth and establish their reputation. Among the Cheyenne and some other Plains Indians, older adolescent boys were expected to join war parties and to be daring and aggressive warriors and raiders. Along with adult males, they were expected to take part in hunts and help supply food for their family. In societies in which warfare is a serious concern, adolescence is frequently a period in which young male associations take part in defending a group's land and livestock against aggressors. By being vigorous and fierce in warfare, a young man could establish a reputation that might endure for the rest of his life.

On the Micronesian island of Chuuk (formerly Truk), most young men in their late teens and early 20s get intoxicated on alcoholic beverages. There is almost no "social drinking"; men drink mainly to get drunk. Chuukese say that a drunken man loses control of himself and goes out of his head "like a sardine" (which come headless in cans). While out of his senses, a man usually acts fierce and often picks fights with other young men. More seriously, he may physically attack a close relative, which ordinarily is normatively forbidden. Mac Marshall, who worked among the people of Chuuk, believes that drunkenness is a *role* most young men adopt. While in the role of a drunk, they get away with actions that ordinarily are not allowed. This phase of their life course proves their manhood—they are fierce, they won't back down, they are someone to be respected. But the role of drunk is a temporary phase for almost all males. Once they have children, almost all men soon become responsible adults, joining the church and giving up the role of drunk. Those who continue to drink are stigmatized.

In American society, as many parents know, adolescence is often a difficult stage of life, filled with experimentation, rebellion against parental authority, mood swings, and the like. Some researchers attribute the problems that arise during this period primarily to physiological changes, but others consider cultural factors to be the major causes. In the 1920s, Margaret Mead examined adolescence in a Pacific culture in her classic study, *Coming of Age in Samoa*. Mead found that adolescence was not a particularly traumatic time in the life of Samoan girls. She argued that the problems Americans associated with adolescence were the result of cultural factors, not physiological changes. In 1983, Derek Freeman challenged Mead's findings in his book, *Margaret Mead in Samoa*, arguing that Samoan adolescents have about as much trouble and conflict as do American teenagers. He went on to suggest that the physiological changes that occur during adolescence have similar effects among all peoples, so this stage of the life course is always stressful no matter what the cultural context. Most anthropologists of today agree that even if physiological changes create problems for adolescents everywhere, these problems are manifested in various ways, depending on the cultural context.

Rites of Passage

How individuals become adults and gain adult rights and responsibilities varies. In the United States, the transition to the adult stage of life is marked by rites of passage, such as graduation ceremonies (from high school or

◄ Some of these Micronesian boys are nearing adolescence. Will their teen years be filled with the same emotional responses as those of American adolescents?

college): one leaves the status of "student" and (the parents hope) becomes an independent, wage-earning adult.

Victor Turner pioneered the modern study of rites of passage. In his study of male initiation rites among the Ndembu of Zambia, Turner noted that most rites have three phases: separation, liminality (transition), and incorporation. The phases are revealed by common cultural themes and behaviors involved in male initiation rituals. The boys are often forcibly taken away from where they live, which represents a rite of separation from their houses and their mothers, and also from their previous role as "children" or "boys."

Turner noted that, once separated from their former homes and roles, boys go through a liminal phase. Typically, they are secluded and subjected to tests of their ability to endure pain without crying out. The rituals themselves frequently include beatings, genital operations, intimidation by threats and frightening stories, social seclusion, fasting, going without water, and so forth. Scarification of face and body is common because it is a visible symbol that a male has gone through the proceedings and is entitled to the privileges of manhood. These pains and traumas are usually considered necessary to strengthen the boys and prepare them for the rigors of adulthood. Such ordeals indelibly mark the transition from boy to man in the minds and usually the bodies of the males.

Turner also pointed out that a simple social structure usually characterizes the liminal period: to symbolize their equal status, the boys are typically stripped of all possessions, their faces or bodies are painted in an identical way, they are dressed alike, and their heads are shaved. All these actions make them look alike and emphasize their common identity and subordination to the elders in charge of the proceedings. (Incidentally, notice that some of these practices are similar to those that new recruits in modern militaries experience during the early weeks of their training, when they too are in the liminal phase of "no longer civilians, not yet full soldiers.")

After their common experience, the youths are reincorporated into the group, usually with new rights and responsibilities. Sometimes, they become eligible to be married or betrothed. They may dress differently or wear new jewelry. Often, the initiation ritual marks their independence from their mother, symbolized by a change in residence. Details vary, but the youths are brought back into normal social life as new persons.

In many societies, the transition from childhood to adulthood is marked by an elaborate set of rites of passage called **initiation rites.** Initiation rites often occur around puberty, so sometimes they are called *puberty rites,* although they do far more than simply mark a person's sexual maturation. During many rituals, the initiates are educated in the intricate responsibilities of adulthood. Elders tell them about the changes that will soon be expected in their behavior and often share ritual secrets.

Some societies have initiation rituals for males only, others for females only, and still others for both sexes. But even those societies that hold initiation rites for both males and females almost always have separate ceremonies for each sex. This generalization suggests that an important function of initiation rituals is to incorporate children not just into adulthood but also into the adult responsibilities culturally appropriate for their sex (see Chapter 11). In fact, the most common theme of initiation rituals is to make girls into women and boys into men.

Male initiation rituals: Highland New Guinea. The interior highlands of the island of New Guinea is one place where male initiation rituals are especially well developed. In many highland cultures, people believe that females can pollute males. In their worldview, a woman's body contains substances that endanger a man's health unless preventive measures are taken. Above all else, men fear contact with women's menstrual discharges, which they believe can cause them to sicken and die. Because of such beliefs, among many New Guinea peoples, women must remain in seclusion during their menstrual periods, either in a menstrual hut away from the main settlement or in a special place in their house, which men never enter.

These pollution beliefs have many implications for women's lives. Women must take precautions to avoid accidentally causing injury to their husbands by polluting the food they serve. In some New Guinea societies, women and men travel on separate paths, lest a man unknowingly step on a female secretion and become polluted. Women have to suffer through having their young sons taken away from them by force because, according to beliefs, continued association with their sons endangers the boys once they reach a certain age.

Finally, it is common for husbands and wives to live in separate dwellings. A man's wife or wives have their own house, where they live with their children. The husband lives in a separate men's house, together with all the older boys and men of the hamlet or village. By the time they are around 10, boys are usually taken away from their mother—because even contact with one's own mother is dangerous for a boy—and brought to live in the men's house. Male initiation rituals usually begin when a boy is taken from the company of his mother and other women and inducted into the men's house.

The details of male initiation vary from people to people in highland New Guinea. One common cultural ratio-

nale for the rituals is to transform a boy into a man: boys do not grow up naturally but must go through a lengthy series of rituals to give them masculine qualities. Masculine courage, strength, aggressiveness, and independence are desirable not only for the boys themselves but for the group as a whole, because most New Guinea peoples traditionally were heavily involved in warfare with their neighbors and so needed warriors to survive. Another goal of the rituals is to protect boys from feminine contamination: initiates learn ritual procedures that will allow them to have sexual relations in relative safety.

The Awa, a New Guinea people numbering about 1,500 who were studied in the 1970s by Philip Newman and David Boyd, illustrate both themes: "maturation" and "protection." Awa believe that if female substances get inside male bodies, the men will become sick or old before their time. When several boys in a region have reached age 12 to 14, they are taken from their mothers' houses. They are inducted as a group into the men's house during an intimidating ritual involving food and water restrictions, beating with stinging nettles to toughen them, and rubbing the inside of their thighs with a coarse vine. In Turner's terminology, this is a rite of separation. This is only the first of five stages of their initiation, which will last until they are well into their 20s.

In the second stage, about a year later, the boys experience the first cleansing of their bodies from female pollution. At a secluded site in the forest, small bundles of sharp-edged swordgrass are jabbed into their nostrils and two small cuts are made in the glans of their penis to bleed out contamination. A vine is looped and thrust down their throat, inducing the vomiting that also cleanses and helps dry out their body—for the Awa believe that bodily desiccation is necessary for boys to achieve maturity. The purpose of these acts is to protect the boys' health and promote their physiological maturity by ridding their bodies of polluting female substances.

The third ritual stage occurs between ages 18 and 20. The initiates again are purged of female contamination by nose bleeding, penis cutting, and induced vomiting. They are also told certain ritual knowledge, known to all adult men but kept secret from women and boys. After they have been through the third stage, the young men are taught why too much contact with women is so dangerous. They learn that menstrual pollution can overstimulate their growth and age them prematurely. Because they have not yet learned to protect themselves from female substances, they are warned to avoid sexual intercourse altogether until they are married.

About five years later, in their mid-20s, men go through the "sweat ceremony," which is the fourth stage

© David Boyd

▲ Beginning in their early teens, Awa boys participate in a prolonged series of rituals intended to strengthen, protect, and instruct them. This second-stage initiate is having his nose bled to remove harmful substances from his body.

of initiation. They sit together next to the fire in the men's house and sweat profusely for a week or more. The older men lecture them about their upcoming responsibilities as husbands and fathers. They are told about how to protect themselves from the dangers of sexual intercourse, and they are emphatically warned about the evils of adultery. When the men emerge from the men's house after the sweat ceremony, they receive new clothes and body ornaments, including a boar's tusk that they wear in their pierced nose as a symbol of their adult status. In Turner's terminology, stages two through four are the liminal period: Awa youths have been ritually separated from their former lives as boys, but they have not yet achieved the full maturation of adulthood, which in the Awa view includes marriage.

The fifth stage—appropriately called the "severe penis cutting"—occurs only a few days later. The young men are again subjected to food and water taboos, to nose-bleeding and vomiting, and to penis cutting. This time, however, canes are driven deep into their nose to cause severe bleeding. Small wedges of flesh are cut from either side of their penis, producing deep gashes in the glans.

The fifth stage is an Awa man's rite of incorporation. Once a man has been through the fifth stage, Awa

believe that he has been sufficiently strengthened by the hardships of initiation to be capable of withstanding feminine pollution, although he continues to undergo periodic bloodletting to protect himself and maintain his strength. After this stage, the men are in their early 20s. To celebrate their manhood, they turn their boar's tusk upside down to show they are ready for sexual relations and marriage. They are usually married soon afterward.

The Awa include several practices common in male initiation rituals: causing physical maturation, strengthening and protecting boys, imparting secret male knowledge, learning the importance of masculine responsibilities, symbolically marking the transition to manhood. We must note that Awa initiation rites are not "typical" of rites in other cultures, which are not usually so severe. But, again, it is interesting to know that male physical maturation—growing into a man—is a cultural as well as a biological process. Indeed, to the Awa, the series of rituals do not just "mark" or "symbolize" the maturation, but they are believed to actually cause the physical changes that make men out of boys. Without male rituals, they believe, boys will never grow up.

Female initiation rituals: Mescalero Apache. Fewer societies make the attainment of adulthood for girls into an initiation ritual. Some say this is because the physical signs of maturity are more obvious in the female body, so it is less essential for them to be socially recognized and proclaimed. Whatever the reason, where they occur, initiation rites for females most often emphasize attainment of physical maturity, instruction in sexual matters and childbearing, and reminders of adult duties as wives and mothers. (In Chapter 1, we discussed the sensitive topic of female genital mutilation, so we will not repeat it here.)

Mescalero Apache are one people who have ceremonies that recognize and celebrate girls' attainment of puberty. Each year, around the Fourth of July, the people celebrate the attainment of womanhood in a ceremony that lasts four days and four nights. Apache girls in the region who have had their first menses in the last year go to a place where a large tepee is erected. During the ceremony, the girls are regarded as reincarnations of White Painted Woman, a spiritual being who gave many good things to the people. The girls are blessed by singers (specialists who have gone through lengthy training to learn the stories and chants) and by their relatives and friends. Those attending participate in traditional songs and dances dedicated to the four directions and the spirits associated with them. The Apache ceremony places a lot of emphasis on the girls becoming the "Mothers of the Tribe," perhaps because the Apache are a matrilineal people. On the fourth day, singers recount the history of the Apache and the girls are reminded of their ancestry and obligations. The ceremony honors the girls as individuals, reaffirms their commitment to the community and vice versa, urges them to act responsibly, and upholds and re-creates Apache traditions annually. According to ethnographer Claire Farrer (1996, 89), "almost invariably, the girls report having been changed, not only into social women but also at a very basic level. They are ready to put aside their childhoods and become full members of their tribe and community." The ceremony thus helps the girls make the social transition to adulthood, with all its rights and responsibilities.

Adulthood

Partly because there are no obvious physiological transformations or psychological indicators of full adulthood, some peoples have no clear idea of when someone becomes an adult. But almost all peoples hold that adults have both more privileges and more responsibilities than adolescents, thus recognizing adulthood (at least implicitly) as a stage of life.

In many preindustrial societies, becoming married most clearly denotes the transition to adult status. This is one reason marriage in most societies is marked ceremonially with a rite of passage. The wedding not only formally ties the couple to each other and publicly recognizes their relationship, but also signifies that the couple is prepared for adult responsibilities.

In most preindustrial societies, the eventual marriage of nearly every individual is expected, and there are relatively few unmarried people. Why should marriage be so important for the attainment of adulthood in so many preindustrial societies?

There are several reasons. Sociobiologists/evolutionary psychologists hold that reproduction is a primary human motive because it is the means by which genes are transmitted. Among most peoples, marriage is the bond by which legitimate reproduction occurs. Marriage legitimizes children in the eyes of others and makes children more likely to receive favorable treatment in inheritance and in social life generally. Both women and men can and do have children outside of marriage, of course, but marriage helps stabilize the female–male bond for purposes of child care and gives children greater standing and rewards in the community.

The evolutionary psychology view is plausible, but it is not very helpful in accounting for why there is a greater expectation of marriage in preindustrial than in Western industrial societies. For that, we need to bring in the economic and social benefits of marriage while recalling that marriage concerns a wide range of people (see Chapter 8), not just the couple.

In preindustrial cultures, marriage is important to an individual because children often provide the only form of economic security available for elderly people; one needs children for support in later life. Relationships created by marriage are also important for various kin groups. Socially, a person's family members usually urge or demand that he or she marry in order to establish useful economic relationships with other families or useful political alliances with other villages. Access to resources is usually enhanced by marriage and by strategic choice of spouses. The desire to establish some degree of economic and social independence is another reason for high marriage rates among preindustrial peoples. Some kind of family unit is usually responsible for producing and processing the food and other products required. Because the domestic tasks performed by wives and husbands are often complementary, each sex requires the goods and services provided by the other. Most people who do not marry remain dependent (and typically low-status) members of someone else's household.

More than among industrialized people, then, marriage in preindustrial societies established a person's prestige, security, and social and economic independence. The importance of marrying and having a family has lessened in many industrialized nations, including Korea and Japan as well as Western nations. That modern industrial nations have relatively high percentages of never-married people, as well as high rates of separation and divorce, is partly explained by the fact that marriage has lost many other economic and security-providing functions it so often performs in preindustrial cultures, as explored in Chapter 8.

Old Age

Gerontology, the study of elderly people, has recently become a major interest of anthropologists. Part of our interest stems from conditions in North American society, in which elderly people are often seen as a burden, both to their children and to those who pay taxes to support elderly entitlements like Social Security and Medicare. (See A Closer Look for more on the care of the elderly in the United States and Japan.)

One popular notion is that the neglect of elderly people in modern American society is something recent.

© Paul Chesley/Stone/Getty Images

▲ Apache girls have a four-day puberty ceremony to publicly acknowledge and celebrate their attainment of adulthood. The initiate is coated in clay to symbolize her identification with a benevolent female spirit.

Sometimes we hear or read statements like "The elderly were respected and admired for their wisdom in tribal societies." As we have emphasized, however, "tribal" peoples are enormously diverse in all respects, including the way they regard and treat elderly people.

Among some preindustrial peoples, adults who can no longer economically contribute to the family because of age, physical injury, or severe illness become burdens to their families and largely dependent on the goodwill of others. Among the Comanche, old men were often the victims of pranks by young boys, who sometimes slashed the prized painted buffalo robes of older men. Little time was spent mourning the death of an old, "useless" person. Intense mourning was reserved for people who died while still physically in their prime because only their death constituted a true loss to their community.

Among some Inuit peoples of Canada, conditions for survival were even more tenuous, and parricide (the killing of close relatives) sometimes occurred. The old or infirm who could no longer keep up with the migratory movements of the group often were abandoned by their families. In some Inuit groups, an elderly person who was no longer able to travel would be abandoned in a sealed igloo with a little food and a seal-oil lamp for warmth.

Such ethnographic cases are not "typical"—no generalization can be made about *the* treatment of elderly people among preindustrial peoples. The cases do show that the attitudes of some people in developed nations toward the elderly are not unique.

Other preindustrial peoples come closer to the romantic ideal some of us have about the elderly: Authority over family and community, control of resources, and the respect one receives increase with advancing age. Senior members of the family and community are elevated to positions of leadership. Knowledge and wisdom gained from experience replace physical strength and stamina as the elderly person's contribution to the well-being of the family and community.

In the United States, as baby boomers (persons born between about 1945 and 1965) retire, people now in their teens and 20s face the possibility of paying sharply rising Social Security taxes to support retired persons. Improved medical technology and increased attention to personal health are leading to average life spans in the high 70s. Today many Americans live another 20 or more years after they leave the labor force. Partly because there are now so many Americans in their 50s, 60s, and 70s, commentators joke that existing Social Security benefits are the "third rail" of United States politics—"touch Social Security and you die." Older people generally need more medical care, so an aging population contributes heavily to rising health care prices. But health care for elderly persons is also widely seen as an entitlement—even by individuals who do not approve of other kinds of entitlements for other kinds of people. Because older people vote in such large numbers, the costs to taxpayers of Medicare (government-funded health care provided for those over 65) are increasing rapidly.

But North America is not alone. Other developed nations face similar issues. Consider Japan. In 2007, its population was around 123 million. Of these, about 22 percent are over the age of 65. Japan's average life span is 82 years (86 for women), the world's highest. An average Japanese woman today has only 1.25 children during her reproductive years, the world's lowest. Just to maintain the current size of the population, women in developed nations with good health care systems must average around 2.1 children. Japan's population size actually began falling in 2005. (The populations of many Europeans nations will soon begin to decline, although immigration probably will make up for most of their declining birth rate.) Fewer children today means fewer workers 30 years into the future, and rising life expectancies mean more dependent elderly. So, if we project these trends into the future, by 2050 about a third of all Japanese will be elderly.

In Japan and East Asia generally, respect for and care of aged parents were powerful cultural values that went beyond the Judeo-Christian commandment to honor one's father and mother. In old China, Korea, and Japan, the Confucian ethical philosophy held that *filial piety* (extreme respect and almost blind obedience to one's parents) was a primary human virtue. Parents made most of the important decisions for their children about matters such as when and whom to marry, education, and daily work activities. In China, many brief stories were told to teach and reinforce these filial values. In one story, the parents of an 8-year-old boy are bitten by swarms of mosquitoes. To spare his parents, the boy allows them to bite his stomach and doesn't even swat at them for fear it will lead them to fly away and feast on his parents. In another, a 70-year-old man amuses his very elderly parents by acting like an infant in front of them, stumbling around and crying like a baby to make them laugh. During the Qing dynasty (1644–1911), many violations of filial piety were considered serious enough to warrant harsh legal punishments. For example, a magistrate (acting as judge) could order the execution of a son who struck one of his parents.

In old Japan, there were strong normative obligations to provide for the needs of one's elderly parents. Because of primogeniture (see the Globalization box in Chapter 8), eldest sons and their wives bore most burdens of parental support. In rural Japan, especially, even into the 1980s elderly persons usually lived in the same household as their eldest son and his wife and family. The resident (usually the eldest) son was often so tied up in farm work and other activities that brought in income that he had little time to take care of his aging parents. Besides, the social realm of house and home was managed primarily by females—the resident daughter-in-law in most of Japan. So, when a woman married in, she took on a substantial duty to care for the parents of her husband as they grew old.

Of course, for decades most Japanese have lived in cities, where old practices like patrilocality and primogeniture seem to matter little. In cities, where people make their living

What are some theories about the care of elderly persons? For evolutionary psychology, at first glance, why people should care for their elderly parents and grandparents at all is puzzling. The benefits of caring for your own children and grandchildren are clear: if you did not do so, their chances of surviving would be small, and if you do so poorly, their chances of succeeding in the wider society (and having offspring themselves) would be lessened. But the biological fitness benefits of care for children do not apply to parents and grandparents: the *fitness* benefits of caring for elders are not obvious, especially if elders are beyond their childbearing years and so cannot even have any more offspring that share some percentage of your genes. In fact, the fitness benefits of even surviving beyond the age of childbearing are not very clear: if your genes are already represented in the next generation, why not just die so there are more resources for the survivors?

from wages and salaries rather than from working the family estate, elder care obligations are more diffuse: sometimes sons take responsibility, sometimes daughters, depending on circumstances. Still, children feel a strong obligation to care for their elderly parents, who brought them into the world and who sacrificed so much for their upbringing and education.

Today in Japan, collectively speaking, there are a lot of "elderly parents," whose care poses a significant cost to millions of family members. (Incredibly, in the eyes of North American youth, in the mid-1990s about half of all people who cared for elderly relatives in Japan were *themselves* over the age of 60!) As the number of Japanese elderly grew, starting in 1989 the government passed laws that provided taxpayer-funded services to qualifying older persons. Today all elder-care services are part of a national long-term-care insurance program. Services include periodic visits by nurses, help with daily tasks like bathing, delivery of meals, adult day care, and short-term stays at public nursing homes. There are co-payments, but they depend on family income and are generally affordable. Most caregivers take advantage of these services, if only because they offer a break from their day-in, day-out responsibilities.

In the 1990s, Brenda Robb Jenike interviewed 32 caregivers in Tokyo and also researched public facilities that offer services to the elderly. She found that Japanese still tended to entrust only one child with the main responsibilities, even if siblings lived nearby. Usually, this child is a son. Partly because of the feeling that management of home and family is primarily a woman's duty, most often the caretaker is the daughter-in-law of the elderly parent. Not surprisingly, many daughters-in-law wanted more assistance from the elderly person's "real children" and felt that their work was underappreciated (as such "family work" so often is).

Jenike also looked at how "real children" and daughters-in-law felt about transferring most burdens of elder care out of their hands to impersonal governmental agencies. Given Japan's traditions of filial piety and the cultural emphasis on the duties of wives to their husbands' families and despite the availability of public services, many Japanese continue to think it is best that elderly parents are cared for in the home for as long as possible. Very old parents, especially men in their 80s or older, are also less willing to accept help from outside the home, and their children are likely to respect their wishes.

So, family-based caregivers (overwhelmingly female) have some misgivings about using public services, both because they were socialized in a culture in which care of parents is a child's and/or daughter-in-law's duty, and because other family members are ambivalent about outsourcing this care. And there is a feeling that it is selfish to complain about one's family work. One way caregivers adjust to these cultural realities is by judging the quality of care given by public services as superior to the care they are able to provide themselves. Professional service providers encourage this attitude by providing occasions for caregivers to meet for public talks and join support groups. They also routinely express gratitude for the years of elderly care services offered by these women. Thus, caregivers have their services acknowledged by professionals and also can justify (to themselves as well as others) their actions as doing what's best for their elderly dependents.

In Japan's elder care arrangements, women who were socialized into the norms and values of their cultural system prove able to alter their behavior as circumstances change. This shows again that human behavior is not related to cultural knowledge in any simple or straightforward way, as noted in Chapter 2.

Sources: Jenike (2003, 2004, n.d.); Norimitsu Onishu, "Japan's Population Fell This Year, Sooner Than Expected," *New York Times* (December 24, 2005)

Evolutionary psychologists have dealt with the puzzle. The reason, they say, that people survive past childbearing is so they can continue to supply resources to their children and grandchildren. For example, elderly persons commonly provide material assistance, adaptively useful knowledge, and care of their grandchildren that free up parents' time to do other things. This is related to the long period of social learning that is necessary for human maturation: if older people are active in socialization and in providing resources, then their fitness might be higher than if they just died. Presumably, evolutionary psychologists would argue that helping the elderly survive and stay healthy keeps their benefits flowing to the next generation, so elder care pays off in increased fitness for the children and grandchildren also. Or, they admit that not *everything* has to be explained directly by genetic fitness, so perhaps there is a generalized human disposition to help those who have helped you (as in

© Noboro Komine, Photo Researchers, Inc.

▲ In many societies, advanced age brings increasing prestige and authority, as in these elders' homeland in Xinjiang, China.

balanced reciprocity). This would be a kind of intergenerational reciprocity.

Cultural materialists try to explain why cultures vary in their regard for and treatment of elderly people. One materialist argument is that the elderly receive the greatest respect and authority in those societies in which they control the land, livestock, and other resources of their family group. Younger family members rely on elders for rights to land and other resources needed for survival and success, so children have economic as well as emotional reasons for acceding to the wishes of their parents and deferring to their judgments. Obedience and deference, though, are not permanent because almost everyone who lives long enough will attain the status of family elder along with the esteem and authority it brings. Rather than fearing old age, many people look forward to it in such settings.

Another contributing factor is the contrast between literate and nonliterate people. In societies without writing, elderly people are the major repositories of historical, religious, and technical knowledge, functioning as the de facto libraries of these societies. Their control of knowledge makes them indispensable to the community and gives them power over its members, enhancing their social value and the respect they receive. In some Micronesian societies, for example, people do not reveal everything they know until near their death, which gives them some control over their children and grandchildren. This might be termed the "knowledge is power" explanation.

Another contributing factor is the rate of change a people is experiencing. In slowly changing societies with relatively stable technologies and organizations, old age is seen as imparting the wisdom that comes from decades of life experiences. Older people are (correctly) viewed as the repositories of community knowledge, so their opinions are valued and their words are often decisive—they are "the deciders."

In contrast, industrialization unleashed rapid changes in the technologies and economies of nations, and existing technologies quickly become obsolete. Therefore, people tend to view knowledge not as fixed but as continually changing. Experience alone does not generate the wisdom necessary for effective decision making. Like yesterday's technology, elderly people may be seen as out of step with contemporary realities. Like the elderly themselves, their knowledge is believed to be antiquated.

If it is true that the value people place on elderly persons varies with the rate of change, then as the globalization of production and markets incorporates more and more peoples, we would expect to see cultural norms and values about the elderly in many nations break down. This would *not* be simply because they are exposed to new "cultural models," but because they are experiencing the same rapid changes unleashed by industrialization as happened in the West.

Summary

1. Cultures differ in their child-rearing practices—nursing and weaning norms, the degree and methods of discipline, toilet-training practices, nurturing, sexual permissiveness, caretaking roles, and so forth. The Aka and Gusii, both African peoples, illustrate some of the diversity in child-care and enculturation beliefs and behaviors.

They also show that child care everywhere is affected by people's circumstances as well as by their ideals and beliefs about how children should best be raised.

2. During their life course, people undergo changes as they mature and age. Age is everywhere a relevant social characteristic used to allocate roles, which partly explains why transitions from one age category to another are so often marked by formal public ceremonies known as rites of passage.

3. Exactly when infancy begins and ends is defined by culture as well as by actual biological birth and physical maturation. Often, as among the Osage, a naming ritual confers human status to an infant.

4. The passage from childhood to adolescence is often accomplished and marked by an initiation ritual, which sometimes involves severe physical and psychological trauma, as illustrated by male initiations among the Awa of highland New Guinea. Among the matrilineal Mes-

calero Apache, female puberty rituals publicly recognize and celebrate a girl's maturity.

5. Exactly when adult status is attained is not always marked by a rite of passage, but among preindustrial peoples, marriage often is an indication that an individual is ready for adult responsibilities and privileges.

6. There are many influences on how a society regards and treats elderly persons. Some influences are: the degree to which elderly people exercise control over important property and its inheritance; whether people are literate (which affects whether elderly people are the main repositories of knowledge); and the rate of technological change a people are experiencing.

Key Terms

life course
rite of passage
initiation rite

Suggested Readings

Farrer, Claire R. *Thunder Rides a Black Horse: Mescalero Apaches and the Mythic Present.* 2nd ed. Prospect Heights, Ill.: Waveland, 1996.

A brief and readable description of the author's experiences with the Apache girl's initiation ceremony. Focuses on the ceremony itself, the roles surrounding it, the symbolism, and the place of the ceremony in the people's culture.

Hewlett, Barry S. *Intimate Fathers: The Nature and Context of Aka Pygmy Paternal Infant Care.* Ann Arbor: University of Michigan Press, 1991.

Fathers among the Aka Pygmies of Central Africa are more involved in the care and nurturing of infants than in any other known culture. An excellent study of Aka paternal care and how the case relates to wider issues of adaptation and gender egalitarianism.

Leiderman, P. Herbert, Steven R. Tulkin, and Anne Rosenfeld, eds. *Culture and Infancy: Variations in the Human Experience.* New York: Academic, 1977.

A volume of 23 articles, mostly dealing with infancy in various cultural settings.

LeVine, Robert A., Suzanne Dixon, Sarah LeVine, Amy Richman, et al. *Child Care and Culture: Lessons from Africa.* Cambridge: Cambridge University Press, 1996.

Examines parenthood, infancy, and childhood among the Gusii of Kenya and compares it to child care and parent–child relationships in the American middle class.

Mead, Margaret. *Coming of Age in Samoa.* New York: Morrow, 1928.

Account of adolescent girls in Samoa and one of anthropology's great classics. Few anthropological studies have been more widely read by the general public.

Turnbull, Colin. *The Human Cycle.* New York: Simon & Schuster, 1983.

A readable summary of life-cycle changes in various cultures.

Media Resources

The Wadsworth Anthropology Resource Center
academic.cengage.com/anthropology

The Wadsworth discipline resource website that accompanies *Humanity: An Introduction to Cultural Anthropology,* Eighth Edition, includes a rich array of material, including online anthropological video clips, to help you in the study of cultural anthropology and the specific topics covered in this chapter. Other material includes a case study forum with excerpts from various Wadsworth authors, map exercises, scientist interviews, breaking news in anthropology, and links to additional useful online material. Begin by selecting Cultural Anthropology to take you to videos, research, and more. From the homepage, you may also select Applied Anthropology, which directs you to essays, glossary terms, the case study forum, and a list of internships and careers in anthropology.

11 GENDER IN COMPARATIVE PERSPECTIVE

Sex and Gender

Cultural Construction of Gender

    The Hua of Papua New Guinea

The Sexual Division of Labor

    Understanding Major Patterns

    Understanding Variability

**Gender Crossing and Multiple
Gender Identities**

    *Cross-Gender Occupation or
Work Roles*

Transvestism

*Associations with Spiritual
Powers*

Same-Sex Relationships

Gender Stratification

    Is Sexual Asymmetry Universal?

    Influences on Gender Stratification

    *Gender Stratification in Industrial
Societies*

The roles, rights, and responsibilities of women have changed considerably in recent decades, as illustrated by this November 2007 photo of Hillary Clinton campaigning for the Democratic presidential nomination. What has anthropological research concluded and not concluded about gender?

Questions addressed in this chapter

What male–female biological differences most affect gender relationships?

What do anthropologists mean by the cultural construction of gender?

How and why do cultures vary in the sexual division of labor?

How do some cultures treat gender crossing and multiple gender identities?

Why is it so difficult to determine whether sexual asymmetry is universal?

What are some important influences on sexual stratification?

All human beings think and act within the framework of a cultural system that affects their interests, concerns, worldviews, social behavior, and so forth. Because anthropologists are humans too, our own research and teaching interests are affected by the changes that occur in our own culture. So, it is hardly surprising that the feminist movement—one of the most powerful social and political forces of the late twentieth century—has led to increased anthropological concern with the role of gender in human relationships and in society generally. In the early twenty-first century, the investigation of issues connected to gender is one of the most popular specializations within ethnology. Even those of us who do not "specialize" in gender now take gender into account in our research on other subjects, due to the recognition that most human relationships are permeated by beliefs about gender.

Like kinship and age, gender is a universal basis for organizing group activities and allocating roles to individuals. Everywhere, your identity as a male or female or as a member of another gender matters: it makes a difference in who you are, what you have, how you interact, and what you can become. But anthropologists have found that in different cultures, gender matters to different degrees and in different ways. These cultural variations and the factors that affect them are the subjects of this chapter.

Research in gender is so vast that we must focus our coverage on only four of the main issues to which anthropologists have made important contributions: (1) the cultural construction of gender, (2) the sexual division of labor, (3) multiple (as opposed to "dual") genders, and (4) gender stratification. Where relevant, we suggest specific ways in which anthropological findings and perspectives help in understanding gender roles and beliefs about gender in contemporary societies.

In any society, gender is a key dimension of a person's *social identity:* how other people perceive you, feel

about you, and relate to you is influenced by the gender to which they assign you and by how your culture defines gender differences. Less obviously, an individual's *self-identity* is affected by cultural beliefs and ideas: your conception of yourself depends partly on how your culture distinguishes masculinity and femininity, allocates roles to one or the other sex, and uses symbols (such as dress, behavior, speech style, and sexual preferences and practices) to help define differences between females and males.

The importance of a person's self-identity as a member of a particular sex is apparent in social relationships. Certainly, you are aware of how important your sexual identity is when you interact with someone of the opposite sex. But even in same-sex interactions, your social behavior is affected by your culture's norms, categories, worldviews, symbols, and other ideas and beliefs that influence your group's conceptions about gender. Cultural conceptions of "masculinity" and "femininity" matter just as much in same-sex as in opposite-sex interactions.

Finally, just as sexual identity affects interactions between individuals, so do beliefs about gender affect behavior in a variety of social settings and contexts: in the workplace, home, school, church, and political arenas, to name a few. Our culture's ideas about males and females—and about masculinity and femininity—permeate most of our personal relationships and our society's institutions, whether or not we are consciously aware of it.

Sex and Gender

The world's peoples differ in how much importance they attach to whether a person is female or male and in what specific behaviors they expect from females and males. To emphasize such cultural variations, anthropologists make a conceptual distinction between *sex*

cultural variation, however, there are some cross-cultural regularities and patterns in the sexual division of labor. What are these patterns, and can they be explained?

Understanding Major Patterns

Table 11.1 summarizes a vast amount of comparative work on the sexual division of labor. It lists some specific tasks and whether they are more likely to be performed by females or males. Those tasks toward the left of the table are more likely to be performed by males; those to the right are more likely to be done by females. The nearer a task is to the left, the more likely it is to be performed by males, and vice versa for females.

A few comments are needed to clarify Table 11.1. First, the table does not portray the sexual division of labor in any specific society. Rather, it represents a composite of information drawn from hundreds of societies in various parts of the world. For example, the tasks listed as "Predominantly Females" should be interpreted as those that are done by women in most societies, although in some specific societies one or another of the tasks are performed mainly by men. Tasks listed as "Exclusively Males" are those that are carried out by men in all or almost all societies, with very few exceptions.

Also, Table 11.1 includes only those activities that produce some kind of material product. Left out of the table are other activities that are predominantly or exclusively male, such as holding political office and fighting in wars. Also omitted are some activities, such as caring for infants, that are predominantly or exclusively women's work in all cultures. Of course, there is a sense in which all activities are "productive" (of social order, group defense, or children, for example), but here our discussion is limited to activities usually considered to be "economic tasks."

Table 11.1 reveals two patterns. First, all human groups divide *some* kinds of labor by sex in similar ways. That is, some tasks are done mainly or nearly exclusively by one sex in most societies. For instance, hunting, clearing land, preparing the soil, working with hard materials, and cutting wood are exclusively or predominantly men's work in the great majority of societies. Gathering wild plants, processing plant foods, and cooking are mainly the work of females in almost all cultures. In short, although the table shows that groups vary in the kinds of tasks allocated to women and men, there are *widespread* (although not *universal*) patterns; consistently, some tasks are more likely to be done by men, others by women. The first thing to explain is: Why are some tasks done mostly by women, whereas others are done mainly or entirely by men?

To see the second pattern, notice the tasks listed in the column headed "Either or Both Sexes." These tasks are not sex-specific; that is, they are about equally likely to be performed by men or women, depending on the particular society. Members of either sex may do them, or both may work cooperatively on them. For example, whether men or women plant, tend and harvest crops, milk animals, or work with skins or leather varies from people to people, with no clear pattern apparent. Which sex performs these kinds of tasks is so culturally variable that we cannot make generalizations; whether they are done by women, men, or both depends largely on local circumstances. The second thing to explain is: What determines the cultural variability in the sexual division of labor? Why are women more heavily involved in

▲ Although there is cultural diversity in the sexual division of labor, some tasks are performed primarily by one sex in almost all societies. For example, males almost always handle carpentry and woodworking, as this Indian woodcarver illustrates.

▲ These Tuareg women from Niger are processing millet, an African grain. Processing and preparing plant foods after the harvest are mainly women's work in the majority of cultures.

agriculture (planting, tending, and harvesting crops) in some societies than in others, for example?

This section focuses on hypotheses that deal with the first question. We put off discussion of the second question until the next section.

What explains why some tasks are nearly always done by men, whereas others are performed by women in most cultures? Biological/physical differences between the sexes—such as sexual dimorphism—provide one possible explanation. Perhaps tasks are assigned in such a way that the members of each sex do what they are physically able to do best.

This notion seems like biological determinism. If understood properly, though, it is not. Physical differences between men and women are only *relevant* in explaining the sexual division, not *determinative*. To claim that biological differences alone account for (determine) similarities would be outrageously wrong. The sexual division of labor *varies* cross-culturally, whereas the biologi-

cal differences between females and males are *similar* everywhere. You cannot explain something that *varies* from people to people by something that is the *same* among all people.

Rather, to say that physical differences between the sexes are relevant is to say something like the following: Because of biological differences, men can perform certain kinds of tasks more effectively than women, and vice versa, and these differences are reflected in the widespread cross-cultural similarities in the sexual division of labor.

Consider an example. Anthropologists used to say that there was one task that was everywhere done by men: hunting. Hunting seems to require certain biological capabilities—such as speed, strength, and endurance—that give men an advantage over women. Hunting also was thought to be incompatible with certain responsibilities universally borne by women for biological reasons: pregnancy, lactation (breastfeeding), and child care. Pregnant

FEMALE/MALE DIFFERENCES AFFECTING THE MAJOR PATTERNS IN THE SEXUAL DIVISION OF LABOR

Fertility Maintenance	Heavy, prolonged physical exercise by women results in lowered body fat and hormonal changes that reduce female fertility, so most strenuous tasks are done by males.
Reproductive Roles	Only a few males are needed to sustain population size, so societies protect their females by assigning hazardous tasks to males.
Physical Strength	Most men are stronger than most women, so tasks requiring greater strength generally are performed by males.
Child Care Compatibility	Women are everywhere the bearers and primary caregivers of young children, so they tend to perform those tasks that can be combined effectively with child care.

women would have a hard time chasing game, and lactating mothers would have to quit the hunt several times a day to nurse their infants. Because men could hunt more effectively than women, in foraging populations men hunted. In contrast, gathering required less strength and endurance. Because men had to spend so much of their time hunting, which women couldn't do as efficiently, gathering became largely women's work.

These arguments are partly valid, but female and male biological differences do not make it physically mandatory that males are the hunters and females are the gatherers in foraging populations. For one thing, not all kinds of hunting, and not all tasks connected to hunting, require superior strength, speed, and endurance. For another, there are questions about whether males typically have more "endurance" than females. Finally, there is no necessary biological reason a woman could not give up hunting only during her pregnancy and lactation and leave her older children in camp under the care of someone else.

In fact, it is just not true that hunting is *universally* a male activity. When BaMbuti Pygmies of the Zaire rain forest hunt animals with nets, the women help by driving game into the nets held by men. In another part of the world, Agnes Estioko-Griffin describes hunting by women among the Agta, a mountain tribe of the Philippines who live on the island of Luzon. Agta men do most of the hunting, but women often accompany them in teamwork efforts, and women frequently hunt together without the company of men. Interestingly, sometimes women take their infants with them on the hunt, carrying the children on their backs. There are some differences between the methods used and types of game hunted by women versus men. Still, people like the Agta and BaMbuti show that the "man the hunter" image is oversimplified.

But such cases do not make the image entirely wrong. The great majority of peoples in which hunting is a significant means of acquiring food are foragers or horticulturalists. In most foraging cultures, women gather most of the wild plants, although men may contribute among the Ju/'hoansi, Aka, BaMbuti Pygmies, and other peoples. Among horticultural peoples, the *pattern* is for women to do most of the planting, weeding, and harvesting of cultivated plants, whereas men hunt to provide meat. These patterns are not *universal* (no pattern is among humanity), but they are *widespread* enough that many anthropologists believe there must be some physical differences between men and women that are relevant in explaining them.

What specific female–male biological differences are likely to be most relevant in explaining cross-cultural similarities in the sexual division of labor? Four main arguments have been proposed, briefly summarized in the Concept Review: (1) the possibility that regular heavy exercise depresses female fertility, (2) the fact that women and men have different roles in reproducing the population, (3) the relative overall strength of the two sexes, and (4) the biological fact that only women give birth to and nurse infants and young children. We discuss each factor, although the first two do not seem very plausible in the view of the authors.

Fertility maintenance. One potentially relevant physical characteristic is that heavy exercise can reduce a woman's fertility. Modern female athletes—especially long-distance runners—often do not menstruate or ovulate monthly. This is because of a combination of a low body fat ratio and hormonal changes in women who engage in prolonged physical exercise. Some anthropologists suggest that work activities requiring heavy exertion would reduce women's fertility. For example, with

▲ The relative average strength of the sexes is one factor in the sexual division of labor, but this Pygmy woman carrying a heavy load of firewood illustrates that strength is not a "determinant."

preindustrial technologies, hunting often requires wielding weapons such as bows and spears that are powered by muscles alone, locating and tracking prey, and running down animals once they are shot. Lumbering and clearing land for planting also involve physical exertion such as swinging heavy axes for hours at a time. Conceivably, female fertility would be so decreased by such strenuous activities that the population would not be sustained over the course of many generations.

However, hunting among most foragers and horticulturalists is not as strenuous as portrayed, nor are many other activities that are exclusively or largely done by males. In fact, women commonly do many tasks that are as physically demanding as those done by men, such as hauling water, gathering firewood for fuel, and planting and harvesting crops. Although fertility maintenance could be relevant among a few peoples, it is unlikely to be a widespread factor and certainly does not account for the widespread patterns in the sexual division of labor.

Reproductive roles of women versus men Another possibility arises from the fact that fewer men than women are biologically necessary to maintain population size. A man produces enough sperm to father many thousands of children (theoretically), whereas a woman can bear a child only every year or so. (See A Closer Look for evolutionary psychology's ideas about how this might affect societies.) Because only a few sexually active men can impregnate a large number of women, the size of the population seemingly depends more on the number of women than the number of men. Also, in all known societies, women are far more involved than men in the care of infants and young children. For these reasons, speaking only of reproduction, fewer males than females are needed to sustain a population. For the sexual division of labor, this biological difference might imply that males are more expendable, which helps explain why so many hazardous roles (most important, hunting and fighting battles) are male roles: the group can afford to sacrifice some of its males but must protect its females as much as possible. If men "have" to perform such dangerous roles, then many other tasks are left to women by default.

Males are expendable only "theoretically," however, and if "all else is equal." In those societies—and there are a great many of them—in which warfare is a serious threat, large numbers of males are needed to protect the entire group. In fact, among many peoples, group survival itself depends on the ability to mobilize many warriors and to make political/military alliances with friendly neighbors. Only in their reproductive role are males "expendable"; in other respects, large numbers of males are essential for group survival. *If* there is a biological explanation for males performing more hazardous activities, it is because they are better equipped physically to do so, not because a group finds many of its males to be expendable.

Relative strength. Another biological factor is the average difference in physical strength between men and women, which allows men to perform tasks requiring great strength more efficiently. In Table 11.1, superior average male strength is *relevant*—once again, no anthropologist claims it is "determinative"—in many tasks under the heading "Exclusively Males" and in some of the tasks labeled "Predominantly Males," such as clearing land and preparing soil. On the other hand, male strength has no obvious relationship to other exclusively

◄ Whether or not a task is compatible with caring for young children seems to be an important influence on the sexual division of labor. This woman from the Malagasy Republic is looking after her baby and harvesting rice at the same time.

or predominantly male tasks, such as trapping, butchering, and working with fibers. Also, note again that women often do tasks that require significant strength, like gathering fuel and fetching water. Relative strength does influence patterns in the sexual division of labor, but other factors also matter.

Compatibility with child care. A fourth biologically based difference is that women are the bearers, nursers, and primary caregivers of infants and young children. This reproductive fact means that women are most likely to perform those tasks that can be combined with pregnancy and child care. Back in 1970, Judith Brown argued that such tasks have four characteristics:

1. They are fairly routine and repetitive, so they do not require much concentration.
2. They can be interrupted and resumed without significantly lowering their efficient performance.
3. They do not place the children who accompany their mothers to the site of the task in potential danger.
4. They do not require women and children to travel very far away from home.

The gathering of various products and the domestic work listed in Table 11.1 are highly compatible with child care. In addition, among horticultural peoples, garden tasks such as planting, weeding and tending crops, and harvesting usually are done by women; these activities, too, generally seem to be highly compatible with caring for children. Notice that child care compatibility is most

likely to be an important factor among peoples with high fertility. Where most couples have few children, this factor becomes less relevant as a basis for allocating productive work.

In sum, biological factors do help explain cross-cultural patterns in the sexual division of labor. Female–male differences in strength and child care roles have the most widespread relevance, although the other two factors might matter among specific peoples. Notice, though, that even if all four factors in combination totally explained the widespread patterns in the sexual division of labor shown in Table 11.1 (which they do not), none of them can explain the *differences*. In fact, no biological difference between males and females alone can explain the cross-cultural diversity in the sexual division of labor. The biological differences between the sexes in strength, reproductive physiology, and ability to care for infants are roughly constant in all human populations. But a condition that is constant in all groups cannot, by itself, account for things that vary between the groups. Constants cannot explain variability and diversity. We need other hypotheses to account for the cross-cultural variability in the sexual division of labor.

Understanding Variability

Here we focus on only one of the most important variations. Comparative studies reveal a fairly consistent pattern in the degree of women's versus men's involvement in certain agricultural tasks, specifically in those tasks labeled "Either or Both Sexes" in the middle column of Table 11.1. Recall the distinction between horticulture and intensive agriculture in Chapter 6. In most horticultural groups, much—and in some societies nearly all—of the everyday garden work is done by women. For example, in traditional cultures in parts of the Pacific, the Amazon basin, tropical Africa, and North America, women do most of the planting, weeding, tending, and harvesting of crops, whereas men participate in farming by clearing new land and preparing the plots or fields for planting. In contrast, among peoples who rely more heavily on intensive agriculture, women's actual work in the fields and direct contribution to the food supply are less important. To phrase the relationship in a few words: Women are more likely to be involved in direct food production in horticultural than in intensive agricultural communities.

There seem to be several reasons for this general pattern. First, in the New World, horticultural Native Americans had few or no domesticated animals, so men's contribution to the food supply focused on hunting. Most routine garden work fell to women because such work is generally compatible with pregnancy and child care. In contrast, most intensive agriculturalists relied on livestock for meat, dairy products, hides, wool, and other products derived from animals, so men spent relatively little time hunting. They had more time for farming.

Also, prior to the twentieth century, in Europe and Asia nearly all intensive agriculturalists used the animal-powered plow to turn the earth prior to planting. Some researchers have suggested that most women are not strong enough to perform the heavy work of plowing efficiently. (You might remember, though, that draft animals provide most of the muscle power for plow agriculture, which makes this suggestion difficult to evaluate. Also note that men are stronger than women only "on average.")

There is another reason women are less involved in direct cultivation in intensive agricultural societies. In Europe and Asia ("Eurasia"), the horticultural and intensive agricultural adaptations tend to involve the farming of different kinds of crops. Roughly half of horticultural societies grow *root crops* like yams, sweet potatoes, manioc (cassava), or taro. In contrast, about 90 percent of intensive agriculturalists rely on *cereal crops* like rice, wheat, corn, barley, and millet.

This difference affects the sexual division of labor. Root crops can be stored in the ground for long periods after they first become ready to eat, so they typically are harvested continuously during the growing season (think of familiar root crops like carrots or potatoes, which gardeners pull or dig up as needed). Either daily or a few times weekly, a woman goes to the garden and returns with root crops for herself, her children, and her husband. In contrast, cereals (because they are the seeds of plants) tend to ripen at about the same time each year, usually near the end of the growing season. They have to be harvested in a short period of time, dried and processed, and stored for the rest of the year.

How does crop type affect the work of men and women? Cereal crops generally require a lot of labor to process (e.g., winnowing, drying, grinding) before cooking. Plant processing labor is women's work in most cultures (see Table 11.1). Further, people who rely on wheat, rice, barley, or other cereal grains usually face periods of intense labor requirements: At the beginning of the growing season and at harvest time, there is a need for laborers who can do a lot of hot, heavy work in a short period that is best not interrupted by other tasks. Such work is generally done by men (see the preceding section). In contrast, root-growing horticultural peoples tend to spread cultivation tasks out more evenly over the entire year, making gardening a day-in, day-out, repetitive task that requires less strength and that is more compatible with child care.

A third reason is warfare. Where war was prevalent, men in horticultural communities defended the local village, neighborhood, or kin group from enemies. In regions such as highland New Guinea and parts of the Amazon, group survival depended on the ability to defend land and resources from attack. Community welfare often was improved by taking over the land of enemy neighbors, so offensive as well as defensive warfare was common. Men were not actually fighting their enemies most of the time, of course, but maintaining community defenses and guarding against surprise raids did require significant amounts of (predominantly male) time.

For most peoples, making alliances with other groups improved the odds of success in warfare. Forming and maintaining alliances required a lot of politicking, mutual visiting, and exchanges, further consuming male time and energy. Also, male solidarity ("male bonding") was advantageous, so in many groups where warfare was prevalent, there were elaborate male-only rituals or social events that strengthened ties between men and helped socialize boys into manhood and the warrior role (see the discussion of the Awa in Chapter 10 for an example). All these pressures related to defensive and offensive warfare led men to concentrate much of their time and resources in fighting, preparing to fight, or maintaining the political relationships needed for success in organized fights. Routine garden tasks were left to women, partly by default.

To summarize, comparative research shows that women are less involved in direct food production in intensive agricultural systems than in horticultural systems. Three of the most important factors that influence female involvement in cultivation tasks are:

1. Among horticultural peoples, men spend more time hunting than they do in intensive agricultural adaptations, so men have less time for cultivating crops.
2. Compared to horticultural communities, intensive agriculturalists are more likely to grow cereal crops, which makes it more likely that men will concentrate more on farm work and women more on domestic work, including processing foods before cooking.
3. Horticultural peoples tend to be subjected to pressure from hostile neighbors, so men are busier fighting, guarding, politicking, exchanging, and creating bonds and relationships among themselves.

In brief, as agricultural systems become more intensive, other factors change that usually lead to reduced women's involvement in direct food production.

It is important to emphasize that these relationships are *generalized,* meaning that they may not hold for any particular people. Horticultural peoples "tend to" be more affected by warfare pressures, intensive agriculturalists are "more likely to" grow cereals than roots, and so forth. Obviously, there are many exceptions to the general patterns.

Consider the Kofyar of Nigeria, for example. They construct terraces, spread goat manure over their fields, use compost, and practice other methods of increasing yields that lead anthropologists who observe them to call their farming "intensive." Yet quantitative studies in the 1990s reveal that Kofyar women work about as much as men in agriculture. The Kofyar and many other peoples do not have the relationship between cultivation intensity and male labor that comparative research says they "ought to have" or "predicts they will have."

The Kofyar and other exceptions to the general pattern illustrate two other points. First, the existence of a general relationship established by comparative research does not tell us what any particular group of people are doing or thinking. The culture of any people is a product of a complex interaction among their history, adaptation, beliefs, and other factors. In any particular group, factors *unique* to that group may be more important than factors that are *generally* important. So, the fact that Kofyar women work the land about as much as men, even though the Kofyar farm the land intensively, does not "disprove" the general point that women's labor becomes less important as land use becomes more intensive.

Second, just because there are exceptions does not invalidate a generalization provided, of course, that the general pattern is well established. If we are interested in the factors that influence the cultural variations in the sexual division of labor, then we must do comparative work to look for general patterns. The fact that particular cultures do not fit the pattern does not invalidate the generalization—at least not until the number of exceptions becomes large enough to make us suspicious of the existence of the general pattern.

The preceding discussion is an excellent example of the materialist theoretical approach discussed in Chapter 4. The way a population acquires food (by horticulture or more intensive methods) greatly affects the kinds of tasks women and men do (given the physical differences between the sexes and given the biological fact that women give birth to and nurse children). So the material conditions of life interact with biological differences between women and men to produce the overall pattern of the division of labor along gender lines. That, at least, is the materialist argument.

Gender Crossing and Multiple Gender Identities

Many of the world's peoples tolerate and even institutionalize diversity in gender roles and sexual orientation. Biologically male or female individuals who, for one reason or another, wish to adopt aspects of the role or behavior of the other sex are allowed to do so, with little or no social stigma or formal punishment. A boy who cannot or does not wish to conform to male roles is not forced to follow norms nor is he socially ostracized, but he is allowed to act like a woman in certain respects or contexts. Conversely, a girl who shows an affinity for activities culturally defined as male is allowed to participate in manly roles when she becomes an adult. In short, in many cultures, people can adopt the behaviors and roles typical of the other sex in features such as clothing, work, and sexual preference without experiencing social or legal punishment from other members of their communities.

These practices or customs are often called **gender crossing,** for obvious reasons. In many cultures, it is expected that a certain number of people are born who will, when they mature into adulthood, become like the other sex in some ways. Rather than stigmatizing such persons or trying to force them to live up to the group's standards of femininity or masculinity, they are accommodated and integrated into social life; that is, their alternative sexual identity is *institutionalized.*

Most North Americans will interpret "institutionalized gender crossing" as a way that cultures accommodate lesbians, gays, and bisexuals. This interpretation is generally correct, but, in fact, there is much more to gender crossing than sexual orientation, as we shall see. First, let's consider briefly how anthropological thinking about gender crossing has changed recently.

Until the 1970s or 1980s, most ethnologists viewed gender crossing in the following way. In any society, some individuals are born who do not fit into the existing sexual identities of "male" or "female." There will always be some boys who do not want to go to war, hunt, or compete in politics, but instead prefer to play with girls, do domestic work, tan skins, or otherwise act in ways culturally considered feminine. Likewise, some girls display an affinity for actions culturally associated with masculinity, preferring to play boy games, use weapons, dress like males, or whatever. In many human societies, such persons eventually learn to outwardly conform to the normal sex roles. If they do not conform, they are considered deviant and punished or stigmatized throughout their lives. In some societies, though, a legitimate role exists that allows them to satisfy their inclinations while serving the group in various ways. In this view, institutionalized gender crossing is interpreted as a cultural mechanism that provides a legitimate outlet for people who otherwise might be unhappy or cause problems in the social life of the community.

Certainly, this is a relatively favorable image of cultures that allow gender crossing. Anthropologists have often seen the institutionalization of gender crossing as a lesson "we" can learn from "them." Some human groups do not insist on rigid conformity to their sexual stereotypes, but allow diversity, in contrast to chauvinistic cultures like the anthropologists' own. Unlike "us," "they" normalize individual variation in aspects such as dress style, sexual orientation, work activities, mannerisms, and the like, rather than rigidly insisting on uniformity. And unlike many of "us"—who view men who act like women and women who act like men as morally degenerate, dangerous to society, or genetically abnormal— "they" do not despise or ostracize such individuals, but provide them with legitimate roles in the community's social life. The usual lessons were two: (1) "We" ought to be more like "them" by tolerating variation and accepting people as individuals whom we value and who can contribute in various ways. (2) Not all peoples in the world require conformity to their society's normal sex roles, so there is no reason to think that our intolerance is universal and, therefore, inevitable. These two lessons are well worth learning or, at least, pondering.

Still, some anthropologists today think that this view somewhat disparages gender-crossed individuals because it assumes that they cannot live up to the expectations of their "real sex," so they are allowed to "alter their sex." Further, the view assumes that, in all cultures, people classify individuals as belonging to one of only two genders (female and male), so that a woman who doesn't want to be completely a woman must become partly like a man, and vice versa. In fact, the term *gender crossing* itself implies that there are only two alternative genders.

In contrast, some contemporary anthropologists argue that many societies have more than two gender identities. Rather than dual genders, they say, such societies culturally construct **multiple gender identities.** Such peoples define a third or even a fourth gender of "man–woman" or "woman–man" (or "not woman–not man," or "half man–half woman," as some indigenous terms often translate). These third or fourth gender identities go beyond Euro-American definitions of homoeroticism, transvestism, transsexualism, or other concepts familiar in the Western cultural tradition.

Multiple gender identities are well documented for many Native American peoples. In his 1998 book, *Changing Ones,* Will Roscoe reports that more than 150 Native American cultures had institutionalized multiple gender identities for males, or females, or both sexes. Males adopted the dress, tasks, family roles, or other aspects of womanhood. Females took on activities usually associated with manhood, such as warfare or hunting. When they did so, they did not become the opposite sex, but took on alternative third or fourth gender identities. Far from being ridiculed, ostracized, despised, or otherwise socially stigmatized, such individuals in most cases were treated with respect and valued for their contributions to their families or group.

Among the Navajo of the Southwest, for example, families and local communities generally welcomed third-gender persons. An anthropologist in the 1930s quoted a Navajo elder:

> If there were no *nadle* [men–women], the country would change. They are responsible for all the wealth in the country. If there were no more left, the horses, sheep, and Navaho would all go. They are leaders just like President Roosevelt. (Quoted in Roscoe 1998, 43)

The elder surely exaggerated, but his statement does indicate the Navajo's recognition of the contributions of men–women. They often managed their family's property, supervised work, and became medicine men or took on other ritual responsibilities. On the other hand, we should assume that Navajo (like other people) vary in their opinions, so there was unlikely to have been unanimous approval or tolerance of *nadle*.

People with female genitals could adopt alternative roles as well, which also were valued in many Native communities. A girl who came to be known as Woman Chief was adopted by a Crow family during the nineteenth century. Like boys, she hunted deer and bighorn sheep while growing up. When the man who raised her was killed, she took responsibility for the family, acting as both father and mother. Later in life, she helped save her camp from an attack by the Blackfoot and went on horse-raiding parties. Eventually, Woman Chief took four wives and participated in council deliberations in her band, a role usually reserved for men.

Most Native tribes had a special word for such roles in their language, but gender identities varied so much from people to people that applying a single English word is problematic. To refer to males assuming an alternative gender, most anthropologists use the term *berdache,* taken from a term used by early French explorers of the Southeast. Some Natives and scholars today find this term inaccurate and offensive because the original Arabic term meant "male prostitute." But the Arabic meaning of *berdache* is not popularly known, so we continue to use it here, along with *man–woman, woman–man,* or *third or fourth gender identity,* depending on context.

As you might expect, most early Anglo observers of Native American men–women or women–men misunderstood these individuals and their roles in society. They overemphasized the sexual orientation of the person, whereas in fact their sexual behavior varied from tribe to tribe and from individual to individual within the same tribe. In most cases, even when *berdache* were homosexual, sexual behavior was not the aspect of the role that was considered the most important element by the people themselves. Further, male *berdache* rarely engaged in homosexual activity with *one another.* Where homosexuality was an aspect of the role, the men with whom relations occurred were not considered homosexuals at all.

A more accurate portrayal of third and fourth genders defines the roles as multidimensional, thus recognizing that practices varied not only from tribe to tribe, but also from individual to individual within the same tribe. Nonetheless, certain patterns are apparent. Serena Nanda identifies several features of gender variants that were widespread (but not universal) among Native American peoples. Four of the main characteristics are:

1. Cross-gender occupation or work activities—a preference for the work of the opposite sex and/or for work set aside for their third or fourth gender identity
2. Transvestism—in most cultures, a dress style different from the style of men and women—most commonly

▲ An old photo of the Zuni *berdache* whose name was We'wha. We'wha was a valued member of his family and community. Here he is dressed as a woman.

cross-dressing but sometimes a combination of female and male garments
3. Associations with spiritual power or a spiritual sanction—possession of special powers derived from spiritual forces, usually combined with a personal experience interpreted by the group as a calling
4. Same-sex relationships—the formation of sexual and emotional bonds with members of the same sex, who were not themselves men–women or women–men

These four widespread characteristics of third- and fourth-gender identities provide a convenient way to organize our discussion, but the variability of the role must always be kept in mind. No single dimension is "typical."

Cross-Gender Occupation or Work Roles

Adopting the work roles of the opposite sex was a widespread feature of men–women or women–men. This aspect often received special attention in various Native communities. Probably more than any other single dimension, occupation/work best defines the role. A famous Navajo *nadleehi* who died in the 1930s was unusually skilled in weaving blankets, a typically female task. In many tribes, individuals who performed the tasks of the opposite sex often excelled at the work, in the opinions of their communities. Sioux *berdache* (called *winkte*) dressed like women and lived in their own tepees at the edges of camps. The quill and beadworks of a *winkte* were often highly valued because of their fine quality. Among the matrilineal, matrilocal Zuni of the American Southwest, a *lhamana* (man–woman) was looked upon favorably by the women of his family because he stayed with the household of his birth rather than leave upon marriage. Matilda Cox Stevenson, a nineteenth-century ethnographer, wrote that Zuni *lhamana* would do almost double the work of a woman because they were not burdened by childbirth or the heaviest duties of child care. In spite of such examples, to say that all gender variants exhibited "sex role reversal" in work performance is simplistic; the most famous Zuni man–woman was We'wha, who participated in both female and male tasks.

Commonly, a child who showed an inclination for the work of the opposite sex was considered by others to be suited for an alternative gender role. For example, girls who acted as though they wanted to go hunting or use weapons were seen as potential women–men. A Mohave adult told a 1930s ethnographer that adults "may insist on giving the child the toys and garments of its true sex, but the child will throw them away" (Roscoe 1998, 139). A child could not control such behavior, in the Mohave view, for the kinds of dreams a child had affected whether the child would become a man, a woman, a man–woman, or a woman–man. Among the Zuni, as children grow up, they experience several rites of passage that initiate them into ceremonial groups and also instruct them in the ceremonial and work duties appropriate for their sex. While a child, one Zuni man–woman underwent the first male initiation ceremony but not the second, making him an "unfinished male" (Roscoe 1991, 144), who could participate in some male activities but not others, such as warfare and hunting.

Transvestism

Transvestism was one of the most common ways in which alternative genders expressed their identity. Wearing the clothing of the opposite sex was especially common and culturally significant among the tribes of the Great Plains, including the Arapaho, Arikara, Blackfoot, Cheyenne, Crow, Gros Ventre, Hidatsa, Iowa, Kansa, Mandan, Omaha, Osage, Oto, Pawnee, Ponca, and speakers of the Siouxan language. Although common, transvestism was not found in all cultures with gender crossing. Sometimes men–women dressed like men, sometimes like women, and sometimes their choice of clothing depended on the situation. Among the Navajo, some *nadleehi* (men–women) wore women's clothing; others did not or only sometimes did so. Woman Chief, the adopted Crow woman, did not wear men's clothes, although she adopted many other aspects of the male role.

After whites began settling the West, most regarded men–women (whom many simplistically categorized as "sodomites") as disgusting or sinful. Because it was a visible manifestation of the *berdache* role, transvestism was especially abhorrent to Anglo government officials, missionaries, educators, and settlers. Due to formal punishments and white ridicule, this symbol of alternative gender identity had largely disappeared by the early twentieth century.

Associations with Spiritual Powers

Usually, communities perceived men–women and women–men as having some sort of unusual powers or abilities derived from spiritual sources. The Cheyenne of the Great Plains used a term that translates "half man–half woman." These people served as masters of ceremony for the important Scalp Dance that followed a successful raid by a war party. They also possessed powerful love medicines, so their services were sought by young men and women who wanted to attract heterosexual partners. Lakota believed that *winkte* could predict future events and could bestow lucky names on children. Osh-Tisch (whose name translates as "Finds Them and Kills Them"), of the Crow tribe, had a vision as a youth and became a powerful medicine person. One Navajo man–woman memorized numerous curing chants and learned to construct dozens of the intricate sandpaintings used in curing rituals (see Chapter 15). He was widely credited with near-miraculous healing powers.

Same-Sex Relationships

The sexual orientation of Native American *berdache* varied from people to people (and from person to person within a single tribe). Understandably, reliable information on the sexual orientation of third- and fourth-gendered persons is rare. Some seem to have refrained from sex altogether. But the most common pattern was for men–women to be sexually active with men and sometimes women, but not with other men–women. These relations (most Anglo-Americans or Canadians would culturally categorize them as "homosexual relations") in most cases were an expected aspect of the third or fourth gender role. Thus, a (genitally) male *berdache* would engage in sex with men of his group, without stigma or punishment for either party. The man would not be considered homosexual because he had not had relations with *another man,* but with a *man–woman.* In some tribes, a man would take a man–woman as a second "wife"—again apparently without stigma.

Even less is known about the sexual practices of women–men, and often early observers just stated that they were women who avoided marriage, or refused to marry. It appears, though, that they most commonly had relations with females. The complications of characterizing a person's sexual orientation are shown by a Mohave woman–man who had three wives (sequentially). All three eventually left her, and later in life the woman–man became very active sexually with men.

After contact with Euro-Americans, multiple gender identities were suppressed in most regions where Native Americans still lived, especially after the confinement of so many Natives to reservations in the 1800s. The majority of whites—settlers, traders, government agents, missionaries, and others—found the existence of a *legitimate* role such as man–woman or woman–man abhorrent. Because most viewed the custom as sinful, as harmful to Indian character, or as an obstacle to Native assimilation into Anglo society, they often imposed legal or social punishments for third and fourth genders. For example, in the 1920s, large numbers of Indian children were taken away from their families and communities—by force when necessary—and placed in on- or off-reservation government-run boarding schools. In these Indian Schools (as they are known today), the explicit goal was to socialize and educate Indian children into Anglo culture. By separating Native children from their families and traditions, the theory was, they could be more quickly and thoroughly assimilated into white society. Of course, young people who showed signs of assuming alternative gender identities were punished.

Through such educational and legal mechanisms, multiple gender identities were suppressed. Even some tribes that had once accepted third and fourth genders came to reject such persons. For instance, in the 1940s, some Winnebago told an ethnographer that "the *berdache* was at one time a highly honored and respected person, but that the Winnebago had become ashamed of the custom because the white people thought it was amusing or evil" (quoted in Roscoe 1991, 201).

In North American society generally, popular ideas about gender crossing and homosexuality changed dramatically in the late twentieth century. Polls show that most U.S. citizens favor giving spousal benefits such as medical care and life insurance to same-sex domestic partners. But the majority of people oppose same-sex marriage. Thus, in the November 2004 national elections in the United States, 11 states had ballot initiatives that defined marriage as a relationship between a man and a woman. The initiatives passed in all states, and by very wide margins. Many large corporations now provide spousal benefits such as health insurance for domestic partners of either sex, partly reflecting the modern realities of the labor market and partly reflecting changes in society's attitudes about sexual preference. Despite such changes in attitudes, however, most North Americans still regard cross-dressing, transsexuality, and homoeroticism as deviant or perverted. Most conservative religious people view these practices as sinful, and even some Protestant denominations generally considered fairly liberal do not allow ordination of gays and lesbians. The Episcopal Church may soon be formally divided by the issue of gay and lesbian ordination.

Cultures such as the Native American examples mentioned here show that attitudes of fear, hatred, and intolerance of transsexuals and homosexuals are not universal. Indeed, acceptance and even appreciation of alternative genders are fairly common among Native peoples. Perhaps the knowledge that there are lots of cultures in which alternative genders are accepted is relevant for our attitudes about diversity in sexual orientation and other gender-related issues in twenty-first-century societies. Knowledge of such cultures must, however, be balanced by noting that there are a great many other peoples whose attitudes toward homoeroticism and gender crossing are highly negative.

Gender Stratification

A fourth main issue in the anthropological study of gender is **gender stratification,** or the degree to which human groups allocate material and social rewards to women and men *based on their gender.* Other sources of unequal rewards include class, caste, family origins, and race (covered in other chapters). Here we discuss only rewards based on whether one is a male or a female. We ignore such complications as third or fourth gender identities.

Gender stratification is also often referred to as "the status of women," with the implied phrase "relative to men." Whatever we call it, gender stratification is difficult to define because it includes many components that interact in complex ways. Here are the main components, including questions whose answers would indicate high (that is, very unequal relationships between women and men), moderate, low, or nonexistent gender stratification for some culture:

- The kinds of social roles men and women perform: Are some roles limited to males only or to females only? If so, which roles, and how are they valued?
- The cultural value attached to women's and men's contributions to their families and other groups: Are men's contributions viewed as more important and more rewarded than women's?
- Female deference to males: Do women defer socially to their husbands or male relatives? How much, and in what contexts?
- Access to positions of power and influence: Do women hold offices in the political arena? Can and do women control family or household members and domestic tasks?
- Control over personal decision making: Do women control their own lives by making marital, sexual, childbearing, work, leisure, and other important decisions for themselves?
- General beliefs and ideas about the sexes: Are men considered to be superior to women intellectually, psychologically, and/or physically?

These are the main dimensions that we consider in evaluating the degree of gender stratification in particular cultures. Think of the list as some of the main features that constitute the overall pattern of gender stratification in particular cultures. Obviously, gender stratification is *multidimensional,* which makes it difficult to categorize as "high" or "low" even within a single culture. Why is it so difficult?

For one thing, some of the components are not consistent with other components. Studies of family life often report that women have a great deal of control in making decisions about child rearing and about the allocation of domestic resources, even though they have little independence outside the domestic context. For instance, in two Andalusian towns of southern Spain, David Gilmore's fieldwork showed that wives have great autonomy in managing household affairs. He believes this is because many women are able to live near their own mothers, so that wives and their mothers frequently "gang up" on a husband. Even in male-dominated societies like traditional Korea, Japan, and China, the eldest female in a household usually had the right to manage household

affairs with a fair degree of autonomy. Yet in these countries, and in many other societies, women hardly participated in public affairs, had barely any property of their own, had little voice about their marriages, and were clearly subordinate to their fathers, husbands, and husband's fathers socially and even legally.

Another factor complicating gender stratification is that, in most cultures, a woman's status changes over the course of her life. For example, most scholars agree that "the status of women" was comparatively low in most of traditional East Asia and South Asia. In these regions, most families were patrilocally extended (see Chapter 8), so when women married, they left their own family and moved into or near the house of their husband's parents. A young wife was subjected to the authority of her husband's mother and was duty-bound to work extremely hard. But, as a woman settled into the household, had a son, and aged, her status improved and she gradually took over control of the household from her mother-in-law. Eventually, she became the everyday manager of the household and was an authority figure over her own daughters-in-law after her sons married. The same pattern of women's status improving with age appears in numerous other cultures.

Finally, in more complex societies like modern nations, distinctions of rank or class (considered in Chapter 13) or of ethnic affiliation (see Chapter 17) often overpower male–female distinctions. That is, inherited wealth or perceived membership in a racial or ethnic category influences inequality more strongly than does gender.

So, avoid thinking of gender stratification as a unitary phenomenon—as a single thing. Like other social relationships, male–female relationships are complex. This is not surprising. Concepts like "gender stratification" are used by contemporary social scientists. They are not universal concepts. The people whose lives anthropologists study may not have such cultural concepts at all. Nor are women's and men's lives in any community so simple that anthropologists (or for that matter, anyone else) can categorize them unambiguously by statements like "Women have low status in culture X." (This point—that simple categorizations are misleading—is one you might remember when a friend bemoans how some region, or country, or religion "suppresses women.")

Is Sexual Asymmetry Universal?

In spite of the complications, there are significant cross-cultural variations in gender stratification. Even those humanistic anthropologists who mistrust comparisons and objective measurements recognize that there is much less gender stratification among the Native American Hopi and Iroquois than among the Yanomamö of the Amazon basin. Gender stratification is a meaningful concept to use for answering certain questions such as: Are there societies in which women and men are equal? Are there societies in which women dominate men?

The answer to the second question is no. Despite the stories we sometimes read or the occasional old adventure movie in which the hero finds himself captured by "amazons," not a single instance of clear female domination over men has ever been found by ethnographers. *Matriarchy*—rule by women over men—does not exist, nor has it ever existed, to the best of our knowledge. Clearly, there have been and are individual women who hold great power, control great wealth, and are held in high esteem. Certainly, there are queens, female chiefs, and individual matriarchs of families and kin groups. But no clear instance of matriarchy—women as a social category holding power over men as a social category—has been documented.

The first question—whether there are cultures in which men and women are equal—has a more uncertain and complex answer. Even anthropologists who have devoted their careers to studying gender cannot agree. On the one hand, some scholars believe that women are never considered fully equal to men. They interpret the ethnographic record as showing that an asymmetry—an inequality based on one or more components of gender stratification—exists between the sexes among all peoples.

Those who believe that male dominance/female subordination is universal point to two fairly well-established generalizations. One applies to the realm of political institutions. In political life, sexual asymmetry always exists. In no known society are the primary political authority roles restricted to females. But, in many societies, all women are denied the right to succeed to political offices. In the majority of cases, even kin-group leadership roles are dominated by men. Male elders of the lineage or clan decide how the group's land and other resources are to be used and allocated, how the group's wealth objects are to be disposed of, whether the group is to engage in a battle to avenge a wrong, and so on. (As we shall soon see, however, women often do have significant influence over these matters, especially in matrilineal societies.)

The other realm of life in which sexual asymmetry occurs is religion. In many societies, women are excluded from performing major religious leadership roles. To be sure, there are societies—lots of them, in fact—in which *particular rituals* are performed by and for women, as in female initiations. But there are many societies in which females are forbidden to participate in the most important *public* rituals. Even among matrilineal peoples like the Hopi and Zuni of the American Southwest, it is men who don the costumes and wear the masks for public dances that benefit the whole community.

According to some scholars, then, the activities of males are everywhere regarded as more important than those of females. Women as a social category are everywhere culturally devalued relative to men as a social category. Women are universally subordinate to men. Sexual assymetry is a culture universal, varying only in degree.

There is another way to interpret the ethnographic record, though. Many scholars note that most fieldworkers—and hence most of the ethnographic data available to shed light on the issue of universal female subordination—have been biased in two ways. The first is the *androcentric* (male) bias. Most of the fieldwork until the 1970s was done by men, most of whom were not very interested in local women's lives. At any rate, simply because they were themselves men, fieldworkers had little access to women's points of view, so they often unwittingly took the men's values, attitudes, and opinions as representative of the entire group. Female points of view were largely unreported.

The second source of fieldwork bias in the study of gender is *Eurocentric* bias. Because of the inequalities in wealth, power, and status in Western (European-derived) societies, Western anthropologists might perceive relationships of inequality, hierarchy, and domination/subordination even among cultures where they are less developed. For instance, when a wife greets her husband by bowing her head or stays behind him while walking, Western fieldworkers may interpret such behaviors as behavioral symbols of female subordination, when in fact they are merely public demonstrations of politeness.

In short, some scholars think that many fieldworkers have been sexually and culturally biased. Because of this bias, the ethnographic record is not objective; it "records" a universal female subordination not justified by the real world. It is worth mentioning, though, that those who accuse others of bias may be biased themselves, and especially if a subject is as politically charged as that of gender.

Some ethnologists who have looked at the "ethnographic facts" have found examples of what they consider sexual equality. Anthropologists who believe that female–male equality does exist in some cultures can point to particular people who they think document their belief. The Iroquois, a matrilineal and matrilocal people

▶ Iroquois women's control over cultivated foods and their distribution gave them relatively high status.

© Stock Montage

of northeastern North America, are the most famous ethnographic example of women achieving equality with men. Iroquois women produced the corn and other cultivated foods, put them in storage, and largely controlled how they were distributed from the storehouses. Iroquois men were away from their apartments in the longhouse much of the time, engaged in warfare or cooperative hunting expeditions. After the introduction of the fur trade into northeastern North America in the seventeenth century, men often were away searching for beaver pelts or raiding their neighbors for pelts. The matrilineally related women of a longhouse influenced their inmarried husbands' behavior by withholding provisions from their hunting trips and war parties. Only men had the right to hold the most powerful political leadership offices because only males could be elected to the great council of chiefs. But it was the older women of the various matrilineages who selected their groups' representatives to the council. These women also had the right to remove and replace men who did not adequately represent the group's interests. Also, women had a voice in the deliberations of the council itself. They could veto declarations of war and introduce peacemaking resolutions.

So, is sexual asymmetry a cultural universal or not? Certainly, some male and Western ethnographers have been biased—but does this bias account for their reports of female subordination? Certainly, the Iroquois, the Hopi (see Chapter 10), and many other peoples demonstrate that women in some cultures have achieved considerable control over their own lives and over public

decision making—but do such cases represent *full equality* of males and females? Indeed, would we know "total equality" if we saw it in a society? What would it look like? Would men and women have to carry out the same kinds of economic tasks before we could say they are completely equal? Is monogamy necessary, or can a society be polygynous and still qualify? Shall we require that women occupy 50 percent of all leadership roles before we say they have equal rights? How should family life be organized before we can say that husbands in culture X do not dominate their wives?

Many questions must be answered before we can say whether sexual asymmetry is universal—the most important of which is how we would know complete gender equality if we were to encounter it!

Why is the question important? Many anthropologists think that the more cultures that exhibit gender equality, the greater the chances that modern societies can achieve equality. At the very least, lots of examples of equality show that patriarchy is not inevitable because so many peoples are not patriarchical. Feminist psychologists, sociologists, historians, biologists, and other scholars have examined ethnographic descriptions of various Other Cultures, looking for equality or even "matriarchy." Their reasoning also is that, if anthropologists have discovered numerous cultures in which women have achieved equality, then women will be more likely to achieve equality in the future. Their hope is that there are many such cultures. Their fear is that there are few or none.

The ethnographic record on the issue of sexual equality—though not silent—is filled with ambiguity and uncertainty. It is ambiguous both because gender stratification is so multidimensional and because total equality would be difficult to recognize. At any rate, how much does it matter for the cause of sexual equality *today* if women are "universally" or "nearly universally" subordinate? Perhaps what matters most is that women and men are a good deal more equal in some societies than in others, which allows us to study the conditions under which future equality is likely to be possible. To argue that because women have always or usually been subordinate, they will forever be subordinate is analogous to pre–twentieth-century arguments that humans will never be able to fly. Just because no human group has achieved some state in the past does not mean that none will achieve it in the future. It does not mean that we should give up trying to achieve it today and for the future. And it certainly does not mean that women alive in the twenty-first century have achieved about all the equality they are likely to achieve.

A more answerable question is: What influences the degree of gender stratification in a society?

Influences on Gender Stratification

So far no one has shown that any small number of factors are the primary determinants of gender stratification in all times and places. Here we discuss only a few generalizations that point to the kinds of influences that are most widespread and important.

Women's contributions to material welfare. Materialists argue that women's role in production strongly influences their property rights, their role in public affairs, their degree of personal freedom, and other dimensions of their overall status. One idea is that, where women produce a high proportion of the food, shelter, clothing, and other necessities of existence, men will recognize their contributions and reward women with influence, property, prestige, dignity, and other benefits. In other words, the sexual division of labor and the proportion of valued goods women produce are strong influences on gender stratification.

Such ideas might apply to some foraging and horticultural peoples, among whom women's gathering or gardening contributes much of the food consumed by their domestic groups. Women's productive labor might give them a status that is closer to equality with men than they have in other forms of adaptation in which their subsistence contributions are not as great. For example, among

the BaMbuti and Aka, two foraging Pygmy groups of the central African rain forest, women's labor is critical for success in net hunting, and ethnographic studies on both these Pygmy peoples report male–female equality or near equality. Among the Ju/'hoansi, too, considerable equality exists between women and men.

But everyone's status is "closer to equality" in most hunter-gatherer and many horticultural populations (see Chapters 7 and 13). So, perhaps the relative lack of gender stratification in these adaptations results not from women's importance as food providers but from some other factor or influence "leveling out" inequalities of all kinds.

Women's control over key resources. A more complex materialist proposal is that women's contribution to production, by itself, is not enough to "earn" them relative equality. It is *necessary* for women to contribute heavily to material welfare to gain resources, rights, and respect, but this alone is not *sufficient*. (To see why, consider enslaved persons.) One specific hypothesis is that women must also own productive resources (land, tools) or have considerable control over the distribution of the products of their labor, or both. If women own productive resources and have a great deal of say over what happens to the goods they produce, then they can have some influence on the activities of men. Overall, this gives them more equality. Peggy Sanday found some support for this hypothesis in a cross-cultural study done in the 1970s.

This hypothesis seems to account reasonably well for some specific cases. For instance, Iroquois women controlled the production and distribution of important resources. They used this control to nominate their kinsmen to chiefly positions and to influence the public decision making from which they were formally excluded. Likewise, Hopi women (see Chapter 10) owned land and had considerable control over the distribution of its products. Women had relatively high status in both these societies, as they did among many other Native American peoples.

Along the same lines, in many West African and Caribbean societies, women are more active than men in market trade in foodstuffs, handicrafts, textiles, and other goods produced by themselves. Sometimes market-trading women are able to transform their independent control over exchangeable resources into more equitable relationships with men. Wives commonly maintain a separate income from that of their husbands, which they are free to spend on themselves and their children. Among the Yoruba of Nigeria, women are active in market trade and in craft production, which gives them access to

▲ Where women commonly earn income for themselves by marketing products, as in Jamaica, their overall status tends to be relatively high.

© R. Krubner/H. Armstrong Roberts

income and economic security independent of their husbands and other men. Many women purchase houses in urban areas and use the rent to improve their own and their children's economic well-being and social autonomy. According to Sandra Barnes (1990, 275):

> Property frees the owner from subordinating herself to the authority of another person in domestic matters. It places her in a position of authority over others and in a position to form social relationships in the wider community that are politically significant. Property owning legitimates her entry into the public domain.

The economic independence that some Yoruba women are able to acquire translates into increased participation in neighborhood associations and other public affairs and allows them much freedom from male authority. A wider generalization would be that control over resources increases women's independence from men and allows women to form associations with other women that have the effect of mutual support networks.

Thus, many ethnographic and comparative studies suggest that controlling resources is one way for women to get respect and independence from their husbands, brothers, and other men. This ability to acquire some measure of control over family resources helps to account for

why many late-twentieth-century North American wives demanded and received more help from their husbands in housework and child care. In recent decades, married women in increasing numbers have acquired wage- and salary-earning jobs by selling their labor and skills to the private or public sector. Between 1970 and 2006, in the United States, the percentage of all married women who were employed doubled. Even the presence of young children does not keep most American women from entering the workforce: between 1970 and 1990, the percentage of married women with children under age 5 who were working for a wage doubled, from about 30 percent to about 60 percent. Since 1990, this percentage has leveled off, to about 65 percent in 2006. Among the reasons so many married women have entered the workforce since the 1960s are the insufficiency of one person's (formerly, the husband's) income to support the family at an acceptable living standard, structural changes to a more service-oriented (less goods-producing) economy, the increasing value women place on personal fulfillment through career advancement (partly because of the feminist movement), and dramatic increases in the numbers of women who have college degrees.

As a result of entering the workforce as wage and salary earners, many American women have gained considerable economic independence from their husbands and other men. The legal system has also helped by increasingly considering family violence more than just a private family matter, as well as by prosecuting or garnishing the wages of "deadbeat dads." Husbands have, therefore, lost considerable economic leverage in the household relative to their wives. In the twenty-first century, working wives have psychological ammunition against their husbands' domestic incompetence or laziness—they've put in a full day's work on the job just like their husbands.

In the early twenty-first century, increasing numbers of North American couples are "role reversed," to use the phrase of sociologists Theodore Cohen and John Durst. Husbands-fathers stay at home with young children while wives-mothers are the breadwinners. Some believe this pattern reverses the natural order of male–female family roles and thus is both immoral and harmful to children, who look up to their parents as role models. However, others believe the feminist movement has helped liberate men as well as women from old cultural attitudes: as economic or familial circumstances warrant, or as couples prefer, parents can reverse, switch, or alternate caretaking and breadwinning roles. They believe that feminism has given both sexes the freedom to choose.

With most women now out in the world of work, and with the families of so many married women now virtually dependent on their income to pay the bills, more women are demanding equal pay for equal work, equal treatment and opportunity in the workplace, equal legal rights, and equal respect. As in other societies, in North America women's success in obtaining control over important resources empowers them relative to men.

Descent and postmarital residence. The form of descent and postmarital residence also influences the degree of gender stratification. Women in matrilineal and matrilocal societies have greater equality in many areas of life. What is it, specifically, about matrilineality and matrilocality that gives relatively high status to females? It is not that "women rule" in these societies. Generally speaking, men hold positions of both political and domestic authority in matrilineal societies (see Chapter 9). The main difference is whom among their relatives men have authority *over*: their sisters and sisters' children in matrilineal systems, versus their sons, unmarried daughters, and sons' children in patrilineal systems.

Other elements of matrilineality and matrilocality benefit women. In a cross-cultural study, Martin Whyte found that women enjoy more authority in domestic matters, have more sexual freedom, and have more worth placed on their lives in these societies. Two factors contribute to their equality. First, because husbands live with the families of their wives, sisters remain with or close to one another throughout their lives. A typical wife thus has her mother, sisters, and other female relatives around to support her in domestic quarrels. Second, in many matrilineal and matrilocal societies, domestic authority over a married woman is divided between her husband and her brother. Alice Schlegel suggests that this arrangement increases her freedom because each man acts as a check on the other's attempts to dominate her.

This situation contrasts markedly with patrilineal and patrilocal societies, such as old China, Korea, Japan, the Middle East, and most of India and Pakistan. In these societies, when a woman married into a family, she was given household tasks to perform for most of her waking hours. Only when she herself bore sons and heirs to her husband's family did her status improve, and only after she herself became a mother-in-law to her sons' wives could she relax a bit. In East Asia, the Confucian social and moral philosophy, which held that women must be submissive to men, affected the way wives and daughters-in-law were treated. Even in modern times, many women feel that marriage results in a loss of freedom and that the heavy duties of family life are burdensome, which in Taiwan affects even wedding practices (see the Globalization box). In the Islamic parts of southern Asia and in the Middle East, the teachings of the Koran generally supported a woman's subordinate status in the home as well as in public. But also important were the social facts that wives became members of the households of their husbands' parents, and the lines of authority over them were clearly and legally redrawn upon their marriage. Socially, a wife had few good alternatives to submission to her husband's family and relatively few sources of support when she was treated poorly. In contrast, in most matrilocal and matrilineal cultures, women do have alternatives to suffering the dominance of their husbands, and they likewise receive support from their own relatives.

Gender Stratification in Industrial Societies

We conclude by bringing together some of the information and ideas covered in this chapter and briefly suggesting how they might be relevant to women living in industrialized, modernized nations.

Anthropological research on gender stratification provides women with a hope and a warning. Part of the hope derives from the fact that women's roles and rights, and the restrictions placed on them, vary from place to

Taiwan, South Korea, Singapore, and Hong Kong are sometimes called East Asia's "Four Little Dragons." (The big dragon, of course, is China, although economically Japan is a bigger dragon still.) In the 1970s, the little dragons developed rapidly by exporting clothing, consumer electronics, toys, and automotive accessories to the United States and Europe. Hong Kong and Singapore for decades have been financial centers. South Korea is now the ninth largest economy in the world, producing ships, motor vehicles, TVs, DVDs, and other high-tech equipment for the global marketplace.

Like the other three little dragons—they are also called Asia's "tigers"—Taiwan is about as modern as any place on our planet. Only 5 percent of its people work in agriculture, and 36 percent are employed in industry, with 59 percent making a living in services, which is about the same as in North America and Europe. Taiwan has three cities with populations greater than one million; the largest is the capital, Taipei, with nearly three million people. Annual income per person in Taiwan is more than $30,000. Of its 23 million people, 96 percent can read and write. Fourteen million households are connected to the Internet, and there are 24 million cell phones. Taiwan, and especially Taipei, is developed, urban, connected, cosmopolitan—global.

Its weddings look global, too. Or, rather, they look global if by *global* you mean "modeled after those of the West," which is exactly what *global* means to many people. Taiwanese young people meet and date, and if they fall in love and marry, their wedding ceremonies are familiar to the eyes of Westerners—at least, to Western secularists. Most weddings include white gowns, tuxedos, flowers, and lots of photos.

What would not be familiar to Westerners is that most couples go to an expensive photo salon *before* their wedding banquet and before the ceremony itself to have pictures taken. Ordinarily, these pictures are displayed at the wedding ceremony itself. And, according to Bonnie Adrian, who studied weddings in Taiwan in the 1990s, in the photos the bride is hardly recognizable as herself. At great expense, the bride visits a professional makeover stylist in a salon. The stylist shapes the bride's eyebrows with a razor, often removing them entirely only to reapply new ones later with an eyebrow pencil. Next she applies foundation makeup to cover any blemishes; usually this is a light color because fair skin is more desirable than a dark, tanned look. Then the stylist attacks the eyes, applying shadow, liner, and false lashes. The goal is to produce a round-eyed look. The lips are next. The foundation makeup has already made the facial features indistinct, so the bride's natural lip color and shape are barely visible. New lip shapes are applied with a brush, depending on the look the stylist wishes to impart, and the lipstick color is added. Finally, the nails are fixed and the hair styled. Typically, all this takes three hours or longer.

What about the groom? He will have his hair cut and styled so that nothing looks out of place, and he may wear a bit of makeup to ensure that his facial features show up properly under the photographic lights. But overall, he is recognizably himself. In the wedding, at least, his appearance is secondary.

Next the couple visits a photographer, who specializes in pre-wedding photos and takes hundreds or thousands of pictures. By the time the photographer has finished, usually a whole day has passed—and several thousand dollars have changed hands. The prints are huge, and on the day of the

place and from time to time. Although it may be very difficult or impossible to say whether women and men are "totally equal" in any culture, we certainly know that sexual equality varies—and varies significantly. So there is reason to think that modern societies can move further toward eliminating barriers to female opportunity and achievement. Patriarchy does not seem to be part of the human genome.

Anthropological work on gender offers another hope. Some of our discussion of gender stratification suggests that any change that improves women's independent access to material resources and to social support will have positive impacts on their status in other realms of life. If married women have their own source of income

independent of their husbands, then they are better able to become empowered within their families and to escape relationships with men who are physically or psychologically abusive. If, as in matrilineal and matrilocal societies, women are able to maintain relationships of "sisterhood" (i.e., support from other women) and/or of extended family ties (i.e., aid from their own relatives), then they can mobilize these supportive relationships in times of hardship. If women have legal recourse to sue discriminating employers and would-be employers, then their opportunities and compensation on the job will be improved by the threat of monetary damages.

And going back to the very first point in this chapter: the knowledge that ideas and beliefs about gender wedding banquet, they are prominently displayed so that all can admire the beauty of the bride.

One interpretation of all this "framing the bride" (as Adrian titles her 2003 book) is that Taiwanese wedding customs have taken on a Western flavor. Consciously or not, it looks like Taiwanese couples have chosen the Western model. Is this yet another example of "cultural imperialism"—the makeover of indigenous customs based on the foundation of the West?

Adrian believes this interpretation is simplistic. In old Taiwan, women viewed marriage not as the fulfillment of romantic dreams, but as the beginning of a life of hard work for her husband's family and for the welfare of the children she would soon bear. This attitude carries over into contemporary Taiwan. Today women and men in love have plenty of opportunities to be intimate before they marry. So they often postpone marriage until they feel ready to have children and undertake the responsibilities of parenthood. When a modern Taiwanese woman marries, she feels she sacrifices a lot of freedom in the interest of her husband and their offspring. The photo, usually hung in the bedroom, will remind her and him of how beautiful and free she was before the trials of family responsibility wore her down.

Weddings, banquets, and photographs also reflect implicit competition—what Americans used to call "keeping up with the Joneses." The more photographs and the more work the photographer must do to make them perfect, the greater the expense, and most of this expense is paid for by the groom and his family. The groom would be embarrassed if the photos were not up to standards, and his wife might remind him of his failure to live up to cultural expectations in future quarrels. At the obligatory wedding banquet, the amount and quality of food must also be up to normative expectations—and so must the quality of the wedding photos. The groom's family would suffer a humiliating loss of face if they did not honor their son's marriage and welcome their new daughter-in-law with an ostentatious banquet and expensive photographs.

These kinds of photographs made before the wedding itself in Taiwan do not document the events of the marriage. They are not records of the ceremony. Rather, they are commemorations of the bride; Adrian (2003, 235) says, "they construct brides," meaning that they build an image of the woman before her marriage so that, after the marriage, her new family can see an idealized image of the woman she once was.

What are the wider lessons of bridal photos in contemporary Taiwan? Consciously or not, Taiwanese take something from the realm of global culture and use it for their own, culturally meaningful purposes. To say it differently, they localize the global by shaping the photos to fit their own traditions and reconfiguring what comes in from the outside world to mesh with their own cultural attitudes and beliefs and social practices. Humanity does not need to become all alike just because we interact with one another in new global settings.

Critical Thinking Questions

1. Do you know any other examples of "localizing the global"? Can you think of things or customs that have come into your nation from another country and have become localized?

2. What are the purposes and functions of photos of ceremonies in your own society? How do they relate to other aspects of your way of life?

Sources: Adrian (2003), CIA (2007), Vogel (1991)

---

are culturally constructed rather than biologically given should—*if taken seriously and understood properly*—lead women and men alike to realize that at least some of the sexual differences they believe exist are differences of our own culture's making. It is a biological *reality* (with minor qualifications) that women have the physical tools to bear and nurse children. But does this biological reality make women generally more nurturing than men? Or is this belief just a cultural construction?

The warning? Anthropological researchers have not yet discovered the key that unlocks the door leading to "total equality" (whatever that might look like) between the sexes. Comparative anthropological work—like most work dealing with human behavior and beliefs—is suggestive, but it is not conclusive. Thus far, we cannot identify the one or two or three things that women can do that will lead to equal treatment in the workplace, in the household, in the bedroom, and in the political arena. No one or two or three male-dominated institutions could be changed to radically improve the position of women in various realms of their lives. For example, outlawing sexual discrimination in the workplace and making comparable pay for comparable work legally mandatory might not translate into greater female–male equality in other contexts such as family life or politics. Even a female CEO or a nation's president or prime minister can be abused by her husband. Therefore, feminists—of both sexes—need to continue to work on a broad front to achieve their objectives.

Summary

1. Physical differences between females and males are recognized and relevant to social behavior in all known cultures, but these differences matter in different ways and to different degrees. Two of the major female–male differences that are most relevant are sexual dimorphism and reproductive physiology.

2. A person's sex is determined biologically (by genes), but gender is a cultural construct. The cultural construction of gender means that cultures vary in how they perceive the physical differences between the sexes, in the significance they attribute to those differences, and in the way those differences are made relevant for self-identity, task and role allocation, access to property and power, and so forth. The Hua of Papua New Guinea illustrate the cultural construction of gender.

3. The sexual division of labor varies cross-culturally. Sexual stereotypes holding that men are breadwinners and women are caretakers are not supported by comparative research. Despite variation, there are certain widespread patterns in the sexual division of labor. Four biological factors that have been proposed to influence the broad cross-cultural similarities are (1) the depression of fertility that seems to occur when a woman engages in heavy exercise; (2) the possibility that women are more necessary than men to maintain population size, so women need to be protected from hazardous tasks; (3) superior male strength; and (4) the degree of compatibility of a task with the care of infants and young children. The last two factors are the most significant cross-culturally. No biological difference between the sexes can account for the variations in the sexual division of labor. Generally, female labor is more important in subsistence tasks in horticultural populations than among intensive agriculturalists. The reasons for this difference are the types of crops grown (root crops versus cereal grains), the amount of time needed for food processing, and the greater prevalence of warfare in horticultural groups.

4. Human groups differ in their tolerance of individual variations in gender identities. Many peoples allow gender crossing, in which males are allowed to enact female roles, and vice versa. Others recognize multiple sexual identities, in which there are not only two, but three or four genders, roughly corresponding to man–woman or woman–man. Native American peoples seem especially tolerant of gender crossing and to allow for multiple gender identities.

5. A fourth issue in gender studies is the causes of cultural diversity in sexual stratification. Anthropologists have yet to discover any peoples who are matriarchical. But even specialists in gender studies cannot agree whether sexual asymmetry is universal or whether there are societies with complete equality between men and women. This is mainly because sexual stratification is so multidimensional and because "complete equality" would be difficult to recognize. Many forces influence women's overall "status" in a culture, including their relative contributions to subsistence, their control over key resources, and the prevalent pattern of descent and postmarital residence. These conclusions have relevance for women in twenty-first-century societies.

Key Terms

sexual dimorphism
cultural construction of gender

sexual (gendered) division of labor
gender (sex) roles

gender crossing
multiple gender identities
gender stratification

Suggested Readings

Brief introductions to the anthropological study of gender include:

Gilmore, David D. *Manhood in the Making: Cultural Concepts of Masculinity.* New Haven, Conn.: Yale University Press, 1990.

Huber, Joan. *On the Origins of Gender Inequality.* Boulder, Colo.: Paradigm, 2007.

Nanda, Serena. *Gender Diversity: Crosscultural Variations.* Prospect Heights, Ill.: Waveland Press, 2000.

The following books are excellent studies of gender identities:

Davies, Sharyn. *Challenging Gender Norms: Five Genders among the Bugis in Indonesia.* Belmont, Calif.: Wadsworth, 2007.

Nanda, Serena. *Neither Man nor Woman: The Hijras of India.* 2nd ed. Belmont, Calif.: Wadsworth, 1999.

Roscoe, Will. *Changing Ones.* New York: St. Martin's Press, 1998.

Roscoe, Will. *The Zuni Man-Woman.* Albuquerque: University of New Mexico Press, 1991.

Some useful edited volumes for introductory students are:

Cohen, Theodore, ed. *Men and Masculinity: A Text Reader.* Belmont, Calif.: Wadsworth/Thomson Learning, 2001.

di Leonardo, Micaela, ed. *Gender at the Crossroads of Knowledge: Feminist Anthropology in the Postmodern Era.* Berkeley: University of California Press, 1991.

Morgen, Sandra, ed. *Gender and Anthropology: Critical Reviews for Research and Teaching.* Washington, D.C.: American Anthropological Association, 1989.

Sanday, Peggy Reeves, and Ruth Gallagher Goodenough, eds. *Beyond the Second Sex: New Directions in the Anthropology of Gender.* Philadelphia: University of Pennsylvania Press, 1990.

Media Resources

The Wadsworth Anthropology Resource Center
academic.cengage.com/anthropology

The Wadsworth discipline resource website that accompanies *Humanity: An Introduction to Cultural Anthropology,* Eighth Edition, includes a rich array of material, including online anthropological video clips, to help you in the study of cultural anthropology and the specific topics covered in this chapter. Other material includes a case study forum with excerpts from various Wadsworth authors, map exercises, scientist interviews, breaking news in anthropology, and links to additional useful online material. Begin by selecting Cultural Anthropology to take you to videos, research, and more. From the homepage, you may also select Applied Anthropology, which directs you to essays, glossary terms, the case study forum, and a list of internships and careers in anthropology.

12 THE ORGANIZATION OF POLITICAL LIFE

In modern urban societies such as England, uniformed police are an important part of the legal system.

Forms of Political Organization
- *Bands*
- *Tribes*
- *Chiefdoms*
- *States*
- *International Governance*

Social Control and Law
- *Social Control*
- *Law*

Legal Systems
- *Self-Help Systems*
- *Court Systems*

Questions addressed in this chapter

Does every society have some form of political organization? What are the different forms of political organization?

Does every society have some form of legal system? What is the relationship between social control and law?

What is the relationship between the legal system found in a society and the political organization of that society?

Every society has some form of political system, meaning those institutions that organize and direct the collective actions of the population. In small societies, political leadership and organization may be informal and even ad hoc. Only when a specific need for leadership arises does some individual assume an overt leadership role. In general, the larger the population, the more formalized the leadership and the more complex the political organization.

Likewise, as mentioned in Chapter 2, all societies demand some minimal degree of conformity from their members. All, therefore, develop mechanisms of social control by which the behaviors of individuals are constrained and directed into acceptable channels. There are always behavioral patterns that are approved or acceptable and patterns that are disapproved or unacceptable. By means of social control, a society encourages normatively proper behavior and discourages unacceptable actions, the objective being to maintain harmony and cooperation. The most serious deviations from acceptable behavior, which threaten the cohesiveness of the group, fall under that aspect of social control known as law, also discussed in this chapter. In the least organized societies, law and political organizations exist independently. As political organization becomes increasingly formalized and structured, governmental institutions take over legal institutions, until legal institutions become part of the formal political structure.

Forms of Political Organization

When we speak of the political organization of a particular society, we frequently are left with the impression that political boundaries and cultural boundaries are the same. But the boundaries of a *polity,* or a politically organized unit, may or may not correspond with the boundaries of a particular way of life. For example, the Comanche of the Great Plains shared a common language, customs, and ethnic identity, yet politically, they were never organized above the local group. Thus, the term *Comanche* refers to a people with a common language and culture who never united to carry out common political activities.

At the other extreme we find highly centralized polities that incorporate several culturally and socially distinct peoples. The United States is unusual in this regard only in the degree of cultural heterogeneity in the population. France, though predominantly "French," also includes Bretons and Basques. India has several hundred different ethnic groups. Russia, China, Indonesia, and the Philippines also integrate highly diversified populations into a single polity. In fact, every large and most small countries in the world today politically integrate several ethnic groups (see Chapter 17).

Political organization may be divided into four basic forms: bands (simple and composite), tribes, chiefdoms, and states. In addition, over the past half-century, a number of international organizations have assumed many governmental prerogatives. Each of these forms of political organization represents a different level of complexity that has developed over time.

Bands

As the least complex form, **bands** were probably the earliest human political structure (see Chapter 6). As more complex political systems developed, band-level societies were unable to compete for resources. Thus, bands survived until the modern period only in regions of the world with limited natural resources. Most known band-level societies were found in the deserts and grasslands of Australia, Africa, and the Americas. A few others lived in the tropical forests of Africa, Asia, and South

America and in the boreal forest and tundra regions of North America and Asia.

Bands consist of a number of families living together and cooperating in economic activities throughout the year. Band-level organization most frequently was found among peoples with foraging economies, which usually dictated low population densities and high seasonal mobility. As a result, only a relatively small number of people could stay together throughout the year. Bands ranged in size from only a dozen to several hundred individuals. The adaptive significance of the band's size and seasonal mobility is described in Chapter 6. In this chapter, we are concerned with leadership statuses and the political organization of bands.

The smallest bands, called **simple bands,** usually were no larger than an extended family and were structured as such. Leadership was informal, with the oldest or one of the older male members of the family serving as leader. Decision making was reached through consensus and involved both adult males and adult females; simple bands operated as families. Because all members of the band were related either through descent or by marriage, they were exogamous units, and members of the band had to seek spouses from other bands. Thus, although an autonomous economic and political unit, every band was, by social necessity, allied through intermarriage with other bands, usually territorially adjacent ones. Simple bands usually had names, although the names may have been informal and may have simply referred to some prominent geographical feature associated with the band's usual territory.

Resource availability influenced the formation of such small groups. Simple bands often were associated with the hunting of nonmigratory game animals, such as deer, guanaco, moose, or small mammals, which occupy a limited territory on a year-round basis and are found either singly or in small herds. The foraging activities of simple bands usually did not generate any significant surpluses of food, which necessitated the year-round hunting of game animals. Effective hunting required only a few male hunters who had intimate knowledge of the seasonal shifts in range of these animals within their territory. The game resources of such areas could be exploited most effectively by a small and highly mobile population. In addition, such bands depended on the seasonal collection of wild roots, berries, nuts, and other edible plants, as well as on limited fishing and shellfish collection.

Composite bands consisted of a larger aggregation of families, sometimes numbering in the hundreds. In contrast to simple bands, composite bands encompassed unrelated extended families. Although leadership in composite bands was informal, it was more defined. Such leaders frequently have been called **big men.** Big men did not hold formal offices, and leadership was based on influence rather than authority over band members. **Influence** is merely the ability to convince people that they should act as you suggest. **Authority** is the recognized right of an individual to command another person to act in a particular way. Thus, a big-man leader could not, by virtue of his position, make demands or impose rules on the members of the band, and his decisions were not binding on others. Because big-man status did not involve a formal office, there was no prescribed process for attaining leadership status. A man might emerge as the leader through a variety of personal accomplishments or qualities, such as his proven ability in hunting or warfare, the supernatural powers he possessed, or merely his charisma. There was no set tenure in the position, which was filled by a man until he was informally replaced by some other leader.

Like simple bands, many composite bands were nomadic groups that moved within a relatively well-defined range. Because of their greater size, composite bands were not as cohesive as simple bands and were politically more volatile. Disputes between families could result in some members joining another band or even the band splitting into two or more bands.

Composite bands formed because economic pressures facilitated or necessitated the cooperation of a larger number of individuals than found in a single extended family. As in the case of simple bands, the behavior of the principal game animals was an important influence. Composite bands were associated with the seasonal hunting of migratory animals that form large herds, such as bison and caribou. Migratory herd animals usually appeared only seasonally in the range of a particular composite band as the herd moved between its summer and winter ranges. Because bison and caribou migrated in herds that sometimes numbered in the tens of thousands, there was no difficulty in locating the herds on the open grasslands and tundra. Unlike the hunters of nonmigratory animals, who secured game steadily throughout the year, hunters of migratory animals took most of their game only twice a year, as the herds passed through their territories during migrations.

Successful hunting of large herds of animals requires maneuvering the herd into situations where large numbers could be slaughtered. Herds might be run over a cliff, into a holding pen, or into a lake where hunters in boats could kill them. Regardless of the method used, all these strategies required a larger group of hunters than was available in a simple band. Thus, composite bands

Form	Characteristics	Associated Equalities and Inequalities
Bands (a) Simple	Local, economically self-sufficient residence group Single extended family, usually numbering 25 to 50 people Family head with leadership based on influence	Egalitarian
(b) Composite	Local, economically self-sufficient residence group Several extended families, usually numbering from 50 to several hundred individuals Big-man leadership based on influence	Egalitarian
Tribes	Several economically self-sufficient residence groups Usually numbering between 1,000 and 20,000 people A few formal leadership positions with limited authority, with access based on inheritance and/or achievements Group cohesion maintained by sodalities	Primarily egalitarian with some societies showing the traits of ranking
Chiefdoms	Several economically interdependent residence groups Usually numbering from a few thousand up to about 30,000 Centralized leadership, with a hereditary chief, with full formal authority	Ranked societies
States	Usually numbering from the tens of thousands up to several million Centralized leadership, with formal full authority, supported by a bureaucracy	Stratified societies

were formed to bring together a sufficiently large number of hunters to control the movements of large herds of animals.

The Comanche of the southern Great Plains of the United States illustrate the nature of composite bands. These horse-raising, bison-hunting people were politically autonomous until the Red River War of 1875. During the early and middle years of the nineteenth century, the Comanche numbered about 6,000 to 7,000, divided between 5 and 13 main bands. Comanche bands had only vaguely defined territories, and two or more bands frequently occupied the same general area or had overlapping ranges. Membership in Comanche bands was fluid: both individuals and families could and did shift from one band to another, or a number of families might join together to establish a new band. Some anthropologists have theorized that there were only five major bands, with a varying number of secondary bands appearing and disappearing from time to time.

A band consisted of a number of families, each headed by an older male member who was "peace chief" or "headman." One of these family heads also served as the peace chief for the entire band. There was no formalized method of selecting either the family heads or the head of the band. As the Comanche say, "No one made him such; he just got that way." A Comanche peace chief usually was a man known for his kindness, wisdom, and ability to lead by influencing other men. Although a war record was important, peace chiefs were not chosen from among the most aggressive or ambitious men. Such men usually remained war chiefs—great warriors who periodically recruited men to raid neighbors—but frequently had little influence outside war and raiding.

A band peace chief was responsible for the well-being of the band. Through a consensus of the family heads, he directed the seasonal movement of the band and the bison hunts. He did have men who voluntarily assisted him. In the morning, the peace chief usually sent out two men to scout the area around the camp for the presence of enemy raiding parties. He also sent a crier through the camp periodically to announce plans for the movement of the camp, an upcoming hunt, or some other cooperative activities. During the bison hunts, the peace chief called on a number of men from the camp to police the hunt and restrain overly eager hunters from scattering the herd and thus spoiling the hunt for others.

In an extraordinarily individualistic and egalitarian society, Comanche band leaders had to strive for and maintain consensus. If a dispute arose and a consensus could not be reached, individuals and families were free either to shift residence to another band or even to form a new band under another leader.

Comanche bands were economically and politically autonomous units. Only seldom did two or more bands come together for any unified action, and never did leaders of the bands come together to discuss issues. At the same time, there was a strong consciousness of common identity—of being Comanche. Comanches freely traveled between bands to visit, marry, and even shift residence. There was an informally reached general consensus on whether relations with a particular neighboring group were friendly or hostile. Comanche bands also usually refrained from attacking other Comanche bands, although on occasion some did ally themselves with foreign groups.

Thus, on the band level of political organization, populations are fragmented into numerous independent political units that operate only at the local-group level. These various communities share a common cultural identity and usually attempt to maintain harmonious relations with one another, but they lack any political structure capable of organizing all the various communities into a single unit for collective actions.

Tribes

Tribes differ from bands in that they have formally organized institutions that unite the scattered residential communities, give the society greater cohesiveness, and make possible a more united response to external threats. These institutions are called **sodalities.** Sodalities take various forms: they may be based on large kin groups, such as clans and lineages; on nonkinship units, such as age sets; or on voluntary associations, such as warrior societies. Regardless of their exact nature, sodalities unify geographically dispersed communities into political units. Although tribal-level societies usually are egalitarian, with leadership dependent in part on the persuasive abilities of individuals, there are formalized political offices with institutionalized authority. Although tribes vary greatly in structure, here we examine only one tribal-level society.

The Cheyenne of the Great Plains numbered between 3,000 and 3,500 during the early 1800s. The Cheyenne, like the neighboring Comanche, were horse-mounted bison hunters. They were divided into 10 main nomadic villages, which averaged between 300 and 350 persons. Village membership was not based on kinship, although the members of a particular village usually were related either by blood or by marriage. Village membership was relatively stable, and marriages between villagers were common. Although a particular village usually frequented a certain range, there was no sense of village territoriality. Periodically and seasonally, family camps and subvillage camps broke off from the main village.

The only time the entire tribe came together was in early summer, when all the widely scattered villages gathered into a single camp at a predetermined location. This crescent-shaped encampment stretched for several miles from end to end, with the open portion facing east. Within the tribal encampment every village had a designated location, and while camped together, they performed the great tribal ceremonies (e.g., the Arrow Renewal, the Sun Dance, and the Animal Dance). At least one and possibly two of these rituals were performed, depending on the particular ritual needs of the tribe at that time. After the performance of the ritual, the tribe as a unit staged the great summer bison hunt. After the hunt, the tribe again scattered into smaller village camps.

Politically, the tribe was controlled by the Council of Forty-Four and the warrior societies. The Council of Forty-Four, which had both political and religious duties, was headed by the Sweet Medicine chief, who was the keeper of the most sacred of the Cheyenne religious bundles. Second to him in importance were four other sacred chiefs, each representing specific supernatural beings. Under these five sacred chiefs were 39 ordinary chiefs.

Chiefs served in their positions for 10 years and could not be removed for any reason. Serving as a chief placed a burden on the individuals. Chiefs usually were selected from among the older men, all of whom had war records. When an individual was chosen as a chief, he was to act like a chief, not an aggressive warrior. A chief was to be generous, kindly, even tempered, and aloof from everyday disputes. In short, he was expected to display ideal human behavior at all times. He was to take care of the poor, settle disputes between individuals, and be responsible for the ritual performances that protected the tribe.

The major sodalities were the warrior societies, of which there were five. These were formal voluntary associations of men, each with its own style of dress, dances, songs, and set of four leaders. As young warriors, men were recruited by the different societies until all had joined one or another. The phrase *warrior societies* is slightly misleading. The heads of the various societies were what some call the *tribal war chiefs.* Although this group planned and led attacks on their enemies, the different societies did not fight or operate as military units in battles. In battles, men fought as individuals, and members of several societies may have been present in a particular raiding party.

Subordinate to the council of chiefs, the warrior societies cooperated as a group only in policing the camps. During the summer tribal encampment, the Council of Forty-Four appointed one of the societies as camp police. Later, when the village scattered into separate camps, the members of the council who lived in the village appointed one of the warrior societies to police the camp. After being appointed, the warrior society usually carried out its function with little direction from the chiefs. Its members scouted the area around the camp to check for the presence of any enemy raiding parties and intervened in any serious disputes between village members.

There are two points to be emphasized about the political organization of tribal societies. First, although there were some formalized political and religious offices that bequeathed some limited authority and prerogatives, on the whole, tribal societies were basically egalitarian (see Chapter 13). Few positions were hereditary, and most leaders were selected on the basis of personal qualities and individual merit.

Second, there was little economic specialization, either individual or regional, among tribes. Except for cooperation in communal hunts, families produced their own food and manufactured their own clothes and other material goods. From an economic perspective, each band or village was capable of sustaining itself without support from other communities; therefore, it was not economic necessity, convenience, or efficiency that led to the supracommunity political organization of tribes. Although sodalities unite tribes at a higher level of cohesiveness than bands, the mere existence of sodalities is not sufficient to generate or maintain the cohesiveness of a tribe. It is likely that external threats, either real or perceived, necessitated the cooperation in warfare of a large group of people and were the major factor that united geographically dispersed communities. Thus, warfare—the existence and activities of hostile human neighbors—was an important force in creating the political integration of separate communities.

Chiefdoms

Like tribes, **chiefdoms** were multicommunity political units. Unlike tribes, chiefdoms had a formalized and centralized political system. A chiefdom (see Chapter 7) was governed by a single chief, who usually served as both political and religious head of the polity. The chief had authority over members of the chiefdom, and the position often was hereditary within a single kin group, which based its rights chiefly on supernatural powers. Thus, a chiefdom was not an egalitarian society but a ranked or stratified society (see Chapter 13) with access to resources based on inherited status. With authority and power conferred by supernatural beings, governing was not by consensus but by decree.

Most chiefdoms were associated with horticultural societies in which craft or regional specialization in production had emerged. There was a need for regularized exchanges of goods either between geographically dispersed communities or, at times, within a single community. This economic exchange was managed through redistribution, with the chief occupying the central position in the flow of goods (see Chapter 7).

In earlier historic periods, chiefdoms probably were found throughout much of the Old World. During more recent periods, such political systems were primarily concentrated in Oceania (Polynesia, Micronesia, and Melanesia) and in the Americas (the circum-Caribbean and coastal portions of South America and the northwestern coast of North America).

The Polynesian-speaking people of Tahiti, an island in the southeastern Pacific, illustrate many characteristics typical of a chiefdom. This relatively large, mountainous, volcanic island had a population of about 100,000 at the time of European discovery. Tahiti was divided among about 20 rival chiefs. Although most of these chiefdoms were about the size of the average tribe and significantly smaller than the largest tribes, their political organization differed significantly.

The economy of Tahiti was based largely on farming. Taro, breadfruit, coconuts, and yams were the main crops, pigs and chickens were also raised, and fish and other seafoods supplemented the food supply. Food production was sufficient not only to meet the needs of the population but also to produce surpluses for export to other islands. Although sufficient food was produced in all regions, there were significant regional differences in the types of food produced because Tahiti varied ecologically.

Tahitian society had at least three and possibly four distinct classes, depending on how finely one wants to divide the units. *Arii,* or chiefs, and their close relatives formed the ruling elite. The *arii* were divided into two groups: the *arii rahi,* or sacred chiefs, and the *arii rii,* or small chiefs. Under these chiefs were the *raatira,* or subchiefs, and the *manahune,* or commoners. The sacred chiefs were viewed as descended from the gods, whereas the commoners were merely created by the gods for their use. The

© Jack Fields/CORBIS

▲ A Samoan chief is pictured here in traditional dress.

subchiefs were the offspring of intermarriage between the sacred chiefs and commoners, whereas the small chiefs were the products of still later intermarriages between sacred chiefs and subchiefs. Once these four classes were established, class endogamy became the rule.

The sacred chiefs, viewed as gods on Earth, evoked both reverence and fear. Whatever the highest-ranking sacred chiefs touched became *tabu,* or sacred, and could not be used for fear of supernatural punishment. Such a chief had to be carried on the back of a servant, lest the ground touched by his feet became *tabu.* He could not enter the house of another individual for the same reason. The lifestyle of the chief's family differed from that of others: they had larger and more elaborate houses, the largest canoes, insignia of their rank, and particular clothing.

Unlike in band and tribal societies, resources in chiefdoms were individually owned. Land was owned mainly by the chiefs and subchiefs, but ultimate authority rested with the sacred chiefs within the polity. Although sacred chiefs could not withhold the title to lands from the families of subchiefs, they could banish an individual subchief. Crafts were specialized, and craftspeople were attached to particular sacred chiefs and produced goods for them. Thus, the sacred chiefs directly controlled craft production and communal fishing. The chiefs could make demands on the property of the subchiefs and commoners. If someone refused, the chief could have the recalcitrant banished or make him or her a sacrificial victim. Theoretically, the sacred chief was the head judicial figure in the polity, but some believe that the chief seldom intervened in disputes between individuals; the chief usually used these powers only against people who challenged his authority.

The sacred chief in each polity was the focal point for redistributive exchanges. The chief periodically demanded surplus production from all his subjects for a public redistribution. Such events were associated with a number of occasions: a rite of passage for a member of the chief's family, the organizing of a military attack, religious ceremonies, or the start of the breadfruit harvest. During such ceremonies, the chief distributed the goods collected to all his subjects.

States

Although they had a centralized political system, chiefdoms were still kinship-based structures. Even in Tahiti, the sacred chief's authority rested in large part on his control over families of subchiefs, each of whom had his own inalienable rights to lands—and thus families—of commoners. As a result, the number of people who could be effectively integrated into a chiefdom was limited. In Polynesia, most chiefdoms ranged from only a few thousand to 30,000 persons. Polities with larger populations require a political structure based on institutions other than kinship.

States, like chiefdoms, have a centralized political structure. States are distinguished from chiefdoms by the presence of a bureaucracy. A chiefdom is basically a two-level system: (1) the chiefs (which in Tahiti included the subchiefs), who have varying levels of authority and power, and (2) the commoners, or the great mass of the populace. A state has three levels: (1) the ruling elite, (2) a bureaucracy, and (3) the populace.

In states, as in chiefdoms, highest authority and power reside in the ruling elite, the formal political head or heads of the polity. States vary greatly in the types of political leaders present and in the basis for the leaders' authority and power. Leaders in the earliest states frequently were considered to be the descendants of gods, and thus themselves gods on Earth. The Inca of Peru and the pharaohs of Egypt were leaders who ruled as gods. Other political leaders, although not claiming to be gods, have legitimated their positions with claims of having been chosen by God. Early European kings legitimated their claims to leadership on such a basis; and as English coins still proclaim, the queen rules *Dei gratia*—by the "grace of God." Other states have evolved political leadership that uses strictly secular ideas to justify its power. In countries where leaders are elected by a vote of the populace, rule is legitimated by the internalized acceptance of such ascendence to office. Even leaders of strictly secular kingdoms, dictatorships, and oligarchies can, if in power for a sufficient time, have their rule accepted by the populace as "legitimate." We have more to say about legitimation in Chapter 13.

Although they differ greatly in political leadership, states all share one characteristic: a bureaucracy that carries out the day-to-day governing of the polity. In simple terms, a *bureaucrat* is a person to whom a political leader delegates certain authority and powers. The bureaucrat thus acts on behalf of the political leader. Lacking any inherent authority or powers personally, bureaucrats depend on the continued support of political leaders. Using bureaucrats as intermediaries, political leaders could expand the size of their polities both geographically and demographically, while strengthening their political control over the population. Bureaucrats could engineer such expansion without threat of revolution and political fragmentation because they lacked any personal claims to independent political legitimacy.

In addition to differences in their political structure, state-level polities differ from bands, tribes, and chiefdoms in two other important ways. First, they can and usually do have multiethnic populations, including members of a number of ethnic groups who not only have distinct cultural traditions but frequently speak different languages as well. One of these ethnic groups is usually the politically dominant group. Second, with few exceptions, states have market economies (see Chapter 7) and depend in varying degrees on external trade with neighboring groups.

Inca Empire. The Inca Empire of ancient Peru was typical of a state-level organization. From the capital of Cuzco, the ruler, or *Sapa Inca*, controlled a multiethnic empire of between 6 and 12 million subjects who spoke dozens of different languages and extended over 2,500 miles from modern-day Ecuador to central Chile.

Dissected by some of the highest mountain ranges and most inhospitable deserts in the world, the Inca Empire existed without a writing system for communication, a monetary system for exchange, or wheeled vehicles for transporting goods. In spite of this limited technology and hostile terrain, the central government was able to organize human labor for massive public works projects, ranging from buildings and terraced fields to a 9,500-mile highway network that stretched the length and breadth of the country.

The *Sapa Inca* was also able to mobilize and supply armies numbering in the tens of thousands for extended periods of time. The Inca Empire was a state created through the military conquest and incorporation of smaller neighboring states. However, it was the administrative abilities of its leaders, more than their military might, that gave the empire its political cohesiveness.

The *Sapa Inca* was believed to be the direct descendant of the Sun God. Thus, the *Sapa Inca* was a divine being, with absolute authority and control over all the people and resources of the empire. Succession was not clearly defined. Any son of the *Sapa Inca* had a legitimate claim to his father's position. To avoid conflict, the *Sapa Inca* usually chose one of his sons as his successor before his death, but the death of the *Sapa Inca* usually resulted in conflicts between potential heirs.

The empire was administratively divided into four geographical regions, each with its own head. The regions were divided into provinces with governors and regional capitals. The provinces were, in turn, organized on the basis of what some have called a "decimal administration" of hierarchically nested administrative units based on population size. The largest, with a population of 10,000 households, was called a *huno*. A *huno* was divided into units of 5,000, 1,000, 500, 100, 50, and finally 10 households. Each unit had an official head responsible to the person above him. Periodically, a census was conducted and adjustments made. This was the ideal administrative model; the actual structure varied somewhat from province to province due to local demographic and ethnic factors.

Regional heads were members of the Incan royal family. In some provinces, relatives of the *Sapa Inca* also filled the position of governor. However, in most cases provincial governors and other provincial officials were drawn from local elite families, and these families even held hereditary rights to these offices. Beneath these officials and their families was the great mass of people, the commoners.

Land was divided into plots used by individual families and households, and land used for the support of

▶ The Inca were able to construct cities such as Machu Picchu despite mountainous terrain.

© Dennis Hallinan/Alamy

public functions. Every household in the empire was given sufficient land to meet its economic needs. Households and local communities were basically self-sufficient. Food and other goods produced on their land and within the family belonged to the family.

The government of the empire was supported by a labor tax, not a tax on production. Every household was required to supply labor for state purposes. Some assignments were for a number of days per year, others were yearlong, and still others lifelong. The major function of provincial officials was to assign tasks, organize work parties, and oversee the work.

The majority of commoners paid their labor tax by working part of the year farming public fields, tending herds of state-owned animals, weaving cloth, making pottery, repairing public buildings, working on public roads, or performing some other local task. In every province, food, clothes, and other utilitarian goods produced by state tax labor were stored in public buildings. State-owned food, clothes, and other goods were used to support the army, visiting government officials, and commoners who had been assigned long-term labor tasks that made it impossible for them to be self-supporting. In return for their services, all provincial officials in charge of

100 households or more were allowed to use tax laborers to farm their fields, tend their herds, build their houses, and make their clothes and other goods.

In the 1530s, the Spanish conquered the Inca Empire and murdered the last *Sapa Inca*. However, the provincial governmental structure and the "decimal administrative" system were incorporated into the government of colonial Peru.

The emergence of states increased the complexity of political units. Bureaucracies not only allowed for specialization in governmental functions but also made possible the effective integration of large land areas and populations into political units. For example, chiefdoms seldom exceeded 30,000 persons, whereas modern states have populations in the millions.

International Governance

Today there are about 200 independent countries or nation-states in the world. These countries vary greatly in resources, wealth, and military power. In population, they range from China and India with more than 1 billion people each to Tuvalu and Nauru with populations of only about 10,000.

Globalization, and particularly the emergence of the global economy, is highlighting many of the inadequacies of the existing state-level political system. What has emerged is a number of separate but interrelated formal global international organizations that have assumed many of the prerogatives that were formerly exclusively those of national governments. These international organizations include groups such as the United Nations, the World Trade Organization, the World Bank, the International Monetary Fund, and the International Criminal Court. These global bodies differ from states in many critical aspects. They have no territory or group of people directly under their control. They have no capital, only administrative centers or headquarters. They have no head of state, only secretary-generals, managing directors, director-generals, or, in the case of the World Bank and the International Criminal Court, presidents. They have no legislatures or parliaments as such, and they enact no laws. They have assemblies, boards of directors, governors and ministerial conferences, and judges that pass resolutions; negotiate treaties, accords, and agreements; make policy decisions; and issue rulings. Unlike state governments, they print no money, levy no taxes, and have no police, prisons, or military. They are international administrative bureaucracies with the key positions filled by individuals appointed or elected by the member states.

Membership in these organizations is "voluntary," and their financial support usually comes in the form of "voluntary" contributions from the member states. The primary purpose of these international organizations is to regulate the relationships among the member states. Within these organizations, NGOs (nongovernmental organizations) and individuals frequently have no direct voice in policy deliberations. In many cases, however, these international organizations have the authority to impose sanctions on the member states or, in the case of the International Criminal Court, on individuals that they decide are not in compliance with international resolutions, treaties, accords, and agreements. These sanctions can directly affect the lives and well-being of the citizens of that member country. What has emerged, in effect, is a new fragmented level of political organization in which much of the sovereignty of the member states has been ceded to international organizations.

There is no doubt that many of the major problems of today's world are global. Problems of health, the environment, conflict, and economic relationships can be addressed only by international governmental organizations. (In the Globalization box, we discuss some aspects of global governance in more detail.)

Social Control and Law

All societies have clearly defined rules that govern the relationships between members. Not all individuals in any society will conform to these rules. There will always be some who behave in a socially unacceptable manner. Thus, among all peoples, there exist formal and informal ways to correct the behavior of individuals. In general, we call these mechanisms social control. One form of social control is the law.

Social Control

Social control refers to the diverse ways in which the behaviors of the members of a society are constrained into socially approved channels. All cultures have certain behavioral norms that most people learn and begin to conform to during enculturation. But all societies have individuals who, to one degree or another, deviate from those norms. Violations of norms usually result in sanctions or punishments for the offender, which serve both to correct the behavior of particular people and to show others the penalties for such deviance. The severity of sanctions and the process by which sanctions are imposed differ greatly, depending on the seriousness culturally attached to the violated norm, the perceived severity of the violation, and the overall political and legal system of the people.

Children who get into mischief usually are corrected by their parents. In our own society, parents may impose sanctions ranging from scolding to spanking to withdrawing privileges. Correcting children trains individuals in proper behavior at an early age.

The community also applies informal sanctions against children and adults who are not behaving properly. Gossip, or fear of gossip, serves as an important method of social control in most societies. Most people fear the contempt or ridicule of their peers, so they try to conform to acceptable behavioral norms. People attempt to hide behavior that would be the subject of gossip, scandal, and ridicule. Individuals whose known behavior consistently violates social norms may even find themselves ostracized by friends and relatives (the severest of informal punishments). Informal economic penalties also may be imposed. A family may withdraw economic support in attempts to modify the errant behavior of a member.

A wide variety of supernatural sanctions may assist in controlling individual behavior, and in some cases these supernatural sanctions are automatically imposed on particular types of behavior. Whether the commission of these acts becomes public knowledge or not, and thus

One of the creations of the global economy has been the transnational corporation. The global economy has allowed corporations to grow in size and economic power far beyond the wildest dreams of their founders. In 1999, the combined sales of the 200 largest global corporations were equal to 27.5 percent of the combined gross domestic products (GDPs) of all the countries of the world. If one looks at the corporate sales and GDPs of the 100 largest economies, 51 would be corporations and 49 would be countries. In the corporate world, globalization has been the avenue by which the big have gotten bigger. In the global economy, the control of economic power is rapidly passing from governments to corporations. The CEOs and boards of directors of the world's largest corporations now have more economic power than the political leaders and governments of all but a handful of the world's countries.

To understand the significance of this shift in economic power, one has to understand that corporations and governments have very different interests and interest groups. The basic function of a government is to promote the collective well-being and economic interests of its citizens. The interest of a corporation, on the other hand, is far more limited. In most cases today, corporations exist only to produce profits for their owners, an ever-changing and anonymous group of stockholders. As a result, there has always been friction between governments and corporations. Ideally, governments attempt to regulate corporate activities so as to increase the economic and social benefits to their citizens. Corporations, on the other hand, attempt to minimize governmental constraints on their activities so as to maximize profits for their owners. As long as corporations were basically domestic corporations, companies whose operations were confined to a single country, there was no question as to the power of the government to regulate corporate behavior. If a corporation or group of corporations acted in a manner that the citizenry opposed, then the government, particularly in democracies, would respond to public pressure and pass laws regulating corporate behavior. The United States and most other countries have a large body of corporate regulatory laws, minimum wage laws, worker safety laws, environmental laws, and product safety laws, to name only some. In almost all cases, these laws are vigorously opposed by corporate groups. The reason is simple: Regulations cost companies, and thus stockholders, money.

With globalization, the relationship between corporations and government is changing. In 1948, the General Agreement on Tariffs and Trade (GATT) talks were established. These talks, initially involving the United States and a few other industrial countries, were concerned with negotiating reductions in tariffs with the eventual objective of achieving "free trade" throughout the world. Free trade is a central element in global economy. Free trade means that goods, raw materials, commodities, and services may be moved and marketed across international borders without regulations or restraints.

Free trade sounds good. But what does it really mean? For a transnational corporation it means that not only can it market its products in any country it wishes, but it can produce those products wherever it wishes. If wages are relatively high in one country, it can simply move its production facilities to other countries where wages are lower. If environmental laws are too stringent in one country, it can move its production facilities to a country with less demanding environmental protection laws. Thus, free trade allows transnational corporations to play countries, particularly underdeveloped countries, against one another, suppressing wages and lowering worker safety and environmental protection standards. It also means that domestic companies cannot develop. Being forced to compete directly with economically powerful transnational corporations, they are either forced out of business or absorbed.

Although GATT agreements have changed, lowered, or eliminated many tariffs and quotas, every country still has some import and export duties as well as trade quotas. World trade is far "freer" than it was 50 years ago, but numerous tariffs and quotas still exist. In 1995, the World Trade Organization (WTO) became the successor to GATT. Headquartered in Geneva, Switzerland, the WTO monitors and enforces existing binding agreements between the 142 member countries, and it is working to develop still other agreements. However, unlike GATT, which was limited to the elimination of import tariffs and quotas, WTO has much broader powers. WTO has the same legal status as the United Nations and serves as a global commerce agency. The stated objective of the WTO is to ultimately create a fully integrated global economic system in which not only do goods, services, and capital flow without any interference or control by local national governments, but also the property rights of corporations, both physical and intellectual, are fully protected.

---

regardless of whether other punishments are inflicted on the individual, the commission still endangers one's immortal soul. Supernatural sanctions can be more specifically directed. In many societies, including some Christian ones, an individual may place a curse on another person by calling on a supernatural being. Fear of sorcery or witchcraft (see Chapter 14) frequently serves as another important form of social control. Most victims are people who offended a witch or sorcerer in some way, often through a breach of social norms.

Many individuals object to the fact that once the government of a country adopts one of these agreements, the WTO has the power to enforce the agreement. Under these agreements, any existing law in any of the member countries may potentially be considered an obstacle to free trade, and thus illegal. The power for determining whether the law of a particular country is "protectionist," and thus a barrier to free trade and illegal, rests solely with panels of appointed bureaucrats of the WTO. Any member country can challenge any law of any other member country if that law presents a barrier to trade or investment. The proceedings of the WTO tribunals are conducted in secret, and only governments, not the public, have a direct voice in these proceedings. If the WTO tribunal finds against a country, that country has one of only three options: (1) change the law, (2) pay compensation, or (3) have trade sanctions imposed. There is no appeal of a WTO decision.

Almost any law has potential economic consequences; thus, most of the existing laws of the 142 member countries of the WTO are subject to WTO review. So far, the WTO's tribunals have made only a handful of binding rulings, while over a hundred additional challenges await action. The few rulings made by the WTO demonstrate the authority it has assumed.

Among other provisions, the U.S. Clean Air Act set cleanliness standards for oil refiners. These requirements were applied to both domestic refiners and foreign refiners who sold their production in the United States. The WTO ruled against the United States, forcing the law to be amended.

The European Union (EU) countries, for public health concerns, ban the sale of beef containing artificial hormones. The United States challenged this ban, and the WTO ruled against the EU, saying that a country cannot ban the import of a food as a precautionary health measure. The EU has to present scientific proof that artificial hormones are unsafe. The EU also has a similar ban on the importation of genetically altered crops, and the United States is challenging this law as well.

Even the threat of bringing a challenge before the WTO has resulted in smaller countries changing their laws. Following guidelines developed by the World Health Organization, Guatemala adopted a set of measures regulating the marketing of infant formula to reduce its infant mortality rate. Citing this law, the Guatemalan government made Gerber stop running an ad stating that Gerber's infant formula was better than mother's milk. Gerber prevailed on the U.S. government to bring this issue before the WTO. The mere threat resulted in Guatemala dropping the regulation.

Supporters of the WTO argue that for the global economy to reach its full potential, there has to be a uniform set of rules and regulations that everyone follows, and sanctions have to be imposed on those who do not. In this regard they are correct. The questions are: Who will set these rules and regulations; who will determine whether they have been violated; and who will impose sanctions? Opponents argue that the WTO consists of 500 publicly faceless and nameless hired trade specialists in Geneva who are exercising governmental and judicial prerogatives. The decisions they reach are based solely on economic considerations, not the cultural, social, health, and environmental concerns and interests of the public whose lives they affect. No one elected these individuals to these positions of power, and they are not directly responsible to the citizenry of the member countries. In fact, individuals and nongovernmental organizations cannot directly bring complaints before the WTO. The WTO responds only to member governments, and these governments usually react only to the requests of transnational corporations.

Critical Thinking Questions

1. Does globalization make some form of world government inevitable?

2. Is the authority of the nation-state and its citizens being eroded?

3. Will the governments of nation-states of the world become increasingly subordinate to the bureaucratic oligarchies of the World Trade Organization, the World Bank, and the International Monetary Fund, or will some new, more representative and democratic form of global governance evolve?

Sources: Chomsky (2000); Public Citizen (n.d.); World Trade Organization, "The WTO in Brief" (n.d.); Globalisation Guide, "Is Globalisation Shifting Power from Nation States to Undemocratic Organizations?" (n.d.) (see the Globalisation Guide web page, www .globalisationguide.org)

Law

Law is the highest level of social control, and legal punishments usually are reserved for the most serious breaches of norms. The question of how law can be distinguished from other forms of social control is not easy to answer. In societies that have court systems, the distinction is formalized, but in societies with no such formalized legal systems, the distinction is not so clear-cut. E. Adamson Hoebel (1954, 28) defined law in the following

▲ Gossip is one of the primary means of social control.

way: "A social norm is legal if its neglect or infraction is regularly met, in threat or in fact, by the application of physical force by an individual or group possessing the socially recognized privilege of so acting." Law so defined was and is present in virtually every society.

In a legal action, some individual or group must have publicly recognized authority to settle a case or punish a violation. In societies with courts the authority is obvious, but in societies that lack courts the authority becomes less clear. What emerges frequently is an ad hoc authority; that is, because of the peculiarities of the case, a particular individual or group becomes recognized by the community as the authority responsible for its resolution. In some cases, the victim may be the recognized authority. In the victim's absence (as in the case of murder), the victim's family, clan, or kin group may be placed in the role of authority. Such ad hoc authority is discussed later in some of the examples.

Implicit in all legal actions is the intention of universal application, which means that in identical cases the sanction imposed is the same. Although one might argue that no two legal cases have been or will ever be identical, the notion of universal application requires that the law be consistent and thus predictable; the arbitrary imposition of sanctions is not law.

Hoebel limited legal sanctions to physical sanctions. However, other scholars have argued that this definition is too narrow. A legal sanction does not have to be some form of corporal punishment, nor does it have to involve the loss of property. Based on his work with the Kapauku of New Guinea, Leopold Pospisil contended that the impact of psychological sanctions can be more severe than that of actual physical punishment. For this reason he stated, "We can define a legal sanction as either the

negative behavior of withdrawing some rewards or favors that otherwise (if the law had not been violated) would have been granted, or the positive behavior of inflicting some painful experience, be it physical or psychological" (Pospisil 1958, 268).

Legal Systems

On the basis of procedural characteristics, two main levels of complexity and formality can be defined: self-help legal systems and court legal systems.

Self-Help Systems

Self-help legal systems, also called *ad hoc systems,* are informal and exist in the absence of any centralized or formalized legal institutions capable of settling disputes. Such systems are associated with band-level societies and most tribal-level societies. In such systems, there is only civil law. All legal actions concern only the principal parties and/or their families. The reason for terming the legal procedure in these societies *self-help* will become clear.

Self-help legal systems may be divided into two main forms: familial and mediator. In *familial* systems, all actions and decisions are initiated and executed by the families or larger kin groups involved. *Mediator* systems add the formal presence of a neutral third party—the mediator—who attempts to negotiate and resolve the dispute peacefully.

In familial systems, legal actions are handled by the families involved. A legal offense only indirectly concerns the community as a whole. When an individual or a family determines that its rights have been violated, the imposition of the proper sanction falls to the plaintiffs; in other words, the offended party assumes the role of authority. Such a system has some problems in implementation, but not as many as one might anticipate. This is not a system of "might makes right." Certainly cases arise in such societies in which the weak are victimized by the strong. In cases of legal redress, however, there is a community consensus in support of the victim and usually a recognized means by which even the weakest members of the community can gather support adequate to impose appropriate sanctions on the strongest.

The Comanche exemplify how a familial legal system operated and how victims weaker than their opponents could nonetheless obtain redress. One of the most frequent Comanche offenses was "wife stealing." Most older Comanche men were polygynous, and some of their wives were significantly younger than their husbands. Among young Comanche men, it was considered prestigious, though illegal, to steal the wife of another man. Under Comanche law, the injured husband could demand either his wife back or some property, usually horses, in compensation. The husband had the responsibility of imposing these sanctions. In such actions, the community played no direct role, but a husband could not ignore the loss of a wife. If he did ignore it, the community would ridicule him, and his prestige would decline. Thus, not only did the community support the husband in pressing his claim, but they informally pressured him to act.

In imposing these sanctions, the husband was allowed to use whatever physical force was needed, short of killing the offender. In cases in which the men involved were physically about equal, the two met to negotiate and discuss the husband's demands. Behind these negotiations was the potential threat that the husband might physically assault the defendant.

In cases where the husband presented little or no physical threat to the defendant, institutionalized means existed whereby the husband could gain physical backing. Although it lowered his prestige in the community, he could call on his relatives for support; with his male relatives present and prepared to support his demands physically, the husband could then negotiate with the defendant. The defendant always had to stand alone. Even if he had asked his kinsmen for support, they would not have responded for fear of community ridicule.

In cases where the husband was an orphan or lacked kinsmen, he could call on any other man he wanted to prosecute his case. He usually asked for the assistance of one of the powerful war leaders in the band. Such a request was so prestigious that a war leader could not refuse. At the same time, such a request was demeaning to the man asking for help and greatly lowered his prestige. As a result, it usually required a great deal of social pressure to force a man to ask for assistance. Once the request was made, the issue was between the defendant and the war leader alone. On approaching the defendant, the war leader would call out, "You have stolen my wife," and then proceed to exact whatever demands the husband had requested. For his action, the war leader received nothing in payment other than the admiration of the community; the husband received the settlement. Although this process was used most commonly in wife-stealing cases, it could be used for other issues as well. Thus, Comanche legal institutions gave any individual the means to marshal overwhelming physical force to protect his rights.

A more formalized type of legal procedure is found in the mediator system. In this system, disputes are still between individuals and families, and the offended party or the person's family has the position of authority. How-

ever, a third party is called on, usually by the offending individual or his or her family, to attempt to negotiate a mutually agreeable solution. The mediator has no authority to impose a settlement. The aggrieved party and/or family must agree to accept the compensation negotiated.

The Nuer, a pastoral tribal society of Sudan, provide an example of how mediator systems operate. The Nuer live in small villages of related families. Although villages are tied together through lineages and clans, there is no effective leadership above the village level. The only formalized leaders who transcend the local units are *leopard-skin chiefs,* who wear a leopard-skin cloak to indicate their positions. These men have no secular authority to enforce their judgments but only limited ritual powers to bless and curse.

The most important function of leopard-skin chiefs is mediating feuds between local groups. The Nuer are an egalitarian, warrior-oriented people. Disputes between individuals frequently result in physical violence, and men occasionally are killed. The killing requires that the kinsmen exact retribution. Any close patrilineal kinsman of the murderer may be killed in retaliation, but at least initially the kinsmen of the victim attempt to kill the murderer himself. Immediately after committing a murder, the killer flees to the house of a leopard-skin chief. This dwelling is a sanctuary, and as long as the man stays in the chief's house, he is safe. The victim's kinsmen usually keep the house under surveillance to try to kill the murderer if he ventures out.

The leopard-skin chief keeps the murderer in his house until a settlement is arranged. The chief will wait until tempers have cooled, which usually requires several weeks, before he begins to negotiate the case. First, he goes to the family of the murderer to see if they are willing to pay cattle to the victim's family in compensation. Seldom do they refuse because one of them might be killed in retaliation. After the murderer's family has agreed to pay, the chief proceeds to the family of the victim, offering so many cattle in compensation. Initially the victim's family invariably refuses, saying that they want blood, that cattle cannot compensate them for the death of their beloved kinsman. The leopard-skin chief persists, usually gaining the support of more distant relatives of the victim, who also pressure the family to settle. The leopard skin chief may even threaten to place a curse on the family if they continue to refuse to settle for a payment rather than blood. The family finally agrees and accepts cattle, usually about 40, as compensation. Even though the matter is formally settled, the killer and his close patrilineal kinsmen will avoid the family of the victim for some years so as not to provoke spontaneous retaliation.

Up to this point, we have examined legal systems that operate without a formalized or centralized political structure capable of resolving disputes. In many of these societies, law, not subordination to a common set of formal political institutions, defines boundaries. To see what we mean, consider the Nuer. The Nuer distinguish among a *ter,* a feud within a tribe that is a legal action subject to arbitration; a *kur,* a fight between members of two tribes that cannot be arbitrated; and a *pec,* a war with non-Nuer people. Nuer believe that disputes within a tribe should be resolved by legal means (that is, peacefully), whereas disputes between individuals who are not members of the same tribe should be resolved by extralegal means, including organized warfare. Legal processes serve to repair and maintain social relations between families; thus, law serves both to maintain the cohesiveness and to define the boundaries of the society.

The Jívaro, a horticultural and foraging people of eastern Ecuador, illustrate how law defines social boundaries. By the 1950s, the Jívaro had been reduced to slightly more than 2,000 persons settled in more than 200 scattered family households. Such households usually consist of a husband, his wife or wives, their children, and possibly a son-in-law or other relatives. Households are grouped into "neighborhoods," which consist of a number of households living within a few miles of one another; the membership of a neighborhood is fluid. Poor hunting, a dispute with other households, or other factors might result in a family's moving away. Neither corporate kin groups nor formalized leadership positions exist. Except for household heads, only a few men are called *unta,* or "big," but their informal leadership role is limited and transitory.

Politically, the Jívaro are organized at a band level. Although they have only limited political institutions, the Jívaro have a strong sense of common cultural identity and territorial boundaries. Living in adjacent or nearby territories are four other "Jívaroan" groups, who speak mutually intelligible dialects, share the same basic customs, and at times trade with Jívaro households. Despite their minimal political integration, there is little question about which households are Jívaro and which belong to the other four groups.

With this political organization, the methods used to settle disputes define the effective boundaries of the society. Disputes between Jívaros are resolved by legal means, whereas disputes with members of other societies are resolved through extralegal means. Like the Nuer, the Jívaro make a sharp distinction between a feud and a war. A **feud** is the legal means by which a sanction is imposed on another family for the murder of a kinsman.

As a legal procedure, a feud proceeds in a manner quite different from a war.

As in most societies, murder is the most serious offense. According to Jívaro beliefs, few deaths are attributable to natural causes; most are the result of physical violence, sorcery, or avenging spirits. Deaths caused by physical violence and witchcraft are considered murders, which have to be avenged by the kinsmen of the deceased. In most cases of physical violence, the murderer is readily identifiable. In cases of poisoning and witchcraft, divination is used to determine the guilty party.

Determination of the guilty party and whether they are Jívaro or non-Jívaro affect how the victim's kinfolk avenge the death. If the guilty party is Jívaro, the kinsmen of the victim attack the household of the murderer with the goal of killing the man himself. If they are not successful in finding him, they may kill a male relative of his, even a young boy. They normally will not harm women or little children, except when the victim was a woman or a child. Even if they have the opportunity to kill more, only one individual will be killed. This is a legal action, and Jívaro law allows only a life for a life.

If the guilty party is determined to be a non-Jívaro, the relatives of the murdered person attack the household of the guilty party, trying to kill as many people as possible. They attempt to massacre the entire family, with no regard for either sex or age. In some cases, they attack nearby households as well, attempting to kill even more members of the group. This is a war, not a legal action.

The Jívaro, the Nuer, and other peoples who lack a centralized and formal political structure nonetheless have definite means of maintaining social control. To those of us who have formal governmental institutions that are supposed to handle our grievances and right the wrongs done to us, self-help systems look rather anarchic. However, rules govern such systems. Some anthropologists believe, in fact, that the best definition of *society* in self-help systems is those individuals whose vengeance-taking activities are constrained by procedural rules.

Court Systems

A number of factors distinguish a **court legal system** from a self-help legal system. First, authority resides not with the victim and his or her family but with a formalized institution, the court. The court has the authority and the power to hear disputes and to unilaterally decide cases and impose sanctions. Authority in legal matters is a component of political authority; thus, fully developed court systems can exist only in societies that have centralized formal political leadership—that is, chiefdoms or states. Second, most court systems operate with formal public hearings, presided over by a judge or judges, with formally defined defendants and plaintiffs. Grievances are stated, evidence is collected and analyzed, and, in cases of conflicting evidence, oaths or ordeals may be used to determine truthfulness. Finally, only in court systems does one find substantive law clearly divided into criminal law and civil law.

Court systems in turn may be divided into three categories: (1) **incipient courts,** (2) **courts of mediation,** and (3) **courts of regulation.** All court systems mediate disputes as well as regulate behavior; however, as societies become increasingly complex, the primary focus of the court shifts from mediating disputes to regulating behavior. This shift results in a qualitative difference not only in courts but in the nature of the law itself. Associated with this shift is an increasing codification of the laws. Laws and their associated sanctions become standardized and rigid, and civil laws are steadily transformed into criminal laws. Court systems begin to emerge with the concept of "crime against society"—the need to control individual acts that might endanger the society as a whole, as opposed to acts that threaten only individuals. Herein lies the distinction between criminal law and civil law.

Incipient court systems. True court systems can be found only in societies that have centralized political systems—chiefdoms or states. However, some tribal societies have what might best be termed *incipient courts.* Although a tribal-level society, the Cheyenne, as described earlier in this chapter, demonstrate the development of an incipient court system. At times, both the Council of Forty-Four and the warrior societies assumed the role of de facto judges and courts. The Cheyenne recognized that certain individual actions threatened the well-being of the group and thus had to be controlled. Some of these actions were purely secular, whereas others were religious. Designated warrior societies were formally empowered by the council to enforce secular laws and regulations. For example, in preparation for a communal bison hunt, camp members would be told to refrain from independent hunting for some days. If the policing warrior society discovered someone hunting illegally, the men present became the de facto judges and court and immediately imposed sanctions on the offender, often beating him with whips, shooting his horses, and slashing his tepee with knives.

Other secular criminal violations were handled just as swiftly. The Council of Forty-Four was responsible for the religious, or sacred, well-being of the tribe; thus, any action that endangered the supernatural well-being of the Cheyenne was their concern. The murder of a Cheyenne by another Cheyenne was the most heinous of crimes. Such a crime was said to bloody the sacred arrows, the most sacred of Cheyenne tribal medicine bundles. The arrows were symbolic of Cheyenne success in hunting (their main economic activity) and warfare. Murder within the tribe polluted the arrows and thus made the Cheyenne vulnerable to their enemies and less successful in their hunting. When a Cheyenne died at the hands of another Cheyenne, the Council of Forty-Four became a de facto court. Although there was no formal hearing, the council met and discussed the case: Was it murder? If so, then the sacred arrows had to be "renewed," or ritually purified. They also decided on the sanction to be imposed—usually exile for a period of years. With the Cheyenne there could be no capital punishment without again polluting the sacred arrows. (See A Closer Look for a further discussion of the Cheyenne.)

Courts of mediation. The key difference between court systems is not how the legal hearings are conducted but the manner in which breaches of the law are determined and suitable sanctions imposed. In courts of mediation, few laws are codified, and the judges follow few formalized guidelines as to what constitutes a legal violation or the sanction that should be imposed. This is not to say that judges act arbitrarily in these matters, but that they have tremendous latitude in their actions. What they apply is a **reasonable-person model.** Using prevalent norms and values, they ask the question: How should a reasonable individual have acted under these circumstances? To determine this, they must examine an individual's actions within the social context in which the dispute occurred: What were the past and present relationships between the parties involved? What circumstances led up to the event? Thus, judges attempt to examine each case as a unique occurrence. Although some sanctions are imposed as punishments, other sanctions are designed to restore as fully as possible a working, if not harmonious, relationship between the parties involved.

One difficulty in attempting to describe courts of mediation is our limited knowledge of such systems. Polities that had courts of this nature were some time ago brought under European colonial rule. Their courts were soon modified by and subordinated to European colonial courts, which were more regulatory in nature.

The killing of one Cheyenne by another was not only a "sin" that "polluted" the murderer and endangered the well-being of the tribe but also a crime against the society. This pollution of the sacred arrows caused the game animals that the Cheyenne depended on for their subsistence to shun their hunting territory. A killing required the ritual purification of the sacred arrows. Not every killing was considered a criminal act, however. On hearing of a killing within the band, the members of the Council of Forty-Four assembled. Exactly how and what they discussed in such cases we shall never know; but the council members had to decide when a killing was to be treated as a murder. Was suicide murder? Was abortion murder? Was a killing ever justifiable? Was drunkenness a mitigating circumstance? If the council determined that a murder had taken place, the chiefs ordered the immediate banishment of the murderer. Such banishment usually included not only the murderer but also the murderer's family and sometimes friends who went along voluntarily. This banishment usually lasted between 5 and 10 years. During the period of exile, the banished individual usually lived with a friendly group of Arapahos or Dakotas.

The act of suicide was not typically considered murder. Several cases are known of Cheyenne women committing suicide for what were considered trivial reasons. Such cases were not considered murder, and as far as can be determined, the sacred arrows were not renewed. In other instances, however, suicide was treated as murder. For example, one mother became infuriated when her daughter eloped with a young man of whom she did not approve. The mother found the girl and beat her with a whip while dragging her home. Inside the tepee, the girl seized a gun and shot herself. In another case, a young girl divorced her husband and returned to her parents' home. At some later time, her mother found the girl participating in a young persons' dance and beat her; the girl subsequently hanged herself. In both cases, the chiefs ruled that the girls were driven to suicide by their mothers, who were thus considered the murderers. In both cases, the sacred arrows were renewed, and the mothers were banished.

Was a killing ever justifiable? In one case, a man attempted to rape his daughter, who resisted and used a knife to kill her father. The sacred arrows were renewed, but the chiefs did not order the girl banished, nor did the people treat her as a murderer. In another case, a man named Winnebago took the wife of another man, who retaliated by taking one of Winnebago's wives. Winnebago was enraged and killed the second man; he was then banished. After his return from banishment, Winnebago argued with and killed a second man, so he was banished again. While living among the Arapaho, Winnebago became involved in a dispute with a Cheyenne named Rising Fire, who knew of Winnebago's murders and therefore shot Winnebago out of fear. Although the facts are unclear, it appears that Rising Fire was not exiled for this killing. Thus, under some circumstances, such as incestuous rape and the fear of a known murderer, the chiefs thought that killing was justifiable. In such instances, the sacred arrows had to be renewed, but the killer was not exiled.

Was drunkenness a mitigating circumstance? During a drunken brawl, Cries-Yia-Eya killed Chief Eagle. In another case, during a drunken party, Porcupine Bear stabbed Little Creek and then called on his relatives to stab Little Creek as well. They did so, killing Little Creek. Cries-Yia-Eya and Porcupine Bear and his guilty relatives were banished by the chiefs; drunkenness was not a defense for murder.

The chiefs were faced with a second issue regarding Little Creek's killers. After their banishment, Porcupine Bear and his relatives continued to stay close to the band camp. When the tribe organized a revenge attack on the Kiowas, Porcupine Bear and his relatives kept their distance but followed along with the other Cheyenne. In the attack on the Kiowas, Porcupine Bear and his six relatives distinguished themselves by bravely attacking first and killing about 30 Kiowas. What about war honors for acts of bravery accomplished during banishment? The council ruled that exiles could not receive recognition for their military acts, no matter how courageous they might be. In a sense, during their period of banishment, they were not Cheyenne.

Was abortion murder? In one case, a fetus was found near a Cheyenne camp. An investigation by a warrior society discovered that a young girl had concealed her pregnancy. The young girl was banished, but only until after the sacred arrows had been renewed. Thus, the chiefs considered abortion a less serious type of murder that required a shorter period of banishment.

The chiefs had to answer many other questions concerning murder and banishment. In about 1855, one of the chiefs, a member of the Council of Forty-Four, killed another Cheyenne. The sacred arrows were renewed, and the chief was banished; but what was to be done about his position on the council? The council ruled that the man could not be removed from office and that he remained a chief even though he could not participate in the council.

From the discussion of these cases emerges some of the reasoning behind Cheyenne legal decisions. The chiefs considered a range of factors in reaching their final determinations. Murder included not merely the cold-blooded killing of one Cheyenne by another but also abortion and acts that compelled another to commit suicide. At the same time, the chiefs thought that, in particular instances, killing was justifiable but intoxication was not a mitigating factor.

Source: Llewellyn and Hoebel (1941)

The example we use is the Barotse judicial system, as described by Max Gluckman. The Barotse made up a multiethnic state in southern Africa that at the time of Gluckman's study in the 1940s had been under British rule for 40 years. The British had removed more serious offenses from the jurisdiction of this court. Despite these factors, the basic Barotse legal concepts aptly illustrate a mediation type of court system.

The Barotse state had two capitals—a northern capital, where the king resided, and a subordinate southern capital, ruled by a princess. All villages in the state were attached to one or the other of these capitals. The capitals were identical in structure; each had a palace and a council house. Courts of law were held in the council house.

The titular head of the court was the ruler; in practice, the ruler seldom was present at trials. In the center at the back of the house was the dais, or raised platform, where the ruler was seated if present. There were three ranked groupings of judges. The highest-ranking group of judges was the *indunas,* or councilors, who sat to the right of the dais. The second-highest-ranking group was the *likombwa,* or stewards, who sat to the left. These two groups were divided into senior members, who sat in the front, and junior members, who sat behind. The third group consisted of princes and the husbands of the princesses, who represented their wives. This group sat at a right angle to the *likombwa.*

A case was introduced by a plaintiff, who was allowed to state his or her grievance at length with no interruption; the defendant was then allowed the same privilege. The statements of witnesses for both sides followed. There were no attorneys for either side; the judges questioned and cross-examined the witnesses. After all the testimony had been heard, the judges began to give their opinions, starting with the most junior *indunas,* followed by the others in order of increasing seniority. The last judge to speak was the senior *induna,* who passed judgment on the case, subject to the ruler's approval.

In judging a case, the Barotse judges used a reasonable-person model. The reasonableness of behavior was related to the social and kinship relationships of the individuals involved. Also, a breach of the law usually did not happen in isolation, and many individuals could be at fault; so one case frequently led to a number of related cases. In passing judgment and imposing sanctions, the judges considered numerous factors. One of the most important was the kinship relationship between the parties. The judges attempted to restore the relationship and reconcile the parties—but not without blaming those who had committed wrongs and not without imposing sanctions. The judges'

opinions frequently took the form of sermons on proper behavior. As Gluckman (1973, 22) notes:

> Implicit in the reasonable man is the upright man, and moral issues in these relationships are barely differentiated from legal issues. This is so even though . . . [they] distinguish "legal" rules, which the . . . [court] has power to enforce or protect, from "moral" rules which it has not power to enforce or protect. But the judges are reluctant to support the person who is right in law, but wrong in justice, and may seek to achieve justice by indirect . . . action.

Courts of mediation have great potential for meeting the basic social purpose of the law, which is the maintenance of group cohesiveness. There is one serious drawback: such a system is workable only in a culturally homogeneous political unit; that is, it works only if the judges and the parties involved share the same basic norms and values.

Courts of regulation. In the second millennium B.C.E., the Code of Hammurabi, the earliest known set of written laws, was created in Babylon. The code covered a variety of laws. One section dealt with physicians. It set the prices to be charged for various types of operations, based on the ability of individuals to pay. It also decreed, among other things, that if a surgeon operated on an individual using a bronze knife and the patient died or lost his eyesight, the surgeon's hand was to be cut off. The laws defined in the Code of Hammurabi reflect the emergence of regulatory laws. The role of the court was no longer to merely arbitrate disputes and strive for reconciliation but to define the rights and duties of members of an increasingly heterogeneous community.

Courts of regulation were a natural outgrowth of state-level polities, which evolved socially and economically distinct classes and encompassed numerous culturally distinct peoples. As relationships between individuals in the population became depersonalized, the law, too, became increasingly depersonalized. This change in the nature of law was compounded by the political incorporation of diverse peoples who frequently had conflicting cultural norms and values. The use of a reasonable-person model is workable only as long as there is a general consensus on what is "reasonable." In increasingly complex and stratified societies, the possibility of such consensus declined. Mediation of disputes works well in small, kinship-based societies, where all parties recognize the need for reconciliation through compromise. In sharply divided societies, the need for mediation is not as great because reconciliation in itself is not seen

Form	Characteristics	Associated Political System(s)
Self-Help		
(a) Familial	Legal concepts based on accepted social norms and behaviors of the society Ad hoc sanctioning authority limited to victim and/or victim's family, with implicit support of other community members	Band
(b) Mediator	Legal concepts based on accepted social norms and behaviors of the society Ad hoc sanctioning authority limited to victim and/or victim's family, with implicit support of other community members Use of a third-party mediator, with limited if any authority, to negotiate a settlement	Composite bands and most tribal peoples
Courts		
(a) Mediation	Legal concepts based on the reasonable-person model Formal judges who have the authority to hear cases and impose sanctions	Some tribal peoples have rudimentary court systems; however, true court systems appear with chiefdoms and smaller states.
(b) Regulation	Laws and sanctions are formally codified Formal judges who have the authority to hear cases and impose sanctions	States

© Royalty Free/Corbis/Jupiter Images

▲ In courts of regulation, the authority of judges is usually limited.

as a gain. Compromise is viewed only in terms of what is lost. Laws were thus created to bring order and stability to the interactions between individuals who were not social equals. With law divorced from social norms and values, justice was no longer simply a moral or ethical issue, but came to be viewed in terms of consistency, or precedent.

The separation of law from social norms and values also opened the door for the "politicization" of the laws. Laws were created to serve political ends, as various groups vied with one another for the creation of laws that would protect, express, or further their own goals, interests, and values. This situation is particularly evident in multiethnic and religious and economically diverse state-level systems such as that of the United States. Given the cultural pluralism, religious diversity, and economic inequality of the United States, it would be impossible to create a code of laws that could equally protect the interests of all classes and that would be consistent with the norms and values of all groups. As a result, many people find themselves subject to laws and sanctions, some of which they judge either immoral or unethical; at times, people find that laws violate their own cultural values. We see this with groups who think that abortion is murder and thus should be made illegal, and with groups who oppose capital punishment on the grounds that the state does not have the right to kill individuals. During the Vietnam War, we saw it with draft resisters who argued that the state did not have the right to order men to fight in a war they considered immoral. Less obvious is the manner in which numerous ethnic minorities, notably Native Americans, subordinate their cultural norms and values to comply with the legal system. With the emergence of states and courts of regulation, law ceased to be an expression of social norms and values and became their molder.

Summary

1. Political organization and social control are distinct but overlapping cultural institutions. Group action—in both economic and social activities—is a prerequisite for the survival of the population. To be effective, group activities must have leadership and organization, which are the basis for political structure. At the same time, individual differences, conflict, and competition within the group must be controlled and channeled in such a manner that the internal cohesiveness and cooperation of the individual members of the group are maintained—thus the need for social control.

2. Four major categories of political organization are bands, tribes, chiefdoms, and states. Found among foraging societies, the band is the simplest and least formal level of political organization. The two forms of band organization are simple bands and composite bands.

3. In simple bands, the highest level of political organization is the extended family, with the highest level of political leadership being the heads of the various families. These simple bands are economically self-sufficient and politically autonomous. Because a simple band has as its core a group of related individuals, band members are forced to seek spouses from outside the band; they are exogamous units. Thus, kinship ties through marriage serve as the primary link between bands. Simple bands most commonly are found among foragers who hunt game animals that are present in small numbers year-round.

4. Composite bands are larger than simple bands and include a number of distinct families. Leadership in composite bands is vested in "big men," or informal leaders, who have influence but not authority. Composite bands most often are found among foragers who hunt migratory herd animals.

5. At the tribal level, institutions transcend local residence groups and bind the geographically scattered members of the society into a cohesive unit. The key element in tribal societies is the sodality, which may be either kinship-based, as in the case of clans, or non-kinship-based, as in the case of warrior societies or age grades. Leadership in such groups is more structured, with formal political offices.

6. Chiefdoms have formal, hereditary leadership with centralized political control and authority. The associated redistributive economic exchange system focused on the chief economically integrates the various communities within the political unit.

7. The state is the most complex level of political organization. States have centralized power and control, but the key characteristic of a state is a bureaucracy—individuals acting on behalf of the political elite, thus enabling the centralized power figures to maintain control of a greater number of individuals.

8. Over the past half-century, a number of international organizations have emerged that are assuming many of the prerogatives that had been exclusively those of state-level governments.

9. Social control consists of the various methods used to control and channel the behavior of individual members of a society into approved behavior. Law and legal systems are merely the highest level of social control. Law is defined as having three attributes: (1) authority, (2) intention of universal application, and (3) sanction. By this definition, all societies have law.

10. In societies with no centralized political systems, legal systems are self-help. In self-help systems, the responsibility and authority for determining a breach of the law and imposing the proper sanction fall to the victim or victim's family (or both). As discussed, this system is not as arbitrary as we might think. In the case of murder or killing, the result may be a feud between families, but a feud—sharply distinguished from a war—is part of the legal process.

11. Law in societies with centralized political systems is handled by courts. Court systems usually can be categorized as either courts of mediation or courts of regulation. In relatively homogeneous societies, most court systems take as their primary objective the mediation of disputes between individuals and the restoration of harmonious social relationships. In more heterogeneous groups, courts usually become more regulatory in nature, with formally defined laws and sanctions.

Key Terms

bands
simple bands
composite bands
big men
influence
authority
tribes

sodalities
chiefdoms
states
social control
law
self-help legal systems
feud

court legal systems
incipient courts
courts of mediation
courts of regulation
reasonable-person model

Suggested Readings

Cohen, R., and Elman Service, eds. *Origins of the State: The Anthropology of Political Evolution.* Philadelphia: Institute for the Study of Human Issues, 1978.

A collection of essays from various perspectives examining the development of state-level political systems.

Fried, Morton. *The Evolution of Political Society.* New York: Random House, 1967.

A theoretical study that traces the development of political systems from egalitarian societies, through ranked, to stratified and state-level societies.

Haas, Jonathan, ed. *From Leaders to Rulers.* New York: Kluwer Academic/Plenum Publishers, 2001.

Making use primarily of archaeological data, the 10 scholars whose papers appear in this volume discuss one of the most critical issues in the evolution of political leadership. How and why did centralized systems develop and leadership shift from informal leaders with only influence, to formal rulers with the authority to command their followers?

Hoebel, E. Adamson. *The Law of Primitive Man.* Cambridge, Mass.: Harvard University Press, 1964.

The first major comparative study of non-Western legal systems. Although somewhat dated, it remains a classic study.

Newman, Katherine S. *Law and Economic Organization: A Comparative Study of Pre-Industrial Societies.* Cambridge: Cambridge University Press, 1983.

A cross-cultural analysis of 60 societies to show that legal institutions systematically vary with economic organization.

The following ethnographies are excellent descriptions of political and/or legal systems within particular societies:

Gluckman, Max. *The Ideas in Barotse Jurisprudence.* Manchester: Manchester University Press, 1965.

Gluckman, Max. *The Judicial Process Among the Barotse.* Manchester: Manchester University Press, 1973.

These two studies of the Barotse of Zambia not only describe a system in a non-Western state but also—and more important—illustrate the legal reasoning used in their court systems. Good description of the political structure and legal system of a band-level society.

Kuper, Hilda. *The Swazi: A South African Kingdom.* 2nd ed. New York: Holt, Rinehart and Winston, 1986.

An excellent short ethnography of Swaziland, now an independent nation. Has a good discussion of recent changes.

Llewellyn, Karl, and E. Adamson Hoebel. *The Cheyenne Way.* Norman: University of Oklahoma Press, 1941.

A classic study of the legal system of a tribal society.

Media Resources

The Wadsworth Anthropology Resource Center
academic.cengage.com/anthropology

The Wadsworth discipline resource website that accompanies *Humanity: An Introduction to Cultural Anthropology,* Eighth Edition, includes a rich array of material, including online anthropological video clips, to help you in the study of cultural anthropology and the specific topics covered in this chapter. Other material includes a case study forum with excerpts from various Wadsworth authors, map exercises, scientist interviews, breaking news in anthropology, and links to additional useful online material. Begin by selecting Cultural Anthropology to take you to videos, research, and more. From the homepage, you may also select Applied Anthropology, which directs you to essays, glossary terms, the case study forum, and a list of internships and careers in anthropology.

13 SOCIAL INEQUALITY AND STRATIFICATION

In stratified societies, large differences in wealth exist and are tolerated and even encouraged. These people of Cape Town, South Africa, seem to be doing well in life.

Systems of Equality and Inequality
   Egalitarian Societies
   Ranked Societies
   Stratified Societies
Castes in Traditional India
Classes in Industrial Societies: The United States

Maintaining Inequality
   Ideologies
   American Secular Ideologies
Theories of Inequality
   Functionalist Theory
   Conflict Theory
   Who Benefits?

Questions addressed in this chapter

What are the three main forms of inequality in diverse societies?

How are castes and classes different?

What are *ideologies* and *secular ideologies*?

How do the functionalist and conflict theories of inequality differ?

"We hold these truths to be self-evident, that all men are created equal, that they are endowed by their Creator with certain unalienable Rights...." As you know by now, whether in fact all "men" are believed to have been created equal depends on which society you happened to be born into. Whether you have certain "unalienable rights," and the nature of these rights, also varies from people to people. In this chapter, we consider another dimension of cultural diversity—the differential allocation of culturally valued rewards.

Systems of Equality and Inequality

Inequality refers to the degree to which culturally valued material and social rewards are given disproportionately to individuals, families, and other kinds of groups. To the extent that inequality exists in a group or whole society, its members receive varying levels of benefits.

Before discussing cross-cultural variations, we must consider the nature of rewards. Rewards are commonly divided into three categories. The most tangible type of reward is *wealth*—ownership of or access to valued material goods and to the natural and human resources needed to produce those goods. The second kind of reward is *power*—the ability to make others do what you want based on coercion or legitimate authority. The final type of reward is *prestige*—the respect, esteem, and overt approval other group members grant to individuals they consider meritorious. Prestige (or *honor*, or *status*) is a social reward, based on judgments about an individual's personal worthiness or the contributions the individual makes to others in the group.

The distribution of each kind of reward varies among societies. Some societies allow ambitious individuals to acquire wealth, power, and prestige, whereas others make it difficult for anyone to accumulate possessions,

gain control over others, or put themselves above their peers socially. For instance, many North Americans admire "self-made" men and women who have supposedly earned higher incomes (wealth) than other people by their own talents and efforts. However, such individuals would be looked down on as self-centered and ungenerous in many other cultures.

To introduce the ways societies differ in inequality, anthropologists often use an influential classification developed by Morton Fried in 1967. Fried identified three basic types of societies based on their level and kinds of inequality: **egalitarian, ranked,** and **stratified.** A description and examples of each type appear later in this section. The differences among the three forms are summarized in the Concept Review. We need to clarify three points about Fried's classification.

First, the categories do not refer to access to rewards based on sex or age. When we call a society *egalitarian,* for example, we do not mean that females and males receive equal or nearly equal rewards, or that elderly people and young people are socially equal. Even in egalitarian societies, there are social distinctions based on sex and age. Essentially, *egalitarian* means that there are few differences in the rewards received by families or other kinds of kin groups within a society. At the other end of the continuum, in societies we call *stratified,* there are major differences in access to rewards between families or kin groups, in addition to any distinctions based on sex or age.

Second, Fried's three categories are merely points along a continuous spectrum of inequality. It is impossible to pigeonhole all human societies into one of these types because most fit somewhere in between the three categories. The terms *egalitarian, ranked,* and *stratified* are useful mainly as short descriptions of the kinds and range of variation in inequality found cross-culturally.

Third, egalitarian–ranked–stratified is the temporal order in which the three forms developed. Until about 10,000 years ago, most people lived in egalitarian societies.

Form	Main Characteristics
Egalitarian	Rough equality across families in access to possessions and wealth objects Wide access to and sharing of productive resources Influence and prestige based on age and personal qualities and achievements
Ranked	Limited number of formal social roles or positions (offices, titles) that grant authority Access to prestigious titles and offices determined largely by hereditary family/kinship ties Rights to resources allocated by those of higher rank
Stratified	Sharply unequal distribution of resources and wealth Large inequalities in access to power and social rewards (prestige)
Caste	Named, endogamous, ranked groups with membership normatively based on birth Occupation and activities constrained by caste membership Interaction between members of different castes governed by social rules (segregation, pollution)
Class	Vague definition and imprecise membership determined by a combination of birth and achievement Class membership broadly determined by occupation and wealth level

Ranked societies developed in a few areas about then, and a few thousand years later, stratification developed in some early chiefdoms and in the great civilizations (see Chapters 6 and 12). Archaeologists have devised some clever means to find out about inequality in prehistoric societies, and there is wide agreement that most of the world's people were essentially egalitarian until the development of agriculture. After that, over the next 4,000 to 5,000 years, stratified societies spread throughout much of the world, as some peoples and nations conquered and ruled over others.

Egalitarian Societies

In egalitarian societies, aside from distinctions based on sex and age, there are minor differences among individuals and families in rewards. People who work hard, or who have attractive personalities or valuable skills, may be rewarded with respect and prestige from other members of their group. Egalitarian groups have various cultural mechanisms to prevent any individual from becoming too "big," however. And, even people who are respected have few, if any, more possessions or power than others.

Mobile hunting and gathering peoples, such as the Inuit, Ju/'hoansi, Hadza, BaMbuti, and Aka, are egalitar-ian. In 1982, James Woodburn identified three reasons rewards are rather evenly distributed among such foragers.

1. Most obviously, the band or camp must move frequently for effective adaptation (see Chapter 6). Mobility makes it difficult to transport possessions and hence to accumulate wealth.
2. The cultural value foragers place on reciprocal sharing (see Chapter 7) prevents individual persons or family groups from becoming wealthier than their bandmates. Because sharing food and most durable possessions is normatively expected, hoarding and accumulation are seen as negative. So, even if someone tried to, he or she would find it difficult to accumulate because other people demand their share, and failure to adhere to the norms of sharing and to live up to egalitarian values is socially punished by public ridicule or worse.
3. Mobile foraging families are not tied to specific territories but have the right to visit and exploit the resources of many areas, often due to extended family ties (see Chapters 8 and 9). If anyone tries to give orders or exercise control, other people have the option to leave and live elsewhere.

In sum, if people move around in their environments a lot, are required to share food and other possessions, and have a range of options about where to live and whom

▲ Like most mobile hunter-gatherers, the Ju/'hoansi are an egalitarian people.

to live with, then inequality in wealth and power does not have much chance of developing. If inequality should develop, it does not have much chance of persisting for very long.

Not all foragers are or were egalitarian, however. The Native Americans of the Northwest Coast, for instance, lived in ranked societies because, in their rich environment, the three conditions just listed did not exist. Northwest Coast people were more sedentary, accumulated wealth in order to distribute it to validate and acquire rank, and formed kin groups that were associated with particular territories (see Chapter 6).

Most hunting and gathering bands have informal leaders whose decisions are respected because others defer to their age or skill at particular activities or because they seem to have some kind of spiritual powers. By and large, such leaders are *headmen,* who have only influence, not authority (see Chapter 12). Only rarely is decision-making authority vested in a formal office or title to which certain individuals automatically succeed. This is the most important difference between egalitarian and ranked societies.

Ranked Societies

In ranked societies, there are a limited number of high-ranking social positions, usually titles or some kind of formal offices that grant authority; people who hold the title can issue commands and expect to have them obeyed. The titles also confer high honor on the people who hold them. In most cases, the privilege of holding a title or occupying an office is largely or entirely hereditary within certain families, lineages, clans, or other kin groups. If you are born into a group that does not have the hereditary right to the title or office, normatively (but not always in fact) you cannot succeed to the office regardless of your talents or ambitions.

In one of the most common types of ranked societies, all kin groups are ranked relative to one another, with each group having its own unique rank relative to every other group. Further, within each kin group, each member is ranked relative to all others, usually on the principle of genealogical seniority (elders being superior in rank to younger people). The highest-ranking individuals of the highest-ranking kin group hold the most valued positions that bring the highest rewards in prestige, power, and, in some societies, wealth. This way of ranking individuals and kin groups is well documented for several ancient Polynesian chiefdoms.

An excellent example of such a ranked society is Tikopia, a tiny Pacific island whose kinship system is described in Chapter 9. When studied by Raymond Firth in the 1920s, Tikopia's 1,200 persons were divided into four patriclans, each with its own chief who exercised authority over his clanmates. Each clan in turn was divided into several patrilineages. Every patrilineage had a head, believed to be the oldest living male descendant of the man who founded the lineage about four to six generations ago. Alongside this ranking of individuals within a single lineage, the various lineages of a single clan were ranked relative to one another. One lineage of each clan, supposedly the original, "senior" lineage from which the "junior" lineages had budded off, was considered the noble lineage. Members of other lineages of the clan had to defer socially to members of the noble lineage, according to Tikopian standards of etiquette. In addition, the noble lineage of each clan selected one of its members to be the chief of the whole clan. Clan chiefs had authority to punish troublemakers and the duty to perform rituals connected to agriculture and other common concerns.

Chiefs and other members of the noble Tikopia lineages had little more wealth than anyone else, however. The nobility received tribute from other lineages of their clan, but they gave away most of it in the many public activities that they organized and financed through redistribution (see Chapter 7). The chief and nobility of each clan had no way to deny access to land and ocean resources to members of other lineages because each lineage was considered to have inalienable rights to certain pieces of land. The Tikopia nobility, then, received much prestige and token tribute from other islanders, but they did not use this tribute to make themselves notably wealthier than lower-ranking people. They were honored, but their wealth and power were not great. It is mainly in this respect that ranked societies contrast with stratified societies.

Stratified Societies

Within a society or nation, a *social stratum* consists of families who have about the same access to rewards. Stratified societies have two distinguishing characteristics:

1. There are marked and enduring inequalities between strata in access to all three kinds of rewards: wealth,

power, and prestige. The inequality may endure because the positions that bring rewards are themselves hereditary or because being born into a certain stratum gives individuals better or worse opportunities in life.

2. Inequality is based primarily on unequal access to productive resources such as the land and tools people need to make their living or the education and training needed to succeed. In some stratified societies, a minority of people control access to the resources other people need to survive at culturally acceptable levels.

Stratified societies vary in their cultural beliefs about the possibilities of social mobility—that is, about movement up and down the social ladder. In some, such as North America and other contemporary democracies, upward or downward mobility is possible through education, special skills, hard work, good luck, or other circumstances. In others, as in European societies before the Industrial Revolution, one's position is considered fixed, often because of beliefs that existing inequalities are hereditary and/or ordained by supernatural beings.

Cross-culturally, we distinguish two major kinds of strata: **classes** and **castes.** Two general differences between class and caste systems stand out. First, by definition, castes are *endogamous* groups: they have cultural norms or laws that require individuals to marry within their caste. As discussed in Chapter 8, rules that mandate marriage within one's own group have the effect of maintaining the distinctiveness of the group relative to other groups. This is because normatively there is no possibility of upward mobility through intercaste marriage, and therefore there are no or few children with anomalous caste membership. In contrast, class societies allow people to marry someone of a different class; in fact, intermarriage between classes is a common avenue of social mobility. It follows from the endogamous nature of caste that one's caste membership is theoretically hereditary: one is born into the caste of one's parents, one marries someone in the same caste, and one's children are likewise born into and remain members of one's own caste. (We say *theoretically* because social reality often differs from cultural norms, in caste societies as in all others.)

Second, caste systems have powerful norms or laws regulating social relationships among members of different castes. For example, norms or laws may prohibit direct physical contact between castes or may forbid members of different castes from eating from the same bowl or drinking from the same wells. In some societies, high-caste members believe they will be spiritually polluted if they touch members of other castes. Indeed, they often must perform rituals to cleanse themselves after accidental contacts.

Both of these general differences mean that castes have more permanent membership and more rigid social boundaries than classes. This does not mean that it is easy to tell whether some particular stratified society "has" castes or classes. Some societies have elements of both. For instance, some scholars have suggested that black–white relations in the American South were more castelike than classlike until the mid-twentieth century. There was no possibility of upward mobility into the white "caste" for blacks because no one could overcome the cultural stigma of dark skin color. Interracial marriage was legally prohibited or culturally taboo, so that the two races were virtually endogamous. Explicit laws against certain kinds of "intercaste" contacts and interactions—known as *segregation laws*—forced blacks to live apart from whites, forbade them to enter certain white business establishments and public restrooms, prohibited drinking from the same water fountains, made them send their children to all-black schools, and so forth. Most whites did not believe that blacks were "polluting" in the spiritual sense of the word, but many whites did believe that blacks were "unclean" in another sense and tried hard to avoid contact with them.

Usually the term *stratification* refers to the differences in wealth, influence, and status within a single society. Of course, there are great inequalities among societies also, such as between nations and even between whole continents in the modern world. Whether future globalization will reduce economic inequalities among nations—and, if so, whether it will be sooner rather than later—is hotly debated. The effect of globalization on inequality *within* nations is also unclear. Many believe that inequality is increasing in both the "developed" and the "developing" worlds. In the former, many working-class people are losing unionized, factory jobs, while the owners of the factories (including stockholders) make higher profits and grow wealthier by relocating their operations overseas. In the latter, some people are better able to obtain new jobs in globalized factories and leap ahead of other citizens who are unable to take advantage of the new opportunities. (See the Globalization box for a discussion of these issues.)

Castes in Traditional India

The best-known caste system is that of India. India's caste system is complex and varies from region to region, so we present only a general picture. Traditionally, the people of India recognized five main social categories, four of which are *varnas*. (A *varna* is not itself a caste.) Each category is ranked relative to the others in honor and degree of ritual purity, and each is broadly associated with certain kinds of occupations.

The highest *varna* is the Brahmins, or priests and scholars; next is the *varna* of nobles and warriors, the Kshatriyas; third are the Vaishas, or merchants and artisans; and ranked lowest are the Shudras, or farmers, craftspeople, and certain other laborers. Although the *varna* are associated with certain occupations, not everyone in a given *varna* follows that occupation. A fifth category—outside and ranked below the four *varnas*—is the untouchables, to whom falls work considered polluting to the *varna*.

The *varnas* (which arose in the second millennium B.C.E. when the Aryans invaded and conquered what is now northern India) are large, inclusive categories into which specific castes are placed. The villages in which most people live are divided into much smaller and specific groupings called *jati* (castes, as the term is usually used). For example, in a particular village, the Shudra *varna* might be represented by several *jati* with names such as weaver, potter, and tailor. There are thousands of these castes in India, distributed among the many thousands of villages, with each village containing a variable number of castes.

To understand Indian castes, we must describe the basic worldview associated with Hinduism, the traditional religion of most of India. (Hinduism is incredibly diverse, so here we present only a simplified depiction of it.) Hindu religion holds that spiritual souls are reborn into different physical bodies at various stages of their existence—this is the doctrine of *reincarnation*. Souls seek an end to the cycle of earthly birth, death, and rebirth, but to achieve this end, each soul must be reborn many times in many bodies, both animal and human. Souls attempt to move from lower forms of life to higher ones: from animals to humans (of various ranked castes) to gods.

The body (be it human or animal) into which a soul is born depends on how closely that soul adhered to proper standards of behavior in previous lifetimes. For souls that were placed in human forms in their previous incarnation, these standards include avoidance of activities that Hindus believe are polluting. Among the most polluting activities are handling and working with animal carcasses or human corpses, touching excrement and other waste materials, dealing with childbirth, and eating meat. Not only are people who regularly perform

Globalization affects the standards of living of most of the world's nations and peoples. Scholars, officers and boards of directors of corporations, leaders of rich and poor nations, and working class people disagree on whether globalization will raise or lower the income and wealth of the poorer nations.

On the positive side, expansion of international trade provides overseas markets for the products of the rich and poor alike, presumably allowing many people in poor countries to produce and sell more than they otherwise would. On the negative side, the richer countries and their companies have advantages due to their greater access to productive technology, shipping and marketing facilities, skills and information, and other resources that give them greater control over prices and other terms of trade.

Some people think that the inequality caused by globalization began in the twentieth century. In fact, global inequality is much older. As early as the 1500s, the products of the two American continents were shipped to Europe. Mesoamerica and the Andes were the homelands of the two great New World civilizations: the Aztec and the Inca, respectively. Like the upper classes in Europe, the Aztec and Inca elite surrounded themselves with treasures, many in gold and silver. The trade of these precious metals produced huge fortunes for some Europeans, helped to finance the Industrial Revolution of the late eighteenth century, and changed the balances of military power and political influence.

By the 1700s and 1800s, products were pouring out of the conquered regions of the Americas and Asia. In the Caribbean, northern Brazil, and the American South, enslaved Africans produced the cotton, tobacco, sugar, and cacao that were worn, eaten, and otherwise consumed by western Europeans. In Asia, spices, tea, porcelain ("china"), and other products produced by peasants and craftsmen were shipped over land or, later, over sea to satisfy European appetites and tastes. Britain's colony in India, for example, provided early English textile factories with cotton and other fibers. In the process, India's own highly skilled textile weavers suffered. Although the costs of transporting goods from Asian, African, and American colonies were high, Europe's climate did not allow the production of tropical crops, and the labor costs of both African American slaves and Asian peasants were a fraction of the costs of production. So, the effects of globalization on world inequality are several centuries old, at least.

During the twentieth century, it is fairly clear that economic inequality among the world's regions and nations widened. The growth of economies in the richer regions of North America, Europe, and East Asia dramatically outpaced growth in Africa, Latin America, and southern Asia. In the twenty-first century economic interdependence among the world's nations seems likely to intensify. Whether future globalization will increase or decrease the economic gap between poor and

these activities polluted themselves, but any members of a higher caste who come into physical contact with them likewise become polluted and must bathe ritually to cleanse themselves. One's present place in society—one's "station in life"—varies with the degree to which one is associated with pure or impure activities. In turn, whether one is associated with pure or impure activities depends on one's behavior in previous lives, including the degree to which one has allowed oneself to become polluted or failed to cleanse oneself in previous incarnations.

India's traditional caste hierarchy is so intimately tied up with Hinduism that the two are almost inseparable. First, the caste into which one is born depends on the actions of one's soul in previous lives. People are born into a low caste either because their soul has not yet been through enough lifetimes to have reached a higher form, or because their sins in a previous lifetime merit reincarnation into a low caste. Thus, all "men" were not created

equal in the Hindu worldview; it is legitimate that some castes have more power and privilege and more status and wealth than others.

Second, each caste is broadly associated with certain occupations. Each village contains a number of castes, most of which are named according to the occupation traditionally performed by their members. Thus, a village might include castes of priests, merchants, blacksmiths, potters, tailors, farmers, weavers, carpenters, washers, barbers, leather workers, and "sweepers" (the last refers to those who remove human waste matter from people's houses). Just as activities are ranked in Hindu beliefs according to their degree of purity and impurity, so occupations and those who perform them are ranked. Working with animal carcasses is defiling, so leather working is a defiling occupation, and leather workers are so polluting as to be untouchable. The same applies to sweeping: people who remove human wastes from houses or spread excrement over village fields are rich nations is hotly disputed. But, within the poorer regions themselves, there is much evidence that inequality increases in the early phases of globalization. This is largely because companies from the richer nations open factories or other enterprises in the poorer countries mainly to lower their production costs. To do so, they hire local managers or contract with local businesspeople. In turn, managers and business owners hire workers at low wages, which is possible because of the high rate of unemployment and the lax labor laws in the host country. People migrate to cities in search of new jobs, higher incomes, and better opportunities for themselves and their families, and many of them benefit significantly. Even as workers earn wages and learn new skills, however, local managers and subcontractors generally benefit disproportionately. Because of factors like geography and educational level, some people are unable to find decent jobs or other income-earning niches like small businesses, so often they fail to gain the benefits entirely or largely.

China, which has experienced the world's fastest growth since the 1980s, is a recent example. China's economic growth rate has hovered between 8 and 12 percent for more than two decades because of its plentiful labor supply, its authoritarian central government, the work ethic of its citizens, and the loosening of restrictions on internal migration and foreign investment. Tens of millions of Chinese have enjoyed a dramatic increase in their living standards by moving from villages to work in factories in Shanghai, Guangzhou, Shenzhen, Beijing, and dozens of other cities. Hundreds of thousands of Chinese factory owners, real estate investors, and market entrepreneurs have become fabulously wealthy. There are 1.3 billion Chinese, however, and hundreds of millions in rural areas have yet to participate significantly in the economic boom. Some have actually lost their livelihood when local Communist Party officials have not compensated them when a new factory takes over the land they have been farming. Hundreds of coal miners have died from mine collapses, and tens of millions of Chinese experience some of the planet's worse air pollution from coal-fired power plants. When will their day come?

Critical Thinking Questions

1. Some think that recent advances in information technology such as e-mail, the World Wide Web, and cell phones will lessen inequality both within and among nations. How might this occur? What other changes will be required if it is to happen?

2. Students from the poorer nations often receive higher education in North America or Europe. What affects whether they take their skills back home or seek jobs where wages are higher, thereby increasing the problem known as the *brain drain* in the countries of their birth?

◄ Hinduism regards certain substances and activities as spiritually defiling or polluting. Ritual bathing—here in the Ganges River—removes the pollution.

© Bernard Wolfe/Photo Researchers, Inc.

polluted, and their touch pollutes those of higher castes. Therefore, members of the leather working, sweeping, and other castes associated with defiling occupations were traditionally untouchable. (Discrimination against people of untouchable ancestry is now illegal in modern India, although it still occurs in many rural regions.) Untouchables usually live in their own special section of the village, separate from members of higher castes. Because they contaminate temples by their entry, they cannot go inside a temple. Their touch contaminates water, so they must use separate wells. These and other restrictions on their behavior are sometimes extreme.

Members of high-ranking castes, however, such as priests, landowners, warriors, and merchants, need the services of low-ranking castes. Again, this is because Hinduism defines some essential activities as polluting, so members of castes who would be defiled by these activities need lower castes to perform these services for them. The bullocks needed for farming die, so someone has to remove dead cattle from the village. Brahmin women give birth just as other women do, so the women of some low-ranking caste have to serve as midwives because handling blood and placentas would pollute other Brahmin women. Everyone passes bodily wastes, so someone must remove these wastes from the houses of high-caste members, lest these substances pollute their occupants. Accordingly, each caste has its proper role and function in the economic, social, and religious life of the village.

In Hindu beliefs, one's soul is reincarnated into a higher or lower form partly according to how well one fulfills the obligations of one's caste in the present life. Leather workers, for instance, cannot do much to improve their lot in this life, but by faithfully fulfilling their obligations to members of higher castes, their souls will attain higher reincarnations in future bodies.

Although the castes are interdependent in that each "needs" the products and services made by the others, one should not conclude that intercaste relations are harmonious, or that the complementary tasks associated with each caste are entirely mutually beneficial. A great deal of friction and outright conflict exist between individual members of different castes. In fact, local castes as a whole group sometimes organize themselves with a council to pursue their common interests.

It is even possible for a caste to improve its rank in the local caste hierarchy, despite the normatively unchanging relative positions of castes. This is done in several ways, including adopting the customs and prohibitions of a higher caste and reinventing the history of one's caste to make it seem that it originally came from a higher *varna*.

Although most castes had names that referred to occupations, in fact, members of a single caste made their living in diverse ways. Most members of lower castes were farmers, regardless of their caste name, and many higher-caste persons engaged in farming as well. Also, there was no simple relationship between caste membership and access to resources or wealth; some Brahmins were poor, some smiths wealthy.

Many people think caste hierarchies and restrictions no longer exist in India. In cities, where people are anonymous, restrictions on behavior clearly are hard to maintain, and many lower-caste urbanites are well-educated, middle-class people. So, caste distinctions have withered in urban areas. In the countryside, however, where most people are still farmers, caste distinctions remain, though in weakened form. For decades, the government of India has given preferential treatment in hiring to members of lower castes, so having an identity as a member of a lower caste may bring some benefits.

Classes in Industrial Societies: The United States

Class societies have strata—the classes—that have different degrees of ownership of productive property and material goods, that have different influence over public decisions made by a government, and that are ranked in the respect or esteem accorded their position in the traditional society or contemporary nation.

An important point to make about classes is that they are seldom organized *as classes*. There are no occasions on which the members of a given class come together for discussion or common action (unlike, say, an extended family or lineage). Indeed, members of a single class do not necessarily believe they have much in common with one another (unlike the members of a labor union). Many people cannot precisely identify the class to which they belong (unlike Indian *jati* or *varna*); about four-fifths of Americans refer to themselves as "middle class." People cannot say how many classes exist in their societies. In fact, there is considerable debate within the social sciences over what the term *class* means, or whether it has any other than the vaguest meaning.

Whether or not the very concept of class is vague, no one can deny the enormous differences in wealth, power, and prestige that exist in many societies. The term *class* refers to all the people in a given stratified society who receive comparable levels of rewards. Members of different classes have different access to the material resources (income, property, wealth), influential relationships (social networks, political contacts), and cultural knowledge (formal education, "social graces") that are positively valued. Unlike caste membership, people are potentially able to move up or down in a class system during their lifetime through interclass marriage, personal talent, hard work and effort, or good luck. More commonly, being born into a given class puts one so far ahead of or behind others that few people rise or fall very far in the class structure during their lifetime.

In this section, we concentrate on the class structure of one industrialized society—the United States. In this country, the kind of work one does (occupation) is often assumed to be the best single overall indication of class membership. ("What kind of work do you do?" or "Where do you work?" is one of the first questions American adults ask of new acquaintances, and the answer gives a lot of information about a person very quickly.) Occupation is generally a good indication of income, and one's income influences so much else: overall lifestyle, access of one's children to education, the kinds of people with whom one associates socially, the kind of church or club to which one belongs, and so on.

Unfortunately for our desire to make societies neat and orderly, the different criteria used to define class membership are not always mutually consistent. For instance, people disagree on the prestige of many occupations—attorneys, physicians, and academicians are despised by some but granted high prestige by others, for example. For some occupations, there is a disjunction between income and prestige—nurses and teachers are held in higher regard than plumbers and assembly-line workers, but often they do not earn as much.

So, it may be difficult to decide to which class some individual belongs. One way around this ambiguity, favored by some sociologists, is to separate the three kinds of rewards from one another and define a separate class ranking for each reward. We can distinguish classes defined on the basis of prestige (*status groups,* as some call them) and on the basis of income or wealth (*economic classes*), for instance. The definitions and methods used for ranking the classes depend partly on our interests.

In the United States, the most widely accepted approach to stratification uses the concept of economic class, in which class membership depends largely on individual and family wealth. Using wealth as the primary basis for assigning class ranking has four major advantages.

1. Wealth is more measurable than other indications of class membership (although cash income alone does not measure it adequately).

2. Wealth is the best single indication of the overall benefits individuals and families are receiving from their citizenship in the nation. Money cannot buy you love, happiness, brains, or many other things, but it can buy you much of what Americans value (including education and consumer goods and, nowadays, better looks and tighter bodies).

3. Extremely high wealth is generally correlated with ownership of productive resources, such as factories, financial institutions, and income-producing real estate. Many wealthy people own the nation's large businesses or made their money in finance. Either they built their companies themselves, or their ancestors made fortunes through business activity and passed their ownership along to the current generation. Many of the wealthiest persons gain most of their income from the stock market, which means either they earn large annual dividends or they get their earnings by buying low and selling high.

4. Wealth levels broadly determine people's access to political power. Through political contributions, the wealthy have a greater say in who gets nominated and elected to important offices, which is why many Americans push for campaign finance reform. Through lobbying efforts, the rich enjoy greater influence on the laws and policies of the nation than their numbers warrant. By providing much of the funding for think tanks and other public advisory groups, the wealthy subsidize the expertise of many economists and other social scientists who advise government. People who serve in the government as elected or appointed officials may later work in the private sector, which covets both their expertise and their political connections.

For these and other reasons, we can learn the most about class inequalities in the United States by focusing on the distribution of wealth.

"Rich Get Richer, Poor Get Poorer—Again" was the headline in the April 1, 2007, Business section of the *Columbus Dispatch.* The article noted that, in 2005, the top 1 percent of Americans received the largest share of national income since 1928. Average incomes for the bottom 90 percent actually fell slightly from the year before.

The article was about *income inequality,* which is one measure of the distribution of wealth. Table 13.1 summarizes income inequality for 2006, the latest year for which the U.S. Census Bureau has published information. In the table, American households are divided into fifths based on their 2006 cash income. For example, the

▼ **Table 13.1** Distribution of Household Income in the United States, 2006

Quintile	Percentage of Income Earned
Poorest fifth	3.4
Second fifth	8.6
Third fifth	14.5
Fourth fifth	22.9
Richest fifth	50.5
Richest 5 percent	20.9

Source: U.S. Bureau of the Census (2007, 5); http://www.census.gov/prod/2007pubs/p60-233.pdf, retrieved November 10, 2007

poorest one-fifth (20 percent) of households earned only 3.4 percent of all income, whereas the richest one-fifth of households earned more than 50 percent of the total income earned by all households. The table also shows that the richest 5 percent of American households earned almost 21 percent of the total family income in 2006.

U.S. Census Bureau data over the past two or three decades reveals that income inequality has been increasing. In 1973, the bottom three-fifths (the "poorest" 60 percent) of American households earned 31.8 percent of all cash income, but by 2006, their share had fallen to 26.5 percent—a *loss* of 5.3 percent. In 1970, the richest one-fifth earned 43.3 percent of all cash income, but by 2006,

their share had increased to 50.5 percent—a *gain* of 7.2 percent. To make the same point more simply, in 1973 the ratio of the incomes of the richest fifth to the poorest fifth was 10.4, whereas in 2006 the ratio was 14.9. So, the relative benefits of economic growth over the last three decades have been distributed unequally, going far more to the affluent than to the poor and even those who view themselves as middle class.

The distribution of income alone does not tell the complete story of inequality in the United States, however, because figures on annual *income* do not show how much *wealth* is owned by families of different classes. Yearly income figures such as those in Table 13.1 greatly underestimate the economic inequality in the United States. People's standards of living are not determined directly by their annual income, nor is their influence on government policies at the local, state, and national levels. If we consider the distribution of wealth, we see that middle-income families, and even families who are generally considered affluent, own little in comparison with the truly wealthy.

Surveys funded by the federal government provide estimates of the net worth (wealth) of American families. *Net worth* includes all the family assets (property) owned minus debts. Assets include material property such as residential homes and other real estate, motor vehicles, household possessions, and the like. Material assets directly affect standards of living. Financial assets include money saved and invested in institutions like banks,

► The income and wealth gap between the very rich and the very poor is enormous in the United States. This family is homeless.

© Viviane Moos/Corbis

"One billion dollars is no longer enough," says the first line of the 2007 Forbes 400 website. For the past 25 years, *Forbes* magazine (whose editor Jack Forbes once ran for U.S. president) has published a list that identifies the 400 wealthiest Americans. In 2006, it took $1.3 billion to be one of the richest 400 Americans.

In 2006, the *Forbes* list included such well-known Americans as William (Bill) Gates (Microsoft, the richest of all with a net worth of $59 billion), Warren Buffet (Berkshire Hathaway, an investment firm, $52 billion), Larry Ellison (Oracle, $26 billion), Michael Dell (Dell computers, $17.2 billion), Paul Allen (Microsoft co-founder, $16.8 billion), Steve Jobs (Apple, the "igod" of ITunes and IPhone, $5.7 billion), George Lucas (movies, $3.9 billion), Steven Spielberg (movies, $3.0 billion), Donald Trump (real estate, $3.0 billion), Oprah Winfrey (talk-show host, $2.5 billion), Ted Turner (former owner of Time Warner and the largest landowner in the country, $2.3 billion), and George Steinbrenner III (New York Yankees owner, $1.3 billion).

People with the historic last names of Walton (Wal-Mart), Rockefeller (Standard Oil), Getty (oil), Hearst (newspapers), Johnson (floor wax and cleaning products), Marriott (hotels), Wrigley (chewing gum), and Disney (media) made the list.

Other members you've probably never heard of but you do know their businesses, like Ty Warner (Beanie Babies), Les Wexner (founder of The Limited and a major owner of Victoria's Secret), Jean Pritzker (Hyatt), Wayne Huizenga (Blockbuster), Frederick Smith (FedEx), James Jannard (Oakley sunglasses), Philip Knight (Nike), Rupert Murdoch (FOX and *The Wall Street Journal,* among other media properties), Charles Dolan (HBO), Pierre Omidyar (eBay), Jeffrey Bezos (Amazon.com), Peter Buck and Fred DeLuca (Subway), and Michael Illitch (Little Caesar's and the Detroit Tigers and Red Wings).

Some lucky members inherited their money. Others made their fortunes in real estate, commercial centers and shopping malls, financial services like banking and mutual funds, newspapers, cruise lines, the stock market, construction supplies, hotels, pro sports teams, auto retailing, gambling casinos, energy, medical supplies and pharmaceuticals, cable and satellite TV, NASCAR tracks, and fast foods.

One of the richest 400 Americans, Michael Bloomberg, is mayor of New York. One, A. Alfred Taubman, spent time in jail for price fixing. One, Henry Nicholas III, has a bad-boy reputation. Some are giving away most of their fortunes to charitable causes, like Bill Gates, Warren Buffet, Ted Turner, and Bernard Marcos.

Altogether, the richest 400 Americans own $1.54 trillion worth of assets. Most people cannot grasp this amount. How much money is this, in terms people can relate to? If $1.54 trillion were divided among the citizens of the United States, then every child, woman, and man would receive about $5,100. Rounding off the numbers, if the wealth of the richest 400 Americans were cashed in and distributed equally, each of the 300 million Americans would receive more than $5,000.

Source: The Forbes 400 (http://www.forbes.com/2007/09/19/forbes-400-introduction-lists-richlist07-cx_mm_0920richintro.html; retrieved November 10, 2007)

bonds, and stocks. Saving and investment assets vastly increase a family's economic security and, of course, can be withdrawn from banks or sold on the stock market to acquire material assets. Savings and, especially, investments also earn additional future income and wealth, although not without risk.

The Federal Reserve Board (the "Fed") is the semigovernmental institution that tries to regulate the economy by affecting interest rates. Every three years, the Fed publishes a *Survey of Consumer Finances* that estimates the wealth held by American families. The most recently available survey is based on information gathered in 2004.

The Economic Policy Institute, a private, nonprofit institution, uses the Federal Reserve surveys to estimate the concentration of wealth in the United States. For 2004, the Economic Policy Institute concluded that the richest fifth of families held 85 percent of the wealth, the middle fifth held 4 percent, and the poorest fifth had negative net worth (they owed more than they owned). The net worth of the vast majority of the population was actually *less* than the amount owned by the top 1 percent: the richest 1 percent of families owned 34 percent of the wealth, whereas the bottom 90 percent owned 29 percent of the wealth. So, the truly wealthy 1 percent owned more than the bottom 90 percent put together. It is revealing to look at how much wealth is owned by the truly, truly wealthy, such as the richest 400 people in the United States (see A Closer Look).

To illustrate how wealth inequality has risen over the last few decades, we can compare the *wealth ratio* for various years: the ratio of the wealth owned by the very richest Americans to the median American wealth. In 1983, the wealthiest 1 percent of Americans owned 131

▶ The difference between the net worths of the very rich and everyone else is much larger than the gap in annual incomes. This couple seems to have the status that used to be called "jet set."

© Sam Bassett/Getty Images/Riser

times the wealth of the median American. In 1998, the wealth ratio grew to 168. In 2007, the figure was 190.

Maintaining Inequality

There are many theoretical issues in studying stratification. One problem is figuring out how such large inequalities first developed long ago, in prehistory. This problem cannot be addressed in this book, other than to note that inequalities between groups of people usually arise from a complex combination of intensive agriculture, control over scarce resources, large-scale cooperation, and conquest warfare. Most archaeologists who study stratification in prehistory agree that significant inequalities (deserving of the term *class*) did not exist until after the evolution of civilization (see Chapter 6).

Further, we know enough about the preindustrial world to know that in most stratified societies, a conquering militaristic group imposed its rule over the indigenous population of a region. This was true in African states such as Bunyoro and Zulu and in the ancient civilizations of the Americas such as the Aztec and Inca. Conquest of the weaker by the militarily stronger was also important in forming the ancient Old World civilizations of East Asia, Mesopotamia, and India. Historically speaking, the lower classes did not consent to their low standing but had it forced on them.

A major question about stratification in contemporary societies is: How do such high degrees of inequality in stratified societies *persist*? As the United States illustrates, a small percentage of the population typically control most of the wealth and wield a great deal of influence over public affairs. Why does the relatively underprivileged majority allow them this power and privilege? Why doesn't inequality produce more conflict? Why don't the "have nots" revolt?

In fact, there is conflict between strata in a wide range of stratified societies. Resentment, rebellion, and occasional attempts at revolution occur in stratified societies in all parts of the world (which is not to say that they are universally present). A great many powerless and poor people do not simply accept their place in the social hierarchy. Inequality is a major source of social unrest. Arguably, global economic inequality and concerns about cultural imperialism are as much responsible for international terrorism as are ethnic conflicts and religious ideologies.

One possible explanation of how stratification persists is that members of the highest stratum (hereafter called the *elite*) use their wealth and power to organize an armed force stronger than that of their opposition. If the elite somehow monopolize control over weapons or organize a loyal army, then they can use coercion and threats to maintain their access to rewards and resources. Elites do sometimes use armed force to put down rebellions,

◀ Elite classes sometimes use armed force to suppress political dissent. In November 2007, Pakistani police tried to control journalists who were demonstrating against General Musharraf's emergency rule, which suspended the constitution and curbed the media.

© Athar Hussain/ Reuters/Landov

and certainly the ever-present threat of coercion and fear of punishment deters resistance to the elite's wealth, prestige, and power.

Yet in most stratified societies, the elite only occasionally find it necessary to actually use force. Use of military might is costly to them. Suppose the elite wait for rebellions to occur and then use police or armies to put them down. Even if no rebellion succeeds, every time armies suppress a rebellion, it produces more hatred and resentment and more awareness of the relative wealth and power of the elite. Increased hatred and awareness caused by suppression can backfire and lead to a greater probability of future rebellion. Notice also that the elite's reliance on brute force and oppression to maintain their wealth and power potentially reduces or eliminates their honor and esteem, one of the three major rewards offered by stratification, and one that they presumably covet. Further, those who supply the military might—the army, guards, thugs, or police—must be paid or otherwise provided for by the elite. Payment requires resources. Either the elite can take these resources from their own wealth, thus reducing it, or they can increase their exploitation of the majority population, thus breeding more hatred and resentment toward themselves. Finally, relying entirely on the loyalty of an army is risky because this allegiance may change, as many modern dictators know or fear. In sum, reliance on threat and armed force alone is both costly and risky.

None of these points deny that armed force is an important way to sustain high degrees of inequality. Probably few elites have remained in power for many generations without using force and periodically suppressing rebellions and dissent. Nonetheless, stratification systems that rely entirely or largely on force seem to be short-lived and unstable and have been replaced by those that use other mechanisms. What other mechanisms are available?

Ideologies

We address this question by noting yet another reason coercive force alone is seldom solely responsible for maintaining inequality. A single rebellion can have many causes, but a persistent *pattern* of rebellion is caused mainly by the lower strata's perception that they are exploited or not receiving their fair share of rewards. Seeking out and eliminating rebels (or, one might suggest, terrorists) do little to change the reasons people rebel. The instigators may be sanctioned or eliminated, but the underlying discontent that causes persistent conflict remains. Imprisoning or killing instigators removes them from rebellions, but sometimes removing one instigator creates several more instigators. Sooner or later, there will be new instigators who organize new rebellions and attacks. Further, while armies or police eliminate rebels, innocents are usually killed, injured, or harmed economically. This can alienate those who otherwise would be passive about their place in the world. For these and other reasons, armed force alone is unlikely to eliminate the perceptions of unfairness, injustice, cultural domination, or other attitudes that cause rebellions.

One means available to the elite to maintain their privileges is to change the perceptions of the underprivileged about why they are underprivileged. For example, if poor people think it is God's will that they are poor, they are less likely to rebel than if they believe they are poor because of exploitation. Or, if they think the elite use their property and power to benefit everyone in the society, they are less likely to challenge the elite. Or, if they think that a concentration of property and power is inevitable because that's just the way human life is, they will be less likely to resist. Or, if they think that they, too, can acquire property, power, and prestige through their own achievements, they are more likely to put their effort into improving their own position rather than into causing trouble. Finally, if "the masses" are divided internally on the basis of values, ethnic identities, perceived racial differences, religious attachments, regional loyalties, and so forth, then they are less likely to unite in the political arena.

If, to state the general point, members of the lower strata adopt a set of beliefs that justifies and legitimizes the rewards received by the higher strata, then they are more likely to try to join the system rather than to beat it. In such beliefs, the elite have a powerful and relatively cheap tool with which to dampen opposition to their power and privileges. Further, these ideas increase the prestige of the elite. If people believe that inequality is God's will, or that the activities of the elite benefit all, or that the elite became elite through intelligence and hard work, then the elite deserve the honor and respect of everyone else. (Not surprisingly, elites themselves find it easy to believe such things about themselves.)

We call those ideas and beliefs that explain inequality as desirable or legitimate **ideologies.** The term *ideology* also has a broader meaning, often referring to any set of ideas held by a group—as in the phrases *leftist political ideology* and *feminist ideology*. Here we use the term in the narrow sense, to refer only to ideas that justify the status quo of inequality.

In many stratified societies, ideologies are based on religion. We are familiar with the notion of the "divine right of kings" from feudal Europe—certainly a handy supernatural mandate for kings and aristocracies! Similar notions are common in non-Western stratified societies. For instance, in Bunyoro, a kingdom in East Africa, the health and welfare of the ruler were mystically associated with the fertility and prosperity of the whole kingdom. Anything that threatened his life was believed to be a threat to everyone. In many ancient civilizations, such as the Aztec, the Inca, the Japanese, and the Egyptian, the ruler himself was believed to be a divine or semidivine being. In pre–twentieth-century China, the emperor had the "Mandate of Heaven," meaning that Heaven itself had granted him secular authority over the vast Chinese Empire for as long as he ruled it wisely and humanely. In traditional India, as we have seen, Hindu beliefs about reincarnation and pollution were so intertwined with the caste system that they rendered its inequities both explicable and legitimate.

In the ancient complex chiefdoms of Hawaii, there were marked social distinctions between the noble and commoner classes. The nobility was viewed as endowed with a supernatural power called *mana*. *Mana* was partly hereditary, and within a single family the eldest child inherited the most *mana* from his or her parents. The highest-ranking noble, the paramount chief, was believed to be descended from one of the gods of the islands. This descent gave him the right to rule because he had more *mana* than anyone in the chiefdom. Other nobles (lesser chiefs and their families) were relatives of the paramount chief and thus also were endowed with *mana*. *Mana* gave chiefs the power to curse those who were disloyal or disobedient or who violated some taboo, which further reinforced their authority. Hawaiians believed that the prosperity of a chiefdom and everyone in it depended on the performance of certain religious rituals held in grand temples. Because commoners did not have enough *mana* to enter a temple, only priests and nobles could perform the rituals needed to ensure prosperity. Everyone in the chiefdom thus relied on the social (and religious) elite for their well-being.

The preceding examples illustrate a few ways religion serves ideological functions in some societies. In stratified societies, religion commonly gives the elite a supernatural mandate, provides them with the supernatural means to punish people, and gives them ritual functions to perform that are believed to benefit the whole population.

American Secular Ideologies

Do similar kinds of religious ideologies exist in modern industrial societies, some of which are as highly stratified as any preindustrial society?

Some people who are critical of the impacts of the Judeo-Christian heritage of the West believe that it supports greed and accumulation. In fact, however, many New Testament passages warn Christians about the accumulation of wealth. The best known are the story of the rich man and Lazarus (Luke 16:19–31) and the passages about the rich man who came to Jesus seeking salvation (told in Matthew 19:21–24, Mark 10:21–25, and Luke 18:22–25). Lesser-known scriptures say that the poor are blessed and the rich are oppressors (Luke 6:20–24, James 2:2–6, and James 5:1–6). Two passages in Acts (2:44–45 and 4:32–37) seem to instruct Christians to hold their possessions in common, which not only does not support wealth accumulation but is a rather anticapitalist teaching.

Further, most citizens do not believe that the richest Americans have a supernatural mandate for their wealth. The wealthiest families do not justify their income and ownership of property and financial assets by invoking religious authority. Religion is not generally used to justify the wealth and power of particular individuals and families. At most, some wealthy claim to be "blessed," but most take credit for their own success or admit that they are "lucky."

Finally, Christian teachings historically have been and still are used to support social and political movements that seek to correct inequalities that are believed to be unjust. The nineteenth-century antislavery movement is one example. More recent examples include the civil rights and liberation theology movements. And a variety of Christian churches and denominations are resolutely against the Establishment in their beliefs. In the political realm, certainly many officeholders attend church and find ways to work their religious faith into their speeches to certain audiences. But few gain politically by claiming they are God's chosen officials. Even suspicion that a politician thinks he or she is carrying out divine will is a political liability (although some citizens will believe it, depending on whether they agree with his or her policies).

In brief, with regard to the issue of who has what and why, most Americans, and Westerners generally, are *secularists:* they explain the unequal distribution of rewards by events here on earth, not by the will of heaven.

Ideologies do not have to be based on religion, however. There are only two essential features of ideologies:

1. They justify (legitimize) inequality by affecting people's consciousness, not by threatening physical coercion.
2. They are believable to large numbers of people, based on existing cultural knowledge.

In the first condition, *consciousness* refers to cultural attitudes, values, worldviews, and so forth. In the second condition, *believable* means that effective ideologies match people's general ideas about how their society works. Ideologies must make sense in terms of existing

▲ Although politicians in the United States appeal to religious values in their campaigns, few claim to have actually been chosen by God.

cultural knowledge, or they will be ineffective. **Secular ideologies** as well as religious ideologies can have both features.

Many social scientists argue that two major secular ideologies exist in the modern United States. One is that the whole nation benefits from inequality. Because a few people are very wealthy, many citizens believe that "the masses" are better off than they would be if wealth were distributed more equally. After all, the chance to get rich motivates people to do their best, and we all win when our fellow citizens perform up to their potential. Besides, the accumulation and investment of wealth are necessary to create jobs, from which poor and middle-class people benefit. Income tax cuts since 2000 have increased the income of the already wealthy and have hardly helped average people at all. In 2005, the top 1 percent of Americans, whose annual incomes averaged $1.2 million, enjoyed an increase in after-tax income of

$65,000 as a result of tax cuts for that year. The bottom half of the population got $234 worth of tax cuts. These tax policies are justified by the claim (ideology?) that the wealthy were previously overtaxed and that they will invest their extra income in expanding businesses, thus creating jobs that eventually trickle down to everyone. Putting more resources into the hands of the rich will "grow the economy," thus benefiting everyone, according to this economic theory (ideology?).

A second secular ideology is that the elite earn their rewards through their own merit and efforts. They are more intelligent, ambitious, hard working, willing to take risks, and so forth. In short, the elite have personal qualities that account for their success. This is, of course, accurate for some members of the elite. Those who inherited their wealth or were lucky enough to buy the right stock at the right time or get into the right housing market early enough, however, receive the same rewards as those who earned their rewards with actual work.

To the extent that they are widely believed, these two ideas fit with Americans' other beliefs about the way people are and how their society works. They are compatible with widespread beliefs about human motivation— people need strong incentives before they will make the effort to get a good education and have a responsible career. They also fit with many American values, such as individual freedom, progress, the work ethic, and private ownership of property.

Of course, many Americans do not believe these two ideas. (If you do not believe them, then they are not effective ideologies for you.) Others believe that these ideas are an accurate portrayal of how the whole nation benefits from economic inequality. (If you fall into this camp, you will think that these ideas are objectively true, rather than merely ideologies.) Your personal opinion depends on your class, upbringing, ideas about human nature, political views, and so forth. Can the comparative perspective of anthropology shed any light on the issue of whether stratification benefits society at large, or mainly members of the elite class themselves? To answer this question, we must first look at the major theories of inequality.

Theories of Inequality

Many sociologists and anthropologists apply one of two theories to analyze stratification. One holds that a high degree of inequality in the distribution of rewards is necessary, morally justified, and beneficial to all members of society. Unless society offers unequal rewards for un-

equal talents and efforts, the most talented people will have no incentive to put their talents to work for the welfare of all. This view is called the **functional theory of inequality.**

A contrary view holds that a high degree of inequality not only is unjust or even immoral but also robs the whole society of the benefits of much of its potential talent, which lies undeveloped in many of those at the bottom of the socioeconomic ladder. Stratification is not beneficial to society as a whole, but only to elites, who use their wealth to influence the passing of laws and regulations that benefit mainly or only themselves. This view is known as the **conflict theory of inequality.** It holds that a high level of inequality offers few benefits to anyone except the elite and, indeed, is harmful to the whole society because of the conflicts it creates and the lack of equal opportunities it entails.

Functionalist Theory

The functionalist theory holds that inequality is necessary for society to motivate its most talented and hardworking members to perform its most important roles. Some roles (including jobs) require more skill and training than do others. Ordinarily, the more skill and training required to perform a job, the fewer the number of people qualified to do the job and the more valuable their abilities are to the whole group. Functionalists argue that unequal rewards are effective ways to recruit the most able individuals into the most socially valuable roles. Unless there are rewards for those with the talents most of us lack, they will have no incentive to put those talents to work in activities that benefit all of us.

Further, in the functionalist view, inequality is not only socially useful but also morally justified. If society as a whole is to enjoy the fruits of the labor of its small number of well-trained, talented, and hard-working individuals, it is only fair and right that it reward these individuals with material goods, respect, and control over public decision making.

The functionalist analysis of inequality makes a lot of sense. People who do the most valuable things often do get the greatest rewards, but note that it is difficult to measure the "value" of various activities. It is reasonable that rewards be proportionate to personal qualities like effort and skill, but note that the two do not always go together.

Two objections to functionalism are possible within the framework of the functionalist theory itself. First, there is no reason to believe that the high degree of inequality that actually exists in stratified societies is necessary to ensure that those with scarce talents will fill the most valuable roles. In industrialized nations, for example, how many dollars does it take to motivate a qualified individual to manage a major company? In the United States, chief executive officers (CEOs) of large corporations enjoy relatively large compensation packages. In 2005, American CEOs earned 262 times the compensation paid to workers. This is part of a 40-year upward trend from the 1965 earnings ratio (24), the 1977 ratio (35), the 1989 ratio (71), and the 1995 ratio (101). (It is interesting that the ratio peaked at 300 in the year 2000 but has declined since then. The decline is due to several factors, two of which are stockholder concerns about the effects of CEO compensation on dividend earnings and share prices and the corporate scandals of the early twenty-first century.)

Comparing the 1977 ratio of 35 to the 2005 ratio of 262, CEOs in 2005 earned 7.5 times more than CEOs earned in 1977. Were the top executives of American companies responsible for a sevenfold increase in productivity and profits between 1977 and 2005? How did they get so much better in 28 years? In 2005, an average worker worked 262 days to earn what a CEO earned in one day. On any given day, is a CEO 262 times more valuable to the company than an ordinary worker?

More generally, is there an actual relationship between the compensation (rewards) of the elite and their contributions to their groups or to the nation as a whole? Obviously, there is no way to measure this relationship. Compensation amounts are mostly set by markets, but markets respond to supply and demand, not to the "value" that some activity or role has for society at large. So, one objection to the functionalist theory is that no one knows how much inequality is needed to motivate people, nor does anyone know how to calculate the benefits that the elite actually offer to their group or to society at large. In brief, there is no reason to think that the *high degree* of inequality that actually exists in some stratified society is necessary for the nation to enjoy the benefits of *some degree* of inequality. Is there any reason to think that America as a whole would be worse off if the wealthiest 20 percent owned only 40 percent of the wealth rather than 85 percent?

Second, functionalists assume that the system of stratification *effectively* places qualified individuals in important roles. It is a large assumption, however, that those who are best able to perform the most important roles are those who are usually recruited for them. In all systems of stratification, there is a powerful element of inheritance of wealth, prestige, and power. Even assuming that most of the elite of the present day actually earned their rewards, many will pass their resources along to their heirs, who may or may not be talented, hard working, and meritorious. And, even if elite families do not transmit wealth to their children, the latter still have a head start in life from the extra help they get in education, job prospects, contacts through social networks, and other privileges. Certainly, children born to poor families can and do succeed, but they must overcome more obstacles than those born to privilege. If every generation were born with nearly equal access to the means to succeed in life, we could be more confident that those who occupy the most important roles are those who are best qualified to fill them. The functionalist theory that those who receive the highest rewards are most deserving would be more plausible if the (metaphorical) playing field in which people compete were leveled.

Suppose there were some way to calculate the amount of inequality that is optimal for a given society. Suppose further that a society could devise some way of beginning each generation with everyone on an equal footing, with truly equal opportunities to compete. (This could be partly accomplished by steep inheritance taxes, which are often opposed by those who claim to believe in equal opportunity.) Then the functionalist theory of inequality might apply. But no stratified society has ever achieved this condition, partly because these questions are unanswerable and partly because the wealthy and powerful would have to consent to such a change, and they have no incentive to do so.

Conflict Theory

The conflict theory takes off from the objections to functionalism, such as the two just given. But it goes much further. Conflict theorists claim that stratification is based ultimately on control over productive resources, such as land, technology, information, and labor. Once the elite gain control over these resources—by whatever means—they get other people to do work that benefits themselves. How this is organized varies among different kinds of economic systems. In ancient preindustrial states and some chiefdoms, the noble class controlled the land and the commoners had to provide tribute and labor to the nobility in return for the privilege of using it. In parts of feudal Europe, the serfs were tied to their estate and ordinarily had strong rights over the land they worked, but they still had to contribute a certain number of days of work or a certain proportion of their harvest to their lord per year.

As for the capitalist economic system, Karl Marx—the nineteenth-century "father" of conflict theory—argued that capitalist societies include only two fundamental classes. Members of the capitalist class (or *bourgeoisie*) own the factories and tools. Members of the working class (or *proletariat*) have only one thing to sell on the market: their labor. To earn their living, workers must sell their labor to some capitalist. This seems like an equitable arrangement: the capitalists buy the labor they need to operate their factories, mines, and fields to sell goods and make profit; the workers get the jobs they need to support their families by selling their time and skills for a wage.

But, Marx noted, the goods the workers produce must be worth more on the market than the workers themselves receive in wages, or there would be no profit for the capitalists. The difference between the amount the capitalists receive for the goods they sell and their costs (including the amount they pay their workers) is *profit*. In Marx's controversial view, profit is based on the exploitation of workers. The belief that workers receive a fair day's wage for a fair day's work is merely an ideology.

Conflict theorists are criticized for being ideologues themselves, though of a different political persuasion than functionalists. If one wants to find exploitation in an unequal relationship, one can usually do so. Critics of conflict theory claim that the value-laden term *exploitation* does not adequately characterize relationships between chiefs or kings and commoners, between lords and serfs, or between capitalists and workers. Conflict theorists play down the valuable services that elite classes perform, such as maintaining social control, organizing the society for the provision of public goods, and accumulating productive resources (capital) put aside to increase future production.

▲ Conflict theorists hold that stratification exists because some groups are able to exploit others. For example, this woman is boxing up clothing for shipment. Is her employer therefore "exploiting" her labor, as Marx claimed?

© William Taufic/Corbis

Many conflict theorists assume that it is possible to organize a complex society without unequal rewards. This is a rather unrealistic view of human nature, according to some critics of the approach, which may be one reason "communism" has collapsed almost everywhere. Complex societies are always hierarchically organized, with centralized leadership. Many critics believe that the functions of leaders, controllers, and organizers are so valuable to society at large that they deserve the rewards they receive.

Who Benefits?

Contrasting the two theories, we see that functionalism emphasizes the positive aspects of stratification, whereas conflict theory emphasizes the negative side. Functionalists say the class structure benefits everyone directly or indirectly—indirectly because of the useful services wealthy people provide. Conflict theory points to the costs of stratification not just to those on the bottom of the social ladder but also to society at large. A country or other form of society loses the undeveloped potential of its underprivileged members. Societies also suffer the periodic violent conflicts (rebellions, revolutions) or the ongoing disorder (crimes, labor strikes, political dissent) that result from a high degree of unjust inequality and inherited privilege.

Conflict theorists argue that many of the problems that have afflicted modern North America in the last couple of decades are caused (or at least made worse) by increasing inequality. Much resentment toward "the system" comes from people's sense that their lives will not get better or are getting worse. Unable to identify the causes of their frustrations, some white conservative groups find scapegoats in African Americans and Jews, immigrants, the United Nations, and all those South Asian and Chinese laborers who work for "peanuts." Unable to make a personally acceptable living in a socially acceptable manner, inner-city youths turn to drug dealing and other kinds of crime. Economic hardship contributes to family breakups. Poorer people need more social programs, funded by taxpayers, who watch stories in the media about people cheating the government and so elect representatives who provide *fewer* services—for the poor, at least. More generally, the sense of national unity and social responsibility is undermined by worsening inequality, according to conflict theorists.

Does the comparative perspective of anthropology have anything to say about who benefits from inequality? In preindustrial stratified societies, elites did indeed perform vital roles for the whole population, just as functionalists claim. For example, elites often organized labor to construct and maintain public works projects, provided relief to regions struck by famine or hardship, and raised a military force to provide for the defense of the political unit (see Chapter 12). Some kind of central authority is useful and may even be necessary for such tasks to be coordinated effectively. Cooperation on a large scale (involving hundreds or thousands of people) requires organization. Organizing hundreds or thousands of people requires leaders and decision makers. Provided they make decisions they believe are in the public interest, decision makers deserve rewards.

On the other hand, elites assumed some roles that probably were created to maintain their positions at the top of society. Thus, ordinary people regarded the religious functions of elites or of the priests they supported as indispensable to the general welfare, but in fact the rituals they sponsored did not bring rain, sustain the fertility of women, or assuage the anger of the gods. The elite's regulation of access to land and other resources might have seemed necessary, but it was partly because they themselves controlled so many resources that other people's access to them had to be "regulated" so severely. The law and order that states governed by elites helped maintain benefited everyone, but the elite's power, wealth, and internal political rivalries produced violent conflicts that otherwise would not have occurred.

With the insight gained from this comparative perspective, we can question whether some of the "functions" carried out by the elite in industrialized nations are imaginary. We also wonder whether some of the "benefits" other people receive from the roles performed by the elite exist only because society's institutions are organized in such a way that the roles of elites are widely perceived as beneficial.

Who does benefit from the inequality in stratified societies? Functionalists are probably correct in assuming that some degree of inequality is needed for motivation. Most people would agree that unequal rewards for unequal efforts and talents is a fair and just standard. We do not know how much inequality is necessary to provide incentives, however, much less whether some particular stratified society—including our own—has approximately the right amount. We do know that power and privilege are partly inherited, and, therefore, the current members of the upper class are not automatically more talented and diligent than everyone else. Looking at other stratified societies, we see that elites do provide some useful services for the population at large. But we also see that many popular ideas about their functions are "just ideologies," and that many of their "essential roles" are useful only under circumstances that previous elite classes had a hand in creating and that present elites help perpetuate by their privilege and power.

Perhaps most citizens in stratified societies would benefit from inequality, if only there were some way to find out what the optimum amount of inequality is for a particular society, if only there were some way to achieve this optimum initially, and if only there were some way to ensure that opportunities to succeed and achieve are equal for children born in different circumstances. But no known human society has ever achieved this utopia.

Summary

1. *Inequality* refers to the degree to which individuals and groups have differential access to the socially valuable rewards of wealth, power, and prestige. Fried's typology of egalitarian, ranked, and stratified societies provides a useful description of the range of cross-cultural diversity in inequality.

2. Most foragers are egalitarian, mainly because their relationship with nature makes it difficult for anyone to exercise control over productive resources and the behavior of others. Egalitarianism is explained by the frequent movements of camps, the ability of individuals to choose their band affiliation, the cultural value placed on sharing and the social pressure against making oneself stand out, and the difficulties of maintaining exclusive access to a territory.

3. In ranked societies, there are a set number of honored positions (chiefs, titles, offices) to which only a small number of people are eligible to succeed. Succession may be determined by genealogical ascription, or membership in a particular kin group may establish a pool of candidates from which one will emerge or be selected. Tikopia illustrates one form of ranking.

4. Stratified societies have marked inequalities in access to all three kinds of rewards. One form of stratification is the caste system. Castes are best known from India, where they were intimately associated with the Hindu doctrines of reincarnation and pollution.

5. Class systems exist in all modern nations. In the United States, the best criterion of class membership is wealth. Studies conducted by scholars and by the federal government reveal an enormous disparity in the distribution of wealth, especially if net worth rather than annual cash income is used to measure a family's wealth.

6. How such a highly unequal distribution of rewards persists in stratified societies is puzzling. The mobilization of armed force by the elite is an insufficient explanation. Cultural beliefs that inequality is inevitable, divinely ordained, legitimate, or beneficial to society as a whole provide ideologies that justify and reinforce the power and privilege of elite classes.

7. Among preindustrial peoples, religious beliefs were the main form of ideology, as exemplified by most ancient states and chiefdoms. In modern countries, ideologies are more secular in orientation because effective ideologies must be compatible with people's overall cultural ideas about how their society works. In the United States, Americans' ideas about the social and economic usefulness of inequality, about the fairness of unequal rewards for unequal talents and efforts, and about how the well-to-do achieved their wealth are often interpreted as secular ideologies.

8. The two major theories about inequality are the functional and the conflict theories. Functionalists hold that societies offer unequal rewards to those individuals who have the scarcest talents and who use them to perform the most socially valuable roles. Conflict theorists claim that inequality is based ultimately on control over productive resources. Comparisons suggest that although elites often do perform valuable services for society at large, many of their "functions" are illusory. Others exist only because past elites have set up the structure of society so that elite "services" are necessary. Although functionalists are correct that some degree of inequality is necessary for incentive, we have no way of knowing whether any society has the amount it "needs," nor has any society ever succeeded in establishing the equal opportunity required for the functionalist theory to be correct.

Key Terms

inequality
egalitarian
ranked
stratified

class
caste
ideology
secular ideology

functional theory of
  inequality
conflict theory of
  inequality

Suggested Readings

Domhoff, G. William. *Who Rules America? Power, Politics, and Social Change*. 5th ed. Mountain View, Calif.: Mayfield, 2005.

This book has become a classic analysis of how the upper class in the United States exerts disproportionate influence over the political process.

Ehrenreich, Barbara. *Nickel and Dimed: On (Not) Getting By in America*. New York: Henry Holt, 2002.

A popular columnist describes her personal experiences in temporarily living like the poor in the United States.

Lenski, Gerhard. *Power and Privilege*. New York: McGraw-Hill, 1966.

A treatment of stratification comparing the range of inequality in preindustrial and industrial societies. Best known as an attempt to reconcile the functionalist and the conflict perspectives.

Newman, Katherine. *Declining Fortunes: The Withering of the American Dream*. New York: Basic, 1993.

Newman, Katherine. *Falling from Grace: The Experience of Downward Mobility in the American Middle Class*. New York: Vintage, 1988.

Written by an anthropologist, the interview and observational data in these two books show the impacts of job loss or declining income on former members of the American middle class and how they cope with downward mobility.

Schepher-Hughes, Nancy. *Death Without Weeping*. Berkeley: University of California Press, 1992.

How poor northeast Brazilian families cope psychologically with high rates of infant and child mortality.

Media Resources

The Wadsworth Anthropology Resource Center
academic.cengage.com/anthropology

The Wadsworth discipline resource site that accompanies *Humanity: An Introduction to Cultural Anthropology*, Eighth Edition, includes a rich array of material, including online anthropological video clips, to help you in the study of cultural anthropology and the specific topics covered in this chapter. Other material includes a case study forum with excerpts from various Wadsworth authors, map exercises, scientist interviews, breaking news in anthropology, and links to additional useful online material. Begin by selecting Cultural Anthropology to take you to videos, research, and more. From the homepage, you may also select Applied Anthropology, which directs you to essays, glossary terms, the case study forum, and a list of internships and careers in anthropology.

14 RELIGION AND WORLDVIEW

The religion of a people includes their traditional ways of communicating and interacting with supernatural powers. These Buddhist monks are praying at a temple in Thailand.

© Paul Chesley/Stone/Getty Images

Defining Religion

Beliefs About Supernatural Powers

Myths and Worldviews

Rituals and Symbols

Theories of Religion

Intellectual/Cognitive Approaches

Psychological Approaches

Sociological Approaches

Supernatural Explanations of Misfortune

Sorcery

Witchcraft

Interpretations of Sorcery and Witchcraft

Varieties of Religious Organization

Individualistic Cults

Shamanism

Communal Cults

Ecclesiastical Cults

Revitalization Movements

Melanesian Cargo Cults

Native American Movements

Questions addressed in this chapter

What are the major characteristics of religion, according to anthropologists?

What are the three main theories of religion, and what are the problems with each?

How might sorcery and witchcraft be useful for society or individuals?

How are variations in societal complexity reflected in religious beliefs and rituals?

What are revitalization movements, and under what conditions are they most likely to occur?

All cultures have some form of religion. The religion of a people is related to their worldview—the conceptions of reality that affect their interpretations and perceptions of things and events and, therefore, how they act in patterned ways. Like other dimensions of culture, religion and worldview vary greatly among the world's diverse peoples. In this chapter, we introduce this diversity. We begin with a description of what anthropologists see as the most important aspects of religion, using examples. Then we cover some of the main theories social scientists use to understand religion. Next we look at some of the major forms of religion that have most interested anthropologists. We conclude by discussing religious movements, which often occur when a society is undergoing rapid change and foreign domination.

Defining Religion

How can we best define religion so as to encompass all the diverse religions of humanity? A nineteenth-century definition that many scholars still use is E. B. Tylor's **animism,** or "belief in spiritual beings." Most modern conceptions follow Tylor's lead: all religions include beliefs that some kind of spiritual or supernatural powers exist. By expanding on Tylor's definition, we present an overview of religion in comparative perspective.

Beliefs About Supernatural Powers

As discussed in Chapter 4, nineteenth-century anthropologists proposed that religion had passed through evolutionary stages. As cultures evolved, the early, rudimentary forms evolved into more complex forms. For Tylor, the three states of religion were animism, polythe-

ism, and monotheism. Monotheism occurs, he argued, in complex ("advanced") societies. But, in fact, even within religious traditions commonly considered monotheistic, there are elements of animism. Christianity, for example, has many kinds of spiritual beings, such as saints, angels, Satan, and the souls of deceased and living humans.

Also, Tylor's "spiritual beings" are not the only kind of powers. The worldview of various peoples includes the belief in other supernatural powers that are more like forces and substances than beings. For example, before becoming predominantly Christian, Polynesians believed in *mana,* a diffuse, incorporeal power that permeated certain people and things. *Mana* lent supernatural potency to objects, which explained unusual qualities such as why some fishing lures worked so well. The gods gave *mana* to certain people, which explained success or why chiefs had the right to receive privileges and issue commands. Specific pieces of land were infused with *mana,* which explained why they produced such fine crops.

Other peoples hold that there are mystical substances that can be transmitted by direct or indirect contact with people or things. An example is pollution, which can be passed between people of different statuses based on differences such as gender or caste (see Chapters 10, 11, and 13). Unlike *mana,* pollution is harmful to individuals who receive it, and cleansing or other forms of purification are required to remove it.

Spiritual *beings* usually have qualities such as the ability to assume a bodily form, a personality with emotions, and a consciousness and will. Usually gods and other kinds of beings respond to human actions in some way: if you communicate with them (by prayer), they will listen, and if your actions displease them, they will react negatively. Some beings have human origins or are associated with living or deceased persons, such as souls, ancestral ghosts, and important people who did such notable things that they became gods. There are numerous other kinds of beings: spirit helpers, nature spirits, demons, zoomorphic spirits, forest spirits, disease spirits, and so on. The characteristics people attribute to supernatural beings vary enormously: they can be unpredictable or consistent, irrational or reasonable, vengeful or forgiving, amoral or just.

In the religious traditions of Western civilization—Judaism, Christianity, and Islam—the supreme being is all-knowing and all-powerful, expects sacrifices or worship, and is mindful of human behavior and morality. The gods that many other peoples believe in have none of these characteristics, however. They can be tricked and manipulated. Often they are commanded more than worshipped. Sometimes people do not believe gods are concerned about the morality of human actions: they do not punish wrongdoing, in either this life or the next. There is no belief that *sin* (violation of a commandment or moral precept) even exists.

In contrast to beings such as gods, supernatural *forces* or *substances* generally cannot take on a physical appearance and have no will of their own. Rather, they are known mainly by their effects: *mana* makes a chief successful; pollution sickens a man. In many cultures, the beliefs about how powers work are indefinite: one performs a ritual and utters an incantation (spell), and the effect that the rite and spell are intended to cause simply happens. This is generally known as *magic* and is discussed later in this chapter.

Myths and Worldviews

Belief in the existence of supernatural powers is only part of religion. Religion also includes **myths**—oral or written stories (narratives) about the actions and deeds of supernatural powers and cultural heroes. Sometimes myths explain how the entire universe was created. They may recount how and why people, animals, plants, and natural features originated. Myths may explain how a people acquired their tools and customs and how they came to live where they do. They often tell why people should or should not act in certain ways, and what happened to someone in the past who did something people are forbidden to do.

North Americans mostly learn their mythology in formal settings: myths are taught at church and, to a lesser extent, at home. (Here we need to emphasize that calling the Bible, Koran, Torah, and other religious texts *myths* is not intended to imply that they are false.) In many societies, however, there are no formal services. Elders re-

count myths more informally, sometimes in moments of leisure. Myths are repeated regularly on days set aside for religious performances. They are sung or chanted while one is doing daily tasks. The fact that myths sometimes are recounted rather casually does not mean that their importance in a people's way of life is negligible. A people's worldview—and therefore their behavior—is affected by their myths.

For example, in the 1960s, historian Lynn White argued that the Judeo-Christian account of creation makes it easy for North Americans to view nature as something to be conquered and used for their own profit and gratification. God gave humans "dominion" over nature and told us to "subdue" the earth and its living creatures (see Genesis 1:26–30). Because of the biblical account of creation, when it suits our purposes and interests, we have no divine prohibitions against polluting the air and water, ruining the habitats of other creatures, destroying the landscape with strip mines and highways, and so forth. According to this argument, because of the religious heritage of Western civilization—which influences the worldview of Europeans and peoples culturally derived from Europe—Westerners are more likely to believe that God gave the earth to humans to conquer and exploit than to preserve and protect. In contrast, Westerners might show more respect for other living things if (as in some cultures) the sacred myths of our religious heritage recounted how some of us are descended from bears or other animals, or that earth is our sacred mother, or that gods instruct us not to waste any resource, or that trees are just as precious to God as humans. In short, if Western scriptures emphasized the importance of living in harmony with nature rather than subduing nature, perhaps the modern ecological crisis would be less of a crisis.

Judeo-Christian scriptures can be interpreted in many ways and used for many purposes, however, not all of which involve the uncontrolled exploitation of resources for profit or material self-gratification. The Old Order Amish of North America, for example, are thoroughly and devoutly Christian, but they reject the materialism of modern society (see A Closer Look).

A people's myths—and this is our general point—are more than stories they tell after dark or recite on appropriate occasions. Myths do more than satisfy curiosity and help pass the time. Myths help to form a people's worldview: their conceptions of reality and the interpretations of events that happen in society and the natural world. Worldview and myths affect people's beliefs about how they ought to relate to the world and to one another (see Chapter 2), and therefore they affect how people behave in their everyday lives.

On October 2, 2006, a milk truck driver entered an Amish school in Lancaster, Pennsylvania. He killed five girls in the school and then committed suicide. Americans were horrified at the senselessness of the attack, but it was the subsequent reaction of the Amish community that left many dumbfounded. Just hours after the incident, an Amish neighbor comforted the family of the shooter. The grandfather of one girl said that people must not think the assailant was evil. Many of the Amish parents forgave the attacker. Clearly, the Amish are outside the American cultural mainstream.

Amish cultural roots lie in Switzerland, where their Christian sect broke off from the Anabaptist movement in 1693. Persecuted and martyred in Europe because of their practices of shunning and foot washing, many Amish migrated to the Americas in the 1700s and early 1800s. They originally settled in Pennsylvania, but because their population grew during the last century, the Amish migrated and established new communities in Ohio, Indiana, Illinois, Wisconsin, and adjacent states, as well as in Ontario, Canada. Judging from their increased numbers and geographical spread, the Amish have done well in Canada and the United States.

The Amish believe they should live by certain values. First, their faith emphasizes humility and submission to the will of the community over individualism and personal freedom. Pride is one of their major sins. Second, the Amish prefer simple living to seeking self-gratification by symbolic consumption. They look down on clothing styles and jewelry that beautify personal appearance and celebrate the self. The Amish consider themselves "plain people." Third, they believe that the scriptures mandate equality, so they dislike differences in levels of wealth and consumption within their communities. Farm sizes should be limited to the acreage that a family can work using equipment that is (literally) horse-powered. Fourth, Amish think that work itself is virtuous. Work builds character and keeps the mind and body away from frivolous concerns; community cooperation in projects helps tie the group together. Tools and other devices that save too much labor (that are "too handy") are unwelcome.

These and other values contrast to the individualism, self-gratification, competitiveness, materialism, future orientation, and other values that the Amish see as characteristic of the surrounding society. Like people everywhere, the Amish have fun, but many activities such as dancing, joyriding, movie and TV watching, and alcohol drinking are too "worldly" and are considered sinful, as is divorce and the use of artificial birth control. Amish people who participate in such activities or who persistently fail to uphold Amish values may be excommunicated and shunned until they repent.

The Amish believe that maintaining their values and religious beliefs requires that, insofar as possible, they keep themselves separate from the influence of the wider North American population (whom they often call "English"). For economic reasons alone, the Amish cannot isolate themselves completely, but they do attempt to minimize their interaction with the outside world. The Amish do various things to maintain their separation. They converse among themselves using an old German dialect. They forbid television and radios, out of concern that access to mass media will corrupt their values. They discourage travel outside the immediate area except for economic necessity, for fear it will expose people to worldly influences and weaken community ties. Amish children are not educated beyond the eighth-grade "basics" (most communities have their own schools with Amish teachers), both because this level is all the Amish consider necessary for their way of life and because children could learn things that might weaken their faith.

Over the decades, Amish leaders have decided that new technologies threaten their "plain" way of life, and so the Amish are not allowed to own and use many things the English consider necessities. Contrary to what many outsiders believe, however, the Amish are not restricted to nineteenth-century technologies. Transportation, household products, and farming technology illustrate how they allow technology in, but keep control over its impacts.

- *Transportation.* The Amish are well known for their horse-and-buggy travel. (In areas with large Amish populations, signs are posted to warn motorists of their presence on the highways.) The Amish are not allowed to own or drive cars or to have driver's licenses. They can ride in cars driven by non-Amish for certain purposes, however, including conducting business, visiting distant relatives, and traveling to medical facilities and auctions.

- *Household products.* Bishops in most Amish communities outlaw the hookup of Amish households to 110-volt electricity carried by public power lines. Leaders think that connections to public power sources will lead to undue dependence on the outside. Also, this prohibition prevents family access to television and other mass media. Families cannot own household conveniences powered by 110-volt electrical current, such as lights, stoves, and refrigerators. On the other hand, most church districts allow access to other sources of power, including propane, kerosene, and electric power that comes from batteries or that is generated by family-owned generators. For example, lightbulbs are prohibited, but homes have gas lanterns; kerosene refrigerators and propane stoves are allowed and widely used.

- *Farm equipment.* Some modern farm machinery is not allowed or can be used for only certain purposes. Farmers are

(continued)

not allowed to use self-propelled tractors to plow, harvest, or do other field tasks. However, they can use tractors with gasoline engines to blow silage into the barn, power hydraulic systems used for tools, and spin ventilation fans. Farmers also are allowed to take mechanical corn binders, hay balers, and some other kinds of gasoline-powered equipment into their fields, provided that the equipment is pulled by horses rather than self-propelled.

These specific technologies are only a sample. Many English and other outsiders are puzzled by the restrictions and allowances. To the mainstream, allowing some things in while keeping similar things out seems curious, and in some cases even hypocritical. The Amish ride in cars for normatively approved visits, emergencies, and work, but they cannot own or drive them. Their neighborhoods have a public telephone or two located in a place where several families have access to it, yet the Amish cannot have private phones in their homes. The Amish prohibit electric stoves and refrigerators, yet propane stoves and kerosene refrigerators are permitted. The Amish use engines in their barns and even in their fields when the equipment is pulled by horses, but using engines to propel farm machinery is not allowed. What's the logic behind these restrictions and allowances?

Sociologist Donald Kraybill has conducted extensive research on just such questions. The Amish have to reconcile two opposing objectives. On the one hand, the economic viability of their communities requires that they adapt to a changing world by adopting efficient technologies. On the other hand, wholesale adoption of these technologies might unravel their way of life, having a negative impact on the purity of their religion, the integrity of their values, and the cohesion of their community. Amish leaders have to walk a fine line. The combinations of restrictions and allowances are compromises between the need to change and the desire to stay the same.

Amish policy toward automobiles is a good illustration. Cars are handy for transportation—too handy for the Amish. The freedom and speed cars offer would take people away from the neighborhood and expose them to worldly things such as movies. In addition to their practical use as vehicles, cars have social and cultural implications. Private ownership of cars promotes individualism and independence from the community. Soon more well-to-do families would buy and drive nicer cars and begin to use them as status symbols, threatening Amish egalitarian values. Finally, car ownership would threaten horses and buggies, which are a key symbol of Amish identity and a visible mark of their separation.

At one time, car use as well as ownership was banned. But, after World War II, population growth led to the formation of new communities that lived too far away for travel by horses and buggies. Soon the Amish hired English drivers to take them to funerals, weddings, barnraisings, and the like. In the 1970s, more and more Amish found it impossible to make a living by farming, and they started their own businesses in areas such as carpentry, cabinetmaking, retailing, and, more recently, retail tourism. Other Amish have jobs in the dairy and other industries. Transportation to and from the business or the job site is required, and many Amish businesses hire cars on a regular basis, leading to the emergence of "Amish taxis" driven by non-Amish. So, under changed economic conditions, the use of cars became a necessity. But the Amish still avoid many negative impacts of cars on their traditions by continuing to ban their ownership.

Similar considerations apply to farm machinery. Using some farm machinery in fields is essential for efficiency, but propelling it by horses keeps farms small and family-run. It also ensures the continuance of the tradition of calling on one's neighbors to help with harvest and other labor-intensive operations. Self-propelled, rubber-wheeled tractors could be too easily used to transport people off the farm, partially substituting for the tabooed car and further undermining the horse and buggy, which is still a main visible symbol of Amish identity.

Banning private telephones but allowing community phones also makes sense as a compromise. Private phones threaten the face-to-face interaction and visiting that are essential for community cohesion. Incoming calls—as the non-Amish know all to well—disrupt family life and studies. Community phones, however, are essential for things like making medical appointments, calling veterinarians, handling emergencies, placing business orders, and calling taxis. Today, a number of neighbors often share the expense to install a phone shanty to place and receive calls for such purposes.

Amish success at keeping most of their traditions intact while *selectively incorporating* new technologies to keep their living standards high is the key factor that explains the twentieth-century growth and spread of their communities. Compared to the "English," Amish families are large: an average couple has six or seven children. Further, Kraybill estimates that four out of five Amish children remain Amish, staying with their communities and retaining their heritage. Large families mean that the population grows rapidly, while a low "dropout rate" means that the number of people carrying Amish culture and transmitting it to future generations grows almost as fast. The compromises that keep communities prosperous have led most young people to choose to remain Amish, so Amish culture is in little danger of becoming assimilated by the "English." If Amish leaders refused to compromise with changing economic forces, how much poorer would their communities become, and how many more Amish young people would abandon their faith?

Source: Kraybill (1989)

© akg-images, London

▲ In this depiction of a biblical myth, Eve offers forbidden fruit to Adam. Their original sin explains the origin of evil in the Judeo-Christian worldview.

Rituals and Symbols

People everywhere believe that gods, ghosts, demons, ancestral spirits, and other supernatural beings take an active interest in worldly affairs, particularly in the lives of human beings. You can ask them for blessings or aid through prayer. Sometimes you can command them to do things for you or for other people. If you become polluted, there are actions you can take to restore your purity. Because people believe that supernatural powers can make natural events occur and can intervene in human affairs, certain human behaviors can control or influence powers. In the context of religion, the organized performance of behaviors intended to influence spiritual powers is known as **ritual.**

Rituals are *stereotyped:* Definite patterns of speech or movement, or definite sequences of events, occur in much the same way in performance after performance. In gen-eral, people performing rituals want supernatural powers to do things on their behalf. For example, some central Canadian Inuit believe that they may fail to locate game animals because an undersea goddess is angry about the misconduct of members of the camp. They persuade the goddess to release the game by performing a ritual in which camp members publicly confess their violations.

Rituals the world over have *symbolic* aspects. These symbolic aspects are so important that some anthropologists define ritual itself as *symbolic behavior.* For example, rituals often occur in *places* that have symbolic significance to the performers. They may be held where some mythological event occurred, or where the women who founded a matrilineage were born. Muslims are supposed to make pilgrimages to the holy city of Mecca at least once in their lifetime. Millions of Hindus journey to the city of Varanasi to pray and bathe in Ganga Ma (Mother Ganges). To die and be cremated in Varanasi and have your ashes mix with the river can help you achieve *moksa,* spiritual liberation. Buddhists may go to the site of the Bodhi Tree, where 2,500 years ago Siddhartha's meditation led to his enlightenment and transformation into The Buddha. In Shinto, the ancient religion of Japan, shrines at which people pray to spirits and to their ances-tors are set apart from other spaces by a Torii, an arch supported by two pillars.

There are other ritual symbols. Rituals often involve the display, touching, and manipulation of *objects* that symbolize an event (e.g., the cross), a holy person (stat-ues of Jesus and Mary), a relationship (wedding rings, the symbol of holy matrimony), and a variety of other things. Buddhist and Hindu temples are filled with statues and relics. The *language* and *behavior* of ritual carry deep symbolic meanings, as in the Christian rituals of wor-ship, hymn singing, prayer, baptism, and communion.

Anthropologists often classify rituals on two bases. The first basis is their conscious purposes—the reasons people themselves give for performing rituals. For ex-ample, some people believe that divination rituals allow them to acquire information from a supernatural power about the future or about some past event. Divination is commonly employed to determine the source of sickness or misfortune or to help people make decisions in uncer-tain situations. Familiar examples include Tarot cards, crystal balls, and palm reading. There are also curing, sorcery, sacrificial, and exorcism rituals. There are ritu-als to renew the world, to make a man out of a boy and a woman out of a girl, to make people and nature fertile, and to free the soul from a dead person's body. Rituals are held for single individuals, for kin groups, for people of similar age, for whole societies, and so forth.

▲ As this Hindu religious pilgrim praying in Varanasi, India, illustrates, rituals include symbolic behavior and objects.

Many peoples use rituals to control the weather. The Hopi of the American Southwest believe that rainfall that fills springs and streams and nourishes crops is brought by supernatural beings. These beings, called *kachinas,* live in the peaks of mountains to the west of Hopi villages. They bring life-giving rain to the Hopi cornfields when they come in the form of clouds. In the spring and summer, the Hopi believe, *kachinas* dwell in the villages. During this period, men wearing masks of the *kachinas* perform ritual dances, impersonating and honoring the spirits. The spirit enters the body of the dancer, who thus becomes the *kachina.* The dances bring rain to the Hopi cornfields.

The second basis of classification is when rituals occur—on a regular schedule (like weekly church services or annual religious holidays) or simply whenever some individual or group wants or needs them (like funerals or prayers for a sick person). If rituals are held regularly (seasonally, annually, daily, monthly), they are called *calendrical rituals.* The Hopi and Zuni, for example, follow a ritual calendar in which certain rituals are performed by certain groups at the same time every year. One ritual begins the sequence, and then other rituals follow in regular sequence. The same cycle is repeated the following year.

In contrast, *crisis rituals* are organized and performed whenever some individual or group needs, wants, or asks for them—for purposes of curing, ensuring good hunting or fishing, burying or honoring the dead, or accompanying other events that happen sporadically or unpredictably. The supernatural curing practiced by shamans, described later, is the most widespread type of crisis ritual.

With this brief and broad overview of religion in mind, we consider some of the major theoretical orientations offered to understand or explain religion.

Theories of Religion

Why do all cultures have religious beliefs, myths, and rituals? With regard to beliefs, people cannot actually prove the existence of supernatural powers such as ghosts, gods, demons, angels, souls, *mana,* and so forth. Although people who follow a particular form of religion may believe that traditional accounts of their past reflect historical events, outsiders to the religion are more likely to consider at least parts of them entirely mythical. Indeed, some people who do not share the beliefs of a given culture think such beliefs result from ignorance or superstition.

As for rituals, people who are outsiders to a religion and worldview may not share the opinion that rituals help achieve the goals the performers have in mind. To them, most rituals may seem like a waste of time and resources. For example, when a Trobriand Islander plants a yam garden, he does some things that "work" in the way he thinks they do: he clears the land, removes the weeds, and so forth, just as anyone should for success. But a Trobriander believes certain acts that many outsiders consider superfluous are also necessary for success in gardening. He hires a magician to perform rites and spells to improve his yam harvest. Outsiders (nonbelievers) to Trobriand beliefs understand what the gardener gets out of the first kind of activity: a yam harvest, if nature cooperates. But what does he get out of the magic rites and spells? How did Trobrianders come to believe that magical rites are needed?

We can look at this behavior in another way to see a main problem in understanding rituals in other cultures.

© David Samuel Robbins/Corbis

From an outsider's perspective, when the Trobriander plants a crop and weeds his garden, his actions are effective in attaining the goal he has in mind—they work in more or less the way he thinks they do. But when the garden magician performs rites and spells, his actions do not achieve the result he has in mind. The magic does not "really work." How, then, did the Trobrianders get the idea that they do?

Speaking broadly, to those who do not share the particular religion's beliefs, rituals do not have the effects performers intend. The crazy woman is not "truly" restored to sanity by exorcizing the demon; no spirits "really" enter the body of the medicine man; there were no "genuine" witches in Salem, Massachusetts, in 1692. Why, then, do so many people believe in the power of ritual?

Some people who consider themselves sophisticated say that religious beliefs and rituals are based on ignorance and superstition. All anthropologists reject (or should reject) this nonanswer to the question, Why religion? Its ethnocentrism is apparent: superstition is something that someone else believes in but you do not. Many of our own beliefs seem superstitious to others, and undoubtedly many of the accepted truths of the twenty-first century will be considered superstitions by the twenty-second century. Even if we think that such beliefs and practices are superstitious, we still have not explained them. Why does one form of superstition develop in one place and another form in another place?

You already have thought of possible answers. If rituals do not work in the way performers believe they do, perhaps they work in some other way. If they do not have the effects people intend, they may have other effects that people find useful or satisfying. If the conscious reasons people give for performing rituals seem inadequate, perhaps their meaning is entirely symbolic: They convey and reinforce deep meanings and values that help people cope with life or that tie people together. As for myths, if they are not accurate historical accounts, perhaps they are symbolic statements that help people make sense of reality and give meaning to real-world things and events. Maybe religious truths are a different kind of truth than scientific truths: they cannot be subjected to tests and experiments to see whether they work the way people think they do, but they nonetheless work on another level.

Social scientists have proposed many theories for why religion exists. Some theories hold that beliefs, myths, and rituals provide benefits that people want or need but cannot acquire without religion. Broadly, social scientists have proposed three types of theories: the intellectual (or cognitive), the psychological, and the sociological.

Intellectual/Cognitive Approaches

Those who posit the **intellectual** (or **cognitive**) **approach** assume that humans seek explanations for the world around them. Religious beliefs help satisfy the uniquely human desire to understand and explain things and events. Without religion, much of the world would be incomprehensible and inexplicable, which (these scholars argue) would be intolerable to the mind of a conscious, reasoning, problem-solving species like *Homo sapiens*. For example, religion satisfies the human demand for understanding by providing explanations for the movements of the sun, moon, and stars. *Origin myths* explain things like the creation of the sky, land, and water; where animals and plants come from; and where people got their language, tools, rituals, and other customs and beliefs. The essential purpose of religion, in the intellectual view, is to provide people with explanations.

Sir James Frazer was an influential scholar who championed the intellectual approach. His most famous work was *The Golden Bough,* published in 12 volumes at around the turn of the twentieth century. Among other things, Frazer was interested in the development of rational thought. He argued that human thinking progressed through three stages that he called magic, religion, and science. The earliest cultures practiced *magic;* they attempted to control the world by performing rites and spells. Later cultures came to believe in the existence of supernatural beings, who demanded that people worship them or make sacrifices to them, giving birth to *religion.* Finally, people realized that neither magical techniques nor worship of imaginary beings enabled them to explain or control events. With the advent of *science,* the errors of magic and religion were replaced with knowledge of true cause-and-effect relationships. In Frazer's view, magic, religion, and science are alternative worldviews: each provides people with an intellectual model of the way the world works and a means to manipulate events and people. Because science is a superior system of knowledge, Frazer thought it was replacing magical and religious beliefs.

The idea of Frazer and others that religious beliefs provide people with explanations for things and events is correct, as far as it goes, but it surely is an incomplete explanation for religion. Religion does satisfy curiosity about the world, but this is not its only function. The people whom Frazer called "savages" possess and use practical knowledge just as "civilized" peoples do—a

Trobriander knows that he must care for his yams as well as perform garden magic. Conversely, many "scientific" people believe in and practice religion—including many of those formally educated persons who make their living practicing the science for which religion supposedly substitutes! Those scientists who go to church apparently find little or no contradiction between their religious beliefs and worship and their scientific knowledge and practice. Religious beliefs do not simply substitute for objective knowledge. People don't "have" religion because they "lack" science. Somehow, the two are complementary.

Although few scholars today hold that religion exists solely or even mainly to provide "prescientific" people with explanations their culture would otherwise lack, the intellectual approach is by no means passé. Clifford Geertz, a leading humanistic theorist (see Chapter 4), argued that religion provides its believers with the assurance that the world is *meaningful*—that events have a place in the grand scheme of things, natural phenomena have understandable causes, suffering and evil happen to good people for some good reason, wrongs will be righted and injustices corrected. Cultural beings (i.e., humans) cannot tolerate events that contradict the basic premises, categories, and worldview of their cultural tradition. Yet such events do occur periodically. Because of religion, people are able to maintain their worldview in spite of events that seem to contradict it. Religion, Geertz believed, reassures believers that the world is orderly rather than chaotic, all within the framework of their existing cultural knowledge.

Stewart Guthrie is another contemporary scholar who views religion in cognitive terms. Guthrie thinks the essence of religion is the belief that natural phenomena have humanlike properties. He points out that people tend to see the world *anthropomorphically:* we tend to attribute human motives, purposes, feelings, senses, and other characteristics to living and nonliving things that are not human. For example, thunder is the voice of the gods, clouds are the spirits of our ancestors, the sun is our life-giving father, Mother Earth is alive, the wind is the breath of a god. Anthropomorphism is natural to human thought, and most of us regularly think this way, as when you think your car or computer hates you or when you interact with your pet as if it were a person.

When we see the world as "peopled" with spirits (as in animism), or think that different gods control various aspects of nature (as in polytheism), or believe that one god created and controls everything (as in monotheism), we are attributing human characteristics to the natural world. In Guthrie's view, this actually is a smart thing to do. If you think there are no humanlike beings mak-

ing things happen, and you are wrong, then the consequences are costly. If the earth is in fact our mother, but we treat her as nonliving, then she might punish us. But if we think anthropomorphically about the earth and take steps to worship and protect her, then no harm is done. If there is a war god, and our enemy sacrifices to him but we do not, we may all be killed, so why take the chance? As Guthrie phrases it, religion is then a "good bet."

However, not all the rituals that result from beliefs that humanlike beings control natural processes are "harmless." In fact, many rituals are quite costly. They require sacrifices to deities or ancestors, and they consume time and energy that could be used in other ways. In some societies, religious beliefs are costly indeed. In some ancient Mesoamerican civilizations, priests pierced their bodies with thorns to make themselves bleed because they believed the gods demanded blood sacrifices. Humans were also sacrificed. Attributing human properties to nonhuman entities is not always harmless: religion often helps motivate individuals and groups of individuals to do horrific things to others—and sometimes to themselves.

Psychological Approaches

The notion that religion helps people cope with times of trouble, stress, and anxiety is a common one. Sicknesses, accidents, misfortunes, injustices, deaths, and other trials and tribulations of life can be better handled emotionally if one believes there is a reason and meaning to them or that one's troubles can be controlled or alleviated by means of ritual. Scholars who make such arguments follow the **psychological approach.**

In anthropology, a well-known psychological theory of religion was proposed by Bronislaw Malinowski, whom we introduced in Chapter 4. Malinowski thought that religion (including magic) serves the valuable function of giving people confidence when they are likely to be unsuccessful despite their best efforts. There are always natural phenomena that people cannot control and that constantly threaten to ruin their plans and efforts. Belief in the power of ritual to control these (otherwise uncontrollable) elements instills confidence and removes some of the anxiety that results from the uncertainties of life. Not only do rituals relieve our worries, but they may also help us be more successful in activities by making us more confident of success.

People grow frustrated—and occasionally violent—when they cannot control what happens to them or those they care about. Our lives are filled with uncertainties and unknowable futures. Our families and friends don't always do what we want or what we think is right for

◄ Psychological approaches hold that religion helps individuals and groups cope with crisis, uncertainty, grief, stress, trauma, and other emotional distress. This Iraqi woman cries at a funeral.

them. Accidents happen. Stock markets fall. Bosses fire us. Crops fail. Professors fail us. We fail ourselves. Religion (and in this context we mean "faith" in a power with more knowledge and power than humans have) is there to offer hope and comfort. Often, it helps us cope with frustrated hopes by telling us what we can do to make things better. For example, during the 2007 summer and fall drought in Georgia, people got together to pray for rain. It did rain later.

Another specific psychological theory of religion holds that, as self-conscious beings, we humans are aware of our own mortality. Knowing that we will eventually die causes us great anxiety and leads us to worry about our own death. Experiencing the serious illness or death of a parent or other relative likewise produces grief and psychological stress for most people. We must have some way of coping emotionally with the grief over the death of our loved ones, and with the anxiety caused by the knowledge of our own mortality. Religion helps us cope by denying the finality of death—that is, by inculcating beliefs about the existence of a pleasant afterlife, in which our immortal souls live forever.

The notion that belief in life after death helps to calm our fears and alleviate our anxieties seems reasonable. This theory is tainted by an ethnocentric assumption, however: Although most religions do include beliefs about some kind of afterlife, in a great many cultures, the afterlife is far from pleasant. The Dobu people of Mela-

nesia believe that human bodies also have a ghostly form, seen as a shadow or a reflection. During life, the ghostly self goes out at night and appears in the dreams of other people. Once the corpse rots after death, the ghosts of people go to a place called the Hill of the Dead, where they have a "thin and shadowy" existence and mourn for their homeland. How are such beliefs about the afterlife "comforting"?

Certainly, religion is psychologically useful. For some people some of the time, it relieves anxieties, calms fears, and helps them cope emotionally with life's uncertainties and hardships. That religion often serves such functions is indisputable. Yet, sometimes religious beliefs actually increase our anxieties, fears, and stress levels. Consider the Kwaio, a people of the Solomon Islands. Kwaio believe that women are polluting to men, so Kwaio wives are expected to take elaborate precautions to avoid polluting their husbands when preparing food for them. If a man dies of an illness, his wife may be blamed, and perhaps killed, for her "offense." Just whose anxieties and fears are relieved by this belief?

The general point of the Dobu and Kwaio examples is that, from a psychological perspective, religion has two faces. On the one hand, it does—for some people, some of the time, in some respects—help us cope emotionally with times of trouble and hardships. On the other hand, beliefs about supernatural powers and what they do often create fears and anxieties that would not otherwise exist.

© Stephanie Sinclair/Corbis

▲ This crowd is gathered for a ritual in Irian Jaya, Indonesia. French sociologist Émile Durkheim proposed that rituals involve gatherings and common activities that enhance social solidarity among a group of people.

Pleasant afterlives ("Heaven") offer us comfort and hope. But what *psychological* benefit does the threat of eternal damnation ("Hell") offer? This question leads logically to the sociological approach.

Sociological Approaches

"Societies need religion to keep people in line," you may have heard people say. The idea of the **sociological approach** is that religion instills and maintains common values, leads to increased conformity to cultural norms, promotes cohesion and cooperation, promises eternal rewards for good deeds and eternal damnation for evil acts, and so forth. Those who champion the sociological approach hold that religion exists because of the useful effects it has on human societies—because of its *social functions.* Religion helps societies maintain harmonious social relationships between individuals and groups. It encourages people to respect the rights of others and to perform their proper duties. It is part of the socialization process that instills deeply held values in children.

Consider the Ten Commandments, for example, which serve as a moral code for the three religions of the West.

Two prescribe how people ought to feel and act toward God and other people, and eight give rules for actions, including the five "thou shalt nots" (see Exodus 20:3–17). Note that five of the divinely ordered prohibitions are against the commission of acts that could result in harm to others, such as killing and stealing. God gave us commandments that will, if obeyed, lead to good relationships with others and therefore promote earthly social order. More general Judeo-Christian moral guidelines are the Golden Rule ("Do unto others as you would have them do unto you") and love of one's neighbor (Matthew 19:19); both are useful prescriptions for harmonious social life.

Religion also enhances the cohesion of society by making people sense their interdependence on one another and on their traditions. Émile Durkheim, a French sociologist of the early twentieth century, was influential in formulating this perspective. Durkheim's view was that the main function of religion in human society is to promote *social solidarity,* meaning that religion has the effect of bringing people together and enhancing their sense of unity, cohesion, and reliance on their society's customs. Groups of people who share the same beliefs and who gather periodically to perform common rituals experience a feeling of oneness and harmony.

The most important social function of religion, Durkheim believed, is to strengthen social solidarity. There also are other versions of the sociological approach. One is that religion helps to maintain social order (that is, religion serves as a social control mechanism—see Chapter 12) by increasing conformity to norms, inculcating shared values in children, reminding people to act responsibly, teaching moral lessons through myths and doctrines, and so forth.

One mechanism by which religion maintains social control is by offering rewards for good behavior and punishments for antisocial behavior. In this life, when people have an accident or get sick, they may think they are being punished for some crime or deviant action, for example. This deters the individual from future deviance and also serves as an example to others, teaching them to act properly in the future. In the next life (the afterlife, which some peoples believe lasts for eternity), gods may reward virtue and punish sinful behavior. Such socially useful effects of religion are widespread.

Not all peoples have such beliefs, however. In some worldviews, gods and other kinds of spiritual beings have little or no interest in the morality or immorality of human actions. There is no concept of "sin" as behavior that violates a doctrine or divine will, and the fate of a person in this life or in the afterlife is not related to her or his moral character or conduct.

There is a relationship between whether spiritual beings punish and reward people according to their character or conduct and the general nature of the cultural system. In his cross-cultural research in the 1960s, Guy Swanson found a striking relationship between the degree of social inequality in a society and the likelihood that its religion includes beliefs that spiritual beings punish wrongdoing. Generally, societies in which there is greater inequality (class societies—see Chapter 13) are much more likely than egalitarian societies to believe that gods or other spirits will reward and punish individuals according to how well they behave.

Like the cognitive and psychological approaches, the sociological theory works in some cases but not in others. At some times, in some places, and in some contexts, religion teaches the difference between right and wrong and thus encourages social harmony. It does strengthen solidarity by bringing people together. It does inculcate the belief that good behavior is rewarded and bad behavior is punished eventually, if not immediately. But also, sometimes religion has effects that few people believe are socially useful. It has contributed to wars and led to persecutions. In stratified societies, its beliefs have supported vast social differences in powers and privileges. Occasionally, as among the Aztec, it has led people to take blood from their own bodies by piercing their bodies with thorns and has led priests to drag war captives to temples where their hearts are offered as sacrifices to the gods. There may be ways in which such impacts are "socially useful," but clearly they are not useful to *everyone*.

Supernatural Explanations of Misfortune

One occurrence that many peoples attribute to the action of spiritual powers is personal misfortune, including death, illness, and events that many Westerners consider accidents. Many beliefs and rituals of various societies are concerned with explaining, preventing, and curing illness and disease.

Cross-culturally, two major complexes of beliefs about misfortune are common. First, as already discussed, many people believe that sickness or some other unfortunate occurrence is caused by the action of spiritual powers. The violation of a taboo can lead some supernatural power to cause sickness. The ancestral spirits of kin groups cause their members to become ill because of conflict or bad feelings within the group. Similar beliefs may apply to accidents that many Westerners attribute to bad luck or carelessness. Drownings, falls, snakebites, prolonged failure to succeed at some activity—such events are likely to be seen as evidence of unfavorable supernatural intervention. The victim has offended a god or spirit, who brings an "accident" as punishment.

Second, many people think that illnesses or other misfortunes are caused by the action of some evil human who is using special supernatural powers against the afflicted person. The belief that certain people, called *sorcerers* and *witches*, have powers to harm others by mystical means is enormously widespread among humanity. Sometimes witches and sorcerers are thought to strike randomly and maliciously against people who are innocent of any wrongdoing. More commonly, they direct their evil magic or thoughts toward those against whom they have a grudge. Sorcery and witchcraft are worth considering in more detail.

Sorcery

Sorcery is the performance of rites and spells intended to cause supernatural harm to others; that is, it is a form of evil magic. In some cultures, almost everyone learns to harm their enemies by sorcery techniques; knowledge of such techniques is widespread. Among other peoples, sorcery is a more specialized practice; only certain people inherit or acquire the knowledge of how to recite spells and perform the rites correctly.

In 1890, Sir James Frazer proposed that magic (including sorcery) is based on two kinds of logical principles or assumptions. Both involve a symbolic identification of something (e.g., an object or action) with something else (e.g., an event or a person).

The *imitative principle* is often stated as "Like produces like." That is, if an object resembles a person and the sorcerer mutilates the object, then the same thing will happen to the person. The so-called voodoo doll is a familiar example. In another kind of imitative magic, the magician or sorcerer mimics the effects she or he wants to produce. Sorcerers among the Dobu of Melanesia cast spells by imitating the symptoms of the disease they want their victims to suffer.

The second logical premise underlying magic and sorcery is the *contagious principle,* which is "Power comes from contact." That is, things that were once in contact with someone can be used in rites and spells to make things happen to that person. By performing sorcery rites and spells on such objects as hair clippings, bodily excretions, nail parings, infant umbilical cords, or jewelry and clothing, one can cause harm to one's enemies. In societies in which sorcery rests on the contagious principle, people must dispose of objects they have been in contact with, including things have come out of or off of their bodies, lest one of their enemies use them for sorcery.

There are many ways in which sorcery beliefs and accusations fit into the social life of a people. One important way is that who accuses whom of sorcery reflects how individuals and groups relate to one another. In all societies, certain kinds of social relationships are especially likely to be beset by conflict. Cowives of a polygynous man may be jealous over their husband's favors or may compete for an inheritance for their children. People who have married into a kin group or village may be viewed as outsiders who are still loyal to their own natal families. Two men who want the same woman, or two women who want the same man, have reasons to dislike each other. Men who are rivals for a political office have conflicts of interest.

These and other kinds of relationships are sources of strain and conflict within a human group. Which relationships are likely to cause strain and conflict depend on the way the society is organized: Brothers-in-law are allies in one society, but their interests regularly conflict in another society, for instance. The relationships most likely to be troublesome are *patterned,* meaning that individuals who have these relationships with one another are most likely to experience conflicts.

Suppose you were brought up in a culture that explained illness or accident by sorcery. If you or a relative became ill or suffered misfortune, you would not suspect just anyone of harming you. You would ask: Who has a motive to perform evil magic against me? Who envies me? Who would profit from my sickness or death? With whom have I recently quarreled? These people are your prime suspects, and they are the ones you or your family are most likely to accuse.

Members of most cultures reason in much the same way. They believe that sorcerers do not strike randomly but harm only their enemies or the people toward whom they feel anger, envy, or ill will. Bad feelings are more likely to exist in certain kinds of relationships than in others, within a single society. Accusations of sorcery, therefore, usually follow the prevalent lines of conflict: because people who stand in the same kinds of relationships are likely to accuse one another again and again, sorcery accusations are patterned.

Witchcraft

Witchcraft is another explanation that people in many societies give for personal misfortune. There is no universally applicable distinction between sorcery and witchcraft. Whereas sorcery usually involves the use of rites and spells to commit a foul deed, here we define **witchcraft** as the use of psychic power alone to cause harm to others. Sorcerers manipulate objects; witches need only think malevolent thoughts to turn their anger, envy, or hatred into evil deeds. (The English language's main distinction between the two—witches are female, sorcerers usually male—is not useful cross-culturally.) Many cultures believe in the existence of both kinds of malevolent power, so sorcery and witchcraft are often found among the same people. Like sorcery accusations, accusations of witchcraft are likely to be patterned because people most often believe that both witches and sorcerers harm only people they dislike, hate, envy, or have a conflict with.

Cultures vary in the characteristics they attribute to witches and in how witches cause harm. The following examples illustrate the diversity.

• The Navajo of the American Southwest associate witches with the worst imaginable sins. Witches commit incest, bestiality (sex with animals), and necrophilia (sex with corpses); they change themselves into animals; they cannibalize infants; and so on.

- The Nyakyusa of Tanzania hold that witches are motivated mainly by their lust for food; accordingly, they suck dry the udders of people's cattle and devour the internal organs of their human neighbors while they sleep.
- The Azande of southern Sudan believe that witches possess an inherited substance that leaves their bodies at night and gradually eats away at the flesh and internal organs of their victims. Witches, as well as their victims, are considered unfortunate because the Azande believe that a person can be a witch without even knowing it. Witches can do nothing to rid themselves permanently of their power, although they can be forced to stop bewitching some particular individual by overcoming their bad feelings against their victim.
- The Ibibio of Nigeria believe that witches operate by removing the spiritual essence (soul) of their enemies and placing it in an animal. This makes the victim sick, and he dies when the witches slaughter and consume the animal. Sometimes Ibibio witches decide to torture, rather than kill, a person. In that case, they remove the victim's soul and put it in water or hang it over a fireplace or flog it in the evenings. The afflicted person will remain sick until the witches get what they want out of him or her.
- The Lugbara, a people of Uganda, claim that witches—who are always men—walk around at night disguised as rats or other nocturnal animals. Sometimes they defecate blood around the household of their victims, who wake up sick the next morning.

Such beliefs, it might appear to someone who does not share them, are logically outrageous; no one's soul leaves his or her body at night to cavort with other witches, for example. It might seem that these beliefs are socially harmful as well. Beliefs about witchcraft, fear of witchcraft, and accusations of witchcraft engender conflict and aggression among a people. Finally, the treatment that many suspected and "proven" witches receive offends our notions of social justice. As we know from the witch hunts of European and American history, the truly innocent victims of witchcraft are usually the accused witches, who sometimes are cruelly executed for crimes they could not have committed.

Interpretations of Sorcery and Witchcraft

Given their seemingly harmful effects and the injustices that frequently result from them, why are beliefs about and accusations of sorcery and witchcraft so widespread?

Why do so many of the world's peoples think that some or all of their misfortunes are caused by the supernatural powers of their enemies?

Many answers have been offered to such questions. In line with the overall theoretical approaches discussed earlier, the answers fall into two categories: cognitive and sociological. (In the following discussion, for simplicity, we use the term *witchcraft* to refer to both witchcraft and sorcery because the ideas presented have been applied to both kinds of beliefs.)

Cognitive interpretations. The most influential cognitive interpretation is that witchcraft explains unfortunate events. The argument is that most people find the idea of coincidence or accident intellectually unsatisfying when some misfortune happens to them or their loved ones, so they search for other causes. Their logic is something like this: I have enemies who wish me harm, and harm just came to me, so my enemies are responsible.

The classic example of how people account for misfortune by reference to the actions of witches comes from the Azande in Africa. The Azande attribute prolonged serious illnesses and many other personal misfortunes to witchcraft. Ethnographer E. E. Evans-Pritchard (1976, 18) describes their beliefs:

> Witchcraft is ubiquitous. . . . There is no niche or corner of Zande culture into which it does not twist itself. If blight seizes the groundnut crop it is witchcraft; if the bush is vainly scoured for game it is witchcraft; if women laboriously bail water out of a pool and are rewarded by but a few small fish it is witchcraft; . . . if a wife is sulky and unresponsive to her husband it is witchcraft; if a prince is cold and distant with his subject it is witchcraft; if a magical rite fails to achieve its purpose it is witchcraft; if, in fact, any failure or misfortune falls upon any one at any time and in relation to any of the manifold activities of his life it may be due to witchcraft.

This does not mean that the Azande are ignorant of cause and effect and therefore attribute every misfortune to some witch who is out to get them. When a man seeks shelter in a granary and its roof falls and injures him, he blames witchcraft. But the Azande know very well that granary roofs collapse because termites eat the wood that supports them. They do not attribute the collapse of granaries in general to witchcraft; it is the collapse of this particular granary at this particular time with this particular person inside that is caused by witchcraft. Don't granaries sometimes fall when no one is sitting inside them? And don't people often relax in granaries without the roof falling? It is the coincidence between the collapse and the presence of a particular person—a coincidence that many other peoples consider bad luck—that Azande witchcraft explains.

Another cognitive benefit is that witches serve as scapegoats. When things are going poorly, people do not always know why. Witchcraft provides an explanation. It also provides people with a means to do something about the situation: identify, accuse, and punish the witch responsible. If, as is often the case, things still do not improve, there are always other yet to-be-identified witches. People can blame many of their troubles on witches—evil enemies conspiring against them—rather than on their personal inadequacies or on bad luck.

Sociological interpretations. One sociological interpretation is that witchcraft reinforces the norms and values that help individuals live harmoniously with one another. Every culture has notions of how individuals ideally ought to act toward others. Witches typically are the antithesis of these cultural ideals. They act like animals or actually change themselves into animals. They mate with relatives. They often put on a false front, pretending to be your friend by day while they eat your liver by night. They have no respect for age or authority. They are in league with the forces of evil (in the Judeo-Christian tradition, witches made compacts with the Devil, agreeing to be his servant in return for worldly pleasures). All the most despicable personal characteristics of people are wrapped up in the personality of witches, whom everyone is supposed to hate. So, witches symbolize all that is undesirable, wicked, and hateful. Just as one should despise witches, so should one hate all that they stand for. In short, by providing a hated symbol of the abnormal and the antisocial, the witch strengthens cultural conceptions of normatively approved social behavior.

Another argument is that witches provide an outlet for repressed aggression, and thus beliefs about witches lower the overall amount of conflict in a society. Writing about the Navajo in 1944, Clyde Kluckhohn argued that Navajo culture emphasizes cooperation and good relationships between members of the same extended household. When bad feelings do develop within the household, Navajo culture encourages people to suppress them. But, pent-up hostilities have an outlet in the form of witches, whom people are allowed to hate and gossip about. Because most of the persons the Navajo believe to be witches are members of distant groups, usually little action is taken against them. Solidarity between relatives of the in-group is preserved by displacing hostility to people of the out-group.

Another sociological interpretation is that witchcraft beliefs serve as a mechanism of social control. This might work in two ways. First, many people believe in the existence of witchcraft but do not know which specific members of their community are witches. This leads individuals to be careful not to make anyone angry, since the offended party might be a witch. Second, individuals who fail to conform to local norms of behavior are most likely to be suspected and accused of being witches. People who are always mad at somebody, who carry grudges for prolonged periods, who always seem envious and resentful of the success of others, who have achieved wealth but selfishly refuse to share it in the culturally accepted manner—such violators of these and other normative standards frequently are believed to be the likely perpetrators of witchcraft. Fear of being accused and punished presumably increases adherence to the norms and ideals of behavior.

Most of our readers will deny that they believe in sorcery and witchcraft. Those who do believe probably have *wicca* (also called *paganism*) in mind, which obviously is different from the way we have used the terms to refer to supernatural powers employed for harmful, antisocial purposes. Of course, we could broaden the definitions of sorcery and witchcraft to include paganism by removing the "antisocial" elements. Then wicca becomes almost the same as *magic,* as anthropologists usually use the term. Or, we could change the definitions in another way. We could remove the part of the definition that refers to "supernatural powers." Then sorcery and witchcraft would include beliefs that unknown persons harm other persons or the members of some group using techniques that cannot be demonstrated or that are not entirely clear. In the United States, in the 1950s Senator Joseph McCarthy played on peoples' fears by claiming that the government and Hollywood were filled with Communists dedicated to overturning all that Americans hold dear. In the 1980s and 1990s, various supremacists blamed certain political factions and minorities for social problems and what they believed to be the degeneration of their nation's values. What does the twenty-first century have in store along these lines?

Varieties of Religious Organization

As we've seen in earlier chapters, to compare cultures ethnologists develop classifications based on differences and similarities. Of course, classifications are simplifications

Form	Major Characteristics
Individualistic cults	Individuals have a special relationship with one or more supernatural powers who serve as personal guardians and protectors.
Shamanistic cults	Shamans have power to contact supernatural beings to help (especially cure) individuals. Shamans may also act on behalf of their band or village to cause harm to enemies.
Communal cults	Members of a well-defined group gather periodically for collective rituals that benefit the group as a whole or some individual member. "Elders" often have special roles in rituals.
Ecclesiastical cults	Groups have full-time religious officials (priests) organized into a religious bureaucracy supported by tribute or redistribution. Priests officiate at calendrical rituals believed to benefit the society or political unit as a whole, making people dependent on priests and rituals for their spiritual and material welfare.

of the real world, and anthropological classifications are no exception. To be useful, classifications must be broad, but that broadness inevitably masks many details. In classifying diverse religions into a relatively few forms or types, we oversimplify and, to some degree, distort, as humanistic anthropologists remind us. Just as we oversimplify a given culture when we classify it as (for example) horticultural, polygynous, patrilineal, tribal, and egalitarian, so do we simplify when we pigeonhole its religion as (for example) shamanistic or monotheistic. Nonetheless, a classification of religion is useful because it gives a general picture of religious diversity among humanity.

In the 1960s, Anthony Wallace proposed a classification of religions that remains influential. In his typology, he used the word *cult*. As Wallace used the term, *cult* does not refer to some exotic, offbeat, and (usually) short-lived set of beliefs that grow up around a "cult leader." Rather, he used the term in a neutral way to refer to an organized system of beliefs and practices pertaining to the control or worship of specific supernatural powers. Thus, rituals intended to help sick people get well might be called *curing cults;* rituals believed to bring precipitation might be called *rain cults;* and so forth.

Unfortunately, the word *cult* has many negative connotations, so it is important to understand that we use it to refer to how people organize their ritual behaviors. The members of a given society can participate in many different kinds of cults, each with its own purposes. The total religion of a people includes many different kinds of cults devoted to different purposes, like curing illness, controlling weather, worshipping gods, foretelling the future, hunting animals, divining the future, renewing nature, protecting people from enemies, saving souls, and keeping ancestral spirits happy.

Wallace distinguished four kinds of cults:

1. **Individualistic cults.** Each individual has a personal relationship with one or more supernatural powers, who serve as the person's guardians and protectors. The aid of the powers is solicited when needed for personal goals.
2. **Shamanistic cults.** Some individuals—shamans—are believed to have relationships with the supernatural that ordinary people lack. They use these powers primarily for socially valuable purposes, to help (especially cure) others in need. They may also act on behalf of their band or village to cause supernatural harm to the group's enemies.
3. **Communal cults.** The members of a particular group gather periodically to perform rituals that they believe benefit the group as a whole, or some individual in it. There are no full-time religious specialists, as is also true of individualistic and shamanistic cults.
4. **Ecclesiastical cults.** The distinguishing characteristic of ecclesiastical cults is the presence of full-time religious practitioners who form a religious bureaucracy. The actual practice of religion is managed or carried out by formal, specialized officials—priests—who perform mainly calendrical rituals. The priesthood is usually materially supported by institutionalized governmental authorities through taxation or redistributive tribute (see Chapters 7 and 12).

The Concept Review summarizes these four forms of religious organization.

Although any given culture has more than one kind of cult, the varieties are not randomly distributed among the peoples of the world. Rather, they occur in a rough evolutionary sequence. For example, in many foraging bands and horticultural tribes—such as the Inuit, Ju/'hoansi, and Yanomamö—shamanistic cults are common, whereas ecclesiastical cults occur mainly in stratified chiefdoms and states. If we consider the religion of a people to be composed of some number of cults, then more kinds of cults are found in states than in tribes.

To be sure, the evolutionary matching of kinds of cults with kinds of economic and political organizations is rough and general. For instance, the aboriginal peoples of Australia had communal cults, although they were foragers and lived in bands. Many tribes of the North American Great Plains had individualistic, shamanistic, and communal cults, although they were primarily foragers.

Further frustrating our desire to "pigeonhole" religious diversity is the fact that many societies have several religions, sometimes at odds with one another. In the

Caribbean nation of Haiti, voudon (voodoo) persists even though the official hierarchy of the Catholic Church has tried to eliminate it for more than a century. Multiethnic nations, of course, have a variety of religions within their borders (see Chapter 17). Even nations that are linguistically and culturally homogeneous are religiously diverse. South Korea, for example, is a heavily industrialized, urbanized nation, most of whose 43 million people are Buddhists or Christians or express no religious affiliation. But many Buddhist or Christian Koreans today seek the services of shamans (who are usually women) to help with illness or difficulties in their personal lives. Many Japanese people have Christian-style weddings and Buddhist funerals, and they may honor their ancestors at Shinto shrines. Some North Americans pay spirit mediums ("channelers") large sums of money to put them in contact with deceased relatives, a practice that is comparable in many ways to shamanism.

These and other complications should not obscure the general pattern, however. The religions of hunter-gatherer

▲ Religious healing aids people in societies at all levels of complexity and development. This South Korean woman is leading a *kut,* a ritual that helps her clients with physical, psychological, and family problems.

bands differ generally and significantly from those of complex chiefdoms and states, as we now discuss. Because one major point is that religious beliefs, myths, and rituals are embedded in the context of a people's entire cultural system, we discuss how they relate to economic and political organization.

Individualistic Cults

The defining characteristic of individualistic cults is that individuals intentionally seek out particular spirits or other supernatural powers to protect and help them. The most well-known example of individualistic cults is the **vision quest.** It is widespread among Native American peoples but is especially important for the Great Plains tribes. To the Plains peoples, the world is charged with spiritual energy and supernatural power. Power exists in inanimate objects, such as rocks or mountains, and in living animals and plants. Humans require the aid of the supernatural in many activities—in hunting, warfare, and times of sickness or other troubles.

Spiritual power most often comes to individuals in visions. These visions play an important role in religious life because it is through them that people achieve the personal contact with the supernatural that is essential in various endeavors. Spiritual powers occasionally make contact with individuals for no apparent reason, coming to them as they sleep or even as they are walking or riding alone.

More often, humans—especially young men—have to seek out these powers through an active search, or quest, whose purpose is to acquire a vision. There are places that supernatural powers are believed to frequent: certain hills, mountains, or bluffs. A young man goes to such a location alone. There he smokes and fasts, appealing to a power to take pity on him. Among one tribe, the Crow, sometimes a man will even amputate part of a finger or cut his body to arouse pity. The vision commonly appears on the fourth day because four is a sacred number to the Crow.

The way the power manifests itself varies. Sometimes the man hears the spirit speak to him. Sometimes the spirit comes in the form of a dreamlike story. In other instances, it simply materializes before his eyes, taking the form of a bear, bison, eagle, or some other large animal. Sometimes small animals like rabbits, field mice, and dogs also appear. The power tells the man how it will help him. It might give him the ability to predict the future, locate enemies, find game, become a powerful warrior, or cure illness. It tells him the things he will have to do to keep his power—what songs to sing, how to paint his war shield, how to wear his hair, and so forth. It also tells the man some things he cannot do; for example, if the power comes from an eagle, the man might be prohibited from killing "his brother," the eagle. As long as the man continues to behave in the prescribed manner, the power will be his supernatural protector, or *guardian spirit.* Through the spirit, the man acquires special powers other men do not have.

There is no known culture in which individualistic cults make up the entire religion. Even among the Plains Indians, among whom the vision quest is unusually well developed, shamanistic and communal cults also exist.

Shamanism

A **shaman** is a person who is believed to have a special relationship to supernatural powers, which he frequently uses to cure sickness. In many societies (especially among foraging peoples), the shaman is the only kind of religious practitioner; that is, he possesses the only kinds of abilities not available to ordinary people. Usually, shamans are not full-time specialists in curing. Rather, they carry out their tasks whenever their services are needed, usually in return for a gift or fee. Otherwise, they live much like everyone else.

Shamans are believed to possess several qualities. They have access to the power of spiritual beings, usually called *spirit helpers.* The effectiveness of a shaman in curing (or causing harm) is believed to derive from the potency of his spirit helpers and from his ability to contact them and get them to do his bidding. A shaman commonly makes contact with spirit helpers by achieving an altered state of consciousness. He reaches this altered state (referred to as a *trance*) in various ways: through the intake of drugs, ritual chanting, or participation in percussive or rhythmic music. The Tungus, the northeast Asian people from whom English acquired the word *shaman,* use tambourines and drums to achieve the trance in which they journey to the spirit world to discover the cause of illness.

Among peoples who practice shamanism, a trance is interpreted as a sign that some spirit, often one of a shaman's spirit helpers, has physically entered (possessed) the shaman's body. The spirit takes over his body and speaks to the assembled audience through his mouth. When possessed, the shaman becomes a *medium,* or mouthpiece, for the spirits—he may lose control over his actions and his voice may change its quality because a spirit is speaking through him. The unusual behavior and strange voice are seen as evidence of genuine possession, which is a sign of a shaman's power.

▲ Healing physical and psychological ailments is a main function of shamanistic religions. These people are Jamaicans.

The way a person becomes a shaman varies from people to people because the details of the role are defined by local cultures. Many scholars argue that shamans are individuals who are unusual in some way: they hear voices, parts of their bodies tremble uncontrollably, they dress or act in strange ways, and so forth. Other members of their community interpret their "difference" as a sign that they have been chosen by a spirit to become a healer. Other observers report that shamans are normal people who act like everyone else when not in the role of shaman. Ju/'hoansi healers use dance and percussion to achieve the trance state that makes them powerful and able to diagnose and cure illness. When not in the role of healer, however, they are indistinguishable from other people. Obviously, whether shamans are believed to be "different" from other people varies cross-culturally.

Shamans are usually considered to have knowledge and powers that others lack. They acquire these in three major ways. In some societies, they undergo a period of special training as an apprentice to a practicing shaman, who teaches the novice chants and songs and how to achieve the trance state. Among other peoples, shamans must endure difficult deprivations, such as prolonged fasting, the consumption of foods culturally considered disgusting, or years of sexual abstinence. Finally, in many societies, shamans are individuals who have experienced some unusual event. For example, they may have miraculously recovered from a serious illness or injury, or they claim to have had an unusual dream or vision in which some spirit called them to be its mouthpiece.

In some cultures, shamans, as healing experts, work alone during the actual cures, although many other people may be physically present. Sometimes, though, shamans have helpers in the curing tasks. Among the Navajo of the American Southwest, shamans (also called "singers") have assistants who fetch objects, help construct the elaborate sandpaintings used in curing, supply food and drink for all-night cures, and perform other duties. Navajo singers need the help: in olden times, some of the curing ceremonials lasted nine nights.

Shamanistic cults can be complexly organized. Among the Zuni, who now live on a reservation in western New Mexico, 12 special groups of people (sometimes translated into English as "medicine societies") were recognized as knowledgeable about curing. Different medicine societies knew the secret techniques for curing various illnesses. If a Zuni became ill with specific symptoms, he or she would go to the appropriate society to be healed. Once healed, the person had learned the secrets of the society and so was usually then initiated into it.

Communal Cults

Like shamanism, communal cults have no full-time religious specialists who make their living as practitioners. Communally organized rituals do have leaders—often an elderly person or someone with a special interest in the results of a ritual—who manipulate the symbolic objects or address the supernatural.

Communal rituals are held to intercede with the supernatural on behalf of some group of people, such as a kin group, an age group, a village, or a caste. To illustrate, we consider two widespread kinds of communal rituals organized by descent groups: ancestral cults and totemism.

Ancestral cults. Almost all worldviews hold that people have a spiritual dimension—a *soul*—that lives on after the physical body has perished. Beliefs about the fate of the soul after death vary widely. Some peoples—such as Hindus and Buddhists—believe that the soul is reincarnated into another person or animal. Others hold that the soul passes into a spiritual plane, where it exists eternally with a community of other souls and has no further effects on the living. Still others believe that souls become malevolent after death, turning into ghosts that cause accidents or sickness or that terrify the living.

Another common belief about the fate of souls after death is that they interact with and affect the living, especially their descendants. The many peoples who hold such beliefs use rituals to induce the spirits of their deceased ancestors to do favors for them or simply to leave them alone. Beliefs and rituals surrounding the interactions between the living and their departed relatives are called **ancestral cults,** or *ancestor worship.*

The Lugbara of Uganda provide an example of ancestral cults. The patrilineage is an important social group to the Lugbara. As the most important members of the lineage, lineage elders oversee the interests and harmony of the entire group. They serve as the guardians of the lineage's morality, although they have no power to punish violations physically. The Lugbara believe that the spirit of a deceased person may become an ancestral ghost of her or his lineage. The ghost punishes living descendants who violate Lugbara ideals of behavior toward lineage-mates. People who fight with their kinsmen (especially their older relatives), who deceive or steal from their lineagemates, or who fail to carry out their duties toward others are liable to be punished by an ancestral ghost. Sometimes this happens because a ghost sees an offense committed and makes the offender ill. More commonly, the ghosts do not act on their own initiative to make someone sick. Rather, the ghosts act on the thoughts of an elder who is indignant because of the actions of some lineagemate. John Middleton (1965, 76) describes Lugbara beliefs about the power of lineage elders to cause illness by invoking ghosts:

> [The elder] sits near his shrines in his compound and thinks about the sinner's behavior. His thoughts are known by the ghosts and they then send sickness to the offender. He "thinks these words in his heart"; he does not threaten or curse the offender. For a senior man to do this is part of his expected role. It is part of his "work," to "cleanse the lineage home." Indeed, an elder who does not do so when justified would be lacking in sense of duty toward his lineage.

In the Lugbara example, we see how elders maintain harmony and cooperation in the lineage by invoking the power of deceased members. This is a common feature of ancestral cults.

Matrilineal peoples often have ancestral cults as well. The Ndembu of Zambia provide an example. When a woman experiences fertility problems, people often say that she is forgetting her ancestress or doing something disapproved by an ancestress. The cure consists of a lengthy ritual in which many members of the matrilineage make the victim "remember" her relative.

Why do some societies have ancestral cults, in which the spirits of deceased ancestors are concerned with the affairs and behaviors of their descendants? Like other "why" questions, this one is controversial. Many anthropologists agree, however, that such beliefs are related to the degree of importance of large kin groups in a society. The greater the importance of kin groups such as lineages and clans in making public decisions, regulating access to resources, allocating roles, controlling behavior, and so on, the more likely a society is to develop an ancestral cult. Someone who follows the sociological interpretation might argue that ancestral cults provide a religious mechanism by which behavior can be channeled and controlled.

Totemism. Another widespread form of communal cult is **totemism,** the cultural belief that human groups have a special mystical relationship with natural objects, such as animals, plants, and, sometimes, nonliving things. The object (or objects) with which a group is associated is known as its *totem.* The group most often is a unilineal kin group, such as a clan. The totem frequently serves as a name of the group—for example, the bear clan, the eagle clan, the sun clan.

The nature of the relationship between the members of the group and its totem varies widely. Sometimes the totem is used simply to identify the group and its members, much like our surnames. Often there is a mystical association between the group and its totem object. People believe they are like their totem in some respects. Or, the totem may be used as a symbol of differences between clans. In many populations—most notably some of the aboriginal peoples of Australia—the members of a clan treat their totem like a clanmate, believing that the totem gave birth to their ancestors in a mythical period. The welfare of the clan is mystically associated with the welfare of the totem, so periodically the clan gathers for rituals that ensure the reproduction of its totem.

Ecclesiastical Cults

In Chapters 6 and 12, we discussed how a high degree of specialization accompanied the development of civilization. Among New World peoples, such as the ancient

Incas, Aztecs, and Mayans, and in the Old World cities of ancient Mesopotamia, Egypt, East Asia, and India, this specialization extended into the religious dimension of cultural systems. Rather than organizing rituals on a communal basis—in which a wide range of people controlled and participated in the performance—a formal bureaucracy of religious specialists controlled many public rituals. The religious bureaucracy probably also had a large voice in formulating the religious laws, which prescribed certain kinds of punishments for those who violated them.

These religious specialists are known as **priests.** It is instructive to compare priests with shamans. In addition to their more specialized status, priests differ from shamans in several respects. First, except for some people like the Zuni, shamans are not organized as a group and cooperation between them is minimal. Indeed, many peoples believe that enemy shamans engage in supernatural battles with one another, with the stronger shaman winning the battle, which leads to the recovery or death of the sick person. In contrast, priests are hierarchically organized and usually subsidized and supported by a formal government, either by the high-ranking chiefs of a large chiefdom or by the state (see Chapter 12). Second, priests undergo a lengthy period of formal training because they must master the complex rituals needed to perform their role. Third, the priests were at or near the top of the social ladder in ancient civilizations, so individual priests lived much better than the population at large. Fourth, shamans typically perform mainly crisis rituals, whenever some person requires their services. The rituals at which priests officiate tend to be calendrical—they occur at regular intervals because the gods that the rituals are intended to appease demand regular praise or sacrifice.

A final difference is especially revealing. With the development of a *priesthood* comes a strong distinction between priest and layperson. The layperson has little control over the timing of religious performances or the content of myths. The population at large relies on the priesthood to keep it in the proper relationship to supernatural powers. This creates a sense of spiritual dependence on the priesthood and on the state apparatus that so often sponsors it, a dependence that reinforces the high degree of stratification found in states.

These state-sponsored cults are called *ecclesiastical* (meaning "of or pertaining to the church") because their priesthood was highly organized and their rituals were usually held in grand buildings that served as temples. The entire ecclesiastical cult was under the control of the government. Officials exacted tribute or taxes to finance the construction of temples, the livelihood of the priesthood, the sacrifices that often accompanied state rituals, and other expenses needed to support and organize religious activities on a fantastically large scale.

There is little question that ecclesiastical cults provided a body of myth and belief that supported the domination of the ruling family or dynasty. (See Chapter 13 for more on ideologies that support the powers and privileges of elite classes.) The content of the cults' beliefs, myths, and rituals almost invariably expressed the dependence of the entire population on the ruler's well-being and on the periodic performance of rituals. A common belief of official state religions is that the ruler is a god-king: He not only rules by divine mandate but is himself a god or somehow has divine qualities. This was true of most of the ancient civilizations and of the states that developed in sub-Saharan Africa. The complex chiefdoms of Polynesia and the Americas had comparable ideas (see Chapter 12).

Many official rituals of ecclesiastical cults are held to keep the entire polity in a beneficial relationship with supernatural beings. For example, the state religion of the ancient Aztecs held that the gods had to be periodically appeased or they would cause the world to end in a cataclysm. To keep the gods' goodwill, the priesthood periodically performed human sacrifice at temples, offering the heart of the victim (usually a war captive) to the deities. The ancient Egyptians believed that their pharaoh would rule in the afterlife—just as in the present world—so when he died, he took much of his wealth, his wives, and his servants into the next world with him. The emperors of Japan were believed to be descended through males from a sun goddess; in later Japanese history, the emperors were so set apart from the mundane world that political affairs were handled by the shogun, who ruled in the name of the emperor. The emperor of old China—who was at various times in the more than two-millenia history of Chinese civilization the most powerful man on the planet—ruled so long as he had the mandate of heaven.

Ecclesiastical cults everywhere consumed enormous resources, but they did not necessarily wipe out other kinds of cults. Common people usually continued to rely on local shamans to cure them, to practice magic, to believe in witches and sorcerers, and to worship their ancestors. In ancient China, Korea, and Japan, for example, each household and lineage continued to revere its own ancestors through communal rituals and to make offerings to them at family shrines.

In medieval Europe, Catholicism was ecclesiastical: the authority of the Church was tightly interwoven with

▲ Ecclesiastical cults feature grandiose temples, awe-inspiring physical symbols, and specialized priests to mediate between laypersons and gods. This Catholic mass is being performed at the Vatican.

the exercise of secular power, although there often was conflict between popes and various kings. Only in the past few centuries has the formal alliance between the power of government and the will of the gods been broken for any length of time. We should not assume that even this official separation between church and state will necessarily be permanent. As the recent history of Iran and Afghanistan suggests, the intermingling of political and ecclesiastical authorities can be reborn in the modern world—perhaps even in democratic nations.

Revitalization Movements

So far in this chapter we have discussed religion in cultures that are changing only slowly. Under conditions of rapid change, many peoples have turned to supernatural beings for aid and protection when their way of life or their very survival is threatened by contact with pow-

erful outsiders. To preserve their way of life or to cope with changing conditions, large numbers of people join organized movements, usually called **revitalization movements.**

Revitalization movements are most likely to occur in a society when three conditions coalesce: (1) rapid change, usually caused by exposure to unfamiliar people, customs, and objects; (2) foreign domination, which leads to a sense of cultural or even racial inferiority; and (3) the perception of relative deprivation, meaning that people think they lack wealth, power, and esteem relative to those who dominate them. Historically, revitalization movements were especially common during colonialism, in which a foreign power subjugated an indigenous people. Colonialism did not always lead to revitalization movements, however.

Revitalization movements usually originate with an individual (a *prophet*) who claims to have had a dream or vision. Sometimes the prophet claims to be a savior (a *messiah*) sent by a spiritual being to save the world from destruction. In the dream or vision, the prophet received a message (a *revelation*) from a god, an ancestor, or another spiritual power.

Revelations typically include two kinds of information given by the spirit or spirits. The first is a statement about what is wrong with the present-day world, about why people's lives have changed for the worse. Prophets and their followers commonly blame the introduction of corrupting foreign objects and habits—such as tobacco, alcohol, money, new religions, formal schooling, the relaxation of old moral standards—for the troubles of today.

Second, prophets' revelations usually include a vision of a new world and a prescription for how to bring it about. In some cases, the message is vague and secular, with the prophet claiming that earthly lives will improve if people do (or stop doing) certain things. However, the message is often *apocalyptic:* the prophet says that the present world will end at a certain time, and only those who heed his message will be saved. The expulsion or death of foreigners is a frequent theme of apocalyptic visions: foreigners will be drowned in a flood, burned in a fire, swallowed up by an earthquake, or killed by deities or ancestors. Another common theme is the reversal of existing political and economic dominance relations: foreigners will work for us, we will have the wealth instead of them, we will tax them and make laws that they must obey. Nearly always, the prophets' revelations are *syncretic;* that is, they combine elements of traditional myths, beliefs, and rituals with introduced elements.

The following examples from two regions illustrate revitalization movements.

Melanesian Cargo Cults

The area called Melanesia in the southwest Pacific experienced numerous revitalization movements in the early to mid-twentieth century. Melanesians placed great cultural emphasis on wealth and its distribution as the means to become a big man or powerful leader. It is therefore not surprising that they were most interested in the material possessions of German, English, French, and Australian colonial powers. Because European wealth was brought to the islands by ship or plane, it became known as *cargo,* and the various movements that sprang up with the aim of acquiring it through ritual means became known as **cargo cults.**

To Melanesians, all Europeans were fantastically wealthy; yet the Melanesians seldom saw them do any work to earn their possessions. The whites who lived in the islands certainly did not know how to make cars, canned foods, radios, kerosene lanterns, stoves, and so forth. In many traditional Melanesian religions, technology was believed to have been made by deities or spirits, so it followed that European objects were made by their God. Further, when the whites who lived in Melanesia wanted some new object, they simply made marks on papers and placed them in an envelope or asked for the object by speaking into metal things. Some weeks later, the object was delivered in ships or airplanes. Surely, the goods were made by spirits, and the acts the whites did to get their spirits to send cargo were rituals. Melanesians therefore believed that they, too, could acquire this wealth through the correct ritual procedure, which they frequently believed the whites were selfishly withholding from them.

Numerous prophets sprang up among diverse Melanesian peoples, each with his own vision or dream, each with his own story to explain why the Europeans had cargo and the Melanesians had none, and each claiming to know the secret ritual that would deliver the goods. The prophet often claimed to have received a visit from one of his ancestors or a native deity, who told him that the whites had been lying to people about how to get cargo.

The Garia, of the north coast of Papua New Guinea, illustrate some common themes of cargo cults. Like most other indigenous peoples, the Garia were visited by missionaries. Also, like many other peoples, the Garia initially adopted Christianity for reasons other than those the missionaries had in mind. They assumed that the whites knew the ritual that was the "road to cargo." The missionaries would give it to the Garia if only they practiced what the missionaries preached: church attendance, monogamy, worship of the true God, and cessation of pagan practices such as sorcery and dancing. Based on their belief that the missionary lifestyle and Christian rituals held the secret of cargo, many Garia converted to Christianity early in the twentieth century.

But the cargo did not arrive. The Garia grew angry as they concluded that the missionaries and other Europeans were withholding the true ritual secret of how to get cargo to keep all the wealth for themselves. In the 1930s and 1940s, two Garia prophets arose. They told the people that the missionaries had been telling them to worship the wrong gods. God and Jesus were both really deities of the Garia, not of whites. The Europeans knew the secret names of God and Jesus and asked them for the cargo with secret prayers. All along, Jesus had been trying to deliver the goods to the Garia, but the Jews were holding him captive in heaven. To free him, the Garia had to perform sacrificial rituals. To show him how poor they were and to make him feel sorry for them, they had to destroy all their native wealth objects. If they did these things, Jesus would give the cargo to the ancestral spirits of the Garia, who would in turn deliver it to the living.

Native American Movements

Revitalization movements also occurred among American Indians, whose sufferings at the hands of white traders, settlers, armies, and administrators are well known to all Americans. Two movements were especially important, both of which were precipitated by a deterioration of tribal economic, social, and religious life.

Handsome Lake. In the 1600s and 1700s, the Seneca of New York were one of the members of the League of the Iroquois, a loose confederation of different tribes who agreed to live in peace and come to one another's aid in case of attack by surrounding tribes. Like other members, the Seneca traditionally were matrilineal horticulturalists. Men hunted, traded for furs, and went on raids against neighboring tribes, while women owned most of the farmland and did most of the planting and harvesting of corn and other crops.

By 1800, the Seneca had lost most of their land to the new state of New York, Anglo settlers, and land speculators. Whites committed many atrocities against the Seneca in the 1780s and 1790s, partly because most Seneca supported the British during the American Revolutionary War. Devastating diseases—such as smallpox and measles, which wiped out millions of Native Americans all over the continent—reduced the tribe to a fraction of its former numbers. Seneca men had been proud warriors, hunters, and fur traders, but all these activities became more difficult because of the loss of land and the presence of whites. The American government waged psychological warfare against them, intentionally corrupting their leaders with bribes and liquor and generally attempting to dehumanize and demoralize them.

Seneca men turned to alcohol and drank up most of what little money they could still earn from the fur trade. Neighboring peoples, who once feared the Seneca and other members of the League of the Iroquois, ridiculed them. Witchcraft accusations increased the internal conflict and divisions within their communities. Many women lost their desire for children and took medicines that caused them to abort or become sterile altogether. A way of life—and perhaps an entire people— was dying.

In 1799, a Seneca man named Handsome Lake lay sick. Three angels cured him and gave him a message from the Creator. Handsome Lake reported that the Creator was saddened by the life of the people and angry because of their drunkenness, witchcraft, and use of abortion medicines. The Seneca must repent such deeds. Handsome Lake had two more visions during the next year. There would be an apocalypse in which the world would be destroyed by great drops of fire, consuming those who did not heed Handsome Lake's teachings. People could save themselves and delay the apocalypse by publicly confessing their wrongs, giving up sins such as witchcraft and drinking, and performing certain traditional rituals.

The apocalypse did not occur, but Handsome Lake was able to give his teachings a new, more secular twist between 1803 and his death in 1815. He continued to preach temperance because, he said, the Creator had never intended whiskey to be used by Indians. He encouraged peaceful relations with both whites and other Indians. He urged that the scattered reservations of the Seneca be consolidated, so that the people could live together as one community. Family morality must be impeccable: sons were to obey their fathers, divorce (commonplace among the matrilineal Seneca in aboriginal times) was no longer to be allowed, and adultery and domestic quarreling were to cease. Most important, Handsome Lake succeeded in changing the traditional division of labor, in which women cultivated the crops and men who worked in the garden were considered effeminate. Seneca men took up farming and animal husbandry and even fenced their fields and added new crops to their inventory.

Peyote religion. Peyote is a small cactus that grows in the Rio Grande valley of Texas and northern Mexico. When eaten, it produces a mild narcotic effect. The ritual use of peyote among northwestern Mexican Indians predated European conquest. However, its consumption as the central element in a revitalization movement dates only from the last two decades of the nineteenth century.

In 1875, two southern Plains tribes, the Kiowa and Comanche, lost their land after they were defeated militarily. During their confinement to reservations in southwestern Oklahoma, the Lipan-Apache introduced them to peyote. By the 1880s, the two tribes had made consumption of the cactus at religious services the central ritual of a revitalization movement. Peyotism was syncretic, adopting many elements of Christian theology and worship along with the consumption of peyote as a sacrament. Like many movements, peyotism subsequently spread, reaching about 19 Indian groups in Oklahoma by 1899. During the early twentieth century, the church spread rapidly to other Indian communities throughout the western United States and Canada.

The peyote movement had no single prophet or leader. Local churches developed their own versions of services and rituals. One early leader was John Wilson, a Caddo/Delaware from western Oklahoma who had learned to ingest peyote from the Comanche. While eating dinner in the early 1890s, Wilson collapsed. Thinking him dead, his family began preparations for the burial. But Enoch Parker, a Caddo, told the family that he had learned in a vision that Wilson was not dead. Indeed, Wilson revived three days later. He reported that a great Water Bird had sucked the breath and sin out of his body, causing his collapse. Jesus brought him back to life three days later, telling him that his sins had been removed and that he was to teach the Indian people to believe in God and to use peyote to communicate with him.

Until his death in 1901, Wilson proselytized the peyote religion among the Osage, Delaware, Quapaw, and other groups. He preached that they needed to believe in God and Jesus, work hard, act morally, and stop drinking alcohol. They were to abandon their traditional religious practices because the spirits that formerly had aided them could be used for evil as well as good purposes. Wilson attracted a large number of adherents among the Osage, who combined the use of peyote in worship services with the Christian teachings they had learned in mission schools.

Peyote provided meaning and moral direction to tribal life during a period of rapid and harmful change. The peyote religion exists today on many reservations, especially in the central and western United States. It was legally incorporated as an official church—now known as the Native American Church—in 1918. Those who follow the Peyote Road eat pieces of the cactus during services, treating it as a deeply meaningful sacrament. Many members of the Native American Church say that the Creator intended peyote to be used by Indians. Periodically, the governments of some states have tried to outlaw the use of peyote because it is a legally banned substance defined by the wider society as a "dangerous drug." So far, the courts have upheld the right of church members to consume peyote as a part of their religious sacraments.

What is the fate of revitalization movements? Many with apocalyptic messages simply disappear when the end of the world does not occur. Other movements have been remarkably tenacious. In Melanesia, certain areas saw the rise and fall of numerous prophets, each claiming to have the cargo secret. People followed again and again because they had no other acceptable explanation for cargo, for why whites had it and they lacked it, or for how they could acquire it. Certainly, their own worldly efforts—working for Europeans in mines and plantations, growing and selling coffee, copra, cocoa, and so

▶ Members of the John Frum cargo cult in Tanna, Vanuatu, perform a ritual march. They await the return of their messiah, John Frum, who will bring them wealth and a new life. This movement, which has also become a political party, has existed on the island of Tanna since the 1940s.

© Lamont Lindstrom

Most modern nations have *religious pluralism,* meaning that followers of many different religions live inside their boundaries. For centuries, India has included Hindus, Muslims, Sikhs, Christians, and Jains among its population. Since 1949, China has been officially atheistic according to its ruling Communist party. Most think that traditional China was Confucian, Daoist, and Buddhist, but in fact for a thousand years it has had millions of Muslims concentrated in its western provinces. Today, about 20 million Chinese are Muslims (less than 2 percent of its population). Most countries in sub-Saharan Africa are religiously plural, partly because of the way colonial powers established their boundaries and partly because of the spread of Islam and, later, Christianity across the continent. Brazil and several other Latin American countries still have hundreds of thousands of indigenous people living in rain forests, not all of whom are converted to Christianity. In these places, religious pluralism is centuries old.

In recent decades, religious pluralism has increased because of global migration patterns. The United States remains predominantly (75–80 percent) Christian, although there are large differences in doctrines and lifestyles between denominations such as Episcopalians and Southern Baptists. Today, however, students from around the world acquire visas to study in American and Canadian universities. Employers are looking for people who have high-tech professional job skills, for which American labor is either insufficient or overpaid, depending on whether you believe labor or management. Except for the Jewish faith (6 million, or about 2 percent), it is difficult to know the numbers of non-Christian religions represented in the United States. According to the 2007 *World Almanac and Book of Facts,* the United States has 4.7 million Muslims (most of them native-born Americans), 2.7 million Buddhists, 1.1 million Hindus, and 1 million Baha'is. We also have the indigenous religions of Native Americans.

The contemporary United States faces many issues about religious pluralism. One is how the nation should accommodate religious diversity. As a recent example, in 2007, the issue of accommodation arose in an American university. About 10 percent of the students at the University of Michigan, Dearborn, are Muslims. Muslims should pray five times a day and, as part of their preparation, they should wash their feet. To accommodate the students, the university installed foot-washing stations in some restrooms. Other students objected to what they claimed was special treatment for members of one religious faith. An outside organization, Americans United for Separation of Church and State, got involved because a public university built a facility to accommodate the followers of a particular religious doctrine, which they held to be a violation of the U.S. Constitution. Supporters of the footbaths responded by saying that the footbaths could also be used by other students, such as athletes, and that many of the university's holidays and the calendar itself accommodate the beliefs of Christians.

Similar issues have arisen in other contexts in universities, including problems about whether cafeterias should be required to prepare special foods for Hindus and whether exams should be rescheduled for a particular religious holiday for a religious minority. Some issues have been around for a long time, but their relevance is magnified by religious pluralism. Should Christian prayers be offered at meetings of city councils? Should Christian crèches be displayed on public properties? In the name of equal time, should intelligent design be taught as an alternative to evolution in the classrooms of public schools? (If the answer is yes, then should public schools also include the intelligent design theories of Native Americans such as Navajos and Zunis, of Hindus, and of numerous other religions?)

Increased religious diversity scares some Americans, including even many of those who do not view themselves as religious persons. For now, the U.S. government is more interested in restricting immigrants from Mexico and other Latin American countries than they are in reducing immigration from places like India. Until recently, the religious affiliation of immigrants has not been much of an issue in whether their numbers should be controlled. It is worth recalling, however, that the Catholicism of Irish and Italian immigrants was an issue when large numbers of those immigrants arrived. Today hardly anyone publicly questions the concept of religious freedom as a basic American value, but does this abstract value mean, practically speaking, that followers of any religion should be allowed to immigrate?

Critical Thinking Questions

1. How far should a nation go in accommodating religious pluralism? Where are the limits?

2. Should religious affiliation be an important criterion for denying or accepting admission into a country?

Sources: World Almanac and Book of Facts 2007, pp. 711–712; Lewin, "Muslims' Footbaths Set Off Debate," *Columbus Dispatch* (August 12, 2007, p. G2)

forth—did not reward them with the fantastic wealth that whites enjoyed with virtually no effort. In some regions, cargo cults became political movements or parties. This was the fate of cargo cults among the Garia, Manus, Tannese, and some Malaitans.

Other movements do not wither away or transform into a more secular, political movement. They retain their religious character, frequently teaching that contentment is to be found within oneself rather than in worldly material things. After his death in 1815, Handsome Lake's exhortations on how to live became codified and still persist as a church—the Old Way of Handsome Lake, also known as the Longhouse religion. Peyotism also became formally organized. Like many other revitalization movements that give birth to new religions, the adherents of peyotism are thus far largely confined to a single ethnic category: Native Americans.

Still other movements grow over the centuries. From humble beginnings, they eventually attract millions of believers. They develop a formal organization, and the religious specialists called priests replace the prophets. The ancient prophets and disciples are seen as the founders of the religion, their lives take on mythical proportions, and their revelations become texts that are considered sacred by believers. Followers become organized into a institutionalized church, which formalizes and codifies the texts so that they become official doctrines. The teachings and rituals cross national and ethnic boundaries. Beliefs and rituals go from being "local" to becoming "national" and sometimes "international." Most of the major religions of the modern world began as revitalization movements, including Judaism, Christianity, Islam, and Buddhism. These religions are sometimes called *world religions* because they have spread outside their original homelands. Today, more and more people are becoming familiar with world religions, not just through books and TV documentaries, but also through firsthand experience. Globalization brings old religions to new places, raising issues of how to accommodate religious pluralism (see the Globalization box).

Summary

1. Defining religion is difficult, but broadly, religion includes three components: beliefs about the nature of supernatural powers, myths about the historical actions of such powers and culture heroes, and symbolic rituals intended to influence them. These components affect wordview and, hence, behavior in the secular world.

2. Religion is a cultural universal despite the facts that beliefs and myths can never be shown to be true or false and that most rituals do not achieve the results people have in mind when they perform them. Most theories of religion fall into three basic categories: intellectual/ cognitive, psychological, and sociological. Among one or another people, religion is probably helpful in all these ways. Not only is each theory incomplete, but for each there are many instances in which religion actually has opposite effects to the theory's principles. It is likely that no single theory can explain religion itself or the great diversity of human religions.

3. Most religions include a belief that supernatural beings or forces cause or influence group or personal misfortune, such as deaths, illnesses, and "accidents." The malevolent powers of sorcerers and witches are blamed for misfortune in a great many societies. Accusations of sorcery and witchcraft tend to be patterned and to reflect prevalent conflicts and tensions in the organization of society. Although beliefs in sorcery and witchcraft might seem to be harmful, anthropologists have argued that they have useful functions.

4. Religions may be classified according to the types of "cults" they include, although any such classification is inadequate to depict the diversity of the world's religions. Cults may be characterized as individualistic, shamanistic, communal, and ecclesiastical. In a generalized way, there is an evolutionary sequence to cults, in that they tend to be associated with different degrees of cultural complexity. Ecclesiastical forms are regularly found in complex chiefdoms and states, where they legitimize and rationalize the powers and privileges of ruling families and elite classes.

5. Revitalization movements aim to create a new way of life to replace current conditions that are intolerable. Most movements originate with prophets who claim to

have received a revelation, which usually is syncretic and often apocalyptic. Twentieth-century Melanesian cargo cults are among the best-studied movements. The Handsome Lake religion among the Seneca of New York and the peyote religion are two of the many North American revitalization movements. Most revitalization movements disappear, but some are transformed and develop into formal churches that evolve into world religions if they eventually attract tens of millions of members.

Key Terms

animism
myths
ritual
intellectual (or cognitive)
   approach
psychological approach
sociological approach

sorcery
witchcraft
individualistic cults
shamanistic cults
communal cults
ecclesiastical cults
vision quest

shaman
ancestral cults
totemism
priests
revitalization movement
cargo cults

Suggested Readings

Four recent textbooks provide basic introductions to the anthropological study of religion:

Bowen, John R. *Religions in Practice*. 2nd ed. Boston: Allyn & Bacon, 2002.

Bowie, Fiona. *The Anthropology of Religion: An Introduction*. Oxford: Blackwell Publishers, 2000.

Crapo, Richley. *Anthropology of Religion: The Unity and Diversity of Religions*. Boston: McGraw-Hill, 2003.

Stein, Rebecca L., and Philip L. Stein. *The Anthropology of Religion, Magic, and Witchcraft*. Boston: Pearson, 2005.

Two recent readers are written for undergraduates:

Hicks, David, ed. *Religion and Belief: Readings in the Anthropology of Religion*. 2nd ed. New York: McGraw-Hill, 2002.

Lehman, Arthur C., James E. Myers, and Pamela A. Moro, eds. *Magic, Witchcraft, and Religion*. 6th ed. Boston: McGraw-Hill, 2005.

The following ethnographies about religion and witchcraft are accessible:

Boyer, Dave, and Stephen Nissenbaum. *Salem Possessed*. Cambridge, Mass.: Harvard University Press, 1974.

Evans-Pritchard, E. E. *Witchcraft, Oracles, and Magic Among the Azande*. Oxford: Oxford University Press, 1937.

Keesing, Roger. *Kwaio Religion*. New York: Columbia University Press, 1982.

Kraybill, Donald B. *The Riddle of Amish Culture*. Rev. ed. Baltimore, Md.: Johns Hopkins University Press, 2001.

Stoller, Paul, and Cheryl Olkes. *In Sorcery's Shadow: A Memoir of Apprenticeship Among the Songhay of Niger*. Chicago: University of Chicago Press, 1987.

These are some of the better-known books dealing with movements:

Anderson, Edward F. *Peyote: The Divine Cactus*. 2nd ed. Tucson: University of Arizona, 1996.

An excellent description of peyote and its religious uses among Native Americans.

Stewart, Omer. *Peyote Religion*. Norman: University of Oklahoma Press, 1987.

A detailed study of the peyote religion, with a historical focus.

Wallace, Anthony F. C. *The Death and Rebirth of the Seneca*. New York: Vintage, 1969.

An account of Handsome Lake, the revitalization movement that first appeared among the Seneca of New York State in the early 1800s.

Media Resources

The Wadsworth Anthropology Resource Center
academic.cengage.com/anthropology

The Wadsworth discipline resource website that accompanies *Humanity: An Introduction to Cultural Anthropology,* Eighth Edition, includes a rich array of material, including online anthropological video clips, to help you in the study of cultural anthropology and the specific topics covered in this chapter. Other material includes a case study forum with excerpts from various Wadsworth authors, map exercises, scientist interviews, breaking news in anthropology, and links to additional useful online material. Begin by selecting Cultural Anthropology to take you to videos, research, and more. From the homepage, you may also select Applied Anthropology, which directs you to essays, glossary terms, the case study forum, and a list of internships and careers in anthropology.

Questions addressed in this chapter

What can we consider art or an art form, and how pervasive is art in our daily lives?

What are the various forms artistic expressions take?

How is art integrated into our secular and religious lives?

How are gender and social status reflected in art?

There is much more to human life than acquiring necessities like food, clothing, and shelter. There is also more to living than producing and using things for their utilitarian value. All peoples have both a sense of and a desire for the aesthetic: those things that appeal to the eye, the ear, the taste, the touch, the emotions, and the imagination. Such sensory experiences are important not only for their functional value but also because their color, form, design, sound, taste, and feel are pleasurable in their own right. Commonly, these experiences are sought after to stimulate our imaginations and emotions by creating feelings of happiness, fear, and even anger. These expressions of the aesthetic are what we generally call art—the subject of this chapter.

Art is one of those elusive terms we all know and use, and think we understand, but it is difficult to define. Some scholars have defined *art* by saying what it is not: It is not utilitarian. The difficulty is, When does something stop being utilitarian and become art? Richard Anderson uses a Tikopean wooden headrest as an example. Any block of wood, even a log of the proper size, might serve as a headrest. A person might go further by cutting away portions of the block or log to form legs, which Anderson argues still serve the utilitarian purpose of lessening the weight of the block. If, however, the person carves designs on the headrest, this carving becomes its artistic component, and the object becomes art. According to Anderson, it is this artistic component, the design, that transforms the object from the realm of the utilitarian to the realm of art. Thus, it is ornamentation placed on the object—not its functional design—that defines it as art.

If this way of defining art seems simple enough, consider the Shakers, a religious communal group that reached its height in the early nineteenth century in the United States. As "plain folk" they emphasized the utilitarian. The qualities of simplicity and function were incorporated into everything they made and used in their communities. Their wooden furniture was simple, delicate, and superbly crafted, but unpretentious with stark straight lines or gentle curves. There were no accessories, carvings, extravagant turning, or inlays. In keeping with their idea of natural purity, wood was usually finished with light stains and varnishes. Their furnishings were very different from those of their neighbors, and some Shakers said that their designs came from heaven, communicated to them by angels.

Extremely functional and utilitarian, Shaker furniture is beautiful in its masterful simplicity of form. Collected today as art, Shaker furniture is among the most highly prized and pricey American furniture. Form and superb craftsmanship, not ornamentation, make Shaker furniture art.

So, at what point is a piece of wood, stone, or ivory transformed into a work of art? When does noise become music? When do body movements become dance, and words become poetry, literature, or song lyrics? When does a shelter become architecture? Are there any limitations on what can be considered art? Can the preparation and serving of food be considered art? Is the painting or alteration of the human body art?

Something becomes **art** when its purely utilitarian or functional nature is modified for the purpose of enhancing its aesthetic qualities and thus making it more pleasurable to our senses. Artists can produce art objects that only they themselves will see or hear, but most of the time art is displayed publicly or used in social events such as gatherings or ceremonies. In such contexts, art objects sometimes take on an additional function: they become material means of communication. Thus, Western artists often claim that they are trying to "make a statement" through their artwork, although we all recognize that the artistic message is in the eye of the beholder. In other cultures, too, artistic creations communicate messages that can have both religious and secular meanings.

Obviously, art is inseparable from the **aesthetic,** and the aesthetic is an elusive quality because it is subjective.

15 ART AND THE AESTHETIC

The Pervasiveness of Art
Forms of Artistic Expression
Body Arts
Visual Arts
Performance Arts

Art and Culture
Secular and Religious Art
Art and Gender
Social Functions of Art

The Shakers of the nineteenth century emphasized simplicity and utility, not ornamentation and aesthetics, in the objects they manufactured. Yet today many of their products are considered works of art. Shaker chairs such as those hanging from the walls of this house are highly prized by collectors.

Anthropologists since Franz Boas have argued that there are no universal standards for art. Something that one society might find beautiful or pleasing, others might consider ugly, disgusting, or even repulsive. As we frequently hear, "There is no accounting for taste."

Aesthetics cannot be separated from culture. Just as we learn other aspects of our culture, so we learn what is beautiful. Beauty is culturally determined. Aesthetics is unrelated to complexity, difficulty, or skill in creation or performance. Although we might appreciate the craftsmanship that went into making a piece of pottery, or the difficulty in performing a particular piece of music, we may or may not find them aesthetically pleasing. During a visit to Scotland, the English writer Samuel Johnson complained about bagpipe music. On being informed that bagpipes were an extremely difficult instrument to play, Johnson replied, "I wish it was impossible."

Not only does every culture, as well as every individual, have its own ideas about what is aesthetically pleasing, but aesthetics change within a culture over time. For example, examining European or Chinese art over the past 2,000 years, one finds dramatic changes in both the nature and the complexity of designs. Thus, the idea of what is beautiful is not only subjective but also volatile and ever changing.

The Pervasiveness of Art

In the urban, industrial world, we usually think of artistic creation as a separate and distinct kind of activity, and artistic objects as a special set of things. We also commonly think of art only in terms of "fine art": painting, sculpture, music, and dance. If pressed, we might add great architecture, literature, and even poetry. We tend to categorize as art only those things whose sole or basic value is aesthetic. Artists, in turn, are those painters, sculptors, composers, writers, architects, performers, and others who produce these things of aesthetic value. Individuals who are not directly involved in the production of "art" are commonly seen as merely the audience or consumers—people who buy, see, and hear art.

The notion that art is a conceptually separate realm of social and cultural existence is not found among all peoples. As anthropologists have long noted, Native American peoples had no word for art in their languages. Similarly, other traditional peoples in other parts of the world frequently lack words for art. The basic reason for this is that art is integrated into virtually every aspect of their lives and is so pervasive that they do not think of it as something separate and distinct. The idea of "art for art's sake" is a recent Western cultural phenomenon that in some ways both distracts and diminishes the reality of human creative expressions. If we define art broadly, then it permeates virtually every aspect of our lives. All of us search for and attempt to create that which is aesthetically pleasing and, thus, we are all "artists." Creative artistic expressions are found in even the most mundane and commonplace acts of the daily lives of all peoples. Consider, for example, three behaviors that most of us think of as "mundane" rather than "artistic": dressing for the day, residing in a particular place, and eating.

We begin the day by ornamenting our bodies. From among our clothes we make choices about what to wear based on colors and styles appropriate for the day's events. We make choices on how to wear our hair and even the color of our hair. We may paint our faces and further adorn our bodies with jewelry of varying kinds, worn on our fingers and arms, around our necks, in our ears, noses, and—in recent years—other parts of our bodies. Some of us have our bodies permanently decorated with tattoos. By these everyday acts, we are artists, attempting to enhance the aesthetic qualities of our persons by making ourselves a work of art. Through these acts we are also adept communicators of messages about ourselves; through hair, makeup, dress, jewelry, and other ways of adorning our bodies, we present to the public certain images of ourselves.

Consider your living space. In finding or building a place to live, we don't just look for something that will meet our physical needs; aesthetic appeal also plays an important role. We alter our homes by changing walls, adding rooms, remodeling the bathroom or the kitchen, and repainting everything in different colors inside and outside. We decorate the inside with furniture, rugs, paintings, posters, mirrors, and a host of knickknacks and smaller things. If we have a yard, we may remove or add trees, shrubs, flower beds, and fences. Even temporary apartment and college dormitory dwellers try to make a place their own. Although some of these additions and changes may be of utilitarian value or need, most serve to enhance the aesthetic appeal of the place where we live.

Finally, think about mealtimes. Whether we eat food raw or cooked, boiled, baked, fried, hot, or cold, and whether we season it with salt, pepper, garlic, or other herbs and spices, we are attempting to create something that is pleasing to our sense of taste. Our quest for new and exciting ways of preparing food seems endless, giving rise to the steady flow of new cookbooks from publishers. Nor is eating food a purely utilitarian act. We set

► Notice the ways the clothing and jewelry of these Maasai women serve to enhance their appearance.

© Barry D. Kass/Images of Anthropology

the table and arrange the repast in bowls and on plates, which have usually been purchased for their aesthetic appeal. In our food preparation and serving, we attempt to create something that is appealing to both the palate and the eye. (Chinese, incidentally, are far more conscious of this artistic quality of food than are most North Americans.)

Even in our daily lives, then, we attempt to immerse ourselves in the aesthetic. The search for the aesthetic is reflected in the appearance of our persons, our homes, and our meals, as well as in our places of worship, recreation, and work. Much of our day is filled with music, song, dance, drama, comedy, literature, and sports, which we listen to, participate in, and sometimes create. Art, anthropologists recognize, is a cultural universal. But beyond this, the artistic impulse is seen in the everyday lives of individual human beings, for we are all both producers and consumers of art.

Forms of Artistic Expression

Although art permeates most aspects of human activity, from clothing and furniture to music and theater, space constraints do not permit us to discuss all these diverse forms of artistic expression. For this reason, we limit our discussion to certain categories: body arts, visual arts, and performance arts.

Body Arts

People around the world are highly creative in altering their physical appearance. Almost anything that can be done to the body is probably being done or has been done in the past. In Euro-American societies, for example, people are piercing parts of the body that few people even thought of as pierceable a decade or two ago. For convenience, we focus on the **body arts** of physical alterations, body painting, and tattooing and scarification.

Physical alterations. In most societies, people attempt to physically alter their bodies. Head and body hair is treated in many different ways. In Western societies, hair is styled and often artificially colored. Some people shave their head, their beard, and even their legs and armpits. Others let their beard and mustache grow and style them in various ways. Still others, particularly middle-aged men, attempt vainly to have replacement hair grow on the top of their head. In most Western societies, these actions are mainly a matter of fashion or personal taste; in other societies, such actions may have deeper cultural meanings.

In parts of Africa, a woman's status—for example, whether she is unmarried or married, or is a mother or a widow—is indicated by her hairstyle. Among the Hopis, adolescent girls of marriageable age wear their hair in a large whorl on each side of the head, creating the so-called butterfly hairstyle. After marriage, they wear their hair long and parted in the middle. Children among the Omahas had their hair cut in patterns indicating their clan membership.

Wearing beards is not always a matter of personal taste and fashion. In many societies, such as Hasidic Jews, Mennonites, Amish, some Muslim sects, and Sikhs, wearing a beard is an act of religious belief. In the ancient world, social status was frequently associated with beards. In Egypt, only the nobility were allowed to wear beards. Not only did noblemen wear beards, but women of the nobility frequently wore artificial beards as well to indicate their social rank. In contrast, in ancient Greece, only the nobility were allowed to be clean shaven; men of commoner status had to let their beards grow.

Hair alterations are usually reversible because hair will grow back. Other parts of the body are altered permanently. Cranial deformation or head shaping has been and is still widely practiced among the peoples of the world. The skull of a baby is soft and, if the baby's head is bound, the shape of the skull can be permanently changed, flattening the back and the forehead or lengthening the head. In parts of France, cranial deformation was virtually universal until the eighteenth century. A baby's face was tightly wrapped in linen, resulting in a flattened skull and ears. In the Netherlands, babies once wore tight-fitting caps that depressed the front portion of the skull. The elite classes of the ancient Andean civilizations elongated the skull, as did the ancient Egyptians. For the first year of its life, a Chinook baby was wrapped on a hard board, with another board bound against the top and front of the head. This technique resulted in a head with additional breadth. Some peoples of central Africa bound the heads of female babies to create elongated skulls that came to a point in the back.

Some peoples permanently altered other parts of the body as well. In China, the feet of female children of high-status families were bound at the age of 5 or 6 to deform the feet and keep them small. Not only were small feet considered attractive, but foot binding was practiced as a visible indication that the family was sufficiently wealthy that its women did not have to do much physical labor. In parts of Africa and among some Native American peoples, holes were cut in earlobes or the lower and upper lips were expanded so that ear plugs and large lip plugs could be inserted. Some of these plugs were up to 3 inches in diameter. Some central African Pygmy peoples file their front teeth into points, which in their culture enhances their attractiveness. In parts of Africa, a series of rings was placed around a girl's neck over a period of time, so that when she reached womanhood, her

shoulders were pressed down, her neck appeared longer, and she could wear multiple neck rings.

Such alterations continue in modern nations. Much of the lucrative work of plastic surgeons in contemporary Western nations is concerned with altering physical appearance by changing the shapes of the eyes, nose, mouth, and jowls, or increasing or decreasing the size of breasts, lips, thighs, hips, or waistlines.

Body painting. Painting is a less drastic and a temporary way of changing an individual's appearance. Some peoples paint only their faces, while others paint almost their entire bodies. Face painting is more common than body painting. Native American peoples commonly painted their faces for war. Among the Osage, before attacking their enemy, the men would blacken their faces with charcoal, symbolizing the merciless fire and their ferocity. In other Native American groups, face painting was individualized, with each man using different colors and designs to create a ferocious appearance. Sometimes the manner in which a man painted his face depended on a vision and his spiritual helpers (see Chapter 14). Not all face painting was associated with war, however. Faces were commonly painted for religious rituals as well. In ritual face painting, the painted symbols usually had religious significance. In addition, many Native American peoples simply painted their faces to enhance their social appearance. Thus, Native Americans painted their faces for a variety of reasons—warfare, religious rituals, and social appearance—just like other peoples in the world.

Body painting refers to painting the entire body, or most of it. Like face painting, body painting is found all over the world. In some cases, body painting has religious significance and meaning; in other cases, it is purely secular, designed to enhance the person's physical appearance. Many peoples in Papua New Guinea cover their faces and limbs with white clay when a relative or important person dies, as a sign of mourning and respect for the deceased. The aboriginal peoples of Australia painted their bodies with red and yellow ocher, white clay, charcoal, and other pigments. During rituals, individuals were painted with elaborate designs covering most of the body. The colors and designs were standardized and had symbolic meaning. Ritual specialists who knew these designs did the painting for religious ceremonies. Outside of ritual contexts, for many Australian peoples, body painting was a secular and daily activity, performed by family members on one another. Individuals were free to use whatever colors and designs pleased them, so long as they were not ritual designs.

▲ These Australian aborigine boys have their bodies painted for a dance. Body painting is commonly used in many cultures for ceremonial and ritual occasions.

Tattooing and scarification. Tattooing and the related practice of scarification are widespread. Tattoo designs, achieved by etching and placing a colored pigment under the skin, have been practiced by diverse peoples. When the skin is too dark for tattooing designs to be seen, people may use scarification, the deliberate scarring of the skin to produce designs on the body.

Tattooing has a long history as an art form. Tattooing was practiced by the ancient Egyptians as well as by the ancient Scythians, Thracians, and Romans in Europe. The ancient Bretons, at the time of the Roman conquest, were reported to have had their bodies elaborately tattooed with the images of animals. In the fourth century A.D., when Christianity became the official religion of the Roman Empire, tattooing was forbidden on religious grounds. Tattooing virtually disappeared among European peoples until the eighteenth century, when it was

discovered in the Pacific and Asia by sailors and reintroduced to Europe as purely secular art.

Robert Brain noted an important difference between body painting and tattooing and scarification: paint is removable, whereas tattooing and scarification are indelible and permanent. As a result, tattooing and scarification are usually associated with societies in which there are permanent differences in social status. In complexity of designs and parts of the body tattooed, peoples differed. Among some people, tattooing was limited to a few lines on the face, chest, or arms. For others, complex designs covered most of the body from the face to the legs. In some cases, every adult had some tattoos; in other societies, only certain individuals had tattoos. The significance and meaning of tattoos varied, but most had socioreligious significance. The more fully tattooed an individual was, the higher the social status.

The adornment of the body by tattoos is most elaborate in the scattered islands of Polynesia. In fact, the word *tattoo* itself is Polynesian. The word, like the practice of tattooing sailors, came into use as a result of the voyages of Western explorers and whalers in the seventeenth and later centuries. Tongans, Samoans, Marquesans, Tahitians, the Maori of New Zealand, and most other Polynesian peoples practiced tattooing, which everywhere was connected to social distinctions such as class or rank, sex, religious roles, and specialization. Polynesian peoples are all historically related, so it is not surprising that marking the body with tattoos is found on almost all islands, albeit to different degrees and with somewhat different styles.

Many Maori had large areas of their bodies covered with tattoos, which could be on the torso, thighs, buttocks, calves, and, most notably, the face. Skilled tattoo artists used several instruments to incise the curvilinear patterns characteristic of most Maori tattoos. One was a small chisel made of bone and etched into the skin with a hammer. Apparently, no anesthetic was used to relieve the pain and, in fact, tolerating the pain of the procedure may have been part of its cultural significance. To make pigment, several kinds of wood were burned for their ashes. After the artist made the cuts, pigment was rubbed into the wounds to leave permanent markings. The most skilled tattoo artists were rewarded with high prestige and chiefly patronage, and their craft was in such high demand that they traveled widely over New Zealand's two huge islands.

Both Maori men and women wore tattoos, although men's bodies were more thoroughly covered. For both sexes, tattoos were seen not merely as body ornamentation or expression of one's personal identity. Having tattoos brought certain privileges. Men who did not

◄ The Maori of New Zealand are well known for their elaborate tattoos. The designs of Maori facial tattoos are important symbols of identity and achievement.

© Paula Bronstein/Getty Images

undergo tattooing could not build canoe houses, carve wood, make weapons, or weave nets. Untattooed women could not help in the gardens with sweet potatoes, the Maori staple vegetable crop.

Maori facial tattoos, called *moko,* have special importance. Women were tattooed on the lips and chin, often near the time of their marriage. Male facial tattoos were designed by splitting the face into four fields—left versus right of the nose, and upper versus lower at roughly eye level. *Moko* were basically symmetrical on the vertical axis, with curvilinear designs on the forehead and eyebrows, cheeks, and mouth regions. In many cases, virtually the whole male face was tattooed. Not just any *moko* design could be worn by just any male; designs were related to factors such as hereditary status, place of birth, and achievement in battle. Social restrictions thus were placed on the wearing of facial tattoos, suggesting that they were important symbols of group identity and personal achievement. North Americans might see echoes of their own styles of clothing, jewelry, hairstyle, and other personal ornamentations in Maori and other Polynesian tattoos.

In other Polynesian islands, tattooing was similar to the Maori in broad pattern but varied in detail. In Samoa,

for instance, a group of boys was tattooed together on the hips and thighs in their early teens, accompanied by much ceremony. The primary recipient of the tattoo was the son of a high-ranking chief, and other boys participated to share his pain and, therefore, publicly show their respect and loyalty. Supposedly, Samoan women disdained men as sexual partners if they did not have tattoos. Traditionally, Samoan girls received tattoos only on the backs of their knees, which they were not supposed to reveal to others. It is interesting that in Samoa greater and more elaborate male tattoos were connected to different sexually based biological functions. There was a saying:

> The man grows up and is tattooed.
> The woman grows up and she gives birth.
>   (Milner 1969, 20)

According to one interpretation, voluntary tattooing gives pain to men just as childbirth causes pain to women. Perhaps the male experience of pain by tattooing is connected to Samoan women's contempt for tattooless men.

In all of Polynesia, it was the people of the Marquesas whose bodies were most covered by tattoos. The highest-ranking chiefs had tattoos on even the soles of their feet.

Alfred Gell argues that this relatively thorough covering of the body in the Marquesas wrapped the body in images in order to protect it from spiritual dangers. Gods and spirits were not tattooed; tattoo images protected the human body from spiritual harm.

Decorating the body by cutting and creating scars, or scarification, is more limited than tattooing among the world's peoples. Like tattooing, scarification is practiced for numerous reasons. Depending on the culture, both men and women may be scarred. Sometimes the scarred design is on the face; in other cases, the chest, breast, back, and even the legs and arms may be elaborately covered with such designs. Sometimes scarification forms part of the puberty rite or some other initiation rite. Among the Nuer of southern Sudan, a series of horizontal cuts is made on the foreheads of men who have completed male initiation rituals. These cuts symbolically mark and communicate a young man's maturity and courage. After the cuts scarify, the scars become permanent symbols of Nuer manhood.

Visual Arts

Visual arts are produced from material, tangible objects, so they are part of the material culture of a people. They may be religious or secular in meaning and use. Usually they are permanent in that they are meant for long-term use, but sometimes they are created for one-time use only and then destroyed. Visual arts encompass a wide range of basketry, ceramics, textiles, clothing, jewelry, tools, paintings, masks, and sculpture, to name only a few examples. Metal, wood, stone, leather, feather, shell, paper made of fibers, pigments, and other materials are used in their creation. The two main factors that transform a material item into a visual art are form and ornamentation.

Form. The physical form or shape of an object is a reflection of its utilitarian function, the materials available, the technical knowledge and skill of the person producing it, and the general lifestyle of the society. Nomadic or seminomadic foraging and pastoral people often produce items that are lightweight and easily transportable. One might think that the visual arts of nomadic or seminomadic people are "less refined" than those of more settled peoples. But Inuit peoples of northern latitudes precisely carved small art objects out of soft soapstone, and decorated many of their portable tools with figures of animals. Shields and hides were elaborately painted among many nomadic peoples of the American plains. Plains Indians heavily decorated their clothing and moccasins with shells and beadwork, thus allowing people to carry their

art along with them. Native Americans of the western United States, especially the Southwest, used pigment to paint or hard stones to etch images of animals, celestial objects, people, mythological beings, and other things on rocks. The prehistoric people who created these images might have moved according to the season, but their art was stationary and long lasting. Today we know these images as pictographs and petroglyphs, also called rock art.

Rock seems like a difficult object to use as a canvas, but the world's peoples have used other unusual materials as well, including sand (as we shall see later). Of course, the availability of wood, stone, clay, hides, and other natural materials does influence what people can create and how. The kinds of tools the artist uses to paint, etch, or sculpt are also important influences on the final artwork. Metal tools have advantages over stone tools in giving artistic form to a raw material. Peoples also differ in their technical knowledge of how to work stone or wood, and how to model clay or metals.

Within these natural and technical limitations, the form of an object is the result of the interplay of utilitarian function and aesthetic style. The function/style debate has long interested archaeologists. Prehistoric stone tools display a bewildering variety of forms. In North American archaeology, extensive typologies have been created to classify projectile point types, which differ in size, relative length and width, and shape (straight, concave, convex, or even serrated). Some are unnotched; others are notched on the bases or sides. Many of these differences are undoubtedly related to function, but others seem to be purely stylistic. Great variability is also present in the vessel shapes and decorations of another archaeological favorite, pottery. Pottery vessels vary tremendously from one group to another, as well as within the same group of people over time.

One does not have to look at peoples remote in time or space to see that the form of an object that has utilitarian purposes is part of the artistic expression of a people. Look at something as mundane and "functional" as the legs of tables and chairs in our own culture. The legs can be straight or tapered, or round, square, or rectangular. The table may have a pedestal base. All are equally functional; they keep the seat or the top off the floor. The differences are a question of aesthetics, not of function. Thus, the physical form of an object may be part of its aesthetic appeal; however, it is sometimes difficult to determine where function ends and the aesthetic begins.

Ornamentation. Ornamentation is design added to the physical form of an object. Humans are highly creative in developing ways of adding ornamentation to material

© Sean Sprague/Panos Pictures

▲ These women in Chaing Mai, Thailand, are producing traditional pottery.

items. Ornamental designs may be woven or carved into an object. They may be painted, incised, molded, or sewn onto an object. Or a combination of these techniques may be used to decorate.

In basketry and textiles, designs are commonly woven onto the item during its construction. For baskets, different colors of plant fibers, either natural or artificially dyed, are used for the designs. The same is true in the weaving of textiles, for which different colored yarns are used. Not all textile designs are created using fibers of contrasting colors, however. By using various techniques, weavers may create different designs in a single color.

Carving refers to creating a design by removing parts of the original form. Wood, stone, clay, ivory, shell, and bone may have carved designs. An object may be carved in three dimensions so that the form itself becomes the design, as in a piece of sculpture. Or the form of the object will remain the same, with only shallow relief carving of a design on the surface.

Painting is certainly one of the easiest and most versatile methods of ornamenting an object. It is possibly the oldest method of ornamentation; European cave paintings are at least 20,000 years old. All one needs to paint is a range of colors. To make colored pigments, a variety of different materials may be mixed with water, oil, or fat, such as charcoal, plant materials, and natural mineral pigments. Paintings can be applied to wood, stone, clay, textiles, paper, or leather. Paintings can be applied to flat surfaces, such as cave walls, exposed rocks or cliff walls, wooden furniture, or canvas. They may be made on round or irregular surfaces, such as pottery, masks, and sculpture.

Incising consists of decorating an object by scratching lines into the surface. Like painting, incising appears to be one of the earliest ways of adding designs to an item. Incising is most commonly used on ivory, bone, and shell. In these cases, the scratched lines are frequently accentuated by adding some type of colored pigment, usually black or a dark color, so one can more readily see the design itself. Incised designs are also occasionally used for decorating clay pots and leather.

Designs on ceramics and metal are commonly modeled by raising certain areas above the surface. There are two ways in which this form of ornamentation can be accomplished. One is by making additions to the object after the surface area is finished. In pottery, for example, designs may be formed by placing little balls or coils of clay on the surface after the body of the pot has been formed. A similar technique is sometimes used in adding designs to metal items, as when metal wires shaped into designs are welded to the surface. More commonly, though, molds are created with designs carved into the surface area. Clay can be forced into these molds, or metal poured into them. After the object is removed from the mold, the design areas stand out as raised areas on the object surface.

Sewing is often used to add ornamentation to cloth or leather. Glass, bone, or shell beads may be sewn onto an item, forming designs, as on moccasins or clothing. Designs may be created by sewing with various colored threads of hair, plant fiber, quills, or metal, or by sewing different colors of fabrics together, as in a patchwork quilt.

This discussion has only touched upon some of the ways in which peoples add ornamentation to and create design on objects. When it comes to ornamenting objects, humans are highly creative. When most people think of artistic creativity, they think of the artist as creating a novel object (e.g., a unique drawing or sculpture) using some medium (e.g., paper or wood). Looking in

The artistic tradition of the Osage of the central United States was, and still is, distinctly different from art in Western societies. Not only was Osage art fully integrated into the everyday material culture of the community, but it was also an expression of their religious beliefs. Even by Native American standards, the Osage were extremely religious. Religion governed virtually every aspect of their lives and their behavior. The Osage believed that everything in the universe was a creation as well as a manifestation of a great invisible force that they called Wah-kon-tah. Collectively, the visible universe was the tangible expression of Wah-kon-tah. Thus, the more one understood the visible universe, and the meanings and purposes of every type of animal, bird, plant, and other nature phenomenon, the more one understood this great mysterious and controlling force. Of course, the Osage realized that no one could ever fully understand the universe in all of its complexity. Thus, no humans could ever fully understand Wah-kon-tah. From their observation of the world about them, the Osage did come to understand certain things. Everything created by Wah-kon-tah was born and would eventually die. Everything created by Wah-kon-tah passed through the stages of birth, maturity, old age, and death. This was true for all animals, plants, birds, humans, and even natural phenomena. It was seen in the passing of the year, in spring, summer, fall, and winter. This was true individually as well as collectively. Someday even the Osage, like all other peoples, would disappear.

Many of the things created by Wah-kon-tah were blessings that had been bestowed on humans for their use. The sun and the associated fire gave warmth and comfort to humans. Certain animals and plants could be used for food and nourishment. The skins of certain animals and the bark, wood, and/or fibers of certain trees or plants could be used for clothing, shelter, and other material wants. Still other plants could be used to heal the sick. Everything created by Wah-kon-tah was for a purpose. Wah-kon-tah did not reveal the purposes of these creations to humans. Humans were unique among Wah-kon-tah's creations in that only they possessed *wa-thi'-gethon,* the power to search with the mind. Thus, humans were responsible for studying the universe about them in a never-ending search to gain ever-greater knowledge of the meanings and purposes of all of Wah-kon-tah's creations. Wah-kon-tah also bestowed on humans the ability to take their knowledge and use it to create new things.

So, endowed with the power to reason and to create, humans were responsible for securing for themselves the continued blessings of Wah-kon-tah. The greatest of these blessings were children, indicative of Wah-kon-tah's will that they as a people would continue to live. To this end, the Osage consciously structured every aspect of their lives and behavior in a manner that showed respect for Wah-kon-tah. Just as all things created by Wah-kon-tah had purpose and meaning, so it had to be with them. Everything they did had to have purpose and meaning, with the ultimate goal of receiving Wah-kon-tah's continued blessings.

Based on their observation of the universe, the Osage noted that there were two main divisions, the sky and the earth. The sky was the source of life, the father, and the earth was the nourisher of life, the mother. All living things existed in a narrow lens between earth and sky, which they called the *hoe-ga,* or snare. The countless other creations, animals, birds, plants, and other natural phenomena of Wah-kon-tah were associated with either the earth or the sky. Based on this cosmic model, the Osage organized their life as a symbolic mirror image of the cosmos. The basic unit was the clan, which symbolically represented a portion of Wah-kon-tah's creations. Collectively, 9 of these clans, acting together symbolically, represented the forces of the sky, while the other 15 clans collectively symbolized the earth. All marriages had to be between a member of a sky clan and a member of an earth clan, with the children belonging to the clan of their father.

The village structure was modeled after the cosmos, with each village having two chiefs, a sky chief and an earth chief. The houses of the sky clan families were placed in a specific clan order along the north side of an east–west street. The houses of the earth clan people were placed in a specific clan order along the south side. The street itself symbolized the path of life, the passage of the sun from east to west, and the *hoe-ga* or snare. Rituals were organized following the same model; priests of the sky clans sat in a precise order on the north, while earth clan priests sat on the south.

Every morning before sunrise, the people of the village would arise and greet the sun with prayers. This ritual was repeated at noon and at dusk. Their lives were organized as one continuous prayer for Wah-kon-tah's blessings. Warfare, hunting, planting, harvests, marriage, death, and the naming of children were all structured as religious rituals.

Everything created by Wah-kon-tah had meaning and purpose, and thus it had to be with all of the material items used in their daily lives and rituals. Every animal, bird, shellfish, and plant had its own behavioral characteristics; bears, mountain lions, and eagles were powerful in different ways; otters could swim; wolves were tenacious; hawks were courageous; pelicans and shellfish lived for a long time; cedar trees did not "die" in the winter like other plants. The hides, feathers, shells, bones, wood, or bark of these and other animals, birds, and plants symbolically represented specific qualities of Wah-kon-tah. Colors also had meanings; red and white as in the sun and fire were colors of birth and life; black as in the night, charcoal, and the fur of the black bear was the color of death and destruction; blue as in the sky on a cloudless day was the color of peace and tranquility; and green as in the cedar tree in winter was the color of everlasting life. Form and designs also had meanings. A disk shape or design was the form of the sun and thus life. A design divided with each side the mirror image of the other represented the sky and earth balanced as in the universe. A line with four lines descending from it was the *hoe-ga*.

Every object created by the Osage consisted of a number of different elements, raw materials, color, and form and/or designs. Each of these elements had a specific symbolic meaning. All objects consisted of several elements, each with its own symbolic meaning, which collectively gave meaning and purpose to the object. Ritual items were the most symbolically complex. A good example of symbolism in Osage art is found with the staff used in the Osage peyote church meetings.

Osage peyotism is an Osage form of Christianity. Established at the turn of the twentieth century, it replaced the traditional religion while retaining much of the traditional symbolism. Unlike other forms of peyotism, each Osage meetinghouse has a permanent concrete altar in the middle of the floor, and a set of ritual interments that have been consecrated for use in that specific church. The most important of these interments was the staff or *mon,* a word that means "arrow." This staff consists of a straight wooden pole about 4 feet long. At the base end, it is carved into a four-sided arrow point. On the top is a crown of eagle and hawk feathers. Attached to the staff are "drop feathers," a narrow strip of otter skin, a narrow strip of opossum hide, and a string of bells. When not in use during the meeting, the staff stands upright in a hole at the head of the altar. During the singing, the staff is passed in a clockwise direction from singer to singer. Each singer holds the staff in one hand while he sings.

Every aspect of the staff has multiple symbolic meanings. Each part has a distinct meaning; however, in association with other parts, new composite meanings are created. The staff in its entirety is symbolic of the ideal man. The upright feather crown, like a war bonnet, and the downward dropping scalp feathers, such as men wear in dancing, mean that this man is "Indian." Some say that the staff represents Jesus Christ, the ideal man, clothed as an "Indian." The arrow point at the end not only gives the staff its name, *mon* or arrow, but also introduces another dimension to this symbolic man. Arrows had traditionally been used in both war and hunting. The arrow in the context of the

Courtesy Thomas Gilcrease Museum, Tulsa

staff introduces the symbolic meanings of spiritual protection and nourishment. The symbolic meaning of nourishment is further enhanced by the carving of the staff out of the wood of a tree that bears fruit, and is thus a source of food. The fact that the wood is from a deciduous tree adds the symbolism of death (loss of leaves in the fall) and rebirth (new leaves in the spring). The feathers add still another dimension to the *mon*. Among all creatures, birds fly in the air and thus come closest to the life-giving powers of the sun. As a result, feathers are spiritually pure and serve to guard one or cleanse one of evil. The fact that there are both eagle and hawk feathers is also of symbolic importance. The eagle was a symbol of power, and the hawk was considered the most courageous of birds. Even a small hawk will attack a large bird in defense of its nest. Together, the eagle and the hawk symbolized the ideal man as both powerful and courageous. The otter is an animal much admired. At home on the land as well as in the water, it moves swiftly and is protective of its young. The otter in its swiftness symbolized the ability to avoid evil and protection. The opossum is a clean animal, pure in its habits. It can also feign death. Thus, the strip of opossum hide conveys the meaning of purity as well as death and rebirth. When the staff is moved, the bell will tinkle, like the sound of raindrops, symbolic of the life-giving rain. Just as the universe consists of land, water, and sky, so symbolic elements of land, the wood and the hides; water, the otter and the bells; and the sky, the bird feathers, are brought together in the construction of the staff. The staff was thus a symbolically constructed, Christ-centered universe, emphasizing the qualities of purity, safety, courage, power, and death and rebirth. Finally, the ordered movement of the staff during the ceremony was symbolic of an ever-moving, changing universe. A traditional Osage ritual involved first the symbolic creation of the universe and then putting it in motion through the use of ritual objects, song, movements, and other acts. Their peyote church ceremonies were structured in the same manner.

To the Osage everything had to have meaning and purpose. Everything in the universe was a creation of Wah-kon-tah. Thus everything was sacred. The Osage, like all humans, had the abilities to alter and change material objects to meet the special needs of humans. To work properly, however, these changes had to be in accordance with the meanings and purposes that Wah-kon-tah had given to the objects they used.

▲ Osage peyote staff.   *Source:* Bailey, Swan, Nunley, and StandingBear (2004) broad cross-cultural perspective, we see that humanity as a whole has also been enormously creative not only in its styles but also in its techniques of ornamentation and in some of the surprising materials used.

Art of the Northwest Coast: An example of style.

In visual arts, some two-dimensional image (e.g., a painting or drawing) or three-dimensional form (e.g., a sculpture or mask) is created. Cultures vary in many ways in their visual arts: the themes or subjects portrayed, the purposes of the artwork, the relationship between the artist and the public, and so forth.

Stylistic conventions are an important variation. In visual arts, stylistic symbolism may be especially important because artists in many cultures are not especially concerned with realistic portrayals of people or nature, but use conventional representations that are understood by themselves and the public. But, even when the intention is a realistic portrayal, symbolic representation may be necessary. In a painting or drawing, for example, three-dimensional reality is portrayed on a two-dimensional surface, and the stylistic conventions of different cultures may handle this problem of representation in various ways.

The art of some of the Native Americans of the Northwest Coast, from southern Alaska to Oregon, is one example of stylistic variation in imagery and two-dimensional representation. Although they were hunters, gatherers, and fishers—rather than cultivators—Northwest Coast peoples were largely sedentary villagers, which was made possible by the abundance and reliability of coastal and riverine food resources, especially fish (see Chapter 6). Their social and political organization included large descent groups, chiefly roles, and hierarchical ranking. Sponsoring the creation of art objects, displaying them, and/or using them in ceremonies were the ways groups and high-ranking people proclaimed their wealth and social position.

Northwest Coast art is famous for its sheer quantity, quality, and style. Many major Canadian and American museums contain substantial collections of masks, wooden sculptures, incised silver jewelry, carved boxes, finely woven blankets, and sometimes larger objects such as "totem poles" and painted housefronts. Animals, humans, and spirits are the most common subjects of the art of these peoples, although many creations represent animal–human–spirit at the same time. Because of the unique style used to represent these subjects, most Northwest Coast art is easily recognizable.

Animals such as beavers, ravens, hawks, frogs, bears, and killer whales were common subjects of the art, but their depiction was not intended to be realistic. Artists created animals by combining design elements representing what was culturally considered their most distinctive body parts. For example, beavers have two large incisors, a scaly (often hatched) tail, a rounded nose, and forepaws (often holding a stick). Hawks are portrayed by emphasizing their distinctive beak, which is turned backward and often touches the face. Frogs are suggested by wide and toothless mouths. Bears usually are identified by paws with claws and a large and heavily toothed mouth. Images of killer whales have a large toothed mouth, a blowhole, and an exaggerated dorsal fin. Using such conventional design elements, Northwest Coast artists carved animals onto boxes, masks used in a multitude of ceremonies, huge cedar tree trunks representing a group's or individual's ancestry (commonly mislabeled "totem poles"), and other three-dimensional objects.

Painters are familiar with the problem of representing the world on flat surfaces. In the Western and many other artistic traditions, three dimensions are represented on two-dimensional surfaces (canvas or paper) by such techniques as relative sizes of images, perspective, and coloration, all intended to create the visual illusion of depth. Northwest Coast artists painted on many two-dimensional surfaces, including the flat sides of boxes and communal housefronts. They also wove representations of animals into blankets and incised lines into bracelets and other metal jewelry. Most often, their work on flat surfaces tried to retain as many as possible of the design elements characteristic of each animal, so that each animal representation would be identifiable. A common technique was to split the animal down the middle and paint profiles on each half of the surface. The result was a representation that distorted the actual shapes of the body and its characteristic parts, but retained the elements that conventionally identified the animal.

Yet another stylistic characteristic of Northwest Coast art is the artists' apparent intolerance of empty spaces. The subject's body, limbs, and even hands and feet were generally filled in by design elements. Most commonly, curvilinear patterns, stylized eyes, or faces were painted or carved inside body parts. Thus, one frequently observes a face on an animal's torso or an eye pattern on a leg joint.

Although meaningful cross-cultural studies of visual arts are difficult, comparative studies have been made of stylistic elements found in ornamental designs. Working with the idea that art reflects the creator's view of society, John Fischer studied the use of stylistic elements in 28 different societies around the world. He divided the societies on the basis of their degrees of social equality and inequality (see Chapter 13), thinking that the artistic

▲ Along the Northwest Coast, houses were elaborately decorated with designs that were symbolic of the family and its heritage. This Tlingit house is in Ketchikan, Alaska.

expressions of egalitarian (primarily foraging) societies would differ from those of socially stratified (primarily intensive agricultural) societies. He examined the stylistic elements in terms of their relative complexity, use of space, symmetry, and boundedness. Fischer found that in egalitarian societies, designs tended to repeat similar, symmetrical elements, with large areas of empty space without enclosures. In more stratified societies, ornamentation was characterized by asymmetrical designs that integrated unlike elements and more fully filled enclosed areas. Fischer interpreted these differences as symbolically reflecting the differing social realities of egalitarian and stratified peoples. Egalitarian peoples tend to live in small, scattered isolated groups, whereas in stratified societies, people live in crowded communities.

Performance Arts

Performance arts encompass music, song, and dance, which use voice, instruments, and movement to delight the senses and communicate. (Theater/drama is also a performance art, but we do not cover it here.) Music, song, and dance are closely interrelated. Dancing is usually to the accompaniment of music, especially rhythms created partly by drumming, clapping, or other kinds of percussion. Singing is often accompanied by instrumen-

tal music. Traditional religious ceremonies and pageants commonly integrate music, song, and dance.

An interesting aspect of performance arts is that not only do we watch or listen to such formal performances but we also frequently perform them ourselves, in many cases for pure pleasure. We play our own pianos or guitars, we sing in the shower or as we drive, and we take part in social dances. The dual dimension of these art forms has been questioned by some anthropologists. Speaking only of dance, Adrienne Kaeppler has asked, "Is participation in rock and roll in any way comparable to watching ballet? Indeed, should 'dances of participation' and 'dances of presentation' be classified as the same phenomenon either in our own or other cultures, let alone cross-culturally?" She further questions whether dance performances for the gods should be categorized with social dancing, since their purposes are so different. Similar questions may be asked of music and song, which so often are part of religious rituals. For example, Osage rituals integrated music, song, physical movements (including dance), and theatrical performances to communicate ideas that could not be expressed by words alone. In his studies of Osage religious rituals, Francis La-Flesche argued that these rituals were not merely prayers for supernatural assistance but were educational as well. They were a manner of recording and transmitting the collective knowledge of the society, communicating social messages to the assembled participants. Thus, even within a society, the purposes of performance arts may differ significantly, depending on whether they are religious or secular in nature.

People raised in the Judeo-Christian religious tradition are quite familiar with the many functions of music in religious services. The lyrics of familiar hymns sung to praise God are an integral part of worship rituals. Music also helps to create the mood and sense of reverence for the service and is capable of altering the emotional state of the participants. The shared experience of singing in unison may help draw the congregation together, enhancing what many Christian denominations call their fellowship. In these and other ways, music is important in making the congregation receptive to the messages delivered by the sermon and prayers.

Music and other forms of performance arts are essential to the religious experience for diverse peoples in all parts of the world. The *voudon* (voodoo) religion of the Caribbean heavily incorporates performance arts into religious ceremonies. Followers of *voudon* consider themselves to be people who "serve the spirits" (*loa*). Many *loa* originated and now live in West Africa, where the ancestors of modern Afro-Caribbean peoples were enslaved during the era of the slave trade beginning in about 1500. *Voudon* temples are elaborately decorated with sacred objects, paintings, and symbolic representations of various *loa,* which show the devotion of the worshippers and make the temple attractive to the spirits. Through drumming, music, and energetic dancing, *voudon* worshippers induce the *loa* to leave their spiritual homes and take over the bodies of those who worship them. When the *loa* possess their human servants, the latter speak with the voices of the *loa,* wear the *loa*'s favorite clothing, eat their foods, drink their beverages, and generally assume their identity. Visiting petitioners with problems can ask questions of the worshipper/*loa,* who may answer with directions about what course of action to take. *Voudon* drumming, music, and dancing are so totally integrated into temple rituals that the religion is unimaginable without it.

Among many peoples, music, dance, and other forms of performance arts are essential elements of curing ceremonials. !Kung shamans (see Chapters 6 and 14) use percussion, song, and dance to induce the trance state they believe is necessary for curing sick people. The power to heal, !Kung believe, comes from a substance called *n!um,* which, when heated up by dancing and trance, allows shamans to draw sickness out of people. While women produce a definite rhythm by clapping and singing, the curers circle the fire in short, synchronous dance steps. The experience of music and dance causes the *n!um* inside their bodies to boil up into their heads, inducing trance. In this spiritually powerful state, shamans heal by placing hands on the sick, shrieking at the same time to drive out the affliction.

Music is essential to the healing process among many other African peoples. The Tumbuka-speaking peoples of northern Malawi combine singing, drumming, and dancing in all-night curing sessions. Some kinds of illness are caused by a category of spirits called *vimbuza.* *Vimbuza* are the powerful spiritual energy of foreign peoples and wild animals (especially lions). *Vimbuza* cause various kinds of illness and even death when they possess someone. Tumbuka believe that health requires a balance between bodily cold and hot forces (similar to the bodily "humours" of old Europe). When *vimbuza* enter the body, they create an imbalance between hot and cold forces, leading to the buildup of heat that is culturally interpreted as sickness.

Tumbuka diviner-healers (curers) both diagnose illnesses and direct elaborate healing ceremonies that include drumming, music, and dance. The most essential part of the curing ritual is a shared musical experience in the context of a group gathering, with every individual present expected to contribute to the music making. Even patients themselves participate in the total experience by singing, clapping, and dancing. As the sick person dances to the accompanying rhythm of drums and music, the heat inside the person's body increases. This leads the possessing spirit to expend excess energy and cool off. By thus restoring the balance between hot and cold, the individual is cured, at least temporarily.

Steven Friedson, who worked among the Tumbuka, briefly summarizes the importance of music and performance to healing among just a few African cultures:

> Africans approach healing through music and dance. Azande "witch doctors" eat special divinatory medicines, activated by drumming, singing, and dancing. In northern Nigeria among the Hausa, the sounds of the *garaya* (two-stringed plucked lute) and *buta* (gourd rattle) call the divine horsemen of the sacred city of Jangare to descend into the heads of *boorii* adepts, thus healing the people they have made sick. Similarly, the various *orisha* and *voudon* spirits of the Guinea Coast, called by their drum motto, mount their horses (possess their devotees). The resultant spirit-possession dance, though religious in nature, is in the first instance often a therapy for those afflicted by the same spirits. Spirit affliction is healed through music and dance in Ethiopia and Sudan, wherever *zar* cults occur. . . . Central, southern, and parts of Equatorial Africa have examples of the *ng'oma* type of healing complex, whose name . . . points to the centrality of music in curative rites. (Friedson 1998, 273–274, references in the original deleted)

In the early 1980s, the authors of this book first heard about a medical practice that involves integrating music into the treatment of both biomedical and psychological disorders. At the time, we thought the field now called *music therapy* was a new mode of treatment and a new occupation. As the preceding examples illustrate, many other cultures have long recognized the connection between music and healing and have integrated the performance arts into their treatments.

Like other forms of aesthetic expression, comparative studies of performance arts are difficult and few. Alan Lomax's comparative studies of dance and song rank with the most ambitious. Lomax and his collaborators analyzed film footage of peoples from around the world, comparing their body movements in everyday activities with their dance movements. They found that dance movements were formalized repetitions of the movements found in daily life. Lomax further argued that the form of dance was correlated with the relative complexity of the society.

Body Arts	Alterations to the physical appearance of the body, including, but not limited to, physical alterations, painting, tattooing, and scarification
Visual Arts	Material, tangible objects that are part of the material culture of a people, including, but not limited to, basketry, pottery, textiles, clothing, jewelry, tools, furniture, painting, masks, and sculpture
Performance Arts	Arts meant to be heard, seen, or personally performed, including music, song, dance, and theater

In his comparative study of songs, Lomax found that differences in song styles were also correlated with societal complexity. The songs of less complex peoples, such as egalitarian foragers, included more vocables (sounds, not words). Words were not enunciated as clearly in their songs, and there was more repetition of vocables and words. The songs of the most complex peoples included fewer vocables, less repetition, and more words, which were more clearly enunciated. Although Lomax's conclusions concerning the correlation between dance and song and relative cultural complexity have been questioned, there are some interesting parallels between his findings and those of Fischer on stylistic elements in ornamental designs.

Art and Culture

Anthropologists are not interested in art simply for art's sake. As we have already seen with the examples of body, visual, and performance arts, art is embedded in a cultural context. Three of many features of this context are religion, gender, and identity.

Secular and Religious Art

In our discussions of the various forms of art, we mentioned that certain artistic products are sacred and others are not. There are both sacred and secular designs, forms, dances, songs, music, and literature. This division between secular and sacred cuts across many forms of art and across most cultures.

In contemporary industrial society, the greatest artistic energies are expended in the creation of secular art, although such art may at times include religious themes. If, for example, you examine the works of the greatest Western painters, architects, and composers of the last century, you will find that most of their work is secular. This was not always true. The great art of earlier periods was for the most part concerned with religion, partly because religious and political authorities so often sponsored artists and their creations. The pyramids and great temples of ancient Egypt were related to conceptions of the afterlife and other dimensions of the supernatural world. While visiting pyramids and great statues of the pharaohs, one must remember that the pharaohs were gods on Earth.

In classical Greece, the cradle of Western European artistic traditions, religion was a central focus for most of the greatest artistic accomplishments. The Parthenon in Athens was the temple of Athena. Most of the greatest Greek public statuary depicted gods such as Poseidon, Zeus, Apollo, and Venus. Much Greek drama had strong religious overtones and was associated with the god Dionysus. In Rome, secular art became more prominent. The great buildings were usually palaces and theaters, while public monuments honoring the triumphs of living or recently dead heroes filled Roman cities. In the Middle Ages, religion regained preeminence. The great buildings of the medieval and Renaissance periods were cathedrals, while the greatest artists of the time labored to fill these buildings with frescoes, mosaics, paintings, statuary, and other artistic works, as well as music, song, and pageantry dedicated to the worship of God.

The 1700s saw an emphasis on reason and science, the Industrial Revolution, the rise of capitalism, and the beginnings of modern political democracy. Ever since, Western art has become increasingly secular. The largest buildings in our cities are no longer dedicated to religion, but to government, commerce, or athletics. Contemporary painters choose secular subjects, from realistic landscapes and buildings to abstract designs and cans of Campbell's soup. The most illustrious composers and performers today seldom produce or perform religious music, but focus on secular and, at times, even irreligious themes. For those of us who learned our culture in a society dominated by secular art, it is important to remember that for most peoples and for most of human history, religion and religious art have been preeminent. The most elaborate artistic achievements of a great many peoples are associated with religious ceremonies: visual arts, music, dances, ornamentations, architecture, and their associated mythologies.

We have already discussed examples of the integration of performance arts like music and dance into African healing practices. Another people for whom art—both visual and verbal arts in this case—is part of curing rituals is the Navajo of the American Southwest. In Navajo belief, the most common cause of illness is the loss of harmony with the environment, often because of the person's violation of a taboo or other transgression. When illness strikes and a diagnosis is made, a Navajo "singer" (curer or medicine man) is called on to organize a complex curing ceremony.

In curing ceremonies (and there were traditionally hundreds of such ceremonies), the singer addresses and calls on the Holy People, who are spiritual beings believed by Navajo to have the power to restore sick people to harmony and beauty. Ceremonies usually occur in a hogan (house) at night, and in theory the procedures must be executed perfectly for the cure to work.

For the ceremony, the singer creates images of the Holy People out of sand, called sandpaintings. Navajo sandpaintings are visual representations of the Holy People that are created, used in a single ceremony, and then destroyed. Most sandpaintings are stylized scenes of events involving various Holy People that occurred in the mythological past. Each sandpainting is part of a ceremony that also includes other sacred objects (such as rattles and prayer sticks) and lengthy songs or chants recited by the singer. The songs/chants that are recited over the sandpainting and the patient may last for hours. Most songs/chants tell of the myths depicted in the specific sandpainting.

In their years of learning to become singers, Navajo singers must memorize the lengthy songs and chants that they recite over sick people to restore their harmony with the world. Singers also learn to make precise sandpaintings that represent specific mythical scenes and events. To make the images, a singer, usually with the help of his family members and/or apprentices, collects and mixes sand and other materials of various colors, including white, red, yellow, black, and blue, with charcoal, corn pollen, and various plant materials. Pictures are created by carefully dribbling fine grains of sand through the fingers onto the prepared floor of the hogan.

There are literally hundreds of sandpaintings. Most ceremonies involve a combination of many sandpaintings used in association with particular chants. Because

some are quite large and enormously detailed, they often take hours to create. But all must be exact representations of the ideal model of the mythical scene or event depicted. The images are stylized drawings of the Holy People, many of whom are depicted with weapons and armor. Most scenes represented in the sandpaintings are from particular myths that are familiar to the patient and audience.

Sandpaintings are made for the express purpose of inducing the Holy People to come to the hogan where the ceremony is held. The Holy People are attracted by their images in the sandpainting and, once consecrated with pollen, the sand images and the Holy People become one and the same and thus holy. This process of transforming the sand figures into actual spiritual beings is termed *transubstantiation* and is a commonly occurring feature of religious art. The very same idea is found in the Eucharist of the Roman Catholic Church, with the conversion of wine and bread into the "blood and body of Christ." During the ceremony, the patient is seated on the sandpainting itself, which is imbued with the power of the Holy People. The singer completes the transfer of power to the patient when he rubs the patient's body with the sand of the images of the Holy People. After each phase of the ceremony is finished, the sandpainting is destroyed and the sand carefully removed from the Hogan.

Navajo sandpaintings certainly are works of art. Some Anglos who have seen them think it is a shame to destroy such beautiful images that the singers and their helpers have worked so hard to create. But in the context of Navajo beliefs, sandpaintings are made for specific curing ceremonials held for particular patients. That is their purpose—not expressing the singer's creativity, making an artistic statement, celebrating Navajo culture, or publicly displaying the singer's talents. For Navajo, fulfilling that purpose requires that the paintings not be permanent.

Navajo sandpaintings and the singing of curers clearly have strong religious overtones, but the division between their secular and religious purposes is not always clear. The kachina dolls of the Hopis are small figures carved out of cottonwood root and painted to look like one of the kachinas or supernatural beings that are a central focus of their religious life (see Chapters 10 and 14). Traditionally, these dolls were given to girls at ceremonial dances by people wearing kachina costumes and masks. The dolls themselves were not ritual items, but rather a way to help the children learn about and recognize the 500 or so different kachina spirits. Similarly, the Hispanic peoples of New Mexico have a tradition of producing *bultos*, which are carved wooden crucifixes and figures of saints, and *retablos,* which are flat wooden boards, painted with images of Christ or saints. Today in New Mexico, there are dozens of artists who produce and sell *bultos* and *retablos.* Some of these paintings and figures of saints find their way into churches or family chapels and altars, but the majority are used in a more secular context as decorative art for the home. Religious symbolism is often used to decorate clothing and other items of everyday use, blurring the distinction between secular and sacred art.

Religious considerations have other effects on secular art as well, frequently placing limits on secular artistic expressions. The use of certain types of motifs or themes may be religiously forbidden. The Koran prohibits the use of human images, which are viewed as idolatry. Thus, many Islamic peoples extended this ban to include any pictorial representation of humans or animals. As a result, much of the art of Islamic peoples is devoid of naturalistic representations, focusing instead on elaborate geometric or curvilinear designs. The Shakers emphasized singing and dancing as important parts of their religious services but prohibited the use of musical instruments.

Art and Gender

Gender differences are often reflected in body, visual, performance, and verbal arts. Colors and designs are sometimes considered male or female, most familiarly reflected in clothing and body decoration. Gender also influences who creates and performs certain types of visual, performance, and verbal arts. The BaMbuti Pygmies of the African rain forest have a ritual performance involving dance and music they call *molimo.* They view the forest as like their parent and, like any parent, the forest looks after its children—themselves. Therefore, when misfortune strikes, it must be because the forest is asleep. To wake up the forest, at night the women and children retire to their huts while the men make *molimo* music. Women are not supposed to know that the *molimo* is just a long, flutelike instrument stored in a local stream, but instead believe it to be some kind of forest animal. (In fact, women seem to know all about the *molimo.*)

As discussed in Chapter 11, men and women are usually involved in the production of different types of durable items, and usually the individuals involved in production decorate the items as well. In many cases, the aesthetic qualities of the items are an integral part of the production process itself, as with the shape of a pottery vessel or metal tool, or the design in a blanket or a basket. In other instances, however, decorative arts are separate and distinct from the production of the basic item, and decorative artists may be defined by gender.

Among the Plains Indians, beadwork and quillwork were produced by women. The only men who produced beadwork and quillwork were *berdaches,* men who dressed and acted as women (see Chapter 11). Although both women and men painted hides, there were distinct differences in subject matter. Women painted only geometric designs. The hide containers called *parafleches* used for the storage of food and clothing were made by women and were painted only in geometric designs. Representational designs of people, horses, and other animals and supernatural beings were painted only by men. Tepees and buffalo robes, though made by women, were painted by either men or women, depending on whether the design was to be geometric (by women) or representational (by men).

Some visual art objects are made for specific rituals or ceremonies. Initiation rites are usually held for only one sex (see Chapter 14). The art produced for them, therefore, is sometimes "sex specific." In many cultures of the highlands of Papua New Guinea, long bamboo flutes are played at male initiation ceremonies. Women are not supposed to know about the existence of the flutes. Many initiation ceremonies also include carved and painted masks, supposedly kept secret from women and uninitiated boys.

Performance arts are often carried out during religious ceremonies. Men have historically played the dominant role in most religions. Not surprisingly, in most societies, men dominate the performance arts associated with religion. For example, even though many of the Hopi kachinas are female, in traditional kachina dances all dancers, even those impersonating female spirits, are men. In ancient Greek drama, the roles of women were played by men. In the West, women were not allowed to participate in certain performance arts long after they had become secularized. The role of Juliet, in the original production of Shakespeare's play, was performed by a young boy because women could not be actors in Shakespeare's time. It was not until the late seventeenth century that women could perform in the English theater.

Social Functions of Art

Does art exist solely to satisfy the human desire for the aesthetic? Perhaps, but if so, why have humans expended such incredible energy in its creation? Perhaps art also has a critical role in human social life and cultural existence. Through the use of art, people can express their identities as members of particular groups, while at the same time demonstrating their individuality. Through the production, consumption, and use of art, we can express our personal individuality, our group identities (including ethnic affiliation), and even our social status.

Individuality. Many of us attempt to express our individuality by creating art or displaying art, as shown by the widespread appeal of handmade goods produced by skilled craftspeople. Since the advent of the Industrial Revolution in the nineteenth century, the attraction of handmade over machinemade goods has been their individuality. This individuality is not solely the result of the differing technical skill of the makers; also, the makers have consciously tried to make every item unique by varying colors and designs. Thus, if one looks at Oriental rugs, Native American jewelry, pottery and baskets, Maya textiles from Guatemala, or wood carvings from New Guinea, rarely does one find two identical items. If they are identical, it is probably because they were produced for the commercial market.

Similarly, our clothing and houses express our individuality. Even though we usually conform to the norms of our society in clothing styles, most of us abhor uniforms, and thus we enhance our clothes in some manner to make them uniquely ours. In their dwellings, people also attempt to express their individuality. Although all Maori dwellings were carved and painted, different designs and images were used. Today in suburban North America, builders of subdivisions usually vary the houses by using a range of floor plans, building materials, and colors. Many residents of older neighborhoods, though, still think the new subdivisions lack character, style, and individuality.

Social identity. As well as displaying our individuality, art is a means of expressing social identity, publicly displaying what kind of person you are or which group of people you identify with. In the 1960s and early 1970s, many young people wore long hair, beads, and baggy clothes decorated with peace signs and upside-down flags. Some traveled the country in old Volkswagen minibuses or school buses that were hand painted in strange colors and designs. The minute you saw them, you knew they were "hippies." Clothing styles, hairstyles, and other art forms are commonly used to indicate social group identity, from the black leather jackets painted with club emblems of motorcycle gangs to the shepherd crook spears and red sashes of the Cheyenne Dog Soldier society.

A widespread use of art to express social membership has to do with ethnic affiliation. In Chapter 17, we discuss ethnic boundary markers in more detail, but here it is important to note that art is one of the common expressions of ethnic identity. Clothing styles and decoration are important visual markers of ethnic identity. Plaid kilts are markers of Scots as much as beaded clothing and feather headdresses are of Native Americans. A woman in Guatemala wearing a *huipuli* is a Maya. If you see a man wearing a cowboy hat and boots in Europe, you can guess that he is an American tourist, even though he has probably never ridden a horse or seen many cows.

Ethnicity is expressed in more than clothing. The full range of artistic forms—body, visual, performance, and verbal arts—is employed to display one's ethnic identity. Thus, we speak of ethnic art, ethnic dance, ethnic music, ethnic songs, ethnic literature, and ethnic foods. Despite our use of the word *ethnic* in such contexts, ultimately, of course, all art is ethnic art because it is associated with a specific ethnic group and everyone is a part of some ethnic group. For various reasons, people value and pay premium prices for the art produced by ethnic groups other than their own.

From an anthropological perspective, much of the multicultural movement in contemporary North America—and particularly in colleges and universities—is really about understanding and appreciating "ethnic" forms of artistic expression. When Anglo-Americans talk about "other cultures," as often as not they are referring to African, Hispanic, Asian, and other "non-Anglo" Americans. When they "celebrate diversity," as often as not they are celebrating differences in literature and other forms of verbal art, interpreting graffiti as a legitimate art form, listening to African or Mexican music, eating South Asian or Vietnamese foods, and so forth. Overall the multicultural movement has had a positive influence on intercultural tolerance and understanding. In fact, multiculturalism is part of what anthropologists have been trying to get across to their students for nearly a century. But perhaps more people ought to realize that appreciating multicultural diversity should mean far more than celebrating diversity in forms of artistic expression.

Social status. Finally, relative social status within societies is reflected in the use of art. As discussed earlier, body arts are frequently an indicator of social status. Other art forms also indicate status. In many ranked and stratified societies, the rights to use certain art forms may be the property of families or status groups. Only certain

The traditional visual arts of different people of the world are integrated into virtually every aspect of life, with some of the most important forms found in the everyday material items they make and use. Depending on the society, these artistic traditions find expression in clothing, pottery, basketry, and other furnishings of their homes. Although these material items may be elaborately decorated, for the most part these items are utilitarian, valued not just for their beauty but for their usefulness as well.

In the global economy, all goods and services have to compete for market share. Thus, as people become economically integrated into larger global markets, local traditional handmade goods must compete with mass-produced imported goods. Mass-produced aluminum, tin, ceramic, and plastic pots, pans, kettles, jugs, jars, plates, bowls, and cups compete with locally made pottery, basketry, hide, horn, and wooden items. Machinemade cloth, blankets, canvas, plastic sheets, and mass-produced clothing compete with traditional woven textiles, bark cloth, felt, and handmade clothing. Both cost and quality are factors in this competition. For the most part, these imported items are more durable and more useful than locally made goods. Because traditional goods are labor intensive to produce, once a group becomes even marginally involved in a cash economy, the handmade items are no longer competitive in terms of costs. As a result, the global economy is resulting in rapid and dramatic changes in the material culture. Throughout the world, local, traditional, handmade goods are being replaced by mass-produced, machinemade items. And, as people stop making their own material goods, many of the artistic traditions associated with making them are disappearing as well.

This is not a new trend. During the Industrial Revolution in Western Europe and North America, the same process occurred as machinemade goods rapidly replaced locally made, handcrafted goods. In reaction, the so-called Arts and Crafts Movement emerged in the late nineteenth century, producing handcrafted furniture, pottery, and other goods.

An example of how quickly such a change can occur is found in northern India with the production of Varanasi saris. Varanasi (Banaras), in the northern Indian state of Uttar Pradesh, has been a center for textile weaving since the ancient period. Originally, the textiles woven here were cotton. During the Moghal (Muslim) period, however, the local people began weaving in silk and became famous for the production of elaborate brocade saris with intricate designs using various colors of silk and gold and silver thread. Highly valued, usually selling for $150 to $1,500 each, these saris have been traditionally prized as wedding gifts for brides and for formal wear for special events throughout northern India.

The production of Varanasi silk saris has been a cottage industry and a livelihood for more than 100,000 weavers and their families. The vast majority of weavers work either independently in their own homes or in small shops for master weavers. Using only simple foot-powered looms and small punch cards as guides for designs, three weavers work together to produce a sari. The most elaborate of these designs are wedding scenes and royal processions with elephants and carriages. A normal sari is 6 yards long and takes the weavers 15 days to a month to finish, but saris with more intricate designs may take as long as six months to produce. Sari weavers are highly esteemed artists/craftsmen, despite the fact that they are usually Muslims, datils ("untouchables"), or OBC ("other backward castes"), the last being an official legal status in India. The Varanasi weavers have, by Indian standards, traditionally earned reasonable incomes, and many of the master weavers have been relatively wealthy.

In the mid-1990s, the Varanasi weavers began to find it increasingly difficult to sell their saris. Changes in government trade policies allowed the importation of Chinese silk yarn and machinemade Chinese silk saris. Not only were the Chinese saris more durable than Varanasi saris, but the Chinese had copied traditional Varanasi designs and their saris were much cheaper. At about the same time, textile mills in Gujarat (western India) and in southern India began to produce machinemade printed copies of Varanasi-style saris. To make the situation even more difficult for the Varanasi weavers, Western influences have had an impact on dress styles. Women, particularly in the more prosperous, high-tech regions of India, have adopted a more Western style of dress. As a result, over the last decade, competition from cheaper machinemade saris and a declining demand due to changes in dress styles have resulted in the improvishment of many of the Varanasi weavers. No longer able to support their families as weavers and lacking any other marketable skills, many have committed suicide; some have become beggars or sell their blood or even their children to wealthy families. Others have joined a mass exodus to other cities to find work as day laborers, or to Gujarat or southern India to work in modern textile mills.

Critical Thinking Questions

1. Does an object have to be handcrafted to qualify as art? Human considerations aside, does it really make any difference whether a "Varanasi sari" is entirely machinemade in China or Gujarat as long as it looks authentic?

2. Does an object have to be "one of a kind" to qualify as art? Can one speak of mass-produced art?

3. Are the traditional ethnic and regional art forms of the world doomed to disappear? Is a homogeneous global art tradition going to replace them?

individuals have the right to wear or use particular colors or designs, sing particular songs, dance particular dances, and even tell particular stories. This control over the use or performance of particular artistic expression is a symbolic indicator of individual social status.

Similarly, in contemporary Western society, we use art to demonstrate our relative status. We display our status in our homes, automobiles, furnishings, and clothing, communicating to the world, "Look what we can afford to buy." We also demonstrate our status in what we hang on our walls, read, listen to, and watch. In our consumption of visual, performance, and verbal arts, the evaluation, of course, is more subjective and difficult to measure. But for many people, opera, ballet, and classical music have higher status than comedy, square dancing, and country and western or rap music. Classical literature has higher status than romance novels, science fiction, and comic books.

Summary

1. All cultures have artistic objects, designs, songs, dances, and other ways of expressing their appreciation of the aesthetic. The aesthetic impulse is universal, although cultures vary in their ways of expressing it and in the social functions and cultural meanings they attach to it.

2. People raised in the Western tradition are inclined to think of art as something set apart from everyday life—as when we use the phrase "fine arts"—yet we all express ourselves aesthetically in many ways, including how we dress, decorate our houses, and eat our meals.

3. In addition to allowing people to express themselves aesthetically, art serves communicative functions by encoding meanings and messages in symbolic forms.

4. Art takes a multitude of forms, including, at minimum, body, visual, and performance arts. People around the world change their bodily appearance by such means as physical alterations, application of body paints, tattoos, and scarification. These decorations of the body are used for a variety of purposes, including beautification, expression of individual or group identity, display of privilege or social position, and symbolic indication of social maturity. The tattooing practices of the Maori of New Zealand and other Polynesians exemplify some of these functions.

5. In the visual arts, humankind as a whole has shown enormous creativity in form, style, design, techniques, materials, and many other features. Ornamentation of tools, clothing, basketry, houses, and practically all other material objects is a universal practice. The Northwest Coast peoples illustrate one way in which art varies in style and two-dimensional representation.

6. Performance arts include the use of sound and movement for both aesthetic and communicative purposes. In preindustrial cultures, performances of music (including song and percussion), dance, and theater often involve audience participation, as they often do in the everyday lives of people everywhere. Often, performance art is tightly integrated into a people's spiritual and religious life, from Judeo-Christian worship services to possession trances in the *voudon* religion of the Caribbean. The integration of music and dance into the healing practices of the Tumbuka of Malawi and many other African peoples shows that using music to help cure both physical and psychological ills is not a recent Western innovation.

7. Perhaps many forms of art began as "sacred" in that they were connected to the appeal to or worship of spiritual beings. Certainly, the religious elements of artistic expression are important not only in the history of Western art but also in the artistic traditions of people the world over. In their complex curing ceremonies, Navajo singers used both visual arts (sandpaintings) and performance arts (chants/songs) in appealing to the Holy People. Distinguishing "sacred" and "secular" art seems like a simple thing, but objects with religious significance are often used for practical purposes.

8. Art is connected to other social and cultural elements such as gender, identity, and status. In many societies, certain arts and art forms are associated with women and others with men. Ethnic identity is commonly expressed in art and serves as ethnic boundary markers. Finally, within societies, relative social status is frequently expressed in the consumption of art.

Key Terms

art
aesthetic
body arts

visual arts
performance arts

Suggested Readings

Bailey, Garrick, Daniel C. Swan, John W. Nunley, and E. Sean StandingBear. *Art of the Osage*. Seattle: St. Louis Art Museum and Washington University Press, 2004.

In this study by two anthropologists, an art historian and an Osage artist/craftsman, Osage art is examined within its cultural historical context. Symbolism in Osage art is shown to be both an appeal to Wah-kon-da (god) for continued blessings and an important mnemonic device for communicating and perpetuating traditional cultural knowledge and beliefs.

Boas, Franz. *Primitive Art*. New York: Dover Publications, Inc., 1955 (original 1927).

The first systematic treatment of the subject by an anthropologist. Despite its original publication date over 80 years ago, this book remains insightful today.

Brain, Robert. *The Decorated Body*. New York: Harper & Row, 1979.

Though written in popular style, this is a well-researched introduction to the broad range of techniques used by humans to decorate their bodies.

Faris, James C. *Nuba Personal Art*. London: Duckworth, 1972.

The Nuba people of Sudan are famous for their body painting. This book presents the classic study of Nuba painting and is a good general introduction to body painting as well.

Kirk, John T. *The Shaker World: Art, Life, Belief*. New York: Harry N. Abrams, 1997.

The Shakers, a communal religious sect, were a small but influential group in nineteenth-century America. This book discusses the evolution of their religious beliefs and practices and how they influenced their distinctive art styles.

Levenson, Jay A., ed. *Circa 1492: Art in the Age of Exploration*. Washington, D.C.: National Gallery of Art, and New Haven, Conn.: Yale University Press, 1991.

The catalog for a museum exhibition at the National Gallery of Art, this is an excellent visual introduction to the range of major artistic traditions present at the dawn of globalization.

Mead, Sidney Moko. *Te Maori: Maori Art from New Zealand Collections*. New York: Harry N. Abrams, 1984.

A museum exhibition catalog, the edited text provides an excellent discussion of Maori art within the broader context of Maori culture.

Nunley, John, and Judith Bettelheim. *Caribbean Festival Arts*. Seattle: University of Washington Press, 1988.

This work focuses on the history and development of festivals in the Caribbean, with particular attention to their elaborate costuming. Although African American peoples form the vast core of the participants, on some islands east Indians and other groups contribute and actively participate.

Parezo, Nancy J. *Navajo Sandpainting: From Religious Act to Commercial Art*. Albuquerque: University of New Mexico Press, 1991.

An excellent study of Navajo sandpainting and how some individuals were able to convert sandpaintings into a commercial form that did not violate religious beliefs.

Phillips, Ruth. *Trading Identities: The Souvenir in Native North American Art from the Northeast, 1700–1900*. Seattle: University of Washington Press, and Montreal: McGill-Queen's University Press, 1998.

In this study, the author discusses early European influences on Native American art in eastern Canada and the northeastern United States, as well as the manner in which some of these arts were commoditized and marketed to Euro-Americans.

Schevill, Margot Blum. *Maya Textiles of Guatemala.* Austin: University of Texas Press, 1993.

The text of this book serves as an excellent introduction to Maya textiles, while the accompanying catalog of the Eisen Collection of the Hearst Museum presents a good visual picture of the diversity of Maya textiles at the end of the nineteenth century.

Media Resources

The Wadsworth Anthropology Resource Center
academic.cengage.com/anthropology

The Wadsworth discipline resource website that accompanies *Humanity: An Introduction to Cultural Anthropology,* Eighth Edition, includes a rich array of material, including online anthropological video clips, to help you in the study of cultural anthropology and the specific topics covered in this chapter. Other material includes a case study forum with excerpts from various Wadsworth authors, map exercises, scientist interviews, breaking news in anthropology, and links to additional useful online material. Begin by selecting Cultural Anthropology to take you to videos, research, and more. From the homepage, you may also select Applied Anthropology, which directs you to essays, glossary terms, the case study forum, and a list of internships and careers in anthropology.

16 GLOBALIZATION

© Dimodia/The Imago Works

The Development of Global Trade

European Expansion

The World and the Industrial Revolution

The Emergence of the Global Economy

Globalization: The Continuing Process

Population Growth and Inequalities in the Global Economy

Consequences of Globalization and the Global Economy

Mumbai, India—with a Worli village temple in the foreground and the modern part of the city in the background—reflects the contrast between poverty and wealth, traditional and cosmopolitan, that is one of the consequences of globalization.

Questions addressed in this chapter

When did globalization begin, and what were its initial social and cultural consequences?

Why is it important to understand European colonial expansion and the effects of the Industrial Revolution?

What political and technological changes occurred after World War II that allowed for the development of an integrated global economy?

What are the social, cultural, and economic consequences of the emergence of the global economy?

Until the violent street protests at the meeting of the World Trade Organization in Seattle in late 1999, few Americans had given more than passing attention to issues of globalization and free trade. To most, globalization seemed to be part of the natural evolution of the world economic system, which, during the decade of the 1990s, had resulted in economic prosperity for the United States. We assumed that globalization was bringing or eventually would bring prosperity to the rest of the peoples of the world as well. Since Seattle, virtually every major international economic meeting or summit has brought increasing numbers of protesters into the streets. At the G-8 meetings in Genoa, Italy, in the summer of 2001, between 100,000 and 150,000 demonstrators filled the streets. What was the problem? The protesters have been variously labeled "anticapitalists," "anarchists," "environmentalists," and even "Luddites." But no single label can be readily applied to these protesters because they range widely in their concerns about the effects of globalization and in their ideologies.

It was not until the 1980s that the term *globalization* first came into common usage. Today, although we hear and use the term almost daily, we might find it difficult to define. Globalization is not a thing or a product, but rather a process. **Globalization** refers to the worldwide changes that are increasingly integrating and remolding the lives of the people of the world. Most commonly, we speak of the *global economy* and think of globalization primarily in economic terms. Although economic changes are certainly the driving force behind globalization, it is having far more profound effects on our way of life than merely what we eat, what we wear, and how we make our living. It is having an impact on our political, social, and cultural institutions as well.

Globalization began 500 years ago, with the voyage of Columbus, and has had two stages of development. The earliest stage, the period from about 1500 to the mid-twentieth century, saw the development of a global trade network, which eventually connected, directly or indirectly, every group of people in the world. The second stage, which began to develop at the end of World War II, saw the development of global marketing of products and the emergence of a global economy.

The Development of Global Trade

Before C.E. 1500, the major world regions were relatively isolated from one another. Most contact was limited to societies that occupied adjacent territories. Trade was minimal, and the long-distance trade that existed between Europe and China or Africa seldom involved direct exchange between members of those societies. Trade was managed by intervening groups whose members acted as middlemen. Thus, although more informed Europeans, Asians, and Africans were aware of the existence of the others, their knowledge was extremely limited and rarely based on firsthand contact. Although innovations in technology and cultural institutions spread from one population center to another, diffusion was slow because there was no direct contact.

Although the terms *Old World* and *New World* are ethnocentric, this distinction is useful from a cultural/historical perspective. The Old World—Europe, Africa, and Asia—did form a unit within which trade and contact, however tenuous and limited, allowed for the spread of technology and institutions, primarily from Asia westward to Europe and Africa. *New World* is a term usually applied only to the Americas, but it could just as well include Australia and most of Oceania because both of these regions were outside this exchange network before 1500.

Thus, before European expansion, the world consisted of two broad geographical regions with peoples who for much of their history had developed technologies and lifeways in isolation from one another.

European Expansion

With the "discovery" of the Americas by Christopher Columbus in 1492, the age of European expansion began. In population and technological achievement, Europe was not the most developed region of the world during the fifteenth century. China and the Mogul (Islamic) states of India were the richest and economically and politically the most powerful countries in the world. Asia had a total population four to five times that of Europe. Compared with the states of Asia, European countries were small. The populations of such soon-to-be-imperial powers as England, Portugal, Spain, and the Netherlands were insignificant in comparison with those of China or the Mogul states. Even the Aztec Empire in the Americas may have had a population equal to the total population of these four European countries.

The major advantage that Europeans had over most other peoples was their military technology. Guns, crossbows, iron weapons, armor, and horses gave them significant advantages over the stone-tool military technologies of the peoples of the Americas and Oceania. To a lesser degree, Europeans also enjoyed a military advantage over most peoples of Africa. The same was not true in Asia: on land, European armies enjoyed no technological advantage. Only in naval warfare were the Europeans superior to the Asian states.

These factors influenced European expansionist policies during the early period and caused the histories of contact with Asia, Africa, the Americas, and Oceania to differ significantly. With some exceptions, principally in the Americas, the expansion of Europe during the sixteenth, seventeenth, and eighteenth centuries consisted of the development of maritime mercantile empires, as opposed to actual overseas colonies and territorial empires.

Because European contact took such different forms from one region to the next, we examine the history of contact region by region (see Figure 16.1).

Conquest of the Americas. In 1492, Columbus found a new world inhabited by numerous peoples, who still had only an advanced stone-tool technology. Initially, the Spaniards were disappointed in their new discoveries because they failed to find the immense treasures of the Indies they were expecting. On the island of Hispaniola, where they first settled, there were no vast riches and most Spanish settlers quickly turned their attention to the development of sugarcane plantations and cattle ranches.

During the first quarter-century after its discovery, the New World attracted only a few thousand Spaniards. In 1519, the Spanish landed on the coast of Mexico, and by 1521, they had completed the conquest of the Aztec Empire. Aztec gold and silver sent back to Spain encouraged the migration of others to search for still more wealth and plunder. Between 1532 and 1534, a Spanish military expedition conquered the Inca Empire and took the wealth of Peru for Spain. By the late 1500s, Spanish expeditions had explored much of the Americas and had located and conquered every major Native American state. In little more than half a century, the Spaniards had conquered the richest and most populous portions of the Americas: the West Indies, Mesoamerica, and Peru.

The Treaty of Tordesillas, signed in 1494, divided the non-Christian world between Spain and Portugal. The easternmost part of South America, Brazil, fell into the Portuguese portion. The coastal regions of Brazil were well suited for sugarcane plantations. Starting in 1500, Portuguese settlers began colonizing Brazil, and by 1550, small settlements were scattered along most of the coast.

The Spanish and Portuguese were able to conquer large portions of the Americas in a surprisingly short time. As the Spanish demonstrated in their conquests of the Aztecs and Incas, their military superiority was so pronounced that their small armies numbering in the hundreds were able to vanquish well-organized native armies whose troops numbered in the thousands.

The main period of conquest and territorial expansion had ended by 1600, and Spanish settlers turned their attention to exploitation of the West Indies, Mesoamerica, and Peru, where they developed silver and gold mines, ranches, and plantations. The Portuguese contented themselves with coastal sugarcane plantations in Brazil.

The cultural impact of the Spanish and Portuguese was most pronounced in those regions directly under their control. Existing native political organizations were either replaced or modified and integrated into a colonial government. European technology and livestock were introduced—iron tools, plows, cattle, horses, sheep, and so forth—as existing economic systems were altered to meet European needs. Indian labor was used in the mines and on the plantations and ranches that were developed. Missionaries flooded the Americas seeking converts. Temples were replaced by Christian churches. In some regions, such as Mexico and Peru, native peoples managed to maintain their languages and Indian social

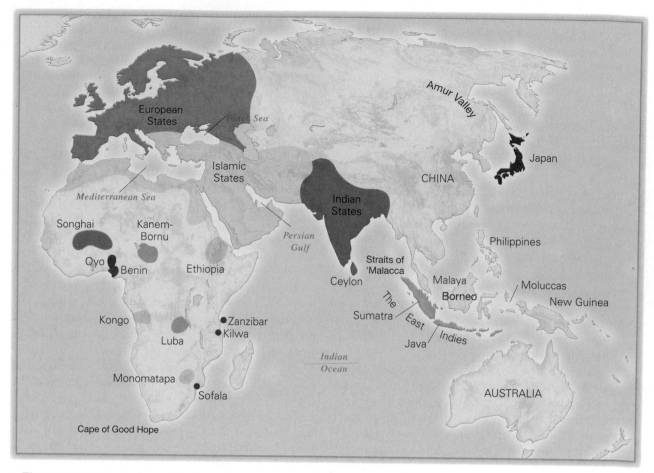

▲ **Figure 16.1** Major States and Regions of Europe, Asia, and Africa (ca. 1500).

and ethnic identity, but even these societies were given a veneer of Christian customs and beliefs. Even Native American peoples beyond direct European control were affected. Old World crops, domesticated animals, and metal tools in limited numbers were diffused to these autonomous peoples. In some regions, the introduction of European items and animals, such as the horse, revolutionized native societies.

As important as these material elements were in altering Native American culture, they were not the only causes of change. Old World diseases such as smallpox, measles, influenza, bubonic plague, diphtheria, typhus, cholera, malaria, and scarlet fever were also introduced by early Europeans. Isolated as they had been, the peoples of the Americas had no natural immunities to these diseases. Because these illnesses spread well in advance of European contact, it is impossible to estimate with any exactness the size of native populations before that contact. The massive population decline caused by European diseases is best documented in regions under direct Spanish and Portuguese control. Father Bartolome de las Casas reported that there were 1,100,000 Indians 14 years of age or older on Hispaniola; even the most conservative estimated a native population of 100,000. Regardless of the original figure, by 1535 only 500 Indians were left on Hispaniola. In Mexico, the decline was also severe. One study places the contact population at 25,200,000 in 1519; with a decline to 16,800,000 by 1532; 2,650,000 by 1568; and 1,075,000 by 1605. Although these estimates are open to question, there is no doubt that Native American societies suffered severe population declines after European contact.

From the very beginning, the Spanish and Portuguese were heavily dependent on Indian slave labor to work their mines and plantations and to perform other menial tasks. As the native populations decreased, the land and mine owners faced a labor shortage. New sources of human labor had to be found to fill the expanding vacuum.

◀ Conversion of native peoples to Christianity was one of the primary interests of the Spanish in the Americas.

Awareness of the rapid and dramatic decline in the Native American population is critical to understanding not only the history of the Americas during the past 500 years but the histories of Africa and Europe as well. The population decline of the Native Americans created a vacuum that was filled by the massive migration of Old World peoples. Because neither Spain nor Portugal sent a sufficient number of emigrants to offset the declining Native American population, another source of labor had to be found. This was the genesis of the African slave trade. Starting in the 1490s, ever-increasing numbers of African slaves were sent to the Spanish and Portuguese colonies. By the eighteenth century, these colonies had more individuals of African ancestry than of European ancestry.

During the late sixteenth and early seventeenth centuries, other European powers—England, France, and the Netherlands—began to contest Spanish and Portuguese dominance of the Americas. For the most part, these countries occupied portions of the Americas outside the limits of Spanish and Portuguese control: some of the small islands in the West Indies and the Atlantic coast of North America. The Native American populations in this region had already suffered the devastating effects of Old World disease and were of little interest to northern Europeans as a source of labor. Unlike the Spanish and Portuguese to the south, northern European settlers were primarily interested in the land the Indians occupied, and they considered Native Americans to be a hindrance and a danger to their settlements, not an economic resource. As these northern European settlers pushed their frontiers into the interior, Native American populations were evicted and forced west.

As early as 1619, English colonists in Virginia were purchasing African slaves. The number of African slaves in the French, English, and Dutch West Indies and in English North America steadily increased during the 1600s and 1700s, paralleling the pattern of growth in the Spanish and Portuguese colonies.

Although Native Americans were seldom enslaved in the northern European colonies, their labor was used indirectly. Unlike the Spanish and Portuguese, the French, English, and Dutch quickly established trading networks in the interior regions, exchanging cloth, metal tools, guns, and other items of European manufacture for hides and furs. By the late 1700s, most of the Native American societies in North America had regular trade contact with these Europeans. By the end of the eighteenth century, virtually every Native American society had been affected by European expansion. Many had already become extinct. Others were under the direct political and economic control of European colonial governments. Even those societies that had been able to retain their autonomy had seen their populations sharply reduced through disease or warfare and their lifestyles changed by the introduction of European material goods and technology. Few, if any, "pristine" societies were left in the New World.

Sub-Saharan Africa. Portuguese explorers first made contact with sub-Saharan Africans in 1444 and 1445. Trade quickly followed, and Portuguese explorer-traders steadily expanded farther south down the west coast of Africa. In the 1470s, they reached the Gold Coast and found the area so rich in gold that in 1482 they erected a fort to protect their trading interests. This fortification was the first of a series of coastal forts that the Portuguese established to keep other European powers out of the region. By 1488, Portuguese explorers had reached the Cape of Good Hope, the southern extremity of the African continent. Between 1497 and 1499, Vasco da Gama successfully sailed to India and back by way of the Cape. By the end of the fifteenth century, the Portuguese had established the basis for a trading empire that stretched along the coast of Africa and all the way to Asia. The problem confronting the Portuguese was how to strengthen and maintain their hold against European rivals. They created trading ports along the African coast not only to acquire gold and ivory but also to serve as way stations for ships bound to and from Asia.

In 1482, the Portuguese discovered one of the largest states in Africa, the Kongo kingdom, near the mouth of the Congo. The Portuguese developed friendly relations with the Kongo, and in 1490 missionaries and various artisans were sent there. The missionaries soon converted the king and many of the people. The capital of the kingdom was rebuilt on a European model and renamed Sao Salvador. Many younger Kongo went voluntarily to Portugal for formal education.

Although gold and ivory were the primary trade items, early Portuguese traders dealt in other commodities as well: slaves, sea lion oil, hides, cotton cloth, and beeswax. Slaves eventually emerged as the most valuable trade item of the African coast, and it was the slave trade that led other European countries to challenge Portuguese control.

Slavery and the slave trade existed in portions of Europe before European expansion. On the Iberian Peninsula in Spain and Portugal, slavery knew no racial or religious boundaries: slaves could be black or white, Christian, Jewish, or Muslim. The number of slaves in Spain and Portugal was extremely limited, however. During the early 1500s, the market for African slaves in the New World grew rapidly.

The magnitude of the African slave trade cannot be determined with any exactness. We know that the slave trade grew steadily during the sixteenth and seventeenth centuries, reached its zenith during the last decades of the eighteenth century, and ended in about 1870. Estimates of the number of African slaves sent to the Americas range from about 10 million to about 50 million, but the actual number was probably closer to 10 million. Likewise, estimates of the number of slaves taken to the Americas during particular centuries vary. Estimates for the sixteenth century range from 250,000 to 900,000; for the seventeenth century from 1,341,000 to 2,750,000; and for the eighteenth and nineteenth centuries from 6 million to 11 million.

The Portuguese were the first major traders of African slaves in the Americas. In the earliest period of the trade, the slaves who were brought to America had already been slaves in Africa. However, as the demand for slaves increased, the Portuguese turned to raiding to acquire them. As early as 1575, Portuguese mercenaries and African "allies" began systematically to stage slave raids throughout much of central Africa.

In the late 1500s, the English and French began competing for a share of the African slave trade and marketing slaves in the Spanish colonies. During the early 1600s, with the establishment of French, English, and Dutch colonies in the West Indies, even more traders attempted to tap this lucrative trade. French, English, Dutch, Swedes, and Danes obtained slaves along the west coast of Africa. For the most part, these new traders concentrated on West Africa, where they established their own fortified trading stations and drove the Portuguese out of many posts. The French, English, and Dutch were not challenging the Portuguese only in Africa; they were also competing for the Asian trade. To reach Asia, they had to circumnavigate Africa, and they needed ports. In 1652, the Dutch East India Company established a colony of Dutch farmers at the Cape of Good Hope to supply their ships.

By the late 1700s, the French, English, Dutch, Portuguese, and Spanish controlled ports scattered along the western coast and much of the eastern coast of Africa. Most of these posts were manned by only a handful of Europeans. Actual European settlements were few and small; the main settlements were the Portuguese colonies in Angola and Mozambique, and the Dutch colony at the Cape. Few Europeans had ever penetrated the interior, and little was known of the peoples of interior Africa. Yet, at the same time, the European presence in Africa had produced far-reaching effects on the lives of all Africans through the slave trade and through the introduction of New World food crops.

Slaves were acquired through raiding and warfare, usually in exchange for guns supplied by the Europeans. In Africa, the gun trade and the slave trade were

◄ The introduction of New World crops greatly changed the lives of many of Africa's farming peoples.

inextricably linked. By the early eighteenth century, about 180,000 guns were being traded annually, and by the end of the century, that figure had climbed to between 300,000 and 400,000.

The slave-for-gun trade shifted trade networks and disrupted the existing balance of power among African societies. Some groups, primarily coastal peoples in contact with Europeans, faced the choice of becoming slave raiders and acquiring guns or falling victim to those who opted for raiding. As slave-related warfare escalated, new states sprang up, and there was a concurrent decline in many older states. In West Africa, the power and influence of the old states of Sudan declined. The Songhai Empire disintegrated, and Kanem-Bornu weakened considerably. At the same time, along the coast of West Africa, many small kingdoms and city-states—such as Oyo, Aboney, Ashanti, and Benin—were undergoing rapid expansion, which can be traced to slave traffic. In west central Africa, the Kongo kingdom refused to be involved in the slave trade and disintegrated because the Portuguese supported and encouraged the development of slave-raiding states. Lunda was the largest and most important of these new states.

At the same time that Africa was undergoing this dramatic escalation in warfare, New World crops brought to the continent by Europeans dramatically changed African farming. During the early 1500s, the Portuguese introduced corn, manioc, sweet potatoes, pineapples,

peanuts, papayas, and some lesser crops. The introduction of these new crops, particularly corn and manioc, greatly increased the productivity of farming in Africa. In the savannas and grasslands, corn produced higher yields than native cereal crops, and in the tropical forest regions, manioc was superior to existing starchy crops. Some researchers have suggested that the introduction of corn resulted in a population explosion that minimized the demographic impact of the slave trade.

Thus, the Europeans' quest for slaves caused an escalation in warfare that resulted in major losses in population and significant restructuring of African political power. However, the Europeans also introduced new crops that increased and expanded African farming. Although we cannot describe exactly what happened, we can say with certainty that the population of Africa underwent major changes. Basil Davidson (1969, 235) provides an excellent summary of the situation in Africa at the end of the eighteenth century: "By 1800 or soon after there were few regions where many polities, large or small, old or new, had not clearly felt and reacted to strong pressures of transition. Widely varying in form and power though it certainly was, the impact of change had been constantly and pervasively at work."

Europeans in Asia. The Portuguese were the first Europeans to reach Asia by sea. In 1498, Vasco da Gama landed on the coast of India. The Europeans soon learned that Asia offered a situation quite different from what they had confronted in the Americas and Africa. The population of Asia far surpassed that of Europe, and Asia was divided into numerous highly developed and militarily powerful states. In economic terms, Asia was a self-sufficient region with only limited interest in outside trade. Although Asia offered such desirable goods as silk, cotton textiles, spices, coffee, tea, porcelain, and so forth for trade, the Europeans had little to offer in exchange other than gold and silver bullion.

Da Gama encountered difficulty trading Portuguese goods in India, but eventually he managed to trade away his cargo. The Portuguese quickly realized that the only significant role they could play in the Asian trade was as middlemen in the inter-Asian trade, particularly between the Far East (China) and India. During the early and mid-1500s, the Portuguese established a series of fortified trading ports extending from India to China. Asian goods flowed through these ports to Europe in exchange for silver and gold coming from the Americas. This trade was extremely limited; during the 1500s, the trade between Europe and Asia averaged only 10 ships annually. Of greater economic importance was the fact that an ever-increasing percentage of the lucrative trade among Asian peoples themselves was being carried by Portuguese merchant ships.

The same treaty that gave Portugal a portion of the Americas (Brazil) gave Spain a portion of Asia (the Philippines). In 1564, the Spanish founded Manila (Philippines). Unlike the Portuguese trade that flowed westward around Africa, Spanish ships sailed between Manila and Acapulco, Mexico. From Acapulco, goods were transported over land to Vera Cruz, and from there shipped to Spain.

It was not until after 1600 that other European powers began to compete for the trade with Asia. The earliest of these new competitors were the Dutch, who in 1602 organized the Dutch East India Company. By the mid-1600s, the Dutch had established bases in the East Indies (modern-day Indonesia) and Ceylon (modern-day Sri Lanka). With fewer ships and less capital, the English were at a disadvantage relative to the Dutch during the first half of the seventeenth century. Early English attempts to establish trading bases in Asia failed. Their first success came in India (Madras) in 1639. By 1665, they had Bombay, and in 1691, Calcutta.

While Western European maritime powers were active on the southern and eastern coasts of Asia, Russia was expanding by land across northern Asia. By 1637, the Russians had reached the Pacific coast of Asia, and by the 1690s, they were trading with China.

On the whole, the initial European influence on Asian society was not significant. European territorial holdings were small, usually little more than port cities. Europeans had little effect on Asian economic life; they were little more than a small, parasitic group attached to an Asian economic system.

The World and the Industrial Revolution

The Industrial Revolution began during the waning decades of the eighteenth century with the production of machine-woven cotton textiles in England. By the early nineteenth century, industrialization included steel production and was spreading to other European countries and the former English colonies in North America, now the United States. The Industrial Revolution dramatically changed the relationship between European peoples and the other peoples of the world. The technological advances that were associated with industrialization rapidly elevated European peoples to a position of military, political, and economic dominance in the world.

As a result, European peoples redrew the political map and restructured the world economy to meet the needs of their new industrial economy. This new European economic system required overseas sources of raw materials as well as markets for finished goods. Technological advancements resulted in the construction of larger and faster ships, which meant that maritime commerce was no longer limited to high-cost luxury goods. The development of railroads opened the interiors of the continents by lowering the cost of transporting goods to the coastal ports.

During the sixteenth, seventeenth, and eighteenth centuries, global trade and cultural exchange had developed. The nineteenth century saw the beginning of a global economy based on regional economic specialization and the production of commodities for export. As in the earlier period, the effects of this change varied from one portion of the world to another.

The Americas. The Americas were the first region to experience this changed relationship because they were more closely tied politically and economically to Europe. Just as the Industrial Revolution was beginning in Europe, a political revolution was starting in the Americas. From the English-speaking colonies this revolution spread to the Spanish-speaking portions of the Americas. By the third decade of the nineteenth century, most areas of mainland America were independent of European political domination. These independence movements did not change the status of Native Americans, however, because the new countries were dominated by Euro-Americans or, in the case of Haiti, African Americans.

Although these new countries had achieved political independence, they maintained strong economic ties to Europe and quickly became the major sources of raw materials as well as markets for industrializing Europe. The West Indies and the United States supplied cotton for the textile mills of England, and the Americas—both the English- and Spanish-speaking countries—served as the earliest major market for finished cotton textiles. The growing European need for raw materials stimulated economic development and territorial expansion of settlements throughout the Americas.

With the initial emphasis of the Industrial Revolution on producing plantation crops, such as cotton and sugar, the African slave trade escalated to unprecedented proportions. Of all the African slaves brought to the Americas, the vast majority came between 1750 and 1850. As industrial centers developed in the northeastern United States and as mining, grain farming, and ranching expanded throughout the Americas during the nineteenth century, the need for slave labor declined. In 1833, slavery was abolished in the British West Indies, and by the 1880s, slavery had been abolished throughout the Americas. As the importation of African slaves declined, the migration of Europeans to the Americas increased. In 1835, there were about 18.6 million individuals of European ancestry in the Americas, compared with 9.8 million people of African ancestry. By 1935, the population of Euro-Americans had jumped to 172 million, whereas the number of African Americans had risen to only 36.5 million.

In 1775, the area of Euro-American and African American settlement in North America was, for the most part, limited to the region east of the Appalachian Mountains. Within a century, however, the territorial limits of these settlements had been pushed across the continent to the Pacific Ocean. During the period of expansion, Native American populations had been quickly defeated militarily and confined to small reservations. A similar pattern of territorial expansion occurred in South America. The grasslands of Argentina initially attracted few European settlers. In 1880, the territorial limits of Euro-American settlements were about the same as they had been in 1590. In the late 1800s, however, Euro-American ranchers swept through the pampas and Patagonia, virtually eliminating the Indian population. By the early 1900s, autonomous or semiautonomous Native American societies were found only in the Amazon basin and in a few scattered and isolated pockets in other portions of the Americas.

Sub-Saharan Africa. The initial impact of European industrialization on Africa was an intensification of the slave trade. During the mid-nineteenth century, as the slave trade declined, European economic interest in Africa changed. Africa had potential as both a supplier of raw materials for industrial Europe and a market for finished goods. This economic potential could not be realized under existing conditions because the slave trade and resulting warfare had destroyed the political stability of the entire region. If the economic potential of Africa was to be realized, political stability had to be reestablished, transportation systems developed, and the economies restructured to meet European needs. These goals were accomplished through direct military and political intervention by European countries, primarily England, France, Germany, Belgium, and Portugal, who proceeded unilaterally to divide up the peoples and resources of Africa. As late as 1879, European powers claimed only small portions of Africa. The Portuguese had the coastal areas of Angola, Mozambique, and Guinea. The British had Cape Colony, Lagos, Gold Coast, Sierra Leone, and Gambia. The French had only Gabon, Senegal, and a few coastal ports. Twenty years later, virtually all of sub-Saharan Africa, with the exception of Liberia and Ethiopia, was under direct European rule. With some exceptions, the imposition of colonial control was accomplished with relatively little bloodshed.

As colonial authority was established, the usual policy was to institute a tax system. Taxation of native populations served a dual purpose. The revenues generated were frequently sufficient to cover the cost of the colonial administration and troops. In addition, native populations were forced either to produce marketable exports or to work for European-owned plantations or mines to raise the money for taxes. Thus, taxation forced Africans into the European economic network.

Although exploitation of native populations characterized all the European colonies in Africa, it reached its height in the Congo basin. In 1885, King Leopold of Belgium claimed the Congo as "Crown lands" and organized it as the Congo Free State. He then sold concessions to companies, which received sole rights to all land and labor within given tracts of land. Africans were forcibly conscripted to work on the plantations and in the mines under armed guards. The labor conditions in the Congo were some of the most brutal and exploitative in world history. Between 1885 and 1908, when protests from other European powers caused the Belgian government to assume control, as many as eight million Africans were killed, or about half the total population of Congo.

By the early part of the twentieth century, the authority of Europeans had been established throughout Africa. Gold, silver, copper, diamonds, palm oil, rubber, cacao, and other raw materials were flowing back to Europe, while Africa became an expanding market for European manufactured goods. Few Europeans immigrated to Africa, and in most regions, the presence of Europeans was limited to a handful of government administrators, soldiers, missionaries, and entrepreneurs.

Asia. The basic pattern of European political and economic expansion in Asia was similar to the pattern in Africa. However, the magnitude of the population and the already highly developed economic system in Asia tempered the European impact. The Industrial Revolution had resulted in major advances in European military technology, which shifted the balance of power in favor of the Europeans. For the first time, they could successfully challenge even the largest and most powerful Asian states. This change became evident during the mid-1800s. China had successfully resisted making trade concessions to European powers. In the Opium War with England (1839–1842), and in a second war with England and France between 1856 and 1858, China saw its navy and army badly defeated and was forced to make humiliating land and trading concessions. During the late 1700s and early 1800s, the British East India Company steadily expanded its territorial control in India through manipulation of internal political rivalries and limited localized wars. The crushing of the Sepoy Mutiny (1857–1858) ended any question about English political dominance of India.

By the end of the nineteenth century, most of Asia had been brought under the control of European colonial governments. England had India, Burma, Malaya, Sarawak, Hong Kong, and Ceylon. The French held Indochina, and the Dutch had extended their control over the Dutch East Indies. Although still politically independent, China, Nepal, Afghanistan, Thailand, Persia (Iran), and most of the Middle Eastern countries were so strongly dominated by various European powers that some historians have called them *semicolonial regions*. Japan stood alone as the only Asian state that truly retained its autonomy.

During the late nineteenth century, as European political control spread over Asia, the economy of the area was steadily modified by various means to meet the needs of industrial Europe. Although Europeans owned and operated plantations, mines, and various industries in some areas, the principal instruments for changing the existing economies were taxes and duties. Taxation encouraged the production of cash crops for export, whereas import and export duties encouraged the production of some goods and commodities and discouraged the production of others. Native industries that would directly compete with European goods were discouraged.

The degree to which the local economy was changed differed greatly from region to region. In some regions, large-scale developments for the production of critical cash crops were associated with massive relocations of populations to supply labor. Such changes were most characteristic of, but not limited to, territories within the British Empire. Ceylon became a tea-producing colony, whereas Malaya focused on rubber, Burma on rice, and Bengal (India) on jute (hemp for rope). To increase production, additional labor was frequently needed. Indians and Chinese were recruited to work on the rubber plantations in Malaya. Tamil speakers from southern India provided the labor on the tea plantations of Ceylon. Rubber, tea, and hemp flowed to Europe, and Indian immigrants in Burma increased rice production ninefold, a surplus that was, in turn, shipped to India, Malaya, Ceylon, and other plantation regions within the empire to feed the workers.

These changes in the political and economic life of Asia occurred despite the relatively small number of Europeans in Asia. For example, in India during the mid-1920s, Europeans numbered only about 200,000 administrators, soldiers, and civilians, compared to a native population of about 320 million—a ratio of 1:1,500.

Oceania. During the latter half of the eighteenth century, French, Russian, and English naval expeditions explored the Pacific, charting and describing the major islands and island groups. These men were soon followed by merchants, colonists, and whalers. In one way, the history of Oceania during the nineteenth century parallels the history of the Americas during the first three centuries after European discovery. The total population of Melanesia, Micronesia, Polynesia, and Australia was estimated at several million at the time of contact. Disease and warfare quickly reduced the population of much of Oceania during the nineteenth century.

In 1785, the English established a penal colony in Australia and laid the foundation for the Europeanization of portions of Oceania. The pattern of white settlement expansion in Australia and New Zealand during this period closely followed that of European settlement and occupation of the United States and Canada. Native populations declined because of disease and warfare, while European settlements expanded, occupying an ever-increasing portion of the land. Surviving native populations were eventually limited to small reserve areas. During the nineteenth century, the population of native Australians declined from about 300,000 to only 60,000. In New Zealand, the native Maori were only slightly more successful in resisting. Numbering only about 100,000 in 1800, by the 1840s the surviving 40,000 Maori were a minority population confined on small reserves.

Aside from Australia, Polynesia (including New Zealand) was the region most affected by Europeans. During the nineteenth century, the indigenous population of these islands declined from 1,100,000 to only 180,000. In 1779, the native population of Hawaii numbered between 300,000 and 400,000. By 1857, only 70,000 native Hawaiians remained. Missionary-entrepreneurs from the United States were able to secure lands for plantations, and as the native population declined, they began importing laborers from Asia to work the fields. This influx of Europeans and Asians reduced the native Hawaiians to a minority population before the end of the nineteenth century. There were major exceptions to these patterns, however. Although the native populations of Samoa and Tonga declined, there was no significant influx of Europeans, and the native populations of these islands eventually recovered.

The islands of Micronesia also suffered from a population drop during the nineteenth century, declining from about 200,000 to about 83,000. However, these small, scattered islands had little to attract large numbers of Europeans. Micronesians were mostly left on their own.

The pattern of contact differed significantly from island to island in Melanesia. The indigenous population of New Guinea was too vast to be displaced by Europeans. The same was not true in Fiji and New Caledonia. The native population of Fiji decreased from 300,000 to 85,000, and New Caledonia's native population declined from 100,000 to a low of 27,000. In Fiji, English entrepreneurs secured land for sugar plantations and began importing laborers from India, until by the twentieth century the Indians constituted a majority of the population.

In the 400 years following 1492, the world was dramatically changed. By 1900, European political domination was complete and the global trade network was well established. Global trade allowed for the exchange of technologies, including domesticated plants and animals, between the various peoples of the world. It also exposed the world's peoples to different ideas, beliefs, and cultural practices. Except for the peoples of the Americas and Oceania, however, the changes did not erode the basic economic, cultural, and social autonomy of most of the world's peoples. Although many societies became extinct, many new societies had come into existence. New technologies, ideas, beliefs, and practices had, for the most part, been adapted and integrated into preexisting economies and cultures. Global trade had dramatically changed the lives of most of the world's peoples, but it had not significantly lessened social and cultural diversity. There had been migrations of peoples, both voluntary and forced, but direct contact between peoples was minimal in comparison with contemporary standards.

The Emergence of the Global Economy

Over the past 50 years, the process of globalization has entered a new and different phase. A global economy has started to evolve. In its essence, the global economy is simple: the creation of a global market and the integration of peoples and communities into this market. **Global trade** involved the exchange of goods between regional markets. In the **global economy,** labor, goods, and services are bought and sold on the global market.

We can readily see some effects of the global economy. The price we pay for a loaf of bread or a gallon of gasoline is determined in large part by the world price for wheat and oil. Similarly, the price we pay for a Ford is no longer influenced only by competition from General Motors, but by Japanese and European auto manufacturers as well. Foreign imports not only place American companies in competition with foreign companies but also put American workers in direct competition with their foreign counterparts. American farmers, oil producers, businesspeople, and workers are now finding that they have to compete on a global market for the prices they can charge for their goods, services, and labor. This has both good and bad points. It has resulted in cheaper prices in the United States for many manufactured goods and services. However, it has also meant the loss of jobs, as companies, in order to compete, have closed their domestic manufacturing plants and offices, laid off their relatively high-paid American workers, and either moved the manufacturing plants overseas or outsourced manufacturing to foreign companies. As a result, many American companies are no longer producing the products or services they market in the United States.

Many scholars argue that the global economy differs qualitatively from global trade in that implicit in the global economy is an underlying and unifying ideology, capitalism, and a single objective, the production of wealth. Capitalism is an ideology based on Western (European) cultural beliefs and values. To survive, let alone prosper, in the new emerging global economy, a people has to adopt Western cultural ideas. Thus, not only is the global economy resulting in the restructuring of the world economic system, but it is having far-ranging cultural and social consequences for the peoples of the world as well. In earlier chapters, we highlighted in boxes many of the potential cultural implications of the global economy. In the last part of this chapter, we discuss the development of the global economy and some of the associated social and economic problems.

The world today, at the beginning of the twenty-first century, is a far different place from what it was in the 1950s. The past 50 years have seen vast changes in the lives of virtually all the peoples of the world. The Second World War was a major watershed in human history. As we have seen, before World War II, the world economic system was dominated by European-controlled colonial empires. The British, French, and Soviet (or Russian) empires were the largest. However, the Netherlands, Belgium, Spain, Portugal, and Italy also had overseas possessions. Global trade existed, but there was no integrated global economy. These empires had been created for only one reason: the economic enrichment of the "home country" or colonial power. The colonial powers were primarily interested in politically controlling the peoples of their colonies while economically exploiting their resources. Colonies were the economic monopolies of the home country. Thus, India, South Africa, Kenya, and the other British colonies served as monopolized sources of raw materials for English factories as well as protected markets for English manufactured goods. Economic development within the English colonies was limited to increasing the production of raw materials needed by English factories and eliminating the production of local goods that would compete with goods made in England. Trade between the colonial possessions of the empire and other countries was highly controlled and regulated from London. A similar relationship existed between the home country and the colonies of other colonial powers.

Even if political barriers had not inhibited trade, the problems of geography and distance remained. International telephone service was extremely limited, and most communications had to be sent by mail. International air travel was in its infancy. The vast majority of international travelers went by train or ship. As for moving raw materials and manufactured goods, compared to today, shipping was slow, expensive, and frequently difficult. Thus, markets were protected by not only trade barriers but also geography. As a result, even within the colonial empires, regions were usually self-sufficient in their basic economic needs. The people raised the food they ate, built and furnished the houses they lived in from locally produced goods, and tailored the clothes they wore from locally produced materials. Imports were usually limited to goods or products that could not be made or found locally, while exports usually consisted of goods or products not needed for local use or consumption. The development of the global economy thus required changes in political structures as well as new technological innovation.

Three major changes have occurred since the end of World War II that have profoundly altered the course of human history and made the developing global economy possible. The most basic of these changes was the disintegration of the colonial empires and the elimination of many of the political barriers to trade. Although the precise number varies depending on how one defines an "independent" or "autonomous" country, at the beginning of World War II, there were at most only about 60 politically independent countries in the world. Following the war, the colonial empires began to disintegrate. Independence movements had already started in many colonial areas prior to the war, and the war had devastated the economies of many of the colonial powers such as England, France, and the Netherlands. Needing to rebuild their home economies, they lacked the resources to suppress the independence movements in their colonies.

The war also resulted in the United States emerging as the strongest economic and military power in the world. After the war, the United States began pressuring its European allies to grant independence to their colonies. There were two reasons behind the actions of the United States. First, the United States was ideologically opposed to colonialism; it granted independence to the Philippines immediately following the war. Second, U.S. companies wanted direct access to the resources and markets of colonial Africa and Asia. As a result, between 1946 and 1980, 88 new countries were carved out of the old colonial empires and given political independence. The collapse of the Soviet Union and Yugoslavia during the 1990s resulted in the creation of 18 additional countries. Today there are about 200 independent countries, more than three times the number that existed prior to World War II.

With the end of colonialism, the peoples of Africa and Asia had the freedom to manage their own economic affairs. These "new" countries could now sell their raw materials and products on the global market and purchase imported goods from any country they wished. Even more important, these former colonies could now establish local industries to compete with those of the industrialized powers of Western Europe and North America.

◄ Container shipping has greatly lowered the cost of shipping of manufactured goods and has played a key role in the development of the global economy over the past 30 years.

© Chuck Place Photography

The second critical change was the development of new technologies associated with production, transportation, and communications. Today we can extract more raw materials and produce more manufactured goods and food using only a fraction of the human labor required prior to World War II. Technology has greatly improved labor efficiency, allowing people to produce a greater surplus of goods. At the same time, the cost of shipping raw materials, food, and manufactured goods, as well as the time in transit, has been dramatically reduced.

The key element in the global economy is the maritime industry because 90 percent of world trade is carried by oceangoing ships. Since the end of World War II, ships have become bigger, faster, and more efficient in loading and unloading cargos. Supertankers, which may be as long as 1,200 feet, can carry 500,000 tons of oil. Bulk carriers, for transporting iron ore, coal, and other raw materials, have gotten larger. But possibly the most important change has been the development of container ships.

Fifty years ago, cargo was loaded and unloaded piecemeal. Starting in the late 1950s, some shippers began loading cargo in 20- and 40-foot boxes, or containers. The containers were loaded at the factory, sent via truck or train to the port, and loaded directly onto the ship by cranes. This greatly increased the speed of loading and unloading. By the late 1960s and early 1970s, container shipping became the norm, and new cargo ships were being designed and constructed to carry standardized containers. A ship that took 10 days to load or unload piecemeal can now be loaded or unloaded in less than a day. Container shipping not only dramatically increased the speed with which goods could be shipped but also drastically reduced labor costs. Container ships require smaller crews and many fewer dockworkers. Today more than 3,000 container ships carry most of the world's manufactured goods.

Between 1980 and 1999, the cost per unit of marine transportation actually decreased. Today, it costs about 2 cents per gallon to ship crude oil from the Middle East to the United States. To ship a ton of iron from Australia to Europe costs only about $12. The shipping costs of manufactured goods from Asia to the United States or Europe are similarly low: $10 for a TV set that will sell for $700, $1.50 for a $200 DVD/CD player, and $1 for a $150 vacuum cleaner.

The best single indicator of the growth in world trade is not dollar value but shipping tonne-miles, or tonnes of goods carried multiplied by distance. Since 1965, world shipping has more than quadruped from less than 6 trillion tonne-miles to 27.5 trillion tonne-miles in 2004.

The past 30 years have been a time of rapid change in information and communications technology. Communications satellites, personal computers, cell phones, and other new technologies have revolutionized our communications systems and our abilities to store, access, and analyze information. Today letters, messages, photos, music, videos, and even whole databases can be sent or accessed, while products can be bought or sold and money transferred 24 hours a day, instantaneously, to or from any part of the world via the Internet. In terms of communication, it does not make any difference whether the other company or branch office of a company is on the other side of town or the other side of the world. In fact, small companies advertise their merchandise on web pages and sell to customers throughout the world via e-mail. Today one can literally create and operate a global business from a home office. Effective communication is a key element in business, and without the Internet, an integrated global economy could not exist. Technological advancement in transportation and communications has not merely made the world smaller; for many purposes, it has made geography irrelevant.

A third factor has been the emergence of international finance. Prior to World War II, the international flow of capital was extremely limited. Foreign investment was highly risky, particularly in underdeveloped poorer countries. Whether the loan was to a foreign government or a foreign company, repayment was always in question. As long as the empires existed, banks and companies would make investments in colonial possessions, knowing that they would have legal protection. With the end of colonialism and the emergence of new countries, however, the problem became greater. Most of the people in the world today live in underdeveloped countries. The economic growth of these countries requires the development of their infrastructures: communications systems, transportation systems, and even education systems to train workers in skills. The development of infrastructure requires capital, which many of these countries do not have. Similarly, companies in these underdeveloped countries find it difficult to secure sufficent local investment capital for their needs.

In 1945, the World Bank and the International Monetary Fund (IMF) were created to help war-ravaged Europe and Japan reestablish their industrial base. These two institutions have played a pivotal role in the creation of the global economy. The World Bank has been the major conduit for economic development loans to underdeveloped nations. The role of the World Bank is now supplemented by numerous European, American, Japanese, and other banking houses that have become international financiers.

Loans provided to these capital-poor countries have allowed them to more quickly adopt high-cost technology and increase their economic productivity. With these funds, underdeveloped countries have constructed irrigation systems, built transportation and communication systems, expanded port facilities, and developed local industries. In the past decade alone, these loans have amounted to hundreds of billions of dollars.

In the global economy, capital or money flows both ways across international boundaries in search of greater profits. Today the total U.S. debt—public (national, state and local) and private (corporate and individual)—amounts to $46.4 trillion, of which $10.4 trillion is owed to foreign governments, banks, and investors. In fact, U.S. debt shows the interconnectedness of the modern global economy. Much of the debt of U.S. corporations and investors is, in turn, used to finance economic development overseas, while credit extended to U.S. consumers allows them to purchase homes and imported goods that they could not otherwise afford. Thus, much of the economic development in China, India, and other developing countries is made possible only because American consumers are able to borrow money internationally to buy foreign imports. Not surprisingly, when the subprime mortgage problem flared up in the United States in 2007, it had ripple effects in Europe and Asia because foreign banks and investors own much of this debt.

Globalization: The Continuing Process

While the global economy is already dramatically affecting the lives of virtually everyone, it is still developing (see Figure 16.2). Some issues remain to be resolved, and some new economic institutions are starting to evolve. The process of globalizing the world market is far from complete.

Although we have a global economy, we still lack free trade. Every one of the 200 or so countries in the world still has regulations concerning imports and exports, as well as its own labor laws, environmental laws, and other business regulations. In addition, almost every country still has its own currency, currency regulations, and laws concerning banking and other financial matters. Regulation of the economy is one of the primary concerns of government. In a fully integrated and operative global economy, however, there can be no local or national differences. The World Trade Organization is in the process of attempting to negotiate the elimination of all import and export laws and controls as well as any other laws that inhibit the free flow of goods or services between countries. The result will be free trade, a world in which companies and individuals may buy and sell any legal goods or services, at any price agreed upon, in

During the Middle Ages in Europe, the canon courts of the Catholic Church declared usury, or charging interest on loans, to be un-Christian. Thus, Christians were prohibited from charging interest, and banking in medieval Europe was in the hands of Jews. During the late Middle Ages, Italian Catholics began founding banking houses, and by clever semantics were able to circumvent the church laws against usury. An individual would be loaned money, interest free, for an unrealistically short period. When the loan was not repaid within this stated time, which it seldom was, the bankers charged "damages."

The Islamic religion also prohibits usury. However, Islam differs in a number of significant ways from Christianity. The Koran is not only a book of religious teachings but also a codified legal system called *sharia*. Courts in traditional Islamic countries use the Koran as the basis for legal rulings, functioning as what are sometimes called *Islamic courts*.

The law courts in much of the Arab world—Saudi Arabia, Kuwait, Bahrain, and the United Arab Emirates—are Islamic courts. Thirty years ago, this fact had little international significance. Relatively poor, these countries had little need for financial transactions and banking institutions. With the discovery of oil and the rapid development of this region starting in the 1960s, however, a need for such institutions quickly developed. A number of European and American banking houses, such as Citibank and Chase Manhattan, opened Middle Eastern branches. Not only did they manage the vast flow of dollars changing hands through the sale of oil and the purchase of imports, but they also began loaning money to local Arab entrepreneurs who organized companies to profit from this economic boom.

Like the medieval Italian bankers, lenders in the Middle East developed semantic ways of circumventing the Islamic prohibition against usury. The word *interest* was never used in loaning money. Instead, these banks charged Islamic borrowers "administrative fees" or "loan initiation discounts." By 1986, it was estimated that the various world banks had between $8 billion and $9 billion in loans to Saudi Arabian companies alone. This system worked well as long as oil income kept rising and all parties made handsome profits. In the

1980s, the price of oil began to decline, however, and in early 1986, the price collapsed, falling from $28 a barrel to (at one point) less than $10 a barrel.

As their income from oil plunged, governments began to slow payments to local contractors and suppliers. Arab companies with a cash flow problem quickly fell behind on loan payments to banks. Many Arab businessmen suddenly rediscovered their religion. A flood of Arab companies and individuals quickly took the banks to court, charging them with usury. These courts correctly found the banks guilty of usury under Islamic law.

In the summer of 1986, a number of international banks cut back on their Middle Eastern operations. Citibank reduced the size of its offices in Bahrain and the United Arab Emirates; Chase Manhattan closed its Jordanian branch. International and Middle Eastern bankers quickly proved themselves to be as adaptive as the medieval Italians. There was a rapid growth of "Islamic banks." Initially most Islamic banks were local, some were branches of large international banks, while others were associated with international banking houses. By scrupulously avoiding charging *riba,* or interest, and operating as *modarebs,* or "money managers," Islamic banks were able to provide profits for their investors while meeting the banking needs of the region. The financial instrument employed by these banks is called a *sukuk,* which is similar to a bond.

The recovery of the oil industry in the late 1980s and the increasing need for capital for development projects stimulated the growth of Islamic banks. Today (2007) there are about 285 Islamic banks and financial institutions worldwide, with more than $300 billion in assets. Still there are problems. Many conservative Muslims question the legitimacy of *sukuks.* Also most Islamic banks are relatively small, given the regional demands for capital. In 2001 the General Council for Islamic Banks and Financial Institutions (CIBAFI) and in 2002 the International Islamic Financial Market (IIFM) were established. The purpose of these nonprofit organizations is to standardize trading rules and regulations and to provide needed capital for economic development in Islamic countries through Islamic banking institutions.

any country in the world, without government regulation. In all disputes, the World Trade Organization, not the governments involved, would be the final judge. As we discussed in the Globalization box in Chapter 12, some scholars see the World Trade Organization evolving into a de facto world government.

The global economy also requires international control of currencies, banking, and other financial transactions. The International Monetary Fund is assuming the role of regulator of international monetary transactions. Most countries have their own currencies. Exchange rates for currencies are complex and volatile. In international

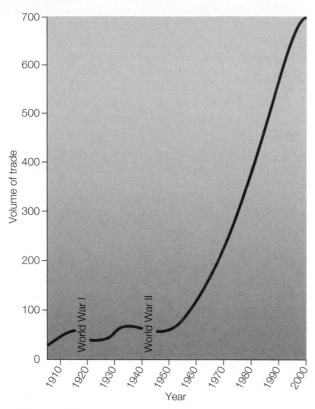

▲ **Figure 16.2** Growth of World Trade: 1905–2000. Between 1990 and 1999, world trade grew at a rate of 6.5 percent per year.

financial transfers, varying exchange rates are an added expense. Recognizing that using different currencies makes it more difficult to integrate economies, most of the countries of the European Union changed to a single currency, the Euro, in January 2002. Some have suggested that a fully integrated global economy will require a single global monetary unit and the elimination of all national currencies.

Traditionally we have thought of corporations, like individuals, as having national identities. Ford, General Motors, and General Electric are "American" companies. These companies are incorporated in the United States, their stocks are traded on the New York Stock Exchange, and their corporate headquarters are in the United States. Companies such as these are increasingly becoming international, however, manufacturing and selling products throughout the world. Globalization is eroding the link between corporations and their countries of origin. This results in the emergence of what are now being termed *transnational corporations*. For centuries, if not longer, some companies have produced goods for export and have had overseas offices and operations. Thus, the dis-

tinction between traditional national corporations and transnational corporations is not precise. A **transnational corporation** is one that has most of its employees, produces and sells most of its products or services, and generates most of its gross revenues outside the national boundaries of its "home" country.

Nokia, a Finnish company known primarily for its cellular phones, is an example of a transnational corporation. Just prior to the collapse of technology stocks in 2000, Nokia had the highest capitalization value (the total value of its stock) of any company in Europe. In 1987, Nokia produced the original handheld portable telephone. The 1990s was a period of rapid growth for the company as it maintained its position as the major producer of cellular phones in the world. Today, Nokia markets products in more than 130 countries, has research and development projects and programs in 15 different countries (including the United States, Canada, Australia, Singapore, Japan, South Korea, Spain, Germany, and England), and produces components and assembled products in 10 different countries (the United States, Mexico, Brazil, Malaysia, China, South Korea, Japan, Hungary, Germany, and England).

Products that are assembled from component parts illustrate the problem of determining the national origin of goods in the global economy. Nokia has six major suppliers: Philips Electronics, a Dutch company, produces their speakers in Austria and display screens in China; Sanyo Electric, a Japanese company, produces their barrier (a component of a phone) in Mexico; Hitachi makes its power amplification modules in Japan; Infineon Technologies makes its semiconductor chips in Germany; and R.F. Micro Devices and Texas Instruments produce their radio frequency integrated circuits and digital signal processors in the United States. Today, most Nokia products are designed by non-Finnish engineers and technicians, manufactured and assembled in countries other than Finland, and sold in 130 countries in the world, in order to produce wealth and profits shared by investors from all parts of the world. Its corporate headquarters may still be located in Finland and its major management decisions are still made in Finland, but is Nokia still a Finnish company? Or, is it a global company with its main offices in Helsinki?

Population Growth and Inequalities in the Global Economy

Probably the least controversial aspect of globalization has been the improvement in the health of the world's peoples. At the end of World War II, the World Health

When we speak of militant religious fundamentalism, we invariably think of Islamic fundamentalism and of Al-Qaeda and the attack of September 11, 2001. The so-called war on terrorism is a war against Islamic fundamentalists. Is Islamic fundamentalism the only source of religiously motivated "terrorism" in the world? What about Christian and Hindu terrorists? Have we forgotten that in the 1990s there were a series of attacks on abortion clinics in the United States, and doctors associated with abortion clinics were murdered in Florida and New York? The so-called Army of God, allegedly Eric Rudolph, in 1997 and 1998, bombed the Atlanta Olympics, a gay and lesbian nightclub, and several abortion clinics. These and numerous other acts of violence were committed by militant Christian fundamentalists. Even Timothy McVeigh, who bombed the Murrah Federal Building in Oklahoma City, though an agnostic, had links to extremist Christian groups. In India, there have been numerous similar acts of violence by militant Hindu extremists against Muslims and Christians. Hindu extremists have attacked mosques and churches throughout India and even destroyed the sixteenth-century mosque at Ayodhya. Hindu extremists have assaulted, and even killed, Indian Muslims and Christians. In 1999, Hindu extremists burned to death a Christian missionary and his two sons, and in 2002, they killed between 1,000 and 2,000 Muslims in Gujarat.

Historically in the United States, there has been a separation between religion and state. For 200 years, the vast majority of Americans, including politicians and religious leaders, have strongly adhered to this principle. In a sermon he gave in 1965, Jerry Falwell summarized the position of most Christian church leaders in America, when he said, "As far as the relationship of the church to the world, it can be expressed as . . . 'preach the word.' . . . Nowhere are we commissioned to reform the externals. We are not told to wage wars against bootleggers, liquor stores, gamblers, murderers, prostitutes, racketeers, prejudiced persons or institutions, or any other existing evil as such" (quoted in Harding 2000, 22). By 1976, Falwell had repudiated this position, stating instead, "This idea of 'religion and politics don't mix' was invented by the devil to keep Christians from running their own country." In 1979, he organized the Moral Majority, a Christian political action group.

During the 1980s and 1990s, Falwell and other like-minded religious leaders encouraged their followers to take an active role in politics, not just by voting for "Christian" candidates but also by donating money, participating in their campaigns, and even running for political office themselves. Through radio and TV talk shows, newsletters, and local churches, Christians were increasingly mobilized for political action. By the late 1990s, an estimated 50 million to 70 million Americans were associated with Christian political action groups, and the so-called Christian Right had emerged as the single most powerful political action group in the country.

Although modern India is predominantly a Hindu country, there is a large Muslim minority (about 120 million) as well

(*continued*)

◄ Hindu fundamentalists in India have become increasingly intolerant of the Muslim minority in the country. Here Hindu militants gather in Ayodhya before destroying the Muslim mosque in the background.

© Feuiers,Bettmann/Corbis

as smaller populations of Sikhs, Buddhists, and Christians. The National Congress Party that evolved under Gandhi and led the fight for independence in 1948 was a secular nationalist movement that included Hindus and Muslims as well as members of other religious groups. In spite of attempts by leaders of the Congress Party to keep the country united, India was partitioned into India (predominantly Hindu) and Pakistan (predominantly Muslim). In Chapter 17, the partitioning of India is discussed in more detail.

The Congress Party, which assumed power over the newly independent and democratic India, emphasizes secularism in government. Following the assassination of Gandhi in early 1948 by a Hindu extremist opposed to the partitioning of India, Hindu nationalist parties were outlawed for more than 20 years. In spite of this, many unofficial "parties" were formed, the largest being the Bharatiya Jan Sangh in 1951. In 1973, this party assumed the name Bharatiya Janata Party (BJP) and together with numerous smaller nationalist parties became increasingly active. After 50 years of rule by the Congress Party, in 1998, the BJP under the leadership of Atal Behari Vajpayee was able to gain control of the government and he became the prime minister. Although in the national elections of 2004 the BJP lost power to the Congress Party, the BJP and other Hindu nationalist parties remain a powerful political force in India.

Both in the United States and in India, religiously based political movements have grown rapidly in strength and influence over the past quarter-century. To understand why, one has first to examine the political concerns they have raised.

Christian fundamentalists in the United States tend to view the country as heading in the direction of moral collapse. They see the primary causes of this moral crisis as being internal, the result of the government and the federal courts being controlled by overly permissive secular individuals whom they usually label "liberals." They oppose the Supreme Court's interpretation of free speech, which has allowed the producing and marketing of sexually explicit magazines, movies, and TV programs, as well as the Court's interpretation of the separation of church and state, which has removed prayer and religious activities from the public schools while allowing evolution and sex education to be taught. At the same time, "liberal" politicians have enacted legislation supporting and encouraging women's rights, the feminist movement, and multiculturalism. The result has been an increasing prevalence of pornography, sexual promiscuity, homosexuality, gay marriage, and abortion, not to mention drug use, crime, and the disintegra-

tion of the traditional family. The basic Christian American values are under attack. Christian fundamentalists think that only by taking direct control of the political, judicial, and educational systems—by the election of Christian legislators, the appointment of Christian judges to the courts, and the election of Christian school board members—can American society be saved.

To the BJP and other Hindu nationalist groups, the ultimate source of the problems of India is what they term "Semitic monotheistic intolerance," the Western world. To them, "the West" includes both Christians and Muslims. To understand the position of the Hindu nationalists, one first has to look at the history of India. Muslim armies first invaded India in the tenth century. Between then and 1948, the Hindu peoples of India were under the domination of first Muslims and later British Christians. Many Hindus converted to Islam. Although only a relatively small number converted to Christianity, larger numbers of Hindus adopted Western cultural values and practices. This was particularly true of the educated elite, who cooperated with the British and, after independence in 1948, dominated Indian economic, social, and political life. They frequently spoke English at home; they dressed like the British, modeled much of their social behavior after the British, and even took up cricket. Some have said that westernized Indians are more British than the British. This westernized elite, through the Congress Party, dominated Indian politics from independence until 1998. The new India that they created was modeled after England. The governmental system, as well as the judicial and educational systems, was based on British models. Adopting a secular ideology, they attempted to accommodate religious and cultural differences within India, allowing, for example, a separate civil code for Muslims. They also outlawed discrimination based on caste, religion, or gender.

In 1998, the BJP came to power advocating the policy of *Hindutva,* or "Hinduness," by which they mean the restructuring of the country based on Hindu, not Western, ideology. Under the concept of *Hindutva* are both general ideas and specific policies. Pakistanis, though Muslims, are really Indians, and Pakistan should be part of India. After the BJP took power, they tested the first Indian nuclear bomb. There should be no separate constitution for the disputed state of Kashmir, which is predominantly Muslim. Nor should there be a separate civil code for Indian Muslims.

Economic policies should focus on developing India for the benefit of Indians, not Western corporations. The BJP also defines as one of its major concerns the corruption of Indian family life, with particular emphasis on women. To them, the immoral Western feminist movement is infecting India, undermining family life by propagating sexual promiscuity, lesbianism, and artificial insemination. Western consumerist culture is resulting in the exploitation of women in Indian society through the sale of pornographic materials. This is leading to a secularization of young people, who no longer have any moral values. According to the BJP, the family structure has already collapsed in Western society, and India has become infected. These corrupting Western influences have to be stopped. Recognizing that many Datils ("untouchable") are converting to Christianity, Buddhism, and Islam, some states, such as Gujarat and Tamil Nadu, have enacted laws making what they term "forced conversions" illegal, enforcing prison sentences and fines for individuals carrying out conversions.

What is surprising is that the underlying ideas fueling the growth of Muslim, Christian, and Hindu fundamentalism are basically the same. All three groups see their societies as morally collapsing. All three cite the same basic concerns: pornography, sexual promiscuity, the changing role of women, immorality, and the erosion of the family. All three think that direct political action is necessary to protect and restore their traditional norms and values. The major difference between these groups is what they define as the source of these morally corrupting influences and how best to deal with them.

To the Christian fundamentalists in the United States, the source is internal. Although there have been isolated acts of terrorism, the vast majority of Christian fundamentalists think they can successfully work within the democratic political system to change the society. To the Hindus in India, the ultimate source of social corruption is external, the West, the Islamic and Christian world. However, there are individuals inside India who are now Muslims and Christians, as well as many Hindus who have adopted Western cultural practices. As a result, their struggle is primarily an internal one. Because of its religious mix, India is far more volatile and acts of religious terrorism are far more numerous than in the United States. Nonetheless, the vast majority of Hindu fundamentalists think they can work within the democratic framework of India to uphold their cultural traditions. To Islamic fundamentalists, the West, by which they mean the United States and Western Europe, is the source of the moral corruption and collapse of their societies. Scattered over numerous countries, Muslims are politically controlled and dominated by undemocratic leaders, who are economically and militarily supported by Western governments and corporations. Lacking democratic political options, Muslim extremists turn to armed revolution, in the form of terrorist acts, as the only recourse open to them to institute social change. Not surprisingly, terrorist acts are directed toward both their existing governments and those countries that support them.

Why these movements differ in their political actions is situational and understandable. The important question is: Why are their basic concerns and issues so similar? In his recent book, *Runaway World,* Anthony Giddens (2000, 22) states, "The battleground of the twenty-first century will pit fundamentalism against cosmopolitan tolerance." By fundamentalists, Giddens means those who are adherents of traditional (non-Western) cultural traditions, values, and practices. In contrast, cosmopolitan peoples are those who have embraced the cultural values and practices of globalization—in other words, people who have or have adopted a Western cultural tradition. Thus, fundamentalism is a response to the rapid changes brought on by globalization—changes that the fundamentalists find disturbing and even dangerous. To Giddens (2000, 67), "Fundamentalism is beleaguered tradition. . . . Fundamentalism isn't about what people believe but, like tradition more generally, about why they believe it and how they justify it. It isn't confined to religion." Thus, Giddens sees fundamentalism not as a true religious political movement but, rather, as a response to the social and cultural changes associated with globalization that non-Western people view as synonymous with the West.

Critical Thinking Questions

1. Giddens's ideas seem to apply to what is occurring in the Islamic and Hindu worlds. Was he unaware of or did he simply overlook the growth of Christian fundamentalism in the United States? Or is the Christian Right qualitatively different from the others?

2. Are the fundamentalist political movements in the United States, India, and the Islamic world the products of social changes resulting from globalization? Is globalization resulting in profound cultural and social changes that are threatening traditional cultures in both the Western and non-Western worlds? Should Giddens have stated that the conflicts in the twenty-first century will pit cosmopolitan against traditional peoples, and dropped the term *non-Western*?

Organization (WHO) was created as part of the United Nations to address global health concerns. Working with private and government health organizations and agencies, WHO defined issues and attempted to direct resources to specific health problems. Of particular concern were infant mortality rates in most of the underdeveloped countries of the world. By improving sanitation systems, nutritional standards, and health care delivery systems in underdeveloped countries, WHO has helped to drastically lower infant mortality rates.

In addition, WHO has developed programs to eradicate epidemic diseases. In 1946, malaria was a major health concern throughout most of the Americas, Africa, Asia, and the Pacific. In India alone, it was estimated that 800,000 people a year died from the disease, while globally several million people died annually. Malaria is an insect-borne disease spread from one infected human to another by *Anopheles* mosquitoes. Using DDT, WHO launched a program in 1948 to eliminate malaria by eradicating mosquito populations. By the 1960s, widespread use of DDT had dramatically reduced the death rate from malaria. In the mid-1960s, India reported no deaths from the disease, and at one time it was thought that malaria might be eliminated altogether. However, the discovery that DDT had numerous environmentally destructive side effects led to limitations on its use as a pesticide. This, together with the evolution of a new DDT-resistant *Anopheles* mosquito, ended the hope of eliminating malaria. Even though the malaria program was not totally successful, tens of millions of lives have been saved.

Smallpox has been a major health problem since ancient times. This virus, spread by human hosts either through the air or by touch, can kill up to 40 percent of an infected population. In the 1960s, there were on average between 10 million and 15 million cases a year, and 2 million deaths from smallpox. In 1967, WHO launched a vaccination campaign designed to eliminate smallpox. In 1980, after three years during which no new cases were reported anywhere in the world, WHO was able to announce that the smallpox virus had been eradicated.

In addition to the malaria and smallpox programs, WHO continues to work to improve health conditions by assisting in the development of health care delivery systems throughout the world. As a result, infant mortality rates have declined dramatically and life expectancies have increased in virtually every part of the globe. In the past 50 years, the world's population has jumped from 2.5 billion to 6.6 billion. WHO's efforts have been the primary factor in this rapid growth.

Although health conditions among all peoples have improved, birthrates differ widely. The most striking differences are between the developed and undeveloped worlds. The birthrates in the developed countries of Western Europe, North America, and Japan have dropped dramatically. In the most extreme cases, some of these countries now have negative growth rates. In Italy, for example, if the present trend continues, the population will decline from 57 million in 2000 to 45 million by 2050. Japan also has a negative growth rate, which, if it continues at its present rate, will result in its population declining from 126 million in 2000 to 101 million by 2050.

In sharp contrast are the birthrates of the peoples of sub-Saharan Africa, Latin America, and most of Asia. The populations of these regions are increasing at a rate averaging almost 2 percent per year or more. In the next half-century, it is projected that the population of India will increase by more than 500 million, while that of neighboring Pakistan will jump by almost 200 million. In 1950, Nigeria, the largest country of sub-Saharan Africa, had a population of only 31 million; by 2000, that population had grown to 123 million. Even given a projected decline in the birthrate, it is still estimated that by 2050, Nigeria will be home to more than 300 million people.

The regional differences in growth rates are rapidly changing the geographical distribution of the world's population. If we compare population changes in the developed and underdeveloped countries and limit our study to only the period from 1950 to 2025, we can see in Table 16.1 how significant the change will be.

▼ **Table 16.1** Population Changes

	1950	2025
Developed countries	33.1%	15.9%
Undeveloped countries	66.9%	84.1%

Source: Adapted from Robbins, (1999, 148).

By 2025, the population of the developed countries of the world will constitute only about one-sixth of the world's population. The rapidly growing majority of the world population is both impoverished and non-Western in cultural heritage.

There is no doubt that the emergence of the global economy has greatly benefited the developed world, and the United States in particular. In terms of tangible material wealth alone, Americans can see a vast change in their lifestyle. In the past 50 years, the size of the average new American home has more than doubled, from 900 square feet to more than 2,000 square feet. The quantity of our material possessions has grown proportionally to fill the new space. Fifty years ago, the typical American family owned only a single automobile; today that same family owns two or more. Today we also eat out more and travel more and farther. The developed countries of Western Europe and Japan have seen similar increases in relative wealth. In contrast, most of the underdeveloped countries of Latin America, Africa, and Asia have not participated in this new prosperity. The result has been increasing inequalities in the distribution of wealth in the world. In 1960, it was estimated that the richest 20 percent of the world's population had 30 times more income than the poorest 20 percent. By 1999, this ratio had risen to 74:1 and was still increasing. It is not just that many people in the world are not sharing in this new wealth; their standards of living are actually declining. Since 1980, per-capita incomes in more than a third of the countries of the world have declined. Today 1.2 billion people, one-fifth of the world's population, are attempting to exist on incomes of less than $1 per day. The distribution of the world's wealth has become so skewed that the total assets of the three richest individuals in the world exceed the annual income of the poorest 600 million, while the richest 200 individuals in the world have wealth that exceeds the annual income of the poorest 2.4 billion people. The problem is not just that a significant wealth gap exists between the rich and poor of the world, but that the gap is increasing.

If we look at the world as a whole, we find that both the global economy and human populations are growing rapidly. If we begin to examine this issue country by country or region by region, however, we quickly discover that there is an inverse correlation between economic growth and population growth. Generally speaking, countries and regions with high economic growth usually have low population growth rates, whereas countries with rapid population growth most commonly have slow or even negative economic growth rates. In Chapter 18, we discuss the reasons for this inverse correlation.

Sub-Saharan Africa in many ways typifies the problems of the underdeveloped regions of the world. The people of this region are basically dependent on agriculture. Relative to their population, they have limited marketable natural resources and little industry. Not only do these countries have poorly developed educational and transportation systems and lack information and communications technology, but they also do not have the financial resources to acquire or develop them. With the highest birthrate in the world, sub-Saharan Africa has already reached the crisis point. For the past two decades, the populations of these countries have grown much faster than their economies. Increasing populations have resulted in an overuse of agricultural resources and a deterioration of the land base. Since the early 1960s, per-capita food production has dropped by 16 percent. As a result, today the people of this region are more than 20 percent poorer in economic terms than they were in the mid-1970s.

With more than 500 million people, sub-Saharan Africa is already overpopulated. It is estimated that about 40 percent of the region's population live on less than $1 per day and are chronically undernourished. In the next 50 years, it is estimated that this population will grow by an additional 1 billion people. The countries of sub-Saharan Africa face the virtually impossible task of developing their economies to meet the needs of this expanding population. Economic conditions are only going to become worse as an ever-increasing percentage of the population goes hungry. Similar, although not as severe, conditions exist in much of Latin America and Asia. Economic development cannot keep pace with population growth, and already impoverished people are becoming even poorer.

There are two possible solutions to the growing economic problems of the underdeveloped world. One answer would be to create massive economic development programs to increase agricultural and industrial production, linked to programs to reduce the population growth rates. However, such programs would cost trillions of dollars and would have to be financed by the developed countries of the world. The only other solution is for a mass migration of people from the underdeveloped to the developed countries of the world. This migration has already started.

The greatest movement of people in human history is already under way. This migration is taking two forms. First is rural-to-urban migration, which is occurring in every country in the world. Second is the migration of people from poorer countries to wealthier countries. Just before World War II, about 50 percent of the total population of the United States and Europe was urban, compared with only about 8 to 10 percent for Africa and Asia and 25 percent for Latin America. Today, about 75 percent of Americans and 70 percent of Europeans are city dwellers. The urban populations of Asia and Africa have jumped to between 25 and 30 percent, and in Latin America the urban population has increased to more than 60 percent. The growth rate of urbanization has thus been highest outside Europe and North America. In fact, the world's most rapidly growing cities are located in underdeveloped nations. In the 1950s, Bogotá had a population of only about 650,000; by 2005, its population was almost 8 million. Similar increases are common. Although most cities in the underdeveloped world lack the large industrial complexes capable of employing the great masses of people migrating into them, their small-scale industries, transportation services, and government jobs, though limited, still offer greater economic opportunities than do the increasingly overcrowded rural regions.

Whereas most migration has been within countries, the growing trend is toward international migration. The United Nations estimates that 191 million people, or about 3 percent of the world's population, now live in a country other than the one in which they were born. Many argue that this is a conservative figure. The main difficulty in discussing international migration is that it takes so many forms. There are legal immigrants who are in the process of becoming citizens of another country; however, not all countries allow such immigrants. There are other immigrants who have temporary legal status to live in another country: guest workers, students, and **refugees.** Then there are illegal immigrants, individuals who have illegally taken up residence in another country. The distinction between these categories is often blurred. In many cases, individuals who come as "students" and "refugees" are in reality coming in search of jobs.

As their industrial economies expanded during the 1950s and 1960s, many Western European countries began experiencing labor shortages. West Germany initiated a "guest-worker" program to actively recruit foreign laborers, first in southern Europe, Italy, and Spain, and later in Yugoslavia and Turkey. Concurrently, French factories began recruiting Arab workers from their then North African colonies, particularly Algeria. In the 1950s, England began experiencing an influx of West Indians from its possessions in the Caribbean. In the 1960s, a wave of Pakistani and Indian immigrants also settled in England. Other Western European countries experienced a similar phenomenon. Today almost 10 percent of the population of Western Europe are recent immigrants.

Since World War II, about 25 percent of American population growth has been the result of immigration, and the number of immigrants is increasing. From only about 300,000 persons per year in the 1960s, the number of legal immigrants to the United States has jumped to about 1,000,000 per year. As the number of legal immi-

grants increased, their origins shifted. From being primarily European in origin, proportionally ever-increasing numbers are now from Asia and Latin America. Between 1980 and 2000, the number of Asian Americans almost tripled, from 3.5 million (1.5 percent) to more than 10.2 million (3.6 percent), while the number of Latin Americans more than doubled, from 14.5 million (6.4 percent) to more than 35 million (12.5 percent).

Although Europe and North America have been the primary destinations for most international migrants, other regions with high incomes, labor shortages, or both have experienced major influxes of immigrants. Many of the oil-rich Arab countries—Libya, Saudi Arabia, Kuwait, Qatar, and the United Arab Emirates—have recruited foreign workers from India, Pakistan, Bangladesh, and Egypt, and from among Palestinian refugees. Indeed, in some of the smaller of these countries, foreign workers outnumber native Arabs. For example, foreign workers constitute almost 60 percent of the population of Kuwait.

Over the past 20 years, international immigration patterns have changed. Whereas in the past most immigrants to the developed countries were from Latin America, East Asia, or South Asia, the numbers of immigrants from Africa, the Middle East, and the former republics of the Soviet Union are growing. Although in recent decades the United States and the countries of Western Europe have increased their legal immigration quotas in all categories, the numbers of individuals wanting to immigrate have increased far more rapidly.

The borders of the developed countries of the world are being overwhelmed by increasing waves of illegal immigrants who will take any risk to escape from their world of hopeless poverty. Illegals from Mexico cross the deserts of the Southwest on foot with no water. Migrants from Nigeria, Ghana, and other West African countries travel across the Sahara on foot, on camels, and in old trucks to try to reach the Mediterranean coast, where, if they are lucky, they might find a small boat that will take them to Europe. Most of the estimated 12 million to 20 million illegal immigrants in the United States are from Latin America; however, they come from all parts of the world. Although the problem of illegal immigration in Western Europe is not so great, it is a growing problem. It is estimated that there are between 3 million and 3.5 million illegal immigrants in Western Europe, and this number is growing by 500,000 a year.

Other developed countries are also facing the problem of growing populations of illegal workers. Japan estimates that about 250,000 Koreans, Filipinos, Chinese,

▲ Illegal immigrants frequently take great personal risks in order to escape the poverty of their homelands. These Haitian refugees are attempting to reach the coast of Florida by sailing a small, overcrowded boat across the open sea.

© Nathan Benn/Stock Boston

and Thais are illegally living and working in Japan. Korea estimates its number of illegals at about 200,000, and Australia estimates that it has an illegal population of about 60,000. However, the country with proportionally the greatest problem is South Africa, which in spite of a high unemployment rate, has an estimated 4 million illegals in a total population of 43 million. The economy of South Africa may not be good by American or Western European standards, but compared to those of the war-torn countries of Central Africa, it is a paradise.

Already many people in the United States and Western Europe are complaining of the growing numbers of immigrants. The same is true in other countries that feel inundated by foreigners. If people think the problem is bad today, they need only wait for tomorrow. If the economic

inequalities of the global economy are not corrected, and the economies of the underdeveloped countries are not dramatically improved, the rate of immigration will only increase. There are hundreds of millions more only waiting for the opportunity.

Consequences of Globalization and the Global Economy

Globalization is multifaceted and its effects and consequences are far-reaching. The global economy is creating an increasing economic interdependence of the world's people, not just in technology, manufactured goods, and clothing, but in food as well. The global economy is producing tremendous new wealth, while at the same time producing poverty and an increasingly skewed distribution in wealth. The global economy is resulting in the greatest migration in human history, which is changing the ethnic mix of all the world's cities, especially the cities of Western Europe and the United States. In Western Europe today, one sees increasing numbers of people from Africa, the Middle East, and all parts of Asia. In the United States, one sees increasing numbers of people from Africa, the Middle East, and Asia, and from Latin America as well. The global media are marketing tools attempting to sell to the world not only material goods but also Western (primarily American) lifestyles, values, and beliefs. Some argue that, whether intended or not, the global media now serve as a means of Western cultural propaganda that is threatening and eroding the cultural traditions of the non-Western peoples of the world.

Globalization has made the world smaller and geography no longer relevant. The oceans of the world no longer separate us or protect us. The problems of one region of the world quickly become the problems of another, and the problems of the Middle East have become the problems of America.

Recent events have raised numerous questions concerning globalization. Is the Western world, led by the United States, attempting, through its control of the global economy and world media, to impose its cultural values, norms, and beliefs on the other peoples of the world? How widespread is the resentment of Western domination, not just in the Middle East but in other regions of the world? If this is a growing problem, what can or should be done about it? In the next chapter, we examine the question of increasing ethnic conflict.

▲ Muslims pray outside the Mosque in the Barbes Rochechouart district of Paris.

Summary

1. The past 500 years have been a period of tremendous change for the peoples of the world. This chapter has discussed globalization, the history of its development, and the recent emergence of the global economy.

2. Globalization started 500 years ago with Columbus. The earliest stage was global trade. The first phase, the time of European expansion and exploration, lasted from about 1500 to 1800. The second phase, during which European empires were created in Africa, Asia, and Oceania, began in about 1800 and lasted until the end of World War II.

3. The age of European expansion and exploration began with the discovery of the Americas by Columbus in 1492. During the three centuries that followed, Europe dramatically changed the world. The Spanish and later the Portuguese, English, French, and Dutch invaded the Americas, conquering or displacing most of the native peoples and gaining control of most of the land and resources. At the same time, these same European peoples were establishing a global maritime trade network that soon brought all of the peoples of the world into contact with one another, directly or indirectly. This global trade network resulted in the exchange of technology, food crops, domesticated animals, diseases, and even people. By the late 1700s, the culture of virtually every people in the world had been affected by this exchange.

4. The Industrial Revolution, starting in about 1800, changed the nature of European contact with non-Western peoples from trade to colonialism and political domination. The nineteenth century was a time of European imperial expansion, as the countries of Europe began claiming the lands and peoples of Africa, Asia, and Oceania. By 1900, the European powers began restructuring the economies of their colonial possessions to meet European needs. The period of Europe's ever-increasing political and economic control continued until World War II.

5. The most recent and current stage of globalization is the global economy. This stage began to develop about 50 years ago, at the end of World War II. The post–World War II period has been a time of continued economic, political, demographic, and sociocultural growth and change. The important feature of this period is the emergence of an increasingly integrated and interdependent global economic system.

6. Three major factors were involved in the emergence of the global economy. First, the collapse of the existing colonial empires allowed the countries of the world to trade directly with one another. Second, developments in technology made geography irrelevant. New technologies in transportation and shipping make it possible to move goods and people faster and at greatly reduced cost, while new information and communication technologies have revolutionized communication with people in different parts of the world. The third factor is international finance and the globalization of world capital.

7. The global economy is still in the process of developing. Two controversial issues are free trade and transnational corporations. The governments of all countries still regulate trade. Pressure is growing to eliminate all government regulations, allowing for free trade, meaning that any company may buy or sell anything in any country, without import or export duties.

8. The population of the world is growing rapidly, in large part due to the efforts of the World Health Organization. In the last 50 years, world population has jumped from 2.5 billion to 6.6 billion. The population growth of the developed countries has stabilized and in many cases started to decline. In the underdeveloped countries, however, populations continue to grow rapidly.

9. While the global economy has greatly benefited the developed countries, many of the countries of Asia, Africa, and Latin America have seen their economies worsen. There is an ever-increasing skewing of wealth, not just between individuals but also between countries and regions of the world. The rich are getting richer, and the poor are getting poorer. Globally, there is an inverse correlation between economic development and population growth.

10. Throughout the world, there is a massive movement of people from rural agricultural areas to urban centers. There is also a massive migration of people from underdeveloped countries to more developed countries.

11. Globalization has resulted in increasing contact among peoples and increasing exposure of non-Western peoples to Western cultural traditions. In many parts of the non-Western world, there is a growing resentment of Western economic dominance and cultural influences.

Key Terms

globalization
global trade
global economy

transnational corporations
refugees

Suggested Readings

There are numerous excellent studies of world history since 1500. The following list includes only studies of more general interest.

Crosby, Alfred W. *The Columbian Exchange.* Westport, Conn.: Greenwood, 1972.

An important and readable study by a historian, discusses some of the cultural and demographic effects of contact between the Old World and New World. The study emphasizes the exchange of food plants, animals, and diseases.

Frank, Andre Gundar. *ReOrient: Global Economics in the Asian Age.* Berkeley: University of California Press, 1998.

An attempt to get us to "ReOrient" our view of history and see the period of Western hegemony in the world as only temporary. Asia was the economic center of the Old World, prior to Columbus, and today is reemerging as the center.

Stavrianos, Leften. *The World Since 1500: A Global History.* 8th ed. Englewood Cliffs, N.J.: Prentice Hall, 1998.

A history textbook that is the best and most readable general description available on world history over the past 500 years.

Wolf, Eric. *Europe and the People Without History.* Berkeley: University of California Press, 1982.

The first major attempt by an anthropologist to describe and analyze global history since 1400. It is one of the classic studies in anthropology.

Over the past few years, numerous books and articles have been published on globalization. Here we list works that reflect various perspectives on the issues.

Chomsky, Noam. "Control of Our Lives." Lecture, February 26, 2000. Albuquerque, N.M.

In this attack on the global economy, Chomsky focuses on the issue of sovereignty and concentration of global economic, military, and political power.

Giddens, Anthony. *Runaway World: How Globalization Is Reshaping Our Lives.* New York: Routledge, 2000.

Seeing globalization as a powerful cultural force reordering societies, Giddens notes an emerging conflict between what he terms fundamentalism and cosmopolitan tolerance.

Hines, Colin. *Localization: A Global Manifesto.* London: Earthscan Publishing, 2000.

Noting many of the negative social, economic, and environmental effects of globalization, Hines argues that globalization as presently conceived (international competitiveness) is not inevitable. He proposes an economic alternative, which he terms localization.

Hutton, Will, and Anthony Giddens, eds. *Global Capitalism.* New York: New Press, 2000.

Bringing together a diverse array of academics and nonacademics (including Paul Volcker and George Soros), this collection addresses both the potential promise of global capitalism and many of its dangers.

Klein, Naomi. *No Logo.* New York: Picador, 1999.

A popular account by a journalist of corporate marketing practices and the growing consumer and anticorporate activism that is emerging in much of the world.

Robbins, Richard H. *Global Problems and the Culture of Capitalism.* Boston: Allyn & Bacon, 1999.

Written by an anthropologist, this work is by far the best general introduction to the history of the development of capitalism and the current related issues and problems of globalization.

Media Resources

The Wadsworth Anthropology Resource Center
academic.cengage.com/anthropology

The Wadsworth discipline resource website that accompanies *Humanity: An Introduction to Cultural Anthropology,* Eighth Edition, includes a rich array of material, including online anthropological video clips, to help you in the study of cultural anthropology and the specific topics covered in this chapter. Other material includes a case study forum with excerpts from various Wadsworth authors, map exercises, scientist interviews, breaking news in anthropology, and links to additional useful online material. Begin by selecting Cultural Anthropology to take you to videos, research, and more. From the homepage, you may also select Applied Anthropology, which directs you to essays, glossary terms, the case study forum, and a list of internships and careers in anthropology.

17 ETHNICITY AND ETHNIC CONFLICT

A city sacred to Jews, Muslims, and Christian, Jerusalem has been and is a major source of ethnic/religious conflict in the world.

Ethnic Groups

Situational Nature of Ethnic Identity

Attributes of Ethnic Groups

Fluidity of Ethnic Groups

Types of Ethnic Groups

The Problem of Stateless Nationalities

Responses to Ethnic Conflict

Homogenization

Segregation

Accommodation

Questions addressed in the chapter

What are ethnic groups, and what are their characteristics and differences?

Why is ethnic conflict so prevalent in the world today, and how is ethnic conflict related to colonialism?

What have been the historical responses to ethnic conflict? What can be done to try to resolve ethnic conflicts?

How does ethnic conflict threaten the global economy and thus all of us?

With the collapse of the Soviet Union and the end of the Cold War, many people thought we had entered a new, safer, and more peaceful era. But instead of peace, we are now faced with growing conflicts that are becoming ever more violent and destructive. In the past decade or so, several million people have fallen victim to wars, while tens of millions more have joined the ranks of refugees. Central governments exist in name only in parts of Africa, Asia, and even Latin America. Large regions of many of these countries are under the control of rebel armies and outlaw groups. Concerns increase about nuclear proliferation and biological warfare. Concerns are also increasing about terrorist groups and their growing capabilities for destruction. New phrases like *ethnic cleansing, failed state, global terrorism,* and *rogue state* have become part of our vocabulary. It is not just that conflict is a problem, but it is a problem that is growing. Most, but not all, of these conflicts are ethnic conflicts.

Globalization has changed the nature of ethnic conflict. In the not too distant past, ethnic conflicts were limited to particular geographical regions or countries. With vastly improved transportation and communications systems, however, together with increasing international migrations of peoples and the emergence of ethnically mixed urban populations, conflicts are no longer localized. Ethnic groups may strike their enemy anywhere in the world. Associated with this increased capability, the tactics of ethnic guerilla warfare also changed—from targeting primarily opposing armies and paramilitary groups to the increased targeting of civilian populations. The first evidence of this change came in 1972, when the Irish Republican Army began bombings in London. The following year, the Black September Organization, a Palestinian militant group, killed 11 Israeli athletes competing in the Olympic Games in Munich, Germany. Since the 1970s, many other groups have become involved in such attacks. In 1985, Sikh separatists allegedly bombed an Air India flight between Montreal and London. In 1995,

Basque separatists began attacking targets, not just in the Basque provinces but throughout Spain. In 2002, Chechen rebels attacked civilian targets in Moscow, almost 1,000 miles from the fighting in Chechnya.

Globalization has also resulted in the emergence of higher and more ominous levels of ethnic identity and conflict, which Samuel Huntington (see the Globalization box) calls *civilizations.* A civilization consists of a large number of otherwise linguistically and socially distinct ethnic groups who share a common, usually religious, cultural tradition that unites them in opposition to members of ethnic groups from other civilizations. By the beginning of the twenty-first century, a multiethnic Islamic identity in opposition to a multiethnic Western (Judeo-Christian) identity has begun to emerge. Al-Qaeda, with members drawn from a wide variety of Islamic ethnic groups and countries, sees Islamic peoples collectively involved in a struggle with Western peoples in general—thus their terrorist attacks on New York City, Washington, London, and Madrid. The U.S.-led invasions of Afghanistan and Iraq, with the military support of other, primarily Western countries, have served to validate Al-Qaeda's assertions in the minds of many Islamic peoples, while also establishing in the minds of many Western peoples the belief that they are in conflict with the Islamic world.

Ethnic Groups

Over the past few decades, the terms *ethnic* and *ethnicity* have become part of our everyday vocabulary, as have the terms *ethnic food, ethnic vote, ethnic conflict, ethnic clothes, ethnic neighborhood,* and *ethnic studies.* In the 1960s, anthropologists began studying ethnicity as a distinct social phenomenon, and since that time literature on ethnicity has proliferated. Part of the increased scholarly interest in ethnic groups came as a result of Nathan Glazer and Daniel Moynihan's study of ethnic groups in

New York City. They found that "in the third generation, the descendants of the immigrants confronted each other, and knew they were both Americans, in the same dress, with the same language, using the same artifacts, troubled by the same thing, but they voted differently, had different ideas about education and sex, and were still, in many essential ways, as different from one another as their grandfathers had been" (1963, 13). These findings contradicted the idea of America as a melting pot. Ethnic differences were far more resilient and significant than had been believed.

What is an ethnic group? First, it is necessary to realize that all peoples, not just minority populations, have an ethnic group identity. In essence, an **ethnic group** is a named social category of people based on perceptions of shared social experience or ancestry. Members of the ethnic group see themselves as sharing cultural traditions and history that distinguish them from other groups. Ethnic group identity has a strong psychological or emotional component that divides the people of the world into the categories of "us" and "them." In contrast to social stratification (discussed in Chapter 13), which divides and unifies people along a series of horizontal axes on the basis of socioeconomic factors, ethnic identities divide and unify people along a series of vertical axes. Thus, ethnic groups, at least theoretically, cut across socioeconomic class differences, drawing members from all strata of the population.

Before discussing the significance of ethnic differences and conflicts in the modern world, we need to examine the varying dimensions of ethnic group identity, including (1) the situational nature of ethnic group identity, (2) the attributes of ethnic groups, (3) the fluidity of ethnic group identity, and (4) the types of ethnic groups.

Situational Nature of Ethnic Identity

One of the more complicating aspects of ethnicity is that an individual's ethnic group identity is seldom absolute. A person may assume a number of different ethnic identities, depending on the social situation. For example, in the United States, an individual may simultaneously be an American, a Euro-American, an Italian American, and a Sicilian American. The particular ethnic identity chosen varies with the social context. When in Europe or among Europeans, the person would assume the identity of American, in contrast to German, French, or Italian. In the United States, the same individual might assume the identity of Euro-American, as opposed to African American or Native American. Among Euro-Americans, the person might take the ethnic identity of Italian American,

as opposed to Irish American or Polish American. When among Italian Americans, the individual might be identified as Sicilian American, as opposed to an Italian American whose family came from Rome, Naples, or some other region of Italy.

The situational nature of ethnic identity demonstrates what some have called the **hierarchical nesting** of identity. A particular ethnic group forms part of a larger collection of ethnic groups of like social magnitude. In turn, these ethnic groups may collectively form still another higher level of ethnic identity, which may be nested in yet another higher level. Thus, ethnic identity does not simply divide the world into categories of "us" and "them" but into varying, hierarchically ranked categories of "us" and "them."

Attributes of Ethnic Groups

Two main attributes help to define and identify an ethnic group: an origin myth or history and ethnic boundary markers.

Origin myth. Each ethnic group is the product of a unique set of social and historical events. The common or shared historical experiences that serve to unite and distinguish the group from other groups and give it a distinct social identity constitute the group's **origin myth.** By *myth* we do not mean to imply that the historical events did not really happen, or that the group is not what it claims to be. We mean only that these particular experiences serve as the ideological charter for the group's common identity and provide the members with a sense of being different from other people. Origin myths play an integral part in creating and maintaining ethnic group identity: they define and describe the origin and collective historical experiences of the group.

Not all historical events are equally important; origin myths make selective references. Wars and conflicts are frequently emphasized because they clearly distinguish "us" from "them." The origin myth imbues the group's members with feelings of distinctiveness and, often, superiority in relation to other groups. What makes an origin myth so powerful is that mythic themes and concepts are embedded in virtually every aspect of the people's popular culture: stories (written and oral), songs, dances, games, music, theater, film, and art. So pervasive are these mythic images in everyday life that members of the group learn them passively rather than consciously. Thus, all members of the group are well versed in the basic tenets of the group myth, and in the minds of most, these ideas become an unquestioned "truth." In larger, more sophisticated groups, the origin myth also takes the form of a written, purportedly objective history that is formally taught in schools. American history as taught in elementary and high school is not merely the objective, factual history of a geographical region; it is also the story of the American people. Thus, it serves as the officially sanctioned origin myth of the American ethnic group. Similarly, English, French, Japanese, and Russian history as taught in their schools is the "authorized" origin myth of those groups.

When you realize that history as taught in schools is, in fact, the collective origin myth of the group, you realize the significance of including or excluding a particular subgroup of the population. Using American history as an example, we can see how historical events play a critical role in the emergence and definition of a distinctively American ethnic identity. Among these events are the landing of the *Mayflower,* the American Revolution, the Civil War, the westward expansion, and the world wars. Certain historical groups, such as cowboys and cavalry, are used as embodiments of American ideals and identity. Americans are the descendants of the various peoples who collectively participated in these and other group-defining events. Thus, it is not surprising that every American subgroup is sensitive to its portrayal in these events. To African Americans, it is important that American history, as taught in the public schools, acknowledge that the first man to die in the American Revolution was an African American, that African Americans fought as soldiers in the Revolutionary and Civil Wars, that a high percentage of cowboys were African Americans, and that African American cavalrymen played an important part in winning the West. Similarly, public acknowledgment and recognition that their groups were active participants in some, if not all, of the major events of American history are equally important for Polish Americans, Italian Americans, Irish Americans, Chinese Americans, and other immigrants in a nation of immigrants. It is inclusion in the collective origin myth that truly legitimates a people's status as members of the group.

Ethnic boundary markers. Every ethnic group has a way of determining or expressing membership. Overt factors used to demonstrate or denote group membership are called **ethnic boundary markers.** Ethnic boundary markers are important not only to identify group members to one another, but also to demonstrate identity to and distinctiveness from nonmembers. Because these markers distinguish members from all other groups, a single boundary marker is seldom sufficient. A marker that might distinguish one ethnic group from a second

group may not distinguish it from a third group. Thus, combinations of markers are commonly used. Differences in language, religion, physical appearance, or particular cultural traits serve as ethnic boundary markers.

As we discussed in Chapter 3, speech style and language are symbols of personal identity: we send covert messages about the kind of person we are by how we speak. Language, therefore, frequently serves as an ethnic boundary marker. A person's native language is the primary indicator of ethnic group identity in many areas of the world. In the southwestern United States, Hopi and Navajo members are readily distinguished by their language alone. However, just because two populations share a common language does not mean they share a common identity, any more than the fact that two populations speak different languages means that they have two distinct identities. For example, the Serbs and Croats of what was Yugoslavia speak Serbo-Croatian. They are, however, distinct and historically antagonistic ethnic groups. Conversely, a person may be Irish and speak either Gaelic or English as a native language. The German government grants automatic citizenship to all ethnic German refugees from Eastern Europe, but a difficulty in assimilating these refugees is that many speak only Polish or Russian. Thus, one does not have to speak German to be an ethnic German.

Like language, religion may serve as an ethnic boundary marker. The major world religions, such as Christianity, Islam, and Buddhism, encompass numerous distinct groups, so that religious affiliation does not always indicate ethnic affiliation. But, in many cases, religion and ethnic group more or less correspond. The Jews may be categorized as either a religious or an ethnic group. Similarly, the Sikhs in India constitute both a religious and an ethnic group. In still other situations, religious differences may be the most important marker of ethnic identity. As we mentioned earlier, the Serbs and Croats speak the same language; the most important distinction between these two groups is that the Serbs are Eastern Orthodox and the Croats are Catholic. Conversely, the Chinese ethnic identity transcends religious differences. A person is still Chinese whether he or she is a Muslim, Christian, Taoist, Buddhist, or Marxist atheist.

Physical characteristics, or phenotypes, can sometimes indicate ethnic identity. It is impossible to identify Germans, Dutch, Danes, and other northern European ethnic groups by their physical characteristics. A similar situation is found in those regions of the world in which populations have been in long association with one another. Thus, physical characteristics do not distinguish a Zulu from a Swazi, a Chinese from a Korean, or a Choctaw from a Chickasaw. However, with the massive movements of people, particularly over the past few hundred years, physical characteristics have increasingly emerged as a marker of ethnic identity. Members of the three major ethnic groups in Malaysia—Malays, East Indians, and Chinese—are readily distinguishable by their physical appearance. The significance or lack of significance of physical characteristics in ethnic identity may also vary with the level of ethnic identity we are considering. The American identity includes almost the full range of human physical types. However, at a lower level of identity—Euro-American, African American, and Native American—physical characteristics do serve as one marker of ethnic identity. Yet within these groups, physical characteristics alone cannot be the only marker. Some Native Americans physically look like Euro-Americans or African Americans, and some African Americans might be identified as Euro-Americans or Native Americans on the basis of their physical appearance alone.

A wide variety of cultural traits, clothing, house types, personal adornment, food, technology, economic activities, or general lifestyle may also serve as ethnic boundary markers. Over the past 100 years, a rapid homogenization of world material culture, food habits, and technology has erased many of the more overt cultural markers. Today, you do not have to be Mexican to enjoy tacos, Italian to eat pizza, or Japanese to have sushi for lunch. Similarly, you can dine on hamburgers, the all-American food, in Japan, Oman, Russia, Mexico, and most other countries. Cultural traits remain, however, the most important, diverse, and complex category of ethnic boundary markers. For the sake of brevity, we limit our discussion to one trait— clothing (see Chapter 15).

Clothing styles have historically been the most overt single indicator of ethnic identity. In the not too distant past, almost every ethnic group had its own unique style of dress. Even today, a Scottish American who wants to overtly indicate his ethnic identity wears a kilt, and a German American may wear his *lederhosen*. Similarly, on special occasions, Native Americans wear "Indian clothes" decorated with beadwork and ribbonwork. These are not everyday garments, and they are worn only in social situations in which people want to emphasize their ethnic identity. In many regions of the world, however, people still wear ethnic clothes every day. In highland Guatemala, clothing, particularly women's clothing, readily identifies the ethnic affiliation of the wearer. Guatemalan clothing styles actually indicate two levels of ethnic identity. If a woman wears a *huipil*, a loose-fitting blouse that slips over the head, she is a Native American. Non–Native American women, called *Ladi-*

© Garrick Bailey

▲ The dress of this woman not only identifies her as a Maya Indian but also indicates that she is from the town of Nabaj in Guatemala.

nas, dress in Western-style clothes. The style, colors, and designs on the huipil further identify the particular Native American ethnic group the woman is from: Nahuala, Chichicastenango, Solola, or one of the other hundred or so Native American groups in highland Guatemala.

Fluidity of Ethnic Groups

Ethnic groups are not stable groupings. Ethnic groups vanish, people move between ethnic groups, and new ethnic groups come into existence.

During the past 500 years, numerous ethnic groups have vanished. Massachusetts, Erie, Susquehannock, and Biloxi were not originally place names but the names of now-extinct Native American ethnic groups. Still other ethnic groups in Asia, Africa, Oceania, Europe, and the Americas have vanished as well. Extinction of an ethnic group seldom means biological extinction, though. In most cases, the members of one group are absorbed into the population of a larger group. The Tasmanians of Australia are typical of what happened to many smaller ethnic groups. Numbering at most 5,000 when the British began colonizing the island of Tasmania in 1802, the population was so ravaged by wars and massacres that only a handful existed by 1850; the Tasmanians as a viable ethnic group had ceased to exist. In 1869, the last full-blooded Tasmanian man died, and in 1888, the last full-blooded Tasmanian woman died. Even today, however, mixed-blood descendants of the Tasmanians can be found among the Australian population.

Both individuals and communities can move between ethnic groups. During the sixteenth and seventeenth centuries, French Protestants, called *Huguenots,* fled persecution in France and settled in large numbers in England and the English colonies in North America. These people quickly became absorbed into the English population. Over the past 200 years, Americans have absorbed numerous immigrant populations.

Ethnogenesis is the emergence of a new ethnic group. Ethnogenesis usually occurs in one of two ways: (1) a portion of an existing ethnic group splits away and forms a new ethnic group, or (2) members of two or more existing ethnic groups fuse to form a new ethnic group.

Probably the most common cause of ethnogenesis is the division of an existing ethnic group. At one time, the Osage, Kansa, Omaha, Ponca, and Quapaw Indians of the central United States were a single ethnic group. The origin myths of these peoples tell how at different times portions broke away, until there were five distinct groups. In the 1700s, small groups of Creek Indians began moving south into Florida, where they eventually developed a distinct identity as the Seminole. Similarly, as Bantu-speaking peoples spread throughout central and southern Africa, they became separated, and new ethnic groups formed. As the Spanish Empire in the Americas disintegrated during the early 1800s, new regional ethnic identities (such as Mexican, Guatemalan, Peruvian, and Chilean) began to emerge among the Spanish-speaking peoples in that region. In 1652, the Dutch began settling near the Cape of Good Hope in southern Africa. These people eventually developed their own distinctive dialect of Dutch, called *Afrikaans,* and their own identity, Boers.

In other cases, members of two or more ethnic groups fuse and a new ethnic identity emerges. In England, the Angles, the Saxons, and the Jutes fused and became known as the English. The original Euro-American ethnic group was not the result of a split among the English people, but rather a fusion of English, Dutch, German, Scots, Irish, French Huguenots, Scotch-Irish, and other European settlers residing on the coast of North America. Most African American groups in the Americas are the result of the fusion of numerous distinct African groups. Intermarriage between French traders and Native Americans in Canada resulted in the emergence of the Metis. Similarly, in South Africa, the Cape Coloured, people of mixed Dutch and Khoikhoi ancestry, are socially and politically distinct from both whites and Africans.

Types of Ethnic Groups

From our discussion and examples so far, it should be apparent that the term *ethnic group* covers a range of social groupings. In general, ethnic groups fall into two main categories: national and subnational.

A **nationality** is an ethnic group that has a feeling of **homeland,** a geographical region over which they have exclusive rights. Implicit in this concept is the assumption of an inherent right to political autonomy and self-determination. In contrast, **subnationalities** lack the concept of a distinct and separate homeland and the associated rights to separate political sovereignty and self-determination. A subnational group sees itself as a dependent and politically subordinate subset of a nationality.

Although it is easy to define the difference between ethnic nationalities and subnationalities, sometimes it is far more difficult to classify particular groups. The ethnic groups in the United States demonstrate some of the difficulties in classification. With some ethnic groups there is no doubt: Italian Americans, German Americans, Polish Americans, Scottish Americans, and Irish Americans are all subnational groups. At a higher level of identity, the same is true for African Americans. None of these groups has a concept of a distinct and separate geographical homeland within the United States. Hence, they are subnational groups that, together with many other groups, collectively constitute the American ethnic nationality.

There are other ethnic groups within the United States whose status is not as clear. What is the status of Native American groups such as the Navajo, the Hopi, the Crow, the Cheyenne, the Cherokee, and the Osage, to name only a few? These groups have a concept of homelands within the United States. They also have histories quite distinct from those of other Americans. In recent years, they have been asserting increased political sovereignty and self-determination within their reservations (homelands). Although there is disagreement, many Native American individuals and groups still consider themselves distinct nationalities. The U.S. government recognizes most American Indian groups as national groups with collective legal and political rights. No other ethnic groups in the United States have officially recognized governments and limited rights of self-determination. There is also some question about the ethnic status of Spanish-speaking people in the southwestern United States. Until the mid-nineteenth century, Texas, New Mexico, Arizona, and California were part of Mexico. Then the United States acquired this region through military conquest. Most of the native Spanish-speaking people in this region still think of themselves as Mexi-

Civilizations	Groupings of two or more distinct nationalities on the basis of a shared or common cultural historical tradition. In most cases, this shared cultural tradition takes the form of religion.
Nationalities	Ethnic groups who collectively own, or feel that they own, a specific geographical region, or homeland, in which they have exclusive rights
Subnationalities	Ethnic groups whose identities are nested within that of a larger national identity
Transnational groups	Ethnic communities that are geographically separated from their homeland and live among members of another nationality

can American or Spanish American, a subnational group. There is, however, a small group who see themselves as "Mexicans" living in a land that is rightfully part of Mexico, a region they call Atzlan.

The distinction between nationality and subnational ethnic group is important because of their different political implications. As we shall see, the demands of subnational groups for equal rights and treatment have long been a source of conflict. But the demands of nationalities for independence and sovereignty in a region carved out of an existing country create a political time bomb.

Globalization has increased our awareness of two additional levels of ethnic identity. Today more than 150 million people live in a country that they were not born in. Among these immigrants is a special category: transnationals. **Transnationals** are members of an ethnic community who live outside their country of origin and homeland. What distinguishes transnational communities from other immigrant communities is that they feel that their true home is still where they came from and that their residence in another country is only temporary. Many transnationals are war refugees; others have come as guest workers, some legally and many illegally. In many cases, they have moved as immigrants and are even citizens of the new country. Although there have always been such communities, eventually either most disintegrated or their members returned home. Today, thanks to improvements in transportation and communications technology, these geographically separated groups can remain in contact with their home communities. Using the Internet, e-mail, and long-distance phone service, they can remain in close, even daily, contact with family and friends at home and be well aware of events at home. Air travel means that they can return home quickly if necessary in case of illness or for family weddings and other important social events. Marriages are even arranged between transnationals and spouses in their home countries. Many transnationals own homes in two countries and,

when possible, acquire dual citizenship and even take an active role in the politics of both countries. There are countless numbers of such communities in the world today, such as the Pakistanis and Indians in Oman, the United Arab Emirates, Kuwait, England, Canada, the United States, and elsewhere; and the Afghani communities in Pakistan, Australia, Iran, England, and the United States. Most of these transnational communities are found in the developed countries of Western Europe and North America, but almost every country in the world has some.

Globalization and the increasing contact and conflict between different peoples have also resulted in the growing significance of a level of identity that transcends nationality: civilization. A **civilization** is a grouping of a number of different nationalities on the basis of a shared cultural historical heritage that collectively distinguishes them from other like groups. Thus, we speak of Western civilization, as opposed to Islamic, Hindu, or Chinese civilization. By Western, we mean those nationalities that are the inheritors of the Judeo-Christian cultural traditions of Europe. Today, Western peoples are found in almost every region of the world. (See the Globalization box for a discussion of civilizations.)

The Problem of Stateless Nationalities

It is difficult for most Americans to understand the causes and bitterness of ethnic conflict in other parts of the world. We think of *nationality* and *nation* as being one and the same. An American is any person who is a citizen of the United States. Most of us think of ourselves primarily as Americans and only secondarily as Irish, Italian, or Chinese Americans. This mind-set about the meaning and significance of ethnicity is due mainly to our history as a nation of immigrants—with the exception of Native Americans, immigrants renounced their

In late September 2001, as the U.S. military prepared to enter Afghanistan in search of Osama bin Laden, Silvio Berlusconi, the prime minister of Italy, remarked in a speech to his parliament that he hoped "the West will continue to conquer peoples, like it conquered Communism." The Arab League demanded an apology. Just three days earlier on BBC television, Dr. Ghazi Algosaibi, the Saudi Arabian ambassador to the United Kingdom, had warned, "We are worried that this has turned from a war against terrorism, which we support wholeheartedly and with no reservation, into a war of America or the West against Islam." The subsequent invasion and occupation of Iraq have only added to these fears.

In 1996, Samuel P. Huntington, one of America's foremost political scientists, published his widely read book, *The Clash of Civilizations and the Remaking of World Order.* In this study, he argues against the position held by many Western and non-Western scholars and writers that the global economy and Westernization go hand in hand and that Western civilization is, as V. S. Naipaul once asserted, the "universal civilization." Huntington suggests that the "Westernization" of the world's people is for the most part superficial. Although other peoples may have adopted many of the overt trappings of Western culture, in their core beliefs and values non-Western peoples have not changed. Thus, in terms of cultural traditions, people have been and still are highly differentiated.

Significant conflicts in recent world history have been what Huntington terms "Western civil wars": wars between competing Western rulers, nation-states, and ideologies. The Cold War, a conflict of Western ideologies, was the last of these "civil wars." According to Huntington, the Western world, by which he means western (Protestant and Catholic) Europe together with the United States and Canada, is now at the height of its political, economic, and military power in the world. Even though the old colonial empires are gone, the West still collectively exercises political and economic control over the world's peoples through the United Nations Security Council and the International Monetary Fund (IMF). In global political affairs, "world community" has become a euphemism to give legitimacy to the actions, frequently military, of the West. Through the control of the IMF and other similar institutions, the West still controls and manipulates global economic growth and development for its own benefit. Relative to the non-Western world, the IMF has been compared by Georgi Arbatov to "neo-Bolsheviks who love expropriating other people's money, imposing undemocratic and alien rules of economic and political conduct and stifling economic freedom" (Huntington 1996, 184). With the United States as the only remaining military superpower, the West has aggressively pursued a policy of limiting the development of advanced military technology, particularly nuclear weapons, in the non-Western world.

claims to their national homelands when they came to the New World. For the most part, the ethnic groups in the United States are subnationalities, not nationalities. Thus, from our common perception, a Russian is a person from Russia, a Nigerian is a citizen from Nigeria, and so forth. Falsely equating country of origin with ethnic nationality, we view ethnic conflicts in other regions of the world as comparable to conflicts between subnational groups within the United States. We think ethnic problems within a country are the result of social or economic discrimination—resolvable and reparable by reforms—and we minimize their political significance. However, the ethnic conflicts in most countries are not between subnational groups, but between distinct nationalities.

The ethnic conflicts in Northern Ireland and in Israel and Palestine have proved particularly bitter. In 1922, after several centuries of British colonial domination and periodic rebellions by the native Irish, the Irish Free State (now the Republic of Ireland) was established. Not all of Ireland was given independence, however. In the seventeenth century, to control the Irish, the British evicted Irish farmers from the northernmost portion of

the island and colonized the region with Scottish Presbyterians, who became known as the Ulster-Scots, or *Scotch-Irish* in the United States. The Ulster-Scots did not identify themselves as Irish and had no desire to become part of an independent Ireland. Recognizing the wishes of the Ulster-Scots, at independence the British partitioned the island. The northern six counties became Northern Ireland and remained part of the United Kingdom. Many Irish did not and do not accept the legality of this partitioning of Ireland. To them, Northern Ireland is part of the Irish homeland and thus should be part of the Republic of Ireland. In 1968, the Irish Republican Army (IRA), a secretive guerrilla army that is illegal in the Republic of Ireland, began waging a guerilla war with the objective of reuniting Northern Ireland with the Republic of Ireland. Bombings, ambushes, and assassinations claimed more than 2,200 lives before the IRA announced in 2005 that it would end its military operations. Several splinter groups have still not agreed, however. The news media frequently report the problems in Northern Ireland as conflict between the British and the Irish or between Catholics and Protestants; in reality, it is

The world has become divided between the West and the rest. Huntington argues that increasing contact between peoples is not serving to lessen cultural differences, but rather to make people more acutely aware of those cultural factors that divide them. People will increasingly identify with others of like cultural heritage. The result will be, according to Huntington, a "political" realignment based on cultural heritage, or "civilizations" as he calls them. The process of de-Westernization is beginning as non-Western peoples try to rid themselves of Western cultural influences. Although de-Westernization is most apparent in the fundamentalist religious movements in Iran, Algeria, and other portions of the Islamic world, it is taking root in many other parts of the non-Western world as well. To Huntington, religious traditions indicate fundamental cultural differences between peoples, and religion forms the cultural core of what he terms "civilizations." He sees the world coalescing into seven or eight "civilizations," which he identifies as Western (Protestant–Catholic), Slavic–Orthodox (Christians), Confucian, Japanese, Islamic, Hindu, Latin American, and possibly African.

Huntington does not see the coalescence of civilizations as replacing existing ethnic identities or ending internal conflicts. He does, however, see these various civilizations increasingly competing with one another, and the boundaries separating these civilizations becoming the "fault lines" along which future conflicts will occur. The intensity of the wars in Bosnia was thus not the result of mere competition between three rival ethnic groups, but rather the result of conflict between three competing civilizations: Western (the Croats), Slavic–Orthodox (the Serbs), and Islamic (the Bosnian Muslims). Ethnic and ideological wars will be superseded by wars between civilizations, and Huntington sees the most imminent of these clashes as between Western and Islamic civilizations.

Critical Thinking Questions

1. Huntington's proposal is highly speculative, and many of his assertions can be questioned. He does, however, present some alarming ideas concerning the nature of future conflicts in the world. Is this present time of rising nationalism and political fragmentation only the prelude to a global political realignment of people based on opposing cultural traditions?

2. Will new supra-ethnic identities emerge as the most potent political forces in the world?

3. Will the attacks on the World Trade Center and the Pentagon and the retaliatory invasions by the United States of Afghanistan and Iraq prove to be isolated events in human history, or will they be the prelude to a clash between Western and Islamic civilizations?

neither. The root of the problem is the conflicting claims of two rival and hostile nationalities: the Irish and the Ulster-Scots. The Ulster-Scots have emerged over the past 400 years as a distinct nationality who claim the northern part of Ireland as their homeland. In contrast, the Irish see the area as an integral and inalienable part of the Irish homeland.

After an absence of almost 2,000 years, the Jews began returning to their historic homeland in Palestine in 1882. During the early twentieth century, Jewish settlements in Palestine grew, and in 1948, the Jewish settlers proclaimed the state of Israel. In the war that followed, the Arab League, Jordan, Egypt, Syria, and Iraq were defeated and the Israelis gained control over most of the area west of the Jordan River and the Sinai. Periodic fighting continued, however. The 1967 War resulted in the Israeli occupation of the Palestinian areas of the West Bank and the Gaza Strip but has not brought an end to the fighting. For the past 60 years, conflict between Israelis and Palestinians has been constant, varying only in the intensity and form of violence. The problem is similar to the problem in Northern Ireland: two nationalities—Israelis and Palestinians—claim the same geographical region as their legitimate homeland. Although some progress has been made recently toward peaceful settlements of the conflicts in Northern Ireland and between Israelis and Palestinians, such agreements are tenuous. These situations remain volatile. In Israel and Northern Ireland, it is impossible to resolve the conflict to the total satisfaction of both nationalities.

These two conflicts vividly illustrate the strength of nationalist sentiments. In both cases, we see groups of educated, rational human beings who are willing to sacrifice their lives and economic well-being in unending conflicts for what they consider to be their nationality's legitimate rights.

Such conflict is more common in the modern world than most of us realize. The world is divided into about 200 countries, but there are 3,000 to 5,000 distinct ethnic nationalities. As a result, the populations of most countries encompass many distinct nationalities. China officially recognizes 56 distinct nationalities. Some estimates are as high as 300 ethnic nationalities in Indonesia. Ethiopia has at least 70 nationalities. Only a handful of

▲ **Figure 17.1** Nationalist organizations use various means to communicate their message of separation. These cartoon panels showing the Basque flag are from a booklet distributed by Basque separatists in northern Spain.

countries are peopled by members of a single nationality and are thus ethnically homogeneous.

The ethnic nationality problem is further complicated because current political boundaries frequently divide members of a nationality from their historic homeland. For example, Hungarians are found not only in Hungary but also in the adjacent portions of Romania and Serbia. Somalis live not only in Somalia but also in the adjacent Ogaden portion of Ethiopia. Large numbers of Albanians live in adjoining portions of Kosovo (Serbia) and Macedonia. Thus, the world is filled with ethnic groups who do not fully recognize the legitimacy of "their" central government and who aspire or may potentially aspire to have political autonomy (see Figure 17.1).

For the most part, nationality problems were not created by the nationalities themselves. The current political boundaries for most of the world are legacies of European colonialism and expansion. In 1884–1885 at the Berlin Conference, European leaders sat at a table and with pens and pencils drew lines on a map of Africa, dividing the resources and peoples of that continent among themselves. Through this agreement, the English, French, Germans, Belgians, Portuguese, and other European powers assumed sovereignty over lands they had never traveled and over peoples who had never seen a white man. Nor was Africa the only continent to have boundaries imposed by Europeans. The national boundaries of most of the world were drawn by Europeans for their own interests, with little regard for the interests of any indigenous peoples or the boundaries of the ethnic groups affected. As a result, most European colonial possessions were a polyglot of ethnic groups, many of whom had long histories of hostilities toward

one another. Sometimes the land and people of an ethnic group were divided between two or more European colonies. To make matters worse, colonial powers frequently moved people from one colony to another to supply labor, introducing groups to new areas. For example, the British settled Indian laborers in Burma (Myanmar), Malaya (Malaysia), Fiji, Sri Lanka, Kenya, Uganda, South Africa, Trinidad, and British Guiana.

The end of the colonial period did not end the ethnic conflicts in the world. As European powers granted independence to their colonies, they made little attempt to redefine political boundaries. In most cases, these newly independent countries had precisely the same boundaries and ethnic composition as the former colonies. Because these political divisions were imposed by European military power, some scholars have termed the former colonies **artificial countries.** In most cases, the basic colonial administrative and governmental structure was maintained after independence; the major departure from the colonial period was that native officials replaced European officials. However, not all ethnic groups were equally represented in these new governments, and most former colonies quickly came under the domination of one or two of the more powerful ethnic groups. Thus, in many instances, European domination was replaced by domination by one or another "native" ethnic group. With this in mind, the political problems endemic in much of the former colonial world become more comprehensible. (See A Closer Look for a discussion of ethnic conflicts in Iraq.)

India is a prime example of ethnic problems in the postcolonial period. Consisting of several hundred distinct ethnic groups as well as major religious divisions, India did not exist—and never existed—as a unified

The conflict in present-day Iraq can be understood only in the context of the region's history. Although the Tigris and Euphrates valleys, ancient Mesopotamia, is one of the ancient "cradles" of civilization, it is also a region that has had an extremely turbulent political history. In the third millennium B.C.E., it was the center of Sumerian civilization, and during the second millennium B.C.E., the ancient city of Babylon dominated the region. Later it was at times part of the Assyrian, Persian, Seleucid, Roman, Parthian, Sassanid, Umayyad, and Ottoman empires, to name only some. In spite of the long history of the region, modern-day Iraq is a recent creation, established by the British following World War I out of three provinces or *wilayat* of the defeated Ottoman (Turkish) Empire. Like many regions long dominated by outside forces and with modern political boundaries drawn by others, Iraq lacks any meaningful sociopolitical cohesion uniting its population. Modern Iraq is an "artificial country."

The native population of Iraq is divided into three main ethnic/religious groups: Kurds, Sunni Arabs, and Shiite Arabs. Of the three groups, the Shiite Arabs are by far the largest, constituting about 60 percent of the total population. The Kurds and Sunni Arabs each number about 20 percent. In addition, there are some smaller ethnic/religious groups: Assyrians, Turkmen, and Arab Christians. About 120,000 Jews lived in Iraq until after the war of Israeli independence, when most immigrated to Israel.

Speaking an Indo-European language, the Kurds are one of the ancient indigenous peoples of the region. Distinguished by dialect differences and highly fractionalized into numerous localized tribal groups, they live primarily in mountain agricultural communities. Kurdish communities are found in Iraq, Iran, Turkey, Syria, Azerbaijan, and Armenia. Numbering between 22 million and 25 million people, the Kurds are the largest stateless nationality in the world. Although the Kurds are predominantly Sunni Muslims, some tribes are Shiite, and a few still practice Yazdani, the pre-Islamic Kurdish religion. Occupying the more mountainous northeastern portion of Iraq, the 3.5 million Iraqi Kurds identify more strongly with Kurdish populations living in adjacent countries than with Arab Iraqis.

Although the Arabic-speaking people of Iraq make up about 80 percent of the population, they are far from a unified group. The Arab population of southern Iraq is overwhelmingly Shiite, while the region of central Iraq around Baghdad is predominantly Sunni. The Sunni and Shiite represent the two major divisions in the Islamic world.

In A.D. 632, the Prophet Muhammad died with no clearly defined manner in which a new successor could be chosen. Some Muslims believed that the Prophet's successor should be chosen from the family of the Prophet. Ali ibn Abu Talib, usually referred to simply as Ali, the cousin of Muhammad and the husband of his only surviving child, Fatima, was the choice of this group. However, most leaders of the new religion thought that the position should be open to others, and Abu Bakr was selected by them to be the first caliph. In the decades that followed Abu Bakr's selection, by conquest and proselytizing, Islam spread rapidly beyond the Arabian peninsula—west into Egypt and North Africa and north into Syria and Iraq. Disputes broke out between the various leaders over the control of the lands being conquered. In C.E. 656, Uthman, the third caliph, was murdered by the son of the first caliph, Abu Bakr. A crisis quickly developed when factional leaders were unable to agree on a successor to Uthman. Many supported Ali, who was now governor of Iraq, but others supported Muawiyah, a cousin of Uthman and governor of Syria. Among the supporters of Muawiyah was Aisha, a widow of the Prophet Muhammad.

The armies of Ali and Muawiyah met on the Plains of Siffin, in what is today Iraq. The battle was indecisive, and Ali attempted to arbitrate their differences peacefully. In 661, Ali was murdered while at prayer in the mosque Al Kufah (Kufah) and buried in nearby Najaf. Muawiyah was able to convince Ali's oldest son, Hassan, to give up any claim to the caliphate, and Muawiyah was declared caliph and established what was to be called the Umayyad Dynasty, with its capital at Damascus (Syria). Shortly after Hassan had renounced his claim, he died. Some say that he died of natural causes, others that he was poisoned. The death of Ali and then Hassan served to strengthen the opposition of Ali's supporters against Muawiyah.

In 680, Muawiyah died and was succeeded as caliph by his son Yazid. Hussain, the second son of Ali, refusing to recognize Yazid, led a revolt. Yazid sent an army against them. On October 10, 680, Hussain and 200 of his followers were killed at Karbala (Iraq) and Hussain's head was sent to Yazid.

The killing of Hussain and his followers created a schism in the Islamic religious community that has lasted until today. The followers of Ali and Hussain became known as the Shiite, with their main shrines at Karbala and Najaf in Iraq. The followers of Yazid became known as the Sunni. Today, only about 16 percent of the Islamic peoples in the world are Shiite, and only in Iraq, Iran, and Bahrain do they constitute the majority of the population. The vast majority, about 83 percent, of the Islamic peoples are Sunni.

There are important theological differences between Shiites and Sunnis. Possibly the most significant difference concerns spiritual leadership and the concept of Imam, or religious leader. Among the Sunni, any righteous and knowledgeable Muslim can act as an Imam, leading prayers and interpreting the Holy Koran. Even the highest-ranking Imams are not and cannot be considered divinely inspired. To suggest such would be considered heresy. For important senior leadership positions, Sunni Imams are usually appointed by political leaders, not chosen by other Imams. In contrast, Shiites believe that the "Twelve Imams," the earliest divinely inspired followers of the Prophet Mohammed, stay in spiritual contact with their followers through the living Imams. The highest-ranking Shiite Imams are called Ayatollahs. The position of Ayatollah is based on agreement of the other Ayatollahs. Shiites further believe that the Ayatollahs (which means "shadow of Allah") receive guidance from the Twelve Imams, and thus their actions in temporal and spiritual matters are divinely inspired.

Although Arab Shiites and Sunnis speak the same language, follow the same cultural traditions, and frequently reside in the same cities and towns, they always live in two socially distinct and separate communities. Conversions from one sect to the other are rare, as are marriages between members of the two sects. Marriage, birth, and death rituals take place within the framework of one or the other of the communities. Frequently, the division between the Shiite and the Sunni communities assumes the same level of sociopolitical significance as ethnic differences.

Under Ottoman Turkish rule, the region now known as Iraq consisted of three separate *wilayat* or provinces: Mosul in the north, which was predominantly Kurdish; Baghdad in the central area, in which the Sunni population was concentrated; and Al-Basrah in the south, where mainly Shiites resided. Soon after the outbreak of World War I, Turkey allied itself with Germany. Quickly moving forces out of India, the British succeeded in capturing Basra and by the fall of 1915 most of the south. In 1917 they took Baghdad, and the following year Mosul. At the peace conference of 1919, the three provinces were made British mandate territories under the supervision of the League of Nations.

At first Iraq, under the British, was to consist of only the provinces of Baghdad and Al-Basrah, the Sunni and Shiite Arab regions. In accordance with the 1920 Treaty of Sevres, the province of Mosul was to be part of a new autonomous Kurdish state that was also to include the Kurdish portion of Turkey. However, in May 1920, fearing continued British control, the Sunni and Shiite communities and leaders joined forces in an armed uprising that failed. The next year, 1921, the new Iraqi government was organized. An individual from Saudi Arabia, Faisal, was named king, and a constitutional monarchy was established with a council of ministers under a British high commissioner. Meanwhile, the Sultan of Turkey was overthrown by Turkish nationalists, who reoccupied the Kurdish portion of eastern Turkey, scrapping the Treaty of Sevres. Recognizing that the area around Mosul contained large oil reserves, which they desired to control, in 1923, the British unilaterally merged the Kurdish province of Mosul with the new Iraq Kingdom. Two years later, the League of Nations approved this change.

The status of Iraq as a British mandate continued until 1932, when Iraq became fully independent and a member of the League of Nations. Although King Faisal was a pan-Arab nationalist, he was not from Iraq, and most local Arabs considered him a foreigner imposed on them by the British. Neither King Faisal nor the government as created by the British had any legitimacy in the minds of the various peoples of Iraq. The Sunni, though smaller in numbers than the Shiite, were better educated. Under the Ottomans, Sunni had filled most of the administrative positions in the regional government. This continued under the British and in the new Iraq government. The Shiite were not pleased by what they viewed as Sunni domination. The Kurds were also unhappy that an autonomous Kurdish state had not been created. There were also problems between the various Arab tribal leaders as well as between pan-Arab and Iraqi nationalists. In addition, the new country faced a wide range of economic problems. With full independence achieved, King Faisal died in 1933, leaving his throne to his 21-year-old, Western-educated son, Ghazi. In 1939, Ghazi was killed in an automobile accident, leaving as his successor a 3-year-old son, Faisal II. A cousin of the new king was named as regent.

Under the "rule" of Ghazi and Faisal II, the government of Iraq quickly degenerated into political bickering and infighting between various tribal leaders, Sunnis, Shiites, Kurds, pan-Arab nationalists, Iraqi nationalists, communists, socialists, military officers, and others. In 1948, Iraq joined the other Arab countries in sending troops to fight against Israel. The defeat of the Arab League and the continued pro-British and pro-Western position of Faisal II and his ministers resulted in a coalescence of the various anti-Western factions in Iraq. As a result, in 1958, a military coup took place, Faisal II was killed, and a republic proclaimed.

The coup and the creation of a republic did not succeed in bringing political stability to the country. During the 1960s and 1970s, there were still more military coups and rapid changes in political leadership. The only constant during this period was that the leaders were all anti-West and pro–Soviet Union. In 1961, Mustafa al-Barzani, with backing from Iran, initiated a Kurdish separatist rebellion. This period of fighting lasted until 1977, when the Iraqi government agreed to give the Kurds greater local autonomy and recognized Kurdish as an official language. The 1960s and 1970s were also a period of increasing oil production and revenue, as well as greater dependence on civilian and military technology from the Soviet Union.

In 1979, two significant events occurred in the region: Saddam Hussein became president of Iraq, and the Shah of Iran was overthrown and the Islamic Republic of Iran was created under the control of Shiite clerics. The following year, the Iran–Iraq War started with the Iraqi invasion of southern Iran. There

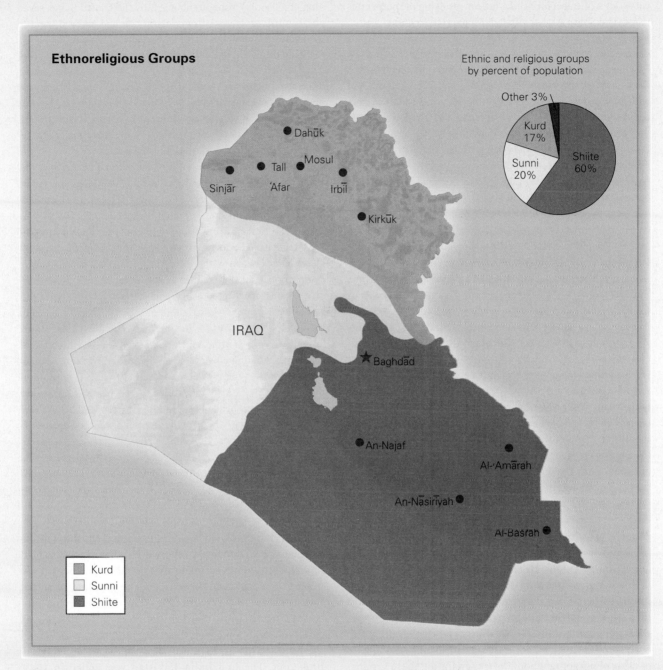

Ethnoreligious Groups

Ethnic and religious groups
by percent of population

Other 3%
Kurd 17%
Sunni 20%
Shiite 60%

- Dahūk
- Tall 'Afar
- Mosul
- Sinjār
- Irbīl
- Kirkūk

IRAQ

★ Baghdād

- An-Najaf
- Al-'Amārah
- An-Nāsirīyah
- Al-Basrah

Kurd
Sunni
Shiite

▲ **Figure 17.2** The Regions of Iraq Occupied by the Kurds, Sunni Arabs, and Shiite Arabs.

appear to have been multiple reasons Hussein ordered the invasion. First, he wished to settle some important border disputes. Second, he feared that the success of the Shiite clerics in Iran would encourage the Shiite majority in Iraq to attempt a similar revolution. Finally, by exploiting the long-standing antipathies between Arabs and Iranians (Persians), Hussein could use the war to help solidify his control over Iraq. The eight years of often-bloody warfare that followed almost bankrupted the two countries while accomplishing little in resolving the border disputes. The Shiite Arabs in Iraq did support the national war effort, however, and the war enabled Hussein to gain a virtually dictatorial control of the country through the military.

During the war with Iran, with weapons supplied by Iran, the Kurds in the north once again revolted. After the war with Iran ended in 1988, Hussein moved against the Kurdish-controlled areas in the north. Nerve gas and mustard gas were dropped on the Kurdish-held cities. Altogether an estimated 200,000 Kurds died in these attacks, but Kurdish guerrillas were able to hold out in some areas.

Iraqi leaders had long claimed that Kuwait should be part of Iraq. In August 1990, the Iraqi army invaded and quickly occupied the country. The United Nations condemned the occupation of Kuwait and ordered the Iraqi army to withdraw by January 15, 1991. When they did not, an allied army led by the United States militarily drove the Iraqis out of Kuwait. The allied army, however, did not attempt to invade and occupy Iraq. Instead, a ceasefire was announced in February, and in April the United Nations imposed restrictions on Iraq.

Hoping to remove Hussein, then U.S. President George Bush encouraged both the Kurds and the Shiite Arabs to revolt. Responding to Bush's call, in 1991 the Kurdish separatists launched a major attack against the Iraqi-held towns, while almost simultaneously Shiites revolted in the cities and towns of the south. The Iraqi army responded quickly with counterattacks both in the north and in the south. Lacking any meaningful military support from the United States, Shiite irregulars in the south were routed, with tens of thousands either killed or executed. Similarly in the north, the Kurds were routed, with almost a million refugees fleeing to Turkey. Only the imposi-

tion of a "no fly" zone in the north by the United States saved the Kurdish separatists from destruction and allowed them to maintain an autonomous region in the mountainous north.

With the defeat of the Iraqi army and the occupation of Iraq by American and coalition forces in 2003, the United States finds itself in an even more difficult situation than Britain did in 1919. The United States is involved in a complex, bloody, multisided war involving a wide range of hostile armed groups, each with different objectives. Each of the three major ethnic/religious groups—the Kurds, Sunnis, and Shiites—is hostile to the others. And, within each of these three ethnic/religious groups are a number of rival factions hostile to the others. The Kurdish groups are in basic agreement on wanting an autonomous region within Iraq, if not an independent Kurdistan. The Sunni and Shiite groups are divided into a complex array of rival factions of nationalists, sectarian zelots, and Islamic fundamentalists. Finally, there is Al-Qaeda, with people drawn from throughout the Islamic world, engaged in a jihad (holy war) against the United States and varyingly allied with different local factions. All of these groups are in the process of positioning themselves for the internal struggle that they think is going to emerge after the United States and Coalition forces leave Iraq. Finding a workable political solution to these internal problems is going to be extremely difficult, if not impossible. The only "stable" government Iraq has had during the past 85 years was headed by Saddam Hussein, and he was able to stay in power only by keeping Iraq on a war footing and using his army to impose draconian measures to suppress any internal dissension. Nevertheless, the oil reserves of Iraq are far too important to the global economy to allow Iraq to descend into anarchy.

country before British domination. As independence approached in the 1940s, hostilities between rival Muslim and Hindu factions became so intense that British officials decided that a unified, independent India was an impossibility. They decided that India had to be divided into two countries: India (predominantly Hindu) and Pakistan (predominantly Muslim). The British drew the borders of these new countries. The problem was the lack of clear geographical boundaries separating these groups; in many regions, the populations were mixed Hindu and Muslim. An East Pakistan and a West Pakistan were carved out on either side, separated by 1,000 miles of what was to be India. After the official announcement of the boundaries, massive migrations began as millions of Muslims and Hindus found themselves on the wrong sides of the borders. These migrations were stimulated

by fanatics on both sides, who massacred Muslims living in what was to become India and Hindus in what was to be Pakistan. Some estimate that as many as one million people were killed in these riots. The granting of actual independence to the two countries in 1947 made the situation worse because neither side was satisfied with its geographical boundaries. The new Indian army occupied the largely Muslim region of Kashmir, and war quickly broke out. The first India–Pakistan war ended in 1949, with most of Kashmir occupied by India.

The creation of two separate states out of British India addressed—but did not solve—only one of the region's problems. Immediately after independence, the Naga people in India's easternmost Assam province revolted and demanded an independent Nagaland. This Naga secessionist movement is still active; for more than

60 years, periodic bloody clashes have occurred between Naga rebels and Indian authorities. More recently, a Sikh separatist movement emerged, demanding an independent homeland in Punjab. The violent tactics of the Sikh nationalists resulted in the Indian army attacking the holiest Sikh religious shrine, the Golden Temple in Amritsar, in 1984. Later that year, two Sikhs assassinated Indira Gandhi, the prime minister of India, causing more violence between Sikhs and Hindus. In 1990, violence again broke out in Kashmir, which continues today. Muslim leaders are demanding either a separate nation or unification with Pakistan. As if India's problems with its religious/ethnic minorities were not sufficient, the Hindu majority is becoming increasingly hostile to non-Hindu minorities (see the Globalization box in Chapter 16).

Pakistan has also experienced ethnic difficulties. Both parts of Pakistan were Muslim, but there were major ethnic differences between the two. East Pakistanis were predominantly Bengalis; West Pakistan was more heterogeneous ethnically but dominated by Urdu-speaking peoples. Although West Pakistan had a smaller population, the capital was located there after independence, and the Urdu peoples gained dominance in the government and the military. In West Pakistan, a separatist movement was started by the Baluchi, who sought an independent Baluchistan. However, the major conflict emerged with the Bengalis in East Pakistan. Although the Bengalis were economically exploited and discriminated against by the Urdu, it was not until the government attempted to impose the Urdu language in the schools of East Pakistan that the situation came to a head. In 1971, the East Pakistanis revolted and, after a short but bloody war aided by India, succeeded in establishing the state of Bangladesh.

Bangladesh is experiencing its own internal ethnic problems. Even before independence from Pakistan, Bengali settlers had begun occupying land in the Chittagong hills, displacing the indigenous tribal peoples. After independence, with official encouragement, the flow of Bengali settlers increased, causing the tribal peoples to rebel and demand local autonomy. The government has refused to halt the settlements, and periodic killings and massacres are continuing. In the realm of ethnic conflict, today's victims can quickly become tomorrow's villains.

Similar secessionist movements have occurred and are still occurring throughout the old colonial world: nationalist separatist movements are active in southern Sudan, the island of Mindanao in the Philippines, Sri Lanka, Burma, Burundi, Congo, and Indonesia—to name just a few. Certainly, it is facile to lay all the blame on colonialism for these and other conflicts in the postcolonial era. But it is undeniable that violence between ethnic nation-

alities, each believing its political and territorial claims are legitimate, is one of colonialism's most unfortunate and long-lasting legacies.

Not all ethnic conflicts are confined to the old colonial world, however. For example, the Kurds (who live in the mountainous regions of Turkey, Iraq, Iran, and Syria) have had an active separatist movement since the 1960s. At different times they have fought the Turks, the Iraqis, and the Iranians (see A Closer Look). In 1950, China invaded and occupied Tibet, a region that the Chinese consider part of China. A Tibetan revolt in 1959 was crushed, but Tibetan Buddhists seek political autonomy under the Dalai Lama, their spiritual leader.

Recently some of the most violent ethnic conflicts have been in Europe and the former Soviet Union. In the early 1990s, Yugoslavia disintegrated as the republics of Slovenia, Croatia, Bosnia, and Macedonia proclaimed their independence. Yugoslavia was reduced to only two of the former six republics: Serbia and Montenegro. Hundreds of thousands of ethnic Serbs found themselves living in Croatia and Bosnia. Supported by the Serb-controlled Yugoslavian army, Serb nationalists in Croatia and Bosnia rebelled, took control of regions in both republics, and demanded unification with Serbia. With more than 100,000 dead and more than one million homeless, the war in Bosnia has been the bloodiest and most destructive war in Europe since World War II. In 1995, the Bosnian Muslims, Croats, and Serbs reached an agreement. Fighting stopped, and NATO troops occupied zones between the warring factions.

Ethnic conflict spread to the Kosovo province of Serbia in 1998, when the Albanian majority in the province organized the Albanian Liberation Army and called for an independent Kosovo. Attempts by the Serbs to crush the rebellion resulted in armed intervention by NATO forces in 1999 and the military occupation of the province. In 2000, ethnic conflict spread to Macedonia as Albanian nationalists rebelled against Macedonian control of their regions of the country. NATO peacekeepers are now in Macedonia. The question remains whether workable political solutions can be found for the ethnic problems in Bosnia, Kosovo, and Macedonia. Will foreign peacekeeping troops have to stay in these areas indefinitely?

This is only a sampling of armed nationalist conflicts. Nationalist movements are difficult to defuse. In most cases, the recognized national governments lack the military resources to defeat them. Even when a government has overwhelming resources, such as the British in Northern Ireland, guerrilla wars are difficult to win decisively. As a result, few separatist movements have been extinguished. In some cases, the central governments have either disintegrated or lost control over most of the country. In other cases, the central governments have adopted policies of geographical containment and lessening of direct conflict. A graphic example of this approach is in Western Sahara, formerly Spanish Sahara. In the early 1970s, Spain committed itself to a policy of independence and self-determination for its colony. However, in 1976, before independence was achieved, Morocco occupied the northern portion of the region, claiming it was historically part of Morocco. In 1979, Morocco occupied the southern portion of the region. The Spanish did not resist the Moroccan occupation. But the local Sahrawi population rejected Moroccan domination, formed the Polisaria Front, and started a guerrilla war. Unable to defeat the guerrillas but unwilling to withdraw, the Moroccan government partitioned the region with a 2,500-kilometer-long sand "wall" equipped with electronic devices to detect movements; the purpose of the wall was to separate the portion Morocco controlled from the area it did not control. In 1989, the Moroccan government agreed to a referendum sponsored by the United Nations, but as of 2007, the status of Western Sahara has yet to be resolved.

Almost yearly the number of unresolved ethnic conflicts increases and the number of peoples and regions affected widens. There are about 150 ongoing armed conflicts in the world today, and 80 to 90 percent of these conflicts may be classified as nationalist movements. Central governments as a whole have been unsuccessful in achieving complete military victories over separatist groups, but nationalist separatist groups themselves seldom have been successful in achieving political victories.

Bangladesh was recognized by the United Nations only because it was a fait accompli, backed by the overwhelming military support of India. In contrast, the United Nations was extremely slow to extend recognition to Slovenia and Croatia. Only when it appeared that Yugoslavia might militarily intervene did the United Nations act, and then only in hopes of preventing a war. The recent problems of chaos and starvation in Somalia have been limited to the southern portion of the country. When the central government of Somalia disintegrated in 1991, the leaders in the north declared their independence and established their state of Somaliland. Although Somaliland is politically stable, it has yet to be granted recognition by any country. The United Nations and the Organization of African Unity have taken the position that northern and southern Somalia will "remain" united, and they act as if no government exists in the north.

One may well ask why separatist movements are seldom extended official recognition. In Chapter 1, Article 1,

of the Charter of the United Nations, the right of a people to self-determination is recognized. The United Nations, however, also recognizes the sovereignty and territorial integrity of existing states. Thus, recognition of a secessionist group would be considered intervention in the affairs of a sovereign state. Other governments have also pledged not to recognize separatist states. In 1964, the Organization of African Unity adopted the policy that "the borders of African States on the day of independence constitute a tangible reality," and thus they firmly oppose any changes in the political boundaries of Africa. The real, unstated reason is that almost every country in the world has one or more minority nationalities that either have or potentially may develop an independence movement. Thus, existing countries make both formal and informal agreements to maintain the current political status quo.

Responses to Ethnic Conflict

How do countries respond to internal ethnic conflicts? The most obvious solution is to divide the country, giving the members of each dissatisfied nationality their own land and independence and allowing them to establish their own country or merge with another country. Peaceful solutions to ethnic questions are rare, however. As Burma, Sudan, and many other countries have shown, governments would rather fight a long, destructive, and inclusive war than officially recognize the independence of a rebellious nationality. Governments take this stance partly because they fear setting a precedent. As a result, most ethnic conflicts have been resolved—and future solutions will probably have to be sought—within the existing political structure. Historically, such internal responses to ethnic issues have taken three forms: (1) ethnic homogenization of the population through the elimination of rival ethnic groups, (2) segregation of ethnic groups, and (3) political accommodation of ethnic groups.

Homogenization

Ethnic homogenization is the process by which one ethnic group attempts to eliminate rival ethnic groups within a particular region or country. Historically, ethnic homogenization has taken one of two main forms: ethnic cleansing or assimilation. The term *ethnic cleansing* entered our vocabulary in reference to the warfare in the republics of what was formerly Yugoslavia. **Ethnic cleansing** is the physical elimination of an unwanted ethnic group or groups from particular geographical areas. It involves genocide and/or relocation.

Genocide is the deliberate and systematic attempt to physically destroy the members of the rival population. The objective may be the total destruction of the group, the reduction of their numbers, or a stimulus for the surviving members of the group to migrate. The process is the same: the indiscriminate slaughter of men, women, and children of the targeted ethnic group. Today, when we think of genocide, we think of the recent events in Bosnia or Rwanda or the killing of millions of Jews and Gypsies by the Germans during World War II, but genocide has been a recurrent event in human history. Only the magnitude of the killing has varied. In the late 1970s and early 1980s, thousands of Native Americans were massacred by the Guatemalan army. The Turks instituted a policy of systematic killing of Armenians during the early years of this century. During the colonial period, the English, Dutch, French, Spanish, Portuguese, Belgians, and Germans were periodically guilty of genocide. Incidents of genocide are found even in American history, beginning with the slaughter of the Pequots in Connecticut in 1637 and ending with the massacre of more than 150 Sioux at Wounded Knee, South Dakota, in 1890. Genocide has been and still is a far too common response to ethnic conflict and rivalry.

Relocation is the forced resettlement of an unwanted ethnic group in a new geographical location. The forced relocation of the target population may be either in conjunction with genocide, as in the Darfur region of Sudan, or separate from it. Sometimes the unwanted group is forced outside the boundaries of the country, becoming what today we term *refugees.* In other cases, an ethnic group is forcibly moved to a new area within the boundaries of the state, where it is assumed that they will pose less of a problem.

At the outbreak of World War II, the Soviet Union was home to several million ethnic Germans who had settled in Russia during the eighteenth century. In 1924, a separate German autonomous republic within Russia was established along the Volga River for the so-called Volga Germans. When Germany attacked the Soviet Union in 1941, Stalin, fearing that the ethnic Germans might join the invaders, ordered all of them moved from Russia and Ukraine to Kazakhstan, Siberia, and other remote areas.

After World War II, the boundaries of much of Eastern Europe were redrawn. That portion of Germany located east of the Oder River was given to Poland, and seven million German residents were forcibly evicted. At the same time, Czechoslovakia evicted almost three million resident Germans from their homes. After independence, many East African countries expelled many East Indians who had settled there during the colonial period.

In American history, Native Americans were regularly relocated as the frontier moved west. The largest and best known of these relocations occurred in the 1830s, when the Five Civilized Tribes were forced to move (along the so-called Trail of Tears) from their homes in the southeastern states to what is today Oklahoma. Most indigenous tribes of the United States experienced similar resettlement programs. In Bosnia and Croatia, the main objective of all the combatants had been the relocation of the other ethnic populations. The killings, rapes, and destruction were the tactics used to force them to abandon their homes.

Assimilation is the social absorption of one ethnic group by another dominant one. Assimilation may be total, in which the ethnic identity of one group is lost, or partial, in which one ethnic group assumes a subordinate identity. Assimilation may be either forced or passive. In **forced assimilation,** the government adopts policies designed to deliberately and systematically destroy or change the ethnic identity of a particular group. The ultimate objective is usually the total absorption of the group into the dominant ethnic group. A key target of a forced assimilation policy is the elimination of ethnic boundary markers: language, religion, modes of dress, and any cultural institution that readily distinguishes the population. If these boundary markers are destroyed, the group loses much of its social cohesiveness. For example, until recently, the Bulgarian government pursued a policy designed to assimilate its Turkish population. Turks were not free to practice their Islamic religion, and they were forced to speak Bulgarian in public and adopt Bulgarian names.

One of the best examples of forced assimilation was the Indian policy of the United States in the latter part of the nineteenth and early twentieth centuries. Federal policy attacked Native American ethnic identity from several directions. Reservation lands, which were owned communally, were broken up, and the land was allotted (deeded) to individual members of the tribe in order to destroy community or village life. Many ceremonies such as the Sun Dance and the peyote religion were made illegal. Traditional or hereditary tribal leaders were not recognized, and tribal governments were either dissolved or reorganized along an American political model. People who worked for the government were commonly forced to cut their hair and wear "citizen's" (Western style) clothes. Native American children were taken from their families and placed in boarding schools, where they were forbidden to speak their native language, had their hair cut, were made to dress in citizen's clothes, were taught Euro-American technical skills, and were indoctrinated with Euro-American Christian values and attitudes. As the head of the Carlisle Indian School said, "You have to destroy the Indian to save the man." Canada and Australia established similar policies for the assimilation of aboriginal peoples.

Assimilation need not be the result of a conscious official policy to solve an "ethnic problem" by incorporating the population into the cultural mainstream. Another form, called **passive assimilation,** occurs without any formal planning or political coercion. Unless strong social barriers prevent assimilation, social and economic forces frequently result in more dominant ethnic groups absorbing members of less powerful groups with whom they are in contact. The dominant ethnic group does not necessarily have to be the largest, but it must be the most socially prestigious and economically powerful group. Many of the governments in Latin America have historically followed a laissez-faire policy toward Native American groups. Guatemala has not had a policy of forced assimilation. In Guatemala, the primary differences between Ladinos and Native Americans are not biological but social and cultural, and people who are technically identified as Native Americans are socially and economically discriminated against. As a result, more ambitious and educated Native Americans frequently have abandoned their native languages, dress, and lifestyles (ethnic boundary markers) and reidentified themselves as Ladinos. During the past 100 years, the Native American population in Guatemala has decreased from about 75 percent of the total population to less than 50 percent; passive assimilation is the primary cause of this decrease.

History shows us that there are other ways of managing ethnic differences. People do not have to resort to ethnic homogenization; they can either segregate or accommodate other ethnic groups.

Segregation

The political, social, and economic **segregation** of different ethnic groups has a long history in human society. In these situations, the dominant ethnic group does not attempt to eliminate the group, but rather places legal restrictions on the actions of the members of the group. In most cases, they have no political rights. They may not be permitted to own land, or they may own land in only certain restricted areas. Marriage between them and members of the dominant group may be prohibited. They may also be restricted to certain economic occupations. Not only is there no attempt to assimilate them into the dominant ethnic groups, but legal restrictions maintain their ethnic identities.

There are two major reasons such ethnic relationships develop: (1) the dependent ethnic group performs a needed economic service, or (2) the dependent ethnic group is so powerless that it presents no threat, economic or political, to the dominant society. The Jews and Gypsies in Europe are examples of groups that survived as segregated ethnic groups. Jews were merchants and craftspeople at a time when most Christian Europeans were farmers. Thus, the dominant society was dependent on them. Gypsies, on the other hand, were a small powerless group that presented no threat to the dominant society.

African Americans performed critical agricultural labor in the American South. After the Civil War and the end of slavery, the southern states passed so-called Jim Crow laws, which placed political, social, and economic restraints on African Americans. These new laws kept African Americans from threatening the continued political and economic dominance of Euro-Americans, while allowing Euro-American farmers and landowners the continued use of their labor. In contrast, government officials segregated Native Americans from the general population by placing them on reservations where their actions could be controlled. It was not until 1924 that U.S. citizenship was extended to all Native Americans, and not until 1948 that Native Americans living on reservations were allowed to vote in state and local elections in Arizona and New Mexico.

Accommodation

An alternative to ethnic homogenization or segregation is some form of political **accommodation** that formally recognizes and supports the ethnic and cultural differences of the population. A number of multinational countries have adopted this strategy of formalized ethnic pluralism. For instance, Canada has two main nationalities: Anglo-Canadians (English speaking) and French Canadians (French speaking). Both English and French are formally acknowledged as official languages. Although Quebec is the only province in which French Canadians are the majority, French speakers are found throughout the other, predominantly Anglo-Canadian provinces. Belgium also has two major national groups: the Flemish (Dutch speakers) and the Walloons (French speakers). Both Flemish and Walloon are official languages of Belgium, and although internal political boundaries closely correspond to ethnic boundaries, neither group is recognized politically. Spain has four main linguistic ethnic groups: Spanish, Gallego, Catalan, and Basque. Although Spanish is still the official language of Spain,

Ethnic homogenization	The elimination of ethnic difference within a region or country
Ethnic cleansing	The physical elimination of an unwanted ethnic group or groups
Genocide	The elimination of an unwanted ethnic group or groups by killing the members of the group or groups
Relocation	The elimination of an unwanted ethnic group or groups by physically moving them outside the boundaries of the region or country
Assimilation	The elimination of an unwanted ethnic group or groups through the process of destroying their social identity
Forced	The process of destroying the social identity of an ethnic group by eliminating their ethnic boundary markers
Passive	The process of destroying the social identity of an ethnic group through conscious or unconscious social and economic discrimination and "voluntary" elimination of ethnic boundary markers
Segregation	The physical separation of an ethnic group and the imposition of social and economic restraints that limit their contact with other ethnic groups
Accommodation	The creation of a balanced political relationship between two or more ethnic groups, with each allowed to maintain its own social identity and cultural traditions

since 1980 both the Basques and the Catalonians have had local political autonomy.

In Canada, Belgium, and Spain, the number of distinct nationalities is limited. Other countries have confronted far more complex ethnic mixes, however. Yugoslavia had eight major nationalities: Serbs, Croats, Muslims, Slovenians, Montenegrins, Macedonians, Hungarians, and Albanians. Separate republics were established for the Serbs, Croats, Montenegrins, and Macedonians. Although no separate republic was created for the Muslims, they were the largest group in the ethnically mixed republic of Bosnia. The Albanians (Kosovo) and Hungarians were given autonomous provinces within the republic of Serbia. Yugoslavia was organized as a confederacy, and a great deal of local autonomy was given to each of the republics.

Having looked at the various means by which people have responded to ethnic differences, we can now examine the results. What are the results of ethnic cleansing? No American can deny that ethnic cleansing does not work. You need only look about you. How many Native American faces do you see? Yet America was once entirely Native American. American Indian peoples were massacred and the defeated survivors driven steadily

westward to lands considered less desirable. Today, most Native Americans live in the western states.

Setting aside the moral issues, ethnic cleansing is seldom a permanent solution. Except for very small groups, rarely has one ethnic nationality been successful in destroying another. Even though it may be greatly reduced in number, the targeted group usually survives. The history of genocidal attacks by the other group becomes an integral part of the origin myth of the victimized group and thus serves to strengthen—not weaken—their identity. Genocide also creates hatred and distrust between groups that can persist for generations after the actual event and make future political cooperation difficult, if not impossible.

Relocation also produces mixed results. As in the case of genocide, the forced removal of a people becomes part of their origin myth and strengthens their cohesion and identity. Among the Cherokee of both North Carolina and Oklahoma, the Indian Removal of the 1830s has become a defining element of their ethnic identity. Removal of a people from their homeland in no way negates their claims to the lands they lost. Four hundred years after the Irish were evicted from Northern Ireland, the Irish Republican Army is fighting to reclaim this portion of the lost Irish homeland. The Jews were expelled from Jerusalem in the first century C.E. and dispersed over Europe, North Africa, and the Middle East. Yet, in the past century, the Jews have returned to Israel and reclaimed their homeland. The collective memory of a nationality is long. Old wrongs are seldom forgotten, and lost homelands are never truly relinquished.

Assimilation—whether passive or forced—is not always effective either. There is no question that throughout history, smaller groups have been absorbed by larger groups, but assimilation is usually a slow and uncertain process. As we discussed, over the past 100 years in Guatemala, Native Americans have slowly declined as a percentage of the total population. We might therefore assume that passive assimilation has proved effective in this case. However, considering absolute rather than relative population, we find that the Native American population actually increased from one million to about four million during the same period. The main problem with passive assimilation, then, is that population growth often creates new members as fast as or faster than members become assimilated.

Another problem is that many people do not want to give up their ethnic identity; if they did, forced assimilation would not be necessary. The forced assimilation policies in the United States were unsuccessful in regard to Native Americans. Loss of language, material culture, and other cultural institutions that functioned as ethnic boundary markers did not destroy ethnic identity or group cohesiveness because new cultural institutions and ethnic boundary markers emerged to replace the old. From a population of only about 250,000 in 1890, the Native American population of the United States has risen to more than two million today, and their major political demands are for greater tribal sovereignty and self-determination. So genocide, relocation, and forced or passive assimilation may be effective to a greater or lesser degree, but none of these practices, under most circumstances, truly resolves ethnic problems. More often, they postpone the formulation of workable policies and are even counterproductive—they worsen rather than alleviate conflicts. Besides these "pragmatic" considerations, genocide and forced assimilation are so morally abhorrent that few modern governments would admit to pursuing such policies. Relocation, likewise, poses ethical dilemmas; most groups are moved against their will, and some other nationality must be relocated to make room for the migrants. In the modern world, there is nowhere to relocate to without violating some other group's rights. Finally, as we have seen, passive assimilation is usually slow and its result is uncertain.

Political accommodation is the only practical and morally acceptable solution. But how well does it work, and what are the problems in maintaining a multinational state? Although the vast majority of countries encompass two or more national groups, few have attempted to politically accommodate multiple nationalities. Most countries are controlled by a single nationality that politically and economically dominates the other nationalities and holds the country together by force or the implied threat of force.

In an effort to understand the problems of political accommodation, we are going to examine the recent history of three such states: Canada, Czechoslovakia, and Yugoslavia. Canada remains a united country as the leaders of both English- and French-speaking Canadians struggle to find a political solution to their ethnic problem. Czechoslovakia peacefully split into the Czech Republic and Slovakia in January 1993. The disintegration of Yugoslavia into six republics in 1991 and 1992 has resulted in a series of bloody ethnic wars. Each of these three cases tells us something about the volatility and problems inherent in multinational states.

Canada. Canada was originally settled by French colonists during the seventeenth century. The British gained control of portions of eastern Canada in 1713 after Queen Anne's War. French settlers were expelled and replaced by British colonists. In 1763, after the French and Indian War, the British took control of the rest of French Canada. Under the Quebec Act of 1774, French settlers were granted the right to have their own language, religion, and civil laws. Then, after the American Revolution, large numbers of American loyalists settled in Canada, which greatly increased the resident English-speaking population. In 1867, the Dominion of Canada was created and the policy of accommodation continued, with both French and English recognized as official languages.

In the 1960s, a separatist movement emerged among the French Canadians in Quebec. The main catalyst for this movement was demographic changes. Originally a small minority, the English-speaking population in Canada grew rapidly during the nineteenth century, and the twentieth century saw an acceleration of this trend. Most immigrants to Canada during the twentieth century chose to adopt English, not French, as their language, thus adding to the English Canadian population. At the same time, the birthrate of French Canadians declined. Thus, the French Canadians see themselves as constituting an ever-smaller percentage of the total population.

French Canadian separatism is not the result of personal animosity toward English Canadians, but rather the collective fear of being overwhelmed by the sheer number of English speakers, the loss of their language, and the erosion of their cultural distinctiveness. In the 1976 elections, the Parti Québecois, the separatist party, won control of the government of Quebec and the next year made French the official language of the province. However, in a 1980 referendum in Quebec, voters rejected separation from Canada. Although 60 percent of the people in Quebec voted against separation in 1980, the issue was not resolved.

Although opposing separation from Canada, the majority of French Canadians remained concerned about the potential loss of French culture and identity. In 1987, the Meech Lake Agreement was negotiated. This agreement would have given Quebec constitutional rights that could be used to preserve the French language and culture. The agreement had to receive the unanimous approval of all the provinces. Two English-speaking provinces rejected the agreement in 1990. In another attempt at reaching a political compromise, a new agreement, called the Charlottetown Accord, was reached in 1992. This new agreement would have weakened the powers of the central government and recognized Quebec as a "distinct society." It also would have permanently given Quebec 25 percent of the members of the House of Commons. Submitted to a national referendum in October 1992, the Charlottetown Accord was soundly rejected, even by the people of Quebec. As a result, in 1995, another referendum was held on Quebec separation, and this time it failed by less than 1 percent. Will there be a third referendum? Will Quebec become a separate country?

Czechoslovakia and Yugoslavia. The early 1990s saw the demise of two multinational states: Czechoslovakia and Yugoslavia. Both had similar histories: they had been created by the Allied powers after World War I; they had attempted political accommodation for their different nationalities and had been controlled by Communists since the end of World War II; and they disintegrated after democratic institutions evolved.

Czechoslovakia was created in 1919 out of a portion of what had been the Austro-Hungarian Empire. It was a two-nationality state that combined both the Czech ethnic regions of Bohemia and Moravia and the Slovak ethnic region of Slovakia. Linguistically, culturally, and socially, the Czechs and Slovaks are closely related peoples. Although rivalry exists, there was no history of any major hostilities or wars between them. Yet, in

January 1993, by mutual agreement, the country peacefully split into the Czech Republic and the Republic of Slovakia. It was the smaller nationality, the Slovaks, who initiated the division, despite the fact that separation would be to their economic disadvantage; the industrial heart of Czechoslovakia had always been in Bohemia. In terms of political and economic power as well as education, the Czechs had always dominated the country. Not surprisingly, many Slovaks thought that the Czechs treated them like poor country cousins. It was ethnic pride, not ethnic hostility, that led to the breakup of the country.

In the dismantling of the Austro-Hungarian Empire after World War I, a new country was also created in the Balkans. Yugoslavia was to be the most ethnically diverse of the central European countries, including within its boundaries Slovenians, Croats, Serbs, Bosnian Muslims, Macedonians, Montenegrins, Hungarians, and Albanians. Unlike other European countries, Yugoslavia had no ethnic majority group. Originally a kingdom, the country was overrun by the Germans during World War II. The local Communist partisan forces under Marshal Tito were able to liberate the country with little direct outside assistance. After the war, Tito created a new political structure for the country in which every ethnic group would have at least some local autonomy. The country was divided into six republics: Slovenia, Croatia, Serbia, Bosnia, Montenegro, and Macedonia (see Figure 17.3). Within the republic of Serbia, two autonomous provinces were created: Kosovo, in which the majority of people were Albanians, and Vojvodina, which had a large Hungarian population. The national capital, Belgrade, was also the capital of Serbia. The army was also dominated by Serbs. With 36 percent of the total population, the Serbs were the largest national group, followed by the Croats (20 percent), the Bosnian Muslims (9 percent), the Slovenes (8 percent), the Albanians (8 percent), the Macedonians (6 percent), the Montenegrins (3 percent), the Hungarians (2 percent), and "others" (8 percent). Members of the other ethnic groups complained that the Serbs acted as if Yugoslavia was "their" country. After Tito's death in 1980, the office of president rotated among the presidents of the six republics.

The Balkans have a history of long and bloody wars among the various ethnic groups. Hatred is particularly deep among the Croats (Catholics), the Serbs (Eastern Orthodox), and the Bosnian Muslims. Genocide has been common, and at one time or another each has massacred members of the other group. During World War II, almost two million Yugoslavians died, but more Yugoslavians

▲ **Figure 17.3** Republics and Autonomous Provinces of Yugoslavia. The individual republics and autonomous provinces more or less correspond with the territories of major ethnic groups.

were killed by members of rival ethnic groups than by Germans.

In June 1991, Slovenia and Croatia declared their independence, with Slovenia leading the way. The wealthiest and best educated of the nationalities, the Slovenians believed that the poorer republics of the country were inhibiting their economic development. The Croats seceded for both economic and nationalistic reasons. With Slovenia and Croatia gone, the ethnic balance in the remainder of Yugoslavia shifted. Serbs now constituted a majority in what remained of Yugoslavia—the country was now a de facto Serb state. In the fall of 1991, Macedonia declared independence, and in early 1992, the Bosnians voted for independence.

The collapse of Yugoslavia did not solve the problem of ethnic conflict, but only made it worse. Croatia, Bosnia, Macedonia, and the Kosovo province of Serbia had large minority populations. Eighteen percent of the population of Croatia was Serbian. Unable to tolerate political domination by the Croats, the Croatian Serbs rebelled, demanding that the areas in which they lived be politically joined to Serbia. The situation in Bosnia was different. With a population that was 43 percent Muslims, 31 percent Serbs, and 17 percent Croats, Bosnia had no

ethnic majority. The resident Serbs rebelled. Historic hatreds aside, there were two main reasons for the rebellion of the Bosnian Serbs. The Bosnian Muslims as a group were more prosperous than the local Serbs, which created economic jealousy. In addition, the birthrate of the Muslims was higher than that of the Serbs. Thus, there was the expectation that in the future the Bosnian Muslims would become the majority and Bosnia would become an Islamic country. The war quickly became a three-sided conflict as the Bosnian Croats joined the conflict, fighting both the local Serbs and the Muslims. Kosovo is the historic homeland of the Serb people. Although 80 percent or more of the population was Albanian (predominantly Muslim), Kosovo was politically controlled and economically dominated by the Serb minority. Albanian nationalists rebelled, wanting either an independent republic or unification with Albania. Twenty-two percent of the population of Macedonia is Albanian Muslims. Politically dominated by the Macedonian (Christian Orthodox) majority, Albanian separatists rebelled.

By examining these three cases, we can see some of the problems that exist in multinational states, even under the best of conditions. The very presence of two or more nationalities within a country creates the potential for political volatility. Historic hatreds between groups increase the potential for conflict and political division. To be successful, political accommodation requires the creation and maintenance of a social, political, and economic balance between the groups. Members of all groups have to feel a collective social equality with members of other groups. They cannot think that their language or cultural institutions are being threatened or eroded by those of another group. They have to believe that their collective political rights are secure. Finally, no group can feel that their collective economic well-being is inhibited or that they are collectively being exploited by other groups. No country has ever existed with a perfect social, political, and economic balance between nationalities. Some differences and inequalities between nationalities always exist. However, these differences and inequalities must not be so great that they threaten any particular ethnic group, and all must believe that political unity is to their mutual benefit. The problems faced by multinational countries are not in their initial creation but in their maintenance over time.

The two factors that most seriously threaten the political stability of multinational countries are differential rates of population growth and relative differences in economic development between the constituent nationalities. If the population of one nationality grows more rapidly than that of another, it threatens the existing social and political balance of the country. The nationality or nationalities whose relative populations are declining may think that their social and cultural institutions are being threatened. They may also think that their collective political influence will decline. Regional differences in resources may result in significant changes in the relative economic status of the different nationalities. Changes in relative economic power can be translated into shifts in relative political power. Attempts to redistribute or divide the new wealth of one nationality among the other nationalities within the country can result in a feeling of exploitation.

The evolving global economy requires close cooperation between countries and nationalities. Rising nationalism directly threatens the global economy. Although we cannot change our basic human feelings, we can more clearly understand those factors that unleash ethnic emotions and attempt to minimize them. In the next chapter, we discuss the critical issues of population growth, world hunger, and the rights of indigenous peoples.

Summary

1. Every individual, not just members of minority populations, belongs to an ethnic group and has an ethnic identity.

2. An ethnic group is a named social grouping of people based on what is perceived as shared ancestry, cultural traditions, and history. Ethnic group identity divides the world into categories of "us" and "them."

3. An individual's ethnic group identity is seldom absolute, but changes with the social context. An individual may assume various hierarchically ranked identities. This characteristic is called the hierarchical nesting quality of identity.

4. The two main attributes of an ethnic group are origin myths and ethnic boundary markers. The origin myth or history describes the common or shared historical experiences that define the social boundaries of the group. Ethnic boundary markers are those overt characteristics that make its members identifiable. Ethnic boundary markers may include language, religion, physical characteristics, and other cultural traits such as clothing, house types, personal adornment, food, and so on.

5. There are two distinct categories of ethnic groups. An ethnic nationality is an ethnic group that shares a feeling of homeland and the inherent right to political autonomy. A subnational group is an identity nested in a larger national identity. A subnationality claims neither a separate homeland nor rights to political autonomy.

6. Some scholars argue that a new level of ethnic identity is now emerging: civilizations. A civilization is a grouping of two or more distinct nationalities on the basis of a shared or common cultural historical tradition, generally religion.

7. Globalization has resulted in the creation of ethnic communities that have become geographically separated from their homelands. These groups are termed transnationals.

8. Much of the conflict in the world today is between ethnic nationalities. There are 3,000 to 5,000 ethnic nationalities in the world, but only about 200 separate countries. Thus, most countries are multinational, and much conflict is the result of nationalities wanting to establish their own independent countries.

9. There is no simple or easy solution to ethnic conflict. Not only are genocide, relocation, and forced assimilation immoral, but history shows that they seldom solve ethnic problems.

10. Passive assimilation is a slow and uncertain process. Segregation reinforces ethnic identities and perpetuates conflict. Attempts by governments of multinational states to accommodate cultural differences and nationalistic aspirations are rarely successful because of differing rates of population growth and regional differences in economic development.

Key Terms

ethnic group
hierarchical nesting
origin myth
ethnic boundary markers
ethnogenesis
nationality
homeland

subnationalities
transnationals
civilization
artificial countries
ethnic homogenization
ethnic cleansing
genocide

relocation
assimilation
forced assimilation
passive assimilation
segregation
accommodation

Suggested Readings

Bodley, John. *Victims of Progress.* 4th ed. Palo Alto, Calif.: Mayfield Publishing, 1998.

A very readable book that is a good overview of tribal peoples in the modern world, with emphasis on how they are being destroyed by industrial civilization.

Burger, Julian. *Report from the Frontier: The State of the World's Indigenous Peoples.* Cambridge, Mass.: Cultural Survival, 1987.

A general survey of the plight of indigenous peoples of the world.

Carmack, Robert, ed. *Harvest of Violence.* Norman: University of Oklahoma Press, 1988.

This collection of 12 original essays is concerned with the war in Guatemala during the late 1970s and early 1980s, and how the war affected and involved the native Maya communities.

Danforth, Loring M. *The Macedonian Conflict: Ethnic Nationalism in a Transnational World.* Princeton, N.J.: Princeton University Press, 1995.

An interesting look at one of the most critical countries in the Balkans. This study provides an excellent background for understanding and interpreting the events that have occurred in Macedonia since the book was published.

Eicher, Joanne B., ed. *Dress and Ethnicity: Changes Across Space and Time.* Oxford: Berg, 1995.

In this collection, dress and changes in dress are examined in a series of case studies of different peoples from throughout the world.

Ember, Melvin, and Carol R. Ember, eds. *Countries and Their Cultures,* four volumes. New York: Macmillan Reference USA, 2001.

This multivolume set, written primarily by anthropologists, is by far the best introduction to the contemporary
peoples and ethnic conflicts in the world. Each country is discussed separately, with every contributor covering the same topics. Focusing on culture and social identity, the topics covered include demography, languages, political history, national identity, and ethnic relations.

Garroutte, Eva Marie. *Real Indians: Identity and the Survival of Native America.* Berkeley: University of California Press, 2003.

This important study addresses the extremely complex issue of Native American ethnic and legal identity in the United States. Who is an "Indian"? There is no single accepted definition. The book discusses various ways in which biological ancestry, sociocultural heritage, and legal statuses have been and are being manipulated by individuals, tribal officials, and the federal government to gain or deny political, social, and/or economic benefits.

Horowitz, Donald L. *Ethnic Groups in Conflict.* 2nd ed. Berkeley: University of California Press, 2000.

The best and most comprehensive study of global ethnic conflict. Originally published in 1985, it has recently been updated.

Huntington, Samuel. *The Clash of Civilizations and the Remaking of World Order.* New York: Simon & Schuster, 1996.

A provocative study that suggests there will be a political realignment of the countries of the world on the basis of civilizations. One of the major fault lines of conflict will be between Western civilization and Islamic civilization.

Moynihan, Daniel Patrick. *Pandaemonium: Ethnicity in International Politics.* New York: Oxford University Press, 1993.

A good introduction to the problem of increasing nationalism and conflict.

Media Resources

The Wadsworth Anthropology Resource Center
academic.cengage.com/anthropology

The Wadsworth discipline resource website that accompanies *Humanity: An Introduction to Cultural Anthropology,* Eighth Edition, includes a rich array of material, including online anthropological video clips, to help you in the study of cultural anthropology and the specific topics covered in this chapter. Other material includes a case study forum with excerpts from various Wadsworth authors, map exercises, scientist interviews, breaking news in anthropology, and links to additional useful online material. Begin by selecting Cultural Anthropology to take you to videos, research, and more. From the homepage, you may also select Applied Anthropology, which directs you to essays, glossary terms, the case study forum, and a list of internships and careers in anthropology.

18 WORLD PROBLEMS AND THE PRACTICE OF ANTHROPOLOGY

Because of anthropology's emphasis on fieldwork, ethnographers often become intimately involved with the people they work among, which makes them more likely than most outsiders to listen to local voices.

Applied Anthropology

Population Growth

Anthropological Perspectives on Population Growth

Costs and Benefits of Children in North America

Costs and Benefits of Children in the LDCs

World Hunger

Scarcity or Inequality?

Is Technology Transfer the Answer?

Agricultural Alternatives

Anthropologists as Advocates

Indigenous Peoples Today

Vanishing Knowledge

Medicines We Have Learned

Adaptive Wisdom

Cultural Alternatives

Questions addressed in this chapter

What is applied anthropology, and why it is so important today to understand the cultures of other peoples?

How can applied anthropology give us a better perspective on the critical question of population growth?

What are the explanations for world hunger? What are some of the possible solutions?

How is globalization changing the lives of indigenous peoples, and what is the potential importance of their cultural knowledge?

Increasing numbers of anthropologists today are using their training to help solve human problems. In the private sector, for example, anthropologists work in a variety of roles—from training international businesspeople to become culturally sensitive when dealing with people from other countries to observing how humans interact with machines. Governmental agencies and international organizations employ anthropological expertise to address problems connected to development, health, education, social services, and ethnic relations. In the first part of this chapter, we show some of the specific contributions anthropologists have made to understanding the problems of population growth and hunger. In the second part, we discuss the anthropologist as advocate.

Applied Anthropology

Applied anthropology is most simply defined as the application of anthropological perspectives, theory, empirical knowledge of cultures, and methods to help assess and solve human problems. The subfield has grown dramatically since the early 1970s, partly because the number of people earning Ph.D. degrees in anthropology has outstripped the number of academic jobs available, and partly because larger numbers of anthropologists want to use their expertise to help people and organizations.

What special talents or insights do applied anthropologists bring to problem solving? What unique contributions can anthropologists make to programs and agencies? One way to answer this question is to think of cultural anthropologists as sharing a certain worldview (see Chapter 2) that differs somewhat from the views of other professional people. Anthropologists' worldview includes how we think about people and groups: the as-

sumptions we share, the categories we use to describe and analyze ideas and behavior, the kinds of information we think it is important to collect to understand a human group, how we believe this information can best be collected, and so on. Anthropologists learn this worldview through our graduate training, our fieldwork and other experiences involving members of other cultures, our interactions with one another, our readings of ethnographies and theoretical studies, and so forth. Not all ethnologists share this worldview, of course, and (like all worldviews) this one changes over time. Nonetheless, its basic features are well engrained in most anthropologists, and the uniquely and distinctively anthropological contributions to problem solving come out of this worldview more than anything else. For applied work, this worldview has five emphases.

1. *Attention to small-scale communities.* Ethnologists pay attention to peoples and cultures that are too often ignored or—what is sometimes worse—known to others mainly by inaccurate or simplistic stereotypes. In applied work, an anthropologist who has worked in a particular small-scale community is often the only outsider who knows enough to provide information about it. Commonly, because of our training in fieldwork methodologies, we are the professionals most qualified to acquire new information relevant to some project about some local community. Through field research, anthropologists provide outside agencies and organizations with information about specific people and cultures.

2. *Insistence on prior detailed knowledge.* Because of anthropology's long-standing emphasis on firsthand fieldwork, we believe it is important to devote time and resources, prior to planning a project or program,

407

to determine what the people affected are doing and thinking. Whatever their goals, almost all projects introduce some kind of change to a group, and prior knowledge of the culture is essential to plan and implement the changes. Many projects fail because those who design them know too little about the "target population" (those whose lives will be affected by the project).

3. *Sensitivity to cultural differences.* Anthropologists try to make themselves aware of the customs and beliefs of a community, to interact with members of the community in culturally appropriate ways, and to treat community traditions with respect. This cultural sensitivity derives partly from anthropology's relativistic, anti-ethnocentric perspective (see Chapter 1).

4. *Appreciation of alternatives.* Anthropologists believe that no one culture's experts know all the answers and solutions. Different people with different histories and traditions have worked out varying solutions to similar problems. What works well in one place and time and among one group may not work well elsewhere. Indeed, local people themselves often know the solutions to their problems but do not have the resources to implement them. More than most other professionals, anthropologists listen to local voices.

5. *Recognition of systematic complexity.* Even the smallest and most homogeneous human groups are enormously complicated. But this complexity is ordered and patterned, and ethnographers have long recognized the importance of trying to determine how the parts of a complex system relate to one another and to the whole. A recognition of systematic complexity allows applied anthropologists to realize that changes introduced into a community may have unforeseen, unintended, and often undesirable consequences. Sometimes making small modifications in a program can avoid some of the potential negative impacts.

In the remainder of this chapter, we describe examples of how these five emphases of anthropological thinking lead to new insights into human problems. Two of our cases deal with major global problems: population growth and world hunger. We show how anthropological work has contributed new insights into these problems. We hope to challenge your conceptions of population growth and hunger and to lead you to think about them in new ways or—at the very least—to question much of what you read and hear in the popular media. We also hope you will think about alternative solutions to these problems.

Quite often, applied anthropologists work in the lesser developed countries (LDCs), which are often collectively known as the Third World. Terms such as *developed, less developed, First World,* and *Third World* convey a certain prejudice resulting from a Western view (e.g., Third World to whom?). Because they are familiar terms, however, we continue to use them as shorthand descriptions of major world regions.

Population Growth

As we discussed in Chapter 16, one of the consequences and problems of globalization is the phenomenal increase in Earth's population. In the last 50 years, world population has more than doubled, jumping from 2.5 billion to more than 6.6 billion. Most of this growth is occurring in the poorer countries of the world, which creates a wide range of problems. Whereas the standard of living in the developed countries of North America, Europe, and Japan is increasing, the standard of living for most of the rest of the world's people is declining, and differences in population growth rates are the primary reason. In addition, overpopulation in Latin America, Africa, and parts of Asia is resulting in increasing ethnic and social conflict, environmental degradation, and massive migrations of people from the underdeveloped to the more developed countries of the world. Why are the poorest peoples of the world continuing to have large families, while the wealthier peoples are having fewer and fewer children? What is the reason for this inverse correlation?

Anthropological Perspectives on Population Growth

Anthropological insight on this issue is twofold. First, anthropologists study human reproductive behavior—including the choices couples make about how many children to have—holistically, meaning in terms of the total system in which people live their everyday lives. By understanding the overall context of behavior, we can understand how the birthrates of a region result from local conditions—especially economic conditions faced by many rural poor. Second, anthropologists have conducted detailed fieldwork in local communities to uncover the major causes of high birthrates in Third World settings.

There is an apparent paradox about the comparatively high birthrates of many underdeveloped countries. An average North American family is able to afford more children than an average Nigerian family. Canadians and Americans have more money to house, feed, clothe, educate, and otherwise provide for their children. Yet they have only two or three children, whereas the Nigerian family averages six or seven. And this is the most puzzling thing about high fertility: It continues despite its adverse consequences for those very nations that are experiencing it and whose citizens are causing it—the LDCs.

Why do these people continue to have so many children? Are Indians, Nigerians, and El Salvadorans too ignorant to realize that they cannot afford to support so many children? Can't they see the strain that all these children put on their nations' educational, health, and agricultural systems? Isn't the refusal of couples in these countries to practice birth control even when condoms and pills are available a perfect example of their backwardness and ignorance?

Not at all.

Costs and Benefits of Children in North America

The March 30, 1998, cover story of the weekly newsmagazine *U.S. News & World Report* was titled "Cost of Children." The article reported on the high monetary expenses of raising an American child born in 1997. Middle-income parents (defined in the article as couples who earn between $35,000 and $60,000 a year) can anticipate paying about $300,000 for their child's day care and education, food and clothing, housing, transportation, health care, and other expenses, between birth and age 18. If parents also finance their child's college degree (not including graduate school), the cost of caring for and educating each new member of a middle-income family rises to around $460,000—close to a half-million dollars! Those numbers are in 1998 dollars, however; adjusted to 2006 dollars, these figures would increase to about $350,000 and $550,000, respectively. Canadians, Japanese, Americans, Europeans, and parents living in other modernized, highly urbanized, industrial, or postindustrial nations are well aware of these monetary costs. Of course, parents in such societies do not have children because we expect our children to bring us future material rewards. For the most part, we do not have children because we expect them to help with chores around the house and yard, or because they will share their income with us when they (finally) get jobs, or because our kids will support us in our old age. Most of us realize all too well that children are an *economic* liability—however *emotionally* gratifying they might be.

Children certainly do cost a lot of money to wage-earning working-class and middle-class couples in an urbanized, industrialized, developed country. Bills for food, housing, doctors, clothing, insurance, and transportation are higher with children—not to mention the costs of day care, babysitting, and education. Nor do most children contribute much economically to their parents as they grow older; retirement plans, Social Security, 401(K)s, and IRAs provide most of the income of the elderly. No wonder that when a young couple read in a newsmagazine that it costs a half-million dollars or more to raise a child and finance a college education, they decide that one or two are quite enough.

The dollar costs of children are not the only factor that leads North American couples to limit their family sizes. There are other relevant factors as well:

- *Cultural norms and social expectations about desirable family sizes.* Not all couples think that one or two or three children are enough, but the majority do agree that seven or eight are too many. Enculturated norms and expectations of friends and families certainly affect how many children we have. Note, however, that these norms and expectations themselves respond to other kinds of societal and economic conditions, so they alone do not explain low (or high) fertility rates.

- *Occupational and spatial mobility.* Many young couples do not know where they will be or how they will be earning a living in the next few years. They want children someday, but they are too unsettled and lack the income to start their family right away. If most couples postpone pregnancy until their mid-20s or 30s, a lower completed average family size results than if most women begin childbearing earlier.

- *Women's employment.* Many women want to have a career and perceive that numerous children will interfere with this goal. The limited time and energy of two-earner households lead to lowered fertility rates.

- *Social burdens of children.* Modern society offers numerous social and recreational outlets that serve as alternatives to devoting one's time and energy to children. A couple may know some friends who have hardly left their house since their baby was born, and they have no desire to be so tied down.

This discussion does not imply that North American couples always have the number of children they choose. Some wind up with more children than they want or with a child sooner than they had planned. And the preceding considerations, to some extent, are class and race biased—they apply more to well-educated, middle-income whites than to African Americans and Hispanics, for example. But we do make reproductive choices, and the result of them—barring infertility and so forth—is that we have about the number of children we desire.

North American couples consider many other factors, of course. But notice the main overall feature of the considerations just listed: they are all things that will affect the deciding couple personally. People consider the benefits and costs to *themselves* of having or not having children, or of having only so many and not more. They do not worry much about whether their children will increase the burden on the American educational system, increase the unemployment rate 20 years in the future, contribute to society's expenditures on public waters and sewers, or overload the nation's farmlands. That is, for the most part, they do not concern themselves with the *social consequences* of their reproductive decisions. They do what they think is best for themselves.

Costs and Benefits of Children in the LDCs

Curiously, although most North Americans do not weigh heavily the future societal consequences when they decide to limit their family size, many of them expect people in the LDCs to be more altruistic by reducing their fertility. Too often, when we learn that rural people in parts of the Third World average six, seven, or more children per couple, we think this is economically irrational. They must be having large families for other noneconomic reasons. Probably "children are highly valued in their traditional culture." Or maybe "men have higher prestige if they have lots of children." Perhaps "they are not educated enough to recognize the effects of having such large families." It could be that "they don't know how to prevent pregnancy."

Part of our error comes from our failure to put ourselves in their shoes—to grasp the conditions of their lives that lead them to bear more children than we do. Just because children are an economic liability in a highly mobile, industrialized, urbanized, monetarized society does not mean that they are a liability everywhere. Many demographers argue that rural people in the LDCs have high fertility not simply because of cultural preferences but because children are economically useful. Village-level ethnographic studies suggest that children do indeed offer a variety of material benefits to their parents in the LDCs.

One such study was done in the Punjab region of northern India by anthropologist Mahmood Mamdani. He researched a family planning project that aimed to reduce the birthrate in seven villages. Mamdani found that in the village of Manupur, people accepted the birth control pills and condoms offered by the staff of the program, but most refused to use them. The reaction of the project's administrators was like that of many outsiders when local people do not behave in ways they seemingly ought to behave: they blamed the "ignorance" and

► Population growth contributes to social problems in the Third World, including unemployment and overcrowding in urban areas. This is a portion of Iquitos, Peru.

"conservatism" of the villagers. To the staff, the benefits of having fewer children seemed obvious. The amount of land available to most people was barely adequate, so by reducing family size, people could stop the fragmentation of land that was contributing to their poverty.

However, the village's parents interpreted their economic circumstances differently. They believed that children—especially sons—were economically beneficial, not harmful. Villagers of all castes and all economic levels reported that children were helpful to a household in many ways. They helped with everyday tasks such as washing, gathering animal dung to use as fertilizer, weeding fields, collecting firewood, and caring for livestock. Even young children supplemented family income by doing small jobs for neighbors. When they grew up, sons were the major source of support for their elderly parents because one or more of them usually continued to live with their parents and farm the land or work in other occupations. Adult sons often went to cities, where part of the money they earned from their jobs was sent back to help their parents and siblings.

In short, Mamdani argued, the residents of Manupur recognized that the benefits of children exceeded their costs to the parents. Outsiders did not recognize this fact because they did not fully grasp the economic circumstances under which people were actually living.

Like people everywhere, however, the people of this region of India proved capable of altering their behavior as their circumstances changed. In 1982, 10 years after Mamdani's study, Moni Nag and Neeraj Kak restudied the village of Manupur. They found that couples had changed their attitudes about desirable family size: about half of all couples were now using contraception or had accepted sterilization after they had two sons. The reason was that changing economic conditions in the region had made children less valuable to families. Parents did not need as much children's labor as before. The introduction of new crops and farming methods had almost eliminated grazing land in the region, so boys were no longer useful for tending cattle. Increasing reliance on purchased chemical fertilizers reduced the value of children's labor in collecting cattle dung to spread on fields. Chemical weedkillers reduced the amount of hand work necessary for weeding. A new crop, rice, did not take as much work to grow as the old staples.

The increased value of formal education also led people to have fewer children. Because more outside skilled jobs were available, parents became more interested in providing a secondary education that would increase their children's ability to acquire high-paying jobs. Opportunities for women increased, and second-

ary school enrollment rates for girls more than doubled between 1970 and 1982. Sending more children to secondary school raised the costs of child rearing. Parents had to pay for clothing and textbooks for their children who attended school, which was a significant expense for poorer families. Accordingly, they wanted and had fewer children.

Finally, most couples believed that having lots of sons was not as necessary as it had been 10 years earlier. People still desired sons for old-age support, but many believed that sons were not as dependable as they used to be. Many sons no longer brought their wives with them to live on the family land, but instead left the village to live on their own. One elderly man said:

> Children are of no use any more in old age of parents. They also do not do any work while going to school. My son in the military does not keep any connection with me. My son living with me has two sons and one daughter. I have advised him to get a vasectomy. (Nag and Kak 1984, 666)

All these and other changes increased the economic costs and decreased the benefits of having large families, and couples reacted to these changes by having fewer children. In this region of northern India, then, ideas and attitudes about desirable family sizes were not fixed by tradition but changed as people adapted their family sizes to changing circumstances.

Researchers in other parts of the world also report that children offer many economic benefits to their parents, explaining why high fertility persists in most LDCs. On the densely populated Indonesian island of Java, rural parents do not have to wait for their children to grow up to acquire the benefits of their labor. Children aged 6 to 8 spend three to four hours daily tending livestock, gathering firewood, and caring for their younger siblings. By the time they are 14, girls work almost nine hours a day in child care, food preparation, household chores, handicrafts, and other activities. Most of the labor of children does not contribute directly to their family's cash income or food supply, so it is easy to see how outsiders might conclude that children are unproductive. However, children accomplish many household-maintenance tasks that require little experience and skill, which frees the labor of adult family members for activities that do bring in money or food. Ethnographer Benjamin White suggests that large families are more successful economically than small families in Java.

Similar findings have been reported by ethnographers working in rural Nepal, Bangladesh, Samoa, and the Philippines. Unlike suburban and urban North

Americans, farming families in the LDCs use much of the time of even young children productively. As children grow older, they are used to diversify the economic activities of a household, earning cash themselves or performing subsistence work that frees their parents for wage labor.

In many countries, the grown children of rural people migrate to a city in their own country or to a developed country. They acquire jobs—which are well paid relative to what they could earn in their own villages—and send much of the cash back to their families. Such remittances contribute half or more of the family income in Western Samoa, Tonga, and some other small nations of the Pacific, both because migrants feel a continuing sense of obligation to their parents and siblings back home and because many of them hope to return to their islands someday. Remittances are also a major source of family income (and, as a by-product, of national income) in West African countries like Nigeria and Ghana, Pakistan, India, Mexico, Central America, and parts of the Middle East.

In most parts of the world, children are also the major source of economic support in their parents' old age because rural villagers lack pension plans and Social Security. As Stanley Freed and Ruth Freed have pointed out, in many parts of India parents prefer to bear two or three sons to ensure themselves of having one adult son to live with them, in case one son dies or moves elsewhere.

In addition to the value of children's labor, remittances, and old-age security, other factors encourage rural families in the LDCs to have many children:

- Relatively high rates of infant mortality, which encourage parents to have "extra" children to cover possible deaths of their offspring
- Extended families, which spread out the burden of child care among other household members, thus reducing it for individual parents
- Low monetary cost of children compared with children in developed countries, partly because many necessities (such as housing and food) are produced by family labor rather than purchased
- The fact that the tasks women are commonly assigned are not as incompatible with child care as wage employment (see Chapter 11)

Such factors mean that children are perceived (in most cases, correctly) as both more valuable and less costly than most citizens of the developed world perceive them. We should not assume that couples in the LDCs are too ignorant to understand the costs of having many children or to appreciate the benefits of small families. Nor should we think that they are prisoners of their "tradi-tional cultural values," which have not changed fast enough to keep up with changing conditions. We should rather assume that they make reproductive decisions just as we do. Then we can begin to understand the economic and other conditions of their lives that often lead them to want more children than affluent couples in urbanized, industrialized countries want. We can also see why birthrates are falling in so many LDCs today. It is not simply the increased family planning education and the recent availability of contraceptive devices. Lowered fertility is also a response to the increased urbanization of most nations, to the growth in wage employment over subsistence farming, to the rising emphasis placed on education for both girls and boys, and to other factors that have changed the circumstances of family lives.

As we have seen, rising human numbers contribute to the resource shortages faced by LDCs today. One of the resources in shortest supply is one of the things people cannot do without: food. Most North Americans see malnutrition and overpopulation as two sides of the same coin. In the popular view, the "fact" that there are "too many people" in the world is the major reason there is "too little food to go around." And the solution to world hunger is "more food"—that is, increased production by the application of modern agricultural technologies. In the next section, we try to convince you that neither the problem (too many people) nor the solution (more production through better technology) is this simple.

World Hunger

The famine in Somalia in the early 1990s is only the most recent reminder of hunger in the world. Hunger is endemic in much of the world today. The World Food Programme of the United Nations estimates that 800 million people go to bed hungry every night and that 24,000 people die of hunger or hunger-related causes every day. Hunger afflicts poor people in parts of southern Sudan, Mozambique, Ethiopia, Chad, Bolivia, Peru, Bangladesh, Pakistan, and India. Even in countries considered "moderately developed" or "rapidly developing," there are regions of extreme poverty and hunger, as in Indonesia, Egypt, Brazil, and Mexico. Women and children constitute the vast majority of the malnourished. Children are especially at risk; if malnutrition does not kill them, it frequently causes lifelong mental and physical disabilities. In this section, we discuss the conditions that contribute to hunger in the Third World. Our focus is on chronic malnutrition or undernutrition on a worldwide scale, not on short-term famine in particular countries or regions. (The reason we focus on *chronic* hunger is that the immediate causes of famine are more likely to be political upheavals and conflicts that disrupt food production or distribution than economic or demographic forces.) First we discuss two alternative explanations for hunger. Then we describe attempts to increase the food supply by modern technological methods, showing why such attempts are so often unsuccessful and counterproductive. Throughout, we suggest anthropological insights into the problem.

Scarcity or Inequality?

What causes hunger? In any given region, people are hungry for a variety of reasons. On a worldwide basis, however, two explanations for hunger are most commonly offered. The first, which we call the **scarcity explanation of hunger,** is that the major cause of widespread hunger in the LDCs is *overpopulation:* in the twentieth century, populations have grown so large that available land and technology cannot produce enough food to feed them. The second, which we call the **inequality explanation of hunger,** holds that the *unequal distribution of resources* is largely responsible for chronic hunger on a worldwide basis: so many people are hungry today because they lack access to the resources (especially land) needed to produce food.

The scarcity explanation holds that there are not enough food-producing resources to provide the poor with adequate nutrition. In countries like India, Bangladesh, El Salvador, Kenya, and Ethiopia, populations have grown so large in the last century or two that there is not enough land to feed everyone. This argument holds that food-producing resources like land, water, fertilizers, and technology are absolutely scarce, meaning that there are not enough resources for the size of the population. In brief, the scarcity explanation holds that hunger is caused by too many people.

Although not our focus here, the scarcity explanation accounts for starvation by saying that chronic hunger turns into outright famine when some sort of disaster strikes. With so many people chronically undernourished, anything that disrupts food production (e.g., droughts, floods, plant diseases, insect infestations, or political disturbances) will reduce food supplies enough to turn hungry people into starving people.

The inequality explanation arose, in part, as a reaction to the excesses of the scarcity explanation, which (some believe) blames the victims of hunger by saying that their own (reproductive) behavior causes their hunger. The inequality explanation holds that resources are not absolutely scarce. In fact, there is enough productive capacity in the land of practically every nation to feed its people an adequate diet, if only this productive capacity were used to meet the needs of the poor. Instead, too many productive resources are used to increase the profits of wealthy landowners and to fulfill the wants of the more affluent citizens of the world.

The inequality explanation says that poor people are hungry because of the way both the international economy and their own national economies allocate productive resources. The international (global) economy allocates resources on the basis of ability to pay, not on need. For example, if affluent North American consumers want coffee and sugar, wealthy and politically powerful landowners in Central America will devote their land to coffee and sugar plantations for export, because this is how they can make the most money. If North Americans want tomatoes and other vegetables during the winter, large landowners in northwest Mexico will produce them, rather than the beans and corn that are major staples for Mexican peasants. The national economies of countries with hungry people work in a similar way. Urban elites have the money to buy luxuries, and urban middle- and working-class families pressure governments to keep food prices low. As a result, too much land is used to produce crops sold to city dwellers at prices made so low by government policy that the rural poor cannot feed themselves. In brief, according to the inequality explanation, hunger is caused mainly by the use of and unequal access to resources.

Which explanation is correct? As is often the case, the two are not mutually exclusive. Both are correct to a certain degree, depending on time and place. The scarcity explanation is correct: all else being equal, the amount of land available per person has been and is being reduced by population growth. Moreover, as the population grows, land of increasingly poorer quality has to be cultivated, reducing its productivity. And as families grow poorer, they have less money to acquire new land or to buy fertilizer or other products that will increase the productivity of their land. These arguments are the kind we encounter regularly in the popular news media. It is hard to see how such conclusions can be wrong.

But these conclusions could be right and still tell only part of the story. The explanation for hunger is more complex than "too many people" combined with "low farm productivity." Hunger is created by human institutions as much as by population increase and unproductive technologies and farming methods. For example, at a growth rate of 3 percent a year, a population will double in less than 25 years. Does this mean that in

We do not attempt to present a complete discussion of the evidence to show that inequality is as important as scarcity in explaining hunger around the world. There are several excellent contemporary studies by anthropologists of the relationships among population, resource distribution, and hunger. Here we discuss a well-known historical example because it personally affected the ancestors of so many North Americans—the Irish potato famine of 1845–1850.

Ireland was in the early nineteenth century an agriculturally diverse country in which large landowners controlled most of the land. Politically and economically, the island was controlled by England. Starting in the last decades of the eighteenth century, large landowners had begun increasingly allotting their land to the production of cash crops for export to England, where the Industrial Revolution was transforming the economy. English mills needed Irish wool and flax in their production of textiles, and England needed Irish wheat, meat, butter, and other food products to help feed the increasing numbers of factory workers. The export of wool, in particular, had resulted in a significant reduction of land available for farming as many wealthy landowners had evicted their tenant farmers to turn their land into sheep pastures. Still other large landowners focused on raising wheat, flax, and other exportable grains. Only a small portion of the population of Ireland worked on the large estates or in the towns or cities. The vast majority of the population survived as small subsistence farmers. Their landholdings, either owned or rented, were so small, usually less than 5 acres, that they had to plant a crop that yielded the most in terms of subsistence value. Thus, they planted potatoes, which, in a normal year, would yield sufficient food to feed their family, with a small surplus that they could sell. The sale of a few potatoes and some irregular wage work produced the only cash income most families had. Malnutrition was common in rural Ireland during the early nineteenth century.

In 1845, the potato blight struck, destroying between a third and half of the potato crop. The severity of the blight varied from one part of the country to another. However, in every region, small farmers quickly found themselves short of food, with little if any cash, little in the way of property to sell, and little chance of finding wage labor. Many families were quickly reduced to starvation. As the blight continued in 1846 and 1847, conditions became increasingly difficult. Several million starving people began wandering the countryside in a desperate search for food or jobs or anything to keep them alive. Many simply abandoned their farms, while others were evicted for nonpayment of rent. Hundreds of

▲ Increasingly, lesser developed countries allocate food-producing resources for the production of export cash crops.

© AAD Worldwide Travel Images/Alamy

25 years everybody will have only half the amount of food? Of course not. Land that formerly was underused will be brought into fuller production, more labor-intensive methods of cultivation can bring higher yields per acre, people can change their diets and eat less meat, and so on. People will adjust their cultivation methods, work patterns, eating habits, and other behaviors to the new conditions rather than tolerate hunger.

Or, rather, they will adjust if they have access to the resources they need to do so. And this is a large part of the problem in many LDCs: it is not just that there are too few resources but that too few people own or control the resources available. In their books *Food First* and *World Hunger: Twelve Myths,* Frances Moore Lappé and Joseph Collins question what they call "the myth of scarcity." They claim that every nation could provide an adequate diet for its citizens if its productive resources were more equitably distributed.

thousands gathered in the port cities, where, ironically, a few found work loading ships with wool, flax, wheat, meat, butter, and other agricultural products for shipment to England. Starvation in Ireland was not the result of a lack of agricultural resources, but rather the people of Ireland did not have money to purchase the food that was being grown and exported. One estimate found that, during the famine, Ireland was exporting to England food sufficient to support 18 million people. In 1845, the population of Ireland had been about 8.5 million. When the famine ended in 1850, only about 6.5 million remained. An estimated 1 million people had died of starvation or related causes, while another 1 million had emigrated to North America, England, or Australia.

The economic relationship between agricultural Ireland and industrialized England that existed during the early nineteenth century is being seen on a global scale today. Poorer, primarily agricultural, countries are increasingly allocating their resources to the production of exports to wealthier, more developed countries, while at the same time their populations are growing rapidly.

There is no denying that population growth contributes to hunger and poverty. But we should not conclude that "too many people" is *the* problem, or that the scarcity explanation is sufficient. Population growth always occurs within a political and economic context, and this context greatly influences the degree to which poor people can adjust to it. In a similar vein, it is fascinating that many economists recognize that famines do not result mainly from an absolute scarcity of food, but rather from the inability of some groups—usually the poorest groups—to gain access to food. There is also increasing recognition that development ought to be measured by more than "income" and ought to mean more than material affluence.

The combination of population growth and increasing land concentration is doubly devastating. Even if they manage to hang on to their land, the poor will get poorer if their numbers grow. If their increased poverty makes it necessary for them to borrow from the wealthy, to sell part of their land to raise cash, or to work for low wages to make ends meet, they are likely to grow poorer still. This "double crunch" is precisely the experience of the rural poor in many LDCs.

Is Technology Transfer the Answer?

One commonly proposed solution for world hunger is to apply modern scientific know-how and technology to areas in which agriculture is still technologically underdeveloped. This solution seems simple: Thanks to agricultural machinery, plant breeding, modern fertilizers,

pest control methods, advances in irrigation technology, genetic engineering, and so on, the developed countries have solved the nutrition problem for most of their people. We have developed science and technology and applied it to agriculture. The LDCs need only adopt our know-how and technology to solve their hunger problems. In this view, the main thing hungry countries need is a transfer of our food production technology.

There are many problems with the **technology-transfer solution.** We can touch on only a few. First, many of the methods developed for application in temperate climates fail miserably when transported to the tropics, where most hungry people live. This is largely because of the profound differences between tropical and temperate soils and climates.

Second, many experts doubt that so-called high-tech solutions to food problems are appropriate to economic conditions in the LDCs. Labor is much more available than capital in these nations, so to substitute technology (machinery, herbicides, artificial fertilizers, etc.) for labor is to waste a plentiful factor of production in favor of a scarce one. Besides, those who need to increase production the most—the poorest farmers—are those who can least afford new technology. And borrowing money for new investments involves risks because many small farmers who borrow from rich landowners lose their land if they default.

Third, new technologies often come as a package deal. For instance, new crop varieties usually require large amounts of water, pesticides, and fertilizers to do well. Small farmers must adopt the whole expensive package for success. The expense, combined with the logistics of long-term supply of each element of the package in countries with uncertain transportation and political regimes, makes many farmers wary of innovations. Further, many new high-yielding varieties of crops are hybrids, which means that farmers cannot select next year's seeds from this year's harvest. Rather, they must purchase their seeds every year from large companies, many of which operate internationally. Is it a good idea to make the world's farmers dependent on a few suppliers of genetic material for their crops?

Fourth, agricultural experts from the developed world often report problems of "resistance" by peasant farmers. Sometimes peasants cling tenaciously to their traditional crops, varieties, and methods of cultivation even when genuine improvements are made available to them. This famed cultural conservatism of peasants seems downright irrational to many technical experts.

But some anthropologists who have conducted village-level fieldwork offer an alternative interpretation of peasant resistance to change. Living in intimate contact with local people, fieldworkers are sometimes able to perceive problems the way peasants do. Subsistence farmers who are barely feeding their families cannot afford to drop below the minimum level of food production it takes to survive. Traditional crops and varieties give some yield even when uncontrollable environmental forces are unfavorable because over the generations they have adapted to local fluctuations of climate, disease, and pests. The new varieties might not fare as well. Because the consequences of crop failure are more severe for poor subsistence farmers than for well-off commercial farmers, the poor farmers minimize their risks by using tried and true crop varieties and methods. Peasant cultural conservatism thus may be a sound strategy, given the conditions of peasant lives.

Finally, the technology that some believe it is wise to transfer to other parts of the world may not be as effective or as efficient as they think. Modern mechanized agriculture requires a large amount of energy to produce its high yields. Studies done in the 1970s suggest that on modern commercial farms in the United States, on average about 1 calorie of energy is required to produce about 2 calories of food. The "energy subsidy" to agriculture goes into producing and running tractors, harvesters, irrigation facilities, chemical fertilizers, herbicides, pesticides, and other inputs. The payoff for this energy subsidy is enormously high yields, in terms of both yields per acre and yields per farm worker. In traditional agricultural systems, however, for every 1 calorie of energy expended in agricultural production, 15–50 calories of food energy are returned (the amount depends, of course, on local conditions, cultivation methods, crop type, and a multitude of other factors). The main reason traditional agriculture is so much more energy efficient is that human labor energy, supplemented by the muscle energy of draft animals, is the major energy input.

Many questions follow from this difference in energy subsidy. Is there enough energy for modern mechanized agricultural methods to be widely adopted around the world? If there is, can the rural poor of the Third World afford them? What will happen if the rural poor have to compete on a local level with the well-off farmers who can afford to purchase and maintain the new technologies? What will be the local and global environmental consequences of agricultural mechanization on such a large scale? The worldwide price of oil was high in 2007, but what will happen to it if tens or hundreds of millions of additional farmers mechanize their operations? Can such methods be used indefinitely—are they ecologically sustainable?

We raise such questions not because the answers are obvious. Some experts—mainly economists—believe that the new problems new technologies create will be solved by even newer technologies. Others say it is too risky to count on a future of uncertain technological salvation, and the consequences of being wrong are too severe to do so. Some believe that whatever future scarcities of energy or other resources occur will stimulate the search for alternative sources, so that the free market will save us. Others claim that we are near the limits of our planet's ability to produce affordable food and other products.

To point out that technology transfers are not economically or ecologically feasible for many regions is not to say that modern food-producing methods are always harmful or should not even be considered as solutions for world hunger. It merely points out that mechanized technologies have problems of their own and that "experts" do not have all the answers. Are there other solutions that avoid or minimize some of the problems with transfers of technology? Some agricultural scientists, anthropologists, and other scholars are researching alternative methods of boosting food production—methods that are productive and sustainable, yet avoid some of the high energy requirements and the problems associated with mechanized agriculture.

Agricultural Alternatives

Since the early 1980s, increasing numbers of agricultural scientists have been taking another look at traditional farming practices—that is, methods of cultivating the soil that have been used for decades or centuries by the people living in a particular region. In the past, technical experts in agricultural development often scorned traditional farming methods, which they viewed as inefficient and overly labor intensive. But today there is increasing awareness of the benefits of traditional methods.

This awareness stems partly from the failure of so many agricultural development programs for the Third World. It also stems from the environmental movement that began in the developed countries in the 1970s, which called attention to the negative environmental impacts of mechanized agriculture. In addition to the high energy requirements of mechanized agriculture previously discussed, some farming practices commonly used in the developed countries cause environmental problems. Such problems include water pollution from fertilizer runoff, poisoning of farm workers and wildlife from agricultural chemicals, soil erosion from failure to rotate crops, and increasing resistance of insects because of exclusive reliance on pesticides.

In addition to negative environmental impacts, technologies such as machinery, pesticides, herbicides, and fungicides are too expensive for many traditional farmers. Sometimes they are inappropriate or uneconomical to use on the small plots that are characteristic of farms in many parts of the world. They may be unfamiliar to local people, who understandably are reluctant to abandon proven cultivation methods for alternatives they perceive to be riskier.

Considerations such as these led some agricultural scientists in the 1980s to ask: Are there *viable* alternatives to mechanized agricultural technologies and practices? Some experts believe there are. The main goals of such alternatives are minimization of negative environmental impacts, affordability to small farmers, reliance on technologies and resources that are locally available, adaptation to local environmental conditions, and long-term sustainability.

Over the centuries, traditional farming systems have evolved that meet many of these goals. Increasingly, agricultural scientists and development agencies look at traditional agriculture not as a system that should be replaced but as a set of farming techniques that they can learn from. Much research on this topic is ongoing; here we present brief descriptions of only two traditional methods: intercropping and resource management.

Intercropping. One method used by traditional farmers in many parts of the world (in the tropics especially) is intercropping, also known as multiple cropping or polyculture. In contrast to monoculture, intercropping involves the intermingling of numerous crops in a single plot or field. It has been practiced for centuries by shifting cultivators, whose plots usually contain dozens of crops and varieties.

Although intercropped fields look untidy, this method offers several benefits, stemming from the diversity of crops growing together in a relatively small space. Many plant diseases and pests attack only one or a few crops, so if there are several different crops, yields may still be good despite an outbreak. In regions where water supply is a problem and rainfall is erratic, some crops suffer during droughts but others will still produce a harvest. The varying growth patterns and root structures of diverse crops have useful ecological benefits: Erosion is reduced because more of the soil is covered, and sun-loving weeds are suppressed by the shade of the crops themselves.

Traditional farmers in some parts of the world have learned over the centuries that many crops grow better when planted together. Leguminous crops, such as beans, peas, and peanuts, take nitrogen (a necessary plant nutrient) from the air and store it in their roots. Intercropping legumes with crops that need lots of nitrogen can increase yields. This is done in Mexico and Central America, where traditional farmers have long intercropped corn, beans, and squash. The stout corn plants provide support for the bean vines to climb, and the ground-hugging squash plants keep the soil covered. African farmers intercrop sorghum with peanuts and millet with cowpea with similar benefits.

Traditional resource management practices. In many parts of the world, traditional farmers actively take steps to control the plant species growing in areas that, to outsiders, look "wild" or "abandoned." They are, in other words, managing their resources so they can continue to use them indefinitely. Two brief examples illustrate these management practices.

The Kayapó of the Xingu River basin of Brazil farm in the forest by shifting cultivation. According to anthropologist Darrell Posey, who has worked among the Kayapó for years, the Kayapó manage the forest carefully. One of their traditional practices is the creation of "islands" of forest in deforested areas. They move composted soil made from termite and ant nests and vegetation into open areas and transplant crops and other useful plants. The created and managed environment provides plant foods, medicines, and building materials and attracts some of the animals hunted by the Kayapó.

The Lacandon Maya of the state of Chiapas in southern Mexico practice slash-and-burn agriculture. Although the staple crop is corn, they plant many other crops in the cleared fields, including several tree species that yield fruits. Lacandon farmers clear and plant new plots frequently, but they do not simply abandon a plot once its main crops are harvested. Rather, they return to it for many years to harvest the long-lived fruit trees and other species they planted. Even while the natural forest is regrowing, the Lacandon continue to use the land. They manage their fallowing fields and thus integrate their exploitation of the land with the natural process of forest regeneration.

We have presented some of the reasons many scientists and others concerned with agricultural development are reconsidering traditional agriculture. It is all too easy to romanticize traditional farmers, to think that they really have had the answers all along and that only recently have so-called experts been forced to pay attention. This view, too, is simplistic. In all likelihood, solutions to the food crisis will require a mixture of traditional and modern technologies. It is, however, encouraging that the knowledge and methods embedded in traditional agricultural adaptations are being taken seriously by the World Bank and other institutions that are in a position to make critical decisions.

Anthropologists as Advocates

Anthropologists do not merely define problems. From the earliest origins of the discipline, anthropologists as individuals have been politically active, using the information gained from their research to voice their concerns about a wide range of public policy issues. Franz Boas (see Chapter 4) took an active role in attacking racist stereotypes during the first decades of the twentieth century and publicly opposed U.S. immigration laws based on racist ideas. Margaret Mead (see Chapter 4) was certainly the best-known advocate for women's rights in the United States during the mid-twentieth century. As individuals, anthropologists have been and still are activists concerned with a wide range of particular and global issues. However, no single issue has concerned anthropologists as a group more than the rights of indigenous peoples.

This should not be surprising. Much of anthropological research has focused on the study of these peoples, and field research is a highly personal experience. As a result, anthropologists as a group more clearly understand the problems of these peoples than other outsiders, and collectively we know them and value them not just as individuals but also as friends. In the late nineteenth century, American anthropologists were engaged in advocating the rights of American Indian peoples. As members of the Lake Mohonk Conference and other Indian rights organizations, they lobbied Congress for changes in the laws concerning American Indian tribes. Throughout the twentieth century and today, at the beginning of the twenty-first century, anthropologists continue to fight for the rights of indigenous peoples. Thus, it is fitting that we end this book by advocating the rights of indigenous peoples to preserve their cultural systems—assuming, of course, that is their choice.

Indigenous Peoples Today

Indigenous may be used to refer to any people who have resided in a region for many centuries. By this definition, the Germans of Germany and the Irish of Ireland are indigenous. However, as **indigenous peoples** is usually used today, the phrase refers to "culturally distinct groups that have occupied a region longer than other immigrant

or colonist groups" (*Cultural Survival Quarterly,* Spring 1992, 73). Generally, indigenous peoples are small-scale societies who make their living by foraging, farming, and/or herding, live in roughly the same region as their ancestors, and are fairly remote from the economic and political centers of the countries that include their territory. Sometimes they are termed *tribal peoples* or, more recently, *Fourth World peoples.* Often their territories cross modern national boundaries.

Indigenous peoples most often survive as ethnic enclaves within a larger nation. The government controlled by the dominant ethnic group of these countries usually claims to have ultimate control over the land and other resources of the indigenous people who live within the officially recognized national borders. For many indigenous peoples, in effect, the colonial world still exists. Because they lack effective political autonomy and are too few to wage successful physical resistance, their remaining lands are constantly threatened by the wider society. Too often their ways of life are destroyed because more numerous and powerful ethnic groups consider indigenous cultures barriers to national progress and development.

The Human Rights Council of the United Nations estimates that there are 370 million indigenous peoples in the modern world. Among them are the Native peoples of the Americas; the aboriginal peoples of Australia and other islands of the Pacific; the Sami (formerly known as the Lapps) and other reindeer-herding peoples of northern Europe and Asia; hundreds of "tribal" cultures of eastern Asia, Southeast Asia, and southern Asia; and numerous ethnic groups of Africa. Estimates can and do vary greatly, however, due to a lack of agreement on which particular groups should or should not be counted as "indigenous."

The legal rights of indigenous peoples became an issue at the time of Columbus's landfall in the Americas. Questions of whether the native peoples of the Americas—or, for that matter, any indigenous people—had any inherent rights to their land, resources, or political autonomy were debated in Spain. Although legal particulars differed from one colonial power to another as well as over time, a basic consensus was reached early in the colonial period: An indigenous people did have some rights based on prior occupancy. However, more "civilized" peoples could unilaterally claim jurisdiction over them and make use of any land and resources that were either not utilized or underutilized. Civilized peoples had both a right and an obligation to uplift indigenous peoples and to act in their "best interest." This responsibility came to be called the "white man's burden."

Civilized peoples also had the right to travel and trade wherever they wanted without interference from indigenous peoples. Finally, if an indigenous people resisted, then the civilized people had the right to use military force against them. Racism, ethnocentrism, and social Darwinist ideas about the inevitability and desirability of progress provided the moral justification for the treatment of indigenous peoples.

Such attitudes and policies affected the governing of most indigenous peoples in the colonial possession of European nations. When independence came to Asian and African countries in the twentieth century, the leaders and dominant ethnic groups of many of the new nations adopted similar attitudes and policies. As discussed in Chapters 16 and 17, the modern boundaries of most existing countries are legacies of European colonization in the sixteenth through the early twentieth centuries. In many cases, the political and legal systems of these countries are also Western-derived or heavily Western-influenced. Such attitudes, governmental policies, and legal concepts are often the basis for the treatment of indigenous peoples and other ethnic groups within a Third World nation itself. In fact, to understand what is happening to most remaining indigenous peoples in the world today, one can start by reexamining American Indian policy during the nineteenth and early twentieth centuries. In Brazil, Indonesia, Sudan, and elsewhere, the same introduction of new diseases, genocide, relocation, forced assimilation, and appropriation of land and resources of smaller indigenous groups by politically dominant ethnic groups are taking place.

Modern governments in parts of Latin America, Africa, and Asia face serious economic, political, and social problems. Many governments—including those that are democratically elected—are under pressure from their dominant ethnic group to pursue policies that lead to the displacement or assimilation of the indigenous peoples whose territories lie within their national boundaries. In many countries aspiring to modernization, indigenous people living in remote, "undeveloped" regions are forced to move aside in the interest of what the dominant society sees as the "greater good" of their nation.

Sometimes this greater good consists of opening up undeveloped areas to settlers. For example, Indonesia resettles peasants from overpopulated Java into its outer islands (such as Sumatra, Irian Jaya, and Kalimantan), now claimed to be "underpopulated." Although often considered a modernized nation, Brazil has some of the poorest people in the world living in its northeastern area. It is also one of the few countries that still has a frontier—the vast tropical rain forest of Amazonia. In the 1970s,

Brazil constructed highways intended to open up Amazonia to resettlement and to mineral, timber, grazing, and agricultural exploitation. One-third of Brazil's Native American tribes have disappeared since 1900, and many others have lost most of their lands to outsiders.

One people who are threatened by the opening up of Brazil's Amazonian frontier is the Yanomamö (mentioned in Chapters 2, 5, and 9). Until the early 1970s, most of the approximately 20,000 Yanomamö were relatively isolated from outside influences. In 1974, the Brazilian government constructed a road through the southern part of Yanomamö territory. Workers involved in forest clearing and road building introduced new diseases such as influenza and measles, and in some regions as many as half the Yanomamö died during epidemics. Dirt airstrips constructed during the 1980s also made Indian territory accessible to Brazilian gold prospectors. In the late 1980s, thousands of gold seekers—most of them impoverished—poured into the area in search of wealth. By early 1990, as many as 45,000 prospectors had invaded traditional Yanomamö lands and extracted gold worth an estimated $1 billion.

The government's National Indian Foundation is charged with protecting Brazil's Native American peoples and territories from invasion and plunder, but it has been unable to control violence against the Yanomamö and other indigenous groups. In 1990, Brazil's former president ordered the landing strips destroyed to reduce future access, and in 1992, a portion of the Yanomamö territory was demarcated by the government as Yanomamö Park. However, by 1996 miners had illegally returned, and by 2001 as many as 2,000 were reported illegally mining land in Yanomamö Park. Not only has the Brazilian government done little to correct this problem, but political pressure is growing to open more areas to mining and timber interests.

Another common justification for the neglect of the territorial rights of indigenous peoples is the desire to improve a country's balance of trade. The Philippines, Indonesia, and other countries earn foreign exchange by leasing rights to harvest timber from their tropical hardwood forests to multinational companies, although much of the "unexploited" forest is needed as fallow by indigenous shifting cultivators. Debts owed to foreign banks and international lending agencies encourage some nations to open up their hinterlands to resource development, pushing their indigenous inhabitants aside. In countries such as Brazil and Mexico, minerals, cattle, timber, vegetables, coffee, and other exports are sold to Europe and North America to earn foreign exchange to help pay off international debts.

▶ The physical and cultural survival of the Yanomamö and other Amazonian peoples is threatened by opening up their traditional lands to mining, logging, ranching, and other extractive industries.

Many indigenous communities are affected adversely by the efforts of well-meaning people to promote environmental causes such as habitat preservation or animal conservation. For some, preservation and conservation of biological resources are interpreted to mean "no resource exploitation" or, in extreme cases, even "no people." Governments of nations with large indigenous populations sometimes react to such concerns by resettling people out of areas they have lived in for centuries. (An irony is worth pointing out here: often the areas deemed appropriate for conservation or preservation efforts are those that are recognized as relatively undisturbed—partly because it is mainly the indigenous peoples who have been using them all along.)

Within the southern African nation of Botswana lies the Central Kalahari Game Reserve (CKGR), which is the second largest game reserve in all Africa. The CKGR was established in 1961, partly to provide the indigenous hunter-gatherers of the region—the San (see Chapter 6 for information on the !Kung, one of several local San groups)—with adequate resources for their subsistence needs. In the 1960s and 1970s, local groups of San used the territory for subsistence foraging, sometimes on horseback. In the 1980s, some environmentalists tried to persuade the European Union to pressure Botswana officials to remove the people from the CKGR and declare the area a game reserve. By the 1990s, the remaining San were encouraged to move outside the reserve by various methods, including failure to repair a needed well, intimidation by selective enforcement of game laws,

and (allegedly) severe physical punishments of accused "poachers."

By 2002, the government of Botswana had resettled nearly all of the resident San, about 1,000 individuals, in two settlements outside the boundaries of the reserve, placing them in an environment that had few trees and wild plant foods and offering them very little compensation. This action was taken partly in the name of conservation. But the San argued that increasing numbers of tourists in four-wheel-drive vehicles were destroying the land and that more cattle were on the reserve. According to an article by Robert Hitchcock (1999, 54) in the journal *Cultural Survival Quarterly,* the San "expressed that the reason they were being removed was so that well-to-do private citizens could set up lucrative safari camps in the reserve." In 2002, the San filed a legal case in the High Court of Botswana. In 2006, the court finally ruled that their eviction was illegal, they had a right to live on the reserve, and the government had to issue them hunting permits. In the summer of 2007, 21 San were arrested for illegally hunting on the reserve. Although the case was dismissed, some questions still remain concerning the use of the reserve by the San.

Perhaps environmentalists in North America and Western Europe should also give more consideration to impacts on the welfare of indigenous peoples when they propose to save wildlife or preserve ecosystems. As these and numerous other cases show, many still consider it legitimate to take land from those who have lived on it for centuries.

The indigenous peoples who remain in cultural communities are learning to protect themselves through political action. In increasing numbers, indigenous peoples around the world are fighting attempts to dispossess them of their traditional territories and resources. Many are resisting efforts to assimilate them into the cultural mainstream of their nations. They are publicly objecting to racist and ethnocentric attitudes about their beliefs and customs.

One people who are resisting are the Kayapó. In the 1980s, the government of Brazil sought World Bank funding for the construction of two enormous hydroelectric dams on Amazon River tributaries. Eighty-five percent of the land that would have been flooded belongs to one or another indigenous Indian population. Organized by leaders of the Kayapó tribe, members of 29 Brazilian Indian groups protested the dams. In early 1988, two Kayapó leaders traveled to Washington, D.C., with anthropologist Darrell Posey to speak against the project to officials of the World Bank and to U.S. congressional authorities. When the World Bank deferred action on the loans, Brazil brought charges against the three protesters under a law that forbids "foreigners" from engaging in political activity harmful to the nation. The courage and sophistication of the Kayapó and other members of threatened communities illustrate how indigenous peoples are organizing themselves to acquire the political power to fight various developments. However, the pressures for the development of indigenous lands are relentless. In 2001, the Brazilian government announced new plans to build three hydroelectric dams on the Xingu River, this time using private and Brazilian governmental funding. The Kayapó and other indigenous leaders held a meeting in the summer of 2004 to resist these new dams. In 2006, representatives of the Kayapó communities met and issued the Declaration of Paiaracu, rejecting the building of the dams and calling for an end to the pollution of the Xingu caused by upstream agricultural activities. In June 2007, Native leaders meeting in Altamira again rejected the construction of the dams.

On September 13, 2007, after more than two decades of deliberations, the United Nations finally passed The Declaration on the Rights of Indigenous Peoples (see A Closer Look).

Vanishing Knowledge

Despite the increased political sophistication of indigenous peoples around the world and the protests of concerned citizens in many countries, there is no doubt that many preindustrial cultures are in danger of extinction. Even if the people themselves survive the onslaughts of lumbering, mining, damming, grazing, farming, and building, their way of life is liable to disappear. Most people would agree that genocide is a crime of the highest degree. But destruction or alteration of a culture is another matter—Isn't it possible that indigenous people themselves would be better off if they joined the cultural mainstream of their nations?

Yes, many peoples do want to acquire formal education, get jobs, improve their living standards, and generally "modernize" their societies. For many peoples and for many individuals within an indigenous culture, contact with the wider world offers new opportunities and new choices. Young people are especially attracted by the material goods, entertainments, new experiences, and sheer variety of activities found in towns and cities. They should have these opportunities and these choices. But indigenous peoples and their ways of life are often overwhelmed by forces over which they have no control. It is not that most indigenous peoples are given the opportunity to carefully weigh the options available to them, so that they make informed choices about whether it is best for them to preserve or to modernize their ways of life. Today, as in the past, their traditions are disappearing more often because powerful national governments want to open up their territory or because private entrepreneurs or corporations want to exploit their resources.

Anthropologists are especially concerned with the rights of indigenous peoples for several reasons. First, because of our interest in cultural diversity, we are more aware of what has happened to non-Western cultures in the past several centuries than are most people. Second, we identify with indigenous peoples partly because so many of us have worked among them. Third, our professional training gives us a relativistic outlook on the many ways of being human, so we can appreciate other peoples' customs and beliefs as viable alternatives to our own. Finally, the fieldwork experience often affects our attitudes about our own societies—deep immersion in other cultural traditions leaves some of us not so sure about our commitment to our own.

Whether one is an anthropologist or not, one can appreciate the rights of any group of people to have their lives, property, and resources secure from domination by powerful outsiders. The most important factors in considering the rights of indigenous peoples to be left alone are ethical ones. Don't people everywhere have the right to live their lives free from the unwanted interference of those more powerful and wealthy than themselves? Does

THE DECLARATION ON THE RIGHTS OF INDIGENOUS PEOPLES

In 1982, the United Nations created the Working Group on Indigenous Populations (WGIP). The purpose of the WGIP was to develop standards for the protection of indigenous peoples. In the decades that followed, the WGIP and then other United Nations bodies worked with indigenous leaders as well as representatives of national governments to draft a declaration concerning the rights of indigenous peoples. On September 13, 2007, the United Nations General Assembly adopted "The Declaration on the Rights of Indigenous Peoples."

The declaration itself is lengthy, containing 45 articles. (For the full text, see http://daccessdds.un.org/doc/UNDOC/LTD/GO6/125/71/PDF/GO612571.pdf.) Here we quote only some of the more important points relative to indigenous rights in general, as well as rights directly related to the political status, landholdings, and cultural traditions of indigenous peoples.

Article 7 states: "Indigenous peoples have the collective right to live in freedom, peace and security as distinct peoples and shall not be subjected to any act of genocide or any other act of violence, including forcibly removing children of the group to another group."

Several articles address the political rights of indigenous peoples: "Indigenous peoples have the right of self-determination [and] by virtue of that right . . . freely determine their political status" (Article 3); "the right to autonomy or self-government in matters relating to their internal and local affairs" (Article 4); and "the right to promote, develop and maintain their institutional structures and . . . in the cases where they exist, juridical systems or customs, in accordance with international human rights standards" (Article 34).

Other articles address the issues of land, resources, and economic development: "Indigenous peoples have the right to the lands, territories and resources which they have traditionally owned, occupied or otherwise used or acquired" (Article 26); "the right to be secure in the enjoyment of their own means of subsistence and development, and to freely engage in all their traditional and other economic activities" (Article 20); "the right to determine and develop priorities and strategies for the development or use of their lands or territories and other resources" (Article 32); and "the right to the conservation and protection of the environment and the productive capacity of their lands or territories and resources" (Article 28).

Finally, the declaration states that "indigenous peoples shall not be forcibly removed from their lands or territories" (Article 10), and it gives peoples "the right to . . . restitution or . . . fair and equitable compensation, for lands, territories and resources which they have traditionally owned or otherwise occupied or used, and which have been confiscated, taken, occupied, used or damaged without their free, prior and informed consent" (Article 28).

The related issues of assimilation and traditional cultures of indigenous peoples are addressed in a variety of ways: "Indigenous peoples . . . have the right not to be subjected to forced assimilation or destruction of their culture" (Article 8); "the right to maintain, protect and develop the past, present and future manifestations of their cultures, such as archaeological and historical sites, artefacts, designs, ceremonies, technologies and visual and performing arts and literature" (Article 11); "the right to manifest, practice, develop and teach their spiritual and religious traditions, customs and ceremonies; the right to maintain, protect, and have access in privacy to their religious and cultural sites; the right to use and control of their ceremonial objects; and the right to the repatriation of their human remains" (Article 12); and "the right to maintain, control, protect and develop their cultural heritage, traditional knowledge and traditional cultural expressions, as well as the manifestations of their sciences, technologies and cultures, including human and genetic resources, seeds, medicines, knowledge of the properties of fauna and flora, oral traditions, literatures, designs, sports and traditional games and visual and performing arts . . . the right to maintain, control, protect and develop their intellectual property over such cultural heritage, traditional knowledge, and traditional cultural expressions" (Article 31).

The United Nations General Assembly adopted the declaration with 143 countries voting in favor, 11 countries abstaining, and 4 countries—the United States, Canada, Australia, and New Zealand—voting against. It is important to note that the declaration is not legally binding; compliance with the declaration is voluntary.

any government, regardless of its "problems," have the right to dispossess people from land they have lived on and used for centuries? Is the demand of citizens in Japan, Europe, North America, or anywhere else for wood, minerals, meat, electricity, or other products a sufficient justification for relocating a people or taking land away from them? (Readers who follow politicians' statements about human rights violations in Iran, Iraq, China, Bosnia, Kosovo, and other countries might wonder why they have so little to say about the rights of indigenous peoples.)

Surely, most of us agree on the answers to such questions. Ethical concerns for the human rights of indigenous peoples, combined with a respect for their cultural traditions, are the primary reasons for granting their rights to survive as living communities.

But if the ethical arguments alone (based on shared values about human rights) are not compelling, there are other arguments (based on practical concerns, and even on the self-interest of the dominant majority). The long-term welfare of all humanity may be jeopardized by the loss of cultural diversity on our planet. Think about the cultural heritage of humanity as a whole. Consider *all* the knowledge accumulated by *all* humanity over hundreds of generations. Imagine, in other words, human culture—here defined as the sum of all knowledge stored in the cultural traditions of all humans alive today.

Some of the knowledge in present-day human culture has been widely disseminated in the past few centuries by means of written language. We may call it *global knowledge* (not meaning to imply that it is "true" or "universally known"). Although some global knowledge will be lost or replaced, much of the knowledge stored in writing (or, more recently, on computer disks) will be preserved and added to over the coming decades and centuries. Other knowledge in human culture is *local knowledge*—it is stored only in the heads of members of particular cultures, many of which are endangered. Most local knowledge will disappear if those cultural traditions disappear—even if the people themselves survive.

How much of this local knowledge is knowledge that may (today, tomorrow, someday) prove useful to all humanity? Of course, no one knows. But no one can doubt that the rest of the world has much to learn from indigenous cultures. (Incidentally, anthropologists have always understood the importance of learning *about* other cultures; recently, there has been increasing emphasis placed on learning *from* them.) In fact, much of what had been only the local knowledge of some indigenous culture has been incorporated into global knowledge, as a consequence of contact with the West and other colonizing peoples. We conclude this book with a small sample of some of the medical and adaptive wisdom of indigenous peoples, whose local knowledge has already contributed so much to the world.

Medicines We Have Learned

"The Medicine Man Will See You Now," proclaimed a headline in a 1993 edition of *Business Week*. The accompanying article described a California pharmaceutical company that sends ethnobotanists and other scientists into rain forests to learn from indigenous shamans. Companies as well as scholars are beginning to understand that the traditional remedies long used by preindustrial

peoples often have genuine medical value. In fact, many of the important drugs in use today were derived from indigenous knowledge. Here we provide only a few examples of the medicines originally discovered by indigenous peoples that now have worldwide significance. An enjoyable source of more examples is the 1993 book, *Tales of a Shaman's Apprentice,* by Mark Plotkin.

Malaria remains a debilitating, although usually not fatal, sickness in tropical and subtropical regions. Its main treatment is quinine, a component of the bark of the cinchona tree. Europeans in the seventeenth century learned of the value of quinine from Peruvian Indians.

The Madagascar periwinkle has long been used in folk medicine to treat diabetes. Researchers first became interested in the plant as a substitute for oral insulin, but it seems to have little value for this purpose. During their investigation, however, scientists discovered that extracts from periwinkle yielded dramatic successes in treating childhood leukemia, Hodgkin's disease, and some other cancers. Drugs based on the plant—notably vincristine and vinblastine—remain the major treatments for these otherwise fatal diseases.

Muscle relaxants are important drugs to surgeons. A popular one is curare, made from the chondodendron tree. Taken in large amounts, curare can paralyze the respiratory organs and lead to death. This property was recognized by South American Indians, who used it as arrow poison for hunting birds, monkeys, and other game, and from whom medical science learned of the drug's value.

The ancient Greeks and several North American Indian tribes used the bark of willows for relief from pain and fever. In the nineteenth century, scientists succeeded in artificially synthesizing this compound that today we call *aspirin.*

There is no way of knowing how many plants used by surviving indigenous peoples could prove to be medically effective. The potential is great. According to pharmacologist Norman Farnsworth, about one-fourth of all prescribed drugs in the United States contain active ingredients extracted from higher plants. The world contains more than 250,000 species of higher plants. Although as many as 40,000 of these plants may have medical or nutritional values that are undiscovered by science, only about 1,100 of these have been well studied. Botanists and medical researchers are coming to realize that indigenous peoples already have discovered, through centuries of trial and error, that certain plants are effective remedies for local diseases. The future value of their medical wisdom to all of humanity is largely unknown, but probably great.

▲ Indigenous peoples, such as these Indonesian "medicine men," commonly have an extensive and potentially important knowledge of the curative powers of plants. How much medical knowledge of healers in indigenous cultures will be lost?

Adaptive Wisdom

Many preindustrial peoples have lived in and exploited their natural environments for centuries. Earlier in this chapter, we discussed the problems of technology in attempting to overcome hunger, and some of the important traditional agricultural alternatives used by indigenous peoples such as the Kalapó and Lacandon Maya. They have learned to control insect pests and diseases that attack the plants on which they depend, and to do so without using expensive and often dangerous artificial chemicals. They have often learned how to make nature work for them while minimizing the deterioration of their environments. They have, in short, incorporated much adaptive wisdom into their cultural traditions. Following are possible benefits that all humanity might gain by preserving the ecological knowledge of indigenous peoples.

Preservation of crop varieties. In all cultivation systems, natural selection operates in the farmers' fields. Like wild plants, crops are subject to drought, disease, insects, and other natural elements, which select for the survival of the individual plants best adapted to withstand these hazards. In addition, crops are subject to human selection. For example, crop varieties that are most susceptible to drought or local diseases are harvested in smaller quantities than drought- and disease-resistant

varieties. Perhaps without knowing it, the cultivator re-plants mainly those varieties best adapted to survive the onslaughts of drought and local diseases. This tuning of plant varieties to the local environment, with all its hazards and fluctuations, goes on automatically so long as the crops harvested from the fields are replanted in the same area. Thanks to the unintentional and intentional selection by hundreds of generations of indigenous cultivators around the world, each species of crop (e.g., beans, potatoes, wheat) evolved a large number of *land races,* or distinct varieties adapted to local conditions.

Over the course of human history, several thousand species of plants have been used for food but less than a hundred of these were ever domesticated. Of all the plants that have been domesticated, today only a handful provide significant amounts of food for the world's people. In fact, only four crops—wheat, rice, maize, and potato—provide almost half of the world's total consumption of food.

Since around 1950, plant geneticists and agricultural scientists have developed new varieties of wheat, corn, rice, and potatoes that are capable of giving higher yields if they receive proper amounts of water and fertilizers. These new strains were developed by crossing and re-crossing native land races collected from all over the world. The aim was to achieve a "green revolution" that would end world hunger by increasing production. Many new varieties are hybrids, which means that farmers must receive a new supply of seeds yearly from governmental or private sources.

Ironically, having been bred from the genetic material present in their diverse ancestors, the new strains now threaten to drive their ancestors to extinction. As farmers in Asia, Africa, and the Americas plant the seeds of artificially bred varieties, the traditional varieties—the land races that are the product of generations of natural and human selection—fall into disuse and many have disappeared.

Why should we care? Increasingly, agricultural experts are realizing the dangers of dependence on a few varieties. If crops that are nearly identical genetically are planted in the same area year after year, a new variety of pest or disease will eventually evolve to attack them. The famous Irish potato famine of the 1840s was directly related to the genetic uniformity of the potato because all the potatoes in Ireland were apparently descended from only a few plants. More than a million people died as a result of the potato blight, and a million more immigrated to North America. The United States has also suffered serious economic losses: the corn blight of 1970 destroyed about 15 percent of the American crop. Losses would have been less severe had most American farmers not planted a single variety of corn.

Many plant breeders are alarmed at the prospect of losing much of the genetic diversity of domesticated plants. Today they are searching remote regions for surviving land races that contain genes that one day might prove valuable. (The seeds are stored in seed banks for future study.) The searchers have been successful, although no one knows how much of the genetic diversity of crops such as wheat and corn has already disappeared.

The knowledge of indigenous peoples is an important resource in the effort to preserve land races. In many parts of the world—the Andes, Central America, Amazonia, the Middle East, and elsewhere—cultivators still grow ancient varieties of crops. They know where these varieties yield best, how to plant and care for them, how to prepare them for eating, and so on. In the Andes, for instance, hundreds of potato varieties survive among the Quechua Indians as a legacy of the Inca civilization. Many have specific ecological requirements, and some are even unique to a single valley. Research is now under way to determine how well specific land races will grow in other areas to help solve food supply problems elsewhere. It is important to preserve the genetic information encoded in these varieties for future generations.

Indigenous peoples who still retain the hard-won knowledge of their ancestors and who still use the often-maligned "traditional crop varieties" are important informational resources in the effort to save the genetic diversity of crops on which humanity depends.

"Undiscovered" useful species. In addition to their familiarity with local crop varieties that have potential worldwide significance, many indigenous peoples cultivate or use crop species that are currently unimportant to the rest of the world. One example is amaranth, a grain native to the Americas that was of great importance to the Indians in prehistoric times. The great Mesoamerican civilizations made extensive use of the plant in their religious rituals. This led the Spanish conquerors, in their anxiety to root out heathenism, to burn fields of amaranth and prohibit its consumption. Otherwise, it—like maize, potatoes, beans, squash, and other American crops—might have diffused to other continents. Amaranth remains an important food to some indigenous peoples of highland Latin America, who retain knowledge of its properties and requirements. Its unusually high protein content might someday make it valuable to the rest of the world.

Other plants used by native peoples have the potential to become important elsewhere. Quinoa, now grown mainly in Peruvian valleys, has twice the protein content

of corn and has long been recognized as a domesticate with great potential. The tepary bean, now grown mainly by the O'odham of the American Southwest, can survive and yield well during extreme droughts, which might make it cultivatable in other arid regions of the world. Another legume, the winged bean, has long been cultivated by the native peoples of Papua New Guinea, and it has helped nourish people in 50 other tropical countries.

Humans use plants for more than food. Indigenous peoples have discovered many other uses for the plants found in their habitats. Scientific researchers today are attesting to the validity of much native knowledge about the use of plants as sources of fuel, oils, medicines, and other beneficial substances, including poisons. Forest peoples of Southeast Asia use the toxic roots of a local woody climbing plant as a fish poison. The root is so powerful that a mixture of 1 part root to 300,000 parts water will kill fish. From the indigenous tribes, scientists learned of the toxicity of these roots, which allowed them to isolate the rotenoid that now is used as an insecticide spray for plants and as dips and dusting powders for livestock.

Scientists no doubt will rediscover many other useful plants that today they know nothing about—if the tropical forests in which most endangered plant species are found last long enough. Their task will be easier if the original discoverers—indigenous peoples—are around to teach them what their ancestors learned.

Cultural Alternatives

There is another kind of practical lesson we might learn from surviving indigenous peoples. Industrialized humans have developed technologies that discover, extract, and transform natural resources on a scale undreamed of a century ago. To North Americans and to many other citizens of the developed world, *progress* is almost synonymous with "having more things." Yet whether our economies can continue to produce ever-increasing supplies of goods is questionable. Many of us are frightened by the thought that economic growth might not continue. The fear that we will be forced to accept a stagnation or even a decline in our levels of material consumption no doubt contributes to the interest today's undergraduates have in careers that they believe are most likely to earn high incomes for themselves and their future families.

On the other hand, some individuals and groups in the affluent, developed world have questioned the value of what most of their fellow citizens call "economic progress." They think that the environmental and familial costs of the unceasing drive to accumulate and

When we think of development, we almost invariably think in terms of economic development. To us, the economic development of a country, a state, or a region is easily measured; it is a matter of dollars and cents. We need only to look at the gross national product (GNP) or the per-capita incomes. If we compare countries in terms of their growth of GNP, then we can determine which are the most economically successful. However, are the gross production figures the only—or even the best—measure of development? Are per-capita incomes the best measure of the standard of living of the society?

The Nobel Prize–winning economist Amartya Sen argues that growth in the GNP alone is not a particularly good indicator of development. As a child in India, he lived through the great famine of 1943, during which three million people died. Perhaps not surprisingly, one of his interests as an economist is in famines. He has discovered that famines were not solely or even primarily the result of food shortages. Instead, famines are frequently the result of market forces that increase the cost of food while depressing incomes to the point that families can no longer purchase adequate food. Just as famines are not necessarily the result of food shortages, the growth in the GNP of a country does not in itself result in increased prosperity. The GNP of a country might be growing, with little economic benefit to many, if not most, of the people.

Sen also questions how we measure standard of living. Is it merely a question of relative income? The Indian state of Kerala is an excellent example that per-capita income figures alone are not always the best measure of quality of life. Covering only 24,000 square miles along the southwest coast of India, Kerala is home to 33 million people. Depending primarily on agriculture, Kerala is a poor state, even by Indian standards. In terms of gross domestic product (GDP), Kerala averages only about $1,000 per capita, $200 less than India as a whole, and only one-twenty-sixth that of the United States. By such economic measures alone, residents of Kerala would appear to have a very poor standard of living. If we look at Kerala in terms of health, education, and other social issues, however, we see a far different picture.

In terms of health, the people of Kerala are better off than most other peoples in India and in countries with much higher incomes. Their infant mortality rate is among the lowest in the developing world. Their life expectancy is 72 years—11 years longer than the average for India, and only 4 years shorter than the United States.

Even more impressive are their achievements in education. Well-maintained schools are scattered throughout the state, and education is virtually universal. As a result, 90 percent of the people are literate—an achievement that places Kerala on the same level as the far more prosperous peoples of Spain and Singapore.

Social discrimination is less of a problem than in other parts of India and most of the world. Protests against the caste system began in Kerala in the middle of the nineteenth century, and in no other part of India has this system been so expunged from social consciousness. Although there are sizable Muslim and Christian minorities in the state, there have not been the religious conflicts that have beset most of India.

However, possibly the major factor that distinguishes Kerala from other parts of India and most parts of the world is its relative equality in income and opportunity. In the 1960s, the state government abolished landlordism and redistributed the land to 1.5 million tenant families. Kerala also has a relatively high minimum wage. This wage has discouraged industrial development and, as a result, Kerala has an unemployment rate of 25 percent. Because most families have land on which they can garden, however, they are shielded from destitution.

Critical Thinking Questions

1. What do we mean by *standard of living*? Can the standard of living of a people be measured in monetary terms alone?

2. Should development take into account not only incomes but also the distribution of wealth, educational levels, health standards, and social discrimination?

3. Do the people of Kerala serve as an example of balanced development? Are they, as Akash Kapur has said, "poor but prosperous"?

4. What do you value more: money or people?

Sources: Sen (1984, 1987); Kapur (1998)

to succeed in a highly competitive environment are not worth the benefits. Some of them believe that material affluence cannot bring happiness because it is gained at the high cost of the emotional gratifications that spring from community relationships, from supportive family and friendship ties, and adherence to what some call spiritual values (see the Globalization box).

Most readers of this book are the beneficiaries of economic progress. At the same time, we should be careful not to become the victims of the mentality of progress—of that unceasing desire to earn more, to have more, to succeed more. If the industrial bubble does not burst in our lifetime, then most of us who live in the developed world will spend our lives in a continuous effort to increase our consumption of goods. We will do so despite the fact that we can never catch up with the Joneses because there will always be other Joneses whom we have not yet caught. We will do so despite the fact that our efforts will never be sufficient to get us all we want because no one can consume goods as fast as companies can turn them out and advertisers can create new desires for them. We will do so despite the fact that many of our marriages and families will be torn apart by the effort and many of us will suffer psychologically and physically from stress-related disorders. Sadly, most of us pursue our dollars and goods unthinkingly because we remain ignorant of any alternative way of living.

The world's remaining indigenous peoples provide us with such alternatives. They do not and did not live in a primitive paradise. Subjugation of neighboring peoples, exploitation by the wealthy and powerful, degradation of women, warfare, and other ideas and practices many of us find abhorrent existed among some preindustrial

peoples, just as they do today. Yet, we also find other cultural conditions that some of us long to recover: closer family ties, greater self-sufficiency, smaller communities, more personal and enduring social relationships, and "more humane," "more moral" values. No anthropologist can tell you whether life is better or worse in preindustrial communities; indeed, we cannot agree on the meaning of *better*. We do know that humanity is diverse. We know that this diversity means that human beings—ourselves included—have many alternative ways of living meaningful and satisfying lives. In the end, it is these cultural alternatives provided by indigenous peoples that might have the greatest value to humankind.

Perhaps a people themselves are the only ones qualified to judge the quality of their lives, to decide what it will take to lend meaning and dignity to their existence. We hope we have convinced you that there are many ways of being human, and we hope you have learned to appreciate some of the alternative ways of living experienced by various human populations. We hope you will agree that some of these alternatives are worth preserving, both in their own right and for the long-term well-being of all humanity.

Summary

1. Anthropological expertise is useful for solving human problems because the way anthropologists look at people and cultures (our worldview) differs somewhat from the views of other professionals. Applied anthropologists have conducted research relevant to both global and local-level problems.

2. Two global problems are population growth and world hunger. Today's high rates of worldwide population growth are caused mainly by advances in medicine and vaccines and by widespread improvements in public health facilities. These advances have reduced death rates and increased life spans in most countries, but in underdeveloped regions, birthrates are still relatively high.

3. Population growth has many unfavorable consequences. It contributes to serious environmental problems, low economic productivity, urban sprawl and shantytowns, political conflicts, and even war. This is

the main paradox of population growth: the high fertility of a country's citizens is mainly responsible for it, yet their high fertility contributes to many of their nation's problems.

4. Having many children is not a simple product of ignorance or irrational cultural conservatism. The fertility rate is a response to the overall economic conditions in a region or country. This is shown by how North American couples choose how many children to have. Our low fertility is a rational response of couples to the conditions of their personal lives. In deciding how many children they want, most modern couples consider the personal, not the societal, costs and benefits of children.

5. High fertility in the LDCs is likewise a consequence of the overall economic and social environment that constrains reproductive behavior. Ethnographic studies suggest that children are a net economic asset rather than a liability in the rural areas of the Third World.

Children are productive family members at a young age. They seek jobs with local people to supplement the family income. When older, they go to the cities or to foreign countries and send money back home. They provide old-age security for their parents. Under such conditions, high fertility exists because large families are beneficial.

6. Population growth is often believed to be the major cause of world hunger. This is the scarcity explanation of hunger, which holds that overpopulation leads to chronic malnutrition and periodic massive starvation.

7. The alternative is the inequality explanation. It holds that land and other food-producing resources are in fact sufficient to provide an adequate diet for the whole world. Hunger is caused by the way local and world economies allocate resources.

8. These two explanations of hunger are compatible: population growth contributes to hunger by increasing the scarcity of food production resources, yet prevalent inequalities in access to productive resources aggravate the scarcity and prevent people from adjusting to it.

9. Technology transfer is a viable solution to hunger in the LDCs, according to many. But there are numerous problems with this solution. Temperate agricultural methods often do not work well in tropical climates and soils. New technologies sometimes harm rather than help the poorest families. Peasants often do not adopt new technologies and crop varieties because they perceive them not worth the costs, or because they cannot afford to assume the risks of failure. Mechanized agriculture requires so much energy to produce food that it may not be affordable to Third World farmers and may not be sustainable in the long run.

10. Agricultural scientists, anthropologists, and others have been researching alternative farming methods that have long been used by traditional peoples of the world. Traditional methods such as intercropping and resource management hold promise for increasing food production sustainably. It is likely that a combination of solutions will be necessary to alleviate problems of hunger and poverty.

11. Globalization and the global economy are threatening many of the smaller groups of indigenous peoples of the world.

12. Ethical considerations alone are a sufficient reason these peoples should be allowed to remain in their communities, on their traditional lands, living in the ways of their ancestors, if that is their choice. Pragmatic considerations are also important because these people still retain a vast body of knowledge—knowledge that is of great potential value to all humanity.

13. Science has already adapted several important medicines and treatments from indigenous peoples. Many other plants with medical value will probably be discovered, if the tropical forests and the cultural knowledge of their indigenous inhabitants last long enough.

14. Adaptive wisdom is to be found in the traditions of indigenous peoples. Land races of important crops still survive and might contain genetic materials from which useful foods might someday be bred. Crops that today are used primarily by indigenous peoples—such as amaranth, quinoa, tepary bean, and the winged bean—might eventually have worldwide significance. Nonfood plants are also important as insecticides, oils, fibers, and other products.

15. Indigenous people provide us with alternative cultural models that should reduce our anxieties about the likelihood of eventual decline in our material living standards. The diversity of the human species shows that we can live meaningful and wholly satisfying lives without the technologies and huge quantities of consumer goods we consider necessary to our economic welfare. The remaining preindustrial cultures allow us to see that there is more than one narrow road to personal fulfillment, cultural health, and national dignity and prestige.

Key Terms

applied anthropology	technology transfer
scarcity explanation of hunger	solution
	indigenous peoples
inequality explanation of hunger	

Suggested Readings

Applied anthropology:

Bodley, John H. *Anthropology and Contemporary Human Problems.* 3rd ed. Mountain View, Calif.: Mayfield, 1996.

A good place to start in glimpsing the relevance of anthropology to modern problems. Provides insights on war, poverty and hunger, population, and environmental destruction.

Durham, William H. *Scarcity and Survival in Central America.* Stanford, Calif.: Stanford University Press. 1979.

This study of El Salvador is one of the most convincing analyses of the scarcity and inequality approaches to hunger and poverty.

Harris, Marvin, and Eric B. Ross. *Death, Sex, and Fertility: Population Regulation in Preindustrial and Developing Societies.* New York: Columbia, 1987.

Two noted anthropologists argue that fertility and other population characteristics of human groups result from material forces. At various times in history, people have successfully controlled (regulated) their numbers. An excellent place to start for an overview of the relationships among population, adaptation, and culture.

Lappé, Frances Moore, Joseph Collins, and Peter Rosset. *World Hunger: Twelve Myths.* 2nd ed. New York: Grove, 1998.

Argues against the scarcity explanation of hunger and provides evidence and analysis in support of the inequality explanation.

Podolefsky, Aaron, and Peter J. Brown. *Applying Cultural Anthropology: An Introductory Reader.* 4th ed. Mountain View, Calif.: Mayfield, 1999.

Contains 41 articles on the applications of cultural anthropology. A good source of case studies for students.

Indigenous peoples:

Bodley, John. *Victims of Progress.* 4th ed. Palo Alto, Calif.: Mayfield, 1999.

A good overview of tribal peoples in the modern world and how they are being destroyed by industrial civilization.

Cultural Survival. *State of the Peoples: A Global Human Rights Report on Societies in Danger.* Boston: Beacon Press, 1993.

Together with other publications of the Cultural Survival organization, an excellent source on the threats to indigenous peoples around the world.

Davis, Shelton H. *Victims of the Miracle: Development and the Indians of Brazil.* Cambridge: Cambridge University Press, 1977.

A study discussing economic development in Brazil and the resulting destruction of Indian communities.

Denslow, Julie Sloan, and Christine Padoch, eds. *People of the Tropical Rain Forest.* Berkeley: University of California Press, 1988.

Written for the general public, this work is a broad introduction to both indigenous and recent peoples living in the tropical rain forests of Latin America, Asia, and Africa. Some articles discuss what can be learned from indigenous peoples about developing the forest in a sustainable manner.

Plotkin, Mark J. *Tales of a Shaman's Apprentice.* New York: Penguin, 1993.

In part an adventure story of an ethnobotanist, this book describes the author's experiences in the Amazon forest while searching for useful medicines. An interesting place to start for an overview of the medical knowledge of indigenous peoples.

Media Resources

The Wadsworth Anthropology Resource Center
academic.cengage.com/anthropology

The Wadsworth discipline resource website that accompanies *Humanity: An Introduction to Cultural Anthropology,* Eighth Edition, includes a rich array of material, including online anthropological video clips, to help you in the study of cultural anthropology and the specific topics covered in this chapter. Other material includes a case study forum with excerpts from various Wadsworth authors, map exercises, scientist interviews, breaking news in anthropology, and links to additional useful online material. Begin by selecting Cultural Anthropology to take you to videos, research, and more. From the homepage, you may also select Applied Anthropology, which directs you to essays, glossary terms, the case study forum, and a list of internships and careers in anthropology.

GLOSSARY

accommodation The creation of social and political systems that provide for and support ethnic group differences.

acculturation The cultural changes that occur whenever members of two cultural traditions come into contact.

aesthetic Qualities that make objects, actions, or language more beautiful or pleasurable, according to culturally relative and variable standards.

affines In-laws, or people related by marriage.

agriculture Intentional planting, cultivation, care, and harvest of domesticated food plants (crops).

ambilocal residence Residence form in which couples choose whether to live with the wife's or the husband's family.

ancestral cults A type of communal cult centered around rituals performed to worship or please a kin group's ancestors.

animism Belief in spiritual beings.

anthropological linguistics Subfield that focuses on the interrelationships between language and other aspects of a people's culture.

anthropology The academic discipline that studies all of humanity from a broad perspective.

applied anthropology Subfield whose practitioners use anthropological methods, theories, and concepts to solve practical, real-world problems; practitioners are often employed by a governmental agency or private organization.

archaeology The investigation of past cultures through excavation of material remains.

art Any human action that modifies the utilitarian nature of something for the primary purpose of enhancing its aesthetic qualities; or actions, objects, or words that are valued largely for their aesthetic pleasure or symbolic communication.

artificial countries Multinationality countries created by external powers; usually applied to former colonies.

assimilation The merging of the members of one ethnic group into another, with the consequent abandonment of the former group's identity.

authority The recognized right of an individual to command another to act in a particular way; legitimate power.

avunculocal residence Residence form in which couples live with or near the mother's brother of the husband.

balanced reciprocity The exchange of goods considered to have roughly equal value; social purposes usually motivate the exchange.

band A small foraging group with flexible composition that migrates seasonally.

big men Political leaders who do not occupy formal offices and whose leadership is based on influence, not authority.

bilateral kinship Kinship system in which individuals trace their kinship relationships equally through both parents.

bilocal residence Postmarital residence in which couples move between the households of both sets of parents.

biological determinism The idea that biologically (genetically) inherited differences between populations are important influences on cultural differences between them.

biological/physical anthropology Major subfield of anthropology that studies the biological dimensions of humans and other primates.

body arts Artificial artistic enhancement or beautification of the human body by painting, tattooing, scarification, or other means.

bound morpheme A morpheme attached to a free morpheme to alter its meaning.

brideservice Custom in which a man spends a period of time working for the family of his wife.

bridewealth Custom in which a prospective groom and his relatives are required to transfer goods to the relatives of the bride to validate the marriage.

cargo cults Melanesian revitalization movements in which prophets claim to know secret rituals that will bring wealth (cargo).

caste Stratification system in which membership in a stratum is in theory hereditary, strata are endogamous, and contact or relationships among members of different strata are governed by explicit laws, norms, or prohibitions.

chiefdoms Centralized political systems with authority vested in formal, usually hereditary, offices or titles.

civilization A form of complex society in which many people live in cities.

clan A named unilineal descent group, some of whose members are unable to trace how they are related, but who still believe themselves to be kinfolk.

class System of stratification in which membership in a stratum can theoretically be altered and intermarriage between strata is allowed.

classifications of reality (cultural constructions of reality) Ways in which the members of a culture divide up the natural and social world into categories, usually linguistically encoded.

cognatic descent Form of descent in which relationships may be traced through both females and males.

cognatic descent group A group of relatives created by tracing relationships through both females and males.

communal cults Cults in which the members of a group cooperate to perform rituals intended to benefit all.

comparative methods Methods that test hypotheses by systematically comparing elements from many cultures.

comparative perspective The insistence by anthropologists that valid hypotheses and theories about humanity be tested with information from a wide range of cultures.

composite bands Autonomous (independent) political units consisting of several extended families that live together for most or all of the year.

configurationalism Theoretical idea that each culture historically develops its own unique thematic patterns around which beliefs, values, and behaviors are oriented.

conflict theory of inequality Theory holding that stratification benefits mainly the upper stratum and is the cause of most social unrest and other conflicts in human societies.

consanguines "Blood" relatives, or people related by birth.

consultant (informant) A member of a society who provides information to a fieldworker, often through formal interviews or surveys.

controlled historical comparisons A methodology for testing a hypothesis using historic changes in societies.

court legal systems Systems in which authority for settling disputes and punishing crimes is formally vested in a single individual or group.

courts of mediation Court systems in which the judges attempt to reach compromise solutions, based on the cultural norms and values of the parties involved, that will restore the social cohesion of the community.

courts of regulation Court systems that use codified laws, with formally prescribed rights, duties, and sanctions.

cross-cultural comparisons A methodology for testing a hypothesis using a sample of societies drawn from around the world.

cultivation Planting, caring for, and harvesting domesticated plants.

cultural anthropology (ethnology) The subfield that studies the way of life of contemporary and historically recent human populations.

cultural construction of gender The idea that the characteristics a people attribute to males and females are culturally, not biologically, determined.

cultural construction of kinship The idea that the kinship relationships a given people recognize do not perfectly reflect biological relationships; reflected in the kinship terminology.

cultural construction of reality See **classifications of reality.**

cultural determinism The notion that the beliefs and behaviors of individuals are largely programmed by their culture.

cultural identity The cultural tradition a group of people recognize as their own; the shared customs and beliefs that define how a group sees itself as distinctive.

cultural integration The interrelationships among the various components (elements, subsystems) of a cultural system.

cultural knowledge Information, skills, attitudes, conceptions, beliefs, values, and other mental components of culture that people socially learn during enculturation.

cultural materialism (materialism) Theoretical orientation holding that the main influences on cultural differences and similarities are technology, environment, and how people produce and distribute resources.

cultural relativism The notion that one should not judge the behavior of other peoples using the standards of one's own culture.

cultural universals Elements of culture that exist in all known human groups or societies.

culture (as used in this text) The socially learned knowledge and patterns of behavior shared by some group of people.

culture shock The feeling of uncertainty and anxiety an individual experiences when placed in a strange cultural setting.

descent group A group whose members believe themselves to be descended from a common ancestor.

domestication The process by which people control the distribution, abundance, and biological features of certain plants and animals in order to increase their usefulness to humans.

dowry Custom in which the family of a woman transfers property or wealth to her and/or her husband's family upon her marriage.

ecclesiastical cults Highly organized cults in which a full-time priesthood performs rituals believed to benefit believers or the whole society, usually in large buildings dedicated to religious purposes or deities; found in complex societies.

egalitarian society Form of society in which there is little inequality in access to culturally valued rewards.

enculturation (socialization) The transmission (by means of social learning) of cultural knowledge to the next generation.

endogamous rules Marriage rules requiring individuals to marry some member of their own social group or category.

Eskimo terminology Kinship terminology system in which no nuclear family kin term is extended to more distant relatives; nuclear family members have unique terms.

ethnic boundary markers Any overt characteristics that can be used to indicate ethnic group membership.

ethnic cleansing The elimination or removal of an unwanted ethnic group or groups from a country or a particular geographical region; usually involves genocide and/or relocation of the population.

ethnic group A named social group based on perceptions of shared ancestry, cultural traditions, and common history that culturally distinguish that group from other groups.

ethnic homogenization The attempt to create a single ethnic group in a particular geographical region.

ethnocentrism The attitude or opinion that the morals, values, and customs of one's own culture are superior to those of other peoples.

ethnogenesis The creation of a new ethnic group.

ethnographic fieldwork Collection of information from living people about their way of life; see also **fieldwork.**

ethnographic methods Research methodologies used to describe a contemporary or historically recent culture.

ethnography A written description of the way of life of some human population.

ethnohistoric research The study of past cultures using written accounts and other documents.

ethnohistory See **ethnohistoric research.**

ethnology The study of human cultures from a comparative perspective; often used as a synonym for cultural anthropology.

evolutionary psychology (sociobiology) Scientific approach emphasizing that humans are animals and so are subject to similar evolutionary forces as other animals; associated with the hypothesis that behavior patterns enhance inclusive fitness.

exogamous rules Marriage rules prohibiting individuals from marrying a member of their own social group or category.

extended family A group of related nuclear families.

feud A method of dispute settlement in self-help legal systems involving multiple but balanced killings between members of two or more kin groups.

fictive kinship Condition in which people who are not biologically related behave as if they are relatives of a certain type.

fieldwork Ethnographic research that involves observing and interviewing the members of a culture to describe their current way of life.

foraging Adaptations based on the harvest of wild (undomesticated) plants and animals.

forced assimilation The social absorption of one ethnic group by another ethnic group through the use of force.

forensic anthropology A specialization of physical anthropology that identifies and analyzes human skeletal remains; forensic anthropologists usually work for or consult with law enforcement agencies.

form of descent How a people trace their descent from previous generations.

free morpheme A morpheme that can be used alone.

functional theory of inequality Theory holding that stratification is a way to reward individuals who contribute most to society's well-being.

functionalism Theoretical orientation that analyzes cultural elements in terms of their useful effects to individuals or to the persistence of the whole society.

gender crossing Custom by which a person of one sex is allowed to adopt the roles and behavior of the opposite sex, with little or no stigma or punishment.

gender (sex) roles The rights and duties individuals have because of their perceived identities as males, females, or another gender category.

gender stratification The degree to which males and females are unequal in dimensions such as status, power or influence, access to valued resources, eligibility for social positions, and ability to make decisions about their own lives.

generalized reciprocity The giving of goods without expectation of a return of equal value at any definite future time.

genocide The deliberate attempt to eliminate the members of an ethnic category or cultural tradition.

global economy The buying and selling of goods and services in an integrated global market.

global trade The direct or indirect exchange of goods and products between peoples from all regions of the world.

globalization The process of integrating the world's peoples economically, socially, politically, and culturally into a single world system or community.

grammar Total system of linguistic knowledge that allows the speakers of a language to send meaningful messages that hearers can understand.

group marriage Several women and several men are married to one another simultaneously.

Hawaiian terminology Kin terminology system in which only sex and generation are relevant in defining labeled categories of relatives.

herding Adaptations based on tending, breeding, and harvesting the products of domesticated animals (livestock).

hierarchical nesting Occurs when an ethnic group is part of a larger collection of ethnic groups, which together constitute a higher level of ethnic identity.

historic archaeology Field that investigates the past of literate peoples through excavation of sites and analysis of artifacts and other material remains.

historical particularism (historicism) The theoretical orientation emphasizing that each culture is the unique product of all the influences to which it was subjected in its past, making cross-cultural generalizations questionable.

historicism *See* **historical particularism.**

holistic perspective The assumption that any aspect of a culture is integrated with other aspects, so that no dimension of culture can be understood in isolation.

homeland A geographical region over which a particular ethnic group feels it has exclusive rights.

horticulture A method of cultivation in which hand tools powered by human muscles are used and in which land use is extensive.

household A dwelling or compound whose composition is culturally variable but lived in by people, usually relatives or fictive kin, who cooperate for some purposes and share some resources; a kin group of one or more nuclear families who live in the same physical space.

human variation Physical differences among human populations; an interest of physical anthropologists.

humanistic approach Theoretical orientation that rejects attempts to explain culture in general in favor of achieving an empathetic understanding of particular cultures.

hunting and gathering *See* **foraging.**

ideology Ideas and beliefs that legitimize and reinforce inequalities in stratified societies.

incest taboo Prohibition against sexual intercourse between certain kinds of relatives.

incipient courts Court systems in which judicial authorities meet, frequently informally, in private to discuss issues and determine solutions to be imposed. Evidence is not formally collected, and the parties involved in these cases are not formally consulted.

indigenous peoples Culturally distinct peoples who have occupied a region longer than peoples who have colonized or immigrated to the region.

individualistic cults Cults based on personal relationships between specific individuals and specific supernatural powers.

inequality Degree to which individuals, groups, and categories differ in their access to rewards.

inequality explanation of hunger Notion that hunger is not caused by absolute scarcity but by the unequal distribution of resources and how these resources are used.

influence The ability to convince people they should act as you suggest.

initiation rite A rite held to mark the transition, usually to sexual maturity, of an individual or a group of individuals of the same sex.

innovation The creation of a new cultural trait by combining two or more existing traits.

intellectual (or cognitive) approach The notion that religious beliefs provide explanations for puzzling things and events.

intensive agriculture A system of cultivation in which plots are planted annually or semiannually; usually uses irrigation, natural fertilizers, and (in the Old World) plows powered by animals.

interpretive anthropologists Contemporary theorists who analyze cultural elements by explicating their meanings to people and understanding them in their local context; generally emphasize cultural diversity and the unique qualities of particular cultures.

interviewing Collecting cultural data by systematic questioning; may be structured (using questionnaires) or unstructured (open-ended).

Iroquois terminology Kinship terminology system in which Ego calls parallel cousins the same terms as siblings, calls father's brother the same as father, calls mother's sister the same as mother, and uses unique terms for the children of father's sister and mother's brother.

key consultant (informant) A member of a society who is especially knowledgeable about some subject, and who supplies information to a fieldworker.

kin group A group of people who culturally conceive themselves to be relatives, cooperate in certain activities, and share a sense of identity as kinfolk.

kin terms The words (labels) that an individual uses to refer to his or her relatives of various kinds.

kindred All the bilateral relatives of an individual.

kinship terminology The logically consistent system by which people classify their relatives into labeled categories, or into "kinds of relatives."

law A kind of social control characterized by the presence of authority, intention of universal application, obligation, and sanction.

levirate Custom whereby a widow marries a male relative (usually a brother) of her deceased husband.

life course The changes in expected activities, roles, rights and obligations, and social relationships individuals experience as they move through culturally defined age categories.

limited-purpose money Money that may be used to purchase only a few kinds of goods.

lineage A unilineal descent group larger than an extended family whose members can actually trace how they are related.

linguistic relativity hypothesis See **Sapir-Whorf hypothesis.**

market Exchange by means of buying and selling, using money.

marriage alliances The relationships created between families or kin groups by intermarriage.

materialism See **cultural materialism.**

matrifocal family Family group consisting of a mother and her children, with a male only loosely attached or not present at all.

matrilineal descent Form of descent in which individuals trace their primary kinship relationships through their mothers.

matrilocal residence Residence form in which couples live with or near the wife's parents.

medical anthropology The subfield that researches the connections between cultural beliefs and habits and the spread and treatment of diseases and illnesses.

monogamy Each individual is allowed to have only one spouse at a time.

morpheme A combination of phonemes that communicates a standardized meaning.

morphology The study of the units of meaning in language.

multiple gender identities Definitions of sexual identities beyond the female and male duality, including third and fourth genders such as man–woman or woman–man.

myths Stories that recount the deeds of supernatural powers and cultural heroes in the past.

nationality An ethnic group that claims a right to a discrete homeland and to political autonomy and self-determination.

negative reciprocity Exchange motivated by the desire to obtain goods, in which the parties try to gain all the material goods they can.

neoevolutionism "New evolutionism," or the mid-twentieth-century rebirth of evolutionary approaches to the theoretical study of culture.

neolocal residence Residence form in which a couple establishes a separate household apart from both the husband's and the wife's parents.

nomadism Seasonal mobility, often involving migration to high-altitude areas during the hottest and driest parts of the year.

nonunilineal descent Form of descent in which individuals do not regularly associate with either matrilineal or patrilineal relatives, but make choices about whom to live with, whose land to use, and so forth.

norms Shared ideals and/or expectations about how certain people ought to act in given situations.

nuclear family Family group consisting of a married couple and their offspring.

Omaha terminology Kinship terminology system associated with patrilineal descent in which Ego's mother's relatives are distinguished only by their sex.

origin myth The collective history of an ethnic group that defines which subgroups are part of it and its relationship to other ethnic groups.

paleoanthropology The specialization of physical anthropology that investigates the biological evolution of the human species.

participant observation The main technique used in conducting ethnographic fieldwork, involving living among a people and participating in their daily activities.

passive assimilation The voluntary social absorption of one ethnic group by another ethnic group.

pastoralism Adaptation in which the needs of livestock for naturally occurring pasture and water greatly influence the movements of groups.

patrilineal descent Form of descent in which individuals trace their most important kinship relationships through their fathers.

patrilocal residence Residence form in which couples live with or near the husband's parents.

patterns of behavior Within a single culture, the behavior that most people perform when they are in certain culturally defined situations.

peasants Rural people who are integrated into a larger society politically and economically.

performance arts Forms of art such as music, percussion, song, dance, and theater/drama that involve sound and/or stylized body movements.

phoneme The smallest unit of sound that speakers unconsciously recognize as distinctive from other sounds; when one phoneme is substituted for another in a morpheme, the meaning of the morpheme alters.

phonology The study of the sound system of language.

polyandry One woman is allowed to have multiple husbands.

polygamy Multiple spouses.

polygyny One man is allowed to have multiple wives.

postmarital residence pattern Where the majority of newly married couples establish their own residence.

postmodernists Those who follow the philosophical viewpoint that emphasizes the relativity of all knowledge, including that of science; focus on how the knowledge of a particular time and place is constructed, especially on how power relations affect the creation and spread of ideas and beliefs.

practicing anthropology The subfield that usually includes anthropologists whose primary employment is in nonacademic organizations, such as corporations, schools, government agencies, nonprofit organizations, and the like.

prehistoric archaeology Field that uses excavation of sites and analysis of material remains to investigate cultures that existed before the development of writing.

priest A kind of religious specialist, often full-time, who officiates at rituals.

primatology The study of primates, including monkeys and apes; subfield of biological anthropology.

psychological approach The notion that the emotional or affective satisfactions people gain from religion are primary.

ranked society Society that has a limited number of high-ranking social positions that grant authority; groups are ranked relative to one another, with the highest rank bringing the highest rewards in prestige, power, and sometimes wealth.

reasonable-person model A model used in legal reasoning that basically asks how a reasonable individual should have acted under these circumstances.

reciprocity The transfer of goods for goods between two or more individuals or groups.

redistribution The collection of goods or money from a group, followed by a reallocation to the group by a central authority.

refugees Individuals and families who temporarily take up residence in another region or country to escape famine, warfare, or some other life-threatening event.

relocation The forced removal of the members of a particular ethnic group from one geographical region to another.

revitalization movement A religious movement explicitly intended to create a new way of life for a society or group.

rite of passage A public ceremony or ritual recognizing and making a transition from one group or status to another.

ritual Organized, stereotyped, symbolic behaviors intended to influence supernatural powers.

role Rights and duties that individuals assume because of their perceived personal identity or membership in a social group. Also, the social and/or economic position a field researcher defines for him- or herself in the community being studied.

Sapir-Whorf hypothesis The idea that language profoundly shapes the perceptions and worldview of its speakers.

scarcity explanation of hunger Holds that there are not enough land, water, and other resources to feed all the people of a country or region an adequate diet, given current technology.

scientific approach Theoretical notion that human cultural differences and similarities can be explained in the same sense as biologists explain life and its evolution.

secular ideology An ideology that does not rely on the will of supernatural powers but justifies inequality on the basis of its societywide benefits.

segregation The enforced separation of ethnic groups, in which the dominant ethnic group places legal restrictions on the actions of the members of the other group.

self-help legal systems Informal legal systems in societies without centralized political systems, in which authorities who settle disputes are defined by the circumstances of the case.

semantic domain A class of things or properties that are perceived as alike in some fundamental respect; hierarchically organized.

sexual dimorphism Physical differences based on genetic differences between females and males.

sexual (gendered) division of labor The kinds of productive activities (tasks) that are assigned to women versus men in a culture.

shaman (medicine man) Part-time religious specialist who uses his special relationship to supernatural powers for curing members of his group and harming members of other groups.

shamanistic cults Cults in which certain individuals (shamans) have relationships with supernatural powers that ordinary people lack.

simple bands Autonomous or independent political units, often consisting of little more than an extended family, with informal leadership vested in one of the older family members.

social anthropology *See* **cultural anthropology (ethnology)**.

social control Mechanisms by which behavior is constrained and directed into acceptable channels, thus maintaining conformity.

social distance The degree to which cultural norms specify that two individuals or groups should be helpful to, intimate with, or emotionally attached to one another.

socialization The process of social learning of culture by children.

society A territorially distinct and largely self-perpetuating group whose members have a sense of collective identity and who share a common language and culture.

sociobiology *See* **evolutionary psychology**.

sociocultural anthropology *See* **cultural anthropology (ethnology)**.

sociolinguistics Specialty within cultural anthropology that studies how language is related to culture and the social uses of speech.

sociological approach The effects of religion on maintaining the institutions of society as a whole by instilling common values, creating solidarity, controlling behavior, and so forth.

sodalities Formal institutions that cut across communities and serve to unite geographically scattered groups; may be based on kin groups (clans or lineages) or on non–kin-based groups (age grades or warrior societies).

sorcery The performance of rites and spells for the purpose of causing harm to others by supernatural means.

sororate Custom whereby a widower marries a female relative of his deceased wife.

state A centralized, multilevel political unit characterized by the presence of a bureaucracy that acts on behalf of the ruling elite.

stereotyping Having preconceived mental images of a group that bias the way one perceives group members and interprets their behavior.

stratified society Society with marked and largely or partly heritable differences in access to wealth, power, and prestige; inequality is based mainly on unequal access to productive and valued resources.

subculture Cultural differences characteristic of members of various ethnic groups, regions, religions, and so forth within a single society or country.

subnationality A dependent subgroup within a larger nationality that lacks the concept of a separate homeland and makes no claim to any inherent right to political autonomy and self-determination.

surplus The amount of food (or other goods) a worker produces in excess of the consumption of herself or himself and her or his dependents.

symbols Objects, behaviors, sound combinations, and other phenomena whose culturally defined meanings have no necessary relationship to their inherent physical qualities.

technology-transfer solution The notion that developing nations can best solve their hunger problems by adopting the technology and production methods of modern mechanized agriculture.

tone languages Languages in which changing voice pitch within a word alters the entire meaning of the word.

totemism A form of communal cult in which all members of a kin group have mystical relationships with one or more natural objects.

transnational corporation A company that produces and sells most of its products or services outside its "home" country.

transnationals Members of an ethnic community living outside their country of origin.

tribe An autonomous political unit encompassing a number of distinct, geographically dispersed communities that are held together by sodalities.

tribute The rendering of goods (typically including food) to an authority such as a chief.

unilineal descent Descent through "one line," including patrilineal and matrilineal descent.

unilineal descent group A group of relatives, all of whom are related through only one sex.

unilineal evolution The nineteenth-century theoretical orientation that held that all human ways of life pass through a similar sequence of stages in their development.

unilineally extended families Family grouping formed by tracing kinship relationships through only one sex, either female or male, but not both.

values Shared ideas or standards about the worthwhileness of goals and lifestyles.

vision quest The attempt to enlist the aid of supernatural powers by intentionally seeking a dream or vision.

visual arts Arts that are produced in a material or tangible form, including basketry, pottery, textiles, paintings, drawings, sculptures, masks, carvings, and the like.

witchcraft The use of psychic powers to harm others by supernatural means.

worldview The way people interpret reality and events, including how they see themselves relating to the world around them.

NOTES

CHAPTER 1—THE STUDY OF HUMANITY

Subfields of Anthropology

Clyde Snow (1995) describes his forensic work in Argentina and northern Iraq. Additional material is in McDonald (1995).

CHAPTER 2—CULTURE

Tylor's definition of culture is from Tylor (1871, 1).

Defining Culture

The distinction between trial and error and social learning is from Boyd and Richerson (1985) and Pulliam and Dunford (1980), who also discuss the advantages of social learning. The material on the Yanomamö and Semai is drawn from Chagnon (1983) and Dentan (1968), respectively.

Cultural Knowledge

Edward Hall's two early books (1959, 1966) were among the first to systematically discuss the importance of nonverbal communication in everyday social interaction. Information on Navajo witchcraft comes from Kluckhohn (1967). Reichel-Dolmatoff (1971) describes shamanism among the Tukano. Aveni (1995) is a wonderful book describing how some cultures experience and measure the passage of time.

The Origins of Culture

Factual material is from Lieberman (2007) and Bouzouggar and Barton et al. (2007). Interpretations and speculations are ours.

Biology and Cultural Differences

Extended coverage of cultural universals is provided in D. Brown (1991).

CHAPTER 3—CULTURE AND LANGUAGE

Five Properties of Language

Information on the five distinguishing features of human language is from Hockett's (1960) seminal discussion.

How Language Works

The examples on Thai aspiration and Nupe tones are taken from Fromkin and Rodman's (1988) textbook. The author's (J. P.) own knowledge is the basis for the discussion of the Kosraen language.

Language and Culture

Concise descriptions and discussions of the Sapir-Whorf hypothesis are in D. Brown (1991). Reviews by Leavitt (2006), Lucy (1997), and P. Brown (2006) helped with the updated material on linguistic relativity.

Social Uses of Speech

See Farb (1974) and Trudgill (1983) on male and female speech and on Javanese "levels" of speech. Chagnon (1983) discusses the Yanomamö name taboo. We thank Kathryn Meyer and Gary deCoker for help with the example of Japanese honorifics.

CHAPTER 4—THE DEVELOPMENT OF ANTHROPOLOGICAL THOUGHT

Main Issues Today

Kuwayama (2004) provided part of the inspiration for this section.

The Emergence of Anthropology

Unilineal evolutionary theory is best known from the works of Tylor (1865, 1871) and Morgan (1877). The times and places of the founding of the first anthropology programs in the United States are from Black (1991).

Anthropological Thought in the Early Twentieth Century

The best single source of writings on Boas is a collection of his articles (1966). The critique of historical particularist assumptions is taken from Harris (1968). Malinowski's ideas about the functions of institutions, behaviors, and beliefs were first presented in a 1944 book, reprinted as Malinowski (1960). Good sources on structural-functionalism are Radcliffe-Brown (1922, 1965) and Nadel (1951).

The Rebirth of Evolutionism in the Mid-Twentieth Century

See Leslie White (1949, 1959). Steward's most influential articles appear in two volumes (1955, 1977).

Anthropological Thought Today: Divisions

The general discussion of the scientific-humanistic division is from our own knowledge and interpretations.

Scientific Approaches

Dawkins (1976) and E. O. Wilson (1975, 1978) were instrumental works that popularized sociobiology. Books by Marvin Harris (1977, 1979, 1985) were influential in the development of modern materialist thought. Harris's work and M. Cohen (1977) emphasized the importance of population pressure. Harris (1999) is an introduction to his own variety of materialist theory. Sanderson (1999, 2007) provides nice summaries of current evolutionary theory and defends it from both old and new critics.

Humanistic Approaches

On interpretive anthropology, good sources are early works by Geertz (1973, 1980).

CHAPTER 5—METHODS OF INVESTIGATION

Ethnographic Methods

The discussion of how to evaluate a particular historical account was influenced by Naroll (1962). See also Hickerson (1970) on ethnohistoric methods. See Fogelson (1989) for a discussion of interpretation of historical events. The discussion of suicide in the Trobriand Islands is derived from Malinowski (1926). The problems of collecting genealogies among the Yanomamö are recounted by Chagnon (1983).

Comparative Methods

The cross-cultural test of the sorcery and social control hypothesis is from B. Whiting (1950). See Adams (1982, 1988) for an excellent example of what can be done with historical data. Data on matrilineal and patrilineal societies are from Bailey (1989). For A Closer Look on Captain Cook, see Sahlins (1981, 1995) and Obeyesekere (1992). For information on ethics, see the website of the American Anthropological Association (www.aaanet.org/committees/ethics/ethics.htm). Information on the Pat Roberts Intelligence Scholars Program can be found on a variety of websites.

CHAPTER 6—CULTURE AND NATURE: INTERACTING WITH THE ENVIRONMENT

Foraging

Dobyns (1983) provided most of the information on the distribution of foragers in North America used in Figure 6.1. Denevan (1992) and Krech (1999) discuss the use of fire to provide habitat for game animals among prehistoric Native Americans. Information on specific foragers is taken from the following sources: BaMbuti (Turnbull 1962), Hadza (Woodburn 1968), Netsilik (Balikci 1970), Western Shoshone (Steward 1938, 1955), Ju/'hoansi (Lee 1969, 1979, 2003), and Northwest Coast (Ferguson 1984; Piddocke 1965; Suttles 1960, 1962, 1968). Information on the recent endangering of the Ju/'hoansi is from Lee (2003); on the Hadza from *The Japan Times,* June 19, 2007, p. 7. Comparative information on foraging working hours is from Sahlins (1972) and Kelly (1995).

Domestication

Smith (1995) is a readable book covering the origins of farming in various world regions. Diamond (1997) summarizes dates and places of plant and animal domestication and also provides reasons for both developments. Recent sources consulted on the origins of plant domestication are Dillehay et al. (2007) and Pickersgill (2007).

Horticulture

M. Cohen (1989) provides an overview of evidence about the health of prehistoric foragers. Sources used to draw the North American portion of the map on the distribution of horticulture are Dobyns (1983) and Doolittle (1992). Material on shifting cultivation is from Conklin (1957), Freeman (1970), and Ruddle (1974). See Bradfield (1971) on dry-land gardening among the Pueblo (mainly the Hopi).

Intensive Agriculture

Differences between extensive and intensive agriculture are described in Boserup (1965) and Grigg (1974). Material on intensive agriculture in the New World is drawn from our general knowledge and from Donkin (1979). On peasant revolts, see E. Wolf (1969). Johnson and Earle (1987) analyze the relationship between intensification and cultural evolution.

Pastoralism

Porter (1965) discusses the subsistence risk-reduction benefit of pastoralism. Schneider (1981) shows the negative relationship between the distribution of the tsetse fly and cattle pastoralism in Africa. A short source on the Karimojong is Dyson-Hudson and Dyson Hudson (1969).

CHAPTER 7—EXCHANGE IN ECONOMIC SYSTEMS

Sahlins (1965) first distinguished the three forms of exchange.

Reciprocity

Malinowski (1922) describes Trobriand *wasi.* The Maring discussion is from Rappaport (1968) and Peoples (1982). Lee (1979, 2003) describes Ju/'hoansi sharing, which he sees as the key to their ability to keep their work levels low and their nutritional status high. Kelly (1995) generalizes some of Lee's points to other foragers in his excellent large-scale synthesis of the foraging adaptation

Redistribution

Alkire (1977), Sahlins (1958), D. Oliver (1989), and Peoples (1985) describe tribute in Micronesia and Polynesia.

Market Exchange

See Neale (1976) on money. Schneider (1981) describes some African monies. Pospisil (1978) discusses the multiple uses of money among Kapauku. Bohannan (1955) describes Tiv exchange spheres. On Philippine *suki,* see W. G. Davis (1973).

CHAPTER 8—MARRIAGES AND FAMILIES

Incest Taboos

Tylor (1888) first proposed the "marry out or die out" theory. "Familiarity breeds disinterest" was originally the idea of Westermarck (1926). On Taiwan, see A. Wolf (1970). On Israeli kibbutz, see Shepher (1971). On Lebanese cousin marriages, see McCabe (1983).

Marriage

The material on Nayar "marriage" is from Gough (1959). Hart, Pilling, and Goodale (1988) describe Tiwi marriage and other aspects of Tiwi culture. J. Goodale (1971) provides information about Tiwi wives. Information on the Na is from Hua (2001).

Marriage in Comparative Perspective

Goldstein (1987) describes Tibetan polyandry and its advantages to husbands and the wife. Chagnon (1983) discusses the importance of marriage alliances among the Yanomamö. The challenges of Tierney (2000) do not alter Chagnon's conclusions about marriage alliances. Kuper (1963) describes Swazi bridewealth. See Lee (1979, 240–242) on Ju/'hoansi brideservice. See Goody and Tambiah (1973) and Harrell and Dickey (1985) on dowry. Material on Indian "dowry deaths" is from our general knowledge and a report in the *Columbus Dispatch* (July 25, 2004, p. A13).

Postmarital Residence Patterns

The frequencies of different residence patterns are as reported in Pasternak (1976, 44). Among those who have discussed the influences on residence patterns are Ember and Ember (1971, 1972) and Pasternak (1976).

Family and Household Forms

Murdock (1949) first suggested how forms of postmarital residence produce various forms of the family and household. Pasternak, Ember, and Ember (1976) suggest an economic hypothesis for why extended families exist.

CHAPTER 9—KINSHIP AND DESCENT

Unilineal Descent

Data on the frequencies of patrilineal and matrilineal descent are from Divale and Harris (1976). Firth (1936, 1965) describes the functions of Tikopian lineages and clans. See Eggan (1950) on Hopi matrilineal descent.

Nonunilineal Descent

Cognatic descent in Polynesia is discussed in Firth (1968), Howard and Kirkpatrick (1989), and D. Oliver (1989). The Samoan *'aiga* is described in M. Ember (1959), Holmes and Holmes (1992), and D. Oliver (1989). Material on the Iban kindred is from Freeman (1968, 1970).

Classifying Relatives: Kinship Terminologies

Aberle (1961) and Pasternak (1976) provide statistical data on the general, but imperfect, correlation between forms of descent and terminological systems.

Chapter 10—Enculturation and the Life Course

Diversity in Child Care

Information on Ju/'hoansi breast-feeding is from Shostak (1983). Howard and Millard (1997) report on the Chagga. Jim Peoples personally observed how Micronesian newborns take attention away from the next-youngest child. Among others, Dozier (1970, 179) reports the Hopi use of "ogre" *kachinas* to frighten misbehaving children.

Two African Examples

The description of the Aka is based on Hewlett (1992). Information about the Gusii is from LeVine et al. (1994). The comparisons of the two are our own.

Life Course

The stages of a Gusii female's life are given in LeVine et al. (1994, 81–82). The Cheyenne concept of abortion is from Llewellyn and Hoebel (1941). Sheper-Hughes (1992) describes the choices poor mothers must make in northeast Brazil. The description of the Osage child-naming rite is based on LaFlesche (1928). The material on whether Samoan young women experience all the stresses and strains typical of American adolescents is based on Mead (1928) and Freeman (1983). Information on drunkenness by young men from Chuuk, Micronesia, is from Marshall (1979), and personal observations by Jim Peoples. Cheyenne adolescence is mentioned in Hoebel (1978). The analysis of the phases known as separation, liminality, and incorporation is from V. Turner (1967). The general information on New Guinea beliefs about feminine pollution and male initiation rituals is synthesized from the case studies of Herdt (1987), Meggitt (1970), Meigs (1988), and Wormsley (1993). Detailed material on the Awa is from Newman and Boyd (1982). On the Apache girls' ceremony, see Farrer (1996). Wallace and Hoebel (1952) provided information on the treatment of the elderly among the Comanche. On the Inuit treatment of the elderly, see Hoebel (1954). Thanks to Brenda Robb Jenike for permission to use her unpublished material (n.d.) on the care of Japanese elderly.

Chapter 11—Gender in Comparative Perspective

Cultural Construction of Gender

The Hua material is from Meigs (1988, 1990). T. Cohen (2000) is an excellent reader on masculinity.

The Sexual Division of Labor

Table 11.1 was constructed from data in Murdock and Provost (1973). On female hunting among BaMbuti Pygmies and Agta, see Turnbull (1962) and Estioko-Griffin (1986), respectively. On the possibility that strenuous exercise inhibits ovulation, see Graham (1985). The influence of female child care responsibilities on the sexual division of labor was first made forcibly by J. Brown (1970a). The discussion of why female contributions to subsistence tend to decline with intensification uses information in C. Ember (1983), Martin and Voorhies (1975), Boserup (1970), Burton and White (1984), and White, Burton, and Dow (1981). The Kofyar material is from Stone, Stone, and McC. Netting (1995).

Gender Crossing and Multiple Gender Identities

The primary source of information consulted on Native American peoples is Roscoe (2000). Nanda (2000) also is a source of the conceptual discussion. Information on the Zuni is from Roscoe (1991). Hoebel (1978) discusses the Cheyenne *berdache.*

Gender Stratification

The general discussion in this section relies on material in di Leonardo (1991), Leacock (1978), Morgen (1989), Rosaldo and Lamphere (1974), Quinn (1977), and Sacks (1982). The information

about Andalusia is from Gilmore (1980, 1990). The suggestion that women's status improves with age in many cultures is from J. Brown (1988). Information on the Iroquois is from Albers (1989), Stockard (2002), and J. Brown (1970b). On BaMbuti and Aka sexual egalitarianism, see Turnbull (1962) and Hewlett (1992). The idea that women's control over key resources frequently leads to high overall status is discussed in Sanday (1973, 1981). Friedl (1975, 1978) was one of the first to argue that women's status in hunting and gathering cultures is positively related to the importance of women's labor in food production and to their ability to control the distribution of the products they produce. Yoruba material is from Barnes (1990). Cotter, England, and Hermsen (2007) provide numerical data on changes in womens' employment between 1970 and 2006. Schlegel (1972) and Whyte (1978) discuss why matrilineality and matrilocality tend to give women high status, all else being equal. Information on Chinese wives is from M. Wolf (1972) and our general knowledge.

Chapter 12—The Organization of Political Life

Forms of Political Organization

The definitions and ideas concerning political structure were influenced by Steward (1955), Service (1962), Cohen and Service (1978), Krader (1968), and Fried (1967). Ethnographic examples were taken from the following sources: Comanche from Hoebel (1940) and Wallace and Hoebel (1952); Tahiti from Goldman (1970); and Inca from D'Altroy (1987), Julien (1988), LaLone and LaLone (1987), LeVine (1987), and Metraux (1969). Information on international governance was taken from the websites of the United Nations (www.un.org), the World Bank (www.worldbank.org), the International Monetary Fund (www.imf.org), the World Trade Organization (www.wto.org), and the International Criminal Court (www.icc-cpi.iut).

Social Control and Law

For the basic definition of law as well as many of the concepts about legal systems, we relied on Hoebel (1954), Pospisil (1958), Fallers (1969), Bohannan (1968), Newman (1983), and Gluckman (1972, 1973). Ethnographic examples were taken from the following sources: Comanche from Hoebel (1940); Cheyenne from Llewellyn and Hoebel (1941); Nuer from Evans-Pritchard (1940); Jívaro from Harner (1973); and Barotse from Gluckman (1972, 1973). The data on global government and the World Trade Organization were taken from Chomsky (2000); "The MAI Shell Game: The World Trade Organization (WTO)" from the Public Citizen Global Trade Watch website (www.tradewatch.org); "The WTO in brief" from the World Trade Organization website (www.wto.org); and "Is Globalization Shifting Power from Nation States to Undemocratic Organizations?" from the Globalisation Guide website (www.globalisationguide.org).

Chapter 13—Social Inequality and Stratification

Systems of Equality and Inequality

The classification of societies into egalitarian, ranked, and stratified was proposed by Fried (1967). Woodburn (1982) discusses reasons for egalitarianism among foragers. The material on Tikopia is from Firth (1936). Berreman (1959) long ago noted the similarity of race relations in the American South to a caste system.

Castes in Traditional India

The Indian caste system and its relationship to Hinduism are discussed in Dumont (1980), Hiebert (1971), Mandelbaum (1970), and Tyler (1973).

Classes in Industrial Societies: The United States

Data on 2006 income inequality are from U.S. Bureau of the Census, Table 1, p. 5 (2007—http://www.census.gov/prod/2007pubs/

p60-233.pdf, retrieved November 10, 2007). Changes in the distribution of income between 1973 and 2004 are derived from DeNavas-Walt, Proctor, and Mills (2004). Information on the distribution of wealth in the United States for 2004 is from Economic Policy Institute (2007).

Maintaining Inequality

Valeri (1985) describes Hawaiian religion. Information on the effects of federal income tax cuts on the wealthiest comes from IRS data reported in the *Columbus Dispatch,* October 13, 2007.

Theories of Inequality

Davis and Moore (1945) originated the functionalist theory. Conflict theory goes back to Marx (1967, original 1867). Dahrendorf (1959) was important in formulating conflict theory in sociology. Lenski (1966) remains an excellent source comparing and evaluating the functionalist and conflict theories. Information on CEO-to-worker income ratios is from Economic Policy Institute (2007).

Chapter 14—Religion and Worldview

Defining Religion

Tylor (1871) defined religion as animism. An excellent summary of *mana* is Shore (1989). The idea that Judeo-Christian mythology helps inculcate a worldview conducive to environmental destruction is taken from Lynn White (1967). The Hopi information is from Frigout (1979) and our general knowledge.

Theories of Religion

The Trobriand magic example is from Malinowski (1954). Frazer's intellectual theory is from Frazer (1963). Geertz (1965) argues that religion provides meaning. The anthropomorphic theory is Guthrie's (1993). Malinowski (1954) argues that magic and religion alleviate anxieties during times of stress and uncertainty. Dobu beliefs about the fate of the dead are discussed in Fortune (1932, 179–188). Kwaio pollution is described in Keesing (1982). The theory that ritual behavior creates social solidarity goes back to Durkheim (1915). Swanson's (1960) cross-cultural study is influential in the sociological approach.

Supernatural Explanations of Misfortune

The distinction between imitative and contagious magic is Frazer's (1963). Fortune (1932) describes Dobu sorcery. The witchcraft examples are from Kluckhohn (1967, Navajo); M. Wilson (1951, Nyakyusa); Evans-Pritchard (1976, Zande); Offiong (1983, Ibibio); and Middleton (1965, Lugbara). Kluckhohn (1967) hypothesizes that Navajo witchcraft beliefs reduce overt, socially disruptive hostilities.

Varieties of Religious Organization

Wallace (1966) formulated and named the kinds of cults. The vision quest material is from Lowie (1954, 1956) and our general knowledge. Middleton (1965) describes the Lugbara ancestral cult. V. Turner (1967) describes women's fertility rituals among the Ndembu.

Revitalization Movements

A general description of cargo cults is in Worsley (1968). Lawrence (1964) describes several Garia movements. On Handsome Lake's movement among the Seneca, see Wallace (1969). Stewart (1980) and E. Anderson (1996) describe peyotism among Native Americans.

Chapter 15—Art and the Aesthetic

Many of the ideas for this chapter came from Hunter and Whitten (1975) and R. Anderson (1989). On Shaker art, we consulted the classic study by Andrews and Andrews (1937) and a more recent study by Kirk (1997). For changes in Chinese art, we consulted the Nelson Gallery (1975). Other sources of general information used in this chapter were

Lipman and Winchester (1974), Hobson (1987), and Harvey (1937). Specific information on art in particular cultures is drawn from Colton (1959, Hopi); Connelly (1979, Hopi); Hoebel (1978, Cheyenne); Kalb (1994, New Mexican santos); and Hail (1983, Plains Indians).

Forms of Artistic Expression

The general discussion of body arts is based primarily on Brain (1979). Information on Polynesian tattooing is from Gell (1993), Hage et al. (1995), and Simmons (1983). A 1998 research paper by undergraduate Maureen McCardel of Ohio Wesleyan University also was helpful on Polynesian tattooing.

Close (1989) provides a good summary of the archaeological debate over style versus function. Material on the Northwest Coast art is from our general knowledge, with specific points drawn from R. Anderson (1989), Boas (1955), Furst and Furst (1982), and Holm (1965, 1972). The comparative information on style in visual arts is from Fischer (1961).

We drew from the studies of Kaeppler (1978) and Lomax (1962, 1968). Good sources on *voudon* are Metraux (1972) and W. Davis's (1985) controversial book. We drew information on !Kung healing from Lee (2003) and Shostak (1983) and on Tumbuka healing from Friedson (1998). A source of case studies on various performances and healing is Laderman and Roseman (1996). An informative and heavily illustrated source for students on Native American dance is Heth (1993). For a discussion of the individual in art, see Warner (1986).

Art and Culture

Information on the use of sandpaintings and song/chants in Navajo curing ceremonials is taken from Sandner (1991), Reichard (1950, 1977), and Parezo (1991). BaMbuti *molimo* is described in Turnbull (1962). The Globalization box on Varanasi saris is based on Wax (2007) as well as on news articles from BBC News (http://news.bbc.co.uk) and the Hindu Business Line (www.thehindubusinessline.com)

Chapter 16—Globalization

The most important single source is Stavrianos (1998). Secondary information is drawn from E. Wolf (1982), Crosby (1972), and—for the period from the fifteenth through the eighteenth centuries—Braudel (1979a, 1979b) and Frank (1998). Data on the demographic effects of contact on Native American peoples are from Thornton (1987) and Dobyns (1976). Specific information on historic changes among Native Americans is from Leacock and Lurie (1971) and Kehoe (1992). Historical data on Africa and the African slave trade are from Davidson (1961, 1969), Oliver and Fage (1962), and Mintz (1986). Data on the effects of New World cultigens on Africa are primarily from Miracle (1966, 1967). Statistics on the number of Europeans in India during the 1920s are from Mayo (1927).

The Emergence of the Global Economy

For information on the global economy, we have drawn from several studies: Chomsky (2000), Giddens (2000), Hines (2000), Hutton and Giddens (2000), Klein (1999), and Robbins (1999). Information on shipping is from an article in the *Washington Post National Weekly Edition* (September 3–9, 2001) and the ShippingFacts website (www.marisec.org/shippingfact/worldtradeindex.htm). Data on U.S. debt are from the Central Intelligence Agency (2007).

Globalization: The Continuing Process

For data on immigration issues, we drew heavily from the *Migration News* (www.migration.ucdavis.edu), the U.S. Immigration and Naturalization Service website (www.ins.usdoj.gov), and the U.S. Census website (www.census.gov). Additional current data on economic, social, migration, and other issues were taken from news reports in the *Washington Post, Christian Science Monitor,* the BBC News website (www.news.bbc.co.uk), and television and radio news reports. For data on fundamentalism, we drew on news accounts as well as Harding (2000), the official website of the BJP (www.bjp .org), Giddens (2000), and the BBC News website (www.news.bbc. co.uk) for information on opposition to the conversions of Hindus to Christianity, Islam, and Buddism.

Population Growth and Inequalities in the Global Economy

Most of the twentieth-century general economic and population data were drawn from Hepner and McKee (1992), Jackson and Hudman (1990a, 1990b), the World Bank (1999), Robbins (1999), and the U.S. Census Bureau, International Data Base (www.census.gov). Data on the changing magnitude of world trade were obtained from Rostow (1978), supplemented with later data from the World Bank (1999) and the World Trade Organization website (www.wto.org). Data on Nokia are drawn from an article in the *Washington Post National Weekly Edition* (July 23–29, 2001) and from the Nokia website (www.nokia.com).

The data on malaria and smallpox are from Gladwell (2001). For data on wealth distribution, see Wealth Distribution Statistics 1999 compiled by the United Nations (www.geocities.com), the World Council of Churches (2000), and the Institute for Policy Studies, "Top 200: The Rise of Corporate Global Power" (www.ips.org).

CHAPTER 17—ETHNICITY AND ETHNIC CONFLICT

There is a vast body of literature in anthropology and sociology on ethnicity and related issues. Because the entire chapter draws on the sources given here, we have not divided these notes into sections. Our ideas on the nature and significance of ethnicity have been most strongly influenced by the studies of Barth (1958, 1969), Vincent (1974), Khlief (1979), Glazer and Moynihan (1963, 1975), Bennett (1975), Himes (1974), DeVos and Romanusci-Ross (1975), R. Cohen (1978), Tax (1967), Nietschmann (1988), Horowitz (1985), and Jackson and Hudman (1990a, 1990b). For discussions of international legal and political issues, see Alfredsson (1989) and Swepton (1989).

For additional data on particular ethnic groups and historical events, we have drawn on a number of sources: Ember and Ember (2001), Gerner (1994), Hajda and Beissinger (1990), Foster (1980), Bodley (1999), E. Wolf (1982), Stavrianos (1998), Davidson (1969), Carmack (1988), Kehoe (1992), McAlister (1973), Handler (1988), and Price (1979), as well as basic reference sources and discussions with colleagues and students from Saudi Arabia, Oman, Bangladesh, Indonesia, and Malaysia.

In addition, one of the authors (G. B.) spent the summer of 1988 in Yugoslavia and the summer of 1989 in Guatemala collecting data on ethnic identity and conflict. For information on current ethnic conflicts, including the events of September 11, 2001, we have had to rely on current news reports from the *Washington Post, Christian Science Monitor,* and BBC News (www.news.bbc.co.uk), as well as television and radio news reports. Materials for A Closer Look on Iraq were taken from news accounts as well as from Marr (1985), Tripp (2000), Izady (1992), and Houston (2001).

CHAPTER 18—WORLD PROBLEMS AND THE PRACTICE OF ANTHROPOLOGY

Applied Anthropology

The ideas about the unique contributions of anthropology to problem solving are our own. The economic interpretation of high birthrates

in the Punjabi villages was presented by Mamdani (1973). The 1982 study of the same area is reported in Nag and Kak (1984). Data on large Javanese and Nepalese families appear in B. White (1973) and Nag, White, and Peet (1978). Nardi (1981, 1983), Shankman (1976), and Small (1997) discuss the importance of remittances in Samoa and Tonga. Freed and Freed (1985) discuss why Indian couples think they need more than one son.

World Hunger

The inequality explanation of hunger is stated and defended in lay terms in Lappé and Collins (1977, 1986). Data on the Irish famine are from O'Grada (1989), Kinealy (1995), and Woodham-Smith (1991). The discussion of the effects of the "green revolution" on Javanese peasants is from Franke (1974). Johnson (1971) discusses risk minimization among peasants. The quantitative data on the energetic efficiency of various food systems are compiled from information given in Pimentel et al. (1973, 1975) and Pimentel and Pimentel (1979).

The potential value of traditional farming methods for the modern world is described in Altieri (1987) and Wilken (1987). The advantages of intercropping and other traditional methods are covered in Innis (1980), Gliessman and Grantham (1990), and Harrison (1987). Traditional resource management is covered by Alcorn (1981) and Posey (1983, 1984, 1985). Nations and Nigh (1980) discuss the potential of Lacandon Maya shifting cultivation.

Anthropologists as Advocates

The anthropologist as advocate is best discussed by Peterson (1974). The early roles of anthropologists in American Indian rights issues are discussed in Mark (1987). For Boas and the issue of racism, see Stocking (1974), and for Mead, see Mark (1999).

For the best general discussion of the evolution of European attitudes to indigenous peoples, see Berkhofer (1978). Germany's policies toward the Herero are discussed in Bodley (1999). S. Davis (1977) discusses the impact on indigenous tribes of Brazil's efforts to develop the Amazon basin. Specific material on the plight of the Yanomamö is from *Newsweek* (April 9, 1990, 34) and from the Commission for the Creation of Yanomami Park (1989a, 1989b), published in *Cultural Survival Quarterly.* On San relocation, see Hitchcock (1999); Hitchcock, Biesele, and Lee (2003); BBC news (http://news.bbc.co.uk/2/hi/Africa/6174709 and /6191185); and Survival (http://www.survival-international.org/news/2498). The Kayapó materials are from T. Turner (1989) and A. Goodale (2003). See also the Piaracu Declaration (www.irn.org/pdf/xingu/Piaracu Declaration). The Maori claim was reported in the June 15, 1996, edition of the *Columbus Dispatch.* The July 22, 1995, issue of the *Economist* reported the claims of Canada's Nisga'a. The *Business Week* issue referred to is from March 1, 1993. The examples of medicines learned about from indigenous peoples are taken from Lewis and Elvin-Lewis (1977). Farnsworth (1984) argues that many more plants will be discovered to have medical uses. A good discussion of the insights of "traditional medicine" is in Fabrega (1975). The discussion of the erosion of the genetic diversity of major food crops is from our general knowledge and Harlan (1975). The material on amaranth is from Sokolov (1986). The material on amaranth is from Sokolov (1986). Information for A Closer Look on "The Declaration on the Rights of Indigenous People" was taken from the United Nations website (www.un.org) and from the BBC news website (http://news.bbc.co.uk).

BIBLIOGRAPHY

Aberle, David F.
1961 "Matrilineal Descent in Cross-Cultural Perspective." In *Matrilineal Kinship*, edited by David M. Schneider and Kathleen Gough, pp. 655–727. Berkeley: University of California Press.

Adams, Richard N.
1982 *Paradoxical Harvest*. Cambridge: Cambridge University Press.
1988 "Energy and the Regulation of Nation States." *Cultural Dynamics* 1:46–61.

Adrian, Bonnie
2003 *Framing the Bride: Globalizing Beauty and Romance in Taiwan's Bridal Industry*. Berkeley: University of California Press.

Albers, Patricia C.
1989 "From Illusion to Illumination: Anthropological Studies of American Indian Women." In *Gender and Anthropology: Critical Reviews for Research and Teaching*, edited by Sandra Morgen, pp. 132–170. Washington, D.C.: American Anthropological Association.

Alcorn, Janice
1981 "Huastec Non-Crop Resource Management." *Human Ecology* 9:395–417.

Alexander, Richard
1974 "The Evolution of Social Behavior." *Annual Review of Ecology and Systematics* 5:325–383.

Alfredsson, Gudmundur
1989 "The United Nations and the Rights of Indigenous Peoples." *Current Anthropology* 30:255–259.

Alkire, William II.
1977 *An Introduction to the Peoples and Cultures of Micronesia*. 2nd ed. Menlo Park, Calif.: Cummings.

Allen, Michael
1984 "Elders, Chiefs, and Big Men: Authority Legitimation and Political Evolution in Melanesia." *American Ethnologist* 11:20–41.

Altieri, Miguel A.
1987 *Agroecology: The Scientific Basis of Alternative Agriculture*. Boulder, Colo.: Westview Press.

Anderson, Edward F.
1996 *Peyote: The Divine Cactus*. 2nd ed. Tucson: University of Arizona.

Anderson, Richard L.
1989 *Art in Small-Scale Societies*. 2nd ed. Englewood Cliffs, N.J.: Prentice Hall.

Andrews, Edward Deming, and Faith Andrews
1937 *Shaker Furniture: The Craftsmanship of American Communal Sects*. New Haven, Conn.: Yale University Press.

Aveni, Anthony
1995 *Empires of Time*. New York: Kodansha America.

Bailey, Garrick
1989 "Descent and Social Survival of Native Horticultural Societies of the Eastern United States." Paper presented at the American Anthropological Association meetings, Washington, D.C.

Bailey, Garrick, Daniel Swan, John Nunley, and E. Sean StandingBear
2004 *Art of the Osage*. Seattle: St. Louis Art Museum and Washington University Press.

Balikci, Asen
1970 *The Netsilik Eskimo*. Garden City, N.Y.: Natural History Press.

Barnes, Sandra T.
1990 "Women, Property, and Power." In *Beyond the Second Sex*, edited by Peggy Reeves Sanday and Ruth Gallagher Goodenough, pp. 253–280. Philadelphia: University of Pennsylvania Press.

Barth, Fredrik
1958 "Ecological Relationships of Ethnic Groups in Swat, North Pakistan." *American Anthropologist* 60:1079–1089.
1969 *Ethnic Groups and Boundaries*. Boston: Little, Brown and Company.

Benedict, Ruth
1934 *Patterns of Culture*. Boston: Houghton Mifflin.

Bennett, John, ed.
1975 "The New Ethnicity: Perspectives from Ethnology." *1973 Proceedings of the American Ethnological Society*. St. Paul, Minn.: West.

Berkhofer, Robert F., Jr.
1978 *The White Man's Indian: Images of the American Indian from Columbus to the Present*. New York: Knopf.

Bernstein, Gail
1983 *Haruko's World: A Japanese Farm Woman and Her Community*. Stanford, Calif.: Stanford University Press.

Berreman, Gerald D.
1959 "Caste in India and the United States." *American Journal of Sociology* 66:120–127.

Black, Nancy Johnson
1991 "What Is Anthropology?" In *Introduction to Library Research in Anthropology*, edited by John Weeks, pp. 1–5. Boulder, Colo.: Westview Press.

Boas, Franz
1955 *Primitive Art.* New York: Dover Publications.
1966 *Race, Language and Culture.* New York: Free Press (original 1940).

Bodley, John H.
1999 *Victims of Progress.* 4th ed. Palo Alto, Calif.: Mayfield.

Bohannan, Paul
1955 "Some Principles of Exchange and Investment Among the Tiv." *American Anthropologist* 57:60–70.
1968 *Justice and Judgement Among the Tiv.* London: Oxford University Press.

Boserup, Ester
1965 *The Conditions of Agricultural Growth.* Chicago: Aldine.
1970 *Women's Role in Economic Development.* New York: St. Martin's.

Bouzouggar, Abdeljalil, Nick Barton, et al.
2007 "82,000-Year-Old Shell Beads from North Africa and Implications for the Origins of Modern Human Behavior." *Proceedings of the National Academy of Sciences* 104:9964–9969.

Boyd, Robert, and Peter J. Richerson
1985 *Culture and the Evolutionary Process.* Chicago: University of Chicago Press.

Bradfield, Maitland
1971 "The Changing Pattern of Hopi Agriculture." Royal Anthropological Institute of Great Britain and Ireland Occasional Paper, no. 30. London: Royal Anthropological Institute.

Brain, Robert
1979 *The Decorated Body.* New York: Harper & Row.

Braudel, Fernand
1979a *The Structures of Everyday Life. Civilization & Capitalism 15th–18th Century,* vol. 1. New York: Harper & Row.
1979b *The Wheels of Commerce. Civilization & Capitalism 15th–18th Century,* vol. 2. New York: Harper & Row.

Brown, Donald E.
1991 *Human Universals.* New York: McGraw-Hill.

Brown, Judith K.
1970a "A Note on the Division of Labor by Sex." *American Anthropologist* 72:1073–1078.
1970b "Economic Organization and the Position of Women Among the Iroquois." *Ethnohistory* 17:131–167.
1988 "Cross-Cultural Perspectives on Middle-Aged Women." In *Cultural Constructions of 'Woman,'* edited by Pauline Kolenda, pp. 73–100. Salem, Wis.: Sheffield.

Brown, Penelope
2006 "Cognitive Anthropology." In *Language, Culture, and Society,* edited by Christine Jourdan and Kevin Tuite, pp. 96–114. New York: Cambridge University Press.

Burton, Michael L., and Douglas R. White
1984 "Sexual Division of Labor in Agriculture." *American Anthropologist* 86:568–583.

Carmack, Robert, ed.
1988 *Harvest of Violence.* Norman: University of Oklahoma Press.

Central Intelligence Agency
2007 *The World Factbook,* https://www.cia.gov/library/publications/the-world-factbook/index.html.

Chagnon, Napoleon A.
1983 *Yanomamö: The Fierce People.* 3rd ed. New York: Holt, Rinehart & Winston.

Chomsky, Noam
2000 "Control of Our Lives." Lecture, February 26, 2000, Albuquerque, N.M. (www.zmag.org).

Close, Angela E.
1989 "Identifying Style in Stone Artifacts: A Case Study from the Nile Valley." In "Alternative Approaches to Lithic Analysis," edited by Donald Henry and George Odell. *Archaeological Papers of the American Anthropological Association,* no. 1, pp. 3–26.

Cohen, Mark Nathan
1977 *The Food Crisis in Prehistory.* New Haven, Conn., and London: Yale University Press.
1989 *Health and the Rise of Civilization.* New Haven, Conn.: Yale University Press.

Cohen, Ronald
1978 "Ethnicity: Problem and Focus in Anthropology." *Annual Review of Anthropology* 7.

Cohen, Ronald, and Elman Service
1978 *Origins of the State: The Anthropology of Political Evolution.* Philadelphia: Institute for the Study of Human Issues.

Cohen, Theodore F.
2000 *Men and Masculinity: A Text Reader.* Belmont, Calif.: Wadsworth.

Colton, Harold S.
1959 *Hopi Kachina Dolls.* Albuquerque: University of New Mexico Press.

Commission for the Creation of Yanomami Park (CCPY)
1989a "The Threatened Yanomami." *Cultural Survival Quarterly* 13:45–46.
1989b "Brazilian Government Reduces Yanomami Territory by 70 Percent." *Cultural Survival Quarterly* 13:47.

Committee for Human Rights, American Anthropological Association
2001 "The Yanomami of Brazil: Human Rights Update," http://www.aaanet.org/committees/cfhr/rptyano10.htm.

Conklin, Harold
1957 "Hanunoo Agriculture." FAO Forestry Development Paper, no. 12. Rome: Food and Agriculture Organization of the United Nations.

Connelly, John C.
1979 "Hopi Social Organization." In *Handbook of North American Indians,* vol. 9, edited by William Sturtevant, pp. 539–553.

Cotter, David, Paula England, and Joan Hermsen
2007 "Moms and Jobs: Trends in Mothers' Employment and Which Mothers Stay Home," http://www.contemporaryfamilies.org/docs/moms_and_jobs_fact_sheet.pdf (retrieved October 28, 2007).

Crosby, Alfred W.
1972 *The Columbian Exchange.* Westport, Conn.: Greenwood.

D'Altroy, Terence N.
1987 "Transitions in Power: Centralization of Wanka Political Organization Under Inka Rule." *Ethnohistory* 34:78–102.

Dahrendorf, Ralf
1959 *Class and Class Conflict in Industrial Society.* Berkeley: University of California Press.

Dalby, A.
2003 *Language in Danger: The Loss of Linguistic Diversity and the Threat to Our Future.* New York: Columbia University Press.

Davidson, Basil
1961 *The African Slave Trade: Precolonial History 1450–1850.* Boston: Atlantic-Little Brown.
1969 *Africa in History.* New York: Macmillan.

Davis, Kingsley, and Wilbert E. Moore
1945 "Some Principles of Stratification." *American Sociological Review* 10:242–249.

Davis, Shelton H.
1977 *Victims of the Miracle.* Cambridge: Cambridge University Press.

Davis, Wade
1985 *The Serpent and the Rainbow.* New York: Warner Books.

Davis, William G.
1973 *Social Relations in a Philippine Market.* Berkeley: University of California Press.

Dawkins, Richard
1976 *The Selfish Gene.* Oxford: Oxford University Press.

DeNavas-Walt, Carmen, Bernadette D. Proctor, and Robert J. Mills
2004 *Income, Poverty, and Health Insurance Coverage in the United States: 2003* (U.S. Census Bureau Current Population Reports P60–226). Washington, D.C.: U.S. Government Printing Office.

Denevan, William M.
1992 "The Pristine Myth: The Landscape of the Americas in 1492." *Annals of the Association of American Geographers* 82:369–385.

Dentan, Robert Knox
1968 *The Semai: A Nonviolent People of Malaya.* New York: Holt, Rinehart & Winston.

DeVos, George, and Lola Romanucci-Ross, eds.
1975 *Ethnic Identity: Cultural Continuities and Change.* Palo Alto, Calif.: Mayfield.

di Leonardo, Micaela, ed.
1991 *Gender at the Crossroads of Knowledge.* Berkeley: University of California Press.

Diamond, Jared
1997 *Guns, Germs, and Steel.* New York: Norton.

Dillehay, Tom, Jack Rossen, Thomas Andrus, and David Williams
2007 "Preceramic Adoption of Squash, Peanut, and Cotton in Northern Peru." *Science* 316:1890–1893.

Divale, William T.
1974 "Migration, External Warfare, and Matrilocal Residence." *Behavior Science Research* 9:75–133.

Divale, William T., and Marvin Harris
1976 "Population, Warfare, and the Male Supremacist Complex." *American Anthropologist* 78:521–538.

Dobyns, Henry F.
1976 *Native American Historical Demography: A Critical Bibliography.* Bloomington: Indiana University Press.
1983 *Their Numbers Become Thinned.* Knoxville: University of Tennessee Press.

Donkin, Robin
1979 *Agricultural Terracing in the Aboriginal New World.* Tucson: University of Arizona Press.

Doolittle, William E.
1992 "Agriculture in North America on the Eve of Contact: A Reassessment." *Annals of the Association of American Geographers* 82:386–401.

Dozier, Edward P.
1970 *The Pueblo Indians of North America.* Prospect Heights, Ill.: Waveland Press (reissued 1983).

Dumont, Louis
1980 *Homo Hierarchicus: The Caste System and Its Implications.* Chicago and London: University of Chicago Press.

Durkheim, Émile
1915 *The Elementary Forms of the Religious Life.* London: George Allen and Unwin.

Dyson-Hudson, Rada, and Neville Dyson-Hudson
1969 "Subsistence Herding in Uganda." *Scientific American* 220:76–89.

Economic Policy Institute
2007 "The State of Working America 2006/7," http://www.stateofworkingamerica.org/.

Eggan, Fred
1950 *Social Organization of the Western Pueblos.* Chicago: University of Chicago Press.

Ember, Carol
1974 "An Evaluation of Alternative Theories of Matrilocal Versus Patrilocal Residence." *Behavior Science Research* 9:135–149.
1983 "The Relative Decline in Women's Contribution to Agriculture with Intensification." *American Anthropologist* 85:285–304.

Ember, Melvin
1959 "The Nonunilinear Descent Groups of Samoa." *American Anthropologist* 61:573–577.

Ember, Melvin, and Carol R. Ember
1971 "The Conditions Favoring Matrilocal Versus Patrilocal Residence." *American Anthropologist* 73:571–594.
1972 "The Conditions Favoring Multilocal Residence." *Southwestern Journal of Anthropology* 28:382–400.

Ember, Melvin, and Carol R. Ember, eds.
2001 *Countries and Their Cultures,* 4 vols. New York: Macmillan Reference USA.

Ember, Melvin, Carol R. Ember, and Burton Pasternak
1974 "On the Development of Unilineal Descent." *Journal of Anthropological Research* 30:69–94.

Estioko-Griffin, Agnes
1986 "Daughters of the Forest." *Natural History* 95:36–43.

Evans-Pritchard, E. E.
1940 *The Nuer.* Oxford: Clarendon.

1976 *Witchcraft, Oracles, and Magic Among the Azande.* Abridged ed. Oxford: Clarendon Press.

Ewers, John
1955 "The Horse in Blackfoot Indian Culture." Bureau of American Ethnology, Bulletin 159. Washington, D.C.: U.S. Government Printing Office.

Fabrega, H., Jr.
1975 "The Need for an Ethnomedical Science." *Science* 189:969–975.

Fagan, Brian M.
1986 *People of the Earth.* Boston: Little, Brown.

Fallers, Lloyd A.
1969 *Law Without Precedent.* Chicago: University of Chicago Press.

Farb, Peter
1974 *Word Play.* New York: Alfred A. Knopf.

Farnsworth, Norman R.
1984 "How Can the Well Be Dry When It Is Filled With Water?" *Economic Botany* 38:4–13.

Farrer, Claire F.
1996 *Thunder Rides a Black Horse.* 2nd ed. Prospect Heights, Ill.: Waveland Press.

Ferguson, R. Brian
1984 "A Reexamination of the Causes of Northwest Coast Warfare." In *Warfare, Culture, and Environment,* edited by R. Brian Ferguson, pp. 267–328. Orlando, Fla.: Academic Press.

Firth, Raymond
1936 *We, the Tikopia.* Boston: Beacon Press.

1965 *Primitive Polynesian Economy.* New York: Norton.

1968 "A Note on Descent Groups in Polynesia." In *Kinship and Social Organization,* edited by Paul Bohannan and John Middleton, pp. 213–223. Garden City, N.Y.: The Natural History Press.

Fischer, John
1961 "Art Styles as Cultural Cognitive Maps." *American Anthropologist* 63:80–84.

Fogelson, Raymond D.
1989 "The Ethnohistory of Events and Nonevents." *Ethnohistory* 36:133–147.

Fong, Vanessa
2004 *Only Hope: Coming of Age Under China's One-Child Policy.* Stanford, Calif.: Stanford University Press.

Fortune, Reo
1932 *Sorcerers of Dobu.* New York: E. P. Dutton.

Foster, Charles R., ed.
1980 *Nations Without a State: Ethnic Minorities of Western Europe.* New York: Praeger.

Frank, Andre Gunder
1998 *ReOrient: Global Economy in the Asian Age.* Berkeley & Los Angeles: University of California Press.

Franke, Richard W.
1974 "Miracle Seeds and Shattered Dreams in Java." *Natural History* 83:10–18, 84–88.

Frazer, Sir James George
1963 *The Golden Bough.* Abridged ed. Toronto: Macmillan (original 1911–1915).

Freed, Stanley A., and Ruth S. Freed
1985 "One Son Is No Sons." *Natural History* 94:10–15.

Freeman, Derek
1968 "On the Concept of the Kindred." In *Kinship and Social Organization,* edited by Paul Bohannan and John Middleton, pp. 255–272. Garden City, N.Y.: The Natural History Press.

1970 "The Iban of Western Borneo." In *Cultures of the Pacific,* edited by Thomas G. Harding and Ben J. Wallace, pp. 180–200. New York: Free Press.

1983 *Margaret Mead and Samoa.* Cambridge, Mass.: Harvard University Press.

Fried, Morton
1967 *The Evolution of Political Society.* New York: Random House.

Friedl, Ernestine
1975 *Women and Men: An Anthropologist's View.* New York: Holt, Rinehart & Winston.

1978 "Society and Sex Roles." In *Anthropology 98/99,* edited by Elvio Angeloni, pp. 122–126. Guilford, Conn.: Dushkin.

Friedson, Steven
1998 "Tumbuka Healing." In *The Garland Encyclopedia of World Music,* vol. 1, edited by Ruth M. Stone, pp. 271–284. New York: Garland Publishing.

Frigout, Arlette
1979 "Hopi Ceremonial Organization." In *Southwest,* edited by Alfonso Ortiz, pp. 564–576. *Handbook of North American Indians,* vol. 9. Washington, D.C.: Smithsonian Institution.

Fromkin, Victoria, and Robert Rodman
1988 *An Introduction to Language.* 4th ed. New York: Holt, Rinehart & Winston.

Furst, Peter T., and Jill L. Furst
1982 *North American Indian Art.* New York: Rizzoli International.

Geertz, Clifford
1965 "Religion as a Cultural System." In *Anthropological Approaches to the Study of Religion,* edited by Michael Banton, pp. 1–46. Association of Social Anthropologists Monographs, no. 3. London: Tavistock Publications.

1973 *The Interpretation of Cultures.* New York: Basic Books.

1980 *Negara.* Princeton, N.J.: Princeton University Press.

1983 *Local Knowledge: Further Essays on Interpretive Anthropology.* New York: Basic Books.

Gell, Alfred
1993 *Wrapping in Images.* Oxford: Clarendon Press.

Gerner, Deborah J.
1994 *One Land, Two Peoples: The Conflict Over Palestine.* Boulder, Colo.: Westview Press.

Giddens, Anthony
2000 *Runaway World: How Globalization Is Reshaping Our Lives.* New York: Routledge.

Gilmore, David D.
1980 *The People of the Plain.* New York: Columbia University Press.
1990 *Manhood in the Making.* New Haven, Conn.: Yale University Press.

Gladwell, Malcolm
2001 "The Mosquito Killer." *New Yorker* (July 2), 42–51.

Glazer, Nathan, and Daniel P. Moynihan
1963 *Beyond the Melting Pot.* Cambridge: Harvard University Press.

Glazer, Nathan, and Daniel P. Moynihan, eds.
1975 *Ethnicity: Theory and Experience.* Cambridge: Harvard University Press.

Gliessman, Stephen, and Robert Grantham
1990 "Agroecology: Reshaping Agricultural Development." In *Lessons of the Rain Forest,* edited by Suzanne Head and Robert Heinzman, pp. 196–207. San Francisco: Sierra Club Books.

Gluckman, Max
1972 *The Ideas in Barotse Jurisprudence.* Manchester: Manchester University Press.
1973 *The Judicial Process Among the Barotse.* Manchester: Manchester University Press.

Goebel, Ted
2007 "The Missing Years for Modern Humans." *Science* 315: 194–196.

Goldman, Irving
1970 *Ancient Polynesian Society.* Chicago: University of Chicago Press.

Goldstein, Melvyn C.
1987 "When Brothers Share a Wife." *Natural History* 96(3):38–49.

Goodale, Ava Y.
2003 "The Kayapo Indians' Struggle in Brazil," www.actionbioscience.org/environment/goodale.html.

Goodale, Jane C.
1971 *Tiwi Wives.* Seattle: University of Washington Press.

Goodenough, Ward II.
1961 "Comment on Cultural Evolution." *Daedalus* 90:521–528.

Goody, Jack, and S. J. Tambiah
1973 *Bridewealth and Dowry.* Cambridge: Cambridge University Press.

Gordon, Raymond G., Jr., ed.
2005 *Ethnologue: Languages of the World.* 15th ed. Dallas, Tex.: SIL International.

Gough, E. Kathleen
1959 "The Nayars and the Definition of Marriage." *Journal of the Royal Anthropological Institute* 89:23–24.

Graham, Susan Brandt
1985 "Running and Menstrual Dysfunction: Recent Medical Discoveries Provide New Insights into the Human Division of Labor by Sex." *American Anthropologist* 87:878–882.

Grigg, David
1974 *The Agricultural Systems of the World.* Cambridge: Cambridge University Press.

Guthrie, Stewart
1993 *Faces in the Clouds: A New Theory of Religion.* Oxford: Oxford University Press.

Hage, Per, Frank Harary, and Bojka Milicic
1995 "Tatooing, Gender and Social Stratification in Micro-Polynesia." *Journal of the Royal Anthropological Institute (N.S.)* 2:335–350.

Hail, Barbara A.
1983 *Hau, Kola!: The Plains Indian Collection of the Haffenrefer Museum.* Providence, R.I.: Brown University Press.

Hajda, Lubomyr, and Mark Beissinger, ed.
1990 *The Nationalities Factor in Soviet Politics and Society.* Boulder, Colo.: Westview Press.

Hall, Edward T.
1959 *The Silent Language.* Greenwich, Conn.: Fawcett Publications.
1966 *The Hidden Dimension.* Garden City, N.Y.: Doubleday.

Handler, Richard
1988 *Nationalism and the Politics of Culture in Quebec.* Madison: University of Wisconsin Press.

Harding, Susan Friend
2000 *The Book of Jerry Falwell: Fundamentalist Language and Politics.* Princeton, N.J.: Princeton University Press.

Harlan, Jack R.
1975 "Our Vanishing Genetic Resources." *Science* 188:618–621.

Harner, Michael J.
1973 *The Jívaro.* Garden City, N.Y.: Doubleday-Anchor.

Harrell, Stevan, and Sara A. Dickey
1985 "Dowry Systems in Complex Societies." *Ethnology* 24: 105–120.

Harris, Marvin
1968 *The Rise of Anthropological Theory.* New York: Thomas Y. Crowell.
1977 *Cannibals and Kings.* New York: Random House.
1979 *Cultural Materialism.* New York: Vintage Books.
1985 *Good to Eat.* New York: Simon & Schuster.
1999 *Theories of Culture in Postmodern Times.* Walnut Creek, Calif.: Altamira Press.

Harrison, Paul
1987 *The Greening of Africa.* New York: Penguin.

Hart, C. W. M., Arnold R. Pilling, and Jane C. Goodale
1988 *The Tiwi of North Australia.* Belmont, Calif.: Wadsworth.

Harvey, Paul
1937 *The Oxford Companion to Classical Literature.* Oxford: Clarendon Press.

Hepner, George F., and Jesse O. McKee
1992 *World Regional Geography: A Global Approach.* St. Paul, Minn.: West.

Herdt, Gilbert
1987 *The Sambia: Ritual and Gender in New Guinea.* Belmont, Calif.: Wadsworth.

Heth, Charlotte, general ed.
1993 *Native American Dance.* Washington, D.C.: Smithsonian Institution.

Hewlett, Barry S.
1992 *Intimate Fathers.* Ann Arbor: University of Michigan Press.

Hickerson, Harold
1970 *The Chippewa and Their Neighbors: A Study in Ethnohistory.* New York: Holt, Rinehart & Winston.

Hiebert, P. G.
1971 *Konduru: Structure and Integration in a Hindu Village.* Minneapolis: University of Minnesota Press.

Himes, Joseph S.
1974 *Racial and Ethnic Relations.* Dubuque, Ia.: Wm. C. Brown.

Hines, Colin
2000 *Localization: A Global Manifesto.* London: Earthscan Publications.

Hitchcock, Robert K.
1999 "Resource Rights and Resettlement Among the San of Botswana." *Cultural Survival Quarterly* 22(4):51–55.

Hitchcock, Robert K., Megan Biesele, and Richard B. Lee
2003. "The San of Southern Africa: A Status Report, 2003," http://www.aaanet.org/committes/cfhr/san.htm.

Hobson, Christine
1987 *The World of the Pharaohs.* New York: Thames and Hudson.

Hockett, Charles F.
1960 "The Origin of Speech." *Scientific American* 203:88–96.

Hoebel, E. Adamson
1940 *The Political Organization and Law-Ways of the Comanche Indians.* American Anthropological Association, Memoir 54. Menasha, Wis.: American Anthropological Association.
1954 *The Law of Primitive Man.* Cambridge: Harvard University Press.
1978 *The Cheyennes.* 2nd ed. New York: Holt, Rinehart & Winston.

Holm, Bill
1965 *Northwest Coast Indian Art: An Analysis of Form.* Seattle: University of Washington Press.
1972 *Crooked Beak of Heaven.* Seattle: University of Washington Press.

Holmes, Lowell D., and Ellen Rhoads Holmes
1992 *Samoan Village Then and Now.* 2nd ed. Fort Worth, Tex.: Harcourt Brace Jovanovich.

Horowitz, Donald L.
1985 *Ethnic Groups in Conflict.* Berkeley: University of California Press.

Houston, Christopher
2001 *Islam, Kurds and the Turkish Nation-State.* Oxford and New York: Berg.

Howard, Alan, and John Kirkpatrick
1989 "Social Organization." In *Developments in Polynesian Ethnology,* edited by Alan Howard and Robert Borofsky, pp. 47–94. Honolulu: University of Hawaii Press.

Howard, Mary, and Ann V. Millard
1997 *Hunger and Shame: Child Malnutrition and Poverty on Mount Kilimanjaro.* New York: Routledge.

Hua, Cai
2001 *A Society Without Fathers or Husbands: The Na of China.* New York: Zone Books. (Translated by Asti Hustvedt)

Hunter, David E., and Phillip Whitten, eds.
1975 *Encyclopedia of Anthropology.* New York: Harper & Row.

Huntington, Samuel P.
1996 *The Clash of Civilizations and the Remaking of World Order.* New York: Simon & Schuster.

Hutton, Will, and Anthony Giddens, eds.
2000 *Global Capitalism.* New York: New Press.

Innis, Donald Q.
1980 "The Future of Traditional Agriculture." *Focus* 30:1–8.

Izady, Mehrdad R.
1992 *The Kurds.* Washington, D.C.: Taylor & Francis.

Jackson, Richard, and Neil Howe
2006 "The Greying of the Middle Kingdom: The Demographics and Economics of Retirement Policy in China." *European Papers on the New Welfare, Paper no. 4,* http://eng.newwelfare.org/?p=91 (retrieved October 14, 2007).

Jackson, Richard, and Lloyd E. Hudman
1990a *Cultural Geography: People, Places and Environment.* St. Paul, Minn.: West.
1990b *Cultural Geography: The Global Discipline.* St. Paul, Minn.: West.

Jenike, Brenda Robb
2003 "Parental Care and Shifting Family Obligations in Urban Japan." In *Demographic Change and the Family in Japan's Aging Society,* edited by John W. Traphagan and John Knight, pp. 177–201. Albany: State University of New York Press.
2004 "Alone in the Family: Great-grandparenthood in Urban Japan." In *Filial Piety: Practice and Discourse in Contemporary East Asia,* edited by Charlotte Ikels, pp. 217–242. Stanford, Calif.: Stanford University Press.
n.d. "From the Family to the Community: Social and Cultural Meanings of Elder Care in Aging Japan." Paper delivered for Japan in Transition Conference, Lawrence University (Appleton, Wisconsin), 2006.

Johnson, Allen W.
1971 "Security and Risk-Taking Among Poor Peasants: A Brazilian Case." In *Studies in Economic Anthropology,* edited by George Dalton, pp. 143–150. American Anthropological Association Special Publication, no. 7. Washington, D.C.: American Anthropological Association.

Johnson, Allen W., and Timothy Earle
1987 *The Evolution of Human Societies.* Stanford, Calif.: Stanford University Press.

Julien, Catherine J.
1988 "How Inca Decimal Administration Worked." *Ethnohistory* 35:257–279.

Jurmain, Robert, Lynn Kilgore, Wenda Trevathan, and Russell L. Ciochon
2008 *Introduction to Physical Anthropology.* 11th ed. Belmont, Calif.: Wadsworth.

Kaeppler, Adrienne L.
1978 "Dance in Anthropological Perspective." *Annual Review of Anthropology* 7:31–49.

Kalb, Laurie Beth
1994 *Crafting Devotions: Tradition in Contemporary New Mexico Santos.* Albuquerque: University of New Mexico Press.

Kapur, Akash
1998 "The Indian State of Kerala Has Everything Against It—Except Success." *Atlantic Monthly,* Sept., 40–45.

Keesing, Roger M.
1982 *Kwaio Religion.* New York: Columbia University Press.

Kehoe, Alice B.
1992 *North American Indians: A Comprehensive Account.* 2nd ed. Englewood Cliffs, N.J.: Prentice Hall.

Kelly, Robert L.
1995 *The Foraging Spectrum: Diversity in Hunter-Gatherer Lifeways.* Washington, D.C.: Smithsonian Institution.

Khleif, Bud B.
1979 "Language as Identity: Toward an Ethnography of Welsh Nationalism." *Ethnicity* 6(4):346–357.

Kinealy, Christine
1995 *This Great Calamity: The Irish Famine 1845–52.* Boulder, Colo.: Roberts Rinehart.

Kirk, John T.
1997 *The Shaker World: Art, Life, Belief.* New York: Harry N. Abrams.

Klein, Naomi
1999 *No Logo.* New York: Picador.

Kluckhohn, Clyde
1967 *Navajo Witchcraft.* Boston: Beacon Press.

Krader, Lawrence
1968 *Formation of the State.* Englewood Cliffs, N.J.: Prentice Hall.

Kraybill, Donald B.
1989 *The Riddle of Amish Culture.* Baltimore, Md.: Johns Hopkins University Press.

Krech, Shepard
1999 *The Ecological Indian: Myth and History.* New York: Norton.

Kunio, Sato
1988 "Wives for Farmers, A Critical Import." *Japan Quarterly,* July–September, 253–259.

Kuper, Hilda
1963 *The Swazi: A South African Kingdom.* New York: Holt, Rinehart & Winston.

Kuwayama, Takami
2004 *Native Anthropology.* Melbourne: Trans Pacific Press.

Laderman, Carol, and Marina Roseman, eds.
1996 *The Performance of Healing.* New York: Routledge.

LaFlesche, Francis
1905 *Who Was the Medicine Man?* Hampton, Va.: Hampton Institute Press.
1925 "The Osage Tribe: Rite of Vigil." In *39th Annual Report of the Bureau of American Ethnology (1917–18),* pp. 523–833. Washington, D.C.: Government Printing Office.
1928 "The Osage Tribe: Two Versions of the Child-Naming Rite." In *43rd Annual Report of the Bureau of American Ethnology (1925–1926),* pp. 23–164. Washington, D.C.: U.S. Government Printing Office.

LaLone, Mary B., and Darrell E. LaLone
1987 "The Inka State in the Southern Highlands: State Administrative and Production Enclaves." *Ethnohistory* 34:47–62.

Lalueza-Fox, Carles, et al.
2007 "A Melanocortin 1 Receptor Allele Suggests Varying Pigmentation Among Neanderthals." *Science* DOI: 10.1126/science.1147417, http://www.sciencemag.org/cgi/content/abstract/1147417 (retrieved November 10, 2007).

Lappé, Frances Moore, and Joseph Collins
1977 *Food First.* New York: Ballantine Books.
1986 *World Hunger: Twelve Myths.* New York: Grove Press.

Lawrence, Peter
1964 *Road Belong Cargo.* Manchester. Manchester University Press.

Leacock, Eleanor
1978 "Women's Status in Egalitarian Society: Implications for Social Evolution." *Current Anthropology* 19:247–275.

Leacock, Eleanor, and Nancy Lurie, eds.
1971 *North American Indians in Historical Perspective.* New York: Random House.

Leavitt, John
2006 "Linguistic Relativities." In Christine Jourdan and Kevin Tuite, *Language, Culture, and Society,* pp. 47–61. New York: Cambridge University Press.

Lee, Richard B.
1969 "!Kung Bushman Subsistence: An Input–Output Analysis." In *Environment and Social Behavior,* edited by Andrew P. Vayda, pp. 47–79. Garden City, N.Y.: Natural History Press.
1979 *The !Kung San.* Cambridge: Cambridge University Press.
2003 *The Dobe Ju/'hoansi.* 3rd ed. Belmont, Calif.: Wadsworth Publishing Company.

Lenski, Gerhard E.
1966 *Power and Privilege.* New York: McGraw-Hill.

LeVine, Robert A., Suzanne Dixon, et al.
1994 *Child Care and Culture: Lessons from Africa.* Cambridge: Cambridge University Press.

LeVine, Terry Yarov
1987 "Inka Labor Service at the Regional Level: The Functional Reality." *Ethnohistory* 34:14–46.

Lewis, Walter H., and Memory P. F. Elvin-Lewis
1977 *Medical Botany.* New York: John Wiley & Sons.

Lieberman, Philip
2007 "The Evolution of Human Speech." *Current Anthropology* 48:39–53.

Lipman, Jean, and Alice Winchester
1974 *The Flowering of American Folk Art.* New York: Viking Press.

Llewellyn, Karl, and E. Adamson Hoebel
1941 *The Cheyenne Way.* Norman: University of Oklahoma.

Lomax, Alan
1962 "Song Structure and Social Structure." *Ethnology* 1:425–451.
1968 "Folk Song Style and Culture." American Association for the Advancement of Science Publication, no. 88. Washington, D.C.: American Association for Advancement of Science.

Lordkipanidze, David, et al.
2007 "Postcranial Evidence from Early *Homo* from Dmanisi, Georgia." *Nature* 449:305–310.

Lowie, Robert H.
1954 *Indians of the Plains.* Garden City, N.Y.: American Museum of Natural History.
1956 *The Crow Indians.* New York: Holt, Rinehart & Winston (original 1935).

Lucy, John A.
1997 "Linguistic Relativity." *Annual Review of Anthropology* 26:291–312.

Malinowski, Bronislaw
1922 *Argonauts of the Western Pacific.* New York: E. P. Dutton.
1926 *Crime and Custom in Savage Society.* London: Routledge & Kegan Paul.
1954 *Magic, Science and Religion.* Garden City, N.Y.: Doubleday.
1960 *A Scientific Theory of Culture and Other Essays.* New York: Oxford University Press (original 1944).

Mamdani, Mahmood
1973 *The Myth of Population Control: Family, Caste, and Class in an Indian Village.* New York: Monthly Review Press.

Mandelbaum, David G.
1970 *Society in India.* 2 vols. Berkeley: University of California Press.

Mark, Joan
1987 *A Stranger in Her Native Land: Alice Fletcher and the American Indians.* Lincoln: University of Nebraska Press.
1999 *Margaret Mead: Coming of Age in America.* New York: Oxford University Press.

Marr, Phebe
1985 *The Modern History of Iraq.* Boulder, Colo.: Westview Press.

Marshall, Mac
1979 *Weekend Warriors.* Palo Alto, Calif.: Mayfield.

Martin, M. Kay, and Barbara Voorhies
1975 *Female of the Species.* New York: Columbia University Press.

Marx, Karl
1967 *Capital,* vol. 1. New York: International Publishers (original 1867).

Mayo, Katherine
1927 *Mother India.* New York: Harcourt, Brace.

McAlister, John T., ed.
1973 *Southeast Asia: The Politics of National Integration.* New York: Random House.

McCabe, Justin
1983 "FBD Marriage: Further Support for the Westermarck Hypothesis of the Incest Taboo." *American Anthropologist* 85:50–69.

McDonald, Kim
1995 "Unearthing Sins of the Past." *Chronicle of Higher Education,* Oct. 6, A12, 20.

Mead, Margaret
1928 *Coming of Age in Samoa.* New York: Morrow.

Meggitt, Mervyn
1970 "Male–Female Relationships in the Highlands of Australian New Guinea." In *Cultures of the Pacific,* edited by Thomas G. Harding and Ben J. Wallace, pp. 125–143. New York: Free Press.

Meigs, Anna S.
1988 *Food, Sex, and Pollution: A New Guinea Religion.* New Brunswick, N.J.: Rutgers University Press.
1990 "Multiple Gender Ideologies and Statuses." In *Beyond the Second Sex,* edited by Peggy Reeves Sanday and Ruth Gallagher Goodenough, pp. 99–112. Philadelphia: University of Pennsylvania Press.

Metraux, Alfred
1969 *The History of the Incas.* New York: Pantheon Books.
1972 *Voodoo in Haiti.* New York: Schocken Books.

Middleton, John
1965 *The Lugbara of Uganda.* New York: Holt, Rinehart & Winston.

Milner, G. B.
1969 "Siamese Twins, Bird, and the Double Helix." *Man* 4:5–23.

Mintz, Sidney W.
1986 *Sweetness and Power: The Place of Sugar in Modern History.* New York: Penguin Books.

Miracle, Marvin P.
1966 *Maize in Tropical Africa.* Madison: University of Wisconsin Press.
1967 *Agriculture in the Congo Basin.* Madison: University of Wisconsin Press.

Moorwood, M. J., P. Brown, et al.
2005 "Further Evidence for Small-bodied Hominins from the Late Pleistocene of Flores, Indonesia." *Nature* 437:1012–1017.

Morgan, Lewis Henry
1877 *Ancient Society.* New York: World.

Morgen, Sandra, ed.
1989 *Gender and Anthropology: Critical Reviews for Research and Teaching.* Washington, D.C.: American Anthropological Association.

Murdock, George Peter
1949 *Social Structure.* New York: The Free Press.

Murdock, George P., and Caterina Provost
1973 "Factors in the Division of Labor by Sex: A Cross-Cultural Analysis." *Ethnology* 12:203–225.

Nadel, S. F.
1951 *The Foundations of Social Anthropology.* London: Cohen & West.

Nag, Moni, and Neeraj Kak
1984 "Demographic Transition in a Punjab Village." *Population and Development Review* 10:661–678.

Nag, Moni, Benjamin N. F. White, and R. Creighton Peet
1978 "An Anthropological Approach to the Study of the Economic Value of Children in Java and Nepal." *Current Anthropology* 19:293–306.

Nanda, Serena
2000 *Gender Diversity: Cross-Cultural Variations.* Prospect Heights, Ill.: Waveland Press.

Nardi, Bonnie
1981 "Modes of Explanation in Anthropological Population Theory." *American Anthropologist* 83:28–56.
1983 "Goals in Reproductive Decision Making." *American Ethnologist* 10:697–714.

Naroll, Raoul
1962 *Data Quality Control—A New Research Technique.* New York: Free Press.

Nations, James, and Robert Nigh
1980 "The Evolutionary Potential of Lacandon Maya Sustained-Yield Tropical Forest Agriculture." *Journal of Anthropological Research* 36:1–30.

Neale, Walter C.
1976 *Monies in Societies.* San Francisco: Chandler and Sharp.

Nestor, Sandy
2003 *Indian Placenames in America: Volume 1: Cities, Towns and Villages.* London: McFarland & Company.

Newman, Katherine S.
1983 *Law and Economic Organization: A Comparative Study of Pre-industrial Societies.* Cambridge: Cambridge University Press.

Newman, Philip L., and David J. Boyd
1982 "The Making of Men: Ritual and Meaning in Awa Male Initiation." In *Rituals of Manhood: Male Initiation in Papua New Guinea,* edited by Gilbert Herdt, pp. 239–285. Berkeley and Los Angeles: University of California Press.

Nietschmann, Bernard
1988 "Third World War: The Global Conflict Over the Rights of Indigenous Nations." *Utne Reader,* Nov./Dec., 84–91.

O'Grada, Cormac
1989 *Ireland Before and After the Famine: Explorations in Economic History 1800–1925.* Manchester: University of Manchester Press.

Obeyesekere, Gananath
1992 *The Apotheosis of Captain Cook: European Mythmaking in the Pacific.* Princeton, N.J.: Princeton University Press.

Offiong, Daniel
1983 "Witchcraft Among the Ibibio of Nigeria." *African Studies Review* 26:107–124.

Oliver, Douglas L.
1989 *Oceania: The Native Cultures of Australia and the Pacific Islands.* Honolulu: University of Hawaii Press.

Oliver, Roland, and J. D. Fage
1962 *A Short History of Africa.* Baltimore: Penguin.

Parezo, Nancy J.
1991 *Navajo Sandpainting: From Religious Act to Commercial Art.* Albuquerque: University of New Mexico Press.

Pasternak, Burton
1976 *Introduction to Kinship and Social Organization.* Englewood Cliffs, N.J.: Prentice Hall.

Pasternak, Burton, Carol R. Ember, and Melvin Ember
1976 "On the Conditions Favoring Extended Family Households." *Journal of Anthropological Research* 32:109–123.

Peoples, James G.
1982 "Individual or Group Advantage? A Reinterpretation of the Maring Ritual Cycle." *Current Anthropology* 23:291–309.
1985 *Island in Trust.* Boulder, Colo.: Westview Press.

Peterson, John
1974 "The Anthropologist as Advocate." *Human Organization* 33:311–318.

Pickersgill, Barbara
2007 "Domestication of Plants in the Americas: Insights from Mendelian and Molecular Genetics." *Annals of Botany* 1–16, http://aob.oxfordjournals.org/cgi/content/abstract/mcm193v1 (retrieved September 22, 2007).

Piddocke, Stuart
1965 "The Potlatch System of the Southern Kwakiutl: A New Perspective." *Southwestern Journal of Anthropology* 21:244–264.

Pimentel, David, et al.
1973 "Food Production and the Energy Crisis." *Science* 182:443–449.
1975 "Energy and Land Constraints in Food Protein Production." *Science* 190:754–761.

Pimentel, David, and Marcia Pimentel
1979 *Food, Energy and Society.* New York: John Wiley & Sons.

Plotkin, Mark
1993 *Tales of a Shaman's Apprentice.* New York: Viking.

Pope, Kevin O., Mary E. D. Pohl, et al.
2001 "Origin and Environmental Setting of Ancient Agriculture in the Lowlands of Mesoamerica." *Science* 292:1370–1373.

Porter, Philip W.
1965 "Environmental Potentials and Economic Opportunities—A Background for Cultural Adaptation." *American Anthropologist* 67:409–420.

Posey, Darrell
1983 "Indigenous Ecological Knowledge and Development of the Amazon." In *The Dilemma of Amazonian Development,* edited by Emilio Moran, pp. 225–257. Boulder, Colo.: Westview Press.
1984 "A Preliminary Report on Diversified Management of Tropical Forest by the Kayapó Indians of the Brazilian Amazon." *Advances in Economic Botany* 1:112–126.
1985 "Indigenous Management of Tropical Forest Ecosystems: The Case of the Kayapó Indians of the Brazilian Amazon." *Agroforestry Systems* 3:139–158.

Pospisil, Leopold
   1958 *Kapauku Papuans and Their Law.* Yale University Publications in Anthropology, no. 54. New Haven, Conn.: Yale University Press.

   1978 *The Kapauku Papuans of West New Guinea.* 2nd ed. New York: Holt, Rinehart & Winston.

Price, Richard, ed.
   1979 *Maroon Societies: Rebel Slave Communities in the Americas.* Baltimore, Md.: Johns Hopkins University Press.

Pulliam, H. Ronald, and Christopher Dunford
   1980 *Programmed to Learn.* New York: Columbia University Press.

Quinn, Naomi
   1977 "Anthropological Studies on Women's Status." *Annual Review of Anthropology* 6:181–225.

Radcliffe-Brown, A. R.
   1922 *The Andaman Islanders.* Cambridge: Cambridge University Press.

   1965 *Structure and Function in Primitive Societies.* New York: Free Press.

Rappaport, Roy
   1968 *Pigs for the Ancestors.* New Haven, Conn.: Yale University Press.

Reichard, Gladys A.
   1950 *Navaho Religion.* Princeton, N.J.: Princeton University Press.
   1977 *Navajo Medicine Man Sandpaintings.* New York: Dover.

Reichel-Dolmatoff, Gerardo
   1971 *Amazonian Cosmos.* Chicago: University of Chicago Press.

Robbins, Richard H.
   1999 *Global Problems and the Culture of Capitalism.* Boston: Allyn & Bacon.

Rosaldo, Michelle Z., and Louise Lamphere, eds.
   1974 *Women, Culture, and Society.* Stanford, Calif.: Stanford University Press.

Roscoe, Will
   1991 *The Zuni Man-Woman.* Albuquerque: University of New Mexico Press.

   1998 *Changing Ones.* New York: St. Martin's.

   2000 *Changing Ones: Third and Fourth Genders in Native North America.* New York: St. Martin's.

Rostow, W. W.
   1978 *The World Economy: History and Prospect.* Austin: University of Texas Press.

Ruddle, Kenneth
   1974 *The Yukpa Autosubsistence System: A Study of Shifting Cultivation and Ancillary Activities in Colombia and Venezuela.* Berkeley: University of California Press.

Sacks, Karen
   1982 *Sisters and Wives.* Urbana: University of Illinois Press.

Sahlins, Marshall
   1958 *Social Stratification in Polynesia.* Seattle: University of Washington Press.

   1965 "On the Sociology of Primitive Exchange." In *The Relevance of Models for Social Anthropology,* edited by Michael Banton, pp. 139–236. London: Tavistock.

   1972 *Stone Age Economics.* New York: Aldine.

   1981 *Historical Metaphors and Mythical Realities: Structure in the Early History of the Sandwich Island Kingdom.* Ann Arbor: University of Michigan Press.

   1995 *How "Natives" Think: About Captain Cook, for Example.* Chicago: University of Chicago Press.

Sampat, Payal
   2001 "Last Words." *World Watch Institute,* May/June, 34–40.

Sanday, Peggy R.
   1973 "Toward a Theory of the Status of Women." *American Anthropologist* 75:1682–1700.

   1981 *Female Power and Male Dominance.* Cambridge: Cambridge University Press.

Sanderson, Stephen K.
   1999 *Social Transformations.* Expanded ed. New York: Rowman & Littlefield Publishers.

   2007 *Evolutionism and Its Critics.* Boulder, Colo.: Paradigm.

Sandner, Donald
   1991 *Navajo Symbols of Healing.* Rochester, Vt.: Healing Arts Press.

Sapir, Edward
   1964 "The Status of Linguistics as a Science." In *Edward Sapir,* edited by David G. Mandelbaum, pp. 65–77. Berkeley: University of California Press (original 1929).

Schlegel, Alice
   1972 *Male Dominance and Female Autonomy.* New Haven, Conn.: HRAF Press.

Schneider, Harold K.
   1981 *The Africans.* Englewood Cliffs, N.J.: Prentice Hall.

Sen, Amartya
   1984 *Resources, Values and Development.* Cambridge, Mass.: Harvard University Press.

   1987 *The Standard of Living.* Cambridge: Cambridge University Press.

Service, Elman
   1962 *Primitive Social Organization: An Evolutionary Perspective.* New York: Random House.

Shankman, Paul
   1976 *Migration and Underdevelopment: The Case of Western Samoa.* Boulder, Colo.: Westview Press.

Shapouri, Hosein, James A. Duffield, and Michael Wang
   2002 *The Energy Balance of Corn Ethanol: An Update.* U.S. Department of Agriculture. Agricultural Economics Report No. 813, http://www.transportation.anl.gov/pdfs/AF/265.pdf (retrieved September 15, 2007).

Sheper-Hughes, Nancy
   1992 *Death Without Weeping: The Violence of Everyday Life in Brazil.* Berkeley: University of California Press.

Shepher, Joseph
   1971 "Mate Selection Among Second Generation Kibbutz Adolescents and Adults: Incest Avoidance and Negative Imprinting." *Archives of Sexual Behavior* 1:293–307.

Shore, Bradd
1989 "Mana and Tapu." In *Developments in Polynesian Ethnology,* edited by Alan Howard and Robert Borofsky, pp. 137–173. Honolulu: University of Hawaii Press.

Shostak, Marjorie
1983 *Nisa: The Life and Words of a !Kung Woman.* New York: Vintage.

Simmons, Dave
1983 "Moko." In *Art and Artists of Oceania,* pp. 226–243. Palmerston North, New Zealand: Dunmore Press.

Small, Cathy
1997 *Voyages.* Ithaca and London: Cornell University Press.

Smith, Bruce
1995 *The Emergence of Agriculture.* New York: Scientific American Library.

Snow, Clyde
1995 "Murder Most Foul." *The Sciences,* May/June, 16–20.

Sokolov, Raymond
1986 "The Good Seed." *Natural History* 95:102–105.

Spoor, F., M. G. Leakey, et al.
2007 "Implications of New Early *Homo* Fossils from Ileret, East of Lake Turkana, Kenya." *Nature* 448:688-691.

Stavrianos, Leften S.
1998 *The World Since 1500: A Global History.* 8th ed. Englewood Cliffs, N.J.: Prentice Hall.

Steward, Julian H.
1938 *Basin-Plateau Sociopolitical Groups.* Bureau of American Ethnology Bulletin 120. Washington, D.C.: U.S. Government Printing Office.

1955 *Theory of Culture Change.* Urbana: University of Illinois Press.

1977 *Evolution and Ecology: Essays on Social Transformation,* edited by Jane C. Steward and Robert F. Murphy. Urbana: University of Illinois Press.

Stewart, Omer C.
1980 "The Native American Church." In *Anthropology on the Great Plains,* edited by W. Raymond Wood and Margot Liberty, pp. 188–196. Lincoln: University of Nebraska Press.

Stockard, Janice E.
2002 *Marriage in Culture.* Fort Worth, Tex.: Harcourt.

Stocking, George W., Jr.
1974 *The Shaping of American Anthropology, 1883–1911.* New York: Basic Books.

Stone, M. Priscilla, Glenn Davis Stone, and Robert McC. Netting
1995 "The Sexual Division of Labor in Kofyar Agriculture." *American Ethnologist* 22:165–186.

Suttles, Wayne
1960 "Affinal Ties, Subsistence, and Prestige Among the Coast Salish." *American Anthropologist* 62:296–305.

1962 "Variations in Habitat and Culture on the Northwest Coast." In *Man in Adaptation: The Cultural Present,* edited by Yehudi A. Cohen, pp. 128–141. Chicago: Aldine.

1968 "Coping with Abundance: Subsistence on the Northwest Coast." In *Man the Hunter,* edited by Richard B. Lee and Irven DeVore, pp. 56–68. Chicago: Aldine.

Swanson, Guy
1960 *The Birth of the Gods.* Ann Arbor: University of Michigan Press.

Swepton, Lee
1989 "Indigenous and Tribal Peoples and International Law: Recent Developments." *Current Anthropology* 30:259–264.

Tax, Sol, ed.
1967 *Acculturation in the Americas.* New York: Cooper Square.

Thornton, Russell
1987 *American Indian Holocaust and Survival: A Population History Since 1492.* Norman: University of Oklahoma Press.

Tierney, Patrick
2000 *Darkness in El Dorado.* New York: Norton.

Trinkhaus, Erik
2007 "European Early Modern Humans and the Fate of the Neandertals." *Proceedings of the National Academy of Sciences* 104: 7367–7372.

Tripp, Charles
2000 *A History of Iraq.* Cambridge: Cambridge University Press.

Trudgill, Peter
1983 *Sociolinguistics.* Middlesex, England: Penguin.

Turnbull, Colin M.
1962 *The Forest People.* New York: Simon & Schuster.

Turner, Terence
1989 "Kayapo Plan Meeting to Discuss Dams." *Cultural Survival Quarterly* 13.20–22.

Turner, Victor
1967 *The Forest of Symbols.* Ithaca, N.Y.: Cornell University Press.

Tyler, Stephen A.
1973 *India: An Anthropological Perspective.* Pacific Palisades, Calif.: Goodyear.

Tylor, Edward B.
1865 *Researches into the Early History of Mankind and the Development of Civilization.* London: J. Murray.

1871 *Primitive Culture.* London: J. Murray.

1888 "On a Method of Investigating the Development of Institutions, Applied to Laws of Marriage and Descent." *Journal of the Royal Anthropological Institute* 18:245–272.

United States Bureau of the Census
2007 *Income, Poverty, and Health Insurance Coverage in the United States, 2007.* Current Population Reports P60-233, http://www.census.gov/prod/200/pubs/p60-233.pdf.

Valeri, Valerio
1985 *Kingship and Sacrifice: Ritual and Society in Ancient Hawaii.* Chicago and London: University of Chicago Press.

Vincent, Joan
1974 "The Structuring of Ethnicity." *Human Organization* 33:375–379.

Vogel, Ezra F.
1991 *The Four Little Dragons: The Spread of Industrialization in East Asia.* Cambridge: Harvard University Press.

Wallace, Anthony F. C.
  1966 *Religion: An Anthropological View.* New York: Random House.
  1969 *The Death and Rebirth of the Seneca.* New York: Vintage Books.

Wallace, Ernest, and E. Adamson Hoebel
  1952 *The Comanches: Lords of the South Plains.* Norman: University of Oklahoma.

Walsh, Michael
  2005 "Will Indigenous Languages Survive?" *Annual Review of Anthropology* 34:293–315.

Warner, John Anson
  1986 "The Individual in Native American Art: A Sociological View." In *The Arts of the North American Indian: Native Traditions in Evolution,* edited by Edwin L. Wade, pp. 171–202. New York: Hudson Hills Press.

Wax, Emily
  2007 "An Ancient Indian Craft Left in Tatters." In *The Washington Post National Weekly Edition,* June 11–17, 2007, p. 21.

Weatherford, Jack
  1991 *Native Roots: How the Indians Enriched America.* New York: Fawcett Columbine.

Westermarck, Edward
  1926 *A Short History of Marriage.* New York: MacMillan.

White, Benjamin N. F.
  1973 "Demand for Labor and Population Growth in Colonial Java." *Human Ecology* 1:217–236.

White, Douglas R., Michael L. Burton, and Malcolm M. Dow
  1981 "Sexual Division of Labor in African Agriculture: A Network Autocorrelation Analysis." *American Anthropologist* 83:824–849.

White, Leslie
  1949 *The Science of Culture.* New York: Grove Press.
  1959 *The Evolution of Culture.* New York: McGraw-Hill.

White, Lynn, Jr.
  1967 "The Historical Roots of Our Ecological Crisis." *Science* 155:1203–1207.

White, Tim, Giday WoldeGabriel, et al.
  2006 "Asa Issie, Aramis and the Origin of Australopithecus." *Nature* 440:883–889.

Whiting, Beatrice
  1950 *Paiute Sorcery.* Viking Fund Publications in Anthropology 15. New York: Viking.

Whyte, Martin King
  1978 *The Status of Women in Preindustrial Societies.* Princeton, N.J.: Princeton University Press.

Wilken, Gene C.
  1987 *Good Farmers: Traditional Resource Management in Mexico and Central America.* Berkeley: University of California Press.

Wilson, E. O.
  1975 *Sociobiology: The New Synthesis.* Cambridge, Mass.: Harvard University Press.
  1978 *On Human Nature.* Cambridge, Mass.: Harvard University Press.

Wilson, Monica
  1951 *Good Company.* Oxford: Oxford University Press.

Wolf, Arthur
  1970 "Childhood Association and Sexual Attraction: A Further Test of the Westermarck Hypothesis." *American Anthropologist* 72:503–515.

Wolf, Eric
  1969 *Peasant Wars of the Twentieth Century.* New York: Harper & Row.
  1982 *Europe and the People Without History.* Berkeley: University of California Press.

Wolf, Margery
  1972 *Women and the Family in Rural Taiwan.* Stanford, Calif.: Stanford University Press.

Wood, Bernard
  2002 "Hominid Revelations from Chad." *Nature* 418:133–135.

Wood, Bernard, and Brian G. Richmond
  2002 "Human Evolution: Taxonomy and Paleobiology." *Journal of Anatomy* 196:19–60.

Woodburn, James
  1968 "An Introduction to Hadza Ecology." In *Man the Hunter,* edited by Richard B. Lee and Irven DeVore, pp. 49–55. Chicago: Aldine.
  1982 "Egalitarian Societies." *Man* 17:431–451.

Woodham-Smith, Cecil
  1991 *The Great Hunger; Ireland 1845–1849.* London: Penguin Books.

World Bank
  1999 *World Development Report 1998/9.* New York: Oxford.

World Council of Churches
  2000 "There Are Alternatives to Globalization." Dossier prepared by the Justice, Peace and Creation team.

Wormsley, William E.
  1993 *The White Man Will Eat You!* Fort Worth, Tex.: Harcourt Brace Jovanovich.

Worsley, Peter
  1968 *The Trumpet Shall Sound.* New York: Schocken.

Yan, Yunxiang
  2006 "Girl Power: Young Women and the Waning of Patriarchy in Rural North China." *Ethnology* XLV(2):105–123.

Peoples and Cultures Index

A

Agta (Phillipines), sexual division of labor among, 241
Aka (Africa), 212–214, 253
Amish communities, 307–308, 337
Apache, 223–224
Arabs, 391–394
Asia
    care of the elderly in, 226–227
    contextual norms in languages of, 60–61
    dowry in, 175
    European colonialism in, 361–362
    gender stratification in, 255
    Industrial Revolution and, 364
    intensive agriculture and, 129
    language in, 48, 49–50
    marriage in, 163, 164
    nonverbal communication and gestures in, 31–32
    religion in, 320
    See also individual nations
Australia
    aborigines, 337, 338, 363–364
    Tasmanians, 385–386
    Tiwi, 166–167
Australian aborigines, 337, 338, 363–364
Awa people of New Guinea, 222–223
Azande of Sudan, 317–318

B

Bambuti (Africa), 253
Barotse (Africa), 277
Brazil, 28, 172–173, 174
    Kayapó, 417, 419–421

C

Canada, French and Anglo-Canadians in, 398–399, 400–401
    See also North America
Chagga (Tanzania), 210, 211–212
Cheyenne, 219, 248
    incipient court systems, 275, 276
    political organization of, 264–265
China, 151–153, 289
    foot binding in, 337
    patrilineality and globalization in, 190–191
    See also Asia
Chuukese (Micronesia), young men of, 220
Comanche, 263–264, 272–273

Croatians, 395, 399, 401–403
Czechoslovakians, 395, 399, 401–403

D

Dobu (Melanesia), 313

E

Ecuador, Jivaro, 274
England
    British functionalism in, 74–75
    colonization by, 357–361, 390, 394–395
    Ireland and, 382, 388–389, 414–415
    Ulster-Scots and, 388–389
Eskimos, 201, 203–204
Europe
    American colonization by, 357–360
    Asian colonization by, 361–362, 390, 394–395
    ethnogenesis in, 386
    Industrial Revolution and, 362–365
    Muslims in, 378, 395
    sub-Saharan Africa colonization by, 360–361
    World War II and, 366

F

Fourth World peoples, 418

G

Gusii (Kenya), 214–217

H

Hawaiians, 201–202, 203–204
Hindus, 287–290, 309, 310, 322–323, 371–373, 394–395
Hispanics and construction of race, 35
Hopi, 193–196, 310
    body art among, 336
Hua (Papua New Guinea), 234–237

I

Ibibio of Nigeria, 317
Inca of Peru, 267–268
India
    British colonization of, 390, 394–395
    caste system, 286–290
    children, 410–412
    globalization and, 426
    Kerala, 426
    Nayar, 165–166
    Varanasi saris, 351

Ireland, 382, 388–389, 414–415, 424
Irish Republican Army, 382, 388
Iroquois, 202, 204, 251–252

J

Jamaica, 254
Japan, 32, 368
    care of the elderly in, 226–227
    language in, 49–50
    marriage and family in, 168–169
    race constructions in, 34
    See also Asia
Jívaro (Ecuador), 274
Ju/'Hoansi (!Kung), 149–150, 174
    exchange practices, 141, 142
    foraging, 115, 118–119, 283, 284

K

Karimojong (Uganda), 132–133
Kayapó (Brazil), 417
Kerala, India, 426
Kofyar (Nigeria), 245
Kosrae (Micronesia), 138
!Kung. See Ju/'Hoansi
Kurds, 391–394
Kuwait, 394
Kwaio (Solomon Islands), 313

L

Lacandon Maya (Mexico), 417
Lugbara (Uganda), 317, 323

M

Malawi, 346
Manupur village, India, 410–412
Maori (New Zealand), 338, 339, 340, 365
Marquesas (Polynesia), 339–340
Melanesia
    cargo cults, 326–327
    Dobu, 313
Mexico, 151–153, 154, 417
Micronesia, 138
Middle East, the
    banking in, 369
    culture, 31, 53
    ethnic and religious differences in, 391–394
    gender stratification in, 255
    Islam in, 103, 104
Mohave, 248
Moroccans, 396

N

Na (China), marriages of, 164
Nandi (Kenya), marriage practices of, 163
Native Americans, 105
    Apaches, 223–224
    bands, 263–264
    body art among, 336–337
    childhood and infancy among, 219
    clothing as ethnic markers, 385
    Comanches, 263–264, 272–273
    ethnogenesis, 386
    European colonialism and, 357–360
    female initiation rites among, 223–224, 225
    foraging by, 113, 114
    forced assimilation of, 397–398, 400
    gender identity among, 246–248
    gender stratification among, 251–252
    Hopi, 193–196, 310, 336
    horticulture and, 123–124
    individualistic cults among, 321
    intensive agriculture and, 126
    Iroquois, 202, 204, 251–252
    kinship, 202–203, 204–205
    languages, 52, 56
    legal systems, 272–273
    matrilineal societies, 193–196
    Mohave, 248
    murder and suicide among, 276
    Navajo, 246–248, 316, 318, 348
    Northwest Coast art, 344–345
    Omaha, 202–203, 204–205, 248, 337
    Osage, 219, 248, 342–343
    Plains, representing, 118–119
    revitalization movements, 327–328
    rights to resources among, 116–117
    same-sex relationships among, 248–249
    sandpaintings, 348
    Seneca, 327
    shamans among, 322
    spirituality, 248, 310, 327–328, 330
    transvestism among, 248
    tribes, 264–265
    visual arts, 340
    Winnebago, 249
    witchcraft and, 316, 318
    Zuni, 247, 248, 322
    See also North America
Navajo, 246–248, 316, 318, 348
Nayar (southern India), 165–166
Ndembu (Zambia), 323
Neanderthals, 5, 7–8
New Guinea, 272, 337
    Awa, 222–223
    Hua, 234–237
New Zealand, 338–340, 364–365
Nigeria
    Ibibio, 317
    Kofyar, 245

    Tiv, 148–149
    Yoruba, 253–254
North America
    Amish communities in, 307–308, 337
    birthrates in, 408–409
    costs and benefits of children in, 409–410
    Eskimos, 201, 203–204
    European colonialism in, 357–360
    Industrial Revolution and, 362–363
    Northwest Coast art, 344–345
    religious diversity in, 329
    secular ideologies in, 296–298
    wealth in, 290–294
    See also Native Americans; Western culture
Nuer (Sudan), 273–274
Nyakyusa (Tanzania), 317

O

Omaha, 202–203, 204–205, 248, 337
Osage, 219, 248
    art, 342–343

P

Pakistan, 394–395
Palestine, 388, 389
Peru, Inca, 267–268
Peyote religion, 327–328
Polynesia
    body arts in, 337–338, 339, 340
    children in, 210
    cognatic descent in, 196–197
    European contact, effects of, 364–365
    political organizations in, 265–266
    ranked societies in, 285–286
    religion in, 306, 324
    respect language in, 60
    tribute payments in, 145–146

S

Samoa, 72, 220, 339
Seneca, 327
Serbia, 395, 399, 401–403
Shakers, 333, 334, 349
Solomon Islands, 313
South America, 357–360, 362–363
    Inca, 267–268
    indigenous peoples today, 419–421
    Yanomamö, 28, 172–173, 174, 419–421, 421
Sudan, 273–274

T

Tahiti, 265–266
Tanzania
    Chagga, 210, 211–212
    Nyakyusa, 317
Tasmanians (Australia), 385–386
Tikopia, 193, 286

    Tiv (Nigeria), 148–149
Tiwi (northern Australia), 166–167
Trobrianders, 310–311
Tumbuka (Malawi), 346

U

Uganda
    Karimojong, 132–133
    Lugbara, 317, 323
Ulster-Scots, 388–389
United States, the
    Amish communities in, 307–308, 337
    birthrates in, 408–409
    costs and benefits of children in, 409–410
    European colonialism in, 357–360
    Hawaiians, 201–202, 203–204
    Industrial Revolution and, 362–363
    Northwest Coast art, 344–345
    religious diversity in, 329
    secular ideologies in, 296–298
    wealth in, 290–294
    See also Native Americans

W

Western culture
    bilateral kinship in, 197–198
    capitalism in, 365–366
    construction of race in, 34–35
    economic independence of women in, 254–255
    emergence of anthropology in, 66–68
    English language in, 55–57
    gender crossing and, 249
    gender roles in, 236–237
    globalization of, 26–27, 256–257
    Judeo-Christian worldview in, 66–67, 69, 96
    marital exchanges in, 173–174
    Native anthropology and, 76–77
    stereotyping and, 95–97
    unilineal evolutionism in, 68–70
    weddings in, 256–257
Winnebago, 249

Y

Yanomamö (South America), 28, 419–421
    marital customs, 172–173, 174
Yoruba (Nigeria), 253–254
Yugoslavia, 395, 399, 401–403

Z

Zambia, 323
Zuni, 247, 248, 322

SUBJECT INDEX

A

Adaptation, 110, *134*
Adaptive wisdom of indigenous peoples, 424–425
Adolescence, 220
Adrian, Bonnie, *256, 256–257*
Adulthood in the life course, 224
Advocacy and anthropology, 418–427
Aesthetics, 334–335
    See also Art
Affines, 158
Africa
    ancestral cults in, 323
    birthrates in, 408–409
    body art in, 336
    European colonialism in, 360–361, 396
    exchange practices in, 141, *142*
    foraging in, 115, 118–119, 212–214
    indigenous people today, 420–421
    Industrial Revolution and, 363–364
    legal systems in, 273–274
    male initiation rites in, 222–223
    marriage in, 163
    pastoralism in, 132–133
    performance arts in, 346
    socialization of children in, 212–216
    witchcraft in, 317–318
    See also individual nations
African Americans and construction of race, *34*
Afterlife, 313–314
Agriculture
    adaptive wisdom of indigenous peoples, 424–425
    alternatives and world hunger, 416–418
    intensive, 125–130, *134*
    prehistoric, 3
    See also Cultivation; Horticulture
Al–Qaeda, 382
Algosaibi, Ghazi, *388*
Allen, Michael, 105
Allen, Paul, *293*
Altruistic behavior, 80
Ambilocal residence pattern, 177–178, 181
American Anthropological Association, 12, *96, 96–97*
American Cultural Resources Association, 12
American Dream, the, 138
American Sign Language, 48
Americans United for Separation of Church and State, *329*

Amish communities, *307–308,* 337
Ancestral cults, 322–323
Ancient cultures, study of, 2–4
Animism, 69
Anthropological linguistics, 8–9, 11
Anthropology
    advocacy through, 418–427
    applied, 11–12, 407–408
    biological/physical, 4–5
    careers in, 12, *96–97*
    corporate, 11
    cultural, 5–8, 79–89
    defined, 2
    development, 11
    early twentieth century, 70–76
    educational, 11
    emergence of, 66–68
    fieldwork, 7–8, 72, 75–76, 89
    forensic, 5, *10*
    humanistic approaches to, 84–88
    interpretive, 85–86
    Judeo-Christian worldviews and, 66–67
    medical, 11
    modern theories of, 78–79
    perspectives on population growth, 408–412
    practicing, 11
    scientific approaches to, 79–84, 87–88
    subfields of, 2–12
    value of, 17–18
    See also History of anthropology
Anthropomorphism, 312
Apotheosis of Captain Cook, The, 103
Applied anthropology, 11–12, 407–408
Arbatov, Georgi, *388*
Arbitrariness of language, 47–48
Arbitrary symbols, 30
Archaeologists, employment of, 4
Archaeology
    contract, 4
    historic, 4
    origins of culture and, 33, 36
    prehistoric, 2–4
    as a subfield of anthropology, 2–4
Argonauts of the Western Pacific, 75
Art
    body, 336–340
    culture and, 347–352
    defining, 334–335
    forms of, 336–347

    gender and, 349
    globalization and, *351*
    performance, 345–347
    pervasiveness of, 335–336
    religious, 347–349
    secular, 347–349
    social functions of, 349–350, 352
    visual, 340–345
Artificial countries, 390
Asia
    care of the elderly in, *226–227*
    contextual norms in languages of, 60–61
    dowry in, 175
    European colonialism in, 361–362
    gender stratification in, 255
    Industrial Revolution and, 364
    intensive agriculture and, 129
    language in, 48, 49–50
    marriage in, 163, 164
    nonverbal communication and gestures in, 31–32
    religion in, 320
    See also individual nations
Assimilation, 397–398, 400
Avunculocal residence pattern, 177, 181, 194–196

B

Balanced reciprocity, 140–143
Balkans, the, 395, 399, 401–403
Bands
    foraging, 114–115, 117–118
    political organization of, 261–264
Bangaldesh, 396
Banking, *369*
Barnes, Sandra, 254
Behavior
    altruistic, 80
    determined by culture, 37–38
    patterns of, 23, 27–29
    social control and law affecting, 269–272
    symbolic, 309–310
    variations, 38–39
Behind the Gates, 12
Bell Curve, The, 35
Benedict, Ruth, 72–73
Berlusconi, Silvio, *388*
Bezos, Jeffrey, *293*
Biblical history, 66
Bilateral kinship, 197–198

Bilocal residence pattern, 177–178, 181
Bin Laden, Osama, *388*
Biological determinism, 39–40
Biological evolution, *6–10*, 67–68
    culture and, 70–76
Biological/physical anthropology, 4–5
Biology and cultural differences, 39–41
Black September Organization, 382
Bloomberg, Michael, *293*
Boas, Franz, 17, 40, 70–72, 75–76, 335
Body art, 336–340
Body painting, 337, *338*
Bosnia, 395, 399, 401–403
Botswana, 420
Bound morphemes, 51
Boundary markers, ethnic, 384–385
Boyd, David, 222
Brahmins of India, 286
Brain, Robert, 338
Brazil, 28, 172–173, 174
Brideservice, 174
Bridewealth, 174
Brigham Young University, 12
British functionalism, 74–75
Bronze Age, 66
Buck, Peter, *293*
Buddhism, 309, 322–323
Buffet, Warren, *293*
Bush, George W., *176, 394*

C

Canada, French and Anglo-Canadians in,
    398–399, 400–401
    See also North America; Western culture
Capitalism, 365–366
Careers
    anthropology, 12, *96–97*, 407–408
    archaeology, 12
Cargo cults, 326–327
Caste systems, 286–290
Catholicism, 324–325, *369*
Causation hypotheses, 101–102
Chagnon, Napoleon, 99
Changing Ones, 246
Chase Manhattan, *369*
Chiefdoms, 265–266, 286
Child Care and Culture, 214
Childhood familiarity hypothesis, 161–162
Children
    adolescent, 220
    in China, *190–191*
    costs and benefits in less developed
        countries, 410–412
    costs and benefits in North America,
        409–410
    cultural views on raising, 209–210,
        217–218
    discipline of, 269
    diversity in care of, 210–218, 243
    grandparents and, 227–228
    hunger and disease among, *211–212*

incest taboos and, 159–162
infant and young, 218–220
in the life course, 218–224
marriage of, 163, 165–166
religion and, 315
rites of passage among, 218, 220–224
socialization of African, 212–216
Chimpanzees, 4, *5,* 6–7
China, *151–153, 289*
    foot binding in, 337
    patrilineality and globalization in,
        190–191
    See also Asia
Christianity. *See* Judeo-Christian traditions
Citibank, 369
Civilizations, 382, 387
    ancient, 3–4
    globalization and clash of, *388 389*
    intensive agriculture and, 127–128
Clans, 192, 194, 286
*Clash of Civilizations and the Remaking of
    World Order, The, 388*
Classes, social, 286, 290–294
Classifications and constructions
    of gender, 233–237
    of kinship, 186–187, 198–205
    of race, *34–35*
    of reality, 32–33
Clinton, Hillary, *231*
Clothing as ethnic boundary markers, 385
Code of Hammurabi, 277
Cognatic descent, 196–197
Cohen, Theodore, 255
Collins, Joseph, 414
Colonialism
    in the Americas, 357–360
    in India, 390, 394–395
    in Northern Africa, 396
    in sub–Saharan Africa, 360–361
Columbus, Christopher, *14,* 356, 357
Coming of Age in Samoa, 72, 220
Communal cults, 319, 322–323
Communication, nonverbal, 31, 51–53
    See also Language
Comparative perspective on human cultures,
    13–14, 301–302
Comparative research methods, 100–106
Composite bands, 262–264
Configurationalism, 72–73
Conflict
    ethnic, 396–403
    theory, 299–301
    warfare, 81, *200–201,* 244
Congregation and dispersal, seasonal, 114
Consanguines, 158
Consultants, 98–99
Contract archaeology, 4
Controlled historical comparisons, 104–106
Conventional symbols, 30
Cook, James, *102–103*
Corporate anthropology, 11

Court legal systems, 274–279
Courts of mediation, 275, 277
Courts of regulation, 277–279
Croatia, 395, 399, 401–403
Crops. *See* Human-nature interactions
Cross-cultural comparisons, 101–104
Cross-gender occupation or work roles,
    247–248
Cross-generational marriage, 166–167
Cultivation
    advantages and costs of, 122–123
    alternatives and world hunger, 416–418
    division of labor and, 243–245
    domestication and, 119–122
    intercropping, 417
    shifting, 123
    See also Horticulture
Cults
    ancestral, 322–323
    communal, 319, 322–323
    ecclesiastical, 319, 323–325
    individualistic, 319, 321
    Melanesian cargo, 326–327
    shamanistic, 319, 321–322
Cultural anthropology
    approaches to understanding human
        cultures, 13–17
    contemporary work in, 12–13, 65–66
    defined, 5–8
    disagreement within, 88–89
    humanistic approaches to, 84–88
    scientific approaches to, 79–84, 87–88
Cultural differences and biology, 39–41
Cultural identity, 25
Cultural integration, 23
Cultural knowledge, 23, 26–27
    classifications and constructions of reality,
        32–33
    individual behavior and, 37–39
    norms, 29
    social uses of speech and, 57–61
    symbols, 30–32
    values, 29–30
    worldviews, 33
Cultural materialism, 81–84, 84–85
Cultural norms and legal systems, 278–279
Cultural relativism, 14–15
Cultural universals, 32–33
Culture(s)
    alternatives demonstrated by indigenous
        peoples, 425–427
    art and, 347–352
    behavior determined by, 37–38
    comparative perspective on, 13–14,
        301–302
    construction of race, *34–35*
    defined, 22, 23, 29
    foraging and, 113–117
    holistic perspective on, 13
    horticulture effect on, 124–125
    humanistic approaches to, 84–88

intensive agriculture effects on, 127–130
language as a reflection of, 53–55
mental and behavioral components of, 23
nature and, 133
necessity for human life, 36–37
origins of, 33, 36
patterns of behavior and, 23, 27–29
relativistic perspective on, 14–17
science of, 69–70
scientific approaches to, 79–84, 87–88
as shared, 24–25
shock, 99
as socially learned, 25–26, 36–37
study of, 22–23
variations in kinship, 186–187
wars and marriage, *176*
See also Cultural knowledge
Czechoslovakia, 395, 399, 401–403

D

Darwin, Charles, 6, 67
Davidson, Basil, 361
Davis, William, 155
Dawkins, Richard, 80
DDT, 374
De Gama, Vasco, 361–362
Dell, Michael, *293*
DeLuca, Fred, *293*
Dentan, Robert, 28
Deoxyribonucleic acid. *See* DNA and
    paleoanthropology
Descent groups. *See* Kinship
Descent of Man, The, 6
Determinism, cultural, 37–38
Development anthropology, 11
Diamond, Jared, 121
Dimorphism, sexual, 233
Discreteness of language, 47
Displacement of language, 48
Division of labor, 111
    fertility maintenance and, 241–242
    foraging and, 114
    relative strength and, 242–243
    sexual, 237–245
    variability in, 243–245
Divorce, 172
Dixon, Suzanne, 214
DNA and paleoanthropology, 5
Dolan, Charles, *293*
Domestic groups. *See* Households
Domestication, 119–123
Dowry, 174–175
Durkheim, Émile, 314–315
Durst, John, 255

E

Ecclesiastical cults, 319, 323–325
Economic Policy Institute, 293
Economic systems, 139–140
    class and, 290–294
    conflict theory, 299–301

emergence of global, 365–368
functionalist theory, 298–299, 301
See also Globalization; Market
    exchanges
Educational anthropology, 11
Egalitarian societies, 283, 284–285
Ellison, Larry, *293*
Ember, Carol, *200*
Ember, Melvin, *200*
Emergence of anthropology, 66–68
Enculturation, 25–26, 36–37
Endogamous rules, 167
England
    British functionalism in, 74–75
    colonization by, 357–361, 390, 394–395
    Ireland and, 382, 388–389, 414–415
    See also Western culture
Enlightenment, the, 67–68, 86
Environment. *See* Human–nature
    interactions
Estioko-Griffin, Agnes, 241
Ethics, fieldwork, *96–97*
Ethnic cleansing, 396–397, 399
Ethnic groups
    accommodation of, 398–399
    attributes of, 383–385
    boundary markers, 384–385
    defined, 382–383
    desegregation of, 398
    ethnic cleansing between, 396–397, 399
    fluidity of, 385–386
    homogenization of, 396–398
    in Iraq, *391–394*
    origin myths, 383–384
    responses to conflicts between, 396–403
    situational nature of ethnic identity
        and, 383
    stateless nationalities and, 387–396
    types of, 386–387
Ethnocentrism, 15, 17, 85, 86
Ethnogenesis, 386
Ethnographic Atlas, 102, 104
Ethnography, 8
    fieldwork, 93–100
    gender stratification and, 251–253
    methods, 93–100
Ethnohistory, 100
Ethnology. *See* Cultural anthropology
Europe
    American colonization and, 357–360
    Asian colonization and, 361–362, 390,
        394–395
    ethnogenesis in, 386
    Industrial Revolution and, 362–365
    Muslims in, *378,* 395
    Sub-Saharan Africa colonization and,
        360–361
    World War II and, 366
    See also Western culture
European Union, *271,* 370
Evans-Pritchard, E. E., 317

Evolution, biological, *6–10,* 67–68
    culture and, 70–76
    modern theories of, 78–79
    neo-evolutionism and, 77–78
    unilineal evolutionism and, 68–70, 76–78
Evolutionary psychology, 80–81, 234–235
Evolutionism, unilineal, 68–70, 76–78
Exchange in economics systems
    marital, 173–176
    market, 139–140, 146–155
    reciprocity, 139–144
    redistribution in, 139–140, 144–146
Exogamous rules, 167
Extended family, 158–159, *168,* 179, 191,
    193–194
Extended households, 180–181

F

Factors of production, 111
Falwell, Jerry, *371*
Family
    disruption hypothesis, 160
    extended, 158–159, 179, 193–194
    globalization and, *168–169*
    and household forms, 179–181
    nuclear, 158–159
    relationships, 54–55, 80–81, 116–117, 150
    See also Kinship
Farming. *See* Human–nature interactions
Farrer, Claire, 224
Federal Reserve Board, 293
Female circumcision, 16
Female genital mutilation, 16
Female initiation rituals, 223–224
Feminism, 254–255, 257
Fertility maintenance, 241–242
Feuds, 274
Fieldwork, 7–8, 72, 89
    developing role and rapport in, 97–98
    ethnographic, 93–100
    history of, 75–76
    identifying and interviewing consultants
        for, 98–99
    interviews, 93–94
    participant observation in, 75, 94–95
    problems and issues in, 95–99
    as a rite of passage, 99–100
    sexual asymmetry and, 251–252
    stereotyping in, 95–97
Firth, Raymond, 286
Fischer, John, 344–345
Fong, Vanessa, *191*
Food First, 414
Foraging, *134,* 212–214
    bands, 114–115, 117–118
    characteristics of, 112–113
    culture and, 113–117
    decline of, 117–119
    egalitarian societies and, 284–285
    reciprocal sharing and, 115–116
    rights to resources and, 111–112, 116–117

Foraging (*continued*)
seasonal mobility and, 114
sexual division of labor and, 239–241
women's roles and, 253
Forbes magazine, *293*
Forced assimilation, 397, 400
Ford Foundation, 11
Forensic anthropology, 5, *10*
Fourth World peoples, 418
Fraternal polyandry, 172
Frazer, James, 311–312, 316
Free markets, 146
Free morphenes, 51
Freed, Ruth, 412
Freed, Stanley, 412
Freeman, Derek, 220
Fried, Morton, 283
Friedson, Steven, 346
Functionalism, British, 74–75
Functionalist theory, 298–299, 301
Fundamentalist religion, *371–373*

G
Gates, Bill, *293*
Gay marriage, *176*
See also Same-sex relationships
Geertz, Clifford, 86, 312
Gell, Alfred, 340
Gender
art and, 349
crossing, 245–249
cultural constructions of, 233–237
fertility maintenance and, 241–242
identities, multiple, 245–249
relative strength and, 242–243
roles in Western culture, 236–237
sex and, 232–233
sexual division of labor and, 237–245
stratification, 249–257
See also Marriage
General Agreement on Tariffs and Trade (GATT), *270–271*
Generalized reciprocity, 140
Genocide, 397, 399
Gerontology, 225
Giddens, Anthony, *373*
Gift giving, 141–143, *145*
Glazer, Nathan, 382–383
Globalization, 13
bridal photos and, *256–257*
clash of civilizations and, *388–389*
consequences of, 377
as a continuing process, 368–377
defined, 356
early development of global trade and, 356–365
emergence of global economy and, 365–368
ethics and field research, *96–97*
the Industrial Revolution and, 362–365
inequity and, *288–289*

language and, *58–59*
lifestyle development and, *426*
localization and, *256–257*
market, *151–153*
marriage and family and, *168–169*
patrilineality and, *190–191*
and Plains Indians representing indianness, *118–119*
political organization and, 269, *270–271*
population growth and inequities and, 370, 374–377
religious diversity and, *329*
religious fundamentalism and, *371–373*
short history of, *14–15*
terrorism and, 382
traditional arts and, *351*
Westernization through, *26–27*
Gluckman, Max, 277
Golden Bough, The, 311
Goodall, Jane, 4, 7, 166
Gorillas, 5, 6–7
Gossip, 269, *272*
Grammar, 48–49
Group marriage, 168, 170
Guthrie, Stewart, 312

H
Hall, Edward, 52
Hamilton, William, 80
Handsome Lake (Native American), 327, 330
Harris, Marvin, 82
Hart, C. W. M., 166
Herding. *See* Pastoralism
Hewlett, Barry, 213
Hidden Dimension, The, 52
Hierarchical nesting of identity, 383
Hinduism, 287–290, 309, *310,* 322–323, *371–373,* 394–395
Hispanics and construction of race, *35*
Historic archaeology, 4
Historical comparisons, controlled, 104–106
Historical Metaphors and Mythical Realities, 102
Historical particularism, 70–74
Historicism. *See* Historical particularism
History of anthropology
British functionalism in, 74–75
early, 66–68
fieldwork in, 72, 75–76
historical particularism in, 70–74
twentieth century, 70–76
unilineal evolutionism in, 68–70, 76–78
Hitchcock, Robert, 420
Hockett, Charles, 47
Hoebel, E. Adamson, 271–272
Holistic perspectives on human cultures, 13
Homeland, 386
Homogenization, ethnic, 396–398
Homosexuality. *See* Same-sex relationships
Honorifics, 60–61

Horticulture, 123–125, *134*
division of labor and, 243–245
See also Cultivation
Households, 159, 179–181
Howard, Mary, 210, *211–212*
Hua of Papua New Guinea, 234–237
Huizenga, Wayne, *293*
Human–nature interactions
culture and, 133
domestication and, 119–123
foraging and, 112–119
horticulture and, 123–125
indigenous people and, 423–425
intensive agriculture and, 125–130
pastoralism and, 130–133
understanding, 110–112
Humanistic approaches to anthropology, 84–88
Humans
adaptation by, 110, *134*
biological evolution, *6–10,* 67–68
biology and cultural differences among, 39–41, 70–76
language and, 45–47
necessity of culture for existence of, 36–37
population pressure and evolution of, *83*
unilineal evolutionism and, 68–70
variation, 4
Hunger, world, 412–413
agricultural alternatives and, 416–418
causes of, 413–415
inequality explanation of, 413–415
scarcity explanation of, 413–415
technology-transfer solution to, 415–416
Hunger and Shame, 211–212
Hunting and gathering. *See* Foraging
Huntington, Samuel, 382, *388, 388–389*
Hussein, Saddam, 5, *392, 392–394*

I
Identity
art and social, 350
cultural, 25
ethnic, 383
gender, 232, 237–249
Illitch, Michael, *293*
Immigrant communities, 12–13, 375–377, 382–383
Inca of Peru, 267–268
Incest taboos, 159–162
Incipient court systems, 275, *276*
Income inequality, 291–292
India
Brahmins of, 286
British colonization of, 390, 394–395
caste system in, 286–290
children in, 410–412
globalization and, *426*
Kerala, *426*
Shudras of, 286
vaishas of, 286
Varanasi saris of, *351*

Indigenous peoples
  adaptive wisdom, 424–425
  cultural alternatives demonstrated by, 425–427
  medicines of, 423
  rights of, *422*
  surviving groups of, 418–421
  vanishing knowledge, 421–423
Individual behavior. *See* Behavior
Individualistic cults, 319, 321
Industrial Revolution, 67–68, 347–348, 350, *351*, 362–365
Inequality, social
  caste systems, 286–290
  conflict theory of, 299–301
  in egalitarian societies, 283, 284–285
  functionalist theory of, 298–299, 301
  globalization and, *288–289*
  ideologies and, 295–298
  in industrial societies, 290–294
  maintaining, 294–298
  in ranked societies, 285–286
  secular ideologies and, 296–298
  in stratified societies, 283–284, 286–287
  systems of equality and, 283–287
  theories of, 298–302
  wealth and, 290–294
Inequality explanation of, 413–415
Infancy and childhood, 218–220
Informants, 98–99
Initiation rites, 221–224
Integration, cultural, 23
Intellectual/cognitive approaches to religion, 311–312
Intensification, population, 82–83
Intensive agriculture, 125–130, *134*
Interaction with nature, 110
Intercropping, 417
International Criminal Court, 269
International governance, 268–269
International Monetary Fund, 269, 368, 369, *388*
Interpretive anthropology, 85–86
Interracial marriage, *168*
Interviews, 93–94
Investigation methods. *See* Research methods
Iran, *392, 394*
Iraq, *391–394*
Ireland, 382, 388–389, 414–415, 424
Irish Republican Army, 382, 388
Iron Age, 66
Islam, 103, *104, 309, 369, 371–373, 378*
  in Europe, *378,* 395
  in India, 394–395
  in Iraq, *391–394*
  terrorism and, *382*

J
Jamaica, *254*
Jannard, James, *293*

Japan, 32, 368
  care of the elderly in, *226–227*
  language in, 49–50
  marriage and family in, *168–169*
  race constructions in, *34*
  See also Asia
Jenike, Brenda Robb, *227*
Jobs, Steve, *293*
Johnson, Samuel, 335
Judaism, 103, *104,* 337, *369*
  Palestine and, 388, 389
Judeo-Christian traditions
  anthropology and, 66–67
  ecclesiastical cults and, 324–325
  fundamentalism and, *371–372*
  music and, 345
  Native Americans and, 327–328
  social inequality and, 296–298
  worldview, 69, 96, 103, *309,* 314
Junkie Business, 12

K
Kak, Neeraj, 411
Keller, Helen, 48
Kelly, Robert, 117
Kenya, 214–217
Kerala, India, *426*
Key consultants, 98–99
Key informants, 98–99
Kibbutzim, 161–162
Kin groups, 158–159, 164, 165, 285–286
Kindred, 197–198
Kinship
  bilateral, 197–198
  cultural classifications of relatives and, 186–187, 198–205
  cultural variations in, 186–187
  diagrams, 177
  Hopi people, 193–196
  matrilineal descent, 187–194, *200–201*
  nonunilineal descent, 196–198
  normative expectations of, 186
  patrilineal descent, 187–193, *200–201*
  study of, 185–186
  terminologies, 198–205
  unilineal descent, 187–196
  ways of tracing, 186
  See also Family
Knight, Philip, *293*
Knowledge
  cultural, 23, 26–27
    classifications and constructions of reality, 32–33
    norms, 29
    social uses of speech and, 57–61
    symbols, 30–32
    values, 29–30
    worldviews, 33
  indigenous, 421–423
Kottak, Conrad, *34*
Kraybill, Donald, *308*

Kroeber, Alfred, 17, 72
Kuwait, *394*
Kuwayama, Takami, *76, 76–77*

L
Labor, division of, 111
  fertility maintenance and, 241–242
  foraging and, 114
  relative strength and, 242–243
  sexual, 237–245
  study of, 237–239
  understanding major patterns in, 239–243
  variability in, 243–245
LaFlesche, Francis, *98,* 345
Land prices, 138
Language
  as an ethnic boundary marker, 384
  anthropological linguistics and, 8–9, 11
  arbitrariness of, 47–48
  components of, 48–53
  discreteness of, 47
  displacement of, 48
  five properties of, 47–48
  globalization and, *58–59*
  grammar in, 48–49
  humanity and, 45–47
  multimedia potential, 48
  Native American, *52,* 56
  nonverbal communication and, 31, 51–53
  perceptions and worldview reflected in, 55–57
  productivity of, 48
  proxemics, 52–53
  as a reflection of culture, 53–55
  social uses of speech and, 57–61
  sound systems, 49–50
  tone, 50
  words and meanings in, 50–51
  See also Speech
Lappé, Frances Moore, 414
League of Nations, *392*
Lee, Richard, 115, 116
Legal systems
  court, 274–279
  cultural norms and, 278–279
  self-help, 272–274
  social control and, 271–272
Less developed countries
  costs and benefits of children in, 410–412
  hunger in, 412–418
  See also individual nations
LeVine, Robert A., 214
LeVine, Sara, 214
Levirate, 173
Life course, the
  adolescence in, 220
  adulthood in, 224
  defined, 218
  infancy and childhood in, 218–220
  old age in, 225–228

Limited-purpose money, 148–149
Lineages, 191–192
Linguistics
    anthropological, 8–9, 11
    relativity hypothesis, 55
    socio-, 57–61
Livestock. *See* Human-nature interactions
Lomax, Alan, 346–347
Lowie, Robert, 72
Lucas, George, *293*

M

Malaria, 374, 423
Malawi, 346
Male initiation rites, 222–223
Malinowski, Bronislaw, 74, 75–76, 82, 312
Manupur village, India, 410–412
Marcos, Bernard, *293*
Margaret Mead in Samoa, 220
Marital exchanges, 173–176
Market exchanges, 139–140, 146
    globalization of, *151–153*
    money in, 146–149
    in peasant marketplaces, 153–155
    principles of market economics in,
        149–153
    work in, 149–150
Marriage, 81, 162–163, 387
    alliances, 172–173
    of children, 163, 165–166
    in comparative perspective, 167–176
    cross-generational, 166–167
    culture wars and, *176*
    defined, 163–164
    function of, 164–165
    gay, *176*
    globalization and, *168–169*
    incest taboos and, 159–162
    marital exchanges and, 173–176
    number of spouses in, 167–172
    polygamous, 168–170
    postmarital residence patterns and,
        177–179, 255
    rules, 167
    unusual forms of, 165–167
    See also Gender
Marshall, Mac, 220
Marx, Karl, 149, 299–300
Materialism, cultural, 81–84, 84–85
Matriarchies, 251
Matrifocal families, 180, 219
Matrilineal descent, 187–194, *200–201*
Matrilocal residence pattern, 177–178,
    180–181
McCabe, Justin, 162
McCarthy, Joseph, 318
McVeigh, Timothy, *371*
Mead, Margaret, 17, 72, 220, 418
Meanings and words, 50–51
Media of exchange, 146
Mediation, courts of, 273, 275, 277

Medical anthropology, 11
Meigs, Anna, 234, 236
Melanesia cargo cults, 326–327
Mexico, *151–153, 154,* 417
Micronesia, 138
Middle East, the
    banking in, *369*
    culture, 31, 53
    ethnic and religious differences in,
        391–394
    gender stratification in, 255
    Islam in, 103, *104*
Millard, Ann, 210, *211–212*
Missing link, 6
Mobility
    livestock, 130–131
    seasonal, 114
Money, 146–149
Monogamy, 168
    serial, 172
Monotheism, 69, 103, *104*
Moral principles, 16
Moral relativism, 16–17
Morgan, Lewis Henry, 200
Morocco, 396
Morphemes, 50–51
Morphology, 50–51
Moynihan, Daniel, 382–383
Multimedia potential of language, 48
Multiple gender identities, 245–249
Murder, *276,* 397
Murdoch, Rupert, *293*
Murdock, George, 102
Music therapy, 346
    See also Performance arts
Muslims, 103, *104,* 309, 337, *369, 371–373,*
    378
    in Europe, *378,* 395
    in India, 394–395
    in Iraq, *391–394*
    terrorism and, 382
Myths and worldviews, 306

N

Nag, Moni, 411
Naipaul, V. S., *388*
Nation-states, 268–269
National Association for the Practice of
    Anthropology, 12
National Historic Preservation Act, 4
National Park Service, 4
Nationalities
    defined, 386
    stateless, 387–396
Native anthropology, *76–77*
Native Anthropology, 76
Natural resources, 110
    domestication and, 119–123
    foraging and, 112–119
    horticulture and, 123–125
    rights to, 111–112, 116–117

Nature–human interactions
    culture and, 133
    domestication and, 119–123
    foraging and, 112–119
    horticulture and, 123–125
    intensive agriculture and, 125–130
    pastoralism and, 130–133
    understanding, 110–112
Neanderthals, 5, 7–8
Negative reciprocity, 143
Neo-evolutionism, 77–78
Neolocal residence pattern, 177
New World crops and livestock, *120–121,*
    121–122, 357–358, 361, 425
New Zealand, 338–340, 364–365
Newman, Philip, 222
Nicholas, Henry, III, *293*
Nokia, 370
Nomadism, 130
Nongovernmental organizations, 269
Nonoverlapping group membership, 185
Nonunilineal descent, 196–198
Nonverbal communication, 31, 51–53
Norms, 29
North America
    birthrates in, 408–409
    costs and benefits of children in,
        409–410
    European colonialism in, 357–360
    Industrial Revolution and, 362–363
    Northwest Coast art, 344–345
    religious diversity in, *329*
    secular ideologies in, 296–298
    wealth in, 290–294
    See also Western culture
Northwest Coast art, 344–345
Nuclear family, the, 158–159
    incest taboos and, 159–162
Nuer people of Sudan, 273–274
Nyakyusa of Tanzania, 317

O

Obama, Barack, *34*
Obeyesekere, Gananath, *102–103*
Oboler, Regina Smith, 163
Observation, participant, 75, 94–95
Oceania, 363–364
Old age in the life course, 225–228
Old World crops and livestock, *120–121,*
    121–122, 357–358
Omidyar, Pierre, *293*
On the Origin of Species, 67
Only Hope, 191
Organization of production, 111–112
    sexual division of labor and, 237–245
Organizations, religious, 318–321
Origin myths, 383–384
Origins of culture, 33, 36
Ornamentation, 340–341, 344
Overlapping membership in kinship
    groups, 196

P

Paganism, 318
Painting, body, 337, *338*
Pakistan, 394–395
Paleoanthropology, 5
Palestine, 388, 389
Participant observation, 75, 94–95
Particularism, historical, 70–74
Partnerships, trade, 141
Passive assimilation, 398
Pastoralism, 130–133, *134*
Patrilineal descent, 187–193, *200–201*
Patrilocal residence pattern, 177–178
Patterns of behavior, 23, 27–29
Patterns of cooperation, 111
Patterns of Culture, 72
Peasants, 129–130
    marketplaces, 153–155
Performance arts, 345–347
Personal space and gestures, 31–32, 53
Peyote religion, 327–328
Phonemes, 49–50
Phonology, 49
Physical characteristics as ethnic boundary
    markers, 384–385
Pilling, Arnold, 166
Planting. *See* Cultivation
Plotkin, Mark, 423
Political organization
    bands, 261–264
    chiefdoms, 265–266
    forms of, 261–269
    globalization and, 269, *270–271*
    international governance and, 268–269
    legal systems in, 272–279
    religious fundamentalism and, *371–372*
    social control and law in, 269–272
    states, 266–268
    tribes, 264–265
Polyandry, 168, 171–172
Polygamy, 168–170
Polygyny, 168, 170–171
Polytheism, 69, 103
Population
    growth and globalization, 370, 374–377
    materialism and, *83*
    migration, 375–377
    size and growth, 82, 374–377, 408–412
    world hunger and, 412–418
Posey, Darrell, 417
Pospisil, Leopold, 272
Postmarital residence patterns, 177–179, 255
Postmodernism, 86–87
Practicing anthropology, 11
Prehistoric archaeology, 2–4
Primatology, 4–5
Primitive Culture, 22, 68
Primogeniture, *168–169*
Pritzker, Jean, *293*
Production of goods
    organization of, 111–112

sexual division of labor and, 237–245
transnational corporations in, 370
Productivity of language, 48
Promiscuity and unfaithfulness, 81
Properties of language, 47–48
Proxemics, 52–53
Psychological approaches to religion,
    312–314
Psychology, evolutionary, 80–81, *234–235*
Puberty rites, 221–224

R

Race, cultural construction of, *34–35*
Radcliffe-Brown, A. R., 74–75
Ranked societies, 283–284, 285–286
Rationality and postmodernism, 86–87
Reality, classifications and constructions of,
    32–33
Reasonable-person model, 275
Reciprocal sharing, 115–116
Reciprocity, 139–140
    balanced, 140–143
    generalized, 140
    negative, 143
    social distance and, 143–144
Redistribution, 139–140, 144–146
Refugees, 376
Regulation, courts of, 277–279
Relationships
    definitions of different, 158–159
    family, 54–55, 80–81, 116–117, 150
    feedback, 82
    human-nature, 110–112
    incest taboos and, 159–162
    marital, 81, 159, 162–179
    postmarital residence patterns and,
        177–179
    reciprocity in, 139–144
    trade, 141
    See also Kinship
Relative strength and gender, 242–243
Relativism, cultural, 14–17
Relativistic perspective on human cultures,
    14–17
Religion
    afterlife beliefs and, 313–314
    in Amish communities, *307–308*
    as an ethnic boundary marker, 384
    art and, 347–349
    Buddhist, 309, 322–323
    cults and, 319–325
    defining, 305–310
    diversity in the U.S., *329*
    fundamentalist, *371–373*
    Hindu, 287–290, 309, *310,* 322–323,
        371–373, 394–395
    intellectual/cognitive approaches to,
        311–312
    in Iraq, *391–394*
    Judeo-Christian, 66–67, 69, 103, 296–298,
        314, 324–325

    Muslim, 103, *104,* 309, *369, 371–373,*
        378, 382, *391–394*
    myths and worldviews, 306
    Native American, 248, 310
    organizations, 318–325
    psychological approaches to, 312–314
    revitalization movements, 325–330
    rituals and symbols in, 309–310
    sociological approaches to, 314–315
    theories of, 310–315
    See also Supernatural, the
Relocation, ethnic, 397
Research methods
    comparative, 100–106
    ethnographic, 93–100
    See also Fieldwork
Residence patterns, postmarital, 177–179,
    255
Revitalization movements, religious, 325–330
Rights to resources, 111–112, 116–117, *134*
Rites of passage
    fieldwork as, 99–100
    in the life course, 218, 220–224
Rituals and symbols in religion, 309–310
Rockefeller Foundation, 11
Roles
    anthropologists fieldwork, 97–98
    cross-gender work, 247–248
    cultural, 28
    gender, 237–245, 249–257
    reproductive, 242
Roscoe, Will, 246
Rudolph, Eric, *371*
Runaway World, 373

S

Sahlins, Marshall, *102–103,* 143
Same-sex relationships, *176,* 248–249
Samoa, 72, 220, 339
Sanday, Peggy, 253
Sandpaintings, 348
Sapir, Edward, 55
Sapir-Whorf hypothesis, 55–57
Scarcity explanation of hunger, 413–415
Scientific approaches to anthropology, 79–84,
    87–88
Seasonal congregation and dispersal, 114
Seasonal mobility and foraging, 114
Secular art, 347–349
Secular ideologies in the U.S., 296–298
Segmentary organization, 192
Segregation, 398
Self-help legal systems, 272–274
Semantic domains, 54
September 11, 2001 terrorist attacks, 16
Serbia, 395, 399, 401–403
Serial monogamy, 172
Sex and gender, 232–233
    See also Gender
Sexual asymmetry, 250–253
Sexual dimorphism, 233

Sexual division of labor
    fertility maintenance and, 241–242
    relative strength and, 242–243
    sexual, 237–245
    study of, 237–239
    understanding major patterns in, 239–243
    variability in, 243–245
Sexual Life of Savages, The, 75
Sexuality
    cultural relativism and, 16–17
    double standards, *234–235*
    puberty rites and, 221–224
Shamanistic cults, 319, 321–322, 324
Shared culture, 24–25
Sharing, reciprocal, 115–116
Sheper-Hughes, Nancy, 219
Shifting cultivation, 123
Shock, culture, 99
Siblings, 159–160
Silent Language, The, 52
Simple bands, 262
Slavery, 360–361, 363
Smallpox, 374
Smith, Frederick, *293*
Snow, Clyde, 5
Social anthropology. *See* Cultural anthropology
Social control and law, 269–272
Social distance and reciprocity, 143–144
Social functions of art, 349–350, 352
Socialization, 25–26, 36–37
    speech and, 57–61
Socially learned, culture as, 25–26
Societies
    definition of, 24
    egalitarian, 283, 284–285
    ranked, 283–284, 285–286
    social classes in, 286
    stratified, 283–284, 286–287, 290–298
Sociobiology, 80
Sociocultural anthropology. *See* Cultural anthropology
Sociolinguistics, 57
Sociological approaches to religion, 314–315
Sodalities, 264–265
Solomon Islands, 313
Sorcery, 101, 315–316, 317–318
Sororal polygyny, 171
Sororate, 173
Sound systems, 49–50
South America, 357–360, 362–363
Speech
    gossip, 269, *272*
    social uses of, 57–61
    See also Language
Spielberg, Steven, *293*
Spirituality. *See* Religion
Standard American English (SAE), 49
Standard of value, 146–147
Stateless nationalities, 387–396
States, 266–268

Steinbrenner, George, III, *293*
Stereotyping
    in fieldwork, 95–97
    of rituals, 309
Stevenson, Matilda Cox, 248
Steward, Julian, 78, 82, 88
Stone Age, 66
Store of value, 147
Stratification, gender
    among different groups, 250–253
    defined, 249–250
    in industrial societies, 255–257
    influences on, 253–255
Stratified societies, 283–284, 286–287
    maintaining, 294–298
    wealth and, 290–294
Subcultures, 24–25
Subfields of anthropology
    anthropological linguistics, 8–9, 11
    applied anthropology, 11–12
    archaeology, 2–4
    biological/physical anthropology, 4–5
    cultural anthropology, 5–8
Subnationalities, 386
Suicide, *276*
Supernatural, the, 101, 269–270, 305–306
    in explanations of misfortune, 315–318
    See also Religion
Surpluses, agricultural, 127
Survey of Consumer Finances, 293
Swanson, Guy, 315
Symbolic significance of money, 147
Symbols, 30–32
    religious, 309–310

T
Tahiti, 265–266
Tales of a Shaman's Apprentice, 423
Tattooing and scarification, 338–340
Taubman, A. Alfred, *293*
Technological determinism, 78
Technology-transfer solution to hunger, 415–416
Terminologies, kinship, 198–205
Terrorism, global, 382
Tone languages, 50
Totemism, 323
Touching and communication, 53
Trade partnerships, 141
Transnational corporations, 370
Transnationals, 387
Transvestism, 248
Tribes, 264–265
Tribute payments, 145–146
Trump, Donald, *293*
Turkey, *391–394*
Turner, Ted, *293*
Turner, Victor, 221
Two-generation households, 179–180
Tylor, E. B., 22, 68–70, 78, 85, 160, 305

U
Ulster-Scots, 388–389
Unfaithfulness and promiscuity, 81
Unilineal descent
    forms of, 187–189
    groups, 189–192
Unilineal evolutionism, 68–70, 76–78
Unilineally extended families, 191
United Nations, 269, 396
    Declaration on the Rights of Indigenous Peoples, *422*
    Development Program, 11
    Human Rights Council, 418
    Security Council, *388*
United States, the
    Agency for International Development, 11
    Amish communities in, *307–308, 337*
    birthrates in, 408–409
    costs and benefits of children in, 409–410
    European colonialism in, 357–360
    Forest Service, 4
    Industrial Revolution and, 362–363
    Northwest Coast art, 344–345
    religious diversity in, *329*
    secular ideologies in, 296–298
    wealth in, 290–294
    See also North America; Western culture
Universals, cultural, 32–33
Unstructured interviews, 93–94
Usary, *369*

V
Values, 29–30, 150, 152–153
Vanishing knowledge about indigenous peoples, 421–423
Variations
    behavior, 38–39
    human, 4
Vision quest, 321
Visual arts, 340–345
Voluntary networks, 185
Voudon (voodoo), 320, 345–346

W
Wallace, Anthony, 319
Warfare, 81, *200–201,* 244
Warner, Ty, *293*
Ways of behaving, 23, 32
Ways of thinking, 23, 32
Wealth, economic, 291–294
Weddings, *256–257*
Westermarck, Edward, 161, 162
Western culture
    bilateral kinship in, 197–198
    capitalism in, 365–366
    construction of race in, *34–35*
    economic independence of women in, 254–255
    emergence of anthropology in, 66–68
    English language in, 55–57
    gender crossing and, 249

gender roles in, 236–237
globalization of, *26–27, 256–257*
Judeo-Christian worldview in, 66–67,
   69, 96
marital exchanges in, 173–174
Native anthropology and, *76–77*
stereotyping and, 95–97
unilineal evolutionism in, 68–70
weddings in, *256–257*
See also North America; United States, the
Wexner, Les, *293*
White, Leslie, 77, 80, 82, 85, 111
White, Lynn, 306
Whiting, Beatrice, 101
Whyte, Martin, 255

Wicca, 318
Wilson, Edward O., *81*
Wilson, John, 328
Winfrey, Oprah, *293*
Witchcraft, 316–318
Wolf, Arthur, 162
Woodburn, James, 284
Words and meanings, 50–51
Work. *See* Labor
World Bank, 11, 269, 368
World Health Organization, *271,* 370, 374
World hunger, 412–413
   agricultural alternatives and, 416–418
   causes of, 413–415
   inequality explanation of, 413–415

scarcity explanation of, 413–415
technology-transfer solution to, 415–416
World Hunger: Twelve Myths, 414
World Trade Organization, 269, *270–271,* 356,
   368–369
World War II, 366–368
Worldviews, 33
   Judeo-Christian, 66–67, 69, 103, 296–298,
      309, 314, 324–325
   myths and, 306
   reflected in language, 55–57

X
Xenophobia, 81